Intelligent Language Tutors: Theory Shaping Technology

Intelligent Language Tutors: Theory Shaping Technology

Edited by
V. Melissa Holland
Jonathan D. Kaplan
Michelle R. Sams
U.S. Army Research Institute

LEA LAWRENCE ERLBAUM ASSOCIATES, PUBLISHERS
1995 Mahwah, New Jersey Hove, UK

Lawrence Erlbaum Associates, Inc., Publishers
10 Industrial Avenue
Mahwah, New Jersey 07430

cover design by Teresa Faella Horton

Library of Congress Cataloging-in-Publication Data

Intelligent language tutors : theory shaping technology / edited by V. Melissa Holland, Jonathan D. Kaplan, and Michelle R. Sams.

p. cm.

Twenty papers based on papers presented at a workshop held in 1993 and sponsored by the Army Research Institute.

Includes bibliographical references and index.

Partial Contents: 1. Text-based language tutors and learning environments — 2. Dialogue-based language games — 3. Graphics-based language tutors and learning environments — 4. Theoretical issues in language tutor design and assessment.

ISBN 0-8058-1502-3. — ISBN 0-8058-1503-1 (pbk.)

1. Language and languages—Computer-assisted instruction. 2. Computational Linguistics. I. Holland, V. Melissa. II. Kaplan, Jonathan D. III. Sams, Michelle R. IV. U.S. Army Research Institute for the Behavioral and Social Sciences.

P53.28.I58 1995
418'.00285—dc20 95-7640
CIP

Books published by Lawrence Erlbaum Associates are printed on acid-free paper and their bindings are chosen for strength and durability.

Printed in the United States of America
10 9 8 7 6 5 4 3 2 1

Contents

Introduction: The Case for Intelligent CALL

V. Melissa Holland
U.S. Army Research Institute

This book offers an argument for intelligent computer-assisted language learning (ICALL), an emerging discipline that seeks to apply advanced technologies, especially natural language processing (NLP), to the problems of language learning and research on learning. The contributors explain how they use NLP to enrich the capabilities of language tutors and learning environments. Where reactions from students are available, these are reported. The argument for ICALL is tempered throughout the book with lessons learned about the limitations of the technology and the complexities of applying it.

NLP technology provides ways of programming the computer with enough information about language, in the form of rules and patterns, that it can analyze the structure of sentences that users put into it, catch or disregard errors, and in some cases appear to understand by carrying out requests or responding conversationally. This technology has evolved primarily through applications like machine translation (Nirenburg, 1993) and automated message extraction (ARPA, 1994). It has only rarely, and relatively recently, been applied to language learning. NLP gives language learners the ability to create original sentences in the language they are learning and enter them into the computer for feedback and response. This is as dramatic a departure from answering the multiple choice and fill-in-the-blank questions of conventional computer-assisted instruction (CAI) as it is from observing other people's use of language in interactive video instruction.

The Neglect of ICALL

At this writing, we know of only one published book on ICALL, edited by Swartz and Yazdani (1992). Their book features European work, whereas this one focuses on U.S. and Canadian contributions. Why is the treatment so limited? Why, in general, do we hear so little about these efforts?

As a program of research, the projects that count as ICALL are scattered in place and time. There is not the critical mass to create a science, whose progress can be charted and whose efforts build on each other to make the cumulative improvements that come with replication and testing. More basically, unlike machine translation or automated message extraction, ICALL has no uniform impetus, no steady source of research funds, and no agreed-on methods for measuring success. Indeed, most systems are not finished enough to support evaluations.

As an application, ICALL suffers from the generally low priority assigned to foreign language education in this country. Where it is a priority, the politics and pragmatics of language education typically call for other kinds of learning tools, such as the lively interactive video and multimedia programs that have captured the public's eye (Fletcher, 1990; Furstenberg, 1992; Hart, 1994; Murray, this volume; Rubin, Ediger, Coffin, Van

Handler, & Whiskeyman, 1991). These programs sometimes become commercial successes: They carry full-blown foreign language lessons that are ready for immediate use. They contrast with NLP-based programs in ways that are significant to implementers.

First, NLP-based programs tend to take a long time to develop and to remain experimental. NLP is hard, as contributors to this book point out. Often there is little concern with, or time to think about, interface—particularly for systems featured in Section I of this book (text-based language tutors). This is partly because the bulk of the work is done by linguists and partly because it takes substantial effort to build smooth, fast NLP engines in multiple languages (see Felshin, this volume). Project resources may be consumed before the interface can be attended to, whereas multimedia programs rely on interface. In addition, many NLP applications currently require large computers that are expensive and difficult to maintain, whereas multimedia is within financial and technical reach of most language lab directors and school media specialists.

Another drawback is that NLP analysis is inherently uncertain; the results are not guaranteed. As Levin and Evans point out (this volume), complete coverage of a human language is impossible, and ICALL must concentrate on sublanguages. Even with a sublanguage covered, false alarms and false positives are likely (where students enter grammatical sentences that the computer will not accept or ungrammatical sentences that are judged correct). These outcomes can be minimized by carefully crafting the constraints on what kinds of sentences students can create. Even so, there are bound to be surprises in what NLP delivers. By contrast, the very rigidity of the response types in conventional interactive video guarantees certainty.

Moreover, NLP applications typically do not produce large curricula. As research projects, they yield lessons that are designed to demonstrate capabilities but that appear impoverished compared with the output of multimedia projects. Although some tutors provide authoring interfaces so that instructors or researchers can design their own lessons, NLP-based lessons may seem daunting to instructors unfamiliar with the technology, especially when they have the choice of editing aspects of NLP representations. This has been the initial reaction of instructors at the National Cryptologic School and at the Foreign Service Institute, even though NLP may save them time in the long run by automating aspects of answer prediction and evaluation (see Levin & Evans and Dorr, Hendler, Blanksteen, & Migdaloff, both this volume). In addition, the initial investment in requisite machinery such as parsers and lexicons is greater, relative to the return in breadth of curriculum, than is the case in conventional multimedia.

Perhaps most important, the politics of language education call for communicative language teaching, and many of the NLP-based systems appear to against that trend (a perspective voiced by Oxford, this volume). The zeitgeist in language teaching encourages environments that contextualize language within culture, which is depicted most authentically through multimedia and which does not dwell on grammatical form (Furstenberg, 1992). Many of the ICALL systems do focus on form because that is what parsers—a core NLP technique—do well.

These are the realities of ICALL applications. The realities often discourage potential users (see Murray, this volume; Sams, this volume), who may prefer the accessibility, certainty, and apparent communicativeness of interactive video.

Why is ICALL Worth Pursuing?

What then, to echo Bailin's (this volume) question, is the point of ICALL? First, we think there is a place for form-focused instruction within communicative language teaching. Otherwise, students may get frozen in an "interlanguage" (Selinker, 1992) of immature syntax that resists change (Hammerly, 1991). We also think that NLP accomplishes this sort of instruction better than other kinds of technology. Confirming this impression are initial studies comparing the effects on syntactic development of language tutors with and without NLP (Nagata, 1992; see also Levin & Evans, this volume). Second, ICALL is beginning to address communicative language teaching in ways that appear to work (DeSmedt, this volume) and that can offer students more flexibility in producing language than does multimedia CAI, as Sections II and III of this book illustrate. Another benefit of ICALL is the automation of response diagnosis and scoring, saving teachers from having to list possible answers, errors, and evaluation messages by hand. This is demonstrated in the use of NLP representations by Levin and Evans and by Dorr et al. to match student answers against target answers. Finally, ICALL offers a unique advantage for studying language acquisition by virtue of its analyzing and tracking the constructions students spontaneously use and the errors they commit in the course of learning a language (as discussed by Bailin and by Garrett, both this volume).

In addition, some of the factors that stymie acceptance—large machines, long and costly development, fragile analyses, narrow scope—are beginning to be alleviated. Many ICALL systems have been or are now being ported to affordable platforms like the personal computer. Some systems are beginning to add huge computational lexicons. For example, the Army Research Institute (ARI) tutor described by Dorr et al. and by Kaplan and Holland has inexpensively developed an Arabic lexicon of over 40,000 words by reusing existing lexical databases and applying automatic techniques for acquiring additional lexical features (Dorr, Garman, & Weinberg, 1994). In this way, ICALL can leverage the advances in NLP fueled by industry and government for machine translation, document analysis, natural language interfaces, and other mainstream applications. Developments are accelerating: Tools for automatic construction of lexicons and knowledge bases, statistical methods for training and testing parsers, and the establishment of repositories for large linguistic databases in multiple languages, can all feed into an ICALL that is more streamlined and cost-effective. Indeed, so many resources are being funneled into NLP from various directions (the private sector, the intelligence community, ARPA), it seems shortsighted to ignore its potential for language tutoring.[1]

---

[1] The same observation applies to speech recognition technology (e.g., Bernstein, 1994; Mostow, Roth, Hauptmann, & Kane, 1993; Waters, 1994).

Other implementation difficulties surrounding ICALL require rethinking the applications. ICALL needs tolerant user groups in the beginning, who can work within the limitations of current technology and help garner a wider acceptance as the technology progresses. ICALL also needs to define more clearly what counts as success. Is it helping all students all the time? Or is it helping some kinds of students with some kinds of problems? Loritz (this volume) counts the initial trial of his grammar checker for ESL (English as a second language) as disappointing because only about one quarter of the students who tried it were able to get any use from it unaided—that is, to make sense of the feedback and correct their essays accordingly. But Loritz also acknowledges that the proportion of beneficiaries could be increased through clearer directions to users. And at the workshop that preceded this book, he advised that, instead of placing such a system in the classroom for general and routine use, it might profitably be set up in a library or language lab, where appropriate students could be directed to it. Part of the problem of defining success, then, is attending to the context of uses and users (see Garrett, this volume; Oxford, this volume). Finally, ICALL needs better marketing. Because interactive video and other forms of CAI attempt less, they succeed more, and their successes have been skillfully promoted.

Organization of the Book: Theory and Technology

ARI sponsored a workshop in 1993 to bring together developers of ICALL in the United States and Canada.[2] This book grew out of that workshop. Each of the systems featured here pays allegiance to some theoretical framework in linguistics, foreign language pedagogy, or cognitive and experimental psychology. That is why they were selected—they stand as more than ad hoc engineering efforts. It is also true that the theory and the technology sometimes go at cross purposes, and this makes for interesting tensions that we have discussed elsewhere (Holland, Maisano, Alderks, & Martin, 1993), for example, how to balance communicative teaching with form-focused feedback (Doughty, 1993; Lightbown & Spada, 1990).

We asked contributors to talk about how theory shaped their use of technology. We found out that the influence runs both ways, and that theory can be significantly molded by the technology.

Theory Shaping Technology

Linguistic theories are key to the design of many of these systems. For example, the CALLE system of Rypa and Feuerman has since its inception (Feuerman, Marshall, Newman, & Rypa, 1987) been driven by a view of lexical-functional grammar as a psycholinguistically valid description of how people understand the structure of their language. By contrast, the BRIDGE tutor's use of a principle-based parser, as described by Weinberg et al., stems from the putative ability of government and binding theory to achieve computational compactness and cross-language extendibility. Comparisons between the major linguistic frameworks and their implications for design and

[2] One workshop participant, Masoud Yazdani, described the LINGER system developed at Exeter University in the United Kingdom.

development are broached by Levin and Evans (this volume) as well as in the introduction to the section on text-based language tutors. Less explicitly influential in ICALL are theories of second language acquisition (as reviewed in Gass & Selinker, 1994, and Larsen-Freeman & Long, 1991), which often draw from linguistic theory. In this book Tomlin, for example, grounds his research in interactionist accounts of acquisition such as Givon (1984).

Theories of second language pedagogy also figure in the design rationales for these systems. Versions of the communicative approach (e.g., Asher, 1977; Kramsch, 1989; Krashen & Terrell, 1983) are prevalent, as in Douglas' LingWorlds, Murray's Athena Language Learning Project, and Hamburger's FLUENT. These systems pay less attention to choices of grammatical framework and more to interface and interactions.

Theories of cognition, psycholinguistics, and learning psychology are sometimes tapped. For example, Frederiksen, Donin, and Décary base the levels of language analysis offered in their learning environment on what theories of discourse processing say about how readers mentally represent text for understanding and remembering. Kaplan and Holland attribute instructional features of the MILT system to what traditional learning psychology shows about the dynamics of practice, feedback, and motivation.

In a more general way, the recent emphasis on communication in theories of second language pedagogy has pushed ICALL technology in new directions—notably, toward the construction of animated computer scenarios, or microworlds, with which learners can interact by using language (see the framework developed by Hamburger, this volume).

We make no assumptions about the correctness of any particular theory. Rather, we see a principled tutor as giving form to theories, so paving the way for refining, comparing, and testing them. A challenge not addressed in these chapters is how to interweave theories from different sources and at different levels—linguistic, cognitive, pedagogical—that are relevant to the design, use, and evaluation of a language tutor.

Technology Shaping Theory

Developers who base their tutors on theories of teaching and learning generally and of language teaching specifically (Douglas; Kaplan & Holland; and Tomlin, all in this volume) admit the inadequacy of those theories to prescribe particular features of a language tutor. Often, the rationalization of design in terms of theoretical principles seems post hoc; the design does not spring inevitably from the theory. Theoretical principles "are not specific enough to fully determine the correct shape of foreign language [tutoring] systems," advises MacWhinney (this volume).

Tutors are therefore useful as testbeds for theory. First, a tutor provides a way to operationalize constructs like "contextualized language learning" and "comprehensible input" that are used loosely in the second language community, as well as a means to specify established learning tenets like "feedback promotes skill acquisition." Second, once these concepts are explicitly defined, the tutor can test their pedagogical effects. According to MacWhinney, "It is crucial for us to conduct new empirical research that evaluates the role of each of these [learning] principles within the context of foreign language tutoring systems." Third, the tutor serves to expose new theoretical issues. For example, Hamburger's attempts to develop a visual microworld to support dialogue led to the formulation of a theory of two-medium (verbal-visual) discourse, laid out in this volume. Similarly, Tomlin's microworld environment led to the discovery of features of effective tutor-student dialogue that help to expand functionalist explanations of grammatical phenomena in second language acquisition (Tomlin, 1994).

Variation in ICALL

The systems featured in this book vary extensively, and we described some of the more important variations in a synopsis of the ARI workshop published in *Computer Assisted Language Learning* (Holland, 1993; Oxford, 1993). Obviously, the languages and skill levels targeted, the scope of the NLP, and the pedagogical approaches all differ widely. Important for assessment, the very purpose of ICALL systems ranges from strictly research (many of the systems presented in Swartz & Yazdani, 1992) to strictly teaching (many of the systems in this volume) to joint goals (e.g., in this volume, Levin & Evans' ALICE-chan and ARI's BRIDGE). Understanding these differences, and the reasons for them, is key to any evaluative comparison of systems. The organizing principle for this book is the aspect of learner knowledge addressed by the tutor—whether language alone (text-based tutors) or language coupled with its visual terrains of reference (graphics-based tutors).

Section I, Text-Based Tutors and Learning Environments, presents systems that have been most influenced by linguistic theory and that tend to provide, in the case of the directed tutors, conventional kinds of language exercises with grammatical feedback. Section II, Text-Based Language Games, presents tutors influenced by communicative language teaching, which provide dialogue games that unfold through purely linguistic interaction. Section III, Graphics-Based Language Tutors, presents tutors that respond to communicative approaches by embedding linguistic interaction in visual microworlds. Section IV gathers discussants who have viewed the systems and read the chapters. They consider—from the perspectives of linguistics, experimental psychology, language teaching, and second language acquisition—what these systems can take from and give back to theory. Preceding each section is this editor's commentary on the chapters included there and the issues that emerge from them.

Beyond Theory: Transferring the Technology

I had planned to devote this introduction to theoretical issues that shape and grow out of intelligent language tutors, but there is another pressing issue.

Many of the ICALL projects described in this book are destined to remain unfinished. They will not have a chance to be integrated into programs of language teaching or research, where their effectiveness can be assessed and strategies for utilization worked out. The story is familiar: Research and development funds are spent on training technology that does not get used because resources are unavailable to complete the job. U.S. Government sponsorship to date has been largely distributed between the Department of Education (systems by Douglas, Loritz, Sanders & Sanders, and Tomlin) and the Department of Defense (systems by Levin & Evans, Rypa & Feuerman, and ARI, with Frederiksen et al.'s system funded in part by the Canadian army).[3] The DoD efforts have tended to be grammar focused, offering students structural exercises and feedback. The Education efforts have tended to be communicatively focused, having students do things with language in a microworld.[4]

This funding has been generally scattered and sporadic. Sponsoring agencies and offices may be unaware of each other's efforts, and, without a unified constituency for ICALL, scarce resources are moved elsewhere. Partly as a result, further progress in this field is at risk. We know that priorities shift. We know that the technology is in many respects unproven. But we have seen firsthand that many of these systems are ready or nearly ready for users and that all brim with ideas about how to exploit NLP to provide creative practice, diagnostic feedback, structural insights, and simulated conversation in a variety of languages, including English. We hope that by demonstrating these ideas, this book will stimulate others to revive and extend them in developing future language teaching systems.

Moreover, this body of work demonstrates the enormous potential of government-funded programs to cross over into schools and business. What can be done to make available to this larger community those systems that are approaching completion? At the workshop that preceded this book, one speaker made a plea for technology transfer: The government, especially DoD, has put significant resources into ICALL, and this technology now has the potential to help civilians. Another participant countered that DoD-developed technology is of dubious value for general use, that it is too narrow and grammar focused, and that the stimulation should flow the other way, from civilian projects to DoD. These counterclaims have merit. However, the larger point remains. Reusable ICALL technologies in the form of parsers, morphology analyzers, large-scale electronic lexicons, and authoring interfaces could be put to use in numerous applications—in creating varied lessons for multiple audiences, in developing on-line assistants and job aids for readers and translators, and in organizing data banks of exploratory language resources. If the core NLP technologies have anything at all to offer the larger community who want to teach and learn languages, and we think they do, some of their richest examples can be found in DoD.

Private companies will not, understandably, undertake technology transfer unless they foresee a profit. It remains a question whether companies will consider the costs of defense conversion, packaging, and promotion worthwhile in the case of educational software. Public schools do not have an established history of returns on R&D investment; they are often hard pressed to pay commercial prices. If schools cannot buy innovative computer programs for what are deemed essential subjects, they are hardly likely to do so for subjects that are considered peripheral, like foreign languages. The obvious market for advanced language training technology is business and industry,

---

[3] In other government funding, aspects of Murray's and Felshin's Athena work were funded by the National Endowment for the Humanities, and aspects of Hamburger's FLUENT, by the National Science Foundation.

[4] This reflects the differing needs of the respective student populations, from intelligence analysts (DoD) to school students (Education).

motivated by international trade and investment opportunities offered by NAFTA and GATT. But how does that help public education?

We can point to a handful of successful efforts to commercialize defense-developed educational software that are also benefitting schools. ARI's Job Skills Education Program (Farr & Ward, 1988), the CIA's multimedia Spanish tutor EXITO ("Federal Language Community," 1994), and the U.S. Air Force Academy's foreign language IVD programs (Heinz, Bishop, & Sutherland, 1994) are all being packaged, publicized, and sold by commercial partners through cooperative research and development agreements (CRDAs) with the government. Prices are adjustable. ARI's CRDA, for example, stipulated that the Job Skills Education Program be sold to nonprofit institutions at substantially reduced cost. In this way the program benefits schools and prisons even as its business sales turn a profit for the developer (B. J. Farr, personal communication, October 12, 1994).

Language and Culture

We do not presume that the technologies described in this book can solve our country's monolingual problem, even if they were widely available to language learners. Computer tutors will not replace classroom communication or real immersion experience. Even the language games and simulations—the "immersion technologies," as they have been called—do not substitute for the real thing. ARI's target users, military language specialists, perform jobs ranging from intelligence gathering to humanitarian assistance. They need help with job-focused language, which has the best promise of being machine-tractable. Even here, I was told by specialists whom I worked with at one army school—who were recognized as the military's most fluent speakers of Arabic or Korean or German, who took pride in their skill and spent hours of their own time reading and practicing it, who competed for overseas assignments, and who obviously loved the language—even here, I was told, there is no substitute for the real thing. As one captain put it, who had mastered her German on location by seeking out Germans and talking to them at every opportunity, "you have to throw yourself into the language, you have to get bloodied and bruised by it, put it, before you can call it your own." Some may prefer a different metaphor, but the message is clear: Immersion is hard, even painful. Yet, real fluency requires a motivation to know other groups (Gardner, 1985). It requires a lived knowledge of culture and language interwoven in infinitely complex ways (Heath, 1983; Hymes, 1972; Karttunen, 1994; Murray, this volume)—a knowledge that goes beyond the wherewithal of computational representation, that takes being there.

We realize this. We offer these technologies as ways to buttress lived experience. Students who are afraid to get bruised in the classroom can try things out with the computer. Students who have difficulty with grammar can get focused on form with a parser. Students with time on their hands can have more fun with computer language games than with workbooks or tapes and are more likely to keep up their skill. Finally, these technologies have a role in the workplace, where foreign language proficiency is likely to go a long way in trading, negotiating, and scientific exchange—where access to advanced technologies for language learning can facilitate national competitiveness and foster global cooperation.

Acknowledgments

The views expressed in this introduction are those of the author and should not be construed as an official Department of the Army position, policy, or decision.

References

ARPA (1994). *Proceedings of the Advanced Research Projects Agency (ARPA) sixth message understanding conference (MUC-6)*. San Francisco: Kaufmann.

Asher, J. (1977). *Learning another language through actions: The complete teacher's guidebook.* Los Gatos, CA: Sky Oaks Publications.

Bernstein, J. (1994). *Speech recognition in language education.* Proceedings of CALICO 94 (Eleventh Annual Symposium of the Computer Assisted Language Instruction Consortium). Durham, NC: Duke University.

Dorr, B.J., Garman, J., & Weinberg, A. (1994). *From subcategorization frames to thematic roles: Building Arabic lexical entries for foreign language tutoring.* Manuscript submitted for publication.

Doughty, C. (1993, March). *Focus on form: What is it? (Research and pedagogical issues).* Paper presented at Georgetown University Roundtable on Languages and Linguistics (presession), Washington, DC.

Farr, B.J., & Ward, J.S. (1988). The Job Skills Education Program: Technology transfer. In *Proceedings of the 1988 Conference on Technology in Training and Education.* Biloxi, MS: U.S. Air Force.

Federal language community receives Hammer Award (1994, winter). *The CALLer* (Newsletter of the Center for Advancement of Language Learning), pp. 1-2.

Feuerman, K., Marshall, C., Newman, D., & Rypa, M. (1987). The CALLE project. *The CALICO Journal, 4*, 25-34.

Fletcher, W.H. (1990). Authentic interactive video for lower-level Spanish at the United States Naval Academy. *Hispania, 73*, 859-865.

Furstenberg, G. (1992). Developing comprehension of spoken French through interaction within an authentic cultural context. In R. Kozma & J. Johnston (Eds.), *Educational computing in the humanities.* Ann Arbor, MI: Institute for Social Research.

Gardner, R.C. (1985). *Social psychology and second language learning: The role of attitudes and motivation.* London: Edward Arnold.

Gass, S., & Selinker, L. (1994). *Second language acquisition.* Hillsdale, NJ: Lawrence Erlbaum Associates.

Givon, T. (1984). Universals of discourse structure and second language acquisition. In W. Rutherford (Ed.), *Language universals and second language acquisition* (pp. 109-136). Amsterdam: John Benjamins.

Hammerly, H. (1991). *Fluency and accuracy.* Clevedon, UK: Multilingual Matters.

Hart, R. (1994). The German Newsroom: Writing German through multimedia. *The Educator's Tech Exchange, 2*, 6-13.

Heath, S.B. (1983). *Ways with words: Language, life, and work in communities and classrooms.* Cambridge, UK: Cambridge University Press.

Heinz, P., Bishop, S., & Sutherland, R. (1994, March). *A new model for government and industry to support language instruction: The cooperative research and development agreement (CRDA) between the U.S. Air Force Academy and HRB-Systems.* Paper presented at the Computer Assisted Language Instruction Consortium (CALICO), Northern Arizona University.

Holland, V.M. (1993). Intelligent computers for learning languages: The view for language acquisition and instructional methodology (Forum II). *Computer Assisted Language Learning, 6*, 179-188.

Holland, V.M., Maisano, R., Alderks, C., & Martin, J. (1993). Parsers in tutors: What are they good for? *The CALICO Journal, 11*, 28-46.

Hymes, D. (1972). Studying the interaction of language and social life. In J. Gumperz & D. Hymes (Eds.), *Directions in sociolinguistics.* New York: Holt, Reinhart, and Winston.

Karttunen, F. (1994). *Between worlds: Interpreters, guides, and survivors.* New Brunswick, NJ: Rutgers.

Kramsch, C. (1989). New directions in the teaching of language and culture. *Occasional Papers of the National Foreign Language Center*, No. 4, Washington, D.C.

Krashen, S., & Terrell, T. (1983). *The natural approach*. New York: Pergamon & San Francisco: Alemany.

Larsen-Freeman, D., & Long, M. (1991). *An introduction to second language acquisition*. London: Longman.

Lightbown, P., & Spada, M. (1990). Focus on form and corrective feedback in communicative language teaching: Effects on second language learning. *Studies in SLA*, *12*, 4.

Mostow, J., Roth, S., Hauptmann, A., & Kane, M. (1994). A prototype reading coach that listens. In *Proceedings of the Twelfth National Conference on Artificial Intelligence* (AAAI-94) (pp. 785-792). San Mateo, CA: Kaufmann.

Nagata, N. (1992). *A study of the effectiveness of Intelligent CALI as an application of natural language processing*. Doctoral dissertation, University of Pittsburgh, PA.

Nirenburg, S. (Ed.) (1993). *Progress in machine translation*. Amsterdam: IOS Press.

Oxford, R.L. (1993). Intelligent computers for learning languages: The view for language acquisition and instructional methodology (Forum I). *Computer Assisted Language Learning*, *6*, 175-179.

Rubin, J., Ediger, A., Coffin, E., Van Handle, D., & Whiskeyman, A. (1991). Survey of interactive language video discs. *The CALICO Journal*, *8*, 65-94.

Selinker, L. (1992). *Rediscovering interlanguage*. London: Longman.

Swartz, M. L., & Yazdani, M. (Eds). (1992). *Intelligent tutoring systems for foreign language learning: The bridge to international communication*. New York: Springer-Verlag.

Tomlin, R.S. (1994). Repetition in second language acquisition. In B. Johnstone (Ed.), *Repetition in discourse: Interdisciplinary perspectives* (pp. 172-194). New York: Ablex.

Waters, R.C. (1994). *The audio interactive tutor* (Technical Report No. 94-04). Cambridge, MA: Mitsubishi Electronic Research Labs.

Contributors

Alan Bailin, PhD
Professor, Department of Effective Writing
Director, Writing Center
University of Western Ontario
London, Ontario, Canada

Scott Blanksteen
Department of Computer Science
University of Maryland
College Park, Maryland

Eleanor Criswell, PhD
Manager, Intelligent Technology Division
Science Applications International Corp.
McLean, Virginia

Michel Décary
Department of Linguistics
University of Montreal
Montreal, Quebec, Canada

William DeSmedt
President, amber productions
Milford, Pennsylvania
and Technical Director, JYACC
New York, New York

Janet Donin, PhD
Professor, Department of Education in Second Languages
and Laboratory of Applied Cognitive Science
McGill University
Montreal, Quebec, Canada

Bonnie Dorr, PhD
Professor, Department of Computer Science
and Institute for Advanced Computer Studies
University of Maryland
College Park, Maryland

Sarah Douglas, PhD
Professor, Department of Computer and Information Science
and Institute of Cognitive and Decision Sciences
University of Oregon
Eugene, Oregon

David Evans, PhD
Professor, Linguistics and Computer Science
Director, Laboratory for Computational Linguistics
Carnegie Mellon University
Pittsburgh, Pennsylvania

Sue Felshin
Head Linguistic Programmer
Laboratory for Advanced Technology in the Humanities
Massachusetts Institute of Technology
Cambridge, Massachusetts

Ken Feuerman, PhD
Principal Member Engineering Staff
Xerox Special Information Systems at Xerox PARC
Palo Alto, California

Carl Frederiksen, PhD
Professor, Department of Educational Psychology
Director, Laboratory of Applied Cognitive Science
McGill University
Montreal, Quebec, Canada

Joseph Garman
Department of Linguistics
University of Maryland
College Park, Maryland

Nina Garrett, PhD
Professor, Department of Foreign Languages and Literatures
George Mason University
Fairfax, Virginia
and Center for Advancement of Language Learning
Arlington, Virginia

Henry Hamburger, PhD
Professor, Department of Computer Science
George Mason University
Fairfax, Virginia
and Naval Research Laboratory
Washington, D.C.

James Hendler, PhD
Professor, Department of Computer Science
and Institute for Advanced Computer Studies
University of Maryland
College Park, Maryland

Melissa Holland, PhD
Senior Research Psychologist
U.S. Army Research Institute
Alexandria, Virginia

Jonathan Kaplan, PhD
Senior Research Psychologist
U.S. Army Research Institute
Alexandria, Virginia

Stephen Kreyer
Intelligent Technology Division
Science Applications International Corp.
McLean, Virginia

Lori Levin, PhD
Research Scientist, Center for Machine Translation
Faculty, Computational Linguistics Program
Carnegie Mellon University
Pittsburgh, Pennsylvania

Donald Loritz, PhD
Professor, Department of Linguistics
Georgetown, University
Washington, D.C.

Brian MacWhinney, PhD
Professor, Department of Psychology
Carnegie Mellon University
Pittsburgh, Pennsylvania

Jeffery Martin
Department of Linguistics
University of Maryland
College Park, Maryland

Paola Merlo, PhD
Professor, Department of Psychology
University of Geneva
Geneva, Switzerland

Barrie Migdaloff
Department of Computer Science
University of Maryland
College Park, Maryland

Janet Murray, PhD
Professor, Department of Humanities
Director, Laboratory for Advanced Technology in the Humanities
Massachusetts Institute of Technology
Cambridge, Massachusetts

Rebecca Oxford, PhD
Professor, College of Education
and Department of English
Coordinator, Foreign Language Education
University of Alabama
Tuscaloosa, Alabama

Marikka Rypa, PhD
Research Engineer, Language Education
SRI International
Menlo Park, California
(formerly of Xerox Special Information Systems at Xerox PARC)

Michelle Sams, PhD
Senior Research Psychologist
U.S. Army Research Institute
Alexandria, Virginia

Alton Sanders, PhD
Professor, Department of Systems Analysis
Miami University
Oxford, Ohio

Ruth Sanders, PhD
Professor, Department of German, Russian, and East Asian Languages
Miami University
Oxford, Ohio

Russell Tomlin, PhD
Professor, Department of Linguistics
and Institute of Cognitive and Decision Sciences
University of Oregon
Eugene, Oregon

Amy Weinberg, PhD
Professor, Department of Linguistics
and Institute for Advanced Computer Studies
University of Maryland
College Park, Maryland

Section I: Introduction

Text-Based Language Tutors and Learning Environments

The Systems

Section I presents systems for intelligent computer-assisted language learning (ICALL) that are largely text-based, both in terms of what the user puts in and in terms of how the system prompts and reacts to it. The emphasis is on the parser and its accompanying lexicon and morphology. This emphasis, capitalizing on the strength of syntactic analysis in current natural language processing (NLP) technology, moves pedagogy in the direction of grammar-focused instruction. The contrast is clear between the systems in Section I and the communicative games and visual microworlds that dominate the succeeding sections of the book.

At the same time, the systems in this section vary widely in goals and methods. They range in pedagogical approach from directed tutors to exploratory learning tools and environments. The directed tutors are represented by Levin and Evans' ALICE-chan for Japanese and by the Army Research Institute's (ARI's) BRIDGE for German, discussed in the chapters by Kreyer and Criswell, by Sams, and by Weinberg, Garman, Martin, and Merlo. The learning environments are represented by the interactive grammar checkers of Loritz, part of the multilingual suite he calls GPARS, and by two reading assistants—Rypa and Feuerman's CALLE for Spanish and Frederiksen, Donin, and Décary's McGill Language Learning Environment for French. The language skills taught by these systems include not only the sentence production that is ICALL's trademark but also text comprehension, fostered by the reading assistants. The linguistic theories applied encompass government and binding (GB) and lexical-functional grammar (LFG), with parsing frameworks ranging from unification approaches to augmented transition networks (ATNs).

Emerging Issues

Choosing a Linguistic Framework: The Relative Benefits of Particular Formalisms
Linguistic theory significantly shapes the BRIDGE, ALICE-chan, and CALLE systems, and to some extent GPARS. The variation in linguistic underpinnings of these systems drives one of the key issues in this section, how to choose grammatical formalisms for ICALL. Weinberg et al. argue for GB theory on grounds of the broad goals of the BRIDGE application, which call for compactness within a language and extendibility across languages. These goals are best addressed, in their view, by a principles and parameters parser. Although not referenced by Weinberg et al., a related argument for GB was made by Matthews (1993) on the basis of explanatory adequacy—that is, its coherence as a theory of second language acquisition. Rypa and Feuerman espouse LFG on grounds of communicative adequacy. They argue that the categories LFG delivers and the relations it reveals convey structural insights they hypothesize as critical to language learning. Loritz favors an ATN-based formalism because of its psycholinguistic

suitability in describing grammatical development as patterns of learned behavior—a connectionist perspective. These choices affect what the systems ultimately look like.

However, at the workshop preceding this book, there was some consensus that, regardless of the criterion applied, the question of linguistic formalism pales against questions of using the formalism to teach. This suggestion is implicit in the discussion by Levin and Evans, who employ LFG and who take up the criterion of compactness from that viewpoint, providing counterbalance to Weinberg et al.

A possible conclusion from these chapters—worth debating—is that the choice of linguistic framework is more a matter of taste and habit than it is of objectively matching theory to criteria for ICALL. The argument for explanatory adequacy by Matthews remains interesting but is not broached by any of the developers in this book, perhaps because adequacy on other grounds—compactness, extendibility, communicativeness, ease of handling—is closer to practice. As Sanders points out in Section II, applied questions tend to supersede theoretical questions in the long-term development of a project. Moreover, even for explanatory adequacy, it is by no means indisputable that GB provides the best account of second language acquisition, as work by MacWhinney and by Garrett suggest (see their discussions in Section IV).

Frederiksen et al. approach the choice of formalism from a different angle in their McGill Language Learning Environment. The levels of language analysis offered to users and the features of each level are the overriding concern; the linguistic frameworks used to represent those features are incidental. The levels of analysis in the system derive from cognitive models of how people process discourse. The resulting design, mapping syntactic structures to discourse scripts and conceptual frames, owes its broad shape to theories of text comprehension which, in turn, have empirical validation in research on component mental processes. Unique in this volume, Frederiksen et al. rely on explicit models of discourse processing to tell them what to put in a language tutor. The authors point out that linguistic theories are not psychological models and suggest that the latter are more pertinent to shaping systems for language learning.

Integrating Instruction with NLP Capabilities

An issue implicit in several chapters is the integration of instructional activities with parsing capabilities. The chapters by Levin and Evans and by Rypa and Feuerman describe two highly focused systems, ALICE-chan and CALLE, whose exercises are designed to respect the parser's limitations while making the most of its possibilities. These chapters provide object lessons in creative response to constraints. ARI's BRIDGE tutor is addressed in three chapters, including introduction to the umbrella ARI program (which includes the MILT system described in Section III). This disproportionate coverage reflects the system's multidimensional focus. Unlike ALICE-chan and CALLE, BRIDGE was developed by a large interdisciplinary team with diffuse ends: a robust and extensible parser, as described by Weinberg et al.; communicative lessons covering a gamut of tasks, as described by Sams; and open-access authoring and lesson structuring, as described by Kreyer and Criswell. To some extent, these ends did not get fully integrated, as suggested by Sams, and the goals of communication were displaced by goals of form-focused instruction. Kreyer and Criswell reveal some of the tradeoffs they confronted in trying to develop a fully authorable tutor that at the same time meets the other goals of the project.

The suite of grammar checkers by Loritz is designed to handle students' freely input sentences and errors, so in some ways it demands the fullest coverage of the least constrained language. To make this task NLP-manageable, Loritz's strategy is to target low-level grammatical phenomena and to select populations whose constructions and solecisms are in theory highly consistent. One such population is deaf learners of English as a second language (ESL). His tactic is to conduct extensive parser training on sizable samples of sentences collected from the designated population (a tactic not discussed in his chapter but in work referenced there).[1] Connectionist theory helped motivate Loritz's choice of the ATN formalism and his corpus-driven approach to parser development.

Exploiting NLP for Instruction

A corollary issue concerns how to exploit NLP for tutoring. The most thoroughly explicated techniques appear in the chapter by Rypa and Feuerman, who describe methods of extracting LFG data from selected text samples not only to support text comprehension but also to deepen learners' structural awareness of the language. They view LFG as a "vehicle for knowledge representation" that designers can mine for information learners need. In this way, LFG serves the goal of knowledge communication that Wenger (1987) articulated for intelligent tutoring systems. CALLE seeks to dispel just those syntactic and lexical confusions that are common in learners of Spanish and that are suited to illumination by LFG—for example, constructions in which the functional roles of words in sentences differ subtly, as in the uses of *se*, or in which they are obscure, as in concatenated clitic structures (*quitarselas*). The adaptability of LFG to communicating functional roles thus influences the phenomena addressed by CALLE and the richness of the information delivered to the student.

The feedback to students in ALICE-chan, which also uses LFG, is equally rich in relational (not just error identification) information. Levin and Evans further deploy the parser in ALICE-chan to assist the instructor in authoring lessons. They demonstrate a matching technique that allows instructors to create free response questions to which they write only single target answers. Each answer formulated by the instructor is then analyzed by the NLP into an abstract representation that handles automatically much of the expected variation in students' responses. Levin and Evans' technique is expanded by Dorr et al. in Section III.

On the other hand, the BRIDGE parser is used for simple error identification, so the feedback to students is more limited as well as more concise. The varying degrees of depth provided by these three systems is influenced by the supporting linguistic theories (LFG versus GB) as well as by the application context. Users of ALICE-chan and CALLE were originally intended to be document analysts and translators, who need structural depth; users of BRIDGE were intended to be military interrogators or interpreters, who must perform quickly. The chapter by Sams shows how BRIDGE taps

---

[1] The NLP community uses the term "training" to mean empirically tailoring a parser to handle a given sample of input language.

the record of parser-derived errors to form a student performance profile on which lesson branching and progression is based. Kreyer and Criswell demonstrate how the rules that govern this branching and progression can be controlled by instructors.

In another kind of exploitation, Loritz taps the capabilities of the parser for instructional assessment and diagnosis. He demonstrates how to derive a map of students' construction usage by elaborating the state diagram on which the ATN parser is based. Teachers or researchers can then use these competency maps to view and compare the sentence patterns prevalent in different groups of learners.

The pedagogical assumption behind these systems is that learning is improved by a conscious reflection on linguistic patterns brought about through explicit instruction. This assumption, however, is not without debate in discussions of mechanisms regulating second language acquisition (Ellis, 1994). Indeed, these chapters largely do not address the status of the designers' assumptions with respect to current debates about learning and pedagogy; nor is much consideration given to how the tutors specifically interact with theories of language acquisition and with the phases and modes of learning posited in the those theories (e.g., Bialystok, 1994).

The problem of lexicon is also given little attention, probably because so few of these systems have passed the concept demonstration stage. A fieldable tutor ultimately requires scaling up from the relatively small, hand-constructed computational vocabularies typical of ICALL systems. To build sizable lexicons efficiently will require leveraging automatic techniques for extracting lexical information from electronic dictionaries or from on-line corpora, techniques used successfully in machine translation (Farwell, Guthrie, & Wilks, 1993; Hovy & Knight, 1993; Ide & Veronis, 1994; McKeown & Passonneau, 1994). ICALL has only recently begun to explore the acquisition of lexicons from machine-readable dictionaries (e.g., Dorr, Garman, & Weinberg, 1994) or the direct deployment of on-line lexical resources in vocabulary learning (Cumming, Cropp, & Sussex, 1994).

Ensuring Reliable Parser Performance

An issue unspoken in most chapters but inescapably shadowing any NLP project is how to ensure the reliability of the parser. This problem is typically of little interest to theorists in linguistics and pedagogy, but addressing it is necessary to put linguistic or pedagogical ideas into practice. Loritz has treated this problem in past work, as we mentioned, by attempting to train the parser empirically on samples of student-produced text. His chapter reports parser accuracy rates arising from that work. The only other developers in this section to report reliability statistics are Weinberg et al. However, their figures apply to only a small sample of sentences; moreover, that sample was created by the system developers, and we do not know how representative it is of what students produce.

We might ask how reliable a parser needs to be for ICALL. Machine translation and message extraction systems can survive on less than perfect accuracy rates because the humans who use those systems understand the limitations and will do postprocessing by hand. ICALL's users are students who, we assume, depend on the parser for something approaching guaranteed results. Errant feedback can at best confuse students and at worst mislead them into mislearning. Many ICALL developers cite the need for robustness in NLP analyses, but they lack an empirical methodology for improving and measuring it, such as has been developed in more traditional NLP applications (e.g., ARPA, 1993).

Increasing the accuracy of parsing involves tradeoffs with other performance factors, like speed, coverage, and automaticity of analysis. A concept for balancing these tradeoffs is explained by Levin and Evans.

Assessing Usability and Effectiveness

The issues of tutor usability and effectiveness are also inescapable and equally unexplored in these chapters. Most systems are not yet complete enough for formal testing. Nevertheless, Sams reports that influential data about the usability and performance of BRIDGE came from even the most preliminary pilot trials. She describes a method of iterative user testing to prevent development of lesson interfaces and forms of feedback that ultimately prove unusable. The need for user trials early and often is echoed by developers who are also teachers, such as Bailin (Section IV), who discusses benefits of beta testing, and Mulford (personal communication, April 14, 1993). Loritz reports usability results more formally obtained. Significantly, the disappointing findings of the first trial of his ESL system are on user interface grounds and not (yet) on parser performance grounds. Indeed, Loritz's conclusion that his system will not help most of the intended population is open to question: Why not improve the system interface, then test whether more students can use it?

We begin to see how the assessment of an ICALL system might be organized. We do not know for any of these systems how well the parser can handle students' language once they start to use it, or how much students will ultimately benefit, but user interface difficulties clearly must be resolved before relevant data can be obtained.

Together, then, the issues raised in this introduction point to the need for a framework for evaluating ICALL designs. We have virtually no data on the utility for language learning of particular linguistic frameworks, feedback strategies, or reliability thresholds. User interface issues are a logical first topic to probe: Can students understand what they are supposed to do? Can they understand and use the feedback given? Parser performance issues follow: Does the parser adequately cover what students type in or, in the case of the reading assistants, what they want to see? Needed are standard ways of collecting a corpus of student language, ensuring its representativeness, and reporting the data. Effectiveness issues come next: Given the theoretically grounded structural representations provided in systems like CALLE and the McGill Environment, how well do those representations actually teach? Do users of any of these systems improve their skills in ways that teachers or the language learning community care about? Compared to what alternative interventions? As Frederiksen et al. note, effectiveness research requires a cyclical agenda. Findings about the pedagogical strategies and conditions involved in successful learning can be used to refine subsequent ICALL, which then undergoes further testing. In addition, effectiveness requires considerations of context. To draw again on Loritz, if a potential help rate of 25% of students is not high enough to warrant classroom use of his system, why not examine the benefits of the system made available selectively in language lab or study hall? A final set of issues involves cost: Can observed gains be brought about in other ways that are less expensive than NLP? How much cost is reduced by steps such as reusing parsers and lexicons from other NLP applications or employing automated acquisition tools? Frameworks for assessment will be revisited in Section IV.

References

ARPA (1993). *Proceedings of the fifth message understanding conference (MUC-5)*. San Francisco: Kaufmann.

Bialystok, E. (1994). Representation and ways of knowing: Three issues in second language acquisition. In Ellis, N.C.

Cumming, G., Cropp, S., & Sussex, R. (1994). On-line lexical resources for language learners: Assessment of some approaches to word definition. *System*, *22*, 369-377.

Ellis, N.C. (Ed.). (1994). *Implicit and explicit learning of languages*. London: Academic Press.

Farwell, D., Guthrie, L., & Wilks, Y. (1993). Automatically creating lexical entries for ULTRA, a multilingual MT system. *Machine Translation*, 8.

Hovy, E., & Knight, K. (1993). Motivating shared knowledge resources: An example from the Pangloss collaboration. In *Proceedings of the 1993 International Joint Conference of Artificial Intelligence*. San Mateo, CA: Kaufmann.

Ide, N., & Veronis, J. (1994). Have we wasted our time? Considering machine readable dictionaries. *Cambridge Language Reference News*, *4*, 1.

Matthews, C. (1993). Grammar frameworks in intelligent CALL. *The CALICO Journal*, *11*, 5-28.

McKeown, K., & Passonneau, R. (1994). Extracting constraints on word usage from large text corpora. In *Proceedings of the ARPA Human Language Technology Workshop*. San Francisco: Kaufmann.

Wenger, E. (1987). *Artificial intelligence and tutoring systems: Computational and cognitive approaches to the communication of knowledge*. Los Altos, CA: Kaufmann.

1

Advanced Technologies for Language Learning: The BRIDGE Project Within the ARI Language Tutor Program

Michelle R. Sams
U.S. Army Research Institute

Language Training in the Military

The post-cold war era of international affairs has seen the United States take military actions in concert with its allies abroad. U.S. soldiers and leaders must be able to communicate with their friends as well as with their foes. Military personnel who need foreign language skills are usually formally schooled in a classroom setting, such as the Defense Language Institute Foreign Language Center, and then proceed to advanced military-specific training that may cover such tasks as how to gather intelligence information. Often this advanced training does not include any further language training, and it is up to the soldiers to maintain their language skills during their off-duty hours. Most training installations provide a language lab for self-study for these purposes. Nevertheless, it has been found that soldiers' language skills, particularly productive skills, decay rapidly during this advanced training period (Jackson, 1994; Lett & O'Mara, 1990).

Fluency in a language incorporates both comprehension (listening and reading) and production (speaking and writing). Military language labs typically have many forms of passive materials to support maintenance of language comprehension, such as periodicals and television news broadcasts from the native countries. There are more active environments in the form of computer-based instruction, especially interactive video disc and hypermedia programs (Bickes & Scott, 1989; Rubin, Ediger, Coffin, Van Handle, & Whiskeyman, 1991). However, the majority of these programs are based on the student's recognition of correct responses (e.g., through selecting multiple choice items) rather than on the student's production of responses. Some programs allow students to produce their responses via typed word or sentence input; however, these inputs are unnaturally constrained due to a reliance on either a string or a keyword matching approach to determine correctness (Burston, 1989).

The Army Research Institute (ARI) believes that the optimal language sustainment and enhancement environments are those in which the student actively participates in the language (including production), practices job-relevant skills, and receives individual tutoring. The Army Research Institute recognized that various emerging technologies could be innovatively combined to create such environments in a cost-effective and portable computer tutor (Swartz & Psotka, 1989). The ultimate goal is for the computer and the human to exchange information much like two humans in a dialogue. Computational linguists, computer scientists, and cognitive psychologists have contributed to this goal through the field of natural language processing (NLP).

The Need for NLP

It can be argued that NLP holds the best promise for communicative language learning in a computing environment. The challenge of ARI's first language tutor project, known as BRIDGE, was to devise a way to use NLP to analyze student input that is not in correct form, identify multiple grammatical errors within a sentence, provide descriptive feedback to the student, build a model of the student's strengths and weaknesses, and then use that information to drive lesson progression and remediation. BRIDGE was developed fully for German, with a parser extension to Arabic. Our second and current project, known as the Military Language Tutor (MILT), is intended to immerse the student more fully in a job-oriented language environment. The target languages are Arabic and Spanish. Building on the BRIDGE foundation, the MILT project adds semantic components that can analyze the meaning, not just the form of students' input. This new semantic capability supports a dialogue module for military intelligence students to practice interrogation skills. It also supports an animated graphics microworld in which students can explore the consequences of their language use. Both generations of tutors are designed to be cost-effective to the military community by providing an easy authoring system for instructors and by operating on a DOS-based (80486) platform.

It may be apparent that BRIDGE is a characteristically text-based tutor, whereas MILT is intended to support both dialogue- and graphics-based language tutoring, a distinction reflecting the organizational divisions of this book. Moreover, several chapters in this book are devoted to aspects of the ARI tutors. Details of the parsing component that underlies BRIDGE and that is being extended to MILT are presented by Weinberg, Garman, Martin, and Merlo. Dorr, Hendler, Blanksteen, and Migdaloff describe the semantic capability being developed for MILT, and Kaplan and Holland describe its instructional design. The authoring interface of BRIDGE is covered by Kreyer and Criswell. This chapter overviews all these aspects, goes into some detail about the instructional functions of BRIDGE, and previews the MILT effort. This is followed by a discussion of lessons learned so far during ARI's research and development effort.

Natural Language Processing: A Brief Look at the Technology

Natural language processing (NLP) has supported foreign language applications in machine translation and in message understanding (extracting pertinent information from texts; ARPA, 1993; Nirenburg, 1993; Slocum, 1985). The NLP mechanisms in these applications are designed with the assumption that the material is in fairly correct grammatical form and is within a well-defined domain. The accuracy of machine translation continues to fall short of human translation, so practical NLP applications require pre- and postediting of target texts by hand. Utilizing NLP in language tutoring presents its own unique set of challenges, not the least of which is analyzing students' free- and ill-formed input with a much higher degree of accuracy than that acceptable in machine translation or message extraction applications. Efforts to incorporate NLP in intelligent computer assisted language learning (intelligent CALL) are fairly recent and primarily take the form of research and development projects (see this volume as well as Bailin, 1991; Swartz & Yazdani, 1992; Underwood, 1987).

There are many grammatical theories and hence different approaches to representing a grammar computationally (Allen, 1987). A brief description of a general approach to parsing follows so that the novice reader may have a better understanding of how NLP can accomplish the necessary tasks of a language tutor.

The main pieces of a typical parsing component are a text preprocessor, a morphological analyzer, a lexicon, and a syntactic parser, as shown in Figure 1.1. A parser used for intelligent CALL often additionally incorporates an error handling facility. These pieces function to identify the words in an input sentence and to analyze the relations between them. First, the written input is submitted to an interactive preprocessor which identifies spelling mistakes to the student. The morphological analyzer then decomposes the words into subparts (roots and affixes) based on information in the lexicon, or computational dictionary. Specific information is drawn from the lexicon about the word subparts (e.g., whether they signify verb or noun, singular or plural). They are then unified back into their original state and passed, along with the descriptive information from the lexicon, to the syntactic parser.

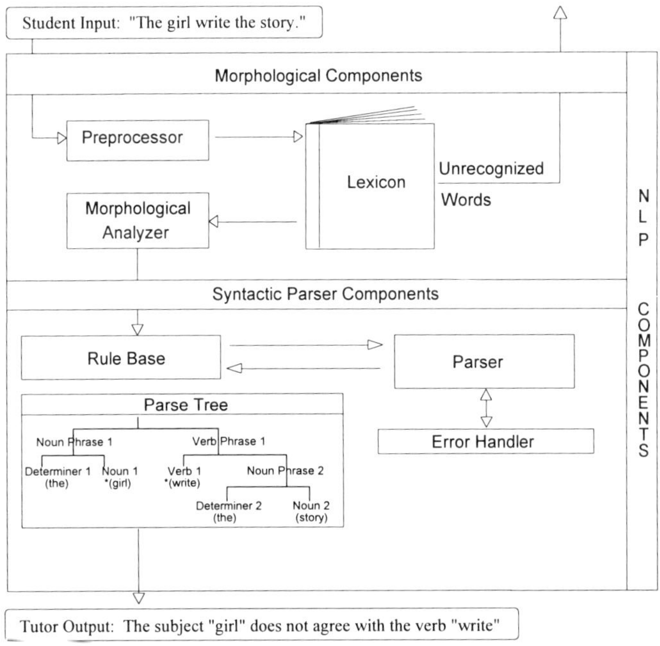

FIG. 1.1. A simplified functional diagram of a typical parsing component in a language tutor.

Based on this information, the parser tries to build a structure, called a parse tree, which reflects the grammatical relations among the words (e.g., which word is subject of the sentence, which is object of the verb). A common approach is to build this structure in a bottom-up process by identifying the smallest word combinations, or phrase units, and then combining these into higher units, ultimately resulting in the tree hierarchy. The parser applies descriptive rules from a set called a grammar (essentially, a representation of the structure of the language) until it finds those that account for the sentence structure.

Let me illustrate (see Figure 1.1) with a simplified example in English, "The girl write the story." All the words and subparts are recognized and passed on to the parser. *Write* is identified as a verb that takes a direct object. The parser looks for a noun phrase in the appropriate position (object of the verb) and thereby constructs the verb phrase branch of the tree (the verb phrase is *write the story*). It continues on in this manner until it completes the parse tree. The error handler records that a subject-verb agreement error (*girl-write*) was made. The parse tree and error report are passed to the tutor. The tutor uses the error data to trigger specific feedback to the student (e.g., "your subject and verb do not agree"). The error data can also be used to build a kind of student model. An error handler provides for robustness, so that the parser does not fail as it encounters each error, and it allows classification of the grammatical error types of importance to the instructional objectives.

NLP in the BRIDGE Tutor

Theoretical Framework

ARI's language tutor required an NLP methodology that would be accurate, tolerant of student errors, compact (for a personal computer application), and extendible across languages (for developing a family of tutors for various languages). As discussed in the chapter by Weinberg et al. (this volume), these goals motivated the choice of government-binding (GB) theory as a framework for parsing, which posits that universal abstract principles form the basic structure of all languages (Chomsky, 1981). The GB approach generates the underlying structures of a language through a small set of interacting modules and constraints, instead of developing an extensive list of specific rules that characterize all the syntactic possibilities of the language. The modular approach, with parameters that are initialized for different languages, in theory promotes both compactness within a language and extendibility across languages. The error handler in BRIDGE works by flagging instances of mismatched features (such as a singular subject with a plural verb) in the course of building a parse tree.

The BRIDGE parser can also handle some reasonable sentence fragments, so that if the tutor asked the student where Heidelberg is located, the student could appropriately type the reply, *to the south of Bonn*. However, every possible sentence construction and grammatical error cannot be captured by the parser. Therefore, determination of the range of input and error types in BRIDGE was made through analysis of language usage by the target audience—military linguists—in their job environments (Criswell, Weinberg, Miller, Byrnes & Blascak, 1989). The most common and critical linguistic problems identified were those which were included in the NLP development.

Construction, Error, and Lexical Coverage

The NLP in the German tutor draws on a lexicon of over 5,000 words (common and military) and can parse many of the basic sentence constructions used by the early intermediate student of German: Levels 1 to 2 on the Interagency Language Roundtable scale (Clark & Clifford, 1987). These types are illustrated in Weinberg et al. (this volume) and include declarative clauses, imperatives, subordination (but not relative clauses), *yes-no* and *wh*-questions, compound tenses and modals, multiple verb embedding, passives, subject inversion, and phrasal conjunction (with exceptions). In addition, the parser's error handler can identify eight classes of syntactic errors, as described by Weinberg et al., including selected errors of agreement, case selection, and word order.

Instructional Design of BRIDGE

Main Features

The BRIDGE tutor was designed to meet the needs of students, instructors, and researchers. It had to challenge students in listening, reading, and writing through a multimedia lesson, provide on-line assistance, and adapt to the individual student's capabilities. For instructors to create new lessons, the authoring interface had to be easy and require no programming. For researchers to study design and pedagogical issues, the tutor parameters (e.g., lesson branching) had to be manipulable. Criswell, Byrnes, and Pfister (1992) related the resulting tutorial design to current pedagogical theory and in particular, the contextualized language learning advocated in a communicative approach. Holland, Maisano, Alderks, and Martin (1993) describe the BRIDGE tutorial design in terms of overall issues in the design of parser-based language tutors. The sections following highlight specific features of the student and author interface.

Exercise types. The tutor has a modular, open architecture design that supports the development of different lessons and instructional approaches by authors (i.e., instructors and researchers). A variety of exercise types are available as building blocks for lessons. These include multiple choice, point-and-click on a graphic (using the cursor), fill-in-the-blanks, free responses (phrases or full sentences) to tutor queries, and sorting text items under appropriate columns. All the exercises except sorting can involve either text or oral queries from the tutor. The fill-in-the-blank and free responses are automatically sent to the NLP component for analysis. Exercises can be presented in a fixed sequence or drawn randomly from a pool of exercises within a set.

Feedback. Students receive feedback as to the correctness of their responses for all the exercise types. The most specific and diagnostic feedback is provided as a result of those exercises sent to the natural language processor. The NLP analyzes the student's input and identifies the specific grammatical errors the student made. The tutor can also classify the grammatical mistakes into primary and secondary errors, a distinction modifiable by authors. Students are automatically presented with details of their primary errors but have the option of viewing details about their secondary errors. This classification scheme was developed to promote language use while not constantly interrupting the intermediate-level student. Therefore, the instructor can determine which errors to bring to the immediate attention of the student and which errors are less important for overall lesson objectives.

Lesson progression. Progression from one exercise set to another can be in a fixed sequence or based on the student's performance. In the fixed sequence, the author determines in advance exactly which exercises the student will attempt. In an adaptive lesson, if the student demonstrates overall proficiency (e.g., answers 80% of the exercise set correctly), then the student can be moved from that set and presented with the next, more challenging exercise set. More sophisticated lesson branching can be accomplished using a student model built on output from the NLP analyses. The student model expresses the cumulative error counts within specified grammatical categories across exercise sets. If it is found that a student is making an unsatisfactory number of errors in a particular grammatical category (e.g., subject-verb agreement), then the student can be automatically branched to an exercise set providing additional assistance and practice in that problem area. After remediation, the student can return to the regular lesson. At any time, students can opt to view a graphic depicting their grammatical problem areas and general progress throughout the lesson.

Help. A variety of on-line help is available for the student through pull-down menu items. Explanations of the tutor's capabilities and exercise procedures are provided. Students may request assistance in the form of oral or written hints as they attempt to respond to each exercise. For vocabulary help, there is a German-English dictionary that can be accessed either alphabetically or through search terms, as shown in Figure 1.2.

Lesson authoring. One of the goals of the tutor was to design a lesson-authoring interface that requires no programming skills and little training. This capability allows instructors and researchers to create new lessons and test alternative instructional strategies. The author needs only to access a template of the desired exercise type and fill in the slots. Creating exercise sets, setting parameters for lesson progression, and defining feedback and hints are all enabled by easy-to-use templates. A full description of the BRIDGE authoring interface is presented in this volume by Kreyer and Criswell.

A Sample Lesson

Overall design. A sample lesson was developed to demonstrate the capabilities of the tutor within a purposeful instructional approach. The focus of this lesson is on expressions of location and direction, which are critical for military intelligence personnel and also problematic for the early intermediate-level linguist. The lesson was designed to move the student progressively from easier to more difficult exercises. Therefore, reading comprehension exercises precede listening comprehension. Recognition-based

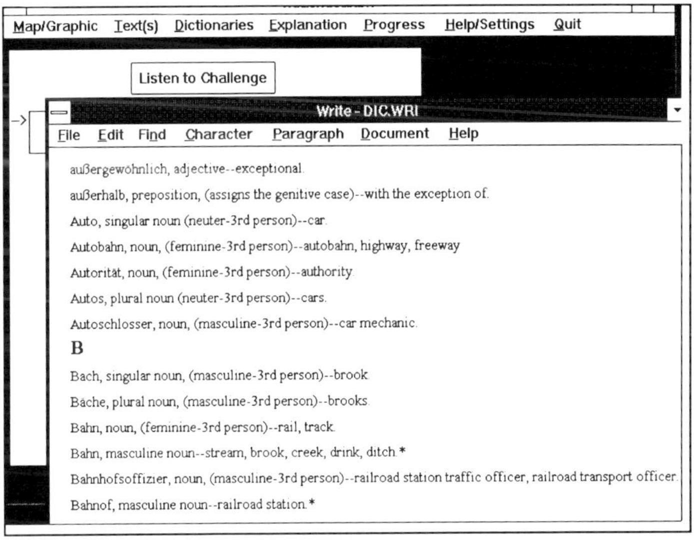

FIG. 1. 2. The pull-down student dictionary in the BRIDGE German tutor.

exercises (e.g., multiple choice) precede productive exercises (e.g., typing free sentence responses). In essence, the student moves from receptive to productive skills, from traditional exercises to more open-ended ones (see Criswell et al., 1992).

The lesson. The student begins by reading a pull-down text about a particular geographical location in Germany. An on-line map depicting the area is available for the student's reference, as is the German-English dictionary. The student can access the text, map, and dictionary at any time during the lesson. The exercises are designed not so much to test the student's knowledge of the geography but to provide a vehicle for language use in a relevant context. Multiple choice exercises touching on overall concepts in the text are presented first. These are followed by a sorting exercise, as shown in Figure 1.3, which gives the student practice in distinguishing between phrases that express direction from those that express location. Next the student interacts with the map graphic. The student points (by positioning a cursor with the mouse) to a location on the map in response to written or oral prompts from the tutor. For example, the tutor may prompt the student to point to "am Zusammenfluß" (the river junction). Following mastery of these exercises, the student begins to use the language more actively, first by producing fill-in-the-blank answers and then by freely typing answers in response to the tutor's written and oral queries about the map. A sample query and response are shown in Figure 1.4, together with the tutor's grammatical feedback.

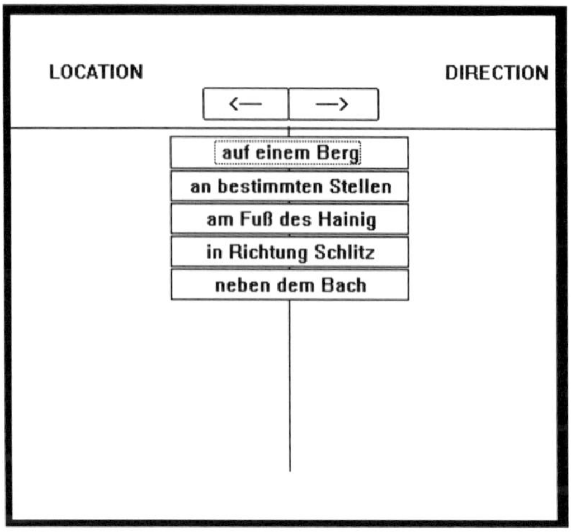

FIG. 1.3. A sample grammar sorting exercise from the BRIDGE tutor.

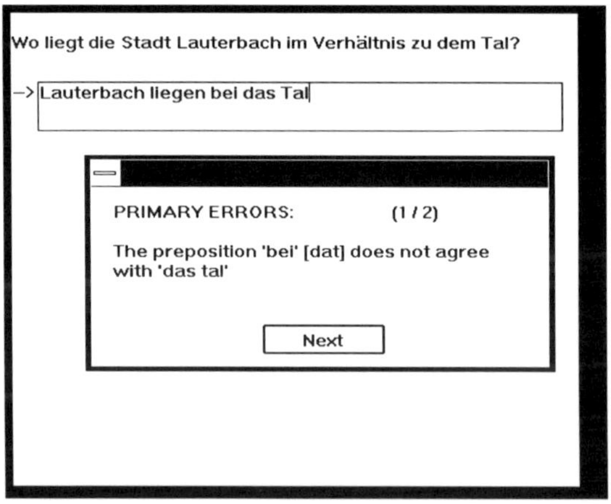

FIG. 1.4. A free response exercise in BRIDGE showing feedback for the student's preposition case error (the subject-verb error is reported in a separate window).

Feedback. The student is allowed two attempts at every exercise. After the first attempt the student may access hints about the proper response. The NLP provides specific grammatical feedback produced by the students in fill-in-the-blank and free response exercises. As explained earlier, instructors may classify errors as primary or secondary, with secondary errors viewed at the student's option. The example in Figure 1.4 shows feedback about a case error after a preposition, an error that has been classified as primary in the sample lesson. The full interaction follows (what actually appears in the tutoring environment is presented in quotations; the remainder is provided for clarification):

> *tutor*: "Wo liegt die Stadt Lauterbach im Verhäeltnis zu dem Tal?"
> (Where is Lauterbach located in relation to the valley?)
> *student*: "Lauterbach liegen bei das Tal."
> (Lauterbach is located near the valley.)
> *tutor*: "Your last response contained 1 primary and 1 secondary error."
> *primary error feedback (automatically displayed)*:
> "The preposition *bei* [dat] does not agree with *das Tal*" [student used accusative case, *das*, when it should have been dative (dat) case, *dem*.]
> *secondary error feedback (displayed at student request)*:
> "Subject and verb do not agree: *Lauterbach* with *liegen*" [student used plural, *liegen*, after the singular subject, *Lauterbach*, when it should have been singular, *liegt*.]

Because the parser is operating, the student's input can take many forms ("Beside the valley lies the city of Lauterbach," etc.) and still be analyzed by the tutor. We lacked resources to develop a semantic analyzer in the BRIDGE project, forcing us to consider alternative exercise and feedback strategies (see Holland, 1994). For example, for free response questions we can handle factual feedback, which tells whether the content of the student's answer is correct, by self-check messages ("Did you put Lauterbach near the valley?" or perhaps "...to the northeast of the valley?"). In a later refinement of BRIDGE, we added a keyword matcher to give the appearance of a meaningful analysis of students' responses. Developed at the University of Illinois (Hart, 1994), this keyword matcher permits authors to specify which words, alternative words, and word combinations should appear in an answer.

User Evaluation

Target users provided valuable input throughout the project; however, the first real "road test" took place six months prior to the end of the contract. There was some concern about presenting an incomplete product, but we felt it was imperative to get user feedback for at least the final revisions. The participants were from the U.S. Army Intelligence Center and School, Fort Huachuca, Arizona, and consisted of three instructors with a German language qualification and four students who were recent German graduates from the Defense Language Institute. While working through the exercises, each participant commented on ease of use, lesson content, and desires for modification or additional features. Instructors also explored the lesson authoring mode. Each participant was assisted when necessary by a system developer and was observed by a human factors psychologist who took notes throughout the session.

The students and instructors had varying degrees of experience with computers, operation of a mouse, and windowing environments. Those with little or no experience seemed to pick up very quickly on how to move through the exercises and access help. Almost every user had difficulty with the sorting exercise interface, and suggestions were taken for modification, some of which were incorporated in BRIDGE as well as in the later MILT (Kaplan & Holland, this volume). Students also expressed a desire to have more control while moving about the lesson material (e.g., to review a previously completed exercise). They wanted to have dictionary words voiced and to have a map more consistent with the kind they use in their jobs. Some aspects of the authoring system were straightforward; others were confusing. Perhaps the most valuable information gained related to the parser. Student entries for parser-based exercises were recorded and areas of unreliability were noted in the parse results. In fact, the data from this evaluation were the impetus for gaining additional funds to add another class of errors, involving word order, to the error handler.

In general, all users were very positive about the tutor and its approach. This was somewhat surprising considering that the tutor was still in development (complete with software bugs) and not yet fully integrated; that is, interaction with the parser had to occur in the DOS environment rather than within the tutor shell. The students seemed to understand that the parser could not handle every possible construction and, in fact, tried different inputs to test the boundaries of the system. Two students asked to see the parse trees to get a better understanding. One student who was fairly computer literate said he had been frustrated in the past with "string matching" programs and could see the benefit of a parser-based tutor. Students said they would like to practice with programs such as the ARI tutor. As pointed out by Holland et al. (1993), this receptivity to parsers may arise from the cognitive traits typical of military intelligence linguists, who tend to be analytical in style of thinking.

Our objectives now are to install the German tutor at selected military sites and to initiate a formal research project to evaluate the tutor.

Beyond BRIDGE: Advances for a Second Generation Tutor

New language interactions. The German tutor is the first product of a multiyear research and development effort. The feasibility of the NLP approach and its integration into an intelligent language tutor was demonstrated, particularly with regard to real-time diagnosis of language form (grammar). However, it is the goal of ARI's language tutor project to develop more communicative interactions for language training. Appropriate language usage in the real world usually results in one of two responses, either a conversational reply or an appropriate action (e.g., execution of a command), as discussed by Hamburger (this volume). Therefore, to support a more realistic language training environment, some major advances are needed in the second generation effort—the Military Language Tutor, which is implemented in Arabic and Spanish.

The capability to analyze meaning is the most critical component of the MILT effort. This capability will support many different types of exercises, ranging from one-turn linguistic exchanges to full discourse. The simplest functioning level will be for those exercises in which the tutor poses a question to the student (about a text or graphic material) and the student types a free response. The NLP will analyze the student's input and give feedback as to the whether the response was appropriate in meaning and factual accuracy as well as in proper grammatical form. The next level of functioning will be for the graphics animation module, in which students type commands and see animated enactments of the commands (e.g., opening a briefcase). The highest level of semantic functioning will be for a dialogue module in which students can freely query a modeled prisoner of war who will respond to the questions in some meaningful way.

Progressing through these various interactional functions (moving toward communicative realism) requires an increasing degree of linguistic proficiency on the part of the student and also requires the support of an increasing degree of software sophistication and deeper levels of NLP analysis. The interactional functions in MILT are described from the user's perspective by Kaplan and Holland (this volume), whereas the NLP mechanisms necessary to accomplish these functions are described by Dorr et al. (this volume). As the latter chapter explains, the key mechanism for semantic analysis in MILT is lexical conceptual structure, which is coupled with a matching routine in the free response exercises to check students' answers against target answers (see Levin and Evans, this volume, for a general discussion of NLP-based answer matching).

Speech recognition. ARI has emphasized that the advantage of our tutoring approach is to support language production. Our work to date has focused on written production; however, our target users desire to produce speech. We initially chose to concentrate the BRIDGE project on written production via NLP since we felt this was a gap few others were addressing and was itself a challenge. We now feel that limited speech recognition for the personal computer is commercially available, robust, and affordable (e.g., "Syracuse Language Systems," 1994). Therefore, in MILT we are including simple speech recognition exercises to give the student practice in pronunciation and in selecting by voice from multiple choice alternatives. These exercises are limited to words and short phrases. It is our future goal to provide more realistic speech-based exchanges in which students create longer utterances that are not selected from displayed alternatives.

Issues: Resolved and Unresolved

It has been said that good research generates more questions than it answers. The same thing can be said of development efforts. During the first generation tutor project, many ideas were generated that could not be incorporated due to time and money constraints. In other cases, hindsight proved better than foresight. We have learned much from our first effort and will try to integrate these lessons into the second generation program. In this section, I address just a few of the issues that are illustrative of those we have faced and will face.

The Design Process and User Involvement

Technical experts often feel that they can conceive and develop the best design for a product. What usually transpires is that each expert concentrates on optimizing his or her own separate piece of the product. Artificial intelligence experts develop ingenious ways to handle complex functions, software programmers design elegant code, and pedagogical specialists concentrate on lesson material. Even if this diverse team manages to work in a closely coordinated effort, they often overlook the most important component of the design team—the intended user of the product. Human factors psychologists (whose specialty is creating effective products) believe that the best way to ensure good design is to involve the target users early in concept design and throughout the development cycle.

Although the BRIDGE tutor project had some user input, particularly for the linguistic needs analysis, users from the target population did not try the tutor until near the end of the project. This meant that very few real changes could be made to the design. In the second generation MILT, users will be part of an iterative design cycle. This means that user input and evaluation of working prototypes (even partial ones) and paper mock-ups (e.g., lesson material) will be obtained regularly and the results folded into the continuing design and development process.

Six months after it began, the MILT project produced a *screen-state* prototype (see Kaplan & Holland, this volume). It gives the functional appearance of the real thing, but there are no actual workings behind the screen. An ARI human factors psychologist and the system developer took this early prototype to Fort Huachuca for an evaluation by military intelligence instructors and students. The purpose of this evaluation was to examine the design of the interfaces for the various exercise types and lesson authoring. Some valuable insights were gained. For example, some users were unsure about what to do next in the microworld, even though they were provided with a goal to achieve. The tutor included a hint icon with a list of allowable actions, yet the users did not spontaneously click on this icon when at a loss for ideas. Therefore, we are considering some possible solutions, such as providing a prompt for a suggested action after a certain amount of time passes with no student input. The advantage of the iterative design approach is that changes can be incorporated before money and time are spent on developing hard code. In addition, soliciting user suggestions and critiques helps foster a sense of product ownership and should facilitate the transfer of the final product to the target community.

Design Tradeoffs

One of the goals of our tutor project is to provide maximum flexibility in lesson design. This applies to instructors who want to develop new lesson material within a variety of instructional approaches and to researchers who wish to investigate language acquisition and training issues. In order to meet their needs, many aspects of the tutor must be capable of being modified. These include feedback, lesson branching, and many aspects of exercise development. The tutor must also capture student data (e.g., entries, response times). It would be easier if we were designing one tutor that put forth a single pedagogical approach, but we are, in essence, building multiple tutors in one.

When faced with a design decision, such as how many attempts at an answer a student should have, we typically tell the developer to have that parameter authorable. However, eventually one arrives at a point at which offering many options gives the author extensive control but at the same time reduces ease of use. This tradeoff is discussed by Kreyer and Criswell (this volume). Our target users are not really interested in designing new types of exercises from scratch, such as is possible through a commercial authoring system. Our current philosophy is to offer many choices within the most communicative interface possible and to deliver a working prototype with default values as a guide. We will have a sample lesson in Arabic and Spanish with lesson-branching rules complete with remediation blocks of exercises that focus on each of the errors captured by the parser. An instructor who is not interested in making new rules or new remediation blocks can simply cut and paste these components into a new lesson.

A parallel tradeoff applies to designing for student use. For example, it is perfectly feasible to allow the student to click on a word in a text and have the translation of the word automatically displayed. However, providing that capability becomes a pedagogical rather than a technical decision. If translations are provided very easily and at no cost, then will the student effectively assimilate that new vocabulary or will it be forgotten after its immediate use? Until an empirical study has answered that question, we have decided to have students look up unknown words in an on-line dictionary.

Feedback

One of the most frequent criticisms of the BRIDGE tutor for German concerns how the error feedback is presented. Early versions presented rather cryptic messages, such as "preposition + case error: bei, das_tal." These messages have been revamped, as shown in Figure 1.4. A key decision in the MILT project is how to further improve grammatical feedback, especially during the more communicative exercises (e.g., graphics microworld, dialogue). Ideally, the feedback would be handled as in the real world. For example, a conversational partner might model the correct usage: If the learner said, "I have two childs," then the native speaker might say, "How nice, two children." However, to handle feedback this way requires that the computer know the intent of the student's utterance. We are not yet able to do this but have decided to make a number of options available in the microworld and dialogue (see Kaplan & Holland, this volume). For example, errors may be reported as they occur, or the report may be saved for an *after-action review* (i.e., the military term for saving feedback until a task has been completed).

Why Parsers?

Parsing technology is quite expensive. How do we know that parsers are any good for language instruction? This question is difficult to answer at this point. The technology has not been fully developed, and we are just making inroads to semantics, which is necessary for comprehensive language instruction. Then there is the question of what is the best way to evaluate this technology. The discussion chapters in this volume offer insights. For example, Bailin says that it is a waste to do comparative studies of parser-based CALL versus traditional instruction. It is tantamount to comparing apples and oranges. Garrett points out that one cannot evaluate a piece of technology separately from the environment in which it is used. MacWhinney proposes that the most sensible evaluation is to compare one bit of technology versus another, for example, comparing the parser-based version of a system to that without a parser. This kind of study was in fact conducted for the ALICE-chan tutor by Nagata, as cited by Levin and Evans (this volume), and appears to us to be a basic step in evaluating intelligent CALL. We are currently making arrangements to conduct a similar type of study for the BRIDGE German tutor.

The Research and Development World

Conducting research on technologies that have yet to be fully proven and accepted in the user community is a challenging task. The R&D community feels they are very successful if they have pushed the technological envelope a bit and have a vision of its full implementation in the future. On the other hand, the user community has very real needs that must be met now. Our target audience (military intelligence students and instructors) have been unusually supportive, even when faced with partially developed prototypes. It just may be that this target population is more suited to dealing with the uncertainty of technology that is still developing. Their main complaint has been that the first generation tutor is largely form-based, there being no semantics to support communicative interactions. It is ARI's goal to develop a language tutor that can be used for both form- and function-based teaching. The most feasible first stage of development, BRIDGE, involved analysis of form. Our subsequent efforts are advancing toward communicative functions. It is sometimes difficult to convey that stretches in technology often take place one step at a time.

Acknowledgments

ARI's prime contractor for the BRIDGE German tutor was Science Applications International Corporation. The MILT is being developed by Micro Analysis & Design of Boulder, CO. The natural language processing components for both phases are developed by the University of Maryland. The views, opinions, and conclusions contained in this paper are those of the author and should not be construed as an official Department of the Army position, policy, or decision.

References

Allen, J. (1987). *Natural language processing.* Menlo Park, CA:Benjamin.

ARPA (1993). *Proceedings of the fifth message understanding conference (MUC-5).* San Francisco: Kaufmann.

Bailin, A. (Ed.) (1991). ICALI research [Special Issue]. *CALICO Journal, 9.*

Bickes, G., & Scott, A. (1989). On the computer as a medium for language teaching. *CALICO Journal, 6,* 21-31.

Burston, J. (1989). Towards better tutorial CALL: A matter of intelligent control. *CALICO Journal, 6,* 75-89.

Chomsky, N. (1981). *Lectures on government and binding.* Dordrecht, Netherlands: Foris.

Clark, J.L., & Clifford, R.T. (1987). The FSI/ILR/ACTFL proficiency scales and testing techniques: Development, current status, and needed research. In A. Valdman (Ed.), *Proceedings of the Symposium on the Evaluation of Foreign Language Proficiency*, Bloomington: Indiana University Press.

Criswell, E., Byrnes, H., & Pfister, G. (1992). Intelligent automated strategies of teaching foreign language in context. In M. L. Swartz & M. Yazdani (Eds).

Criswell, E., Weinberg, A., Miller, L., Byrnes, H., & Blascak, D. (1989). *Applications of artificial intelligence to foreign language learning: Analysis, design, and initial prototyping*. Phase I technical report (ARI contract MDA903-89-C-0033). McLean, VA: Science Applications International Corporation.

Hart, R. (1994). *ERRATA: Response analysis and error diagnosis tools* (Technical report no. LLL-T-23-94). University of Illinois: Language Learning Laboratory.

Holland, V.M. (1994). Lessons learned in designing intelligent CALL: Managing communication across disciplines. *Computer Assisted Language Learning*, 7, 226-256.

Holland, V.M., Maisano, R., Alderks, C., & Martin, J. (1993). Parsers in tutors: What are they good for? *CALICO Journal*, 11, 28-46.

Lett, J., & O'Mara, F. (1990). Predictors of success in an intensive foreign language context: Correlates of language learning at Defense Language Institute Foreign Language Center. In Perry, T.S. & Stansfield, C.S. (Eds.), *Language aptitude reconsidered* (pp. 222-260). Englewood Cliffs, NJ: Prentice Hall.

Jackson, G. (Ed.). (1994). *Final report series from the Language Skill Change Project*. Reston, VA: PRC, Inc.

Nirenburg, S. (Ed.). (1993). *Progress in machine translation.* Amsterdam: IOS Press.

Rubin, J., Ediger, A., Coffin, E., Van Handle, D., & Whiskeyman, A. (1991). Survey of interactive language video discs. *Calico Journal*, *8*, 65-94.

Slocum, J. (1985). A survey of machine translation: Its history, current status, and future prospects. *Computational Linguistics*, *11*, 1-17.

Swartz, M.L., & Psotka, J. (1989). *AI tools for foreign language training* (Research report no. 1533). Alexandria, VA: U.S. Army Research Institute.

Swartz, M.L., & Yazdani, M. (Eds.). (1992). *Intelligent tutoring systems for foreign language learning.* New York: Springer-Verlag.

Syracuse Language Systems ships language training software (September, 1994). *Speech Recognition Update*, p. 1.

Underwood, J.H. (1987). Artificial intelligence and CALL. In W.F. Smith (Ed.), *Modern media in foreign language education: Theory and implementation*, Lincolnwood, IL: National Textbook Company.

2

A Principle-Based Parser for Foreign Language Tutoring in German and Arabic

Amy Weinberg, Joe Garman, and Jeffery Martin
University of Maryland

Paola Merlo
Université de Geneve

We have designed and implemented a parser for German and Arabic, developed to support a language tutor called BRIDGE, whose aim is to reinforce language skills of early intermediate students of these two languages (between skill levels 1 and 2). This tutor is being developed for military linguists in the U.S. Army and is sponsored by the Army Research Institute (ARI). Other chapters in this volume—by Sams and by Kreyer and Criswell—discuss the tutorial aspects of BRIDGE from the perspectives of the student and the instructor/author, respectively. The necessary components for natural language understanding by machine, known as natural language processing (NLP), include decomposing words into their meaningful subparts (morphological analysis), representing possible patterns of combination for sentence formation (syntactic analysis), and mapping these patterns onto an appropriate meaning (semantic analysis). This chapter focuses on the lexical and syntactic components that comprise the NLP system in the BRIDGE tutor. The principles behind these components are being applied in the development of a Spanish and Arabic parser for a second generation ARI system, the Military Language Tutor, described by Kaplan and Holland (this volume).

Goals for Natural Language Processing Driven by a Tutoring Application

It is clear that tutoring applications in general and this project in particular impose rather stringent requirements on a parser, which must be robust, flexible, portable, and efficient. We discuss each requirement in turn.

The parser must be robust because students, particularly at the early intermediate level, are bound to make errors when using a new language. Therefore, the system must be able to parse incorrect input. Because the student is not a native speaker of the language, input of the type in (1) must be processed—namely, input that contains misspelling, as in the German example (1)a and the Arabic (1)c, or grammatical errors, as in the German (1)b and the Arabic (1)d.[6]

[6] The Arabic is written in a transliterated form. The script form of the grammatical version of (1c-d) is كاءحجطألمطريق تقع.

(1) a. *Der Fluss flest auf das Tal.
'The river flows to the valley.'
b. *Der Fluss fliessen auf dem Tal.
c. *at tariiqu taqa9u...
'The road is located...'
d. *aT-Tariiqu taqa9aayna...

If the parser is unable to process erroneous input, it must at least degrade gracefully, possibly giving informative messages on what went wrong.

Our processing system is able to detect the differences in ungrammaticality between (1)a and (1)b. In (1)b the verb form *flest* is an incorrect spelling and should be *fliesst*. In (1)b the verb form *fliessen* is an incorrect inflection (that form occurs with a plural subject); moreover, the prepositional phrase *auf dem Tal* is in the wrong case (dative) and should be *auf das Tal* (accusative). A similar pair from Arabic appears in (1)c and (1)d. In (1)c the word for *road* should have an emphatic consonant (signified by an upper-case letter in the transliteration). This appears to be a spelling mistake of the type in (1)a. In (1)d there is an agreement error between the subject, which is specified as third feminine singular, and the verb, which is third feminine plural. The first type of mistake in these examples, a misspelling, must be corrected by the user for the parser to continue. This correction is done on the model of a spell checker, with the system pointing out the word that is misspelled. The latter kind of error, an error in agreement of two otherwise correct word tokens in German and in Arabic, can be bypassed in the parser through a special mechanism of defaults that enables the parser to analyze some kinds of incorrect input, thus supporting the criterion of robustness.

We also wanted the system to be flexible in its ability either to ignore or to detect errors. That is, we wanted instructors to determine whether a student was ready for feedback on a particular error and what form the feedback should take. Flexible detection of errors is crucial to developing lesson strategies that deal with problems of individual learners. To this end, the parser finds and classifies errors, but the tutor can be set either to withhold or to report this information to the student (see Kreyer & Criswell, this volume).

Because the intended users of this parsing system are language specialists in the U.S. Army, who must receive instruction in a variety of foreign languages (Sams, this volume), there was a strong desire to make the design of our system portable. Portability here refers to a design that can be reused for different languages without fundamental changes. The dictionaries and some of the grammatical information will be different, but it is desirable to design the NLP component in the most general way possible. In the best case the design is parameterized so that it specifies a family of parsers. Arabic and German are good bounding cases to test the portability of the parser design to different languages. The two languages share some similarities in being heavily case marked and in having various forms of grammatical agreement. They are different enough, however, to provide a fair test of whether we can use the same system to handle more than one language.

Finally, our system is meant to run on the kind of hardware that one could expect to find in a language laboratory; in this case, a desktop computer of the class 80486, which is found in some army school and field sites. Because the parsing system is only part of an overall language tutor, it must be able to share computing resources with other software; therefore, it must be compact and efficient. Ideally, it must be able to parse a sentence, detect the errors, and produce an output in something close to the amount of time it would take a human tutor to perform the same task. Long time lags can decrease the student's attention and motivation.

We believe that these requirements for a parser extend to language tutoring applications in general and apply to most of the systems described in this volume. Meeting all these requirements constitutes a real research challenge.

Principle-Based Parsing as a Framework to Support a Tutoring Application

We propose that a principle-based design is suited to satisfying simultaneously the four kinds of needs for a language tutor described above. The principle-based design has its origins in recent developments from linguistic theory, discussed in the following sections.

Language-Universal Descriptions of Syntax

A parser must match the strings it receives against a representation of the grammar of a language. A sentence is grammatical if it can be analyzed according to the parser's internal rules and is incorrect otherwise. Previous grammatical formalisms (Chomsky, 1965, 1973, 1977, among others) assumed that every construction of a language was syntactically represented by a grammatical rule. Thus, big, monolithic grammars were stored and consulted for any parser with reasonably wide linguistic coverage. Recent developments in grammatical theories have succeeded in identifying the unifying principles of many, apparently unrelated, linguistic phenomena. In particular, the government and binding (GB) framework (Chomsky, 1981) provides construction-independent formulas that are grouped into interacting modules that are parameterized. By modifying these modules to a small degree, one can generate the patterns associated with a variety of languages, each language corresponding to a parameter setting on various modules across a range of constructions.

We provide an example of this approach to give the reader a feel for the grammatical basis of our system. Consider the contrast between modern and previous attempts to handle word order in German, Arabic, and English. German is classed as a *head-final* language. That is, the category that determines the identity of phrases (the verb of a verb phrase, the noun of a noun phrase, etc.) appears on the right edge of the phrase in most cases. A common example in German is a subordinate clause, where the verb goes last in (i.e., is on the right edge of) the verb phrase, as in the clausal fragment (2)a. German differs from English, which is *head-initial* and in which relevant categories appear at the left edge of phrases, as in (2)d, where the verb goes first in the verb phrase. German also differs from Arabic, which not only allows the English order, as in (2)c, but also allows the verb to appear at the beginning of a sentence, as in (2)b. The examples in (2) each have verb phrasal heads underlined.[7]

(2) a. ...daß Hans [$_{VP}$ ein buch gelesen] hat.[8]
...that Hans a book read had
'{I know} that Hans had read a book.'

b. taqa9u markazu l-gayši šamaala l-mityaahati.[9]
located center of army north of Mityahaa
'The army center is north of Al-Mityaaha.'

c. Ad-dibdibba taqa9u 9alaa bu9di thamaaniyat amyaalin januuba min Al-mityaahati
Dibdibba located distance eight miles south of Al-Mityaaha
'Al-Dibdibba is eight miles south of Al-Mityaaha.'

d. John [ate the cake].

As an additional complication, German obligatorily exhibits the English-like order in simple clauses with main verbs, as in (3)a, but continues to show its head-final status when an auxiliary and main verb are present, as in (3)b. In these cases, the auxiliary verb must move to a position where it is the second constituent in the sentence, but the verb remains in final position.

(3) a. Ich lese ein Buch.
I read a book
b. Ich habe ein Buch gelesen.
I have a book read

X-bar conventions in language-universal descriptions. Clearly, we want to develop a system that can handle all types of ordering both within a language and across languages in a maximally general way. Syntactic theory contains a component known as *X-bar* that allows us to accomplish this task. According to syntactic theory, all phrases in a language are organized into heads and complements, and the head of a category (e.g., the verb of a verb phrase) determines that category's type. Languages are classed with respect to whether they are head-initial or head-final. If a language has a verb appearing before its objects (i.e., is head-initial), it will also have a noun appearing before its objects.

This means that we can replace rules like the following,

[7] In (2) and elsewhere, the word-for-word English gloss appears directly below the foreign sentence; below the gloss, a well-formed English translation appears in single quotes.
[8] In the German and English examples, the verb phrase (VP) is in brackets.
[9] In the Arabic examples, the copula (*to be*) verb is not expressed, nor is the definite determiner (*the* in English), which is indicated in the English gloss by the symbol *df.*

(4) NP $\rightarrow$ det N
VP $\rightarrow$ aux V (adv)
AP $\rightarrow$ Q adj [10]

which must be written individually for each category in the language (noun phrase, verb phrase, etc.), with the more compact, generalization-capturing representation in Figure 2.1. Here, the left-hand side corresponds to the general template for English and the right-hand side to the general template for German.

FIG. 2.1. Phrase structure templates in X-bar theory, with English on the left (head-initial structure), and German on the right (head-final structure). The template for a given language applies across all the phrase types (noun, verb, adjective, etc.) in the language.

The objective of the representation in Figure 2.1 is to characterize the basic phrase structure of the language. For English and German, a representational system must admit sentences in which the subject precedes the verb and disallow sentences in which it follows the verb for normal cases. This is done in two steps. First, the basic, or underlying, word order is determined by using a common X-bar schema and setting the word order parameter to head-initial or head-final. Then, a simple rule of movement moves categories from basic to nonbasic positions. Jackendoff (1977) showed that templates like these can describe the basic word order for all of the world's languages, including those that allow for free word order.

A system based on this approach is obviously much more supple than the list of rules in (4) in that it applies cross-linguistically. We set the parameter to head-final for German and head-initial for Arabic and English. This leads to the basic Subject Object Verb (SOV) order for German and Subject Verb Object (SVO) order for English and Arabic. A parsing design based on this theory stores the basic templates together with a capability to choose the head-initial or head-final setting as the language requires. The remaining SVO order for simple sentences in German and the Verb Subject Object (VSO) order for Arabic are derived by applying a general transformation that moves the verb from German and Arabic into either the second position (German) or initial position (Arabic). The syntactic derivations for the various structures are given below each example in (5).

---

[10] In (4), *NP* corresponds to noun phrase, *VP* to verb phrase, *AP* to adjective phrase, *det* to determiner, *aux* to auxiliary verb, and *Q* to a quantifier (e.g., *more* or *less*).

(5) a. taqa9u markazu l-gayši šamaala l-mityaahati.
located center of army north of Al-Mityaha
'The army center is north of Al-Mityaaha.'
[[$_{S}$taqa9u $_{i}$[$_{NP}$markazu l'gayshi[$_{VP}$[e_i] [$_{NP}$ shammala l'Mityaahati]]][11]

b. Ich denke daß ich habe ein Buch gelesen.
I think that I have a book read
'I think that I have read a book.'
...[ich [$_{V}$pein Buch [$_{V}$ gelesen]] habe] *(basic order)*
...[$_{S}$ ich$_{i}$ habe$_{j}$ [$_{S}$ [e_i] [$_{VP}$ [ein Buch] [gelesen] [e_j]]] *(surface order)*

In (5)a, the Arabic verb for *located* has moved from its basic position following the subject to the phrase initial position. In (5)b the German auxiliary *habe* has moved from the basic position (verb-final) seen in all embedded clauses (the upper set of brackets) to the verb-second position (the lower set of brackets). These movements are indicated by the coindexation of the verb with the *e* symbol (called a trace), where the subscripts (i, j, etc.) are indexes. The *e* trace remains in the position where the verb is found in basic order, before its relocation by the general movement transformation.

In earlier theories, the fact that these movements were the only possible ones would have been handled either by adding extra rules that matched each of the moved patterns or by adding specific transformational rules that mapped the basic phrase structure patterns onto these surface structures. These rules encoded all features of the conditions in which these movements could apply. In modern theory, these numerous variations are handled by a small set of constraining conditions that apply to the output of the rule component and that can be set differently for different languages. Legal (grammatical) constructions are thus identified through the interaction of simple modules rather than being hand-coded as features on many grammatical rules. This feature of GB theory appears to meet the needs of tutoring systems for compactness and efficiency as well as the need for portability across languages (through the mechanism of parameter switching). The case filter described next illustrates a constraining condition that interacts with the X-bar module (Figure 2.1) to weed out ungrammatical structures generated by that module.

Case assignment as a universal constraint on sentence generation. According to GB theory, there is a universal principle called the case filter that regulates the distribution of noun phrases in natural languages. This filter, which is part of a case checking module that constrains productions of the X-bar module, can be defined simply as follows: Every lexical noun phrase must receive a grammatical case.

Grammatical cases are overt in many languages of the world. They are normally morphologically marked as nominative, accusative, dative, genitive, and so forth. In all the languages discussed here, case is assigned to particular positions in the structure. This is shown in (6) and (7) by the contrasting marking on the pronoun (nominative, or

[11] In addition to the symbols defined in footnote 3, *S* corresponds to sentence and *V* to verb.

NOM, vs. accusative, or ACC), which depends on whether the noun phrase is pre- or postverbal.

(6) *English:* He (NOM) looked at him (ACC).
*Him (ACC) looked at he (NOM).

(7) *German:* Ich (NOM) erkenne Hans.
I recognize Hans
*Mich (ACC) erkenne Hans.

Case is assigned by verbs, prepositions, or the tense or agreement marker. These simple assumptions explain why the following sentences are unacceptable, given that the underlined phrase is not in the appropriate position to receive a case:

(8) a. *The destruction <u>Rome</u> was pervasive.
b. *<u>Mondale</u> to have lost was not unexpected.

In (8)a the noun *destruction* cannot assign case because it is not of the appropriate category. In (8)b there is no tense marker in the subject, so *Mondale* does not receive a case. This theory also explains why the insertion of a semantically null preposition (*of*, *for*) renders these sentences grammatical, as shown in (9).

(9) a. The destruction <u>of Rome</u> was pervasive.
b. <u>For Mondale</u> to have lost was not unexpected.

The prepositions in (9) can assign case to the underlined noun phrases, and thus the entire structure will pass the case filter in each example.

The configurations in which case can be assigned are parameterized across languages. Categories like verbs and prepositions can normally assign case to noun phrases that appear inside phrases of which the verb or preposition is the head—a configuration known as *government.* Government is a technical notion that we can informally think of as obtaining when two categories appear inside the same phrase and are not separated by any intervening phrasal categories. Thus, in (10) the verb (*ate*) and the object (*the cake*) appear inside the verb phrase, so the verb governs the object; the verb does not govern the subject (*John*) because a verb phrase intervenes.

(10) [$_S$ John [ate the cake]]

Paralleling government, categories like tense normally mark case under the configuration of grammatical agreement. That is, in many languages, the nominative subject shows gender and number agreement with the verbal inflection, and this defines a configuration in which case can be assigned. In some instances, however, as in Arabic, a verb can also mark the subject under government.

Dual methods of case assignment allow the dual options of SVO and VSO in Arabic. In the former situation, case is assigned to the subject under agreement; in the latter, case is assigned to the subject under government. English does not have this option. Thus, English does not allow a verb to move to the front of the sentence (except in questions and in emphatic constructions, where case marking behaves differently). Further details and examples from German, in which the verb cannot assign case under government, are given by Garman, Martin, Merlo, and Weinberg (1993).

Besides the case filter, a GB-based system applies agreement constraints, which enforce person, place, and number agreement, and argument structure constraints, which link syntactic positions with the number of arguments associated with the predicate. Argument structure constraints, for example, handle the distinction between transitive and intransitive predicates. Grouped as the *theta-criterion*, these constraints are discussed in a later section of this chapter ("Conditions"). A complete list of constraints and their use in parsing is given by Fong (1991).

Summary: How a GB Framework can Address the Needs of Language Tutoring

The intricate possibilities of order in the three languages considered here are handled by a universal template that can produce radically different orders by setting a switch to head-final or head-initial. This parameter switching is coordinated with the case-checking module, which itself can be parameterized by setting case assignment as under agreement and government, under government alone, or under agreement alone. These functions work with the simplest grammatical rule, a rule that says "move anything anywhere." The overgeneration that this rule produces is handled by passing its outputs through constraints like the case filter. This filter regulates much more than just the operation of verb movement. Not only does it regulate the placement of prepositions, as discussed previously, it crucially regulates the formation of correct passives and other constructions. This filter ideally interacts with the phrase structure rules and a small number of other conditions to generate all and only grammatical sentences in the world's languages. In other words, a small set of interactions exhausts the space of possible languages.

Because the number of rules is so small and because each of the filters handles a wide range of construction types, the resulting grammar is compact and efficient. Because the design can be parameterized to deal with cross-linguistic variation, the same design can be used across different language types, ensuring portability. Because the system is modular, various subparts can be turned off, thus allowing easy error suppression and diagnosis, aiding flexibility. In these ways, the GB framework for parsing supports several of the expressed needs of language tutoring. The specific implementation of this framework in a working parser is discussed next.

A Principle-Based Parser for German and Arabic: Implementation of the Theory

Adopting the approach outlined, we have developed a parser for German and Arabic that is embedded in the BRIDGE tutor. The parser is programmed in Prolog and draws on a German lexicon of over 5,000 words. The Arabic lexicon for this project was intended for demonstration only, but in the succeeding project to BRIDGE (Kaplan & Holland, this volume), we have adapted a large preexisting two-level Arabic lexicon and morphology that yields the equivalent of tens of thousands of English words (Dorr, Garman, & Weinberg, 1994).

The next section of this chapter summarizes the BRIDGE NLP system. The succeeding sections illustrate the routines for recovery of phrase structure, use of conditions, and error handling, respectively. The final section presents an evaluation and illustration of parser coverage, with concluding remarks.

Overview: The Input-Output

The input to the parser is a German or Arabic sentence, followed by a period or a question mark. The output consists of a parse tree, which encodes the hierarchical and linear relations between the elements of the sentence (which can be passed to a semantic analysis) and a (possibly empty) list of errors in the sentence, which is passed to the tutor. For instance, the sentence in (11) is a correct declarative German sentence.

(11) Das Schloss Eisenbach liegt in dem Tal.
'The castle of Eisenbach is situated in the valley.'

This sentence is parsed, and because the sentence is correct, the error list is empty. The sentence in (12) is similar to (11) but contains two agreement errors. These are indicated in the error list returned by the parser, shown below the sentence. The list of errors tells the tutor that the phrase *die Schloss* is incorrect; specifically, there is a mismatch between the noun *Schloss* (neuter singular) and the determiner *die* (neuter plural or feminine singular). The list also indicates that the verb *stehen* (plural) does not match, or agree with, the subject *die Schloss* (singular).

(12) Die Schloss Eisenbach stehen in die Stadt.
ErrorList:[det_noun_mismatch,die,schloss,num_pers_mismatch,die_schloss,steh+en]

The error list categorizes each error and isolates where each occurs in terms of the words involved. Of course, in all cases the error codes are translated by the BRIDGE tutor into feedback messages that can be understood by students (for examples, see Sams, this volume). Moreover, the authoring interface in BRIDGE (Kreyer & Criswell, this volume) permits instructors to develop their own student messages, in the form of templates into which word tokens from the error lists can be inserted. Thus, the first component of the error list in (12) might be communicated in a number of ways, depending on the terminology the student is assumed to be familiar with and the instructional strategy of the tutor (e.g., minimal vs. rich feedback). An example of such feedback is seen in (13).

(13) The modifier *die* does not agree with the noun *Schloss* in person or number.
You need to change the form of the determiner to agree with *Schloss*.
Correct your error at *die Schloss*.

The main components of the parser are a morphological analyzer, a syntactic parser, and an error handling facility. The general overview of the system is shown in Figure 2.2.

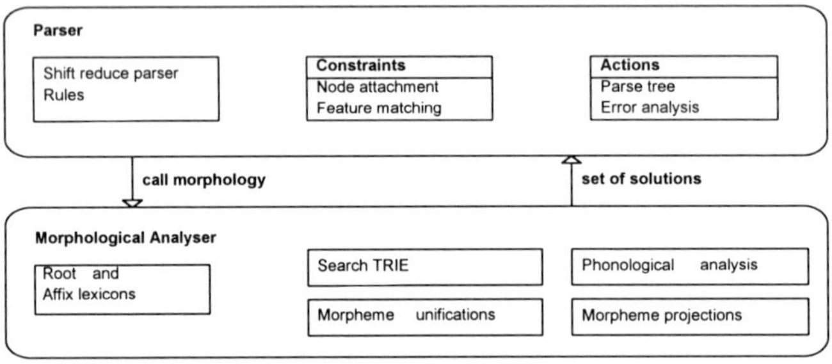

FIG. 2.2. Major components of the parser developed for BRIDGE.

The sentence can be thought of as an input stream, which is received and preprocessed before being passed to the parser token by token (word form). An interactive preprocessor partitions the input stream into word tokens, expands possible contractions (such as *zum* into *zu dem*), and checks whether the input is correctly typed. Once the input is successfully partitioned, it is passed to the parser. The input is consumed token by token. For each token the parser calls the morphological analyzer to hand words (i.e., analyzed tokens) to the parser one by one. (For more details on the preprocessor, routines for lexical search, and morphological analyses, see Azadegan et al., 1993).[12]

Parsing and morphological analysis occur in a single pass on an input sentence. Each call to the morphological analyzer returns a set containing all the morphological analyses of the next input token. Because there may be several possible morphological analyses of a given word (e.g., *marches* in English can be a plural noun or a third person singular verb), it may not be possible to determine which analysis is correct at the point when the morphological analyzer is called. Note that if only one analysis were selected, it might not be the right one. This would cause the parser to fail in a later state and require another call into the morphology.

When the morphemes are correctly identified, the word is passed to the syntax. Before entering the syntax, each token is associated with a syntactic category (e.g., noun,

[12] The morphological analyzer for German differs from that of Arabic owing to the differing morphological features of the two languages.

verb). The parser is a *shift-reduce parser* whose design is discussed in the next section (see also Felshin, this volume; Loritz, this volume). It operates according to the very small set of previously mentioned rules, which store a limited amount of hierarchical information. Other kinds of information to build the right parse tree (see "node attachment" in Figure 2.2) and annotate it correctly ("feature matching" in Figure 2.2) are stored in a set of constraints that must be satisfied before a rule can apply, as illustrated by the case filter. Subsets of these constraints are indexed in the rules, as described next.

The Recovery of Phrase Structure

To analyze the syntax of an input sentence, the parser must derive a basic phrase structure for the sentence. For a sentence like "Where are you," this means deriving a structure in which the sentence subject is in canonical position: "You are where." This section gives computational details on how this recovery is accomplished in our system.

The design of the structure-building component of the parser (i.e., the component that builds a parse tree) is an augmented shift-reduce algorithm. It differs from standard shift-reduce algorithms in using an X-bar module, parameterized for word order, to index a set of grammatical constraints. In addition, a *move-x module* is added to the shift-reduce cycle to connect moved phrases to the positions from which they moved. This section discusses each modification in turn.

The Shift-Reduce Parsing Algorithm Modified Through an X-Bar Module

Some modifications of the basic shift-reduce method of parsing (Aho & Ullman, 1972) are necessary to make it suitable for the grammar framework we are assuming. One modification involves maintaining a very minimal X-bar system within the grammar framework. Most work in parsing consists of constraint checking rather than manipulating X-bar rules, which constitute the backbone of a set of grammar constraints. To separate constraints from phrase structure, we use rewrite rules of the form shown in (14).

(14) $X \rightarrow Y\ Z\ ,\ \underline{f}(X,Y,Z)$

This rule tells the parser that the constituents Y and Z can be rewritten as the superordinate constituent X (i.e, in tree-building terms, that Y and Z can be collapsed, or reduced, into X; for example, a determiner plus noun can be rewritten as a noun phrase). The left-hand side of (14) is an expression of X-bar theory. The right-hand side indicates that the rewrite rule applies given the satisfaction of constraints on the features Y and Z that are specified in the formula $\underline{f}$ (satisfaction of these constraints is said to license the production $X \rightarrow Y\ Z$). The form of these constraints and the way they are applied are discussed in a later section ("Constraints").

The complete X-bar system employed by the German parser is given by the set of clauses in (15), written in Prolog. The parameterization of these rules that gives us Arabic follows directly.

(15) *German:*

x(2,C) → [x(2,C1),x(1,C), prespecifier].[13]
x(1,C) → [x(0,C),x(2,C1), postcomplement].
x(1,C) → [x(2,C1),x(0,C), precomplement].
x(1,C) → [x(2,C1),x(1,C), premodifier].
x(1,C) → [x(1,C),x(2,C1), postmodifier].
x(2,C) → [x(2,C1),x(2,C), preadjunct].
x(2,C) → [x(2,C),x(2,C1), post adjunct].
x(1,C) → [x(0,C), nonbranching1].
x(2,C) → [x(1,C), nonbranching2].

Arabic:

x(2,C) → [x(2,C1), x(1,C), specifier]
x(1,C) → [x(0,C), x(2,C1), complement]
x(1,C) → [x(1,C1), x(1,C), premodifier]
x(1,C) → [x,(1,C), x(1,C1), postmodifier]
x(2,C) → [x(2,C1), x(2,C), preadjunct]
x(2,C) → [x(2,C), x(2,C1), postadjunct]
x(1,C) → [x(0,C), unary1]
x(2,C) → [x(1,C), unary2]

Each right-hand side of the rules in (15) contains a head (i.e., *x* in these rules), which shares the category variable with the left-hand side; a constraint label (e.g., prespecifier, specifier), which is used to index constraints and tree-building predicates so they can be appropriately called on; and possibly a satellite, which is a specifier, complement, adjunct, modifier, or other material that completes the rule. For example, x(2,C) could underlie phrases of the type NP, VP. The parameterization of the German rules that gives us Arabic involves switching the order of satellites in relation to heads and some of the relevant constraints. It is evident from (15) that the same set of rules can handle the phrase structure of both languages and that the grammar in both languages is compact. This demonstrates the cross-language portability that we hoped to gain through use of the parameterized X-bar module. It is a transparent implementation of the principle-based grammatical theory discussed in the previous section: Rules are kept as bare as possible and all other information is checked on-line.

Our parser uses three primary data structures: the *main stack*, which contains word and categories already analyzed, the *buffer stack* of incoming words, and a *hold store* that contains copies of moved phrases. The parser must build a parse tree from the string of input words. In the shift-reduce method, words are successively reduced to grammatical categories and categories are reduced to successively higher phrases, forming a tree. The parser performs reductions by attempting to match the top two elements on the stack with the right-hand side of a rewrite rule. If a match is found, the two elements are reduced to

---

[13] In these rules, *x* is a variable representing the head of a phrase; *0*, *1*, and *2* are phrase structure level, with *0* indicating the lexical level, *1* indicating the combination of head with complement, and *2* indicating the phrasal level. *C* is the packet of relevant constraints that indicate whether a category of the type indicated in the rule can be legitimately formed.

the category named on the left-hand side of the rule. The rule label is used to index the constraints that must apply to the feature sets of the elements on the stack (e.g., that features must agree) if the rule is to succeed. If a rule matches but the constraints for that rule fail, then an attempt is made to match other rules. If the constraints succeed, tree-building actions are performed and the parse continues with the reduced phrase on top of the stack. An unconditional shift simply moves the next word into the parser's field of attention.

It is common in shift-reduce parsing to enter a configuration from which several operations are possible. For example, the parser could shift a new token into the buffer indicating that a rule is not finished, or it could reduce a rule. An instance of this would be *I believe John*, which could end here or continue with *is a fool*. We have adopted various techniques to help us pick the right alternative, but if we make a mistake, we must reparse. This backtracking has not lead to unreasonable parse times. (However, note that in the succeeding project to BRIDGE, which deals with Spanish and Arabic, we have replaced backtracking with an ability to share all possibilities for ambiguous structure, so as to better handle the ambiguities inherent in input sentences, particularly those likely to be entered by students using Arabic script without vowels.)

Techniques we have adopted to help us pick the right alternative include giving priority to some operations over others so that the parsing algorithm has a basis for choosing from among available operations. To choose the operation to apply in a given configuration, the algorithm uses Prolog's control strategy (depth-first search) to select the highest priority operation that matches the configuration. The system also includes a movement clause that determines whether a movement rule should apply in a configuration, discussed in more detail in the next section.

The Shift-Reduce Algorithm Modified Through a Move-X Module

Another modification to the shift-reduce method is necessary to express movement rules; these relate overt categories to empty categories (or gaps) in a different position, as in the verb movement exchanges illustrated in (5), where the *e* trace indicates a gap left by a moved constituent. Our design separates movement rules from X-bar rules. We introduce a move-x operation into the parse cycle, whose purpose is to relate gaps to their fillers. The use of gaps achieves a degree of generalization in the treatment of superficially different constructions and allows the phrase structure module to handle questions (as in (5)), topicalizations, relative clauses, and so forth. In order to maintain compactness however, the computation of gaps is performed on-line by specific routines rather than being precompiled into the rules.

Two basic types of movement rules are implemented. The first involves movement of a phrase. The most common instance of this type is movement of a question phrase to the sentence-initial position, as in the German (16)a as well as in its English translation. The same algorithm generates Arabic question types like (16)b. Again, the question word is moved to the front of the sentence (both examples in (16) show the moved constituent in brackets). This type of movement can also generate topicalizations, clefts, and some relative clauses in both Arabic and German.

(16) a. [In welcher Richtung]$_i$ fliesst die Donau e$_i$?
'In what direction flows the Danube?'

b. [Ayna]$_i$ taqa9u maHaTTat š-šurTati$_i$ binisbati l T-Tariiqi?
'Where is the police station in relation to the road?'

The second type of movement rule is movement of a single word, like a verb, which occurs in the German yes/no question in (17)a, in which the verb *darf* (must/may) has moved. This type of movement is also used frequently in Arabic, where along with the standard SVO word order, we generate the equally frequent VSO order by moving the verb to the front of the sentence. An example is given in (17)b, in which the subject begins in verb-phrase internal position and the verb can move to the front of the sentence.

(17) a. Darf ich hier bleiben?
b. Taqa9u maHaTTaatu šurTati d-dibdibbati 9alaa Tariiqin ?ilaa januubi l'mityaahati
located df police station to the South of on a road Al-Mityaaha
'The police station is located on the road to the south of Al-Mityaaha.'

To form a yes-no question, as in (17)a, the verb is first moved to second position and from there to clause-initial position. To recover the basic phrase structure, the parser uses the two steps in (18) to construct a move-x relation. Each type of movement rule uses the hold store (Woods & Kaplan, 1971), which provides for temporary storage of the moved element.

(18) a. Stack-to-Hold Rules: put a trace of the moved category onto the hold store.
b. Hold-to-Stack Rules: move a trace from the hold store into the position it would occupy in basic word order.

For the Stack-to-Hold operation, we must identify when a phrase is not in its underlying position. Because the types of positions to which a phrase may move are limited and predictable, the parser consults a table of move-x configurations to determine that a phrase is not in its underlying position. The rule applies, for example, in a configuration like (16)a in which the stack contains the single wh-phrase *in welcher Richtung* and the buffer contains the verb *fliesst*. In such a configuration, a trace of *in welcher Richtung* is placed on the hold store. When a moved category is identified, a trace is constructed that is identical to the category in all features except spelling, because the trace does not appear in the surface form (recall that in the output structures, we label traces as *e*). For the Hold-to-Stack operation, we must find the underlying position of the trace on the hold stack. Again the parser consults a table of configurations that determines whether the trace should be moved from the buffer to the stack. For instance, this rule would apply in a configuration in which the verb *fliesst* is on top of the stack, and the trace of the phrase *in welcher Richtung* is in the hold store. A condition on the rule requires that the moved phrase be a possible complement of the verb. This condition is satisfied since *in welcher Richtung* is a possible complement of the verb *fliessen.*

We should underline once again that we have adopted a direct implementation of the principles of the theoretical grammar. Other approaches (Dorr, 1990; Fong, 1991) precompile the possible positions where an empty category can occur. Clearly, our approach could lead to frequent postulation of empty categories in many positions that are not licensed by the grammar. Thus, this method of recovering phrase structure information must be coupled with a method to check conditions that allows us to generate only correct sentences.

The Use of Conditions in Parsing

Using conditions is crucial to guaranteeing the correctness and compactness of our system. For instance, consider the following grammar where restrictions of number agreement (i.e., between subject and verb) and case assignment (to subject of the sentence or to object of the verb) are expressed by the set of phrase structure rules in (19).[14]

(19)
S → NPSingNom I'Sing
S → NPPlurNom I'Plur
S'Sing → ISing VPSing
S'Plur → IPlur VPPlur

VPSing → VSing NPSingAcc
VPSing → VSing NPPlurAcc
VPPlur → VPlur NPSingAcc
VPPlur → VPlur NPPlurAcc

Compare (19) with the much more succinct grammar in (20) that disassociates the conditions on the number and case features from the phrase structure rules.

(20)
S → NP I' Spec Head Agree
I' → I VP Case Assignment
VP → V NP Case Assignment

The set of rules in (20) is more compact. To each of these rules we associate a subset of the universal conditions (those bearing on feature agreement and case assignment) that form the grammar. This association is done by the convention "Recovery of Phrase

[14] In these rules *S* refers to sentence, *NP* to the sentence subject or object, *I'* to the verb and inflections, *VP* to verb phrase, *Sing* and *Plur* to specific number features, *Nom* and *Acc* to the nominative and accusative case features.

Structure," whereby rules are indexed into a set of conditions by means of the rule labels (see (15)).

One of the conditions we use is the case filter discussed earlier. Another condition is *theta marking*, which checks the subcategorization of the verb in terms of the number and types of arguments it can take. The X-bar rules without theta marking will generate:

(21) *er schlaft das Hund
he sleeps the dog

Theta marking rules out (21) because the structure does not match the restriction that *sleep* can only be intransitive. Table 2.1 lists the types of conditions we have discussed (see Garman et al., 1993, for a list of all conditions that are part of our system and for details on indexing of rules into constraints).

Table 2.1.
A Subset of Conditions that Apply to Phrase Structure Rules to Constrain Sentence Generation

CONDITION	FUNCTION
agree	• checks case assignment and person and number agreement between verb and subject • percolates intersection of features to mother node in parse tree
theta marking	• checks availability of sister node for argument assignment • assigns an argument role • modifies the predicate-argument structure
percolate	• checks number, gender, and person
features	• percolates features to mother node

The use of conditions has several advantages. This approach is compact because it reduces the number of rules needed to parse a language. Moreover, it achieves language-independence because it uses highly abstract rules. It is modular because it separates the principles that determine the phrase structure skeleton from those conditions like theta that determine the shape of the tree. It is flexible because it separates those features that guide the parse from the features that annotate the tree. We discuss in the next section why this property of our system is crucial for error tolerance and error detection. Essentially, it allows theta and other conditions to be turned off. If, for example, the tutor wanted to focus on argument selection but not on whether verbs and subjects agree, the theta condition would be left on but agreement would be turned off.

Error Handling

Because the parser is to be used for tutoring, one very important component is the error handler, which must obey precise specifications: It must be able to tolerate, detect, and diagnose errors, and it should be flexible in reporting errors.

Error tolerance is important because the typical user of this system is likely to make mistakes of several kinds: misspellings, wrong or nonexistent words, agreement errors (such as wrong declension for nouns or wrong conjugation for verbs), syntactic errors (such as putting words in the wrong order), and semantic errors (such as using the movement verb *legen* instead of the static verb *liegen* to mean *being located*). The parser must be robust in order not to fail at every instance of incorrect input. At the moment, the parser correctly fails at but does not diagnose many word order errors, nor does it issue error reports for semantic errors. It does correctly diagnose errors of spelling, use of words not in the lexicon, and most agreement errors. The error types are summarized in the next subsection. The requirement for error tolerance is supported by the strong modularity of the design seen so far, particularly the separation of conditions from phrase structure rules. Recall that although some conditions, like theta, can affect the way the parser attaches nodes to the already-built structure (i.e., can affect the shape of the tree), other conditions, like agreement, do not. They simply annotate the nodes of a tree already built. Thus, even if the latter conditions are not met (e.g., verb and subject disagree), the parse tree can still be constructed for semantic analysis.

Error detection and diagnosis are also important features of a tutoring system. They provide the necessary data on the mistakes of the user of the system, which are sent to the tutor and processed. The data are used to provide direct feedback to the student, as illustrated by the error messages we saw in (13). The data are also used to create a performance record for the student with summaries per error type (i.e., a kind of statistical model of the student). These summaries can be matched against thresholds preset in the tutor to determine when the student should be branched to extra practice related to the error type (for details, see Kreyer & Criswell, this volume; Sams, this volume).

Finally, the error handler must be flexible so that it can detect and diagnose errors at different levels of restrictiveness. This flexibility permits the instructor to decide what errors are important for what groups of students—perhaps lower level students suffer from being penalized for mistakes more than do intermediate or advanced students. The tutor can reconfigure the level of tolerance of errors in the parser to determine whether a particular error that is detectable will actually be reported. This can be done in two ways—within the NLP component by a mechanism to set the parser's error flags individually or within the tutor by arranging that all flags be passed to the tutor but that only some of them trigger error messages to the student. Details are given in the following section.

Error Types Supported by the BRIDGE Parser

At present the error handler for German can detect the classes of errors listed here:

- subject-verb agreement (person, number, gender)
- case of sentence subject
- article-noun agreement (gender, number, case)
- preposition-noun agreement

- verb-preposition agreement
- word order errors:
  position of finite verb in main clause (verb second)
  position of finite verb in subordinate clause (verb final)
- auxiliary selection in compound tense (*haben* vs. *sein*)

The errors in these categories are illustrated next. The handler for Arabic is still under development, and selected examples of the Arabic errors we are incorporating are also provided.

Subject-verb agreement. This class of mistakes can be split into two main subclasses: mismatch of number, person, or (in the case of Arabic) gender between subject and verb, as in (22)a for German and (22)c for Arabic; and failure to assign the subject to nominative case, as in (22)b for German.

(22) a. *Ich liebt dich
I loves you (1st person subject, 3rd person verb)

b. *aT-Tariiqu yaqa9u.... (feminine subject, masculine verb)
the road located

(23) *Mir liebe dich
me love you (accusative case subject)

Complements. This class of errors encompasses two cases: mismatch of preposition and complement and mismatch of determiner and complement. We consider an error to fall into the former class if the object of the preposition is in the wrong case for the preposition (i.e., in terms of the grammar, the case assigned by the preposition is not the case of the noun phrase that the preposition dominates), as in (24).

(24) *Sie wohnen auf des Landes (*auf* never takes genitive case)
they live in the country

The latter class reflects disagreement in gender, number, or case between the determiner (i.e., article, demonstrative adjective, or possessive pronoun) and noun:

(25) *Das Mutter liebt das Kind (neuter determiner, feminine noun)
the mother loves the child

Modification. This kind of error (implemented for Arabic only) arises when adjectives and nouns have mismatching features of case, gender, number, or declension:

(26) *Al-kitaab Al-kabiira....(masculine noun, feminine adjective)
the book the big
'The big book.'

Selection of prepositional phrase. This error arises when prepositions that can assign multiple cases, such as *auf, an*, and *neben*, assign a case that is legal for the preposition but illegal for the verb that dominates the prepositional phrase. For example, bimodal prepositions like *auf* assign either dative or accusative case, depending on whether the verb is one of movement like *gehen* (to go), which requires accusative case in the complement prepositional phrase, or a stative verb like *wohnen* to live, which requires dative case.

(27) *Sie wohnen auf das Land (accusative case in prep phrase)
Sie wohnen auf dem Land (dative case in prep phrase)

New additions to the error handler. In addition to including this original set of errors, the parser has been enhanced to trap errors of auxiliary verb selection (*haben/sein*) to form the present perfect tense of the verb (I have gone). Other enhancements include two kinds of word order errors common in English speakers learning German: failure to put the verb at the end of an embedded clause (see correct example in (5)b and failure to put the verb second given an introductory adverb or prepositional phrase, as in

(28) *Morgen ich komme
Morgen komme ich.
'Tomorrow I arrive.'

Mechanisms of Error Handling

The error handling facility consists of three logical parts:

1. Error detection and production of default values on failure of feature matching.
2. Production of error lists to be output to the tutor, with retrieval of lexical items.
3. A set of control switches managed by the tutor to determine the restrictiveness of the error handler.

Producing error lists for the tutor. Error lists delivered by parser to tutor, illustrated in (12), consist of an error name (signifying subject-verb mismatch, etc.) and two lexical items or phrases that precipitated the error. This error list (the output list) is produced by a predicate that receives an input list of error codes and the subtrees built so far in the parse. The error name in the output list derives directly from the error codes; the lexical items are retrieved by traversing the subtrees. If the input list contains more than one error code, then more than one error name is included in the output list, as was illustrated in (12). The codes are generated as the parse is proceeding and accumulated in a list until the end of the parse, at which point they are output to the tutor, which can deliver them in raw form to the user or can translate them into student-friendly messages, as illustrated in (13).

Control switches. The third component of the error handler is a set of control switches that can be set through the tutor. These switches, called flags, determine how restrictive the parser will be in detecting errors. If all the possible flags are set, the parser runs in its most restrictive version; otherwise, it recovers from mistakes whose flags are not set through a mechanism of producing default values on failure of feature matching. These mistakes are not considered errors. The flags now implemented correspond to the error types described above. For example, in the German parser, a preposition-noun-flag detects mismatches between prepositions and their complement noun phrase, and a nominative-flag checks that nominative case is assigned to the subject of the sentence. Upon detection of an error in parsing, the error predicate checks if the flag for that kind of error is set. If so, the error is included in the output list sent to the tutor.

This mechanism of flags makes the parser flexible. For example, agreement errors are not reported if the flags are not set. This might benefit beginning students, who could enter partially ill-formed sentences without penalty, allowing them to concentrate on other issues in the language. Another way to suppress error reporting is outside the parser through the authoring interface to the tutor. As described by Kreyer and Criswell (this volume), instructors can selectively set the tutor to show or withhold feedback for specific error types in each exercise. The two methods of manipulating error reporting are functionally indistinguishable from the user's viewpoint. The advantage of the latter method is that the tutor can keep the errors passed by the parser in a performance profile, even if the student is not told immediately about each error. The latter method is the one used in the current version of BRIDGE because it is easily accessible to instructors who are not programmers.

Evaluation and Future Work

In this section we assess how much the initial design goals of robustness, flexibility, portability, and efficiency have been met in our system. There are two sides to the definition of robustness: first, what the linguistic coverage of the NLP system is, and second, how tolerant the system is of incorrect input. We have already discussed error tolerance in some detail. Errors detected include typos and misspellings, syntactic errors that involve agreement, and (in the German parser) some word order errors that involve deformation of the parse tree. The main features of syntactic coverage are listed and exemplified in Table 2.2 for German and Arabic. Additionally, the Arabic parser handles subjectless sentences, differing word orders in simple declarative sentences, wh- and yes/no questions, simple relative clauses, noun construct constructions (known as *idafa*), simple embeddings, and sentences with unexpressed verbs, which are common in Arabic and must be distinguished from fragments. In both languages, the parser accepts sentence fragments as well as full sentences, a measure intended to support exercises like answering questions, where sentence fragments are typical and appropriate.

Table 2.2.
Constructions Covered by BRIDGE Parser (Arabic below German in example cells)

CONSTRUCTION	EXAMPLE
Simple Locative	• Ihr liegt im Sueden. • Al-Mityaahatu laysat 9alaa Tariiqin. *(Al-Mityaha is not on a road)*
Simple Predicative	• Ihr frau ist klug. • Yuujadu maa'un fii l-mityaahati. *(There is water in Al -Mityaha)*
Simple Transitive	• Ich habe die Antwort gefunden. • da9naa nufakkiru bimandharinTabii9iyyin namuuthajiyyin fii gharbi l-bilaadi. *(Let's consider a prime natural landscape in the west of the country)*
Simple Intransitive	• Rechts neben dem Bach verlaeuft die Landstrasse.
Conjunctive Phrases	• Ich blicke nach links, nachNorden und nach Osten. • SaHrawiyaatun wa Hajariyaatun. *(desertlike and stony)*
Simple Questions	• In welche Richtung waechst die moderne Stadt Lauterbach? • Maa huwa 9adad iT-Tariiqi l-mawjuudati fi-d-dibdibati? *(How many road are found in Al-Dibdibba?)*
Imperatives	• Beschreiben Sie die Umgebung der Stadt! • Sifa l-buyuuta fii d-dibdibbati. *(Describe the houses in Al-Dibdibba)*
Modals	• Man kann ein Burg erkennen.
Inversion	• Oestlich von Lauterbach liegt Angersbach.
Embedded Constructions	• Ich denke daß Angersbach in Deutschland ist.

We underline the fact that handling error-filled input does not involve the addition of extra routines, as in rule-based systems. By taking advantage of the modular design of the system, we can modulate the exactness of the match between grammatical pattern and student input.

We tested the parser on 200 correct and incorrect German sentences, which we constructed to incorporate likely constructions and errors of early intermediate students. The parser appropriately parsed 135 out of 141 (96.4%) correct sentences and 61 out of 64 (95.3%) incorrect sentences (that is, generated the appropriate error messages for these examples). Testing on more extensive corpora is necessary for judging the true robustness of the system. We are constructing batch test suites for the Arabic parser that will be more extensive and will have an empirical basis in a student corpus.

Flexibility is a different way of looking at the features that support robustness. Our parsing system is flexible in the sense that it is modular and that given modules may or may not be incorporated in the parser. For example, we can support a restrictive version of the NLP system (i.e., all error flags set) and a permissive one (i.e., flags selectively set). Finally, our system is portable in the sense that many parts of this implementation, we believe, can be used for other languages. This is based on our application of a modular design and a theory of grammar that encodes universal principles. Of course, the stored words must be different from language to language, but the same design and indeed entire pieces of software can be reused. Several modules of this parser have already been ported to an English parser with a different design (Merlo, 1992). The adaptation of the entire system to a very different language, Arabic, has been demonstrated. Work is now underway to adapt the system to Spanish.

Acknowledgments

This parser was developed under a contract from the U.S. Army Research Institute (ARI). The Bridge tutor of which the parser is part was a joint effort of a team at the University of Maryland and Science Applications International Corporation (SAIC). We are currently extending our approach under a new contract from ARI, with help from MicroAnalysis and Design, Inc. (Boulder, Colorado).

References

Aho, A.V., & Ullman, J.D. (1972). *The theory of parsing, translation and compiling.* Englewood Cliffs, NJ: Prentice-Hall.

Azadegan, S. et al. (1993). *A government-binding parser for foreign language training.* UMIACS Technical report, University of Maryland.

Chomsky, N. (1965). *Aspects of the theory of syntax.* Cambridge, MA: MIT Press.

Chomsky, N. (1973). Conditions on transformations. In S. Anderson & P. Kiparsky (Eds.), *A Festschrift for Morris Halle.* New York: Holt, Reinhart & Winston.

Chomsky, N. (1977). On wh-movement. In P. Culicover, T. Wasow, & A. Akmajian (Eds.), *Formal syntax.* New York: Academic Press.

Chomsky, N. (1981). *Lectures on government and binding.* Dordrecht, Netherlands: Foris.

Dorr, B.J. (1990). *Lexical conceptual structure and machine translation.* Unpublished doctoral dissertation, Massachusetts Institute of Technology.

Dorr, B.J., Garman, J., & Weinberg, A. (1994). *From subcategorization frames to thematic roles: Building Arabic lexical entries for foreign language tutoring.* Manuscript submitted for publication.

Fong, S. (1991). *Computational properties of principle-based grammatical theories.* Unpublished doctoral dissertation, Massachusetts Institute of Technology.

Garman, J., Martin, J., Merlo, P., & Weinberg, A. (1993, August). *A parameterized principle-based parser for foreign language training.* Paper presented at the Third International Workshop on Parsing Technologies of the Association for Computational Linguistics, Tilburg, Netherlands.

Jackendoff, R. (1977). *XO syntax: A study of phrase structure.* Cambridge, MA: MIT Press.

Merlo, P. (1992). *On modularity and compilation in a government-binding parser.* Unpublished doctoral dissertation, University of Maryland.

Woods, W., & Kaplan, R. (1971). *The lunar sciences natural language system* (Technical report). Cambridge, MA: Bolt, Beranek, & Newman.

3

Instructor as Author in an Adaptive, Multimedia, Foreign Language Tutor

Steve Kreyer and Eleanor Criswell
Science Applications International Corporation

The BRIDGE project was a multiyear research and development effort encompassing the design, development, and evaluation of an adaptive tutor for foreign languages. Part of a program in advanced language technologies sponsored by the U.S. Army Research Institute (ARI), BRIDGE integrates natural language processing (NLP) components into tutor and author interfaces. The name, BRIDGE, describes the tutor's function of providing language practice to military personnel between the time they graduate language school at the Defense Language Institute and the time they use their language on the job, often many months later. During this interval, filled with job-related training but with limited resources to maintain language skills, student foreign language proficiency typically drops off. Thus, there is a serious and widespread need for effective language maitenance training and, moreover, for methods that make that training easy to develop.

The BRIDGE project had three interrelated goals. The first goal was technology demonstration: the integration of adaptive multimedia instruction with a natural language parser for analysis of grammatical errors in students' free text input, all on a portable computer (PC) platform with software running under Windows. The structure of the parser and measures to ensure its compactness for the PC environment are by Weinberg, Garman, Martin, and Merlo (this volume). The second goal was to develop effective student interfaces for language learning, especially for the intermediate student. These are described by Sams (this volume) and in more detail by Criswell, Kreyer, Blascak et al. (1992), Criswell, Byrnes, and Pfister (1992), Criswell, Kreyer, Weinberg, and Sams (1992), and Kreyer and Criswell (1992). The third goal was to develop authoring interfaces that could be used by instructors and researchers to develop lessons quickly and easily. This chapter focuses on the authoring interfaces.

Authoring Features

Author Characteristics and Needs

Authoring multimedia language lessons should be a team effort, as is the case with most courseware (Criswell, 1989). Skilled instructional designers are important. If they are not fluent in the target language, a native or fluent speaker is needed to review and refine instructional material. Clerical personnel can perform routine data entry, scans of text and graphics, and maintenance of lesson archives. Sometimes the team develops a lesson on paper, then passes it off to a programmer for implementation on the computer. This latter approach has been inefficient and expensive in the past, and modern authoring systems attempt to eliminate the need for a sophisticated programmer. In fact, the

BRIDGE tutor was developed in ToolBook with the idea that instructors and researchers could learn to use that system to add their own lessons. However, we soon learned that language instructors, especially in military field settings, often do not have the time or inclination to learn new multipurpose authoring systems, such as ToolBook, Authorware Professional, LinkWay, IconAuthor, or HyperCard. For this reason, we designed an authoring interface for the BRIDGE tutor (overlaid on ToolBook) that is intended for use by instructors without specific training and with a minimal set of directions. The authoring interface also had to meet the needs of researchers at ARI who wanted to manipulate various features of the tutor (e.g., feedback messages) to study design and instructional approaches.

Authoring Components

To meet the characteristics of our target authors, several important features are incorporated into the BRIDGE authoring system. Lesson building is based on exercise templates and other configurable tutor features (e.g., lesson branching) using short entry text fields and selectable button options. The tutor automatically provides default entries so that an author does not have to specify every parameter and every field for each lesson and exercise. The use of the graphical, direct manipulation interface provided by the Windows environment fosters ease of use and cross-function consistency.

The authoring component consists of interfaces that allow a nonprogrammer to log in, create practice exercises using templates, implement a sequence of exercises called a set, define up to fifteen sets of practice exercises and their presentation sequence within a single lesson, and specify criteria for graduation and remediation across sets of exercises. In addition, authoring can be applied to libraries of instructional objectives, directions, hints, and explanations, as well as to the wording of feedback messages. The idea behind these features is to allow authors to apply principles from adaptive computer-assisted instruction, which has demonstrated dynamic branching and lesson progression based on statistical summary characteristics of students' performance (Criswell, 1989). Most computer-assisted language learning, including the systems featured in this volume, have not sought to incorporate this kind of adaptivity (see Kaplan & Holland, this volume).

Creating or Modifying Exercises

Exercise types, described by Sams (this volume), include multiple choice, sorting, point-and-click on a graphic, fill-in-the-blank, and free response questions. The exercises revolve around a text and a background graphic (e.g., a map), both of which can be changed. Two key steps are required to create or edit an exercise: definition of the exercise type and specification of hints and explanations. Each exercise type has a definition template, such as that for a multiple choice question shown in Figure 3.1. Common to all exercises, the top fields of the template contain identification data, such as a unique exercise number. The rest of the template has fields specific to the exercise type.

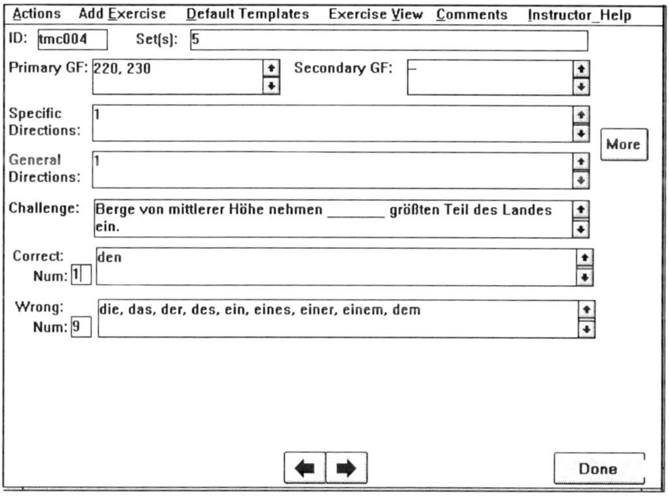

FIG. 3.1. Template for creating a multiple choice exercise in the BRIDGE tutor.

The use of these templates is best shown through examples. The template in Figure 3.1 has been filled at the top with the unique identifiers of the exercise—its number, the exercise set in which it will appear, and designation of instructional objectives (signified by numerical codes in the "GF," or good-for, fields). Numerical codes for directions correspond to prespecified instructions that are displayed to students along with the question. Next the author has typed in the multiple choice challenge (or question) to be presented to the student. Below that, in the "correct" field, the author has entered the correct response (*den*) and in the "wrong" field has entered the distracter items. The author can specify a pool of alternative distracters, and the alternatives are drawn and sequenced randomly from this pool each time the exercise appears (the number of distracters to be drawn is given by the "num" field beside the distracter set and can vary from 1 to 9). Thus, different versions of the same exercise are generated by one template.

Another exercise type is point-and-click, in which the student is asked to use the mouse to click on a described location on a map or other graphic (new ones can be scanned in). The author uses the template shown in Figure 3.2 to define the point-to challenge—for example, *am Zusammenfluß* (at the river junction)—which can be written or voiced (the example shows a voiced challenge, which calls on a prestored sound file). The template also provides for a description of the correct location and for the file name of the map or graphic (e.g., *newgerm.bmp*). The "correct button location" field is automatically filled with map coordinates when the author specifies the target location on the map. The author uses the mouse to click and drag an existing "hot spot" over the desired map location,

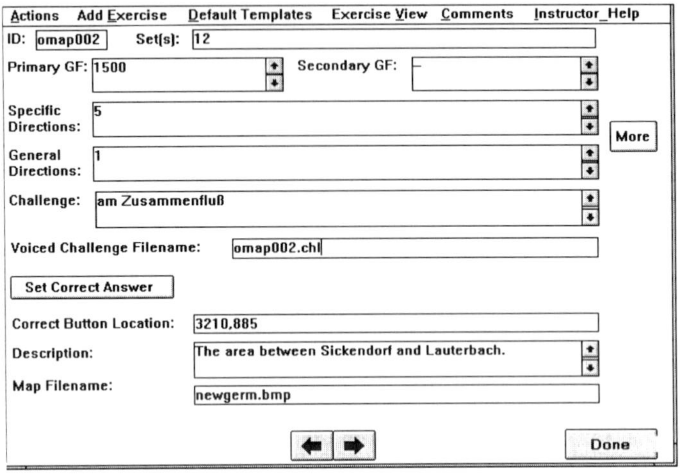

FIG. 3.2. Template for creating a point-and-click exercise.

as shown in Figure 3.3, and the coordinates (3210 and 885 in the example) are inserted into the template. When a student subsequently responds to the point-to challenge, that response is compared to the prestored correct location. Any click inside the predefined box is then counted as correct.

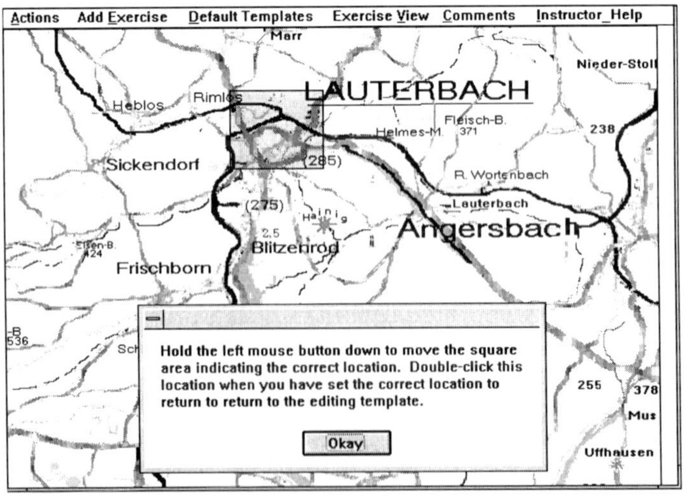

FIG. 3.3. Prespecifying a correct location for the point-and-click exercise (from Figure 3.2).

The multiple choice and point-to exercises do not use the parser. One advantage of incorporating a parser in a language tutor can be seen when authoring a fill-in-the-blank and a free response exercise, as shown in Figure 3.4. The instructor does not have to anticipate all the possible correct and incorrect responses that students may make, as in conventional computer-assisted language learning, because the parser evaluates the student's answer and returns grammatical feedback automatically. The author simply needs to type in the text challenge that is intended to prompt a response from the student.

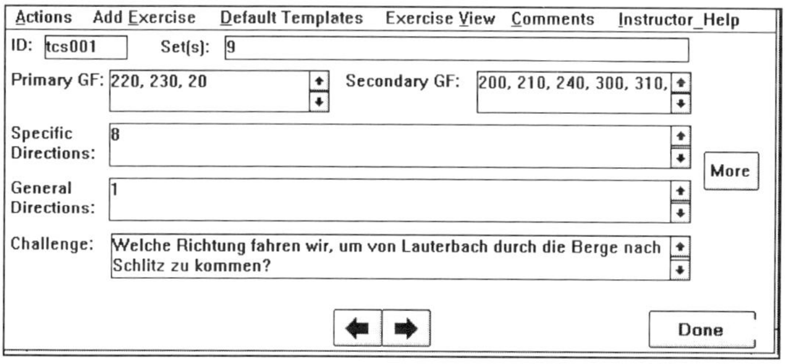

FIG. 3.4. Template for creating a free response exercise.

This way of using the parser can be compared with the authoring methods in ALICE-chan (Levin & Evans, this volume) and MILT (Dorr Hendler, Blanksteen, & Migdaloff, this volume; Kaplan & Holland, this volume). The latter tutors couple a parser (and other NLP analyses) with a matcher to enable a more tailored and semantically relevant evaluation of students' input. The matcher allows the author to prespecify the features that should be present in the student's answer. These features can range from keywords to abstract semantic structures. In BRIDGE we did not have the resources to complete a semantic matcher, so the tutor evaluates only on absolute grammatical accuracy. This means, for example, that in response to a question about where something is located, the student can type *guten tag* (good day) and be counted as correct because the grammar is sound. Two ways around this limitation are to employ hand-coded semantic self-check messages for each question and to present purely grammatical exercises in which the student does not expect meaning to be noticed (as discussed by , this volume, and by Holland, 1994). In a refinement of BRIDGE, ARI has added its own keyword matcher, developed at the University of Illinois (Hart, 1994), to give the appearance of a meaningful analysis of students'input.

Building Lessons out of Exercises

Exercises can be combined into a set, and any number of sets (up to 15) can make up a lesson. To develop a set, the author clicks on and highlights the desired exercises from the list of ones already developed, as illustrated in Figure 3.5. The existing exercises are seen listed under each of the nine exercise types (e.g., oral multiple choice and text multiple choice). In Figure 3.5 the author has selected four exercises, which have been highlighted and automatically placed in the "Exercise Sequence" box at the lower right. When the author creates a new exercise, it is added to the existing exercises under the appropriate type. In addition, bits of lessons can be pieced together by appending a new sequence to an existing one.

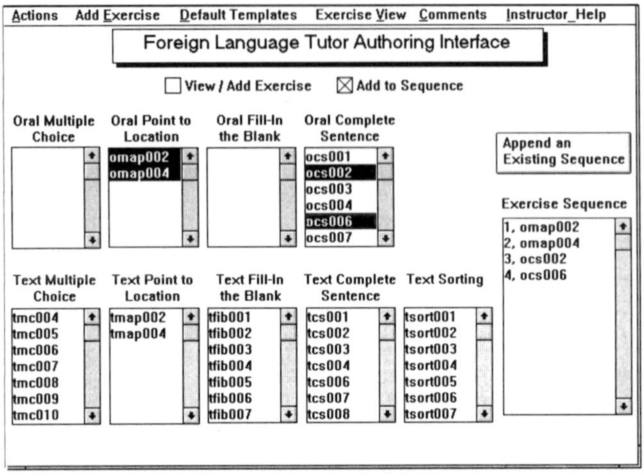

FIG. 3.5. Building a lesson sequence for BRIDGE.

We learned in trying to use this design that the author still has to do a good deal of bookkeeping on paper to keep track of the exercises. No markers are available on the sequence-building screen, and the numbering scheme does not indicate the principles behind a specific exercise. There is no way to tell, for example, which are new fill-in-the-blank exercises and which are old, or what they deal with, without entering into the templates to view each one. This problem is dealt with in ARI's MILT project in part by using a top-down flowchart approach to design (Kaplan & Holland, this volume).

Authoring Lesson Progression and Branching (Adaptive Tutoring)

Instructors may choose to develop lessons that adapt to the individual student's abilities. The BRIDGE tutor accomplishes this in two ways, forward progression and branching to focused practice sets.

Forward progression is a way to move students through the lesson material automatically at a pace based on their performance. Students who demonstrate proficiency complete fewer exercises within sets; they graduate early. Those who make errors stay longer within sets for more practice. Forward progression is defined along three levels (tracks): satisfactory, intermediate, and accelerated. The instructor determines the criteria for each track and the scores the student must attain in order to graduate from one exercise set to another.

Authors can also plan for sets of exercises to be used as extra practice if a student has difficulty progressing forward in the regular lesson. Branching to extra practice is based on identification of grammatical errors captured by the natural language processor. For example, an instructor can develop a separate set of exercises that give the student focused practice on subject-verb agreement. If the student produces an unacceptable number of subject-verb errors (as defined by the instructor), then the student is advised and automatically moved to this practice set. After extra practice, the student returns to the regular lesson. At any time during the lesson, students can check their scores and view their progress through the lesson.

Manipulable Parameters (a Researcher's Tool Kit)

Many of the tutor's parameters can be changed fairly easily. These include items such as feedback messages, directions, hints, and even button labels (see Figures 3.7 and 3.8). This arrangement is intended to help researchers manipulate variables useful for studying instructional approaches. It also allows instructors to customize the tutor to fit their instructional point of view.

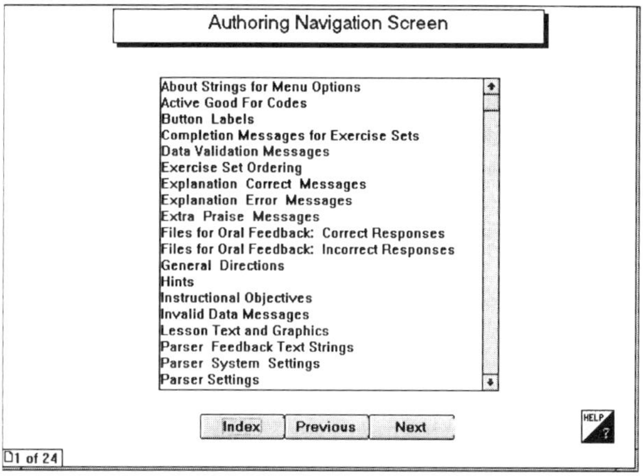

FIG. 3.7. Entry screen for changing tutor parameters.

Note that particular text items, like the feedback messages shown in Figure 3.8, can be phrased in German. Upon the student's entry to the tutor, a switch is available that sets all screen directions and feedback in German or in English. The student can toggle this switch, or the instructor can set it in advance.

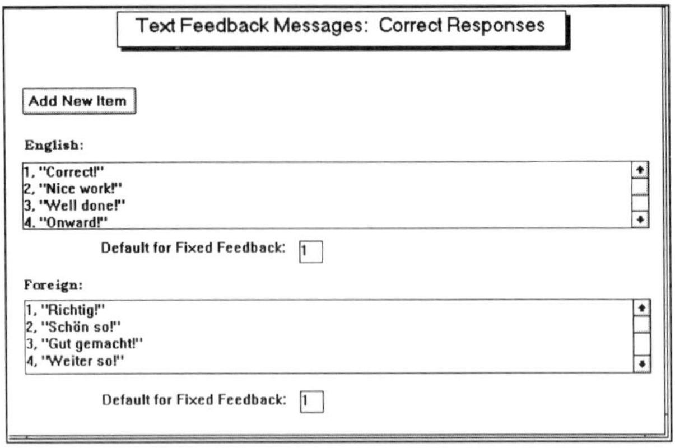

FIG. 3.8. Focused screen for editing feedback messages.

Lessons Learned About Functionality, Execution Speed, and Ease of Use

In designing and developing the BRIDGE authoring system, we learned lessons about the tradeoffs between functionality, execution speed, and ease of use. First, there is a temptation to make every possible parameter and field authorable by a nonprogrammer. In this and the MILT project, the sponsor, ARI, sought as much flexibility as possible by applying a simulation modeling approach, which gives the author ultimate bottom-up control over the configuration of the model or system. However, this flexibility is not without cost. The system runs slower with each value and field made authorable. This problem could have been lessened somewhat by using a programming language like C++, but considerable development effort had already progressed under Toolbook for Windows before the sponsor requested a template design for authoring. Although computer scientists can do things to maintain execution speed, at some point increased functionality is not worth the decreased speed. In the case of BRIDGE, we had to make difficult decisions about which parameters would be authorable and which would be preprogrammed.

Second, in order to maximize the dollars we had to spend for development, we included, wherever possible, commercially available software with free run-time licenses. User interfaces for these products may need to be optimized for project-specific users. As an example, the BRIDGE tutor uses a commercial sound board for recording audio files for use in listening comprehension exercises and in aural feedback. Resources of the BRIDGE project did not permit rewriting the user interface to the commercial sound board for easier use by language instructors. Therefore, someone wanting to make new audio recordings in lessons must either learn how to record using this board or enlist the help of someone who already knows how. The same is true of incorporating new graphic files into the tutor. We did, however, streamline the interface between the audio and graphic files and the exercises by including fields in the exercise templates where authors can designate the location of particular audio and graphic files (e.g., Figure 3.2), which are then automatically presented with the exercises.

Future Directions

We see improvements for authoring evolving in two general directions. The easiest improvements are straightforward modifications or enhancements of capabilities already available (e.g., incorporation of color coding, providing additional pull-down menus for authoring options, better integration of authoring options while creating exercises). One new capability that appears important is the quick creation of new types of exercises beyond those defined by the existing templates, perhaps by reusing code from those templates. In general, there are more different types of exercises used in language textbooks than are implemented in BRIDGE. In addition, we have done some work that will allow an author to specify correct and incorrect answers in advance for languages in which there are no appropriate NLP components, using techniques such as keywords and pattern matching.

Another direction for improvement involves significantly reducing the time it takes to author new lessons, thereby allowing instructors to incorporate timely materials into their lessons rapidly. The ultimate solution is to have the tutor evaluate text and graphic lesson materials, generate its own mix of practice exercises to go along with the lesson materials, generate a set of correct and incorrect answers for prestorage or calculation during run time, and produce relevant explanations and hints. For example, Levin, Evans, and Gates (1991) described a plan for automatic indexing of foreign language corpora for problematic constructions, so that these constructions can be retrieved in context and shown to students having difficulties. SAIC has begun to make incremental steps toward the goal of automatic exercise generation, and we have experimented with ways to generate practice exercises from a knowledge base (Criswell & Blanks, 1989). Exploration should continue along this line, involving automated analysis of lesson text and graphics and production of formatted exercises.

Acknowledgments

Development of the BRIDGE project, "Applications of Artificial Intelligence to Foreign Language Training," was funded by the U.S. Army Research Institute, contract MDA-903-89-C-0033, to Science Applications International Corporation, McLean, Virginia.

References

Criswell, E. (1989). *The design of computer-based instruction.* New York: Macmillan.

Criswell, E., & Blanks, M. (1989). *Intelligent computer-assisted instruction.* (Final Internal Research and Development Report). McLean, VA: Science Applications International Corporation.

Criswell, E., Byrnes, H., & Pfister, G. (1992). Intelligent automated strategies of teaching foreign language in context. In M. Swartz & M. Yazdani (Eds.), *The bridge to international communication: Intelligent tutoring systems for foreign language learning.* New York: Springer-Verlag.

Criswell, E., Kreyer, S., Blascak, D., Azadegan, S., Garman, J., Martin, J., Merlo, P., Weinberg, A., & Byrnes, H. (1992). *Integration of intelligent tutoring and natural language processing to teach foreign language* (Final technical report). McLean, VA: Science Applications International Corporation.

Criswell, E., Kreyer, S., Weinberg, A., & Sams, M. (1992). *Evaluation of a prototype intelligent tutor for foreign language.* (Final technical report). McLean, VA: Science Applications International Corporation.

Hart, R. (1994). *ERRATA: Response analysis and error diagnosis tools* (Technical report no. LLL-T-23-94). University of Illinois: Language Learning Laboratory.

Holland, V.M. (1994). Lessons learned in designing intelligent CALL: Managing communication across disciplines. *Computer Assisted Language Learning, 7*, 226-256.

Kreyer, S., & Criswell, E. (1992). *Forward progress and error correction in an intelligent foreign language tutor* (Final technical report). McLean, VA: Science Applications International Corporation.

Levin, L., Evans, D., & Gates, D. (1991). The ALICE system: A workbench for learning and using language. *Computer Assisted Language Instruction Consortium (CALICO) Journal, 9*, 27-56.

CALLE: An Exploratory Environment for Foreign Language Learning

Marikka Rypa and Ken Feuerman
Xerox Corporation

This chapter reports on the development of the CALLE (Computer-Assisted Language Learning Environment) prototype language training tool. CALLE supports foreign language learning by giving assistance in understanding and analyzing foreign language texts, such as documents and articles on a given topic. The system offers a window-based environment in which learners are presented a text for translation, analysis, or some other practical task. When learners encounter language they do not understand or complex constructions or usage patterns they want to know more about, they can query the text for relevant linguistic information. Learners can query text at the word or sentence level to elicit morphological, syntactic, and semantic information. By aiding the comprehension of complex linguistic constructs, this information is designed ultimately to improve learning of the target language.

CALLE's testbed language is Spanish at the level of an intermediate college course (or, more precisely, Level 2 Spanish according to the scale of the U.S. Interagency Language Roundtable). The underlying theoretical and implementational framework is lexical-functional grammar (LFG), which has been widely applied for parsing text and for representing linguistic knowledge (e.g., Levin & Evans, this volume). This chapter presents the goals and architecture of the most recent version of our system, CALLE90, and a description of its capabilities for support of language training and language reference.

CALLE stands in contrast to many of the language tutoring systems featured in this volume, which focus on eliciting language from students and analyzing it by a parser. The approach in CALLE has been to concentrate not on students' production but on their comprehension, focusing on a communications component that allows students to explore constructs in a predesignated foreign language text.

Theoretical and Pedagogical Issues

Objectives

CALLE90 represents one stage in the ongoing effort to study LFG as the theoretical and computational basis for constructing interactive language training tools (for a discussion of this issue, see Feuerman, Marshall, Newman, & Rypa, 1987; Kaplan & Bresnan, 1982). The current work builds on exploratory efforts earlier in the CALLE project to investigate LFG grammar representation both as a basis for dialogue-based interactive tutoring environments and as a vehicle for representing sophisticated linguistic constructs. Feuerman et al. (1987) described the dialogue-based prototype that resulted from initial efforts, which allowed students to produce language in a constrained conversational context. Our objectives in the CALLE90 phase of the project are to:

1. Isolate a pivotal subset of intermediate Spanish linguistic issues and construct an extensible core of language representation by exploiting the power of LFG to parse Level 2 Spanish;
2. Study and design methods of extracting LFG linguistic data to support instruction of learners trying to comprehend target Spanish text;
3. Construct an extensible interactive prototype linking the representation and extraction modules from Objectives 1 and 2 with a lookup interface designed to support comprehension of new text in Spanish.

In fulfilling these objectives, the CALLE90 project has produced a comprehension-based prototype system that gives feedback on lexical, syntactic, and graphic levels. The creation of the prototype system has resulted in the following components, corresponding respectively to the objectives just listed:

1. Intermediate LFG Spanish grammar representing Level 2 constructs;
2. Detection software that extracts relevant linguistic information from text;
3. A user interface that allows the student to query the knowledge data base for lexical and syntactic information about portions they have selected from the target text.

A final objective in the design of the CALLE tutor was to allow for tailoring and expansion of the parts of the system by the instructor. Here, the project has taken exploratory steps. Mapping tools have been developed to permit an instructor to tailor a response message, and a core capability exists to allow an instructor to add some vocabulary items by template. The significance of this capability is that it allows the system to be used as a syntactic engine and permits an instructor to slide in a new text with the same syntactic constructs, at the same level of linguistic difficulty, but in another subject area. To support the capability of instructors to extend the vocabulary either manually or automatically, the attribute-value and constraint system of lexical representation used in LFG may afford a way to posit templates that can be accessed either through menus or, eventually, through a screening of a digitized corollary lexicon. The CALLE lexicon currently contains more than 500 entries and should eventually permit tailoring and expansion suited to subject areas of interest.

The Model: Assumptions About Learning and the Learner

As a learner's environment, the CALLE90 system plays three roles. It is a reference tool in the sense that it is a repository of information. It is a tutoring tool in the sense that there is an a priori focus on specific syntactic constructions in the target language, which are to be addressed through messages to the learner. It is a discovery tool in the sense that it allows the student to infer a model of linguistic relationships by querying various manifestations of syntactic constructs in varying linguistic environments.

Our basic assumption is that the insights about linguistic relationships that comprise this learner's model can aid acquisition of the second language, or L2. Moreover, we assume that the kinds of data found in LFG representations are particularly well-suited to communicating information relevant to the learner's model. Specifically, the access to information about a queried text in CALLE exploits three types of data in LFG representation that are potentially relevant to L2 learners. First, *word lookup*, which occurs when users query an individual word, derives lexical and morphological information from lexicon files by mapping this information onto messages that use ordinary grammatical terminology. The second access option, *sentence lookup*, occurs when users select a whole sentence for query. The system then produces an explanatory message about target syntactic constructs that are detected by the parser within that sentence. The third type of information that can be presented to the user is a *core sentence diagram*, or pruned parse tree. This tree illustrates the basic predicate-argument relationships in a sentence. As additional graphic information, linguistic features such as subject of the sentence can be highlighted.

In the tradition of tutoring as the act of "clarifying a body of knowledge" (Cunningham, Iberall, & Woolf, 1986), we assume that the student has had exposure to Spanish and comes to use CALLE with a base of L2 knowledge. In particular, we assume that students are adult learners with English as their source language. We further assume that students are familiar with common grammatical and linguistic terminology. Most critically, we assume that adult learners will benefit from accessible linguistic information about a text they are trying to understand and that reflection on the structure of the L2 enhances both the immediate comprehension task and the ultimate acquisition of the language.

Implicit in our model of communicating knowledge to the student is the value of utilizing mechanisms to guide the student in exploring grammatical classes or functional relationships in the target language. For example, explanations of lexical items can be phrased and graphically structured to induce patterns of thinking about the target language that we hypothesize will enhance learning. These patterns, we contend, map directly onto the structure of the underlying knowledge representation in LFG.

CALLE in Context of Intelligent Tutoring Systems

Many intelligent computer-assisted language learning (ICALL) systems have been organized around the classical architecture of intelligent tutoring systems (ITSs) and consist of some configuration of the following four modules:

1. An *expert module* usually contains linguistic domain knowledge and some procedural curriculum plan (i.e., topics and practice exam-

ples); it may incorporate a diagnostic capability based on expected areas of difficulty.

2. A *student model* keeps track of information about the student, goals successfully met, and strategies for repair.
3. A *tutoring component* maintains information about the states of the tutor and transition rules that determine tutor responses.
4. A *communication module* represents the interface between tutor and student. In an interactive tutor, student input is accepted and some computationally based response is provided.

Examples of language tutoring systems built around this model are CALEB (Cunningham et al., 1986) for teaching basic Spanish utterances and the ET system (Fum, Giangrandi, & Tasso, 1989), which elicits the correct form of an English verb given a context. The German tutoring system of Schwind (1990) incorporates tutor-student dialogue capabilities that allow for various levels of feedback about errors and for grammatical questions. These systems, focusing on eliciting phrase- or sentence-length L2 input from the student, depend ideally on some dynamic model to determine the type of evaluation and feedback to present to the student. Currently, the complexity inherent in such systems must constrain the scope of linguistic constructs to be treated. In contrast, the approach in the CALLE project has been to concentrate not on the student model or the tutoring component but on the expert module (i.e., representations of L2 knowledge) and on the communications component. This has allowed us to focus on the extent to which LFG can efficiently capture Level 2 Spanish constructs at a highly sophisticated level as well as on what detection mechanisms can be developed to extract dynamically and flexibly, directly from the linguistic data base, those concepts relevant to learning and understanding written language.

Scope of the Linguistic Domain

Clitics assume a primary role in CALLE's domain of syntactic constructs to be taught, with emphasis on various manifestations of the *se* particle. The impersonal/passive forms of *se*, the true reflexive forms, the intrinsic reflexive and inchoative reflexive forms, and some manifestations of the emphatic use of this particle are all part of the linguistic domain. Prepositional particle usages, both in form and function, are also represented. Particular attention is given to the *a* particle in Spanish in its varying grammatical occurrences, both as verb particle and as personal *a* as well as those uses that parallel English. Also addressed are certain constructions that shift focus when translated into English, for example, the class of verbs known as *psych-verbs* (Belletti & Rizzi, 1988). With psych-verbs, the sentence object or experiencer in Spanish (e.g., *me* in *me gusta*) is translated as the sentence subject in English (e.g., *I* in *I like*), as in the verbs *faltar*, *gustar*, and *importar* (examples appear later in Figures 4.7 and 4.8). This focus shift between Spanish and English is called *subject-object reversal* by Dorr et al., this volume, who account for it by a parameter added to psych-verbs in the Spanish and English lexicons.

Expansion of the CALLE grammar has taken place on other levels. Dependent clause types such as relative, nominal, and subordinate clauses are now handled by the grammar rules, as are introductory adverbial constructions, constrained prepositional modifiers, participial verb tenses, and concatenated forms of verbs.

Along with the effort to formulate linguistic representations of these constructs, work has continued on the formulation of LFG templates, illustrated later in this chapter. These templates represent the major patterns of verbal predicate-argument relationships to be mastered by students of Spanish at an intermediate level (e.g., sentence patterns using transitive, intransitive, and inchoative verbs as well as psych-verbs). These templates could, therefore, serve a potentially important teaching function.

Project Motivations

The CALLE project was motivated both by available resources in the LFG linguistic environment and by cognitive design considerations.

Resources in the computational environment. The motivations behind the development of CALLE reflect two aspects of the computational environment. One motivation was to construct an interactive interface operating on immediate context and feedback, with records of student queries maintained for use in subsequent instructional analysis. A second motivation was to address a readily exploitable knowledge representation environment (the NLP representations) that allows easy access to information in the system containing the knowledge bases.

Cognitive design: The* se *issues. From a cognitive perspective, our design of sample text as a testbed reflects the realistic occurrence and distribution of problematic constructs in authentic Spanish text. An illustrative construct is the Spanish particle *se*, as in "Se vende el libro," which may mean "He sells the book to himself"—a true reflexive—but is more commonly interpreted as passive ("The book is sold") or impersonal ("One sells the book"). A review of the treatment of *se* in grammar texts and Spanish reference works (Holt & Dueber, 1973) reveals that this particle is most often introduced as a reflexive, whereas nonreflexive uses, such as passive or impersonal, are lumped together in a single category with little guidance or explanation as to usage. Moreover, the reflexive use of *se* is commonly introduced first, while its other manifestations are treated later. Consequently, the mental model of *se* inferred by students probably rests on the reflexive usage, with the other manifestations as secondary and/or arbitrary.

Such a model can pose considerable confusion in view of the actual empirical usage of *se*. A review of textual concordances reveals that the true reflexive form of the particle does not occur in the majority of manifestations. We studied a data sample of 130 pages of running journalistic text on the topic of a global health epidemic. Our aim was to target a representative domain-centered corpus in Spanish reflecting the distribution of various linguistic constructs in common newspaper prose. We found the breakdown of *se* usage in this sample as shown in Table 4.1.

Table 4.1.
Incidence of *Se* in a Sample of Spanish Text

Type	#	%
Passive/Impersonal:	212	65
Inchoative:	50	15
Intrinsic:	49	15
Reflexive/Reciprocal:	11	3
Emphatic:	3	1
Total	325	99

It can be noted from Table 4.1 that the reflexive use of *se* comprises only a small percentage of the total uses of *se* in the corpus we analyzed. This would suggest that a more realistic approach to instruction not start with the reflexive role of *se* but rather present *se* in its various manifestations so that the student can formulate a more realistic model of its roles.

In the CALLE grammar the roles of *se* are represented both as reflexive (or technically, as pronominal, functioning as a governable object, either as direct or indirect object) and as a grammatical marker in various functions, including markers for passive, impersonal, emphatic, and intrinsic. This distribution of roles in the LFG reflects the data in Table 4.1. The need to present learners with target sample text that presents a realistic distribution of *se* and of other advanced linguistic constructs guided our thinking in selecting interactive L2 paragraphs for CALLE.

The CALLE System: Architecture and Functionality

The Interface

Educational literature has long supported the view that context solidifies learning and retention. The Windows system in InterLisp Medley affords facilities to present a text on a particular subject so that the student can process and understand the foreign language in a meaningful context, such as a paragraph on a subject of interest. This meaningfulness is enhanced by the immediate feedback offered by the system. The interface allows the student to access Spanish text with mouse clicks and to receive immediate feedback on the word level, the syntactic level, and the core sentence diagram level (i.e., graphic parse tree representations). Any word or sentence in the text is immediately accessible in this way without requiring the student to consult references that distract from the text. Individual tracking is another feature of the system. Tracking focuses on the linguistic areas problematic for the student and provides a trace of queries that can serve as guideposts for individual attention by the instructor.

The LFG Environment

Lexical-functional grammar is a theory of natural language, a vehicle for knowledge representation, and an environment for parsing. As such, it provides a readily exploitable linguistic environment as a basis for constructing a tutoring tool. The main resources available for knowledge representation are a morphological table, a rule set, a lexicon, and template mechanisms. Each resource represents a repository of knowledge that can be tapped by detection methods, allowing the system designer to mine the information that has been structured by the language expert and to present it in a form that will communicate to learners.

Characterizations of linguistic relationships in LFG map into instruction as representation structures that are accessible and potentially useful to a language student. These representation structures reveal pedagogically important relationships such as linguistic classes (e.g., part of speech, verb categories), morphological derivations, and functional relationships (e.g., which words serve as subject or object in a specific context). Consequently, these representations offer the potential for the student or the system to initiate exploration of linguistic phenomena and relationships, thereby leading students to a deeper awareness of structures in the target language.

Approach

Contrastive analysis. Our approach to isolating which Spanish language issues to treat was informed by contrastive analysis as a model of language learning (Lado, 1957; Schuster, 1985). In this approach, the native language grammar acts as a student model. Thus, acquiring a second language is a unique kind of learning in that the learner comes to the endeavor with domain patterns already acquired from the native language, some of which may aid in learning and some of which may interfere. One of the tasks in language teaching is to make the student aware of new structures so as to facilitate their use. Therefore, in determining what should be represented at the intermediate level grammar of CALLE, we were guided by considerations of contrastive syntax and unfamiliar constructions in Spanish that often constitute stumbling blocks for the native English speaker.

In designing a text for comprehension, however, we paid particular attention to those areas in which difficulties stem from contrasts *within* the target language itself, as opposed to pairs of contrasts between source and target language. We concentrated on three areas of within-language contrast:

1. Those constructions in which both syntactic context and underlying functional structure differ in the manifestation of the same verb (e.g., *tratar*, see Figure 4.10);
2. Those constructions in which syntactic appearance varies but the underlying functional structure matches (e.g., *dejo de comer* vs. *quiero comer*);
3. Those constructions whose lexical appearance is identical but whose underlying functional relationships differ (e.g., the *se* construction illustrated earlier). The correct lexical and syntactic interpretations

are arrived at by parsing sentences and detecting possible correct interpretations in syntactic context.

These areas are illustrated in terms of syntactic environments and functional descriptions later in this chapter.

System design. In the course of the CALLE effort, emphasis on representational power shifted from interest in breadth to interest in depth. The focus was constrained to specific issues in comprehension of Spanish. A data extract was culled from the newspaper corpus that was the basis for the analysis in Table 4.1. This extract was constructed so as to include and focus attention on issues problematic for a student at Level 2 Spanish.

Simultaneously, principled detection mechanisms were developed to extract relevant linguistic information from LFG data files and parses. In later sections of this chapter we discuss the range of LFG representation and how the detector mechanisms find and formulate various kinds of linguistic information to be transferred to the student. Mappings between LFG representation conventions and grammatical terminology familiar to the student were then established to facilitate communication of linguistic concepts to the student.

Effort was then directed toward developing a clean, window-based interface that would provide a cognitively supportive environment to aid in comprehension of the sample Spanish paragraph.

The System

The diagram in Figure 4.1 represents a conceptual overview of the major components of the CALLE system prototype. Given a source text, the student (who may be performing as a translator) can query selected text at three levels: a lexical or word lookup, a syntactic construction or sentence lookup, and a core sentence diagram operation. In the case of word lookup, the morphological and lexical information on the selected word is compiled by LFG and passed on to the Linguistic Feature Extraction module. Detectors determine the type and format of information to be passed on to a Help Message Transcript, which is then displayed on the screen. Before being displayed, however, linguistic symbols are mapped into instructional terminology by the Abbreviation Table.

During sentence lookup, the selected sentence is analyzed by the LFG parser, and the results are passed on to the Linguistic Feature Extraction module. Again, detectors transform this linguistic information into instructional information, which is sent to the Help Messages Transcript via the Abbreviation Table (see messages in Figures 6 and 8). In the core sentence diagram operation, the sentence is parsed by the LFG system, and the results are passed on to the Sentence Core Extraction unit, which constructs a pared diagram extracting and depicting the basic predicate-argument relationships in a sentence. The diagram is then displayed in a separate window (see Figure 9).

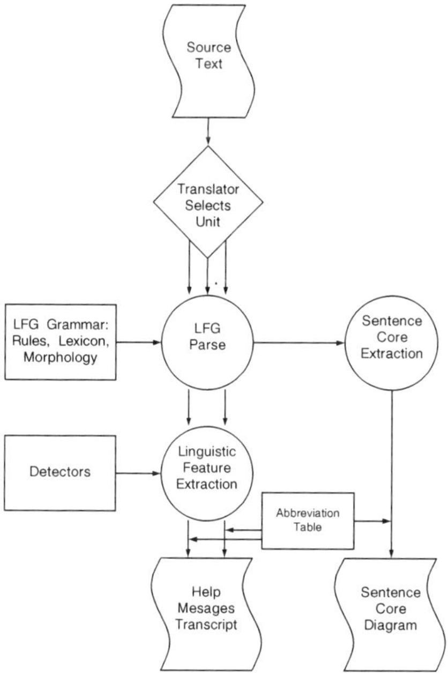

FIG. 4.1. System architecture for CALLE.

System Interactions

In this section we illustrate the surface or *constituent structure* and the underlying or *functional structure* that result from an LFG parse of an input sentence. The detectors simultaneously provide linguistic information in a help window.

Word lookup. When a lexical item in the text is selected by the student, the detection software calculates and extracts the relevant information from the lexical data files together with the morphological tables used in the LFG parse. Concatenated clitic structure, as in the *quitárselas* form following, serves as an example of how the software detects the grammatical structure of a lexical item that cannot in its concatenated form be found in a dictionary:

Se trata de quitárselas.
'They [impersonal] tried to take them away from them.'

Although the constituent structures in Figure 4.2 reflect only the linear relationships of the nodes comprising the *quitárselas* concatenation, the concomitant functional structures in Figure 4.3 reveal the full set of grammatical information.

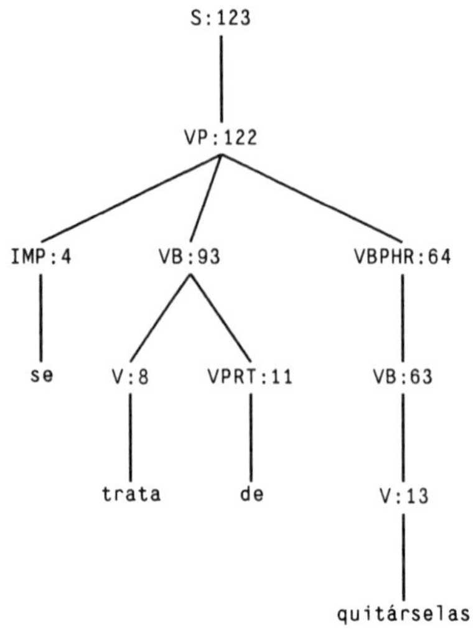

FIG. 4.2. Sentence constituent structure, or C-Structure, from Lexical-Functional Grammar analysis of "Se trata de quitárselas."

An examination of the functional structure in Figure 4.3 shows that the information needed to complete the verbal predicate-argument structure of the verbal unit *quitárselas* is included in the OBJ (direct object) and the OBL-OBJ (oblique object) attributes of the INFCOMP (infinitive complement), with values indicating number, person, and gender where applicable. This information about how the clitic elements relate to each other can be extremely useful to a student trying to interpret the sentence, but the information needs to be converted to a more comprehensible form. The type of information illustrated in Figure 4.3, automatically compiled as the result of a parse, provides the data for the detector software so that comprehensible student messages, such as the one in Figure 4.4, can be formulated.

Sentence lookup. When a sentence is selected by the student, the detector software translates information about syntactic phenomena of interest or difficulty as derived by the LFG Extraction module.

The se *constructions.* As an illustration of multiple interpretations based on variant underlying functional structures, an LFG parse of the following Spanish sentence results in three distinct tree structures, represented by the English interpretations a-c:

Se vende el libro.

a. 'He sells the book to himself.' (*se* as reflexive indirect object)
b. 'One sells the book.' (*el libro*, the book, as OBJ object to the impersonal subject *se*, as in Figure 4.3)
c. 'The book is sold.' (*el libro* as the NP subject of the passive sentence)

```
     ┌PRED        'TRY-TO<[142:PRO],[64:TAKE-AWAY]>'
     │VERBPART   DE
     │VERBROOT   tratar
     │            ┌NUM     SG┐
     │IMPERS     4└PERSON  3 ┘
     │             ┌PRED          'TAKE-AWAY<[142:PRO],[143:LAS],[144:SE]>'┐
     │             │INF           +
     │             │VERBROOT      quitar
     │             │              ┌PRED    'LAS'┐
     │             │OBJ           │GENDER  FEM
     │             │              │NUM     PL
     │             │           143└SUFFIX  LAS  ┘
     │INFCOMP      │              ┌PRED     'SE'┐
     │             │              │CL        +
     │             │OBL-OBJ       │PERSON    3
     │             │              │PREPSEM   FROM
     │             │           144└SUFFIX    SE ┘
  123│           64│              ┌PRED    'PRO'┐
  122│           63│SUBJ          │NUM     SG
   93│           13└           142└PERSON  3    ┘
   11│
    8└SUBJ        [142:PRO]
```

FIG. 4.3. Sentence functional structure, or F-Structure, from Lexical-Functional Grammar analysis of "Se trata de quitárselas."

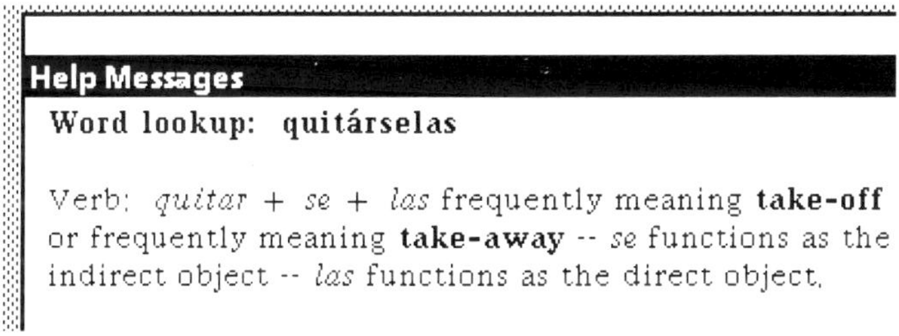

FIG. 4.4. Help message given to student for word lookup of *quitárselas*.

The C-Structures for these interpretations are shown in Figure 4.5. Upon selection of the sentence in question, "Se vende el libro," the lookup window presents information based on the C-structure shown in Figure 4.6. The first interpretation of this sentence (i.e., 'He sells the book to himself') is less likely than the latter two, but choice of interpretation is left to the system user, who can judge by context, which, of course, can vary depending on the particular paragraph the user is viewing.

C-Structures:

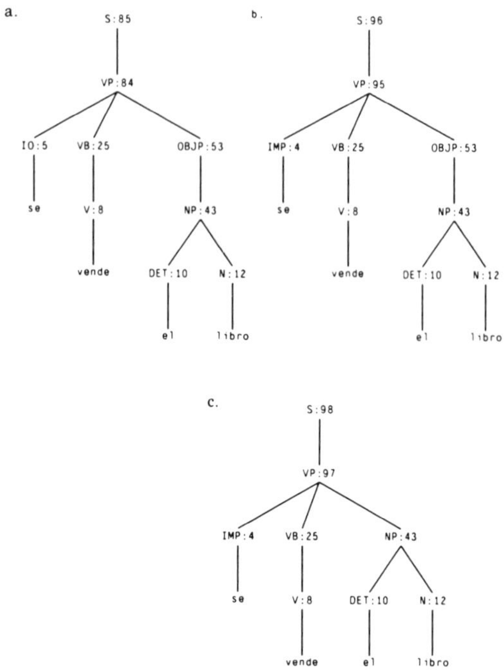

FIG. 4.5. Multiple constituent structures for "Se vende el libro."

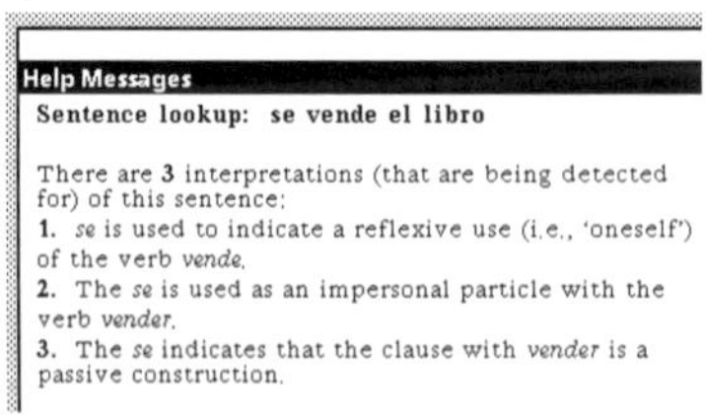

FIG. 4.6. Help message for sentence lookup for "Se vende el libro."

Psych-verbs. A class of verbs particularly problematic for English-speaking students learning Spanish is the class of psych-verbs referred to earlier. These verbs are defined as having an experiencer object and a thematic subject, as in

Me gustan los libros (I like the books).

Confusion often arises because the component that normally translates to the subject (*I*) in English is the indirect object in Spanish (*me*). The functional structure derived by the LFG provides the information that this is a psych-verb and presents a grid of the functional arguments to the verb, as shown in Figure 4.7.

```
  [PRED      'PLEASE<[47:BENEFIT],[4:me]>'  ]
  [PSYCHV    +                               ]
  [VERBROOT  gustar                          ]
  [            [PRED       'me'    ]         ]
  [            [ANIM       +       ]         ]
  [            [CL         +       ]         ]
  [OBL-OBJ     [NUM        SG      ]         ]
  [            [PCASE      OBL-OBJ ]         ]
  [            [PERSON     1       ]         ]
  [           4[PSYCHPRED  +       ]         ]
  [            [PRED        'BENEFIT']       ]
  [            [ANIM        -        ]       ]
  [            [CASE        NOM      ]       ]
  [SUBJ        [GENDER      MASC     ]       ]
49[            [NUM         PL       ]       ]
48[          47[PERSON      3        ]       ]
25[          12[SPEC        DEF      ]       ]
 7[           9[SUBJSTATED  +        ]       ]
```

FIG. 4.7. Psych-verb functional Information for "*Me gustan los libros.*"

The detection software translates these F-structure representations into a message, shown in Figure 4.8, that directs student attention to these differences.

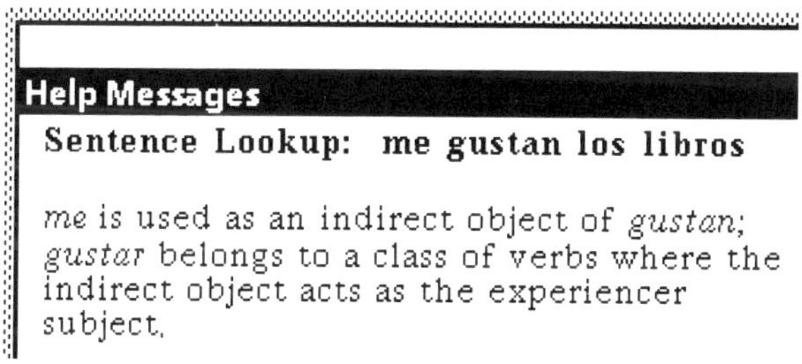

FIG.4. 8. Help message for psych-verb sentence from Figure 4.7.

Core sentence diagram operations. With constructions containing psych-verbs, the third lookup capability proves helpful in presenting a graphic representation of the sentence. We have developed a core constituent parse that isolates only the core sentence and salient relationships for the student. The core tree for the psych-verb sentence "Me gustan los libros," is shown in Figure 4.9, with the subject in bold print to clarify the contrasting relationships in Spanish.

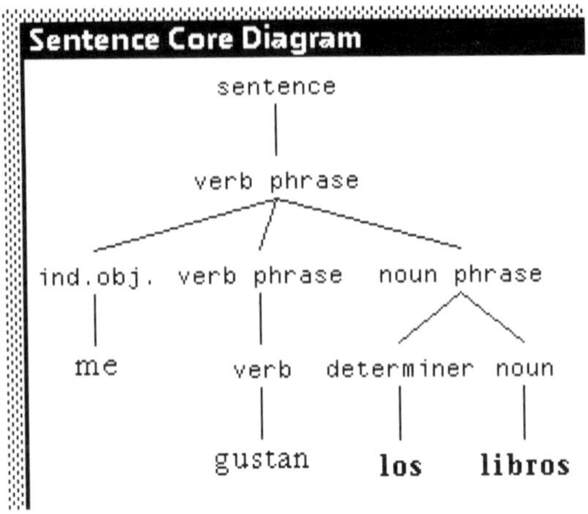

FIG. 4.9. Sentence core diagram for *Me gustan los libros.*

Semantic contrasts determined by syntax. One very important area for the student learning syntax is the recognition that lexemes may have varying semantic content depending on syntactic context. The verb *tratar*, with three distinct meanings, illustrates this point:

a. El médico trata a los pacientes (The doctor is treating the patients).
b. El médico trata de curar a los pacientes (The doctor is trying to cure the patients).
c. Se trata de una pacientes muy enfermos grave (It is a matter of very ill patients).

If the student encounters one of these sentences and is confused, the CALLE Spanish grammar detects these differences in meaning on the basis of syntax and can hand off this information to the detection software. The selection of the verb *tratar* in the translation text window results in the feedback shown in Figure 4.10.

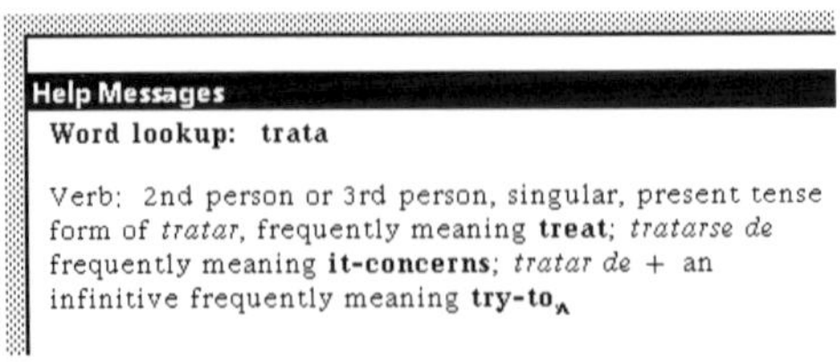

FIG. 4.10. Help message for the verb *tratar.*

The detectors extract from the linguistic data base appropriate information to convey the choices of expression in syntactic context to the student.

Detectors

In this section we discuss the detector technology that was developed to extract information relevant to instruction from LFG parse solutions.

Purpose of Detectors

Detectors form the component of the CALLE system that serves to convert linguistic information from an LFG parse of a sentence into language instruction. Currently, this language instruction takes the form of textual templates, which can be instantiated with information from the sentence parse and formatted for display in a Help Messages window. The text of the these templates is arbitrary; an instructor can compose whatever informative message is desired in order to convey relevant information to the student.

We envision that future designs will generalize this form of language instruction from textual templates to a number of instructional devices. Examples of such devices include pointers to hypertext components and calls to Lisp functions that could invoke other tutorial modules and programs.

Detector use. Each detector searches for a pattern in the solution structures generated by an LFG parse of a sentence. By composing a detector, an instructor determines which pattern to search for. The presence of a target pattern indicates the occurrence of a particular linguistic construction. Thus, for each detector, the instructor can compose a message that serves to point out the occurrence of a phenomenon in the context of actual use. That message can then be displayed for the student.

Anatomy of a Detector

A detector consists of four parts: a version and language indication, a detector label, a detector pattern, and a detector message, as schematized in Figure 4.11.

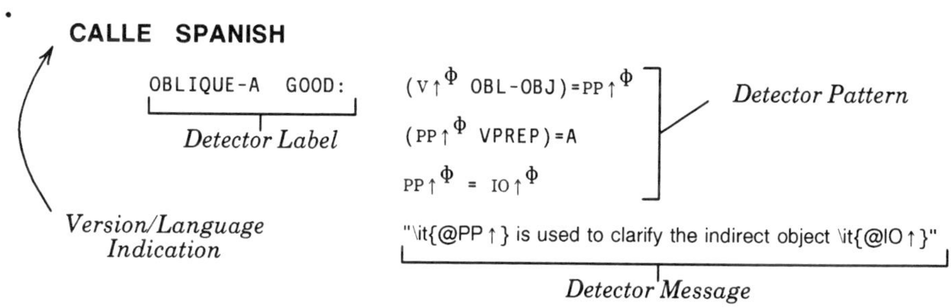

FIG. 4.11. Detector components in CALLE.

Version and language indication. This is an implementation convention. It consists of two words that serve to identify a group of detectors as a logical unit in the CALLE system. The version/language indication of a detector plays a role identical to the version and language of LFG rules, lexical entries, or any other component in the LFG system.

Detector label. The label consists of two parts, the detector name and the detector type. The name is a word that, together with the version and language indication, uniquely identifies the detector in the system. The detector type currently is the word *GOOD*, indicating that this is a feature detector. Error detectors, not yet implemented, will use the detector type to indicate a particular type of error.

Detector pattern. The pattern is a template to be matched against the parse solutions. Its purpose is to find the occurrence of constructions predefined as problematic. The pattern consists of an equation, a constraint, or a Boolean combination of equations and constraints involving constituent variables. Each equation and constraint either makes a statement about the attributes and values of the image of constituents under LFG projections or expresses a relationship between those images. The result of matching a detector pattern against a parse solution is a set of constituent variable bindings for which the pattern's expression holds true (or the empty set if no binding of variables can be found for the pattern). If the result is a nonempty set, the detector's message is displayed for the student, thereby indicating one linguistic phenomenon present in the selected sentence.

A constituent variable has a special form that resembles metavariables in LFG theory. The general form of a constituent variable is *Cat*↑, where ↑ indicates that the symbol is a variable and *Cat* indicates the category of the constituents (e.g., V or verb, NP or noun phrase, PP or prepositional phrase) to which this variable may be bound. For example, the expression

$$(\mathrm{NP}{\uparrow}^{\Phi}\ \mathrm{PERSON}) = 3$$

would result in a variable binding of NP↑ with a noun phrase constituent if that constituent's image under the functional structure projection Φ had a PERSON attribute with a value 3. The binding of variables becomes important when considering logical conjunctions of equations and in constructing the actual message to be displayed in the Help Messages window.

In addition to specifying the constituent category to which a variable may refer, an asterisk (*) may be used to indicate that the variable may stand for any constituent regardless of category. Thus the expression

$$({*}{\uparrow}^{\Phi}\ \mathrm{REF}) = +$$

would result in a set of bindings of the variable *↑ to any constituent whose image under Φ had a REF feature equal to +.

As with the LFG system, when the projection is omitted from the expression, the functional structure projection f is assumed. Consider the following detector pattern:

$$(V\uparrow \text{ OBL-OBJ}) = PP\uparrow$$
$$(PP\uparrow \text{ VPREP}) = A$$
$$PP\uparrow = IO\uparrow.$$

Figures 4.12 and 4.13 show the solution structures produced by the LFG parse of the sentence, "Le doy a ella los libros" (I give her the books). In these figures the numbers on the constituents serve to identify each constituent uniquely, and the corresponding number on the functional structures indicates the image of that constituent under Φ.

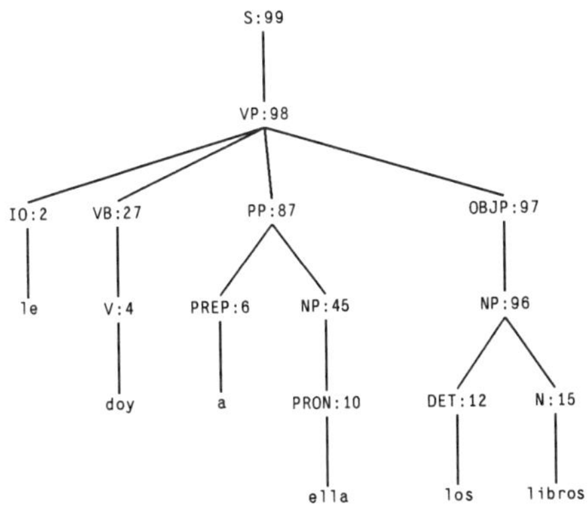

FIG. 4.12. Constituent structure for "Le doy a ella los libros."

```
  ┌PRED       'GIVE<[158:PRO],[97:BOOK],[87:TO-AT]>'┐
  │...         ...                                  │
  │           ┌PRED   'TO-AT<[45:SHE-HER]>'┐        │
  │           │...     ...                 │        │
  │           │PCASE  OBL-OBJ              │        │
  │OBL-OBJ    │VPREP  A                    │        │
  │         87│                            │        │
  │          6│POBJ  45┌PRED 'SHE-HER'┐    │        │
  │          2└        10└...    ...   ┘   ┘        │
  │         97┌PRED    'BOOK'┐                      │
  │         96│...      ...  │                      │
  │OBJ      15│GENDER  MASC  │                      │
  │         12└NUM     PL    ┘                      │
99│           ┌PRED    'PRO'┐                       │
98│SUBJ       │CASE    NOM  │                       │
27│           │NUM     SG   │                       │
 4└        158└PERSON  1    ┘                       ┘
```

FIG. 4.13. Functional structure for "Le doy a ella los libros."

The result of matching the detector pattern against this particular solution is as follows:

Variable	**Binding**
V↑	V:4
PP↑	PP:87
IO↑	IO:2

The detector pattern finds a match in the sentence analysis because (a) the functional structure that is the image under Φ of V:4 has an OBL-OBJ attribute whose value is $(PP{:}87)^{\Phi}$; (b) the structure $(PP{:}87)^{\Phi}$ has a VPREP attribute whose value is A; (c) the images under Φ of PP:87 and IO:2 are equal.

Detector message. The detector message is the explanation string that is displayed in the Help Messages window of the CALLE system when the detector pattern matches the parse solution. The variable bindings resulting from the detector pattern match can also be used to include parts of the parsed sentence or specific information found in the solution structures. In addition, some elementary font indications can be specified by using a TEX-like macro notation. For example, given the variable bindings from the sample above, the message

\it{@PP↑} is used to clarify the indirect object \it{@IO↑}

is displayed to the student as

a ella is used to clarify the indirect object *le*.

Before the detector message is displayed in the Help Messages window, it is examined for indications of textual substitution and font specifications. There are two substitution notations that can be used in the message. These notations depend upon the variable bindings resulting from the detector pattern match and can therefore take advantage of the results of the LFG parse of the sentence, as shown:

1. The symbol & followed by an LFG application expression is replaced by the resulting evaluation of the application expression in the parse solution (with constituent variables replaced by their bindings). For example, with the variable V↑ bound to V:4 in the sample given previously, an expression &(V↑ OBJ GENDER) in the detector message would be replaced by the term *MASC* when the message is displayed in the Help Messages window. This notation is especially useful in lexical detectors. (The result of this evaluation process is looked up in an abbreviation table before displaying in the Help Messages window. Thus, the abbreviation *MASC* can be converted to the word *masculine*.)
2. The symbol @ followed by a constituent variable is replaced by the lexical descendants of the constituent to which the variable is bound.

> That includes all words that are dominated in the constituent structure by the constituent to which the variable refers. In our example, @IO↑ is replaced with *le* because the word *le* is a daughter of the constituent IO:2 in the constituent structure and the variable IO↑ is bound to IO:2. Because PP↑ is bound to PP:87 and the constituent PP:87 dominates the words *a ella* from the sentence, *a ella* is substituted for @PP↑.

Lexical Detectors

In addition to sentence-level lookups, students may request an individual word when they desire lexical information. The same methodology of performing syntactic detection at the sentence level can be applied at the word level. The lexical entry for an individual word allows one to begin building the standard LFG structures that arise as a result of parsing a sentence with that word. These structures can serve as the basis from which to create detectors that transmit lexical information to the student.

As an example, consider the lexical entry for the word *comprobados*:

```
CALLE  SPANISH
 comprobados
      ADJ NREGO (↑ PRED)='CONFIRMED'
            (↑ NUM)=PL
            (↑ GENDER)=MASC.
```

Figure 4.14 presents the functional structure that is constructed as a result of parsing *comprobados* in a sentence.

```
[PRED    'CONFIRMED']
[GENDER  MASC       ]
[NUM     PL         ]
```

FIG. 4.14. Functional structure for *comprobados*.

Based on the structure shown in Figure 4.14, one can write a lexical detector of this form:

```
ADJECTIVE  GOOD: (ADJ↑ GENDER)
      (ADJ↑ NUM)
            (ADJ↑ PRED)
    "&(ADJ↑ GENDER), &(ADJ↑ NUM) form, commonly meaning \lc{\bf{&(ADJ↑
PRED)}}".
```

A word lookup on *comprobados*, after passing through the abbreviation lookup, would produce the following message in the Help Messages window:

masculine, plural form, commonly meaning **confirmed**

The drawback of this approach is that there may be adjectives in the lexicon that do not specify a gender or number feature. Such adjectives would fail to trigger the ADJECTIVE lexical detector. One solution to this problem is to write three different detectors, each one to detect a different feature. The detector messages for each feature that is specified are then collected and concatenated. Because it is desirable to have the features of a lexical item mentioned in a particular order (e.g., gender, number, meaning), an additional # notation followed by a number can be used to specify this order. Thus, one may write the three adjective lexical detectors as

```
ADJ-GENDER  GOOD: (ADJ↑ GENDER)
        "#1 &(ADJ↑ GENDER),".

ADJ-NUM  GOOD: (ADJ↑ NUM)
        "#2 &(ADJ↑ NUM) form,".

ADJ-PRED  GOOD: (ADJ↑ PRED)
        "#3 commonly meaning \lc{\bf{&(ADJ↑ PRED)}}".
```

Because all three of these detectors match the structure for *comprobados*, all three messages are concatenated, in the order specified, to produce the same message as before:

masculine, plural form, commonly meaning **confirmed**

If an adjective does not specify one of these features, that part of the message is omitted.

Future Directions

A number of areas of further research have been suggested by the advances in the CALLE interactive training environment. Most promising are four areas:

1. implicit instructional guidance mechanisms based on structural language patterns;
2. tailoring and channels of instructor access to the system;
3. error diagnosis;
4. automatic lexical augmentation.

Structural Language Patterns

Present access to CALLE explanatory messages is through manipulation of strings that appear in the student help window. Markers can be strategically placed in these messages to indicate that additional information can be explored. Several types of links from these messages to additional linguistic information already present in the LFG representation have suggested themselves in the course of our work. The pattern groups to which a particular lexeme belongs (or the functional grid(s) into which that lexeme fits) can be exploited to induce patterns of thinking about the target language.

The way in which the system interacts with the student can represent an implicit model of classifications and functional relationships (e.g., the functional relationship between inchoative verbs and transitive verbs). As an example, the selection of junctures with expansion nodes leading to further information or explanation types inherently suggests a model of linguistic categorization or hierarchy.

Methods of linkage between certain elements in an explanatory message and linguistic information encoded in LFG can be investigated. For example, when a verb form such as *falta* is chosen for linguistic query, the ensuing message could include button features that may be selected for further information, as shown in Figure 4.15.

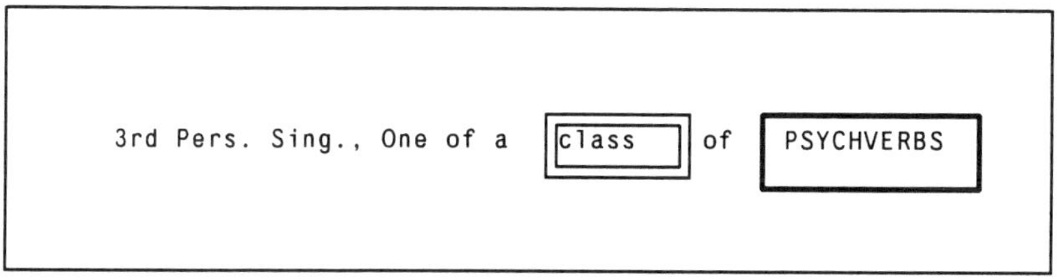

FIG. 4.15. Envisioned *falta* help message.

Moreover, the system might automatically construct a list of morphological or functional items indexed by the same verb subcategorization structure as *faltar*. When the student selects the item "class," for example, those verbs listed in in that class in the lexicon (e.g., *faltar*, *importar*, and *gustar*) would appear in the help window. When PSYCH-VERB is selected, an explanation of why these verbs are a class and why they merit special attention would appear. Many other patterns can be targeted. Transitive verbs allowing reflexivization, transitive verbs that can be inchoativized, or reflexive intrinsics are but a few.

Instructor Access

Methods of part-of-speech subcategorization in LFG also lend themselves to the construction of access channels so that a language instructor who is not a programmer can augment vocabulary in the computational lexicon. A further area of investigation is determining the subset of LFG attributes and features and the types of subcategorizations that are best addressed. Another is identifying the interfaces (such as menus and windows) that are best suited to allowing access to the lexicon by an instructor.

Error Diagnosis

Another potential for continued work is in error diagnosis. A major component of the original CALLE project (Feuerman et al., 1987) was error detection and diagnosis of sentences created by students. At that time, extensive Lisp programming was required to determine the error present in a parse of a student-composed sentence. The new feature detectors from the CALLE90 project can be utilized to detect errors in students' language, thereby eliminating the need for programming Lisp code for this purpose. One could thus express error detection routines in a manner more closely associated with typical LFG grammar rules and lexical entry equations. When certain inconsistencies exist or constraints fail to hold in a parse, one could use the detectors to determine what is at fault with the sentence and make recommendations about how to repair it. Error detection of student input would enrich the tutoring environment and add the dimension of language production and evaluation.

Grammar and Lexical Acquisition

Further research should also be conducted on automating some of the grammar acquisition functions in CALLE, to help the parser extend beyond the limitations of the preprogrammed rules. One approach is to take advantage of preexisting on-line lexicons when a word that is not currently in the LFG lexicon is encountered. Those features that are available from the on-line source would be incorporated into the parse of a sentence; other features required by the LFG grammar may then be induced from the sentence context when the input is known to be grammatically correct.

References

Belletti, A., & Rizzi, L. (1988). Psych-verbs and Q-theory. *Natural Language & Linguistic Theory*, 6.

Cunningham, P., Iberall, T., & Woolf, B. (1986). CALEB: An intelligent second language tutor. *Proceedings of the IEEE International Conference on Systems, Man, and Cybernetics.* Los Alamitos, CA.

Feuerman, K., Marshall, C., Newman, D., & Rypa, M. (1987). The CALLE project. *CALICO Journal, 4*, 25-34.

Fum, D., Giangrandi, P., & Tasso, C. (1989). Tense generation in an intelligent tutor for foreign language teaching: Some issues in the design of the verb expert. *Proceedings of Fourth Conference of the European Chapter of the Association of Computational Linguistics* (pp. 124-129). Manchester, England: University of Manchester.

Holt, M.P., & Dueber, J. (1973). *1001 pitfalls in Spanish.* Woodbury, New York: Barron's Educational Series.

Kaplan, R.M., & Bresnan, J. (1982). Lexical-functional grammar: A formal system for grammatical representation. In J. Bresnan (Ed.), *The mental representation of grammatical relations.* Cambridge, MA: MIT Press.

Lado, R. (1957). *Linguistics across cultures.* Ann Arbor, MI: University of Michigan Press.

Schuster, E. (1985). Grammars as user models. *Proceedings of the Ninth International Joint Conference on Artificial Intelligence.* Palo Alto, CA: Kaufmann.

Schwind, C. (1990). An intelligent language tutoring system. *International Journal of Man-Machine Studies.* London: Academic Press.

5

ALICE-chan: A Case Study in ICALL Theory and Practice

Lori S. Levin and David A. Evans
Carnegie Mellon University

Intelligent computer-assisted language learning (ICALL) presents challenges along several dimensions. First, there are many design and implementation issues related to the use of artificial intelligence and natural language processing (NLP) technologies in instructional systems. ICALL programs must be able to respond to input noisier than that used by other NLP programs. Second, there are pedagogical and associated cognitive issues. ICALL systems must be able to model the learning situation to some degree of granularity—at least to be able to offer an analysis of what might go wrong or what might constitute progress toward a goal. Finally, there are practical issues in the actual use and reuse of systems. The designers are not typically the instructors who use the system, but they must anticipate the changing needs of the curriculum and students. They must also embed sophisticated technology in a computing environment that is usable by those who do not understand the technology. Furthermore, because of the long development time of NLP software, ICALL systems must be built for reuse and reapplication, without having to repeat the initial effort.

The ALICE project has attempted to focus on each of these dimensions in the development of the ALICE system. This is illustrated in the design of ALICE-chan,[15] a version of the ALICE system for use with first- and second-year Japanese instruction. ALICE-chan is a language-training environment for Japanese that uses NLP as a basis both for assisting instructors in preparing exercises and for evaluating student responses to exercises. In this work, we have had the opportunity to assess NLP as a tool in an ICALL system. We have been concerned especially with the problems of making NLP accessible to language instructors and using NLP selectively to render it effective for analysis of learners' language. In this chapter we report our observations and evaluations of the effectiveness of NLP in the ALICE-chan system.

In the second and third sections of this chapter, "The ALICE Project and the ALICE-chan System" and "NLP in ALICE-chan," we briefly describe the ALICE-chan interface and NLP components. The fourth section of this chapter, "What ALICE-chan Teaches NLP," focuses on what we have learned about designing an ICALL system with an NLP engine. We enumerate the strengths and weaknesses of NLP and describe how we have attempted to find a balance. The chapter's final section includes an outline of our plans for embedding ALICE-chan in a broader computer-based language learning environment.

---

[15] ALICE is an acronym for Automated Language-Instruction/Curriculum Environment; *chan* is a diminutive suffix in Japanese.

The ALICE Project and the ALICE-chan System

Project Goals and Design Principles

The ALICE project mission is to develop a multimedia foreign-language learning environment that supports the development and evaluation of many different types of language learning activities (Evans & Levin, 1990; Levin, Evans, & Gates, 1991; Levin, Evans, Gates, & Delon, 1991). The ALICE approach is not tied to any particular pedagogical theory, except perhaps that language learning requires some combination of explanation, exposure, and practice, the exact form and amount of which remain to be determined. In fact, the primary function of ALICE is to be a tool for research in second language acquisition, with the requirement that the research be carried out in the context of normal language learning activities, not in separate laboratory experiments—hence the goal of developing high-quality authoring and instructional software that can serve as the setting for such research.

In developing ALICE-chan we have concentrated on basic NLP capabilities for error analysis and have employed a modular design that can easily be adapted to other languages. Our future plans include further development of NLP, extension to other languages, design of pedagogical strategies based on research, and implementation of other components of the ALICE environment such as multimedia exploration environments, reading assistant programs, and writing assistants.

ALICE-chan conforms to four general design principles. The first is that teachers and students who use the system should not have to know about linguistics or NLP. Thus, the linguistically sophisticated processing that takes place in the system remains essentially hidden from the user. Users need to have only basic linguistic knowledge, such as the amount typically presented in beginning-level language textbooks. Another important feature of ALICE-chan is that it does not enforce a programmed curriculum but rather provides various resources that can be molded freely into different curricula. The resources include Japanese text editing, an authoring interface for exercise creation, an extended on-line dictionary, and a student interface for exercise execution. In the future, however, we may add a curriculum authoring system to allow a teacher to orchestrate a sequence of student activities. The third design principle is that students and authors should be protected from having to learn programming-language-like notation. Interactions with ALICE-chan, therefore, are supported by a graphical user interface (GUI). Except for writing text, all communications can be carried out using a mouse to navigate through dialog boxes and menus. Finally, the design of ALICE-chan is modular so that it can easily be adapted to different languages and different levels of instruction. Changing the system involves changing the grammar rules and lexicons used by the NLP software; the NLP programs themselves and the interface programs remain the same.

Examples of an ALICE-chan Exercise

Figure 5.1 shows an ALICE-chan exercise in which the student must answer a question about a list of historical events. The student's answer must contain a positive or negative sentence using the adverb *moo* or the adverb *mada*. The use of *moo* and *mada* is difficult to master because the words take on different interpretations in negative and non-negative sentences. For example, *moo* with a non-negative predicate means roughly *already* or *yet*, and *moo* with a negative predicate means roughly *no longer*; *mada* with a positive predicate means roughly *still*, and *mada* with a negative predicate means roughly *not yet*. The correct use of these adverbs is also dependent on the presence of other verbal inflections.

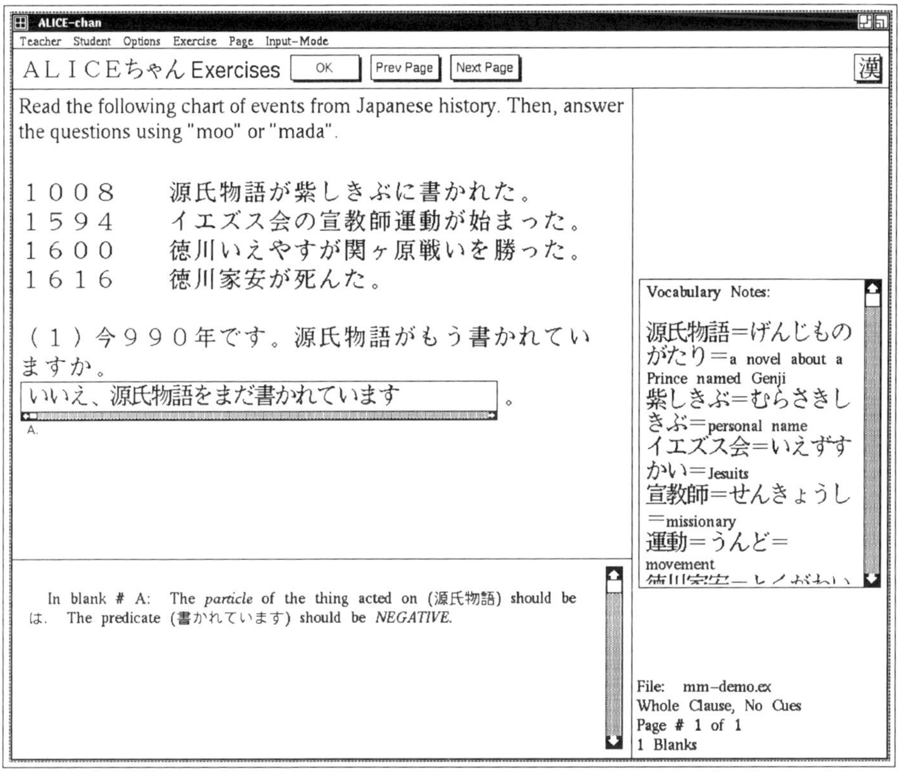

FIG. 5.1. Sample ALICE-chan exercise. (Background information and question written in *kanji*).

The screen in Figure 5.1 reads:

1008 The Tale of Genji was written by Murasaki Sikibu.
1594 The Jesuit missionary movement began.
1600 Tokugawa Ieyasu won the battle of Sekigahara.

1616 Tokugawa Ieyasu died.

(1) It is now the year 990. Has The Tale of Genji been written yet?

The box labeled *A* under Question 1 contains the student's answer. The student can type the answer in *kanji*, *katakana*, *hiragana*, or *romaji*.[16] When the student clicks the OK button at the top of the screen, the answer is sent to the NLP programs, which analyze the student's words or sentences and automatically generate feedback. In Figure 5.1 the student is trying to say "No, The Tale of Genji hasn't been written yet" but has made two errors. The case-marking particle on *The Tale of Genji* is incorrect, and the verb in the student's answer is not in the negative form. These errors are reported to the student at the bottom of the screen. In addition to the example shown here, many other types of errors can be detected by the NLP components of ALICE-chan. We return to a discussion of ALICE-chan's error-detection capabilities in a later section of the chapter.

ALICE-chan can deliver many types of exercises in addition to the type shown in Figure 5.1. The only limitations on the type of exercise are that the answers must be single words or sentences and that it must be possible to limit answers to those that fall into a range of grammatical and stylistic variants of the author's answer. An imaginative author can come up with many interesting exercise types, including cloze, translation, transformation drills, or questions about a chart or story (as in Figure 5.1). Each exercise type can be implemented as multiple choice, fill-in-the-blank, or full sentence response. To accommodate different teaching styles, exercises can contain either a mixture of English and Japanese or just Japanese.

Exercise Authoring

Figure 5.2 illustrates the use of the ALICE-chan authoring system. The first step in authoring an exercise is to enter a text into the ALICE-chan text editor, which provides full text editing capabilities in *kanji*, *hiragana*, *katakana*, and *romaji*. Note that the text of the exercise contains the background information, the question, and the correct answer to Question 1. The sentence under Question 1 means "No, the Tale of Genji has not been written yet." The text is next read into the authoring system, where the author makes it into an exercise. This is the step illustrated in Figure 5.2. This is done by identifying the words and sentences that will be blanked out for the student to fill in. In Figure 5.2, the answer to Question 1 has been selected for blanking out. This was done simply by clicking the mouse on the first and last character of the sentence. The system draws a box around the selected text and sends it to the NLP programs. The NLP programs automatically analyze the selected material and display the analysis as a *feature structure* at the bottom of the screen (as shown in Figure 5.2).

---

[16] Japanese writing is typically a mixture of *kanji* (Chinese characters) and the *hiragana* and *katakana* syllabaries. Japanese children and adult learners often use the *hiragana* syllabary alone while they are in the process of learning *kanji*. Some courses in Japanese use *romaji* (Roman characters) for beginning students.

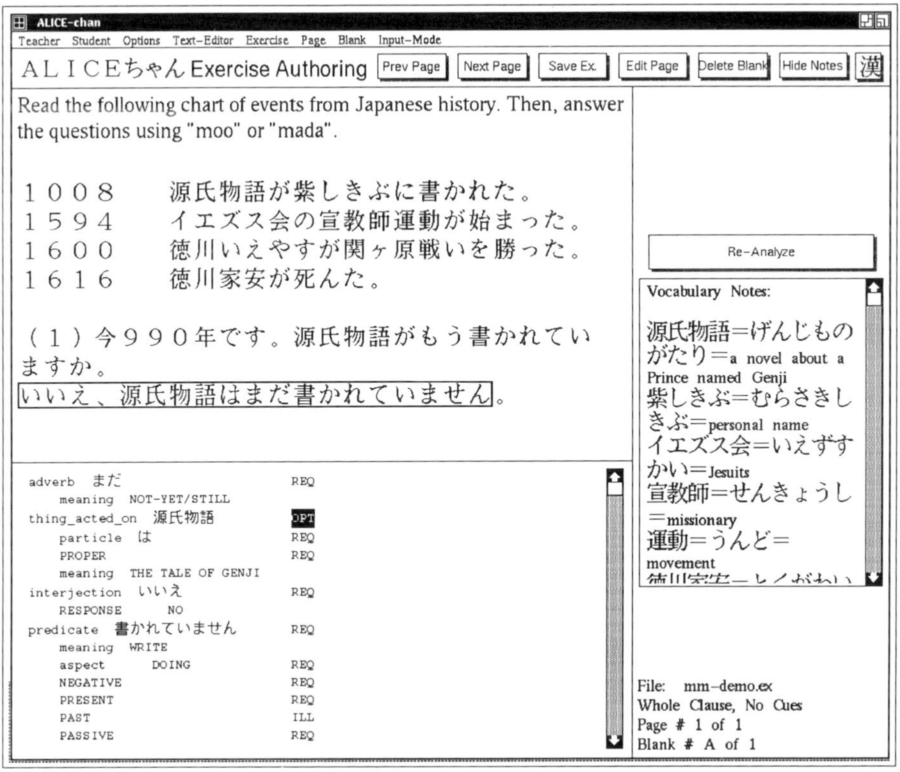

FIG. 5.2. Sample of exercise authoring in ALICE-chan (showing the creation of the exercise in Figure 5.1).

The feature structure represents the words in the Japanese sentence, their meaning in an English gloss, their grammatical features such as tense, aspect, and voice, and the semantic roles of noun phrases, such as *actor* or *thing-acted-on*. This information is intended to be clear to people who are not trained in linguistics. It is abstracted from the output of the parser, which is actually much more detailed.

The feature structure is stored as part of the exercise and compared to a feature structure of the student's answer during error detection. Any mismatches in the analyses of the author and student feature structures are pointed out to the student via error-analysis statements, as shown in Figure 5.1. Matching of author and student feature structures is one of three error detection methods used by ALICE-chan (the others are described in "Error Detection").

The matching of feature structures proves to be more flexible than matching the sentences themselves because the feature structure abstracts away from the surface form of the sentence. ALICE-chan can therefore accept sentences that have the same grammatical features and semantic roles even if they use a different word order or a different but equivalent inflectional marking. The teacher may optionally adjust the flexibility of feature structure matching by editing the feature structure. For example, the tag REQ (required) associated with most of the features and constituents in Figure 5.2 can be toggled to OPT (optional) or ILL (illegal). It is also possible to add more particles (e.g., to add *ga*, the subject marker, as an alternative to *it wa*, the topic marker) or to add alternative open class lexical items. These capabilities increase the range of student responses that can be accepted as correct in order to allow for natural variation in the wording of sentences. However, there are limitations to the flexibility of feature structure matching, which we discuss next.

NLP in ALICE-chan

Character-Independent Processing

The NLP system[17] is designed to accept any combination of *romaji* and Japanese characters as input and can return a mixture of English and Japanese in its output. For Japanese-character entry, ALICE-chan utilizes a common method whereby *romaji* characters (keyboard Roman letters) are converted to *hiragana* automatically as the user types. *Romaji*-to-*hiragana* conversion is carried out by a finite-state transition process written in the cT programming language, which can handle all the standard romanization schemes. The user then may press a key to request that the *hiragana* be converted to *kanji*, if desired. *Hiragana*-to-*kanji* conversion is carried out by external function calls to WNN, a public domain *kanji* server containing a full set of *kanji*. Other functions include scrolling through alternative *kanji* and stretching or shrinking the fence that determines how many *kana* syllables will be grouped together for conversion into *kanji*.

The NLP Lexicon

The NLP lexicon contains information that allows the system to recognize words in all of their morphological variants and to identify syntactic and semantic features of each word. Optionally, lexical entries can contain other kinds of information (on usage, expected error-variant forms, pragmatics, etc.) that may be useful in subsequent processing. Currently about 1,500 entries are in the ALICE-chan NLP lexicon.

Each lexical entry consists of two main parts, a list of keys in *romaji*, *kana*, and *kanji* and a list of syntactic and semantic features. The keys indicate possible orthographic realizations of a word. Figure 5.3 shows the lexical entry for the word *hon* (book) with keys in *romaji*, *kana*, and *kanji*. The second part of a lexical entry contains a

---

[17] A more complete description of the NLP components of the ALICE-chan system can be found in Evans et al. (1993).

list of feature–value pairs. The feature S stands for *sense.* Its value is a short English gloss indicating the meaning of the word. The feature M (morpheme) is a *romaji* spelling of the citation form of the morpheme. The special features L and R are discussed in the next section.

```
(("hon" "ほん" "本")
 (S "book" M (hon) COUNT volume CAT noun INANI-SUBJ +
  BL + R (FINAL PART) L (BEGIN G-HON)))
```

FIG. 5.3. The NLP lexicon entry for the Japanese word *hon* (book).

In addition to the features S, M, R, and L, which every entry contains, there can be potentially many other features. An example in the entry for *hon* is the feature COUNT, which indicates that *hon* is a count noun and determines the appropriate classifier.

Morphological Analysis and Segmentation

Morphological analysis of Japanese is complicated by the fact that there are no spaces between words in written Japanese. Correct morphological analysis depends on correct segmentation—dividing the sentence into separate words. For reasons of simplicity and speed, morphological processing in ALICE-chan is combined with segmentation as a single initial pass over the input string. Both processes are completed before the sentence is sent to the parser for syntactic analysis.

Morphological analysis is guided by the special features L and R, whose values are names of states in a nondeterministic finite-state transition network. The value of L is the starting state for a transition and the value of R is a set of possible ending states. The keys of the lexical entry are the input strings required for the transition. Figures 5.4 through 5.6 show lexical entries involved in the analysis of several forms of the verb *kaku* (write).

```
(("ka" "か" "書")
 (S "write" M (ka) WO-PATIENT + NI-GOAL + COMP + CAT verb BL +
  ROOTKEYS dummy UNUM dummy SUFKEYS ("ku" "く" "く") L (BEGIN HON) R (K)))
```

FIG. 5.4. The NLP lexicon entry for the stem of the Japanese verb *kaku* (write).

```
(("ki" "き")  (M (ki) L (k) R (P-NI mas ASPV VHON DESIDER)))
```

FIG. 5.5. The NLP lexicon entry for the Japanese verb morpheme *ki.*

```
(("masu" "ます") (M (masu) STYLE formal TENSE present L (mas) R (FINAL)))
```

FIG. 5.6. The NLP lexicon entry for the Japanese present formal verb morpheme *masu*.

For example, processing of *kakimasu* starts at the state *hon* and uses the input *ka-* (or the *hiragana* or *kanji* variants) to get to state k. From state k, the input *-ki-* (or the *hiragana* symbol) allows a transition to state *mas*. From state *mas* the input *-masu* (or the *hiragana* symbols) allows a transition to state final.

The processing algorithm involves a left-to-right generation (i.e., detection) of words, followed by a right-to-left filtering of the generated words. The first pass identifies all words that are part of a valid segmentation of a prefix of the sentence string (prefix segmentation), that is, words either beginning at the first position or themselves following a prefix segmentation. Note that if the first left-to-right pass does not reach the last sentence position, no segmentation in the current morphology is possible. The right-to-left filtering of words eliminates words that are not part of a suffix segmentation. Clearly, a segmentation of the sentence must be both a prefix and a suffix segmentation.

During morphological analysis a simple feature structure is built from the feature–value pairs associated with each morpheme in the lexicon. This information is converted into a form used by the parser but can also be used by later application-specific processes (for instance, to facilitate user feedback). Because the morphological processor lacks the ability to do even simple checks based upon the built-up features and values, this information is not used during morphological processing to enforce morphological constraints but could be used by the parser to enforce morphological or syntactic constraints.

Analysis of Syntactic Structure

The goal of syntactic analysis is to identify the predicate of each clause, the predicate's syntactic and morphological features, and a grammatical function and/or semantic role for every other element of the clause. Simplified parser output is illustrated in Figure 5.2. Syntactic analysis is used during authoring and during student exercises. In authoring, it is used for analyzing correct answers so that the syntactic analysis of the answers can be stored and later compared to student answers. In student exercises, it is used for analyzing student answers so that they can be compared to previously stored authored answers. There are three stages in syntactic analysis: parsing, mapping, and disambiguation.

Syntactic analysis is driven by a Generalized Left-Right (LR) Parser with pseudo-unification (Tomita, 1986; Tomita & Knight, 1987; Tomita, Mitamura, Musha, & Kee, 1988). Our approach to syntax is, therefore, based on the theory of lexical-functional grammar (Kaplan & Bresnan, 1982; see also the LFG application of Rypa & Feuerman, this volume). However, in designing the syntactic analyzer, we have had to confront several hard problems in NLP—ill-formed input, ambiguity, robustness of coverage, and human-computer interaction—which have led us to augment and modify a basic LFG approach in two ways. The first innovation concerns terminology. Because grammatical function names like *subject* and *object* are misleading to untrained users, we have replaced them in most instances with semantic role names like *actor* and *thing-acted-on*. The second change is in the method of function assignment. In free word-order languages such as Japanese, syntactic rules can associate phrases with their syntactic function based on case markers. However, because case marking particles are one of the main sources of error in student input, we resort to heuristics rather than syntactic rules for the assignment of functions or roles.

The ALICE-chan Japanese grammar consists of about a hundred rules written in a pseudo-unification formalism, with some calls to Lisp functions. The grammar covers basic mono-clausal sentences and some sentences involving embedded complement clauses, gerund clauses, and sentential modifiers of nouns. A range of noun phrase structures is also allowed, including noun phrases with adjectives, modifiers marked with *no*, and conjuncts marked with *to* and *ya*. Coverage is sufficient for a first-year Japanese course and extends to some of the more complex structures associated with a second-year course.

In addition to the grammar, which contains knowledge about the structure of Japanese sentences, ALICE-chan uses a *mapper* to apply rules and heuristics for assigning a function to each phrase that the parser identifies. The job of the mapper is to determine the best way to fill the predicate's subcategorization frame (which contains slots for subject, object, etc.) with the phrases in the sentence. Such role assignment is complicated by the fact that student Japanese contains many errors in the use of case marking particles. There is also some ambiguity caused by the use of the topic marker *wa* or the conjunctive particle *mo*, which can replace other particles.

The most recent version of the mapper is written in Lisp and Transformation Kit, a pseudo-unification language for specifying transformations of feature structures (Tomita & Nyberg, 1988). The mapper is called from the grammar rules that attach noun phrases to sentences. Each phrase can match zero or more roles in a predicate's subcategorization frame on the basis of its particle and its semantic class. During analysis of student sentences, there are often phrases that do not match any subcategorization slots. If such a phrase is identified, the mapper searches for the meaning of the phrase in the feature structure that was stored during authoring. The role of the phrase in the authored feature structure is hypothesized as the intended role in the student sentence; any error in particle use is flagged. Phrases that still do not have a role after this procedure are given the role *extra*. Phrases without particles are given the role *nominal*. At this point, each phrase is labeled with the names of the zero or more roles it can have. Two phrases may have the same role, and any given phrase may be able to have more than one role. The mapper then identifies all the possible ways of filling the predicate's subcategorization frame given this information, relegating more phrases to the extra role if necessary. The output at this point is potentially ambiguous.

Because ALICE-chan currently employs only minimal semantic analysis, there can be many unresolved ambiguities may occur during parsing. A disambiguator mechanism resolves syntactic ambiguities interactively with the user. First, it detects certain types of ambiguities in the output of the segmentation program, parser, and mapper. Then it formulates questions, which are presented to the user. Sometimes several questions are asked about the same ambiguity so that the user can answer the one that is most clear. Currently, the disambiguator can detect ambiguities in segmentation, homographs, grammatical function/semantic role assignment, nesting of noun modifiers marked with *no* and conjuncts marked with *to* and *ya*, and structural ambiguities involving the attachment of phrases to main and embedded clauses.

An example of a disambiguator question is shown in Figure 5.7. The ambiguous sentence is "kyou gakkoo e itte tomodachi to denwa shimashita," which can means "I went to school today and talked (on the phone) with my friend" or "I went to school and talked (on the phone) with my friend today." The ambiguity has to do with whether the word *kyou* (today) attaches to the main clause, as shown in the first bracketing in Figure 5.7, or to the embedded clause, as shown in the second bracketing. The disambiguation dialogue involves querying the user about which meaning is intended.

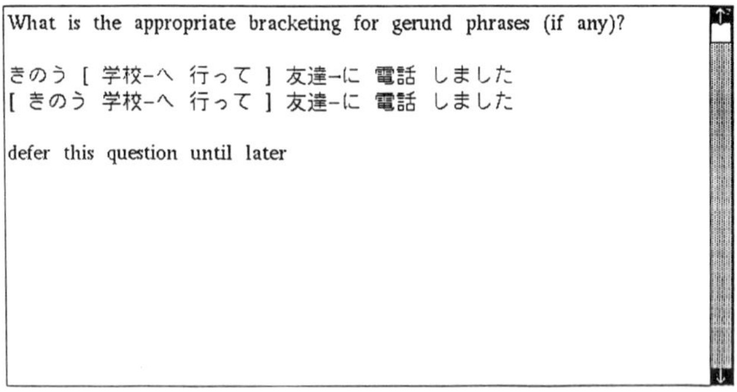

FIG. 5.7. Sample disambiguation dialogue in ALICE-chan.

Error Detection

Errors in student responses are detected at three stages, as illustrated schematically in Figure 5.8. During parsing, special grammar rules are designed to parse errorful structures and raise error flags. During mapping, the mapper may detect phrases whose grammatical function or semantic role cannot be determined. Note that the mapper provides a general mechanism for detecting any failure to satisfy the predicate's subcategorization requirements. It is a general subcategorization checker and does not require knowledge about specific subcategorization errors. During matching, contextually inappropriate features of the student's response are detected by comparing the analysis of the student's response to the prestored analysis of the authored response. Errors are reported if required features or phrases are missing, if extra features or phrases are used, or if the values of any features differ.

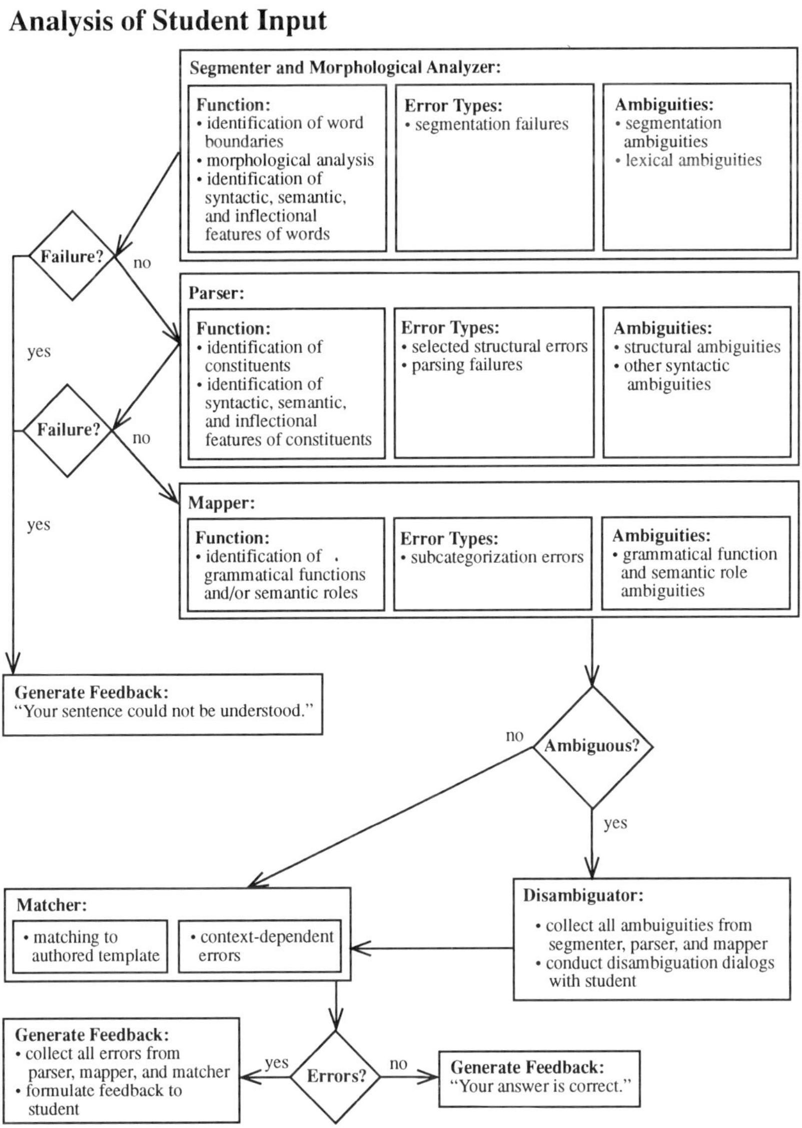

FIG. 5.8. Error detection architecture in ALICE-chan.

Figure 5.9 categorizes and gives examples of some of the types of errors that ALICE-chan can currently detect. Figure 5.10 shows feedback resulting from each type of error detection.

Errors detected by the Parser

Wrong past tense of adjective:

Wrong	Right
takai desita	*takatta desu* it was expensive

Wrong use of adjective:

Wrong	Right
akai ni suru	*akaku suru* make it red
akai no hon	*akai hon* red book

Wrong structure for "na nominal" modifying noun:

Wrong	Right
kirei da mati *kirei no mati*	*kirei na mati* pretty town

Wrong negation of noun:

Wrong	Right
kirei ku nai	*kirei zya nai* not pretty—informal
genki zya nakatta da	*genki zya nakatta desu* wasn't peppy—formal
genki zya arimasen desu	*genki zya arimasen* isn't peppy—formal
genki zya nai desita	*genki zya nakatta desu* wasn't peppy—formal

Disagreement of noun and classifier:

Wrong	Right
hon ni hon	*hon ni satu* two books

Errors detected by the Mapper

Many cases of wrong particles or missing particles:

Case making with stative predicates:

Wrong	Right
sushi o suki desu	*sushi ga suki desu* like sushi

Case marking with passives:

Wrong	Right
kuruma o kodomo ga nusumareta	*kuruma ga kodomo ni nusumareta* the car was stolen by the child

Location with action verbs:

Wrong	Right
kyoositu ni kakimasita	*kyoositu de kakimasita* wrote it in the classroom

Location with stative verbs:

Wrong	Right
kyoositu de armasu	*kyoositu ni arimasu* is in the classroom

Errors detected by the Matcher

Disagreement of adverb and verb tense:

Wrong	Right
kinou benkyou simasu	*kinou benkyou simasita* studied yesterday
asita benkyou simasita	*asita benkyou simasu* will study tomorrow

Backwards modification:

Wrong	Right
biiru no nihon	*nihon no biiru* Japaneses beer
ue no teeburu	*teeburu no ue* on top of the table

Negative polarity item with positive verb:

Wrong	Right
zenzen benkyou simasu	*zenzen benkyou simasen* never study

Wrong formality:
Informal form in a context that requires a formal form.

Wrong giving verb:
Using ageru for giving to the speaker or the speaker's in-group.

Wrong family term:
Using *haha* for someone else's mother.

Missing and extra elements:
Nouns that are present, but are more naturally dropped in context.

FIG. 5.9. Samples of error types covered in ALICE-chan.

- First, Special grammar rules are designed to parse errorful structures and raise error flags

Student:	*watasi wa akai no hon o kaimasita* I bought a red book
ALICE-chan:	*Error:* An adjective (*akai*) modifies a noun (*hon*) without the particle *no* in between.

- During mapping, the mapper may detect phrases whose grammatical function or semantic role cannot be determined.

Student:	*Watashi wa kodomo ga yasai o takusan tabesasemashita.* I made the children eat lots of vegetables.
ALICE-chan:	*Error:* The particle on the actor-causee (*kodomo*) should be *ni*.

- During matching, contextually inappropriate features of the student's response are detected by comparing the analysis of the student's response to the pre-stored analysis of the authored repsonse.

Student:	*sensei ga watasi ni hon o kuremasita* The teacher gave me a book
ALICE-chan:	*Error:* The predicate (*kuremasita*) should be *exalting*

FIG. 5.10. Summary of error detection procedures.

What ALICE-chan Teaches About NLP

NLP offers potential advantages to ICALL but also has many potential pitfalls. Its potential advantages for authors include automation of exercise creation and feedback. For students, it offers better explanations of errors and more chances for communication. However, NLP-based software has a relatively long development time and may have very limited coverage even after several years of development. In many cases, improvements are in a delicate balance; increasing coverage may decrease speed or automation. In this section we report on what we have learned about maximizing the advantages and avoiding the pitfalls of NLP-based software.

Balancing Compromises

As in many other applications of NLP, the state of the art in ICALL does not provide systems that are fully automated, have full coverage, and produce high quality output. Any NLP-based system will have to compromise along one or more of these parameters. ALICE-chan stands out from other ICALL programs in allowing for semi-automatic processing in which the student user guides the system to a correct analysis using the disambiguator and a parse editor. Another ALICE-chan compromise is to restrict coverage syntactically to constructions covered in a first-year course. This is in contrast to those systems that restrict coverage semantically to meanings that can be expressed in a microworld (e.g., Douglas, this volume; Kaplan & Holland, this volume; Murray, this volume; and the dialogue microworld of DeSmedt, this volume). We chose these compromises and not others in order to achieve two goals. The first is to produce high quality, accurate syntactic analysis and error detection (even at the expense of full automation). The second is to create a completely general tool that can be adapted to any part of any first-year curriculum. The path that we navigate through the advantages and pitfalls of NLP is determined by such compromises.

Automation of Authoring

One of the promises of NLP is to automate the authoring process. Because NLP systems contain rules that characterize sentences of a language, an author should not have to list correct and incorrect answers for each authored exercise. Furthermore, because error detection is based on analysis of the language and not just string matching, feedback should be insightful and helpful as well as automatic, thereby relieving the author of specifying feedback for each possible answer. Our goal in designing the ALICE-chan authoring interface was to enable the creation of sophisticated exercises with as high a degree of automation as possible. Although NLP provides a useful degree of automation, we have also learned about its limitations and have begun to explore strategies to overcome them.

In the simplest case, a high level of automation is achieved: The author needs only to type one correct answer for each exercise item. The NLP system analyzes that sentence for structure, grammatical relations, and morphological features and stores the analysis as a feature structure. That structure characterizes a class of correct answers having similar features. Wrong answers are implicitly the complement of the set of right answers. Therefore, wrong answers do not have to be listed; nor do additional right answers. The author does not have to specify any feedback either; detailed feedback can be automatically formulated in terms of the linguistic information stored in the feature structure.

Unfortunately, full automation is not possible for all sentence types. One problem that arises is ambiguity. Sentences may have multiple meanings that must be represented by different feature structures. When the NLP programs do not have enough information to resolve the ambiguity, they must resort to interactive disambiguation dialogs with the user, as we have described. This requires a bit of extra work from the author but ultimately allows the rest of the authoring process to remain automated and accurate.

The second limitation of automated authoring is that the range of correct answers that the system can accept is constrained by the capabilities of the NLP software. In ALICE-chan correct answers are characterized in terms of grammatical relations, semantic roles, and inflectional features. This allows some flexibility in accepting alternative correct answers. As pointed out earlier, ALICE-chan can recognize variants of a sentence with different word orders. Additional flexibility is provided by allowing authors to edit feature structures. However, many sentences that should be recognized as equivalent do not have feature structures that are identical or that fall into the range of variation allowed by the feature structure editor. Horiguchi (1993) discussed one circumstance under which this arises, namely, when different syntactic constructions are used to express the same pragmatic information, such as a speech act ("I want the salt" versus "Pass the salt") or some other feature like evidentiality. Our solution in this case is to add a level of pragmatic structure at which such sentences can be matched. Other types of sentences require further semantic analysis. For example, a natural alternative to "Yamadasan to Tanakasan ga hon o kakimasita" (Mr. Tanaka and Mr. Yamada wrote a book) is "Tanakasan ga Yamadasan to hon o kakimasita" (Mr. Tanaka wrote a book with Mr. Yamada). However, these sentences do not match in the current version of the system because they have different syntactic structures in the LFG representation.

Error Detection and Feedback

Another expectation of NLP-based ICALL is that error feedback based on linguistic analysis, in addition to marking the locations of errors, will provide insightful information. Ideally, this information would be put to use to speed or improve the student's acquisition of the second language or at least be recorded and studied in order to deepen our understanding of second language errors. ALICE-chan lives up to this expectation not only in finding the location of errors but also in explaining the errors in terms of linguistic relations. In Figure 5.10, for example, ALICE-chan explains that the particle *ga* should be *ni* because the noun *kodomo* (child) is the *actor-causee* (i.e., the person who was caused to act) and not the *causer* of the sentence. This type of feedback has been shown to be instructionally effective (Nagata, 1992), at least in the acquisition of case marking particles. However, the role of explanation, timing of feedback, and type of feedback are still active research questions in second language acquisition. We do not claim that ALICE-chan's feedback is pedagogically optimal (for example, it contains many technical terms that may be confusing), but we regard it as providing a basic capability that we can now manipulate and evaluate to determine approaches to feedback that may be optimally effective.

Coverage

A potential problem for NLP-based ICALL systems is that no NLP system has complete coverage of any natural language. This means that some input will be incorrectly analyzed or missed entirely. However, NLP can be used effectively if the application is designed to circumvent dependence on complete sentential analysis and the user does not expect exhaustive coverage. Such an approach was taken on the MINA project (Hull, 1986), where students were not led to expect that all of their errors would be detected. Another solution is to provide heuristics that force a complete analysis of each input, as was done in the old ELIZA program (Weizenbaum, 1966). At a more sophisticated level, the CRITIQUE system (Jensen, Heidorn, Miller, & Ravin, 1993) includes heuristics that produce a complete structure even when parsing fails. In designing ALICE-chan, we took a third approach, limiting coverage to a *sublanguage*. A sublanguage can be defined in two ways—as the language required to talk about a microworld or as a limited set of structures (and meanings) to be covered. Microworld-based sublanguages have the drawback that only the microworld can be discussed. Therefore, in the interest of creating a tool that can be adapted to any curriculum, we have defined the ALICE-chan sublanguage structurally to include the constructions that would be learned in the first semesters of a Japanese class. We have found that teachers can learn the sublanguage easily and prepare exercises that exploit the full power of the system, without being practically limited.

Ambiguity

Ambiguity is one of the most pervasive problems in NLP. Humans resolve ambiguity naturally using background knowledge to determine the interpretations that are appropriate in particular contexts. In fact, most of the time such processing is so automatic that people are not even aware that sentences are ambiguous. NLP systems, on the other hand, do not have the wealth of linguistic knowledge, world knowledge, and understanding of a text that allows people to identify the correct reading of a sentence. These systems mechanically produce many (sometimes hundreds of) structures for even the most simple sentences. The results are that processing becomes impractically slow and that analyses are indeterminate. One solution to ambiguity resolution involves limiting the meanings that can be expressed in a constrained microworld. This can effectively narrow the possible interpretations for sentences. However, as noted previously, systems based on microworlds may not be flexible enough to adapt to new curricula and new language learning activities. Other solutions to ambiguity resolution are available in NLP systems that are not based on microworlds. ALICE-chan uses two approaches—interaction with the user and elimination of implausible structures.

The primary treatment of ambiguity in ALICE-chan is interaction with the user, as described in the prior discussion of the disambiguator. The drawbacks to interactive ambiguity resolution are that it reduces automation and that it requires some training on the part of the user. The advantage, however, is that it almost always results in correct resolution of ambiguity (assuming that the parser has provided the correct options). This ultimately results in a system that is flexible and adaptable because one does not have to work around its mistakes and limitations. Having control over the system is, in many cases, better than settling for whatever it produces on its own.

As a secondary approach to ambiguity resolution, ALICE-chan takes advantage of the sublanguage and the instructional situation (with its implied limits and prescriptive targets) to eliminate unlikely and intrusive alternative interpretations of words and structure. For example, the grammar specifically prevents the adverbial *sore de* (so, therefore, that being the case) from being analyzed literally as a clause consisting of a pronoun and a gerundive copula. In other cases, ALICE-chan requires punctuation for purposes of disambiguation when normally puntuation would be optional.

Size and Speed: The Compactness Criterion

NLP systems can be quite large because of the amount of memory required to search the grammar rules and lexicons for appropriate analyses of sentences. They can also be slow because the search for a suitable analysis of a sentence can involve considering and rejecting hundreds of alternatives. To make matters worse, increasing the coverage of the system can make processing much slower by increasing the number of analyses that the parser will have to try. However, as in all computational systems, it is possible to trade space and time requirements to achieve optimal performance. NLP in ALICE-chan is moderately space-intensive by the current standards of personal computer users[18] but not unreasonably slow. Some sentences are processed in real time; others require several seconds.[19]

Weinberg, Garman, Martin, and Merlo (this volume) suggest the criterion of compactness as a desirable quality for grammars. Compact grammars use only a few rules that generalize over a wide range of data. In theory, a grammar based on fewer rules should run faster than one requiring many. This is a desirable goal, but the reasoning does not hold for the ALICE-chan system. NLP in the ALICE-chan system is based on generalized LR parsing, which compiles a grammar into a parsing table whose entries each describe a state that the parser can be in and actions it can take from that state. Because the table is accessed by hashing algorithms, speed of access does not depend on the size of the table. This means that the speed of the parser is not directly influenced by the size of the grammar. The speed of parsing does depend on how many actions are taken (i.e., how many rules are applied) in parsing a sentence. Parsing will be slower if the sentence is more complex or more ambiguous or if there are many intermediate analyses that are considered in the course of parsing. It is important to notice, however, that parsing complexity is independent of whether the rules are general or specific. Regardless of whether the nodes are labeled *NP* and *VP* or *X-double-bar*, the same number of nodes will be in the tree, and the same number of actions will be taken by the parser in building the tree. In fact, the generalized LR parser typically runs faster when there are more context-free rules, each having fewer constraints and well-formedness conditions, than when there are fewer rules, each with more constraints. Processing context-free grammars is much faster than processing constraints.

Development Time and Portability

Another possible disadvantage of NLP-based CALL systems is that they take longer to develop than simple CALL systems because of the complexity of NLP programs and the size of grammars and lexicons. The time and cost of an initial development effort would be offset if the resulting system were easily adapted to other languages without requiring

---

[18] The PC version of ALICE-chan currently requires a minimum of 16 megabytes of RAM. The workstation version uses 32 megabytes of RAM.

[19] Our speed could be improved by re-implementing some components. For example, the mapper would be faster if it were translated from Transformation Kit to Lisp or C.

significant additional development or adaptation time. Portability is therefore a desirable quality of an NLP-based system.

Most NLP-based systems are portable to some extent because of separation of data (i.e., grammar rules) and programs (i.e., the parser). The ALICE-chan parser, for example, does not contain any specific knowledge of Japanese. Instead, the parser only knows how to apply rules to sentences. If it is given Japanese rules, it will apply Japanese rules. If it is given Spanish rules, it will apply Spanish rules. The same parser can therefore be used for any language. Only new grammars and lexicons need to be provided. The morphological processor and many parts of the interface are also generally applicable to other languages. Our plans include rewriting the mapper, matcher, and disambiguator as fully language-independent programs.

The use of language-independent programs is important in the reduction of development time. However, the bulk of development time in an NLP program is spent on acquisition of linguistic data such as lexical entries and grammar rules. It is therefore also important to reduce data acquisition time. This can be done to some extent by factoring out parts of language that are universal or parameterizable so that those parts do not have to be recoded for each language (Dorr et al., this volume; Weinberg et al., this volume).[20] Reducing data acquisition time by factoring out language universals is an important area of research. However, generalizations must be evaluated—and applied—carefully. Often the language-specific details that are removed from one component of the grammar must be re-expressed in another. For example, information that is removed from phrase structure rules might show up in the lexicon or in a set of constraints somewhere else in the system. Also, based on our experience with systems that process large amounts of free text,[21] we estimate that only a small percentage of linguistic data can be reduced to universal or cleanly parameterizable information. Language consists of a backbone of predictable structure (i.e., the universals and parameterizable elements) and hundreds of thousands of special cases (including lexical constructions and formulaic expressions). Each special case by itself is rare, but taken as a group, one occurs in almost every sentence.[22] Therefore, they cannot be ignored. This does not mean that it is useless to factor out universals, only that it is necessary to be realistic about exactly how much work is saved in doing so.

---

[20] Another way of reducing data acquisition time is to have tools for automated or semi-automated data acquisition. This is an active area of research in computational linguistics (e.g., Dorr, Garman, & Weinberg, 1994).

[21] Two examples are the CLARIT system (e.g., Evans, Lefferts et al., 1993; Evans & Lefferts, 1994), which uses NLP in information-management tasks involving millions of documents, and KBMT-89 (Goodman & Nirenburg, 1991) and subsequent projects at the Center for Machine Translation, which use NLP to translate diverse text types, such as newspaper articles, instruction manuals, and spoken dialogue.

[22] An analogy can be drawn to the performance of part-of-speech taggers. State-of-the-art taggers operate at 95% correctness. However, the 5% error rate (one word in 20) means that there is an error in almost every sentence.

Future Plans

Our future work is defined both by the need to address the sorts of problems we have noted—improving and extending NLP—and by our desire to complete the original goal of the ALICE project, to develop a multimedia instructional environment. In parallel, we aim to hone ALICE-chan as an instrument for research in second language acquisition.

Extensions to New Modes and Languages

Our immediate plans call for the development of a reading assistant using ALICE-chan processing strategies. As with current exercises, an author (instructor) would enter (or scan in) a text to be read. The author will be able to review ALICE-chan's analysis of the reading passage sentence by sentence, to accept or modify the analysis, and to add notes, if desired. All analyses and notes will be stored with their associated text. When reading, the student will be able to click on words, phrases, or sentences and receive variable degrees of information about the passage. Some of the information will derive from the stored notes and analyses; some (such as lexical meanings) may be derived on the fly via morphological analysis and lexical lookup. As a supplement to reading, we plan to add authorable video sequencing and the general ability to script lessons (and the interaction of instructional modes and media) and to deliver curricula. In the near future, we plan to extend the NLP coverage to several new languages, including Korean, Spanish, German, and English.

Second Language Acquisition Research

ICALL in general and ALICE-chan in particular have great potential in supporting second language acquisition research. Data can be collected while the students are engaged in language-learning activities instead of in separate laboratory experiments. Although keyboard input and analyses collected in the course of using an ICALL program will not reveal all the details in students' language learning processes (e.g., what they are thinking or talking about or looking at while using the program), the information is in a form that can be more easily processed than audio or video tape. ALICE-chan has already shown itself to be a useful research tool in the thesis research of Nagata (1992).

We intend to deploy ALICE-chan in first- and second-year Japanese classes at several universities and to collect student/system interaction records to begin refining the use of ALICE-chan as a research tool.

Conclusion

We believe we have identified an appropriate and powerful use of NLP in language instruction: to analyze the lexical, phrasal, and sentential forms of the language to identify features (including errors) in morphology, constituent structure, and grammatical relations. We do not attempt language understanding; we aim for language analysis. In addition, we believe we have developed a practical method for instructors and students to interact with the NLP components of a language-analysis program. Results (thus far) indicate that the design is serviceable and extensible. Our hope is that it will help us realize the goal of an automated CALL system that can both instruct students and gather scientific data on second language acquisition.

Acknowledgments

ALICE-chan has been funded by the Department of Defense. We would like to thank our sponsors at the Department of Defense for helping us to design and refine the ALICE-chan system. We also extend special thanks to Dr. Mary Kim for her suggestions and contributions, which have given us direction and greatly improved our work. ALICE-chan was developed by a team of programmers and computational linguists. The members of the team include Martin Thurn, Keiko Horiguchi, Steven Handerson, Chris Scarpinatto, and Deepa Varma. We are also grateful to Dr. Michael Harrington for testing the system.

References

Dorr, B.J., Garman, J., & Weinberg, A. (1994). *From subcategorization frames to thematic roles: Building Arabic lexical entries for foreign language tutoring.* Manuscript submitted for publication.

Evans, D.A., Lefferts, R.G., Grefenstette, G., Handerson, S.K., Hersh, W.R., & Archbold, A.A. (1993). CLARIT TREC design, experiments, and results. In D. Harman (Ed.), *The First Text REtrieval Conference (TREC-1)* (pp. 251-286; 494-501). (NIST Special Publication 500-207) Washington, DC: U.S. Government Printing Office.

Evans, D.A., & Lefferts, R.G. (1994). Design and evaluation of the CLARIT-TREC-2 system. In D. Harman (Ed.), *The Second Text REtrieval Conference (TREC-2)* (pp. 306-335). (NIST Special Publication) Washington, DC: U.S. Government Printing Office.

Evans, D.A., & Levin, L.S. (March, 1990). Toward the design of natural-language instructional systems: Notes from ALICE. In *Working notes of the 1990 AAAI Symposium on Knowledge-Based Environments for Learning and Teaching* (pp. 58-62). Palo Alto, CA: Stanford University.

Evans, D.A., Levin, L.S., Thurn, M., Handerson, S.K., Horiguchi, K., Scarpinatto, K.C., & Varma, D. (1993). *An overview of NLP in ALICE-chan* (Technical report no. CMU-LCL-93-3). Pittsburgh, PA: Carnegie Mellon University, Laboratory for Computational Linguistics.

Goodman, K., & Nirenburg, S. (Eds.). (1991). *The KBMT project: A case study in knowledge-based machine translation.* San Mateo, CA: Kaufmann.

Horiguchi, K. (1993). *Extraction of pragmatic information in a CALL system* (Technical report no. CMU-LCL-93-5). Pittsburgh, PA: Carnegie Mellon University, Laboratory for Computational Linguistics.

Hull, G. (1986). *Using cognitive research and computer technology to improve writing skill in low-performing college students* (Final project report to the Ford Foundation, Grant 830-0355). Pittsburgh, PA: University of Pittsburgh, Learning Research and Development Center.

Jensen, K., Heidorn, G., Miller, L., & Ravin, Y. (1993). Prose fitting and prose fixing. In K. Jensen, G.E. Heidorn, & S.D. Richardson (Eds.), *Natural Language Processing: The PLNLP Approach* (pp. 53-64.). Boston, MA: Kluwer.

Kaplan, R.M., & Bresnan, J. (1982). Lexical-Functional Grammar: A formal system for grammatical representation. In J. Bresnan (Ed.), *The mental representation of grammatical relations.* Cambridge, MA: MIT Press.

Levin, L.S., Evans, D.A., & Gates, D. (1991). The {\small ALICE} system: A workbench for learning and using language. *Computer Assisted Learning and Instruction Consortium (CALICO) Journal*, 27-56.

Levin, L.S., Evans, D.A., Gates, D., & Delon, L. (1991). Capturing context in a computer-based foreign language assistant. In D. Ross & D. Brink (Eds.), *Association for Computers and the Humanities/Association for Literary and Linguistic Computing 91: Making connections—Conference handbook* (pp. 279-284). Tempe, AZ: Arizona State University.

Nagata, N. (1992). *A study of the effectiveness of Intelligent CALI as an application of natural language processing*. Unpublished doctoral dissertation, University of Pittsburgh.

Tomita, M. (1986). *Efficient parsing for natural language*. Boston: Kluwer.

Tomita, M., & Knight, K. (1987). *Pseudo-unification and full-unification* (Technical memo CMU-CMT-88-MEMO). Pittsburgh, PA: Carnegie Mellon University, Center for Machine Translation.

Tomita, M., Mitamura, T., Musha, H., & Kee, M. (1988). *The generalized LR parser/compiler version 8.1: User's guide* (Technical memo CMU-CMT-88-MEMO). Pittsburgh, PA: Carnegie Mellon University, Center for Machine Translation.

Tomita, M., & Nyberg, E.H. (1988). *Generation kit and transformation kit version 3.2: User's manual* (Technical memo CMU-CMT-88-MEMO). Pittsburgh, PA: Carnegie Mellon University, Center for Machine Translation.

Weizenbaum, J. (1966). ELIZA—A computer program for the study of natural language communication between man and machines. *Communications of the Association for Computing Machinery*, *9*, 36-45.

6

A Discourse Processing Approach to Computer-Assisted Language Learning

Carl H. Frederiksen, Janet Donin, & Michel Décary
McGill University

In this chapter we explore an integrated approach to computer-assisted language learning (CALL) that addresses both general language competence and specialized discourse processing expertise in the development of communicative competence in a second language. *General language competence* refers to general language knowledge and processing skills that are needed to comprehend and produce well-formed sentences and coherent multisentence texts or discourse in a second language. *Specialized discourse processing expertise* refers to proficiency in using particular types of texts and discourse effectively in the second language within specific practical contexts.

Our aim is to create an interactive multimedia CALL environment that can be used to supplement normal classroom instruction. The environment will assist second language learners by providing them with opportunities for guided practice and instruction with a variety of discourse tasks while giving tutorial assistance to help them develop both general and specialized communicative competence. The environment will also help the language teacher by providing a set of supplementary learning tools and activities, a means of monitoring students' learning and performance, a resource for teaching that supports many levels and components of language skill development, and a tool for networked teaching and communication with students.

In developing our system, we use theoretical models and discourse analysis methods from current psychological research on text and discourse processing to model the types of representations that are constructed by competent language users in discourse comprehension and production tasks. These representations include, for example, syntactic structures, propositions, semantic relations, coherence and contextual inferences, referential and thematic relations, discourse scripts, and conceptual frames. The computer environment provides tutors that use these representations to assist language learners in acquiring general language processing skill (e.g., at morphological, syntactic, semantic, and discourse levels). The assumption is that learners benefit from instruction based on constructs from explicit and psychologically valid models of discourse competence.

In addition to addressing general processing skill, these tutors are integrated into authentic discourse environments (e.g., researching a scientific topic using articles in a second language). These environments are designed to help a learner develop specialized discourse processing expertise by providing practice and assistance in using various types of discourse in typical contexts of use.

One objective of the work reported here is to explore the potential benefits of interactive multimedia CALL environments that are based on current research and theoretical models of discourse representation and processing. A second objective is to use interactive multimedia CALL environments to study the processes involved in language learning under authentic yet controlled conditions. Through empirical studies of learning and performance in CALL environments that incorporate different conditions of language learning (e.g., particular pedagogical strategies, types of discourse materials and tasks, contexts of language use, or types and degrees of guidance and assistance to the learner), we can identify information about the cognitive processes and strategies involved in successful language learning and the instructional conditions that facilitate them. This information can then be used to refine and improve subsequent CALL environments.

Discourse Processing Theory and Second Language Instruction

General Language Competence

Approaches to second language instruction focusing on general language competence traditionally emphasized the teaching of vocabulary, phonology, morphology, and syntax, but in recent years emphasis has shifted to the development of discourse communication skills in the second language (e.g., Krashen, 1982; Widdowson, 1978). However, when viewed from the perspective of psychological research on the cognitive representation and processing of text and discourse, it is apparent that this communicative approach to second language instruction has not yet taken advantage of relevant results—in particular, models of the multilayered processes and representations that have been found to be involved in processing extended discourse (see Frederiksen, Bracewell, Breuleux, & Renaud, 1989; Frederiksen & Donin, 1991; Mross, 1990; Van Dijk & Kintsch, 1983, for summaries of two current models).

This lack of attention to the multilevel processes involved in understanding and producing discourse has resulted in difficulty in effectively relating instruction in language processing at the lexical, morphological, and syntactic levels (the traditional emphasis of instruction) to instruction favoring the development of conceptual and semantic processes known to be crucial to understanding and producing connected multisentence discourse (important in the communicative approach). The assumption in the communicative approach is that syntactic competence in the second language will be acquired naturally within the communicative situation. However, it is not obvious that such incidental learning of morphosyntactic rules in a second language would be efficient or complete. Nor is it clear how systematic instruction in morphosyntactic processing can best be integrated into instruction that promotes the development of discourse processing competence in the second language (Frederiksen, Donin, Décary, Edmond, & Hoover, 1992; Spada, 1987).

Recent research on second language discourse processing has demonstrated not only the relevance of cognitive discourse analysis methods and models to this area but also the need to view second language learning as requiring the acquisition of complex interactive processes that involve multiple levels of representation and processing of language and meaning (e.g., Cumming, Rebuffot, & Ledwell, 1989; Donin & Silva, 1993; Eskey & Grabe, 1988). Similarly, assessment models of second language competence now reflect multiple levels of language processing (e.g., Bachman, 1990). Thus, it has been recognized that instruction in a second language must not only develop language processing skills at the lexical, morphological, and syntactic levels. Instruction must also relate these processes to the semantic, inferential, and conceptual processes that are required for comprehension and production of coherent extended discourse (Frederiksen et al., 1992).

Specialized Discourse Processing Expertise

Research on discourse comprehension has clearly established the importance of context to the comprehension process. Context includes relevant prior domain knowledge as well as characteristics of the situation within which discourse is understood or used. It is now generally accepted that discourse comprehension involves the construction of a conceptual representation (or *situation model*; Van Dijk & Kintsch, 1983) by a listener or reader that is appropriate to a communicative context. These constructive processes are based on (a) propositional information that is represented in sentences or other segments of natural language discourse, (b) an individual's prior conceptual knowledge, and (c) other information that is available in the situation within which a text or discourse occurs.

Moreover, current psychological models of discourse production, particularly of written communication, view discourse processing as translating conceptual knowledge structures into rhetorical discourse structures that are appropriate to a communicative situation and setting (Donin, Bracewell, Frederiksen, & Dillinger, 1992; Frederiksen & Emond, 1993; Scardamalia & Bereiter, 1991). One key component of such translation is the construction of a *conceptual situation model* to be communicated to a listener or reader. A second component is the construction of a *propositional text base* to specify precisely the semantic content to be expressed through segments of text or discourse.

Attention within cognitive science has been increasingly directed to the issue of situated cognition, that is, the question of how and to what extent situations, especially social situations, support and constrain complex learning and cognitive functioning in real-world domains of knowledge and activity (e.g., Brown, Collins, & Duguid, 1989; Greeno, 1989, 1991). The comprehension, production, and use of natural language discourse are prominent aspects of most natural situations of cognitive activity and learning. Consequently, discourse competence is an important prerequisite for effective cognitive functioning and learning within many complex situations (Frederiksen & Roy, 1993). Our concept of discourse competence, therefore, should be broadened to include an ability to make effective use of discourse in relation to a variety of specific functions that discourse can serve within situations.

Although these functions of discourse include communication, discourse may also serve other cognitive functions within situations (see Frederiksen & Donin, in press): (a) informative functions (a document functions as an external source of information that can be referred to within a situation), (b) representational functions (text is used as a medium for representing conceptual information during the performance of a task), (c) trace functions (discourse is produced during reasoning or performance of a task and provides an external trace of one's internal cognitive activity for other participants in the situation to observe and evaluate), (d) instrumental functions (text or discourse is produced or used as a tool or means for accomplishing a task), and (e) metacognitive functions (discourse is produced during planning, evaluation, monitoring, or other types of metacognitive activity).

Thus, specialized discourse processing expertise refers to the specialized language knowledge and discourse processing abilities that enable an individual to comprehend, produce, or use discourse effectively for specific purposes within particular situations, settings, and domains of specialized knowledge and skill. The development of specialized discourse processing expertise is a growing focus of instruction and research in the field of second language learning (e.g., Brinton, Snow, & Wesche, 1989; Swales, 1990). Within this focus second language discourse expertise is viewed as being acquired in and for specific contexts, such as the situations, settings, and subject matter domains in which learners must use second language discourse.

Implications for Computer-Assisted Language Learning

Psychological research on discourse processing has identified many aspects of language knowledge and cognitive processing that must be acquired to comprehend, produce, and use connected discourse effectively in a second (or a first) language. Therefore, CALL environments that are designed to make use of explicit models of these processes for instructing students ought to have a valuable role in facilitating the development of communicative competence in a second language.

Intelligent tutoring systems (ITSs) in the field of second language learning have generally consisted of applications of particular linguistic theories or approaches to parsing within computational linguistics. Consequently, the ITS approach has tended to focus on the development of grammar, spelling, or vocabulary tutors. As syntactic theories and parsing techniques have become more concerned with the semantic functions of syntactic and lexical information, tutorial applications have begun to reflect a greater concern with how semantic (propositional) content is expressed by means of natural language structures as well as a concern for how to develop discourse-level skills. Among the unanswered questions that pertain to the design and potential effectiveness of such applications are the following:

1. How should syntactic and semantic knowledge appropriately be communicated to a learner?
2. What is the relationship of the computational and representational formalisms employed in a particular tutoring system to the cognitive processes and representations that are actually used by competent language users when they comprehend or produce sentences?
3. How does one integrate focused instruction in vocabulary, morphology, and syntax into more authentic functional environments of discourse comprehension, production, and use?

An alternative to the ITS approach is to develop *interactive multimedia CALL environments* in which a language learner can interact with and explore a large data base of learning tasks, language exercises, texts, and discourse tasks. Such CALL environments usually incorporate a variety of pedagogical materials, exercises, and approaches already in use in second language instruction. However, beyond the pedagogical orientation, interactive multimedia CALL environments can be practically oriented to provide those discourse experiences that exemplify the types of language and the natural situations of language use in which a learner will be functioning in the second language—for example, job settings.

This practical orientation, from the standpoint of discourse processing research, has many potential advantages. A key advantage is the authenticity of the discourse environment and the opportunities it offers for guided practice and interaction with language in natural situations of comprehension, production, and use. Such an environment is not only deemed important in prevailing literature on second language instruction (see Oxford, this volume; Murray this volume); it can also be highly motivating to learners. This is particularly likely if learners perceive the discourse materials and tasks employed in the environment to be relevant to their needs and if they perceive themselves to be in control of the learning situation.

A common weakness of CALL systems that follow the comunicative approach is the lack of any explicit psychological model of the language knowledge, representations, and cognitive processes employed by competent language users in performing the discourse tasks exemplified by the systems. Ideally, such models would be required to provide a language learner with assistance, explanations, and instruction in the knowledge and processing required to understand and produce well-formed sentences and discourse in the second language. Moreover, a CALL environment should ideally be designed to develop this knowledge and skill by providing guided practice with authentic and varied discourse tasks (i.e., specialized expertise) while giving assistance and instruction in the component processes required to perform these tasks (i.e., general competence). Such assistance could be provided by specialized tutors or by tools and tutorials available online while learners do practical (not pedagogical) discourse tasks. The tools could help learners with, for example, analyzing word morphology, obtaining information about specific lexical items, analyzing the syntactic structure of sentences, obtaining explanations of grammatical structures and their functions in conveying propositional meanings, understanding how language structures are used at the discourse level, and seeing how discourse is organized to convey coherent propositional meanings, guide a reader's or listener's inferences, or represent conceptual information.

In line with these ideals, the project we describe seeks to develop an interactive multimedia CALL environment for supporting the acquisition of discourse competence in a foreign or second language within the context of authentic discourse tasks. In so doing, the project draws on research-based models of text and discourse representation and processing. It also draws on research in second language learning, instruction, and assessment. Moreover, the environment emphasizes practical discourse competence through the use of guided practice and instruction with authentic tasks. At the same time, it offers focused tutorial instruction and on-line assistance toward acquisition of those components basic to communicative competence: lexical, morphological, syntactic, semantic, and discourse knowledge as well as processing skill in the second language. This CALL environment is thus designed to support development of either general language competence or specialized discourse processing expertise, or both.

Within this environment we follow two directions of research. We study the contributions of guided practice and instruction focused on specific subject matter domains and practical communicative situations to the development of specialized discourse expertise. We also study the development of general language and discourse processing skills through both situated and focused tutorial instruction. To accomplish this research, our general approach is to create a flexible CALL environment that enables us to conduct experimental studies of the effectiveness of theoretically motivated pedagogical strategies and discourse representations in facilitating students' acquisition of discourse competence in a second language. The results provide specific information needed to refine and improve subsequent CALL environments and contribute to our general knowledge of the cognitive processes and strategies involved in second language learning.

Design Requirements

To support this general approach to system development and testing, an interactive multimedia CALL system must satisfy a number of specific design requirements. First, the system should allow us to specify explicit models of (a) the multiple levels of language knowledge, (b) representations of language and discourse structures, and (c) language processing skills and strategies that a learner must acquire to comprehend and produce discourse effectively in a second language. Moreover, these models must be specified as formal data structures so that they can be accessed and used by CALL system software. These models constitute the expert knowledge base for the system, in terms of ITS architecture.

Second, the system should support the development of specific modular language tutors to help students acquire general language knowledge and develop proficiency in the component processes (i.e., phonology, morphology, syntax, semantics, discourse structure) necessary for effective discourse comprehension and production. Although the system should allow a language learner to use these modules as stand-alone tutors that provide directed instruction using their own examples, the tutors also should be available to a language learner as tools to provide expert assistance during comprehension or other discourse tasks using externally provided texts. In the latter capacity, modular language tutors should serve as resources for analyzing and explaining particular discourse structures in context and for providing context-sensitive instruction on language knowledge and processes relevant to those structures. In this manner, tutorial instruction focused on language knowledge and skill can be integrated into learning environments in which students engage in activities involving authentic use of discourse (e.g., reading or translating a medical article or procedural instructions in the second language).

Third, the system should support the implementation of interactive multimedia CALL environments that allow language learners to practice using discourse within varied functional and communicative contexts. These language learning environments should simulate tasks and situations in which particular types of discourse are used for specific purposes. These situations should be representative of those in which a student will need to function in his or her second language. These language learning environments, moreover, should be designed to provide assistance to a learner, both through access to language tutors and through guidance, instruction, and feedback pertinent to the specific discourse environment.

Fourth, the system should be capable of monitoring and evaluating student performance and learning. The program should keep a complete record of students' actions while using the system. This ability to monitor actions and performance is required to construct models of students' current knowledge and processing skill and to provide appropriate guidance and feedback. It is also required for studies of students' learning processes, strategies, and use of instructional resources in the CALL system, as well as evaluations of the effectiveness of particular pedagogical strategies or resources.

Finally, the system should be designed to facilitate and encourage experimentation with different pedagogical strategies or approaches to helping students acquire communicative competence in a second language. This requires that the system include authoring tools that allow a developer to create a variety of interactive discourse tasks, create multimedia structured documents for these tasks, configure the system to use particular pedagogical strategies, experiment with different formats for representing discourse information, and control access to modular language tutors during performance on discourse tasks in the language learning environment. Authoring tools are also needed to create specific CALL curricula as the system begins to be used to supplement normal classroom instruction.

Components of the McGill Language Learning Environment

Our overall goal is to develop a flexible CALL environment that can be used to meet the design requirements specified above. Before describing the components of our system, we briefly review the main features of the system from the standpoint of how they address each of these design requirements.

Overview of System Features

Multimedia database of structured documents. Defining an expert knowledge base, the first requirement identified in the previous section, was a fundamental problem in developing the CALL environment. It was necessary to determine how to represent language knowledge and discourse representations as explicit data structures in the system. (Here, we refer to cognitive representations that are constructed in understanding or producing a particular discourse together with their underlying principles.) Language knowledge covers principles of phonology, morphology, syntax, semantics, and discourse. Discourse representations consist of the particular phonetic, morphological, syntactic, propositional, and conceptual representations that are associated with a particular text. Our approach to this problem was to expand the notion of a text model taken from research on text and discourse comprehension. A text model typically consists of five components:

1. A text divided into segments (e.g., words, sentences, paragraphs), with representations of the syntactic structure of text sentences.
2. A list of propositions explicitly encoded in text sentences (i.e., the text base).
3. Propositions that are derived from the propositional text base according to particular kinds of inference rules.
4. Connected semantic network representations.
5. Various types of conceptual representations (e.g., frames, scripts, situation models).

In research on discourse comprehension, text models have been used routinely to study text processing at multiple levels. By matching subjects' protocols to the various components of a text model, researchers have found evidence of syntactic or semantic processing of text segments, various types of inferences, integrative semantic processing, and the construction or use of conceptual frames, scripts, or situation models. Our challenge was to expand this notion of a text model to cover multimedia documents in which textual, graphic, video, and auditory information may be linked together as well as associated with formal models of language and discourse representations.

To develop such explicit text models in a form that can be used by CALL software, we developed an interactive computer program called the *Structured Document Editor* (Décary & Frederiksen, 1993). This editor is designed to assist a system developer in analyzing documents to create expert knowledge data bases. We refer to such data bases as *structured documents*. Structured documents are complex data structures that link text segments, multimedia information, multiple discourse representations (defined as computer data structures of various types, e.g., lists, trees, networks, frames), and formal rules (e.g., grammar rules, associative links, frames) that define particular types of discourse representations.

The Structured Document Editor allows a system developer to edit and develop rules, to input, edit, and segment multimedia documents, and to apply rules to analyze a document. The output of the program is a structured document file that is structured according to a formal protocol. This program also acts as a server to interpret structured document files for other software applications that need to use them, as described next.

Interactive learning environment for guided practice with authentic discourse tasks. The next problem was to develop a user interface that could be used to implement a flexible Language Learning Environment that meets the requirements specified previously. In designing a user interface, we decided to adopt an apprenticeship learning metaphor (Collins, Brown, & Newman, 1989). In this metaphor students can learn through guided practice and instruction with authentic discourse, tasks, and contexts, with available assistance and tutoring in component processes and representations. In the current Language Learning Environment, schematized in Figure 6.1, students choose themes, discourse tasks, and texts for a particular session by means of menu selections. They can obtain guidance and assistance through communication with a main tutor (by means of menus and dialogue boxes), or they may receive specific help with particular language subsystems (e.g., syntax) through selection of specific language tutors from a tutor palette. The main tutor and the language tutors can access information contained in structured documents by communicating with the server, and they can display or interpret this information for a language learner.

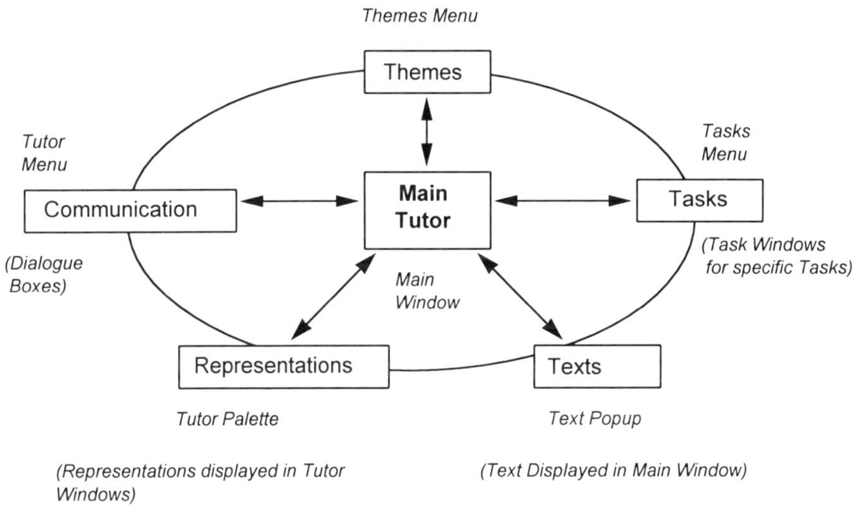

FIG. 6.1. Structure of the main Language Learning Environment.

For example, a learner can elect to read or hear a text, view videos or graphic information associated with it, perform various activities involving the text, receive advice and feedback from the main tutor, or obtain help, explanations, and tutoring on particular language subsystems for any selected segment of the text.

Available language tutors for instruction in component language skills. To meet the requirement for modular language tutoring, the system includes the specific language tutors referred to previously. These are intended to develop knowledge and processing skill with respect to specific language subsystems (phonology, morphology, syntax, semantics, and discourse). These language tutors can be used either for stand-alone instruction or as tools to provide assistance during the performance of practical discourse tasks in the learning environment. In a learning session, language learners may elect to work with a particular language tutor in stand-alone mode by selecting it from the tutor palette and then selecting Topics, Tasks, and Examples from menus, as schematized in Figure 6.2. Learners may communicate directly with the language tutor by means of a tutor menu and dialogue boxes to receive advice, guidance, and feedback on their performance. As aids to acquiring knowledge of linguistic subsystems, learners may also view graphic representations and explanations of language structures (e.g., syntactic trees, propositions) associated with text examples. An example from the syntax tutor appears later in Figure 6.6.

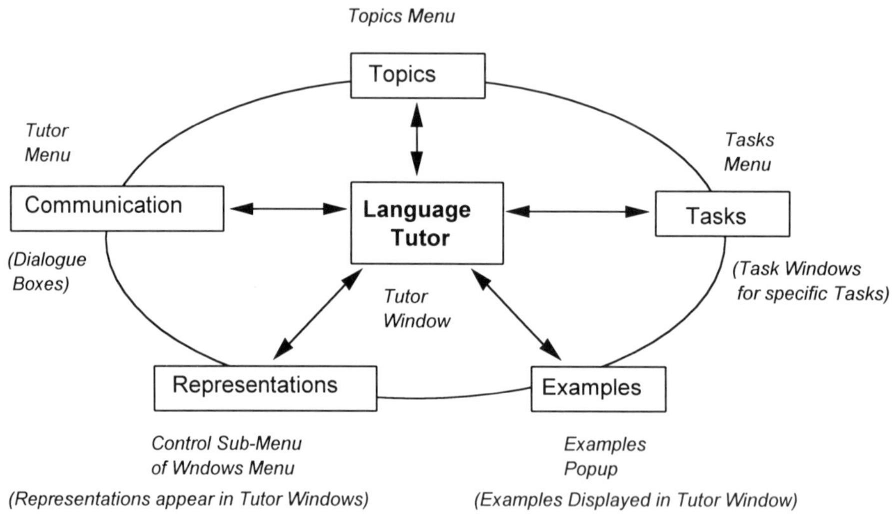

FIG. 6.2. Structure of the language tutors.

Because the examples are themselves represented as structured documents, tutors have access to structures associated with examples (e.g., syntactic parse trees) and the rules that were used to generate the structures.

Language tutors are also available to learners as resources in the discourse learning environment, to assist with comprehension or other discourse tasks (e.g., providing help in analyzing the syntactic construction used in a text segment selected by a learner). They can even be used as embedded tutors in a practical environment to provide focused, systematic instruction on topics for which a tutor is called (e.g., a student may want help on particular syntactic constructions encountered in a document in the second language).

Immediate feedback on progress with practice in self-monitoring by students. To monitor students' developing language knowledge and cognitive processing in the Language Learning Environment, we are adopting an approach to assessment that is based on methods used to evaluate cognitive processing in psychological studies of discourse behavior (Frederiksen & Breuleux, 1990; Frederiksen & Stemmer, 1993). In this approach, students' responses are evaluated in relation to explicit text models (i.e., structured texts). Simple responses (e.g., choices, limited verbal productions) can be evaluated directly by the system. To evaluate students' complex verbal productions, we are experimenting with system-guided self-evaluation. In self-evaluation, students learn to monitor their own discourse processing by comparing their productions to those provided by the system. The system assists the students in this comparison, guides their analysis, and records the results.

In addition, the program keeps a record (called a *dribble file*) of all actions taken by each learner in each session. This record provides information about the choices made by students and a record of their activities while using any selected discourse environment or language tutor. Students receive immediate feedback on their performance, and they can review their records of performance and receive guidance in the selection of learning activities and topics based on their previous performance and selection of topics.

Flexible strategies for pedagogical interaction and guidance. A central requirement of software to support our research program is an authoring system. We need a way of creating a database of authentic texts and situations of discourse activity to provide the learner with a variety of themes, tasks, discourse functions, and texts. In addition, we need to be able to implement various pedagogical strategies in the Language Learning Environment, such as demonstrations, modeling, help, explanations, questions, evaluation, and suggestions. We also must be able to implement more global pedagogical strategies typically used in cognitive apprenticeship teaching. Examples of global pedagogical strategies are guiding the student in the selection of texts and tasks, fading (i.e., gradually withdrawing) the extent and kinds of assistance provided to the student, initial instruction guided by the tutor followed by increased exploration and control of learning activities by the learner, and use of feedback on past performance to advise the student. In addition, scripts or plans may be used to structure the interactive sessions in which the student acquires communicative competence through coaching and practice on authentic discourse tasks. Our intention is to make the authoring system sufficiently user friendly that it can be used by a curriculum developer or researcher.

Facilities for communication with the student. Because our aim is to use our interactive CALL environment to supplement normal classroom instruction or as a part of a remote teaching network, it is important to have resources for communication between a teacher and students using the system. To provide such resources, we are developing a teacher environment. The teacher environment is a program that allows the teacher (or a researcher) to inspect the progress of each student through a continuously updated report created by the learning environment. The teacher can leave messages and provide guidance that will be available to students either during their next session with the system or immediately if both teacher and student are connected to the system at the same time. Also, student responses to open-ended tasks and messages can be examined by the teacher directly, with the results sent back to the student through the system. The learning environment can use these evaluations to update students' profiles and provide students with appropriate guidance and feedback.

The Structured Document Editor

The Structured Document Editor helps developers create the structured documents—the texts and associated data structures—with which language learners interact when comprehending, producing, or using texts in the Language Learning Environment or within the language tutors. The editor provides tools for defining four types of formal structural representations—lists, frames, trees, and associative networks; for generating types of structural representations for a text; and for linking text segments to other types of objects, such as sounds, images, sequences, or symbols. This program not only enables texts to be input for instruction but also allows for the integration of a text with related information, such as pictures and graphics, sound recordings of sentences, links from words to dictionary entries, translations of words and sentences, grammatical analyses of sentences, links between expressions and grammar explanations, semantic analyses of sentence meanings, analyses of inferences relating sentence meanings, analyses of discourse organization, and other potentially useful aspects of language.

Structured documents. Formally, a structured document is a complex multimedia document to which explicit structural information about its contents has been added. It contains displayable objects (e.g., text, pictures, sound, video) that are related to one another in terms of layout and relative location within the document. Document objects are segmented into their logical constituents. For instance, texts are segmented into words, sentences, and paragraphs; pictures are segmented into component parts or zones; and sounds and video sequences are segmented into temporally organized units and sequences that can be related to one another in a hierarchy. Other kinds of information comprising a structured document are described in the following sections.

Links among document units. Document objects or segments may be linked to one another either with automatic links or with author-defined hyperlinks. Automatic links are derived directly from the segmentation of a document and the relations among the objects in the document. Examples of automatic links are inclusion links (e.g., words can be linked to the sentences of which they are a part), equivalence or mapping links (e.g., words can be linked to a segment of a sound file that corresponds to the spoken version of the text), and description links (e.g., a zone of a picture can be linked to a segment of text that describes it). Author-defined hyperlinks with arbitrary labels can be created between units within a document. For example, a word can be linked to its translation.

Representations associated with document objects. Representations can be created and linked to objects and their segments. For example, syntactic parse trees can be linked to sentences, and semantic structures (e.g., a taxonomy, a planning net for a procedure) can be linked to multimedia information. Representations are intended to reflect structures and relations that are understandable to a user and that therefore provide a meaningful basis for structuring document information. These representations are created by applying formal definitions (e.g., grammar rules, associative links, frames) specified by the author.

Components of the editor. The Structured Document Editor includes modular components (functions) that accomplish several objectives.

Object definition and segmentation. Facilities are provided for defining and entering the displayable data objects that comprise a structured document. Objects are of four types: text, pictures (BMP files with 256 colors), sound (WAV files), and video (AVI files). Text can be segmented automatically into words, sentences, and paragraphs, but there is also a utility to give the author some control over the segmentation. Pictures can be segmented into various zones and organized hierarchically. A time-based tool can be used to segment sound and video objects into logical units that are organized hierarchically.

Formal definition of structure representations. Representations associated with document objects must be created from formal definitions. General and powerful tools are provided to define formally the particular types of representations to be associated with (i.e., linked to) objects and their segments. These tools include the following editors:

1. *The BNF grammar editor* allows the creation of recursive production grammars that are expressed by means of BNF (i.e., Backus-Naur-Form notation; Wirth, 1976), as shown in Figure 6.3. For instance, a grammar can be defined that will permit syntactic or semantic descriptions of sentences to be constructed.

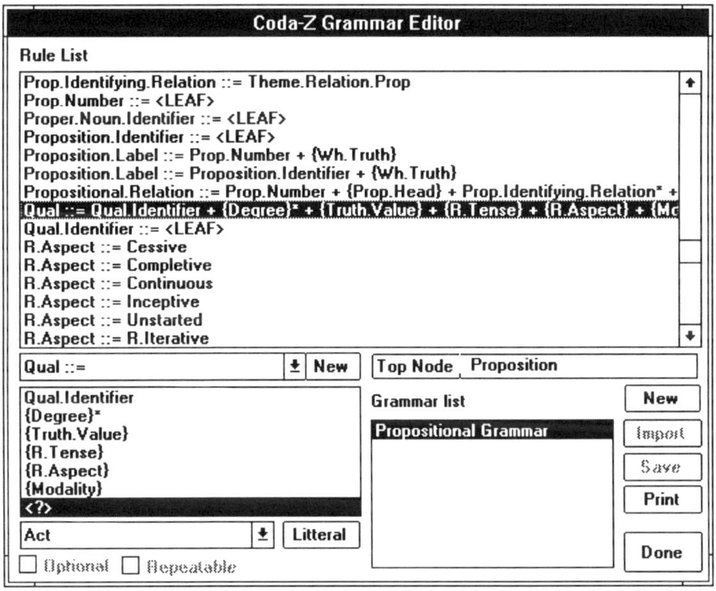

FIG. 6.3. Example of a BNF grammar editor window.

2. *Frame and list definition editors* allow users to define frames (i.e., sets of labeled knowledge structures) or lists (by specifying the number and kinds of elements the list contains).
3. *The General network rule editor* allows the creation and editing of well-formedness rules for trees and networks to allow a user to define representations that are not easily defined by means of grammars. For example, an author can specify the types of nodes in a network, the types of leaves in a tree, the labeling of arcs (links) in a network or tree, and more general constraints on these structures.

Creation and editing of representations. Once a particular type of representation has been formally defined, it can be used to create structures that are linked to units within the document. These structures can be created with a number of different editors. The outline tree editor can be used to create and edit trees by applying production rules from a BNF grammar while operating on an indented outline format for representing a tree structure (see Figure 6.4).

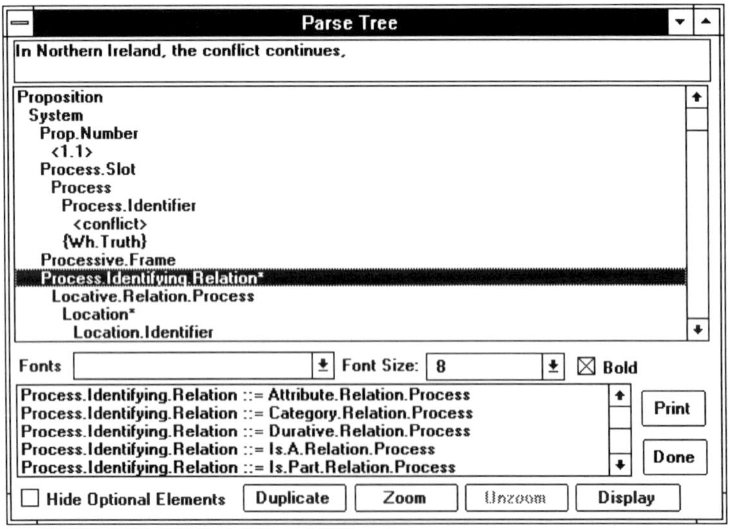

FIG. 6.4. Example of an outline tree editor to create a tree structure.

The graphic tree editor can be used to create trees by following production rules in a grammar while operating on a graphic representation of the structure. The link-based network editor can be used to create and edit trees and networks by specifying individual links between nodes. The frame editor is used to instantiate frames, and a list editor is used to create lists from formal definitions.

Link definition and creation. Authors are also provided tools for defining arbitrary hyperlinks between document units or representations.

Server for structured documents. The Structured Document Editor can be called by other programs to function as a server of structured documents. This is achieved through DDE (Dynamic Data Exchange) in Windows 3.1. A complete but simple DDE protocol is defined. Applications acting as clients can send the editor queries to open a structured document, get the list of objects, display an object, get the list of structures and links available for an object at a specific position, display a structure representation, or synchronize the playing of a sound file with the movement of the cursor in a text transcription.

The Language Learning Environment

The language learning environment is the program with which the student interacts directly (see Figure 6.5).

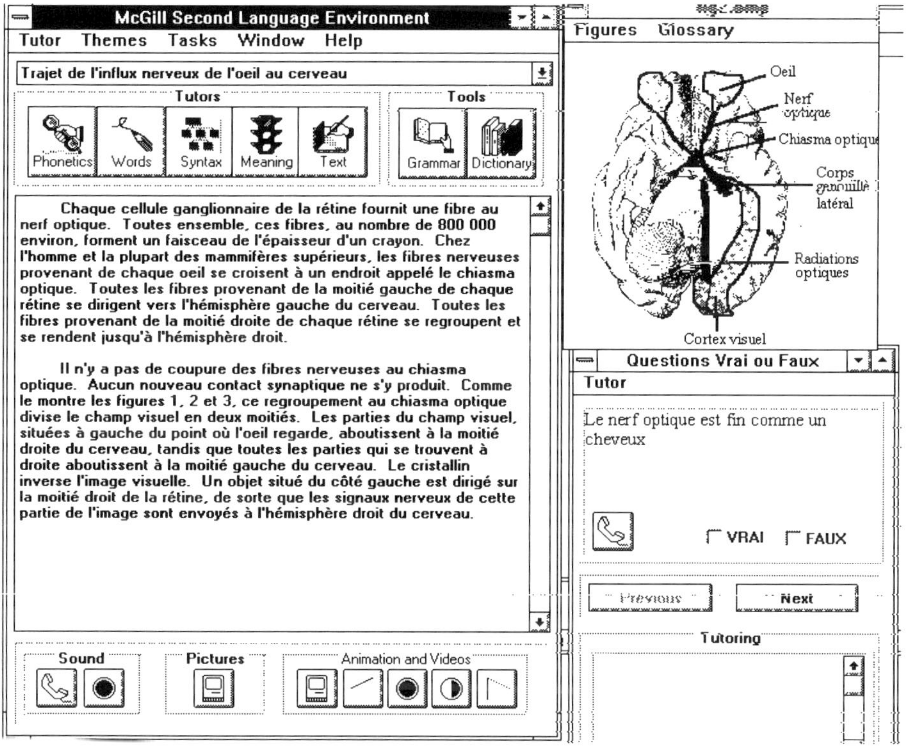

FIG. 6.5. Example of the main language learning environment interface.

Students can select themes and documents following their personal interests. They can explore different aspects of the selected documents (e.g., text, images) and perform learning tasks and activities while using these documents with guidance and feedback from the system. To assist them in reading, revising, and using texts, students have access to many on-line tools such as dictionaries, grammar references, translations, paraphrases, and analyses of sentence structure or meaning.

Students also can elect to use any of five specialized interactive language tutors that develop different aspects of language skill, such as pronunciation (with a phonetics and phonology tutor), word formation (with a morphology tutor), grammar and sentence construction (with a syntax tutor, as in Figure 6.6), expression of meaning and language functions (with a semantics tutor), and text structure and organization (with a discourse tutor).

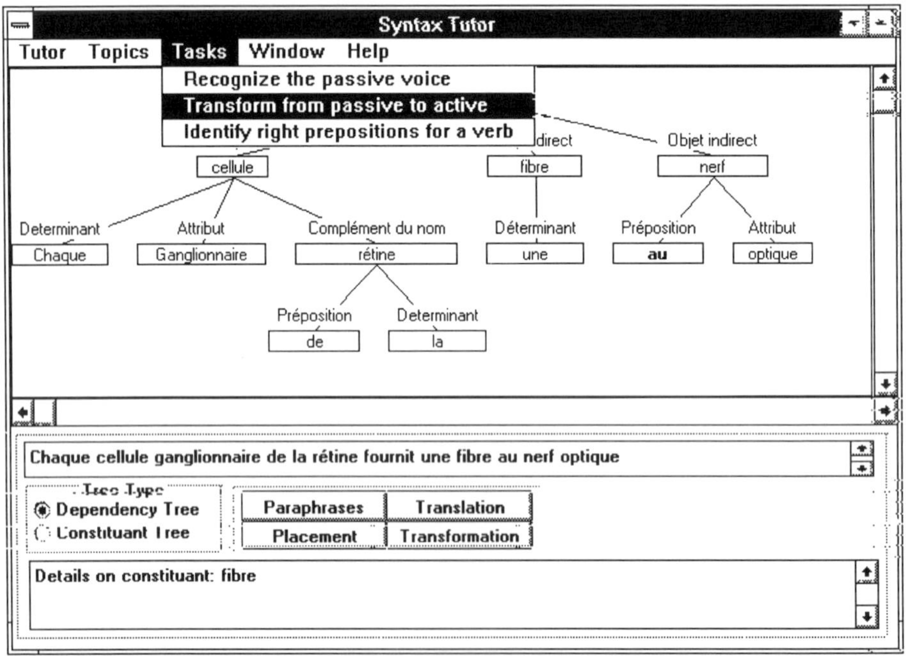

FIG. 6.6. Example of syntax tutor interface (for sentence selected in Figure 6.5).

Students can use the language tutors in two distinct ways. First, they can use these tutors as tools to obtain help with any unit of a text (i.e., a word, sentence, expression, paragraph, etc.) that they are working with as part of another task and that they find difficult or want to understand better. For example, they can see graphic intonation curves, word segmentations, or diagrams of grammatical or semantic relations within a sentence, logical relations between sentences, and the topical organization of a paragraph or an entire discourse. They can also receive an explanation of the representation that is shown. To illustrate, suppose a student working with the French text in Figure 6.5 selects the first sentence of the text and then selects the syntax tutor. That tutor presents a diagram of the sentence, shown in Figure 6.6, with grammatical relations in the form of a dependency tree. The second way students can use each tutor is as an interactive learning environment in its own right, providing systematic instruction, skill-building activities, and explanations of particular components of knowledge and skill needed to master a language. Note, for example, that the syntax tutor illustrated in Figure 6.6 enables students to work on tasks such as paraphrasing, translating, and transforming sentences. The similarities or differences in the tree diagrams that result from sentence transformations such as active-passive are intended to help students grasp the systematic structural relationships between sentence patterns in the language. In addition to themes, documents, tasks, tools, and specialized Language Tutors, students have access to a profile showing their progress in learning, communication with the teacher through a mail system, and on-demand advice and guidance from the system.

The Authoring System

The authoring system is used to create a specific discourse learning environment or an entire curriculum (see Figure 6.7).

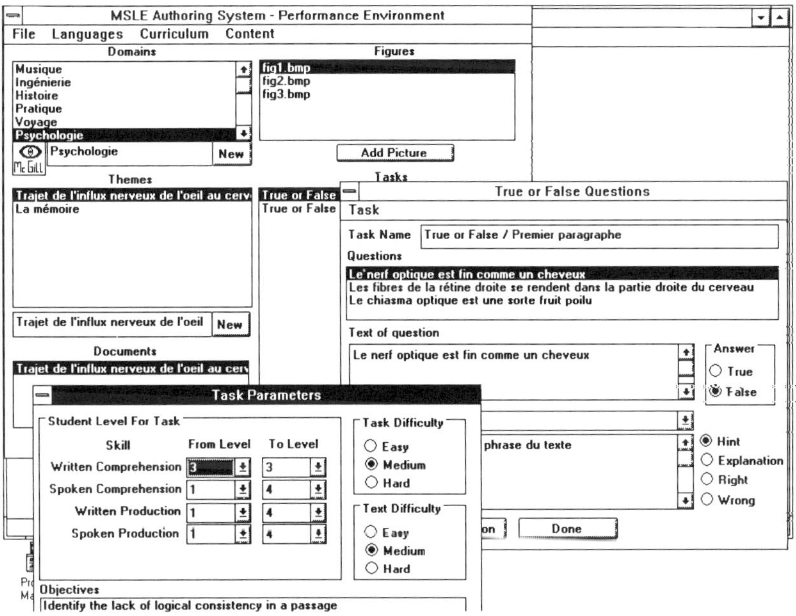

FIG. 6.7. A window used in the authoring system.

Authors define a series of themes that correspond to particular subject matter domains in the second language. A theme is composed of a set of documents and a series of learning tasks and activities. A document is a text created with the Structured Document Editor and can include static pictures, sound, animation sequences, and eventually, video sequences. Learning tasks and activities include both natural discourse activities and skill-building activities that are designed for specific pedagogical functions. Natural discourse activities are intended to simulate uses of language in everyday situations, including a variety of written or spoken comprehension and production tasks. Pedagogical functions that can be authored include defining instructional objectives, obtaining evaluations of students' learning, defining characteristics of various groups of learners or levels of learner proficiency, and defining guidance, assistance, and feedback for learners while they use the system.

A Cycle of Research and Development

Controlled Naturalistic Learning Environments

One advantage of a well-designed and flexible CALL environment is that it can be used as a research laboratory to study many of the current issues in second language teaching and learning. This environment allows the researcher to overcome a major difficulty with classroom-based research, that is, the lack of researcher control inherent in the classroom situation. At the same time, by embedding research within CALL environments that simulate naturalistic situations and domains of language use, one can avoid the artificial nature of many performance tasks used in language research.

In addition, a computer environment should provide a laboratory for studying issues relevant to the design and improvement of CALL systems themselves. Many features of computer-assisted learning environments appear to be based on their authors' beliefs rather than on the outcomes of research. Numerous issues with respect to the design of CALL systems need to be studied and properly evaluated. Thus, we view the environment that we are developing as just one stage in a continuous process of research and development.

Some Examples of Issues to Explore

A general issue from the second language acquisition literature that can be studied within our CALL environment concerns the notion of comprehensible input. Teachers and other native speakers addressing the second language learner appear to modify their language automatically in many ways. It has been theorized that this modification makes the language more comprehensible for the learner and that comprehensible input supports language acquisition (e.g., Chaudron, 1985; Krashen, 1980; Long, 1983). However, the literature does not define what constitutes comprehensible input for a given learner. What are the particular features of the language that are important for defining comprehensibility? This is an area of research that requires more systematic study. Our CALL environment will allow us to look at particular aspects of input modification within naturalistic texts that are being read or listened to by a reader for a specific purpose. In particular, the CALL environment with its analytic tools allows us to focus not only on syntactic complexity, the primary focus of research in this area, but also on issues relevant to text organization, text content, the reader's knowledge, and the interaction of these various aspects both in comprehending the texts and in using those texts as vehicles for supporting language learning.

As stated earlier, we set out to create a CALL environment that would enable us to conduct experimental studies of the effectiveness of theoretically motivated pedagogical strategies and discourse representations in facilitating students' acquisition of discourse competence in a second language. Research suggests that, at least in the case of languages that are of the same language family, second language text comprehension is highly related to first language comprehension (e.g., Cummins, 1991; Donin & Silva, 1993). However, links between one's first and second languages are rarely made explicit in the classroom, partly because of the philosophy that the learner's first language should not be used in the second language classroom. Consequently, one of the pedagogical issues that we plan to address with our environment is the use of the first language as a tool for making explicit the semantic-syntactic links in the second language and how these may be different from those of the learner's first language. It is an issue requiring empirical investigation as to whether such use of the first language aids, or perhaps hinders, second language acquisition. Studies conducted in a realistic yet controlled CALL environment are well suited to addressing this issue.

Second language instruction focused traditionally on the teaching and production of correct syntactic forms. A discourse approach to language learning suggests that syntactic forms are acquired as a vehicle for expressing meaning within a discourse context (Hatch, 1978). Such an approach suggests that, at least for the adult language learner, a tool that allows one to begin with a particular meaning or semantic structure and then translate that structure into its various syntactic realizations might prove beneficial. The CALL environment that we describe will allow us to investigate a number of research questions regarding the design, use, and effectiveness of such a tool. Related to these specific questions is the more general issue of how to make effective use of representational systems within instructional contexts. Although this has relevance to the classroom as well, it is of particular importance in the development of CALL environments. For example, is it advantageous for the learner to be able to access a syntactic tree for a particular sentence or phrase being read? If so, what particular form should that tree have in order for it to be an efficient aid for the learner (i.e., what constitutes an effective pedagogical grammar)? These are critical empirical questions.

Also, we have developed and employed a system of semantic representation that has proved to be a highly effective research tool (e.g., Frederiksen, 1975, 1986; Frederiksen & Donin, 1991). It has been suggested that this system would also prove effective as a tool to aid learners in better understanding what is being expressed in both their first and second languages. Again, empirical tests are required to determine how best to use such a tool and in what contexts.

We began by saying that we wanted our system to function in a manner similar to that of an expert language teacher in a one-to-one apprenticeship tutoring situation. However, within such situations many questions need to be answered. For example, is it advantageous to the student for the tutor to provide tutorial assistance while that student is attempting to understand a particular text? Perhaps this would interfere with the student's own attempts to construct meaning from the text. How important is it that the student control the situation? How and to what extent should the student's learning experiences be directed or assisted by the tutor? There are many different ways that language tutoring can occur within a CALL environment. It is important that alternative pedagogical strategies and approaches be tested, not only with respect to outcome measures but also with respect to how they might affect language learners' strategies and cognitive processing during learning.

The above issues are but a few of those that can and should be addressed within the CALL environment. No pedagogical system should be static. A pedagogical system should be continually evolving to encompass within it the results of well-designed research. This is particularly true of a computer learning environment. We plan to use research results obtained from studies employing the CALL system described here to refine and improve subsequent CALL environments. These subsequent environments would then themselves become the basis for further research, part of a continuing cycle of research and development.

Acknowledgments

This research was supported by grants from the Centre de Recherche Informatique de Montréal (CRIM), the Ministère de l'Enseignement Supérieur et de la Science, Direction Générale de l'Enseignement de de la Recherche Universitaires, Québec (MESS), and the Fonds pour la Formation de Chercheurs et l'Aide à la Recherche (FCAR), Québec. We acknowledge Dr. Jacques Rebuffot and Dr. Carolyn Turner for the many contributions they have made to this project.

References

Bachman, L.F. (1990). *Fundamental considerations in language testing.* New York: Oxford University Press.

Brinton, D.M., Snow, M.A., & Wesche, M.B. (1989). *Content-based second language instruction.* New York: Newbury House.

Brown, J.S., Collins, A., & Duguid, P. (1989). Situated cognition and the culture of learning. *Educational Researcher*, *18*, 32-42.

Chaudron, C. (1985). Comprehension, comprehensibility, and learning in the second language classroom. *Studies in Second Language Acquisition*, *7*, 216-232.

Collins, A., Brown, J.S., & Newman, S.E. (1989). Cognitive apprenticeship: Teaching the craft of reading, writing and mathematics. In L.B. Resnick (Ed.), *Knowing, learning and instruction: Essays in honor of Robert Glaser* (pp. 453-494). Hillsdale, NJ: Lawrence Erlbaum Associates.

Cumming, A., Rebuffot, J., & Ledwell, M. (1989). Reading and summarizing challenging texts in first and second languages. *Reading and Writing*, *2*, 201-219.

Cummins, J. (1991). Interdependence of first and second language proficiency in bilingual children. In E. Bialystok (Ed.), *Language processing in bilingual children* (pp. 70-89). Cambridge, England: Cambridge University Press.

Décary, M., & Frederiksen, C. H. (August, 1993). *Human-computer interface design to access and control complex multimedia documents in learning environments.* Paper presented at HCI International 93, Orlando, FL.

Donin, J., Bracewell, R. J., Frederiksen, C. H., & Dillinger, M. (1992). Students' strategies for writing instructions: Organizing conceptual information in text. *Written Communication, 9,* 209-236.

Donin, J., & Silva, M. (1993). The relationship between first- and second language reading comprehension of occupation-specific texts. *Language Learning, 43,* 373-401.

Eskey, D., & Grabe, W. (1988). Interactive models for second language reading: Perspectives on instruction. In P. Carrell, J. Devine, & D. Eskey (Eds.), *Interactive approaches to second language reading* (pp. 223-238). New York: Cambridge University Press.

Frederiksen, C.H. (1975). Representing logical and semantic structure of knowledge acquired from discourse. *Cognitive Psychology, 7,* 371-458.

Frederiksen, C.H. (1986). Cognitive models and discourse analysis. In C.R. Cooper & S. Greenbaum (Eds.), *Written communication annual: An international survey of research and theory, vol. 1: Studying writing: Linguistic approaches* (pp.227-267). Beverly Hills, CA: Sage.

Frederiksen, C. H., Bracewell, R. J., Breuleux, A., & Renaud, A. (1989). The cognitive representation and processing of discourse: function and dysfunction. In Y. Joanette & H. Brownell (Eds.), *Discourse ability and brain damage: Theoretical and empirical perspectives* (pp. 69-110). New York: Springer-Verlag.

Frederiksen, C.H., & Breuleux, A. (1990). Monitoring cognitive processing in semantically complex domains. In N. Frederiksen, R. Glaser, A. Lesgold & M. Shafto (Eds.), *Diagnostic monitoring of skill and knowledge acquisition* (pp. 351-391). Hillsdale, NJ: Lawrence Erlbaum Associates.

Frederiksen, C.H., & Donin, J. (1991). Constructing multiple semantic representations in comprehending and producing discourse. In G. Denhière & J.P. Rossi (Eds.), *Texts and text processing* (pp. 19-44). New York: North-Holland.

Frederiksen, C.H., & Donin, J. (in press). Les contextes fonctionnels de l'expertise discursive: Implications pour l'évaluation (Functional contexts of discourse expertise: Implications for evaluation). In J.Y. Boyer & G. Fortier (Eds.), *L'évaluation du savoir-lire.* Paris: Editions Logique.

Frederiksen, C.H., Donin, J., Décary, M., Emond, B., & Hoover, M. (1992). Semantic discourse processing and tutoring systems for second language learning. In M.L. Swartz & M. Yazdani (Eds.), *The bridge to international communication: Intelligent tutoring systems for foreign language learning* (pp. 103-121). New York: Springer-Verlag

Frederiksen, C.H., & Emond, B. (1993). La représentation et le traitement cognitif du discours: Le rôle des modèles formels. In J.-F. Le Ny (Ed.), *Intelligence naturelle et intelligence artificielle* (pp. 165-195). Paris: Presses Universitaires de France.

Frederiksen, C.H., & Roy, M. (1993, June). *Modeling the situation in discourse communication: The conceptual basis for discourse activity.* Paper presented at the Society for Text and Discourse, Boulder, CO.

Frederiksen, C.H., & Stemmer, B. (1993). Conceptual processing of discourse by a right hemisphere brain damaged patient. In H. Brownell and Y. Joanette (Eds.), *Narrative discourse in neurologically impaired and normal aging adults* (239-278). San Diego: Singular Publishing Group.

Greeno, J.G. (1989). Situations, mental models, and generative knowledge. In D. Klahr & K. Katovsky (Eds.), *Complex information processing: The impact of Herbert A. Simon* (pp. 285-317). Hillsdale, NJ: Lawrence Erlbaum Associates.

Greeno, J.G. (1991). Environments for situated conceptual learning. *The International Conference on the Learning Sciences: Proceedings of the 1991 Conference* (pp. 211-216). Charlottesville, VA: Association for the Advancement of Computing in Education.

Hatch, E. (1978). Discourse analysis and second language acquisition. In E. Hatch (Ed.), *Second language acquisition: A book of readings* (pp. 402-435). Rowley, MA: Newbury House.

Krashen, S. (1980). The input hypothesis. In J. Alatis (Ed.), *Current issues in bilingual education* (pp. 168-180). Washington, DC: Georgetown University Press.

Krashen, S. (1982). *Principles and practice in second language acquisition.* Oxford: Pergamon.

Long, M. (1983). Native speaker/non-native speaker conversation in the second language classroom. In M. Clarke & J. Hanscombe (Eds.), *On TESOL '82* (pp. 207-225). Washington, DC: TESOL.

Mross, E.F. (1990). Text analysis: macro- and microstructural aspects of discourse processing. In Y. Joanette and H. H. Brownell (Eds.), *Discourse ability and brain damage: Theoretical and empirical perspectives* (pp. 50-68). New York: Springer-Verlag.

Scardamalia, M., & Bereiter, C. (1991). Literate expertise. In K.A. Ericsson & J. Smith (Eds.), *Toward a general theory of expertise: prospects and limits* (pp. 172-194). Cambridge, UK: Cambridge University Press.

Spada, N. (1987). Relationships between instructional differences and learning outcomes: A process-product study of communicative language teaching. *Applied Linguistics*, *8*, 137-161.

Swales, J. (1990). Nonnative speaker graduate engineering students and their introductions: Global coherence and local management. In U. Connor & A. M. Johns (Eds.), *Coherence in writing: Research and pedagogical perspectives* (pp.187-206). Alexandria, VA: TESOL.

Van Dijk, T.A., & Kintsch, W. (1983). *Strategies of discourse comprehension.* New York: Academic Press.

Widdowson, W. G. (1978). *Teaching language as communication.* New York: Oxford University Press.

Wirth, N. (1976). *Algorithms + Data Structures = Program.* Englewood Cliffs, NJ: Prentice Hall.

7

GPARS: A Suite of Grammar Assessment Systems

Donald Loritz
Georgetown University

The GPARS system is a multilingual suite of computer-assisted language teaching programs built around Generalized Transition Network parsers. To date, most of these systems have been developed as interactive grammar checkers, but the focus of these systems is more upon assessment, diagnosis, and modeling of students' language development than upon direct student instruction.

The first section of this chapter presents a brief history of the GPARS project. The second section includes instructional results that have been obtained for deaf students of English using the English version of the GPARS parser and its grammar checker, Ms. Pluralbelle. The third section, a technical endnote, briefly describes implementation details of GPARS systems intended to improve parsing robustness and efficiency. The final section discusses planned research and applications of the GPARS system.

The GPARS system had its origin in 1978 at Boston University in an attempt at computational modeling of the linguistic development of language-delayed children. In the course of that study, it became apparent that hand-coded developmental data were too labor-intensive and too unreliable for teachers to use with confidence. Advanced computational methods promised more reliable and automatic empirical assessments of language data. At that time, however, such assessments required computers that were not educationally affordable.

By the early 1980s microcomputers had begun to develop the capacity to deliver such automatic assessments. One of the first demonstrations of this capacity was Henry Higgins (Loritz, 1983), an intonation tutor that extracted fundamental frequencies (F_0) in learners' speech and digitally recorded, played back, and graphically displayed learner intonation patterns together with intonation patterns of a model speaker.

Shortly after Henry Higgins was developed, both Lisp and PROLOG became available for microcomputers. The GPARS project adopted the augmented transition network (ATN) formalism (Bates, 1978; Bobrow & Fraser, 1969; Winograd, 1983; Woods, 1970) because, among other considerations, Grossberg (1972) had demonstrated that language learning must be a case of massively parallel pattern learning. Although any serial computer parsing system is ultimately rule based, the ATN formalism seemed especially well suited to analyzing grammatical development as patterns of learned behavior. Accordingly, a series of ATN parsers was developed.

GPARS Tutorial Systems: Evolving Choices of Platform, Programming Language, and Target Foreign Languages

The first GPARS ATN system, Ms. Fidditch (Loritz, 1984), was developed for the Apple II personal computer and for the computer chip known as the 6502 microprocessor. Ms. Fidditch was envisioned as a purely reactive, purely syntactic, broad-coverage grammar checker. It was conceived as reactive, as opposed to a directive tutor with a planned curriculum, because, in the absence of ATN diagrams expressing normal developmental patterns, there existed no reliable model by which Ms. Fidditch could tell the student what to learn next. In addition, Ms. Fidditch made no serious attempt at semantic understanding of learner input.

The 6502 computer chip was the first widely available RISC microprocessor, and it was expected that the next-generation 65816 chip for the Apple computer would support evolving Ms. Fidditch systems. In 1985, however, the 65816-based Apple IIgs personal computer was brought out as a dumbed-down, 1-megahertz, educational computer. Ms. Fidditch was then ported to the IBM personal computer environment under the TLC-Lisp programming language (Allen, 1978, 1985) and renamed *Ms. Grundy*.

Sponsored research and development of GPARS systems was first obtained for a Chinese grammar checker, Xuejiu, running over the Chinese version of the GPARS parser (CHIPARS), and a Russian grammar checker, Russkii Sintaksis, running over the Russian version of the GPARS parser (RUSPARS). Classroom testing of these grammar checkers and the development of others have been delayed.

In the case of Chinese, instruction at Georgetown has eschewed pinyin, which is the standard system for romanizing Chinese ideograms, in favor of going directly to character-based instruction. Although character-based output was developed for Xuejiu (with assistance from the Army Research Institute), the difficulties of character-based input for both learner and computer precluded classroom testing of Xuejiu until its grammar could achieve at least intermediate-level competence. With continued doctoral research in linguistics (Chen, 1993; Yen, 1992; Zhang, 1993), that level of parsing has now been achieved. Character-based assessment is still much more complicated than assessment based on pinyin, but research on character-based input is now finally beginning.

More generally, there has been a nationwide decline in interest in foreign language learning and research. This caused Georgetown University to close all foreign language graduate programs except for Spanish, and GPARS research to focus more on English as a second language (ESL).

In 1988 funding was obtained to develop Ms. Grundy for deaf ESL students at Gallaudet, and it is from this study that we have obtained our first instructional results. Since then, Ms. Grundy has been ported to a protected-mode implementation on an 80386 microprocessor (in the 386 personal computer) and runs under the TLC-Lisp386 programming language (Wagner & Tran, 1989). The system has been renamed *Ms. Pluralbelle*. Additionally, several dissertation-level Chinese, Japanese, and Korean extensions of the 386 version of GPARS have been completed.

Instructional Results: Diagnostic and Interactive Uses of GPARS

This section reports two kinds of studies employing the GPARS system: a diagnostic analysis of a user corpus and an interactive user test. In the Gallaudet project, "Using Artificial Intelligence to Teach English to Deaf People (AITED)" (Loritz, Parhizgar, & Zambrano, 1990; Parhizgar, 1991), we used GPARS to analyze some 12,000 sentences of deaf ESL learners drawn from nearly 1,000 passing and failing college-entrance English essay examinations (see "Diagnostic Results"). The essays ranged in level of ESL proficiency from beginning to advanced, but our target group was intermediate learners. Two classes of intermediate learners (24 students) beta tested the GPARS interactive grammar checking system (Ms. Pluralbelle) for one semester (see "Interactive Results").

Diagnostic Results: Using GPARS to Reveal Patterns of Grammatical Usage in a Student Corpus

The ATN parse analysis used in the English version of GPARS (ENGPARS) defines a *parse path* through the parse rules, or grammar, for each sentence under analysis.[23] These parse paths can be statistically aggregated and represented on an ATN state diagram, which graphically depicts phrasal states and transitions between words in a sentence. We can then present this diagram to teachers as a diagnostic grammar map. An advantage of grammar maps based on transition networks is that they can summarize many parse trees in a single diagram. This enables us to derive competency map assessments, such as the map shown in Figure 7.1, representing the particular sentence patterns employed by student users of the parser.

The map in Figure 7.1 is based upon a standard augmented transition network diagram. According to the map, the operation of the ATN parser in parsing a noun phrase kernel (NPK) can be described by the following example (an NPK is a simple noun phrase, like *the big house*, without attached prepositional phrases or relative clauses).

A sample parse: How the ATN analysis works. To parse the following NPK,

the two little, green men,

the parser begins in the state NPK/, the top left box of Figure 7.1 (read as "parsing an NPK from the starting point"). The arcs or paths emanating from NPK/ are tried in alphabetical order. (Many possible paths in Figure 7.1 are not diagrammed because they were never used by the learners in this cohort.) The word currently under analysis, *the*, is neither a pronoun nor the word *all*, so paths B and C from NPK/ in Figure 7.1 are not taken (these paths are referred to as *NPK/B* and *NPK/C*). *The* is a determiner, so eventually path NPK/D is followed to the state NPK/DET (read as "parsing an NPK having found a determiner"). In traversing this path, the word currently under analysis is advanced to *two*.

---

[23] The parse path shows which rules in the entire store of rules, or grammar, of the language (as represented in the parser) apply to describe the sentence under analysis.

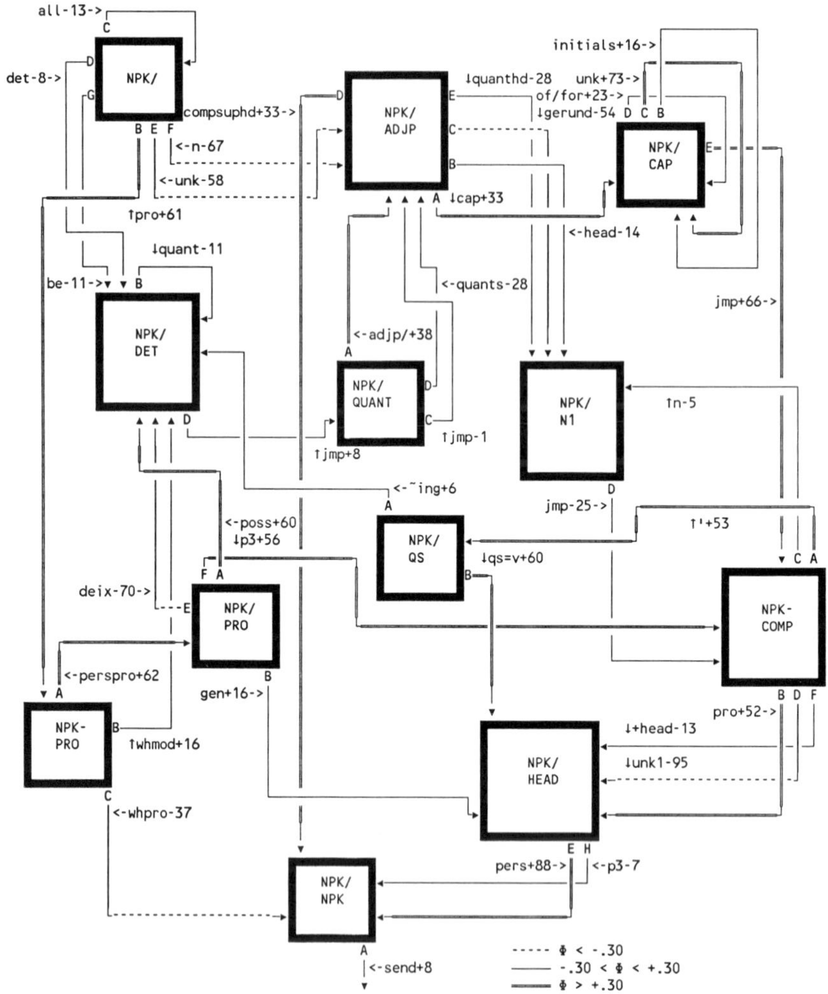

FIG. 7.1. Competency map assessment based on augmented transition network analysis of deaf students' essays. Map shows noun phrase kernel (NPK) constructions used comparatively often by passing students (double-line paths, phi > +.3) or by failing students (dashed-line paths, phi < -.3) and equally often by both (single-line paths, -.3 < phi < +.3). Note that NPK/DET indicates use of determiner; PRO, use of pronoun; ADJP, use of adjective phrase; QUANT, use of quantifier, and so on.

In the state NPK/DET, *two* is a quantifier that matches path NPK/DET_B. This path returns to NPK/DET, and the current word advances to *little*. There being no more quantifiers, path NPK/DET_D is followed to state NPK/QUANT. Path NPK/QUANT_A enters another network (not shown), where *little* and *green* are identified in an adjective phrase.

$NPK/QUANT_A$ then returns to state NPK/ADJP with the current word advanced to *men*. Analysis proceeds in like manner until the state NPK/NPK is reached. At this point the NPK has been parsed. Its distinctive structure can be traced in the paths the analysis has followed.

Competency mapping: Using the ATN analysis to compare grammatical patterns in passing versus failing essays. The parse paths in Figure 7.1 are annotated to represent data about the frequency of usage of noun phrase kernel constructions found in essays in the AITED project. The data are aggregated from two subsamples of the AITED essays corresponding to low-fail (the low end of failing scores) and high-pass cohorts. The two cohorts together contributed 83 learner essays containing a total of 1,102 sentences. A particularly large percentage of the low-fail cohort's sentences were ungrammatical, so only 28% of its sentences (n=131) could be parsed. In the end, only 519 grammatical sentences, containing 1,218 NPKs (233 from the failing cohort, 985 from the passing cohort), contributed to the final data analysis. Because the proportions of grammatical constructions contributed by each cohort were not equal, a phi statistic was calculated to estimate significance of frequencies of usage. The phi statistic estimates the probability that the two cohorts' usages of any path were not equal; its value ranges between -1 (characteristic of failing) and +1 (characteristic of passing).[24] Phi is reported, multiplied by 100, on every path label in the map in Figure 7.1. The double-line paths in Figure 1 (where phi > .3, $p < .05$) represent grammatical structures that were found significantly more often in the NPKs of the subsample of passing AITED essays. Dashed lines (with phi < -.3, $p < .05$) represent grammatical structures that were used significantly more often in the NPKs of the failing essays. Solid lines represent structures of roughly equal incidence in the two groups.

We used this analysis to compare the grammatical patterns used in the passing versus failing student cohorts. The distinctive paths in Figure 7.1 tell the teacher that failing students used significantly more of the following features:

- noun phrases consisting of only a single noun (path $NPK/_F$, phi = -67);
- deictic pronouns (e.g., *this*, *that)*, possibly reflecting transfer from American Sign Language to English (path NPK/PRO_E, phi = -70).

Passing students, on the other hand, used significantly more of these features:

- adjective phrases (e.g., *little, green*; path $NPK/QUANT_A$, phi = + 38);
- contracted copulas (e.g., *I'm)*, a phonologically-conditioned feature of English syntax that might be difficult for deaf learners (path NPK/QS_B);
- third person noun phrases (e.g., *the man*, path NPK/PRO_F);

[24] The phi statistic is a conservative measure of correlation which follows Pearson's *r* when marginal frequencies are equal but cannot attain maximal values of 1.0 when this condition is not met.

- pronouns (path $NPK/_B$), especially personal pronouns (e.g., *I*, *she*; path NPK/PRO_A).

The finding of more pronouns, particularly more personal pronouns, in passing essays has two nonexclusive interpretations. First, it suggests that passing essays exhibited greater linguistic cohesion, at least insofar as cohesion is affected by pronouns: Personal pronouns often express anaphoric reference, tying one clause or sentence to a preceding clause or sentence. At the same time, however, this finding suggests a test bias that favored students who could write about familiar, familial topics in which personal pronouns were appropriate (e.g., referring to family members) and that disfavored students who had no siblings. In helping to expose this bias, ENGPARS analysis has already proved useful. However, the recognition of such topical biases means that grammar maps must be researched in larger studies before ENGPARS results can be considered generally valid.

ENGPARS competency maps can be produced directly from ASCII text with no precoding or other hand coding. ENGPARS' syntactic accuracy rate for identifying intermediate AITED sentences as grammatical or ungrammatical was 93%. In subsequent reanalysis of the AITED corpus, Parhizgar (1991) found that, at least in cross-sectional analyses where the number of sentences exceeded 200, ENGPARS achieved 99% external reliability, even in advanced samples where the accuracy rate of identifying sentences as grammatical or ungrammatical fell to 85%.[25]

Competency maps versus error analysis. In diagnosis and assessment, competency analysis is theoretically preferable to error analysis, although the latter is the more typical use of parsers in language tutors (see, e.g., DeSmedt, this volume; Levin & Evans, this volume; Weinberg, Garman, Martin, & Merlo, this volume). As Schachter (1974) observed, error analysis fails to account for linguistic constructions that students avoid. Historically, error analysis has been used because competency analysis requires detailed comparative norms that heretofore have been impossible to obtain. In their stead, error analysis has generally used standard, adult grammar as its normative reference. This fails to place student errors in the proper, developmental context of the learner's emerging grammar. Competency analysis does not have these weaknesses.

In our present implementations, an error is detected in a sentence and the sentence is classified as ungrammatical when no path can be found through a map. Because no parse path is followed, no diagnostic map is drawn. In theory, it is not always necessary for the parse of an errorful sentence to fail. Error maps or interlanguage maps could be drawn, but without the same high accuracy and reliability of competency maps. Instead of error maps, we approached error analysis in the AITED project using the interactive Pluralbelle grammar checker, as reported in the next section.

---

[25] External reliability, as defined here, provides a finer measure than syntactic accuracy. Roughly, it indicates agreement between the parser and a human rater on just those sentences parsed as grammatical.

Interactive Results: User Testing GPARS as a Grammar Checker

Ms. Pluralbelle is an interactive grammar-checking environment, a word processor that runs over the ENGPARS parse engine. In interactive use, when a sentence or essay is grammar checked, the system responds by alerting the user to errors. It is similar to the SYNCHECK grammar checker for German (Sanders & Sanders, 1987, this volume) and to parsers in more directive foreign language tutors (e.g., Levin & Evans, this volume; Weinberg et al., this volume) in that it performs deep, structural analyses of input sentences.

Under the AITED project, we beta tested Ms. Pluralbelle using two classes of intermediate learners (24 students). The main result of this subproject was discouraging. We had hoped that students at Gallaudet would be able to use Ms. Pluralbelle to formulate and test their own hypotheses about English syntax. Unfortunately, only about 25% of the learners were sufficiently autonomous and motivated to do this. Another 25% of the students indicated they did not want to be in English class in the first place, and they barely tried to use the system. Another 25% were not computer literate. These students tried to use the system, but they did not progress significantly beyond learning to use the backspace key.

We characterized the final 25% of these students as poor learners, whom we subdivided into two groups: dependent learners and irresponsible learners. In response to detection of an error such as the following:

(1) *I want to go to big city.

Ms. Pluralbelle generates the error message and suggestion:

(2) Try "a ... city."
Press <y> for further suggestions.

Dependent learners did not modify the starred sentence until a sign language interpreter assisted them to the point of facilitated communication.

Irresponsible learners made corrections, perhaps responding to (1) with (3):

(3) *I want to go to big a city.

They then would either not try to reparse the sentence or give up when (3) failed to parse. This occurred despite the fact that "pressing <y>" in response to (2) would have produced the suggestion:

(4) Try "a big."

In other words, the help facility could potentially have clarified the apparent misunderstanding had students used it.

This was a disappointing result. Although improvements in student training and the Ms. Pluralbelle user interface could make the system accessible to perhaps half the students, no such straightforward technical fixes seemed likely to motivate the unmotivated students or to teach the poor learners. Of course, in many educational settings teachers can simply flunk poor students and give unmotivated students who are athletically inclined a social promotion. In survival ESL contexts like Gallaudet, however, these strategies are not defensible, and we have consequently deemphasized development of interactive GPARS systems.

Generalized Transition Network Parsing: Computational Features

This section focuses on some of the implementational features of the parser developed for GPARS. Key problems include achieving robustness, speed, and wide coverage in the face of ambiguous or potentially ambiguous input, in which there may be multiple solutions to a sentence parse before the analysis is complete. Conventional parsing technology has developed a number of strategies for achieving these goals. Those adapted for GPARS are discussed in the following paragraphs.

After all their standard features have been implemented, ATN parsers are still usually syntax-centered, nondeterministic, right-branching, depth-first, top-down, and rule-driven. Generalized Transition Network (GTN) parsers allow the preceding parsing strategies to be intermixed with cascaded, deterministic, left-branching, breadth-first, bottom-up, and data-driven strategies. These strategies have been incorporated in GPARS.

Because ATN parsers are potential Turing machines, these latter strategies have always been available within the formalism. Some, if not all, have been implemented and reported previously (e.g., Kaplan, 1973, Woods, 1980). We call GPARS systems GTN parsers to distinguish them from parsers that exploit less fully the potential Turing machine power of the ATN formalism.

Cascaded Parsing

English has little inflectional morphology, so morphological parsing has received little attention in the English-dominated parsing literature. In virtually all other languages, however, morphological parsing presents significant problems, especially if, as in Chinese and other languages, the conjoint morphosyntactic analysis is potentially nondeterministic. GPARS GTN systems use *cascaded networks* (Woods, 1980) to accomplish nondeterministic morphological and syntactic analyses (see the following discussion of deterministic parsing versus backtracking).

Most recently, we have begun to cascade nondeterministic semantic parsing into the GPARS system. Yen (1992) described such a use of case frame supernetworks in the GPARS Chinese parser (CHIPARS), resulting in a dramatic increase in parsing efficiency for Chinese.

Deterministic Parsing

Backtracking is one way to handle the multiple parse problem. That is, if a parse path is pursued based on a partial sentence analysis and subsequent analysis calls for a different path, the parser then backtracks to the point at which the path requires alteration. Because backtracking is costly, Marcus (1980) argued for deterministic parsing. He designed a shift-reduce system, PARSIFAL, that replaced backtracking with a look-ahead buffer of three elements. Although GPARS also incorporates a shift-reduce mechanism, we consider fully deterministic parsing an unrealistic objective for Chinese and other languages, so the cost of backtracking in GPARS GTN systems is limited in other ways.

First, GPARS tried to optimize backtracking speed through maximal use of TLC-Lisp's native-code control stack and binding operators. Second, GPARS implements a set of deterministic *cut functions*, described later. If such a function fails, the entire state fails, eliminating local backtracking. That is, all subsequent arcs leaving the present state are ignored.

The shift-reduce mechanisms, breadth-first parsing, and well- and ill-formed phrase lists described in the following sections also increase determinism and speed parsing by substituting look ahead for backtracking, implementing a maximum-likelihood strategy for parsing nonterminals, and eliminating the need to reparse nonterminals that have already been parsed or rejected. By using these mechanisms, GPARS systems rarely back up more than three words unless an unanalyzable learner error is encountered.

Shift-Reduce Mechanisms for Left-Branch Parsing

GPARS systems implement left-right (LR) mechanisms, especially shift-reduce mechanisms for left-branching constructions and languages (cf. Allen, 1987; Sato, 1988). GTNs implement shift-reduce as a mechanism that can be intermixed within a predominantly right-branching grammar to handle left-branching constructions like the English possessive (*John's red hat*) or the more frequent and therefore more troublesome Chinese relative *de*-clause. As noted previously, this approach also eliminates considerable backtracking (see also the look ahead, left to right parsing mechanisms described by Felshin, this volume).

Breadth-First Parsing

English relative clauses can begin with virtually any part of speech (e.g., an adverb, as in "The shoes nicely dressed people wear are clean"). Because English learners often avoid using relative clauses (Schachter, 1974), the GPARS function of SEEKing a relative clause (in applying grammar rules) usually results in a wild goose chase terminated by bootless backtracking. However, a rigorously top-down parser without full backtracking must SEEK a relative clause before exiting a noun phrase (NP) because once the governing NP node is popped from the control stack, the parser can never again return to it. To allow premature provisional SEND functions that admit subsequent backtracking into a provisionally popped network, the GPARS SEEK function copies its arc's remaining tests and actions into a virtual state and pushes this virtual state onto a NEXT_STATE_STACK.

The NP network can then exit by applying the JMP function to the top of NEXT_STATE_STACK before a relative clause has been sought. The main control stack continues to store the original calling state. Only if this virtual analysis fails must the parser backtrack through the control stack into the provisionally sent NP to SEEK a relative clause.

The Well-Formed Phrase List

GPARS systems normally keep a well-formed phrase list. When a network SENDs, the registers of the just-parsed constituent are preserved on the well-formed list. Later, after backtracking, constituents that were previously parsed correctly do not need to be reparsed. Without a well-formed list, sentences with conjunctions and prepositional phrases are particularly prone to time-consuming backthrashing because of the many possible attachment points these structures can have.

The Ill-Formed Phrase List

Well-formed lists have been standard features of parsers since the work of Earley (1970). Somewhat more innovative is the GTN ill-formed phrase list. Because this list is maintaned, posited constituents rejected once in the course of a parse can be rejected out-of-hand during subsequent backtracking and reparsing. The ill-formed list, an obvious extension of Earley's idea, was independently implemented by Tomita (1987). However, where as both the Earley and the Tomita algorithms are context-free, the GPARS mechanisms are sensitive to morphological and semantic as well as syntactic context.

Bottom-Up Parsing

A chart is a well-formed phrase list that holds all successfully parsed phrases, more or less regardless of how, or even whether, they ultimately contribute to the final parse tree. Several GPARS systems maintain an analogous chart to accommodate the relatively free word order of Chinese and Russian, as compared with English.

In the case of Chinese, for example, (5)-(7) are semantically equivalent, meaning "Zhangsan ate (the) eggplant."

(5) Zhangsan chiguole qiezi.
Agent Verb Patient
Zhangsan ate eggplant

(6) Zhangsan qiezi chiguole.
Agent Patient Verb
Zhangsan eggplant ate

(7) Qiezi Zhangsan chiguole.
Patient Agent Verb
Eggplant Zhangsan ate

On the basis of syntax alone, there is no way for the parser to avoid the following interpretation:

(8)	Qiezi	Zhangsan	chiguole.
	Agent	Patient	Verb
	Eggplant	Zhangsan	ate

In CHIPARS, *Qiezi* and *Zhangsan* are simply placed on a chart until postverbal case frame analysis, using semantic features, can assign the structure of (5)-(7).

Data-Driven Parsing

Declarative programming languages and techniques advocate keeping program and data clearly separated; however, many lexical items control idiosyncratic syntax. Consider, for example, "The more...the more" constructions shown in example (9).

(9) The more John grows up, the more he looks like his father.

Rather than burden the grammar with details of such idiosyncratic lexical items, GPARS defines a *demon* in the lexical entry of *more*. This demon is a piece of virtual grammar code that activates only when *the more* appears in an input sentence. Intermixing such procedures with the lexical database keeps the main grammar concise and synoptic.

Lexico-Semantic Controls

As mentioned previously, the GPARS lexicon is a semantic network that is maintained by an expert system. The network consists of two major classification taxonomies known as ISA-hierarchies (e.g., a flower is a plant): a noun hierarchy and a verb hierarchy. These two hierarchies are related by case frames specified on verbs. The case frame specifications default to inheritance from Cook's case matrix system (Cook, 1989). We have just begun more detailed semantic specifications in order to support cascaded semantic processing in the Chinese, Korean, and English systems.

Summary and Future Research

The GPARS system has evolved to support computer-assisted assessment and diagnosis of students' language learning. The main form of such analyses is the grammar map, an elaboration of the grammar diagram on which the underlying GTN parser is based.

This assessment does form a kind of learner model, but the extent of the model is limited to morphology, syntax, and case semantics. This kind of model does, however, answer many immediate needs of the classroom language teacher, so research has begun to partition the topical variance found in ENGPARS analyses, referred to earlier, and to model additional types of learner language. We have, for example, begun pilot research on the CHILDES corpus of children's language (MacWhinney & Snow, 1985). Although the extant ENGPARS grammar performs satisfactorily on the adult-to-child speech contained in CHILDES, the child-to-adult speech requires quite a different grammar. How different grammars representing different speaker populations can best be reconciled, as they must be for the processing of child-adult dialogue or for simulated learner-teacher dialogue, remains an open issue.

Similar problems confront further lexicon development. For applications such as English grammar mapping, in which no semantic mapping is called for, a sparse dictionary with a robust capacity to accommodate words not in the lexicon is convenient and efficient. For applications such as instructional machine translation, however, it is necessary to have a detailed dictionary with multiple senses per word entry (e.g., the word *run* subsumes the senses of running a race, running a machine, and running a stocking, among others); however, parsing efficiency decreases in exponential proportion to the average number of senses per word. Again, the question of how such disparate requirements can be met by a single system remains quite open.

Computational grammars have not yet had an appreciable impact upon the classroom, where traditional, nineteenth-century grammar, with descriptions that are intuitive and incomplete, is still used. Computational grammars are much more rigorous than traditional grammar, and the most difficult future task facing instructional language processing will probably be teaching teachers to use this new and demanding technology while we also adapt the technology to their needs.

Acknowledgments

This effort was principally supported by U.S. Department of Education grants #G008740399 (Office of Postsecondary Education, International Research and Studies Program), #G08720150 (Secretary's Discretionary Fund for Critical Foreign Languages), and #H180P80020-89 (Office of Special Education and Rehabilitative Services, Technology, Educational Media, and Materials for the Handicapped Program).

References

Allen, J. (1978). *The anatomy of LISP*. Englewood, NJ: Prentice-Hall.

Allen, J. (1985). *TLC-LISP/86*. Redwood Estates, CA: The LISP Company.

Allen, J.(1987). *Natural language understanding*. Menlo Park, CA: Benjamin.

Bates, M. (1978). The theory and practice of augmented transition networks. In L. Bolc (Ed.), *Natural language communication with computers* (pp. 72-105). New York: Springer-Verlag.

Bobrow, D.G., & Fraser, B. (1969). An augmented state transition network analysis procedure. *International Journal of Computer Assisted Instruction, 1*, 557-567.

Cook, W.A. (1989). *Case grammar theory*. Washington, DC: Georgetown University Press.

Chen, L. (1993). *Reducing lexical ambiguity in the Chinese language with a relational semantic model.* Unpublished doctoral dissertation, Georgetown University, Washington, DC.

Earley, J. (1970). An efficient context-free parsing algorithm. *CACM, 6*, 451-455.

Grossberg, S.(1972). A neural theory of punishment and avoidance II: Quantitative theory. *Mathematical Biosciences, 15*, 253-285.

Kaplan, R. (1973). A general syntactic processor. In R. Rustin (Ed.), *Natural language processing*. New York: Algorithmics Press.

Loritz, D. (1983). A digitized speech laboratory for under $2,000. In K. Odwarka (Ed.), *Methods II*. Cedar Falls, IA: University of Northern Iowa.

Loritz, D. (1984). *The parsing of learner sentences*. Demonstration presented at the 18th Annual TESOL Convention, Houston, TX.

Loritz, D., Parhizgar, A., & Zambrano, R. (1990). Diagnostic parsing in CALL. *CAELL, 1*, 9-13.

MacWhinney, B., & Snow, C. (1985). The Child Language Data Exchange System. *Journal of Child Language, 12*, 271-295.

Marcus, M. (1980). *A theory of syntactic recognition for natural language*. Cambridge, MA: MIT Press.

Parhizgar, A. (1991). *Evaluating the diagnostic component of the ENGPARS parsing system*. Unpublished doctoral dissertation, Georgetown University, Washington, DC.

Sanders, A., & Sanders, R. (1987). Designing and implementing a syntactic parser. *The CALICO Journal, 5*, 77-86.

Sato, P. T. (1988). A common parsing scheme for left- and right-branching languages. *Computational Linguistics, 14*, 20-30.

Schachter, J. (1974). An error in error analysis. *Language Learning, 24*, 205-214.

Tomita, M. (1987). An efficient augmented context-free parsing algorithm. *American Journal of Computational Linguistics, 13*, 31-76.

Wagner, R., & Tran, T. (1989). *TLC-LISP/386*. Minneapolis, MN: Seeker Technologies.

Winograd, T. (1983). *Language as a cognitive process. Vol. 1: Syntax*. Reading, MA: Addison-Wesley.

Woods, W.A. (1970). Transition network grammars for natural language analysis. *Communications of the ACM, 13*, 591-606.

Woods, W.A. (1980). Cascaded ATN grammars. *American Journal of Computational Linguistics, 6*, 1-12.

Yen, W. (1992). *Resolution of syntactic and semantic ambiguity in a Chinese instructional system*. Unpublished doctoral dissertation, Georgetown University, Washington DC.

Zhang, Y. (1993). *A practical design for an interlingual machine translation system based on a case grammar model*. Unpublished doctoral dissertation, Georgetown University, Washington, DC.

Section II

Dialogue-Based Language Games

The Systems: Theoretical Background and Technology Reach

This section covers two systems that bridge the text-based tutors of Section I and the graphics-based tutors of Section III. These are the dialogue-based language teaching games—Sanders and Sanders' spy game, Spion, and DeSmedt's detective game, Herr Kommissar. The pedagogical goal is to give students conversation-like practice in the target language. The medium is textual, as in Section I; there is no significant pictorial component. Each system uses the convention of the mystery scenario to constrain the dialogue, following the model of commercial electronic adventure games. The scenario, with its ration of objects and actions, limits the language expected of students and simplifies the job of the natural language processor.[26]

The chief concern in these two systems is to develop an enticing game that naturally constrains input at all levels. Absent are the linguistic theoretical considerations of Section I. The linguistic frameworks applied, categorial grammar and predication-driven parsing, are based on ease of use (Sanders & Sanders) and on practical value in handling anticipated learner language (DeSmedt). The language teaching games are instead shaped by two basic notions from pedagogical theory, the construal of language as communication and the view of games as intrinsically motivating. The motivational view of games combines with an interpretation of second language skill as a "high-performance domain," in DeSmedt's words, whose subskills must become automatized through systematic practice before real conversation goes smoothly. The assumption is that students will be self-motivated to practice language if they are given an interesting problem to solve through language.

Because language games require the appearance of meaningful responses from the computer, these systems couple parsing with semantic mechanisms, in contrast with the reliance on parsing seen in Section I. In Herr Kommissar the semantic mechanisms are expansive and include case frames, selectional restrictions, a concept ontology, a propositional knowledge base, and mechanisms to manage discourse, such as heuristics for resolving anaphoric reference.

While computer-assisted language instruction has previously applied a variety of external game formats (Crookall & Oxford, 1990), in Spion and Herr Kommissar the game is inherent in the simulated discourse—directing a spy or interrogating a criminal. Removed from real crime or espionage, the discourse becomes play.

Pertinent to this section is the dialogue element of the MILT system (Dorr, Hendler, Blanksteen, & Migdaloff, this volume; Kaplan & Holland, this volume), in which text-based interactions follow a structured interrogation format. Discussion of that

---

[26] Mulford (1989) has also described a dialogue-based system that has been used in college language labs.

system is placed in Section III because the component mechanisms are also used to drive graphical actions in a pictorial microworld.

Emerging Issues

Integrating Language Activities with NLP Capabilities: The Role of Constraints

Notable in the dialogue-based tutors is the creative use of game conventions both to achieve pedagogical goals and to reduce computational complexity. For example, Spion labels as *forbidden to students* those words that are not available in the lexicon and semantic network. This conceit is authentic to spy activity and explains to students why the system will not process some game-related terms. In the same spirit, Spion restricts students' sentence input to imperatives on computational grounds, while the restriction appears to be motivated by the student's role in directing the spy. This work foreshadows Murray's use of the poltergeist convention to shape microworld interactions, as described in Section III.

Herr Kommissar derives its constraints from the detective game format. Fundamentally, as in Spion, the system as suspect never queries the student and therefore avoids having to incorporate new information, keeping the semantics closed and tractable. DeSmedt explains the computational difficulty of trying to support dialogues in which the user answers questions and thus potentially provides new and unpredicted information.[27] DeSmedt's account also explains why it is inordinately difficult for nonprogrammers to augment or change a dialogue-supporting knowledge base, an issue to which we return in the introduction to Section III.

The dialogue games mimic the dynamics of communication in specialized, highly structured genres. However, they are not serious attempts to model conversational knowledge and process such as expressed in computational and formal models of discourse (Carberry, 1990; Kamp & Reyle, 1993). Those models require sophisticated discourse planning mechanisms that involve resolution of reference, generation of bridging inferences, tracking of topics and style, and modeling of conversants' mutually held beliefs and plans as well as influential aspects of the conversational context. Therefore, these games do not enable the free, creative discourse that characterizes the immersion classroom (Bernhardt, 1992). Yet, enabled by NLP, they do let students move beyond the memorized dialogues and repetitive drills that define the audiolingual classroom.

The Role of Grammar: Theory or Technology

Grammatical feedback is a built-in feature of the language teaching games, even as they promote communication. The tension between form and function is never clearly resolved. The NLP version of Spion demands grammatically correct input because the original parser had no error detector. Students making syntactic errors have to re-enter their commands. Thus, the game serves more to motivate students than to advance a pure

[27] In the question-answer exercises described by Levin and Evans and by Sams (Section I), the system's queries are discrete and independent, so students' answers can be handled by question-specific templates rather than by general reference to a knowledge base, as needed in coherent dialogues.

communicative agenda. Although Sanders and Sanders invoke philosophies of prescriptive language instruction, it appears that technology more than theory determined this feature of the tutor. Herr Kommissar, on the other hand, recovers from simple syntactic errors; but it still reports them automatically to the student whenever they occur. DeSmedt notes the "understated nature" of this grammatical instruction overlaid on the dialogue. However, without either a guiding theory or empirical research, we do not know how effective this continual grammatical feedback is or to what extent it interrupts the communication that is seen as the student's main goal.

To resolve this issue will require better articulation of the communicative approach in foreign language pedagogy and clearer expressions of the trend toward form-focused instruction within a communicative curriculum (e.g., Doughty, 1993; Lightbown & Spada, 1990; Shelly, 1995). Indeed, systems like Spion and Herr Kommissar, if they were equipped with ways to manipulate grammatical feedback, could help to operationalize theoretical positions and provide proving grounds for varying mixes of form and function in instructional sessions.

Viability of NLP-Based Games

Spion, begun in 1981, is one of the earliest systems featured in this book. Sanders and Sanders originally looked to NLP to permit free sentence input, and they developed and tested an NLP-based prototype. However, the version now implemented in many language labs and available from the authors as shareware lacks NLP. Students type in sentences that have been partially prespecified and that are evaluated by pattern matching. Sanders and Sanders trace the history of the game's development and the reasons for their eventual rejection of NLP in the near term. This decision was made largely on grounds of students' usage strategies, discussed below, not on the basis of parser performance (which we assume was satisfactory). Murray (this volume) also decided to postpone NLP applications in the Athena Language Learning Project, but primarily on grounds of parser performance—that is, the parsers did not reach a robust enough state to permit observation of usage strategies.

Sanders and Sanders went on to develop an NLP-based grammar checker out of components of the Spion parser, into which they have incorporated error detectors (Sanders, 1991). They conclude that grammar checking is a more effective use of an instructional parser.

DeSmedt reaches a different conclusion for Herr Kommissar. We do not, for this system, have the kinds of close user observations reported by Sanders and Sanders because DeSmedt is an independent developer and not a professor designing for his students. We do know that Herr Kommissar is set up in several college language labs, that it has some reliability in handling students' errors, and that new customers continue to request the product.

Assessing Usability and Effectiveness

Parser performance data are usefully provided for Herr Kommissar, but there is no information on the size of the test suite or its representativeness. Moreover, we know little about how students use or gain from it at this point in its dissemination.

Anecdotal evidence is provided on the usability of NLP-based Spion. Students appeared daunted by the freedom of expression enabled by a parser and relied on a help facility to tell them what to say. They then tended to copy from help and thus did not reap the benefits intended. This led the developers to employ a non-NLP version of the game. However, the copying response calls for cautious interpretation. First, controlled observations are needed before we can draw firm conclusions about the usefulness of the system. Next, because the difficulty appears to lie in the interface, an accommodation could be tried that provides hints rather than full sentences or that gradually reduces sentence-making help through the principles of scaffolding and fading developed in cognitive approaches to instruction (Collins, Brown, & Newman, 1989; Reiser, Beekelaar, Tyle, & Merrill, 1991; see the introduction to Section III). Finally, individual differences should be assessed because they may influence who benefits from parser exercises, as observed by Loritz (this volume) and discussed by Oxford (this volume). Individual differences may explain the contradiction between Sanders and Sanders' finding that students used help too much and Loritz's finding that they did not use help enough: Loritz's students were apparently less familiar with computers and with written language generally.

Thus, the discouraging observations of Sanders and Sanders, reflecting those of Loritz, need not be taken as discrediting the technology but as cautioning its application. It is critical to consider what kinds of learners—with what kinds of preparation and given what kinds of help—will get the best use out of language games and other NLP applications. As in Section I, the need is clear for an organized assessment framework that includes a process of iterative refinements to the interface based on observing students' difficulties (the importance of progressive beta testing is underscored by Bailin and by MacWhinney in Section IV).

Assessments of effectiveness must also untangle the contributions of different key features of a system like Spion. It would help to have precise comparisons of the two versions of Spion, with and without NLP, in terms of their cognitive task requirements and their instructional effectiveness. Both versions require comprehension of German passages, and in that may lie their benefit and interest. On the production side, it is unclear what are the differential effects of created commands (in the NLP version) versus partially copied commands (in the non-NLP version), or what either adds to purely receptive practice (see MacWhinney's discussion of how to evaluate ICALL, this volume).

Herr Kommissar provides an array of tools for recording constructions and errors as they occur in dialogue and for analyzing the data. In this way, the system can serve as its own measure of effectiveness in improving language skill. It can, additionally, provide raw error and usage data as a source for theory construction in second language acquisition research. DeSmedt proposes that tracing surface errors is preferable to employing a student model that records theoretically interpreted errors in the intelligent tutoring systems sense. A different point of view is expressed by Garrett (this volume) and by Matthews (1993), who seek an ICALL that classifies performance patterns in light of one or another explanatory theory of SLA. It is arguable that the prima facie error classification provided in Herr Kommissar and espoused by DeSmedt ensures faster development and yields a system that is ready for users sooner.

References

Carberry, S. (1990). *Plan recognition in natural language dialogue*. Cambridge: MIT Press.

Collins, A., Brown, J.S., & Newman, S. (1989). Cognitive apprenticeship: Teaching students the craft of reading, writing, and mathematics. In L.B. Resnick (Ed.), *Knowing, learning, and instruction: Essays in honor of Robert Glazer*. Hillsdale, NJ: Lawrence Erlbaum Associates.

Crookall, D., & Oxford, R.L. (Eds.) (1990). *Simulation, gaming, and language learning*. New York: Newbury/HarperCollins.

Doughty, C. (March, 1993). *Focus on form: What is it? (Research and pedagogical issues)*. Paper presented at Georgetown University Roundtable on Languages and Linguistics (presession), Washington, DC.

Kamp, H., & Reyle, U. (1993). *From discourse to logic: Model theoretic semantics of natural language, formal logic, and discourse representation theory*. Dordrecht: Kluwer.

Lightbown, P., & Spada, M. (1990). Focus on form and corrective feedback in communicative language teaching: Effects on second language learning. *Studies in Second Language Acquisition*, *12*, 4.

Matthews, C. (1993). Grammar frameworks in intelligent CALL. *The CALICO Journal*, *11*, 5-28.

Mulford, G. (1989). Semantic processing for communicative exercises. *Computers and the Humanities*, *23*, 31-44.

Reiser, B., Beekelaar, R., Tyle, A., & Merrill, D. (1991). GIL: Scaffolding learning to program with reasoning-congruent representations. In L. Birnbaum (Ed.), *The International Conference of the Learning Sciences: Proceedings* (pp. 382-388). Charlottesville, VA: Association for the Advancement of Computing in Education..

Sanders, R. (1991). Error analysis in purely syntactic parsing of free input: The example of German. *The CALICO Journal*, 9, 72-89.

Shelly, S.L. (1995). Reinventing 'grammar' for the foreign language classroom. In M. Haggstrom, L. Morgan, & J. Wieczorek (Eds.), *The foreign language classroom: Bridging theory and practice*. New York: Garland.

8

History of an AI Spy Game: Spion

Ruth H. Sanders and Alton F. Sanders
Miami University of Ohio

Spion is a German-language adventure game for college language students, first programmed in 1981. Its designers intended to use its parser as a platform for the development of more extensive and more sophisticated tutorial German parsers. Although Spion and its daughter versions were indeed used by many college students of German, the program's phrase-structure-based syntactic element and its lexical-semantic element ultimately proved impractical for further development. More capacious machines, more flexible programming languages, and changed goals superseded Spion's parser. Syncheck, the designers' subsequent comprehensive syntactic parser of German, has little in common with Spion. Yet the experience gained from several years of working with Spion, discussed in this chapter, has proved illustrative of certain problems and solutions for interdisciplinary teams working on artificial intelligence (AI) applications for language learning.

The Rise of the Personal Computer

In the fall of 1981, when we began our work, microcomputers were still a novel idea, and adventure games, strictly verbal puzzles without action graphics, were a kind of underground amusement for computer users, especially young ones. The computer world was intrigued that as much as 64 kilobytes of memory, or 64K (the kind of storage capacity previously associated with computers taking up a roomful of space), could be packed into a desktop machine and that a few programming languages were becoming available for the little machines.

In the academic world these small wonders were causing a revolution. Computing power was extending to those who previously had no access to mainframe computer accounts. Almost overnight, the word *computer* began to mean not a behemoth in a special building but a piece of single-user equipment in a laboratory booth or even on a student desk.

The microcomputer market was producing scores of brands, many named after fruit, hoping to emulate the Apple computer in success, if not in design or in operating system. *IBM* still meant a mainframe, for Big Blue was not yet a major player in microcomputing. Floppy disks were eight inches in diameter, and, except for the Apple computer, the commonest operating system was CP/M. Computer hobbyists liked to build their own machines (called *homebrew*) from mail-order components. Many a university computer lab director or systems operator put together a microcomputer lab the same way because the new manufacturers could not yet be relied upon as long-term vendors. But one way or another, the age of microcomputing had begun, and we, along with thousands of other university researchers, began to explore the capacity of the new desktop marvels.

With access to a 64K microcomputer and a license for the programming language PL/1, we (a linguist and a computer scientist) began a collaboration to research natural language parsing techniques for German using microcomputers. We mapped out a multi-year plan to design first a small syntactic and semantic parser, then larger and larger systems, culminating in a comprehensive parser. *Spion* (German for *spy*), a parser-based adventure game in German, was to be the first program in the series.

The Initial Plan: Designing a Game for Language Learners

Our programming language for the first version of Spion was Digital Research's implementation of PL/1 running under the CP/M operating system on a homebrew Z80 system (Sanders & Sanders, 1982). The computer had 64K of main memory and two 8-inch floppy disks capable of holding 128K each. Our original intent was to use the application of beginning language learning as a convenient vehicle for studying the processing of natural language. Our research paradigm, in pseudocode, may be stated as follows:

```
Create simple model of language
Implement adventure game using that model
Do forever
        Allow students to use game
        Extend game based on feedback from users
        Repeat
                Try to extend model to allow for game extensions
                If successful then implement new game
                Else reduce complexity of game extensions
        Until new game implemented
```

One general approach to language processing is to have some sort of dialogue between a computer and a person. This was the approach taken by Winograd (1972) in his AI program, SHRDLU, which assembles blocks in response to natural language commands. The difficulty of such a model is that generally humans and machines do not have much to talk about. Hence, there is not generally a large community of users to test a working system thoroughly. One of our colleagues, observing that his daughter spent hours at the keyboard playing one of the early adventure games, suggested that an adventure game format might be a useful vehicle for language processing. At first we considered it impractical to devise a really interesting adventure game (that is, rich and complex, with lots of language) using implementable models of language comprehension. The state of the art in parsing at that time required mainframe capacity, and many now-common techniques for representation of syntactic and semantic models were as yet not developed. Commercial adventure games available for small machines used a dehydrated form of language unacceptable to us: "Go boat" and "Open door" are samples of the kind of verb-object fragments, lacking function words, found in these games. Moreover, we were concerned that our research would be thought frivolous if we concentrated on games without some higher goal.

By aiming our adventure game at language learners, we addressed both of these problems. We could create a small microworld using closed world semantics for simplicity. The microworld could be accessed with the same type of relatively simple language used by second-year college language students. Moreover, as part of the language learning process, students would be likely to use the system extensively. Because as learners they were uncertain in their grasp of the language, they would have to play the game over and over to "get it," thus serving as meticulous bug detectors for us. We hoped the intrinsic interest of the game would repay them for their efforts, and that their repetitive play would teach them German as effectively as an equally repetitive but less absorbing drill program.

Within these constraints, we were able to use the PL/1 language to develop a low-level, phrase-structure-based syntactic element to represent the German imperative and interrogative forms expected from students, and a simple lexical semantics to represent the knowledge base underlying the game world. By requiring correct input from students, moreover, we avoided having to develop error detection and processing mechanisms.

The Game

A syntactic parser and a semantic network are the basis of Spion, whose plot concerns spies in the East and West Berlin of pre-unification Germany. Finally completed in 1987 after several interim versions, Spion has been used by hundreds of students of German at Miami University of Ohio and elsewhere, either in its AI version or in its nonintelligent variant, Pilot-Spion.

To play the game, students communicate by means of written commands or requests to the spy, Robotky, who describes events and objects through messages on the screen (with place names and locations of the real Berlin). The player must question Robotky for information, move him to various locations, and tell him what actions to take. To win, the player must find secret information in a West Berlin chocolate shop, cross the border into East Berlin, exchange the information with Frieda, a second spy, for other information, and return this to the spymaster, Max. A screen from Spion (Figure 8.1) shows a scene description by Robotky and a prompt for the player to tell Robotky what to do. Robotky accepts free response from the player, but it must be in correct German. Commands or questions that Robotky understands bring a change in the game state or information. Those that contain an unknown word bring a message informing the player of that fact. Those that make no sense or are not possible logically or in the game world are rejected and a reason is given. Grammatically incorrect German brings a request to reformulate correctly. Understood statements either advance the player toward winning the game or cause the player to lose, immediately or later. Clues to the solution as well as false leads appear in the environment, as is traditional in adventure games. Close reading of the scene descriptions, as illustrated in Figure 8.1, is required for successful play, and, because this is a language teaching game, players are allowed to borrow Robotky's on-screen dictionary to find the meanings of words used.

> Ich bin jetzt in der Stadt Berlin-West, an der Ecke Kurfürstendamm-Fasanenstraße. Ich sehe eine Bushaltestelle mit Zeichen: BAHNHOF ZOO. Auf der Straße steht ein großes Plakat: LESEN MACHT SPASS. Ich sehe auch einen kleinen Buchladen.
> Was soll ich tun?

FIG. 8.1. A screen from Spion with a message from the spy agent Robotky. The syntactic/semantic processor accepts free input, so the player is not constrained to respond by preprogrammed choices. Robotsky says (translated into English): "I am in West Berlin, on the corner of the Kurfürstendamm and Fasanenstraße. I see a bus stop with a sign: *Train Station at the Zoo*. In the street is a large poster reading *READING IS FUN*. I also see a small book shop. What should I do?"

Thus, Spion is a microworld-based system like those described in this volume by Hamburger, by Douglas, by Tomlin, and by Murray, but unlike those microworlds, Spion lacks a visual graphics context. As in DeSmedt's Herr Kommissar (this volume), the primary interaction with the microworld is text-based.

The Research Environment: Evolving Goals in an Interdisciplinary Team

Academic research is seldom carried out in a single plan-to-goal manner. Nor are the principal researchers usually the only people involved in the research activities. Certainly, in the case of Spion, there were many associated trial efforts and many other people connected indirectly with the project. In 1980 at Wright State University, a group of researchers that included the authors formed a joint research group entitled FLITE (for Foreign Language Instructional Technology Engineering). The research group intended to examine all aspects of the computational problems associated with using computers to assist in language instruction. These aspects included particular applications like Spion, programming languages suitable for implementing such applications, and architectures suitable for such languages. At each level, there were theoretical and philosophical issues that were also relevant. The group at its largest included five computer scientists, three philosophers, one linguist, one mathematician, and several computer science graduate students. Regular weekly seminars with this group provided us with many ideas with which we experimented. Some were partially implemented, some were fully implemented, and many more were shelved, perhaps to be considered further later.

The primary purpose of the Spion project originally had been to study models of language understanding by computer. As time went on, however, our focus gradually changed, and applications to computer-assisted language learning (CALL) became our primary goal. As we became more and more involved with CALL, we viewed the Spion project more as an engineering problem than as basic research. This perspective probably emerged first when we began to polish Spion as a product. Because end users (students) were required by our research paradigm as testers of our program, we had to provide a finished, usable product for them. It turned out that this requirement had a considerable effect on our work.

Producing finished products for users involves additional problems not necessarily directly related to a project's research purpose. Solving these problems can be very time-consuming but is necessary to the success of the project. For example, decisions concerning screen design and what kind of information or help should be available to users were matters of some importance. Problems such as printing German characters (umlauts and ß) on the screen, or deciding what keys the user must press to get them, or differentiating between lower-case and upper-case letters in the input, may seem trivial to designers who think of themselves as working in higher realms than this. However, if these questions are not taken care of, the program will look amateurish on the screen no matter how sophisticated the linguistic or computer expertise behind the design. Students who use the program must be asked for their reactions, and these reactions must be listened to. User friendliness is essential, and when users find a program difficult to use, it must be changed no matter how deeply the developers feel that the program is in fact not difficult to use.

These concerns are essentially engineering problems rather than basic research problems. We found them interesting and challenging, and ultimately they captured more of our interest than the original research problem. We redefined ourselves as a CALL or ICALL (Intelligent Computer-Assisted Language Learning) applications team.

Early Designs

Design Choices to Support Form-Focused Pedagogy

Language processing for language learners poses quite different problems from those posed by other natural language processing interfaces. The prescriptive nature of language instruction prohibits the acceptance of ill-formed sentences (at least for some purposes and under some philosophies of teaching), even if those sentences are understandable. Taking a strong stand concerning input errors, we required the student to retype an errorful input sentence so as to correct the error, even if the program could determine with a high degree of certainty what the input sentence was supposed to be. For example, it was easy for the program to detect when a student forgot to end an imperative sentence with an exclamation point, but we chose for pedagogical reasons to require retyping of this and other erroneous sentences, even where the error was a small one. In that sense, Spion retained some of the rigidity that has come to be associated with drill-and-practice programs.

Design Choices to Accommodate Lexical Limitations

Some design decisions were possible explicitly because of the artificial context provided by the game format. For example, the language used by the fictitious agent, Robotky, was generally much richer and included many more words than we wished to include. (Though it sometimes happens in commercial adventure games, too, that the program claims not to know a word, even when that word has been used earlier by the agent, we did not want to do the same in Spion, because it is frustrating to the user.) Even though we knew that a student was likely to parrot Robotky's words back to him, we were not able to make our receptive lexicon large enough to include complete semantic information on every word used by Robotky. We sidestepped that problem by labeling certain words as forbidden (*verboten*) to the player but permissible to Robotky, presumably because of the latter's higher rank as a spy. A message to that effect, in German, was presented to a player who used one of the out-of-lexicon words:

> [Word] ist ein verbotenes Wort: das heißt, verboten für Sie.

This selective restriction may have been equally as frustrating to the student user as a general claim not to know a word, but it had, in our view, at least the virtue of being more or less candid.

Design Choices in Anticipation of Hardware and Software Developments

While working on our first design, we always anticipated that the program ultimately would run on a machine faster and bigger than our initial Z80. Thus, we were unconcerned when our first version ran slowly, with a noticeable wait from the input to the response. We also proceeded with an artificial design to work around the lack of memory. The first version of Spion was actually two completely separate programs, each of which demanded close to the maximum from our small machine. Because we expected that computers with increased speed and capacity would soon be available, we assumed that we could join the programs later, when the technology caught up to us. We were criticized at the time for this assumption and for being in general too ambitious. However, it turned out that we had been too cautious and that our caution had cost us quite a bit of time.

First, we greatly underestimated the rapidity of technology development. Within only a year or two of our initial work, commonly available microcomputers provided all the capacity we needed for a full version of Spion. In the meantime we had spent a great deal of time and energy devising memory allocation and speed-up mechanisms that were unnecessary almost as soon as we completed them.

Moreover, in 1981 microcomputers were (by today's standards) small and slow, but the unsettled computer market was an even greater impediment to our work. We spent quite some time and effort selecting a computer language for the Spion project, eventually settling on PL/1 for reasons having to do not with the nature of the language but with the practicality of its compiler. At that point, it was not clear which operating system or which disk format would become dominant, and there were very few reliable compilers that produced acceptable code for any of the systems. We experimented with a number of languages, compilers, and interpreters. We needed to be able to provide a compiled version or a version with a public domain interpreter because we intended to give away our program and did not want to have to deal with distribution fees or licensing. Additionally, we wanted a mature and reliable product. Our preference would have been some variant of Lisp, but we were unable to locate an implementation that performed satisfactorily, even if we had been willing to work with an interpreter. We experimented with Pascal, Lisp, Forth, and PL/1 under CP/M. Digital Research's PL/1 compiler was clearly the best choice of the ones we tested. We guessed (incorrectly) that Digital Research would port that compiler to whatever system ultimately won in the marketplace. PL/1 disappointed us on this and several other scores. We abandoned all of the initial program fairly early on.

Later Designs: Research Versus Engineering (Developing a Nonintelligent Spion)

The second and most ambitious version of Spion's design was started, but never finished, in TLC-Lisp (Allen, 1978). Here, our model was the linguistic framework known as categorial grammar, and we took some ideas from Sowa (1984). Our closed world was represented by a semantic network modeled after Sowa's. As syntactic reductions occurred via the categorial grammar's cancellation mechanism, a graph transformation was constructed in the form of a pair of pattern graphs. Well-formed sentences would produce well-formed transformations that would alter the semantic network to reflect the state change required by the sentence. In a categorial grammer, each word is represented as a series of symbols indicating which kinds of other words it is allowed to precede or follow; for example, nouns may follow articles or adjectives. In parsing, or grammatically analyzing a sentence, the symbols representing each word in the input are combined and canceled like an algebraic equation. What remains is the parsing solution, which is then sent to the semantic element as shorthand for what should happen in the environment as a result of that input. For example, if the input is "Read the newspaper," the newspaper's message is displayed to the player. If the input is "Eat the apple," the apple disappears from the scene description, and so forth. Actually, because the output buffer was part of the state, even ill-formed sentences produced a state change, but no graph transformations were involved. The network modification was carried out by mapping one of the pattern graphs onto the network and replacing the image of that pattern within the network with a copy of the other pattern graph. In effect, we used a categorial grammar for our syntactic model and a graph grammar for our semantic model.

This design was very flexible and, of all the designs we considered, offered the most promise as a research vehicle. It had the potential of limited concurrent processing (one of our interests) and was straightforward to extend. Unfortunately, seemingly it would be years before a genuinely usable product could be produced with this design. There were many problems to be solved; some were technical problems, but others appeared to be basic research questions. That was the moment of truth with regard to the research versus engineering issues. We ultimately chose on the side of engineering: We abandoned the design for a simpler one that could be implemented immediately and used effectively.

While the second version was underway, a separate, nonintelligent version of the game was programmed in the authoring language PILOT and named *Pilot-Spion* (Sanders, 1984). In that version, students were given at each decision point a list of choices and were asked to write a request based on one of the alternatives. This is illustrated by the screen from Pilot-Spion in Figure 8.2, which can be contrasted with the screen from Spion in Figure 8.1.

> Ich bin jetzt in der Stadt Berlin-West, an der Ecke Kurfuerstendamm-Fasanenstrasse. Es gibt hier viel Verkehr und viele Leute. Ich sehe eine Bushaltestelle mit Zeichen: "BAHNHOF ZOO". Auf der Strasse steht ein grosses Plakat: "LESEN MACHT SPASS". Ein grosses Hotel—das Hotel Kempinsky—steht auf dem Kurfuerstendamm, und ich sehe auch ein winziges Schokoladengeschaeft und einen kleinen Buchladen. Es gibt hier viel zu tun! Soll ich den Bus nehmen, ins Hotel gehen, ins Schokoladengeschaeft gehen oder den Buchladen besuchen?

FIG. 8.2. A screen from Pilot-Spion. The player formulates a command from the alternatives given by the spy agent Robotky. This version lacks umlauts and the ß. Robotky says: "I am in West Berlin, on the corner of Kurfuerstendamm and Fasanenstrasse. There are a lot of people here, and a lot of traffic. I see a bus stop with the sign: *Train Station at the Zoo*. In the street is a large poster: *READING IS FUN*. A large Hotel—the Kempinsky Hotel—stands on the Kurfuerstendamm, and I also see a tiny chocolate shop and a little bookstore. There's a lot to do here! Shall I take the bug, go into the hotel, go into the chocolate shop, or visit the bookstore?"

Pilot-Spion provides a kind of multiple choice, although students were still required to write their requests rather than simply selecting an alternative. There was no parsing of these written productions and no updating of a semantic network, although a list of variables and switches might be altered to reflect changes to the scene so that even in the absence of a true semantic network, apples would disappear when the order was given to eat them, and so forth.

Although Pilot-Spion was not an AI program and had no parser, the game itself was a much more complex version of the simple game of Spion. It featured eighteen locations (i.e., geographical stations, such as a candy shop or a border crossing, where actions take place), whereas Spion used only six. Pilot-Spion seemed to challenge second-year students, taking them an average of two and a half hours to complete successfully. Used in second-year German at Miami University every year since 1984, this computationally simple program showed that the adventure game format could prove quite useful as a learning tool. It has been provided free of charge on request to about fifty universities in the U.S. and Europe.

The Final Design: Incorporating User Findings Into Intelligent Spion

Experience with the unfinished Lisp version of Spion and the nonintelligent Pilot-Spion caused a return to the simplicity of the original design with only a small portion of the second design included. In effect, Pilot-Spion became the initial version in the terms of our research paradigm, the one that would provide us with user reaction on which we could build for subsequent versions. We did, in fact, learn a great deal about the needs of the user interface and incorporated what we learned into our next version. A graduate student, Steven Molla, programmed that version in C-Prolog on a VAX 785 computer system. It became the first all-in-one complete intelligent version of Spion (Molla, 1987). We then ported that program to an IBM-AT personal computer and modified it according to the experience gained from Pilot-Spion. That program runs in a stand-alone compiled version and (on a 16MHz 386 machine) produces a response to a user's input sentence with no perceptible delay (Molla, Sanders, & Sanders, 1988a, 1988b).

The final design had a language model—a phrase-structure-based syntactic element, representing simple imperative sentences, its syntax limited to simple imperatives and questions, and its semantics limited to a small vocabulary and simple relationships. It was far simpler than it had to be, for the marketplace soon provided more than enough capacity for a much richer language element and game than the one we had designed. By this time, however, we had learned that, from a user's point of view, a more complex game was far more interesting than a complex language model. Our nonintelligent version, Pilot-Spion, thus supplanted the intelligent version for classroom use.

Ironically, the six-location intelligent Spion, with its requirement for student-created, full-sentence responses, seems to be much more difficult for second-year German students than does the eighteen-location Pilot-Spion, which requires full-sentence responses that are partially copied from a multiple choice set. As was illustrated in Figure 8.1, the player of Spion is presented with the situation and left to his or her own devices in talking to Robotky. In contrast, Pilot-Spion presents several clear choices, as was shown in Figure 8.2, and these choices include the vocabulary and partial sentence structure for a response. The user needs only to make a correct choice and formulate the corresponding command to advance the game. Thus, when Pilot-Spion's Robotky asks (in German), "Should I take the bus, go to the hotel, [etc.]," the student chooses from these alternatives and types, "Go to the hotel" (or some other choice).

Because students appeared to have difficulty with freely created commands in Spion, we revised the program to provide a help facility that might be consulted at any time for suggestions on what to type. In practice, this resulted in student players' using the help option at every turn of play, so that the freedom of input we had worked so hard to make available was never actually used by the students. It appears that the open-ended Spion tends to intimidate many early language learners, whereas the delimited possibilities of Pilot-Spion give them confidence.

Future Designs

Although we believe our original paradigm had merit for studying language models, we are now more interested in new products associated with language learning. Although we may well produce another product with a game format, we are unlikely to extend Spion's microworld for yet another version of Spion.

We intended at the outset to use Spion's German parser as the basis for our next project, called *Syncheck*, a parser-based writing aid whose input would be the flawed compositions of intermediate and advanced German language learners (Sanders, 1991; Sanders & Sanders, 1989). During Spion's development, microcomputer capacity advanced yet again, and we began working in Prolog because it offered a formalism that both of us found congenial. This decision facilitated our work greatly. Earlier, transformation of a single grammar clause into computer code using PL/1 often took the two of us several hours of work together because the linguist understood only vaguely the language of the computer scientist, and vice versa. Prolog, on the other hand, with its user-friendly logic formalism, provided in effect an interlanguage for us. Large pieces of the linguist's formal grammar could be coded into Prolog with very little change, and the program could be optimized for computational efficiency afterwards. The comprehensive parser we designed for Syncheck proved so different from the limited parser of Spion that virtually nothing of Spion survived in the later project.

Conclusions

Although we began our collaboration with the idea of basic research into natural language processing techniques, we found that the requirements of producing finished products demanded an increasing amount of our time and effort. It is clear why researchers who design laboratory prototypes do not generally provide user-ready versions of their programs. The challenges of final implementation are sometimes wholly unrelated to the challenges of design. However, from our point of view, these engineering aspects of user products are interesting and satisfying, and we intend to continue this line of work.

One of these engineering challenges has been massaging the hardware to provide the effects we have sought. In our case, the technology appeared to provide capacity faster than we could redesign to compensate for its lack originally. However, we find looking into the future no easier now than it was in 1981, and we cannot be sure of avoiding the error of underestimating technology a second time.

Additionally, we have experienced at first hand the principle that a more sophisticated program (Spion) is not necessarily more effective in practical use than a simple program (Pilot-Spion). Although we conducted no formal comparison of the two programs, we did observe that students failed to make use of the free input capability that should in theory give the sophisticated, parser-based program the advantage. Unquestionably, artificial intelligence and parsing have much to offer to foreign-language teaching programs, but computational complexity in itself is no guarantee of usefulness in application.

References

Allen, J. (1978). *The anatomy of LISP*. Englewood, NJ: Prentice-Hall.

Molla, S. R. (1987). *Prolog Spion*. Unpublished master's thesis, Wright State University, Dayton, OH.

Molla, S. R., Sanders, A. F., & Sanders, R. H. (1988a). Artificial intelligence in a German adventure game: Spion in PROLOG. *The CALICO Journal*, *6*, 9-23.

Molla, S. R., Sanders, R. H., & Sanders, A. F. (1988b). *Spion: An intelligent adventure game for students of German* (Technical Report No. WSU-CS-87-4). Dayton, OH: Wright State University, Department of Computer Science.

Sanders, A.F., & Sanders, R. H. (1982). Spion: Intelligent computer games for German language teaching. *Proceedings of Foreign Language Instructional Technology Conference* (pp. 141-146). Monterey, CA: Goethe Institute and the Defense Language Institute.

Sanders, A. F., & Sanders, R. H. (1989). Syntactic parsing: A survey. *Computers and the Humanities*, *23*, 13-30.

Sanders, R. H. (1984). Pilot-Spion: A computer game for German students. *Unterrichtspraxis*, *1*, 123-129.

Sanders, R. (1991). Error analysis in purely syntactic parsing of free input: The example of German. *The CALICO Journal*, 9, 72-89.

Sowa, J. F. (1984). *Conceptual structures: Information processing in mind and machine*. Reading, MA: Addison-Wesley.

Winograd, T. (1972). *Understanding natural language*. New York: Academic Press.

9

Herr Kommissar: An ICALL Conversation Simulator for Intermediate German

William H. DeSmedt
amber productions

A Functional Overview of Herr Komisar

Herr Kommissar® ("Mr. Inspector") is a German-language intelligent computer-assisted language learning (ICALL) environment masquerading as a role-playing detective game. On entering Herr Kommissar's microworld, intermediate German students assume the identity of a visiting police inspector, or *Kommissar*, asked to solve a murder mystery by interrogating five (simulated) German-speaking suspects (Figure 9.1).

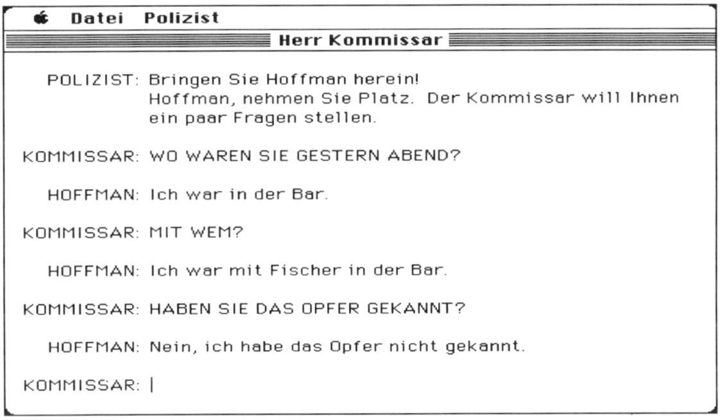

FIG. 9.1. A sample page of dialogue from Herr Kommissar. The learner, playing the role of the inspector (*Kommissar*), is about to ask "Hoffman" the next question.

Immersed in this task, a learner has the experience of carrying on a natural, unself-conscious dialogue, free from constraints on style or subject matter, entirely in the target language. Behind the scenes, however, there is a good deal more going on, as Herr Kommissar commits the resources of a full-functioned natural language processing (NLP) system to holding up its end of the simulated conversation.

Lexical Identification

Herr Kommissar begins by looking up each word of the learner's input query in its on-line German lexicon. In so doing, it detects and corrects most garden-variety misspellings, as depicted in Figure 9.2.

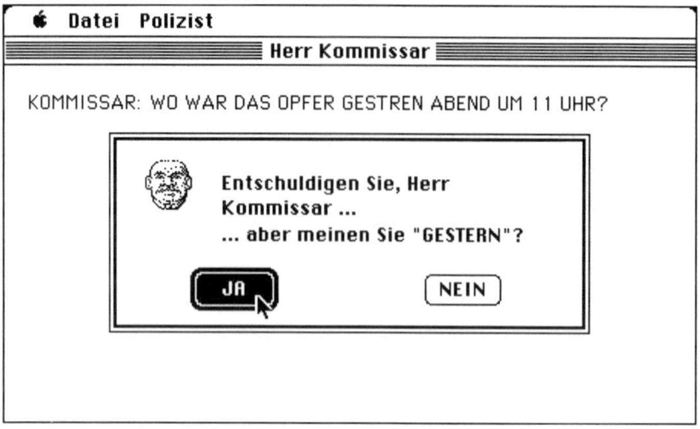

FIG. 9.2. "Sergeant Schulz," Herr Kommissar's tutelary spirit, reporting a spelling error.

In cases where the learner mangles the spelling beyond recognition (or simply uses a term not found in the lexicon), Herr Kommissar recovers gracefully, specifying the word it was unable to find. Not that Herr Kommissar is found wanting all that often; at almost 3,100 entries (representing about 2,300 words), its lexicon compares favorably with the end vocabularies of introductory college-level German textbooks, which average about 1,950 terms (Tussing & Zimmermann, 1977).

However, the lexicon is far from being just a vocabulary list. In addition to an English translation, each entry contains a full syntactic and semantic specification for the word in question. All of this comes in handy in the next stage.

Syntactic Analysis

Herr Kommissar next performs a full-sentence parse on the learner's input. Its parser covers most aspects of basic and intermediate German grammar, including:

- declension and pluralization of nouns and noun phrases,
- agreement of adjectives to nouns in gender and number,
- strong, weak, and mixed declension of adjectival phrases,
- pronominalization of noun phrases,
- government of case by prepositions, including bimodal prepositions governing either the accusative or the dative,
- government of case by verbs,
- agreement of verbs to subjects in person and number,
- present and past indicative conjugation of weak and strong verbs,
- formation of the future indicative,
- formation of present and past modal-auxiliary constructions,

- formation of the perfect and pluperfect indicative, including the appropriate choice of auxiliary (*sein* or *haben*),
- formation of passive voice constructions in present, future, past, and perfect,
- use of coordinate, subordinate, and relative clauses.

If its analysis of the sentence detects one or more grammatical errors, Herr Kommissar coaches the learner in the correct usage, as shown in Figure 9.3.

FIG. 9.3. "Schulz" reporting a grammatical error—use of the accusative case in conjunction with a verb that governs the dative.

If the learner uses a grammatical construction that the parser cannot decipher, Herr Kommissar again recovers gracefully, identifying the problem to the user and continuing the conversation.

Semantic Interpretation

Herr Kommissar then maps the results of its lexical and syntactic analysis onto an internal model of the input's meaning. In the process, it addresses such discourse-level phenomena as paraphrase, ellipsis, and anaphoric or deictic reference. Relative clauses are resolved at this stage, and selectional constraints are applied to bar nonsensical (albeit grammatically correct) formulations, such as use of the verb *to drink* with a nonliquid object.

The resulting semantic interpretation of the learner's input is next tested against Herr Kommissar's knowledge representation schema (KRS), which models the current state of the microworld. More specifically, it is tested against that subset of the KRS that makes up the simulated world view of the suspect under interrogation at the moment. This test determines which one, if any, of that world view's component facts or beliefs matches the meaning behind the learner's original query to the suspect.

Response Formulation

The results of this reality check are then projected onto a new semantic structure, representing a confirmation or contradiction of the proposition contained in the learner's original query. Because it derives from a stable underlying world view, this response model manifests the coherence and consistency of viewpoint that are the sine qua non of any sustained conversation.

The KRS world view itself is updated as each response model is formulated, simulating a memory of what has been discussed. This memory trace makes it possible to mimic certain dynamics of natural discourse, such as chiding the learner for repeating questions that have already been answered (Figure 9.4).

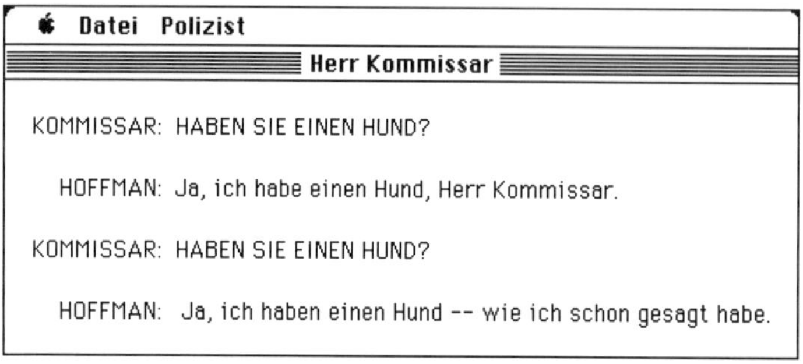

FIG. 9.4. "Hoffman" complaining that he's already answered the learner's question about whether or not he has a dog.

Language Generation

Finally, Herr Kommissar feeds the resulting semantic model of its response through a language generator to yield a grammatical German sentence comprising the suspect's literal reply to the learner. This reply takes the form of written text and, optionally, of audible (synthesized) speech as well. If speech is enabled, discourse analysis is used to set the intonation pattern of the synthesized utterance so as to focus the learner's attention on whatever new information it contains.

Performance Tracking

While all this is going on, Herr Kommissar is at work in the background recording the salient aspects of the learner's target-language interactions with the microworld's denizens. To begin with, as an interrogation session proceeds, every keystroke of every interchange between the learner and the system is captured verbatim in a permanent protocol file that is available for subsequent review by the instructor and/or the learners themselves.

Moreover, Herr Kommissar continually monitors critical performance phenomena (e.g., errors, use or avoidance of complex grammatical constructions) throughout the session, categorizing them according to a reconfigurable set of performance criteria. Its findings are available on demand at any point during the session itself and are also posted to a cumulative history, or performance profile, maintained on each learner for purposes of charting the individual's progress over time.

Operational Characteristics

This cycle of lexical identification, syntactic analysis, semantic interpretation, response formulation, language generation, and performance tracking executes in near real time, so as to sustain the illusion of a natural and free-flowing conversation. Herr Kommissar does this while running on any Apple Macintosh® computer with a megabyte of available memory, a hard disk (or two 800K drives), and any version of Macintosh system software from System 4.1 through System 7.1. As a stand-alone executable, programmed in Pascal (the assembly language of artificial intelligence), Herr Kommissar is entirely self-contained, running without the need of any special utility software, such as HyperCard®.

Two external programs, Magister™ and Dramatiker™ (Dramatist), augment the Herr Kommissar learning environment. Magister is an instructor's utility for conducting qualitative and quantitative analysis on the cumulative profiles of learner performance created in Herr Kommissar sessions and for reconfiguring the criteria by which that performance is assessed. Dramatiker is an authoring tool for creating and editing the characters and plot lines that make up Herr Kommissar's microworld, enabling nonprogrammers to write entirely new mysteries. Both are dealt with in more detail in the next section.

Theoretical Principles and Practical Concerns Behind the Design of Herr Kommissar

In general, Herr Kommissar's design has been driven less by theoretical considerations than by a practical commitment to building a working instructional environment for second language acquisition. As the preceding overview indicates, Herr Kommissar does draw extensively on existing natural language processing and knowledge representation theory, but it adapts the theory to the pragmatic requirements of processing the kind of language produced by learners, as distinct from native speakers.

The difference in emphasis can be illustrated by the lowly spelling checker. A *proof-of-principle* NLP system need not include one, and—at least until recently—many did not, relying instead on the orthographic competence of the native speakers for whom they were designed (e.g., Tennant, 1981). In second language acquisition, however, misspellings are a fact of life (I am tempted to say "a way of life"). Far from being a luxury, a robust and resourceful spelling checker becomes an indispensable item for any ICALL system.

Consider also the issue of how much lexical and syntactic coverage to provide. Clearly, an NLP used solely by students just beginning a language will not encounter the same breadth of vocabulary and grammar as would one intended for native speakers. In particular, many of the studied ambiguities that are used to probe the limits of standard natural language processing systems are beyond the reach of the language learner, and an

ICALL system will consequently never have to deal with them. On the other hand, ICALL must be far more tolerant of ungrammatical input in all the areas it does cover.

Predication-Driven Parsing

Utilitarian considerations like these, rather than philosophical preferences, led to the choice of a somewhat unconventional parsing strategy—one based on predication case-frames rather than production rules. Recall that the typical parser begins from a collection of production rules specifying, for some nontrivial subset of the target language, how to generate all the syntactically correct sentences and only those sentences. It proceeds by applying various interpretations to the input, searching for one that can be derived from (and wholly accounted for by) these rules. If and when that search terminates successfully, the input is considered to have been parsed, and the roles and parts of speech of its component words are taken to be those dictated by the successful interpretation (cf. Matthews, 1993).

The problem with this approach, from the perspective of second language acquisition, is its tacit assumption that the input itself is correct and that the parser need only determine which rules are embodied therein. There is, in other words, a presumption of grammaticality built into production-rule parsers at a fundamental level. This presumption can make dealing with the productions of someone just learning a language—for whom the norms of syntax and usage are as often as not honored in the breach—a nontrivial exercise for standard NLP systems. Their parsers can certainly detect ill-formed input (by the simple device of running out of applicable rules without finding a match), but error diagnosis and recovery can be serious issues.

These difficulties can be addressed, of course, typically by means of adjunct *error grammars* or *relaxation techniques* for easing restrictions on the grammar rules in some principled way. But the end result is still a rule-based system, and, as the authors of IBM's Epistle system note (Jensen, Heidorn, Miller, & Ravin, 1993):

> It is questionable whether such a strategy alone can ultimately succeed in the face of the overwhelming (for all practical purposes, infinite) variety of ill-formedness with which we are faced when we set out to parse truly unrestricted natural language input. If all ill-formedness is rule-based..., it can only be by some very loose definition of the term "rule"...(p. 63).

Rather than starting down this path of piling rule system upon rule system, Herr Kommissar circumvents the issue entirely by not using a production-rule parser in the first place. Instead, it employs a case-grammar technique that I think of as *predication-driven parsing* (DeSmedt, 1991; cf. Cook, 1989; Fillmore, 1968; McCord, 1980; Winograd, 1983). This approach proceeds by first identifying the operative verb and then attempting to interpret the remainder of the input in terms of its complements. Given a transitive verb, for instance, the parser begins looking for a noun phrase that could function as the predication's direct object. Predication-driven parsing is straightforward, it runs in near real time, and, most important, its scope and accuracy for well-formed input is equivalent to that of a production-rule parser.

The real difference lies in predication-driven parsing's potential for diagnosing and recovering from erroneous input. For example, in cases where the verb mandates a complement with syntactic features to which no input element fully conforms, the parser can initiate a search for the unassigned noun phrase that comes closest to meeting the requirements dictated by the case slot in question. Remediation then reduces to closing the remaining gap between the actual and the correct formulation. Such least-distance heuristics are the key to Herr Kommissar's ability to cope successfully with what Mulford (1989) has characterized as "the chaotic disarray that student production displays in precisely those surface markers (case endings, articles, prepositions) that would be important to a [production-rule based] syntactic analysis" (p. 42).

Beta tests conducted at Carnegie Mellon University and at the University of Maryland's Language House in 1990 confirm the suitability of predication-driven parsing for analyzing the real-world productions of second language learners. Herr Kommissar was able to detect and correct 92.8% of all errors committed by students, with a false correction rate (i.e., detecting an error where none is present) of only 1.1%.

Knowledge Representation

Practical considerations also motivated Herr Kommissar's knowledge representation schema. To entice the learner into a simulated conversation, Herr Kommissar needed something to talk about and some means of maintaining the coherence and internal consistency of discourse over time. These requirements can best be met by an underlying model of reality to which both the learner and the system can refer. Without such a shared microworld, the illusion of being immersed in an authentic experience is swiftly dispelled. With one, the learner's involvement can reach a point at which the focus is no longer on the language itself, but on using the language to achieve second-order goals—providing the kind of unself-conscious, automatized exercise that is a hallmark of effective learning in "high-performance" instructional domains (Regian, 1991). To create such a reality model, Herr Kommissar has been endowed with the following complementary formalisms.

Concept ontology. The cornerstone of Herr Kommissar's KRS is an ontology of over 2,500 concepts, embedded in a virtual hierarchy of categories. The hierarchy itself is a partial ordering defined over the set of concepts (see Sowa, 1984, for a formal definition). This concept hierarchy supports the resolution of synonyms, generic references (e.g., "Mount Everest...the mountain"), and paraphrases because any two formulations that map to the same underlying concept are treated as semantically identical.

A separate cross-referencing capability extends the hierarchy into a pseudonetwork for purposes of handling certain simple inferential relationships between ideas. One of the semantic associations realized via this mechanism is that between actions or experiences and their resulting states (e.g., the experience of dying and the state of being dead).

Comprehensive as it is, this concept ontology is essentially static and hence is ill-suited to capturing the dynamic interrelations among the objects making up Herr Kommissar's microworld. As Jolley (1973) remarked regarding the inherent limitations of a not wholly dissimilar taxonomic scheme, "It has a place for lions, and a place for bravery, and even a place for the bravery of lions, but no place for the statement that lions are brave" (p. 39). In order to provide a consistent representation, not only of the objects in its universe of discourse but also of the interactions in which they may participate, Herr Kommissar employs two higher level formalisms, predication constraints and postulations.

Predication constraints. Predication constraints are the negative side of the equation. By imposing common-sense restrictions on the kinds of things that may take part in a given category of action or event, they define what can or should *not* be said (Dahlgren, 1988). Such constraints come in two varieties, ontological and conventional.

Certain actions are subject to ontological predication constraints. They may not be predicated of other than a narrow class of objects, lest they assert a physical impossibility or a logical contradiction. The verb *to drink*, for example, presupposes an animate subject and a liquid (preferably potable) object, as in "John's cat drinks a lot of milk." "Mary's car drinks a lot of gas" stretches this rule but remains at least metaphorically interpretable. A statement like "Fred's honesty drinks a lot of wood," on the other hand, has no referent in any possible world where wood is a solid and virtues have no throat.

Other predications, though not meaningless per se, are precluded by the usage conventions of the language in question. Some of these taboos operate across linguistic and cultural lines. A formulation like "The horse married the donkey" will raise eyebrows in almost any society that recognizes the concept of marriage as such. Others, however, can be more language-specific. Whereas English has a single verb to express the concept of eating, for instance, German has two, depending on whether this action is performed by a human (*essen*) or an animal (*fressen*). Russian mirrors this distinction (*есть* vs. *жрать*) but goes it one better, also using different verbs to denote the experience of dying as undergone by humans versus animals (*умирать* vs. *сдыхать*). Whether general or specific, the effect of violating these usage conventions is much the same. The improprieties that result, while understandable in some sense, just sound funny.

Herr Kommissar implements the requisite constraints against both impossible and inappropriate predications by means of a second-order semantic language. Whereas the concept hierarchy identifies each concept uniquely in relation to the universe of discourse, this second-order language describes the commonalities that unite otherwise unrelated concepts—linking, for example, such disparate categories as human beings and computers through a (putatively) shared quality of cognition. Herr Kommissar's second-order semantic specifications of the objects in its microworld make it possible to observe these and many other constraints and commonalities without compromising the integrity of the backbone concept hierarchy in the slightest.

As the previous examples imply, these second-order semantic descriptions are not associated with concepts per se but are an attribute of individual words as entered in the lexicon. The terms *murder* and *kill*, for example, both map back to the same underlying concept but have differing second-order descriptions regarding both the moral status of the act itself and the nature of its appropriate objects. Murder is an evil that sentients perpetrate upon other sentients (e.g., "The mugger murdered the debutante"), whereas killing is an act that any agent and many instruments can perform on any living organism, without necessarily incurring blame (e.g., "Last night's frost killed the begonias").

In and of themselves, constraints on predication only tell us what might and might not be asserted about the objects and events in the universe of discourse. They provide no clue as to the state of affairs actually obtaining in Herr Kommissar's microcosm. Instead, a separate knowledge representation formalism, the postulation, is marshaled to capture the facts pertaining to a given state of the microworld.

Postulations. As opposed to the general, negative rules of thumb embodied in predication constraints, a postulation is a data structure designed to represent a concrete, individual, and positive datum. It is by means of these postulation structures that the events and relationships that comprise Herr Kommissar's microworld(s) are explicitly defined and maintained.

Postulations themselves are embodiments of the principle of semantic compositionality, whereby the meaning of the whole is taken to be a systematic function of the meaning of its parts (Hirst, 1987). As such, they take the form of a framework into which individual concepts can be inserted at various points corresponding to the roles they play in the event being represented (e.g., agent, action, patient). The semantic interpretation of the postulation as a whole is then taken to be composed from the values of its constituent concepts and the relationship among them implied by their relative role-positions within the postulate framework.

Take the two statements, "The dog bit the boy" and "The boy bit the dog." When reduced to postulations, their difference in meaning is represented not in the values of their individual elements (derived in both cases from the concepts for *dog*, *boy*, and *biting*) but in the locations of these elements within their respective frameworks. Thus, the *dog* concept is slotted as the agent of the first postulation but the patient of the second, and so on. On the other hand, if two superficially different statements actually express the same underlying thought (e.g., "The dog bit the boy" vs. "The boy was bitten by the dog"), they will both map to a single postulation. In this case, the *boy* concept is always slotted as the patient, despite its being the direct object of the active-voice sentence and the subject of its passive-voice counterpart.

The final component of Herr Kommissar's postulatory semantics is a mechanism for translating from natural language formulations to KRS postulations (and back again). This is provided by establishing a correlation between the grammatical categorizations used in analyzing a sentence's syntax and the semantic slots of the equivalent postulation. For example, the words occupying the subject, verb, and direct object categories in the parse of a given (active-voice) sentence are mapped to concepts in the agent, action, and patient roles, respectively, of the postulate framework, with analogous operations for passive constructions. This transformation from a syntactic to a semantic formalism yields a sentence's meaning that is capable of undergoing validation within the framework of Herr Kommissar's knowledge representation schema.

Model-Theoretic Evaluation

As hinted at in the overview, the validation process relies on principles of model-theoretic semantics (Dowty, Wall, & Peters, 1981), according to which a postulation's truth is evaluated not by a formal logic of deduction and inference but by reference to some possible model of reality—in this case, Herr Kommissar's KRS database. So, the truth value of postulating that "the dog bit the boy" is ultimately determined by our success or failure in finding an equivalent master postulation among those database entries that define the state of the currently operative microworld.

A world (even a microworld) is no more made up of unrelated events than of isolated objects. In order to simulate the complex situations and interactions required for an immersive learning environment, multiple individual postulations must be synthesized into a coherent whole—a world view. Each such world view comprises an ordered set of postulations, in which the ordering is realized by means of space-time indices embedded in the postulations themselves. Spatiotemporal indexing, in turn, enables a world view to represent chronological sequences of events—the past, present, and future of the microworld as the individual character sees it.

Because each such world view is formulated not in words but in the concepts underlying them, Herr Kommissar can respond meaningfully when learners use different turns of phrase to reference the same item of information. Rather than parroting back canned answers to previously anticipated questions, the simulated suspects can improvise extemporaneous replies to whatever line of investigation, in whatever mode of expression, the learner chooses to pursue.

The end result of all this is a system that supports meaningful and engaging dialogue with the second language learner and is focused on tasks and interactions that make the exercise and improvement of communicative skills a means, rather than an end in itself. It is a system that, although solidly grounded in theory, is less concerned with abstract proofs of principle than with the practical application of natural language processing and knowledge representation technologies to the specific task of second language instruction.

Potential Contributions to Language Acquisition Research and Theory

Insofar as Herr Kommissar can be said to embody a theoretical perspective on the process of second language acquisition, it is simply this. Mastering a new language involves more than just learning its rules, structures, and vocabulary; it also involves using the language itself to the point at which it becomes second nature. This is a very old insight, but recent work in the branch of learning theory concerned with intelligent tutoring systems (ITSs) has lent it renewed credibility by drawing a crucial distinction between knowledge-rich and high-performance instructional domains (Regian, 1991; cf. Elsom-Cook, 1990).

A high-performance domain is one in which the basic skills must become "automatized," leaving the individual "free to concentrate on other, more cognitively demanding issues." This, in turn, presupposes "very different ITS designs" capable of "imparting not only a certain amount of knowledge, but also of drilling the student in the use of this knowledge to the point where the student no longer needs to concentrate on the actual problem-solving task" (Fink, 1991, pp. 204-205). By this definition, mastery of a foreign language is a high-performance task par excellence, being measured less by one's ability to recite a verb's entire conjugation paradigm than by a facility at inflecting it correctly on the fly without losing sight of the message being conveyed. Accordingly, this domain, too, demands a very different ITS design, focusing less on inculcating new formal knowledge than on activating and internalizing what has already been learned. This is accomplished by providing opportunities to exercise and extend creatively what has been learned—in a word, a microworld learning environment.

This concept of language proficiency as a high-performance skill, requiring a new kind of intelligent tutoring system, permeates every aspect of Herr Kommissar's design. Its role-playing motif and game-like dynamics, the extralinguistic, goal-oriented nature of the challenge it sets for the learner (i.e., solving the mystery), its emphasis on target language conversational interaction as the sole means of attaining that goal, the understated nature of its formal instructional (i.e., remediative) component—all these combine to create a learning environment that exemplifies and serves as a testbed for an extension of the high-performance hypothesis into the field of second language acquisition. For all its self-avowed focus on the pragmatic, then, Herr Kommissar is—from this broader perspective, at least—a research project in both conception and execution, an enterprise theoretical down to its core.

Student Modeling

Although Herr Kommissar resembles a traditional intelligent tutoring system in embodying a theory of language acquisition and implying a research program, there is at least one respect in which it breaks the standard ITS mold. It does not incorporate an explicit, generative student model. To see why not, let us digress for a moment to consider the role of the student model in traditional intelligent tutoring system design.

Separate and apart from its research implications, the rationale for student modeling in ITS theory is to better simulate the approach taken by a human tutor, who (it is held) maintains a mental model of the capabilities and state of mind of a generic learner. There is no question that such a model would be useful—to humans or to machines. Among other things, it could help in assessing progress toward instructional objectives, in analyzing surface errors in terms of the underlying misunderstandings they betray, and in determining the most effective mode of presentation and explanation. The real question is, how does a machine go about acquiring such a model?

The time-honored answer has been to begin with a specification of the correct procedure (or the "ideal student"), representing "the instructional objectives of the text and the tutor," and then apply a "bug catalog" (or "set of incorrect rules that reflect known misconceptions") in an effort to anticipate students' real behavior (Corbett, Anderson, & Patterson, 1990, pp. 90-91). This approach has been formalized in repair theory, which creates a predictive (generative) model of student errors in an elementary arithmetic operation by systematically deleting fragments of the original algorithm and then attempting to patch or repair the resulting holes (Brown & VanLehn, 1980; Burton, 1982). As this suggests, however, we need an exhaustive model of the right way to do things before we can introduce the systematic distortions (or mal-rules) that characterize the student model. That, in turn, means that "the mal-rule approach is, in principle, only possible...in closed-world, formal domains (such as subtraction and Lisp programming) for which a complete algorithmic description is available" (Self, 1990, p. 116; cf. Feurzeig & Ritter, 1988). Even here, "containing the combinatorics of the modeling task is a formidable challenge" (Wenger, 1987, p. 191).

Language is far from being such a closed-world domain, however, and the errors observed during second language acquisition proliferate beyond the power of any merely rule-driven repair generator to reproduce. They certainly exceed the generative capacity of contrastive analysis, with its behaviorist mechanisms of transference or interference from native language habits (e.g., Jakobovits, 1970; Lado, 1957). Even such suggestive explanatory paradigms as interlanguage or learner varieties, which call attention to the constructive, rule-hypothesizing aspects of the transition to competence in a second language (e.g., Corder, 1981; Klein, 1986), have so far failed to manifest much in the way of predictive power. On the contrary, as Bley-Vroman (1988) points out, "no systematic grammar has yet been produced for any substantial portion of any learner's language" (p. 23). Not that there is any shortage of other contenders. One recent survey of the field cataloged no fewer than seventeen distinct theories, models, or hypotheses of second language acquisition (Ferguson & Huebner, 1989), but this evident failure to converge on a single omnicompetent paradigm of the process is part of the problem, rather than its solution.

Its putative applicability to second language learning aside, repair theory has recently come under fire as an adequate generator of student models even on its own home turf of elementary arithmetic (Hennessy, 1990; Laurillard, 1990). What makes this especially worth noting here is the nature of the critique. Generative student models are being faulted for focusing only on those aspects of erroneous student performance that can be produced by syntactic transformations of a correct procedure while ignoring errors arising from a semantic misunderstanding of that procedure. If it is judged necessary to simulate aspects of meaning (as opposed to mechanical manipulations of formal rules) for tutoring subjects like arithmetic, how much more important and more difficult might it be when the discipline being taught is language itself, whose whole purpose is to convey meaning?

There are grounds, then, for entertaining serious reservations about the relevance of generative student modeling to the domain of second language acquisition. Those reservations transcend the immediate issue. Not only does it seem doubtful that an ITS really needs a predictive model of student performance to tutor foreign languages, it seems equally unlikely that human language instructors do either. To begin with, it cannot be an absolute prerequisite that language teachers be able to form such a mental model. Not, at least, if the phonological, morphological, and syntactic rules of students' native language(s) are an essential component of that model, as most would hold. For then it would become problematic in the extreme whether one person could teach another a second language without knowing that other person's first language, and effective ESL (English as a second language) instructors would be a rare commodity indeed.

Of course, it is a great advantage for a language teacher to be familiar with his or her students' native language(s), but not for purposes of generative modeling. Here, Lakoff (1987) offers a useful distinction between "principles that *motivate*, or *make sense of*, a system, and...principles that *generate*, or *predict*, the system" (p. 96). For all the undeniable benefits that would accrue from an ability to forecast erroneous student performance, it seems that most language teachers, including those who know their students' native tongues (indeed, most teachers generally), do well enough to understand and amend the misconceptions underlying that performance after the fact.

If what we really need are motivational, rather than generative, models of the second language learner, Herr Kommissar can help. Building such models demands volumes of raw data about the kind of performance students actually exhibit, as opposed to that imputed to them by a repair generator—and Herr Kommissar provides a platform for collecting such data. As it runs, Herr Kommissar conducts a fine-grained syntactic analysis of all the input it receives and then stores the results in a cumulative record, along with protocols listing every keystroke—every question, every answer, every recourse to grammatical or lexical help information—entered by the learner in the course of the conversation. Over time, this cumulative record of interactions with Herr Kommissar builds into a profile of learner performance, with obvious application to longitudinal studies of the second language acquisition process. Bear in mind that what is being captured here is the student's spontaneous performance. The immersive, nonjudgmental, and task-oriented nature of the learning environment tends to minimize self-consciousness (and self-monitoring) even as it maximizes target-language production.

Performance Profiles

Analysis of the resulting performance profiles is facilitated by a stand-alone utility: Magister. Using Magister, researchers and instructors (Magister tends to blur the line between the two) can verify and refine their evolving motivational student models by reviewing a sort of notebook of detailed diagnostics (see Figure 9.5). They can also step back to take a longer, statistical view of the same student's performance over any time frame, down to any level of granularity (see Figure 9.6).

In either case, Magister delivers not abstract models of ideal versus fallible learners' competence, but evolutionary models of real learners' performance, as revealed through the tutorial interaction itself. The learners plot their own curves, rather than being force-fitted to data points predicted by theory. With enough such data, the phenomena of second language acquisition could begin to serve as "the source for theory construction" rather than as an after-the-fact corroboration (Ferguson & Huebner, 1989, p. 3; cf. Ferguson, 1989).

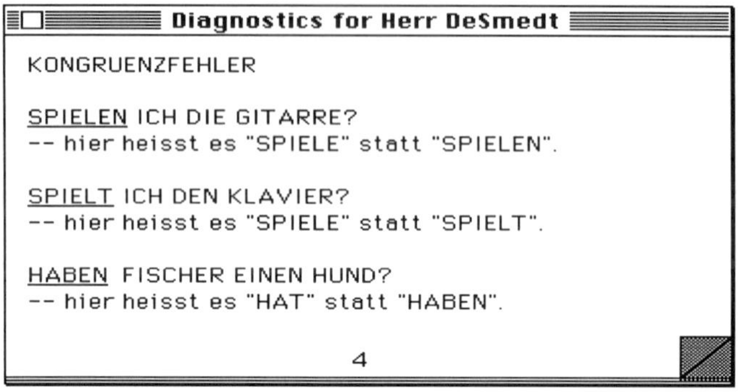

FIG 9.5. A leaf from the diagnostic notebook, showing one student's performance record for subject-verb agreement.

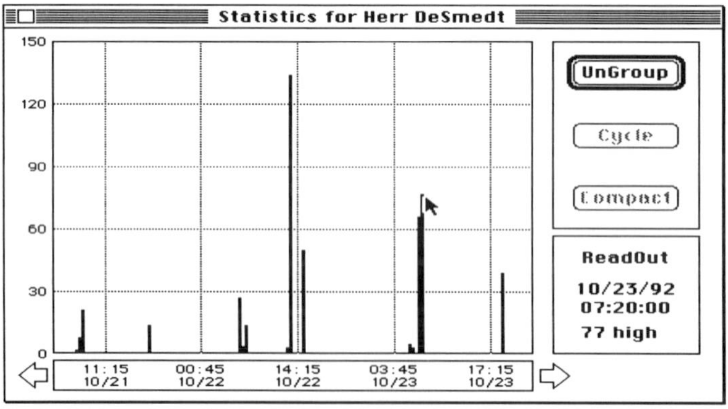

FIG. 9.6. A statistical view of the performance of the student from Figure 9.5, showing total errors plotted in half-hour intervals.

Using Magister, researchers can reconfigure the cumulative performance analysis itself after the fact, redefining its criteria by means of so-called *performance primitives*. The new analytical filter can then be applied against the entire corpus of student production in order to test hypotheses about second language acquisition. On the practical side, instructors can use the same facility to search for an optimal fit between observed learner performance and the operative remediation categories. Once the criteria most relevant to an individual student or an entire class have been found, they can be reimported back into the Herr Kommissar learning environment itself. There they will be used to customize all subsequent performance-coaching interactions.

With performance primitives facilitating the refinement or even the wholesale redefinition of all Magister's analysis criteria, the variety of well-thought-out, rigorous evaluation paradigms that can be described and applied—and the empirical research on pedagogy that can be conducted—is truly limited only by the imaginations of the researchers themselves.

Problems, Tradeoffs, and Lessons Learned in Development

Any ICALL system that aims to go beyond syntactic analysis and engage learners in a simulated dialogue must face the question of just how much background knowledge and common-sense inferencing to support. Here, the tradeoff is between the range of conversational topics the system can cover and the lag introduced by the length of the knowledge-base scan that must be conducted for each new reply. Exhaustively modeling the world view of even a moderately knowledgeable colocutor in KRS postulations could create a search space of daunting proportions, with unacceptably long retrieval times for the simplest responses. No wonder, then, as Dahlgren (1988) noted, "the magnitude and complexity of conceptual knowledge has been dealt with in linguistic semantics chiefly by ignoring it" (p. 69).

Implicit Versus Explicit Knowledge Representation

Fortunately, as has become apparent in the course of grappling with this issue, not all world knowledge need be manifested in formal propositions. There is a second tradeoff operative here—between explicit and implicit knowledge representation—that can mitigate the effects of the first. On reflection, a great deal of implicit common knowledge turns out to be there for the asking. It is embedded in the ontological underpinnings of the system and therefore imposes no additional load on the KRS itself.

The concept hierarchy furnishes a prime example. Although not composed of KRS postulations (quite the reverse; as we have seen, it provides the building blocks out of which such postulations are themselves composed), its structure embodies much of the information needed to address routine issues of taxonomy and typology. All such questions as "What is a man?" or "Is a duck a reptile?" can be answered by reference to the nested categories of the concept hierarchy, thereby saving the KRS storage space (and search space) that might otherwise be needed to accommodate the equivalent postulations.

The second-order semantic language used to represent selectional constraints on verbal complements serves a similar function. In addition to playing a key role in syntactic analysis, predication constraints also prove invaluable in detecting and rejecting assertions that violate either natural law (e.g., you cannot drink a piano) or social taboo (e.g., horses do not get married) without loading down the KRS with extraneous postulations.

This strategy of sharing the knowledge representation burden between explicit postulations and the broader framework within which the KRS itself operates has much to recommend it. In addition to the searching and storing efficiencies this strategy affords, it can also claim a certain measure of psychological realism, as attested by the insights of situated-cognition theory regarding the way the human mind offloads cognitive complexity onto its environment (Brown, 1990). Nonetheless, this strategy can only take us so far.

Discourse Constraints Versus Knowledge Modification

Much of the remaining distance turns out to be covered by the detective-game format itself. Because the object is to figure out "whodunnit," learners tend to concentrate on uncovering the facts of the case at hand—all readily representable as literal KRS postulations—and to steer away from extraneous lines of inquiry that might require more extensive knowledge engineering. Because this constraint on the domain of discourse is embedded in the structure of the exercise itself, it is both unobtrusive and quite effective at keeping the conversation within the limits of Herr Kommissar's current knowledge representation capabilities.

The conventions of the detective game come to the rescue again in dealing with another related issue. It is no coincidence that the simulation is structured so as to place the learner in the role of interrogator, with the computer playing the part of a suspect under questioning. Herr Kommissar's conversational capabilities are, in fact, at their most impressive when answering questions. Its capacity to respond coherently and consistently to statements or commands from the user is considerably more limited.

However, this predisposition toward question-answering dialogues should not be taken to imply a limitation in the natural language processing per se. The parser itself can accept and analyze input in any modality: declarative, imperative, or interrogative. Rather, the difficulty is that statements, in particular, carry with them the unspoken expectation that the individual on the receiving end will learn from them—that is, that the information contained in them will be incorporated into the recipient's world view and taken into account in the subsequent course of the conversation. This is one aspect of human discourse that, by and large, Herr Kommissar does not as yet simulate.

To be sure, as we have seen, Herr Kommissar does deal with other aspects of discourse dynamics that involve an ability to follow the conversation. It can, for instance, remember whether a question has been asked before or track the focus of discourse for purposes of resolving a pronominal reference. What it does not yet do is to respond to the input of novel information by fashioning a new postulation and updating the current suspect's KRS world view with it—at least, not while the session is still in progress. In principle, there is no reason why this could not be done. A world view is just data, after all, and no reprogramming is required to change one—just a set of operations analogous to database management. In fact, the raw ability to perform such world view updates exists now in the form of the previously mentioned KRS-authoring utility Dramatiker.

Even in its current implementation, Dramatiker already supports most of the required world view editing capabilities. As depicted in Figure 9.7, it guides an author through a series of who-what-when-where questions to create a new postulation or amend an old one. As each prompt is answered with a word or phrase in German, a grammatically correct German sentence verbalizing the postulation takes shape in a separate window. The only drawback is that Dramatiker does all this as a separate utility, operating

FIG. 9.7. Dramatiker's postulation entry screen. The author has just augmented the postulation that "Fischer was drinking a beer at 8 p.m. yesterday" by entering "in a bar" as the locale and is now being prompted to specify what kind of bar.

entirely outside the confines of the Herr Kommissar conversational environment. So, even though the revisions to the characters' world views will become available for the learner's very next interrogation session, they cannot take effect while an interrogation is in progress.

Again, there is nothing to prevent us from integrating Dramatiker's capabilities into Herr Kommissar proper. After all, the existing parser can already analyze the syntax of declarative statements, and the existing knowledge base can already assimilate the new information they contain. The only thing missing is an internal KRS-updating capability, and Dramatiker already has that. It would appear that by incorporating a single module from Dramatiker, Herr Kommissar could dispense with its questions-only constraint altogether.

Appearances deceive; the real difficulty is not in accepting new information, it is in knowing which information to accept and which to reject. Until Herr Kommissar can apply common-sense inferencing to a learner's statements, it cannot be sure that the new information contained therein is not in conflict with one or more of the prevailing world-view's master postulations. If the KRS's world views were updated without such a sanity check, they could readily fall into self-contradiction. Here, at last, is the fundamental issue with letting Herr Kommissar engage in a true two-way exchange of information. In the absence of an inferential integrity-checking capability, this kind of exchange opens the door to random corruption of the knowledge base.

The question-and-answer dialogue, by contrast, is safe enough, being one of the few modes of discourse wherein the transfer of information is expected to run only one way: from answerer to questioner (cf. Lehnert, 1978). The only problem was how to get learners to adhere to that conversational convention. The solution, as noted, was the murder mystery format, in which asking questions is the only way to catch the culprit. The lesson to be learned from all this is just how binding such a simple contextual constraint can be without being in the least obtrusive. Caught up in the dynamic of the interrogation, learners seldom if ever notice that Herr Kommissar is not absorbing any new information because they are not providing any.

Conclusion: Where Do We Go from Here?

Herr Kommissar's development could take any number of directions from this point. One possible extension of present capabilities would be to internalize aspects of the motivational student modeling now supported by Magister. This would enable Herr Kommissar to analyze the student profiles it creates and use the results to customize its interactions with individual learners. Expansion into additional languages also beckons. Although currently focused on German instruction, the syntactic/semantic engine that powers Herr Kommissar has been designed for ready adaptation to other languages as well. Yet a third avenue would be the enhancement of Herr Kommissar's current text-oriented user interface in the direction of a direct manipulation environment. This would enable learners to explore and change the microworld as well as talk about it.

Given world enough and time (and an easing of resources constraints), all this may yet come to pass. For the foreseeable future, however, Herr Kommissar's research and development agenda must remain focused on the fundamental objective of providing an intelligent, conversational learning environment for second language acquisition. Here, the best prospects for further progress lie in two enhancements to the core NLP and KRS technologies: *concept matching* and *on-line learning*.

Concept Matching

Addressing issues of psychological reality has never ranked among Herr Kommissar's top development priorities. The cognitive processes that go on in humans as we acquire and use language, although fascinating as objects of theoretical inquiry, have seemed all but irrelevant to the practical challenges of increasing the parser's efficiency, reliability, and robustness. That is about to change. What is causing this change is a suspicion that syntax-oriented approaches to ICALL, even those based on case grammar, are reaching a point of diminishing returns. Contemporary parsing theory has opened the door into a large room, yet no general solution to the ill-formedness problem has so far been found within its confines, and its far wall is already coming into view. Steady, incremental improvement in parsing technology will doubtless continue, but dealing with ill-formed input in all its overwhelming (and for all practical purposes, infinite) variety calls for an order of magnitude breakthrough. It is in the search for such a breakthrough that the model of human cognition takes on renewed relevance, for it suggests that the answer may lie in shifting the balance between syntax and semantics.

There is no denying that syntactic analysis plays a major role in human language understanding. Introspection aside, recent studies tracking the eye movements of German native speakers as they read prose shows a direct correlation between the difficulty of the passage and the amount of time spent on the function words (vs. those conveying content) as the key to interpretation (Berkemeyer & Bernhardt, 1991). This apparent primacy of syntax over semantics (in humans as well as machines) presupposes, as hinted at previously, well-formed input. The further the actual input strays from this ideal, the more the analysis must refocus on its intended meaning in context.

What eventuates at the margin of human language processing resembles a throwback to the syntaxless string-matching operations first employed by ELIZA at the very dawn of computational linguistics (Weizenbaum, 1976). Here, however, the match is being performed not on strings of words but on clusters of concepts. When syntactic analysis does fail us, in the language classroom or elsewhere, we fall back on sifting through whatever isolated chunks of meaning we have been able to extract and trying to fit them into any one of a number of preexisting templates—in other words, concept matching.

If something like such a mechanism underlies the human language instructor's ability to recognize the intent behind a student's garbled productions, could it work for ICALL as well? At a minimum, a concept-matching strategy might enable a conversation simulator like Herr Kommissar to continue the dialogue in a meaningful manner, even when what the learner means to say is less than clear. That is, in any case, the goal.

On-Line Learning

Much as concept matching promises to improve Herr Kommissar's natural language processing performance, it is on-line learning that represents our highest development priority, comprehending as it does the entire constellation of issues and tradeoffs in knowledge representation cited previously. This capacity to learn in real time, to update the knowledge base with new information during the conversation itself, is crucial to Herr Kommissar's further progress toward the goal of maximum-coverage discourse simulation. With on-line learning, it will be possible to move from the current interrogation scenario to simulating modes of communication that rely on a full, two-way exchange of information. Such next-generation simulations might include interviews, cocktail parties, perhaps even—with some additional plan recognition capabilities (Carberry, 1990)—commercial or diplomatic negotiation. To get there, however, we will have to meet many of the challenges that have so far simply been circumvented.

In particular, one sine qua non of on-line learning is a true common-sense inferencing mechanism. Without this mechanism, it is hard to see how to implement a faculty for discriminating between incoming information that can be safely incorporated into the operative world view, and incoming information that conflicts with one or more of the world view's master propositions and should thus be summarily rejected. At a minimum, the desired faculty, christened *a cognitive-dissonance averter* in homage to Festinger (1957), must handle an explicit contradiction between a new assertion and some aspect of the prevailing reality model. It must be able to reject, for example, the statement that "X is alive" if the postulation that "X died yesterday" is already part of the knowledge base. Ideally, it would go beyond this to infer that two apparently unrelated propositions are at odds in terms of their logical consequences. In this case, it would also reject the proposition that "X had pancakes this morning" on the same grounds that X died yesterday and dead men eat no breakfast.

This work has barely begun. It is still too early to say where it may ultimately lead, yet even now, hovering at the very edge of sight, looms at least one wholly unanticipated prospect. If the inheritance structure implicit in the concept hierarchy were conjoined with a more generalized postulation formalism, the two might yield something approaching a KRS-based simulation not just of common-sense or background knowledge but of physical objects and their environmental surrounds as well—in other words, a semantics-based direct manipulation environment! In the meantime, Herr Kommissar is already out there in the field—a working product currently installed at scores of educational institutions.

References

Berkemeyer, V., & Bernhardt, E. (1991, November). *The reading behaviors of native German readers.* Paper presented at the Annual Meeting of the American Council on the Teaching of Foreign Languages, Washington, DC.

Bley-Vroman, R. (1988). The fundamental character of foreign language learning. In W. Rutherford & M. Sharwood Smith (Eds.), *Grammar and second language teaching: A book of readings* (pp. 19-30). New York: Newbury House.

Brown, J.S. (1990). Toward a new epistemology for learning. In C. Frasson & G. Gauthier (Eds.), *Intelligent tutoring systems: At the crossroad of artificial intelligence and education* (pp. 266-282). Norwood, NJ: Ablex.

Brown, J.S., & VanLehn, K. (1980). Repair theory: A generative theory of bugs in procedural skills. *Cognitive Science*, *4*, 379-426.

Burton, R.R. (1982). Diagnosing bugs in a simple procedural skill. In D. Sleeman & J.S. Brown (Eds.), *Intelligent tutoring systems* (pp. 157-184). London: Academic Press.

Carberry, S. (1990). *Plan recognition in natural language dialogue.* Cambridge, MA: MIT Press.

Cook, W.A. (1989). *Case grammar theory.* Washington, DC: Georgetown University Press.

Corbett, A.T., Anderson, J.R., & Patterson, E.G. (1990). Student modeling and tutoring flexibility in the Lisp intelligent tutoring system. In C. Frasson & G. Gauthier (Eds.), *Intelligent tutoring systems: At the crossroad of artificial intelligence and education* (pp. 83-106). Norwood, NJ: Ablex.

Corder, S.P. (1981). *Error analysis and interlanguage.* New York: Oxford University Press.

Dahlgren, K. (1988). *Naive semantics for natural language understanding.* Dordrecht: Kluwer.

DeSmedt, W.H. (1991). *Herr Kommissar instructor's guide.* Milford, PA: amber productions.

Dowty, D.R., Wall, R.E., & Peters, S. (1981). *Introduction to Montague semantics*. Dordrecht: D. Reidel.

Elsom-Cook, M. (Ed.). (1990). *Guided discovery tutoring: A framework for ICAI research*. London: Paul Chapman.

Ferguson, C.A. (1989). Language teaching and theories of language. *Proceedings of the 1989 Georgetown University Round Table on Languages and Linguistics* (pp. 81-88). Washington, DC: Georgetown University Press.

Ferguson, C., & Huebner, T. (1989). *Foreign language instruction and second language acquisition research in the United States*. Washington, DC: National Foreign Language Center.

Festinger, L. (1957). *A theory of cognitive dissonance*. Stanford, CA: Stanford University Press.

Feurzig, W., & Ritter, F. (1988). Understanding reflective problem solving. In J. Psotka, L.D. Massey, & S.A. Mutter (Eds.), *Intelligent tutoring systems: Lessons learned* (pp. 435-450). Hillsdale, NJ: Lawrence Erlbaum Associates.

Fillmore, C. J. (1968). The case for case. In E. Bach & R.T. Harms (Eds.), *Universals in linguistic theory* (pp. 1-90). New York: Holt, Rinehart, & Winston.

Fink, P. K. (1991). The role of domain knowledge in the design of an intelligent tutoring system. In H. Burns, J.W. Parlett, & C.L. Redfield (Eds.), *Intelligent tutoring systems: Evolutions in design* (pp. 195-224). Hillsdale, NJ: Lawrence Erlbaum Associates.

Hennessy, S. (1990). Why bugs are not enough. In M. Elsom-Cook (Ed.), *Guided discovery tutoring: A framework for ICAI research* (pp. 173-195). London: Paul Chapman.

Hirst, G. (1987). *Semantic interpretation and the resolution of ambiguity*. Cambridge, England: Cambridge University Press.

Jakobovits, L.A. (1970). *Foreign language learning: A psycholinguistic analysis of the issues*. Rowley, MA: Newbury House.

Jensen, K., Heidorn, G., Miller, L., & Ravin, Y. (1993). Parse fitting and prose fixing. In K. Jensen, G.E. Heidorn, & S. Richardson (Eds.), *Natural language processing: The PLNLP Approach* (pp. 53-64). Dordrecht: Kluwer.

Jolley, J.L. (1973). *The fabric of knowledge: A study of the relations between ideas*. New York: Harper & Row.

Klein, W. (1986). *Second language acquisition*. Cambridge, England: Cambridge University Press.

Lado, R. (1957). *Linguistics across cultures*. Ann Arbor, MI: University of Michigan Press.

Lakoff, G. (1987). *Women, fire, and dangerous things: What categories reveal about the mind*. Chicago, IL: University of Chicago Press.

Laurillard, D. (1990). Generative student models: The limits of diagnosis and remediation. In M. Elsom-Cook (Ed.), *Guided discovery tutoring: A framework for ICAI research* (pp. 42-53). London: Paul Chapman.

Lehnert, W.G. (1978). *The process of question answering*. Hillsdale, NJ: Lawrence Erlbaum Associates.

Matthews, C. (1993). Grammar frameworks in intelligent CALL. *CALICO Journal*, *11*, 5-27.

McCord, M.C. (1980). Slot grammars. *Computational Linguistics*, *6*, 31-43.

Mulford, G.W. (1989). Semantic processing for communicative exercise foreign language learning. *Computers and the Humanities*, *23*, 31-44.

Regian, J.W. (1991). Representing and teaching high performance tasks within intelligent tutoring systems. In H. Burns, J.W. Parlett, & C.L. Redfield (Eds.), *Intelligent tutoring systems: Evolutions in design* (pp. 225-242). Hillsdale, NJ: Lawrence Erlbaum Associates.

Self, J.A. (1990). Bypassing the intractable problem of student modeling. In C. Frasson & G. Gauthier (Eds.), *Intelligent tutoring systems: At the crossroad of artificial intelligence and education* (pp. 107-123). Norwood, NJ: Ablex.

Sowa, J.F. (1984). *Conceptual structures: Information processing in mind and machine*. Reading, MA: Addison-Wesley.

Tennant, H. (1981). *Natural language processing*. Princeton, N.J.: Petrocelli.

Tussing, M., & Zimmermann, J. (1977). Vocabulary in first-year German texts. *Die Unterrichtspraxis*, *10*, 65-73.

Weizenbaum, J. (1976). *Computer power and human reason.* San Francisco: Freeman.

Wenger, E. (1987). *Artificial intelligence and tutoring systems: Computational and cognitive approaches to the communication of knowledge.* Los Altos, CA: Kaufmann.

Winograd, T. (1983). *Language as a cognitive process, Volume I: Syntax*. Reading, MA: Addison-Wesley.

Section III

Graphics-Based Language Tutors and Learning Environments

The Systems and an Integrative Framework

Section III presents systems that seek to integrate language with the physical, visual world that is its context. That world is represented mainly by computer graphics and digitized sound. Some of the systems presented earlier, like Herr Kommissar (Section I) and BRIDGE (Section II), use still graphics as generic backdrops or as specific question prompts. But these graphics do not react to what students say, do not depict the realistic consequences of language use. The systems in Section III, by contrast, employ microworlds in which animated objects respond to requests, descriptions, or actions by the student—responses enabled by NLP analysis and other artificial intelligence (AI) mechanisms. These systems typify the immersion approach to language learning. They are shaped by theories of language learning that stress engagement in motivating, authentic communicative activity (see Oxford, this volume). They capitalize on the trend in instructional technology away from directed tutors and toward reactive and exploratory learning environments (Lawler & Yazdani, 1988).

Because of the technical and conceptual complexity of these systems, each is described in two chapters—one describing tutoring functions and interfaces, another explicating either computational mechanisms or research underpinnings. The chapter by Douglas on the LingWorlds system is followed by Tomlin's chapter on the precursor FlatLand, a research environment for studying tutoring strategies to put into LingWorlds. The Athena Language Learning Project (ALLP) described by Murray spans several NLP applications, notably, the poltergeist-inhabited LINGO microworld. A companion chapter by Felshin covers the NLP mechanisms built to support the dialogues anticipated in the ALLP applications. The Military Language Tutor (MILT) described by Kaplan and Holland features an intelligence-gathering graphics microworld as well as text-based dialogue and question-answer exercises. The semantic formalisms designed to support these exercises are described by Dorr, Hendler, Blanksteen, and Migdaloff.

As the lead chapter in this section, Hamburger provides a framework for integrating verbal and visual aspects of microworlds—the "two-medium dialogue." Hamburger's FLUENT-1 environment incorporates manipulable visual objects, and his plan for FLUENT-2 is to capture the range of ways that people interact through language in a jointly viewed world. The theory that accounts for this interaction is necessarily complex. Interlocutors can describe actions, request actions, respond to requests, and so forth, yielding a system of interaction types that correspond to roles humans play when they talk and act. Also essential is a scheme of "situation viewpoints": the views of events and scenes that account for how we can describe the same thing in different ways. The poet Wallace Stevens offered 13 ways of looking at a blackbird as a particularization of metaphor. Hamburger's scheme for ordinary description accommodates more ways than that and gives some predictability to description based on what else has gone on during the conversation and what else is expected. Any tutoring system that purports to evaluate how students describe pictures should anticipate the kinds of referentially equivalent characterizations defined by Hamburger. Although his theory is not in its entirety implementable now, it can be expected to organize future systems as computational capabilities catch up with designers' ideas.

Each system presented in Section III can be located within the framework of Hamburger's interaction types, as is noted in each chapter. This framework also applies to the two systems from Section II: Users interact with the text-based games by single-medium dialogue, with the tutor largely in the role of servant (i.e., carrying out commands) or oracle (i.e., answering questions). Murray goes on to analyze roles of microworld characters into tutoring functions, such as coach and informant, which apply across ICALL systems.

Emerging Issues

The Role of Constraints

The technical problems of designing moving, talking microworlds lie not just in semantically analyzing what students say but in linking that analysis to appropriate physical changes in the microworld. This is harder than assessing students' responses to discrete questions where the question closely molds the answer, as in ALICE-chan and BRIDGE (Section I). To make the linkage from word to world manageable requires prudent constraints on what can be said. *First-order constraints* stem from the microworld itself, a limited domain whose boundaries restrict what students are likely to say and what they expect will be understood. For example, in LINGO (Murray) and MILT (Kaplan & Holland) only the objects in the displayed rooms are expected to enter the conversation, and the system can legitimately exempt itself from dealing with references to outside objects. In LINGO the convention of the poltergeist accounts for why an invisible agent magically cleans up (or messes up) a room, and therefore eliminates the complexity of coordinating a visible agent into the scene. In *No recuerdo*, another NLP application from the ALLP, the system's failures to process certain input language are explained in terms of an amnesiac interlocutor, a conceit independently motivated on dramatic grounds. These inherent constraints may not be enough, however. The LINGO world is supported by an expansive NLP built not only to parse but to handle anaphora, focus, and pragmatic phenomena as well as spatiotemporal inferences, as described by Felshin. Still, students in test trials continued to produce commands that the NLP could not treat. In an example given by Murray at the workshop preceding this book, one user typed "thank you" after LINGO had correctly executed a request. This kind of noninformative, purely polite exchange had not been predicted, and the system responded, "I do not know how to thank myself." The solution to such difficulties is either to expand the NLP or to narrow students' input, as by specifying sentence frames or permissible vocabulary. The latter measures can be called *second-order constraints*.

Other kinds of second-order constraints are described for the dialogue exercise in MILT (Dorr et al.; Kaplan & Holland). This exercise is accompanied by a half-screen display of a report form that users are asked to fill in as they query the system. Modeled on a real artifact of the soldier's job, this form guides the topics to be probed and the depth of the probes.

The Search for Motivating Theories

Most systems in Section III draw on various communicative approaches to language teaching, whose common premise is that language is best learned by using it to solve authentic and interesting problems. Hamburger cites Asher's total physical response theory. Douglas and Tomlin both cite Krashen's influence and approaches like Asher's that espouse developing comprehension before teaching production. Murray calls on the communicative framework of Kramsch. Kaplan and Holland draw not from theories of language teaching but from general learning principles dealing with practice, motivation, and feedback. These various approaches and principles are consistent with, if they do not fully determine, the use of microworld formats for teaching. Moreover, in the cases of Douglas and of Tomlin, it is clear that invoking the comprehension approach to language teaching shapes a tutor that has students listen and act before they ever produce.

However, at least some of these authors (see the chapters by Douglas, Kaplan & Holland, and Tomlin) admit the inadequacy of current theories to guide the specifics of how to teach—an argument begun in Section I by Frederiksen et al. and elaborated in Section IV by MacWhinney. Frederiksen et al. note the lack of explicit cognitive models in theories of communicative language teaching. In response, they turn to theories of the knowledge and processes involved in understanding and producing discourse, theories with detailed models that represent communicative competence. By contrast, the response of Douglas and of Tomlin is to derive their own theoretical principles by observing experienced human tutors and analyzing what they say in terms of rhetorical functions vis-à-vis the changing task context.[28] Using the FlatLand research protocol, Tomlin extracted tutoring strategies that are expressible in discourse theories (e.g., Searle, 1969) and that appear to contribute to learning. These strategies in turn have design implications for LingWorlds, as realized in Douglas' Lifeboat simulation. Tomlin's analyses of tutoring utterances are motivated by functionalist explanations of syntax, which give weight to pragmatic aspects of the visual context and are naturally suited to microworld investigation. Thus, theoretically guided empirical discovery helps shape the instructional strategies used in LingWorlds while also enriching theories of tutoring discourse.

In general, in the work of Douglas, Tomlin, Frederiksen et al., and Hamburger, we see how conversants' mutually held (and presumably universal) assumptions about discourse become a resource for ICALL.[29] Douglas and Tomlin address the shared beliefs between learners and tutors about what a learner needs to know to carry out instructions. Giving back to theory, their LingWorlds project may be the first step toward operationalizing Krashen's (1982) notion of *comprehensible input* because the computer implementation demands strict definitions of complexity and incremental comprehensibility that

---

[28] In terms of architectures for intelligent tutoring systems, the models of discourse processing invoked by Frederiksen et al. inform representations of domain expertise; the analyses conducted by Douglas and Tomlin inform representations of teaching strategy. As a reading resource for maturing language learners, the environment of Frederiksen et al. leaves strategy to the learner; as an environment for zero-proficiency learners, LingWorlds encodes ways of guiding students through the world.

[29] Hamburger and Tomlin both interrelate the visual and the verbal in dialogue. Hamburger covers the social or discourse roles available globally in dialogue; Tomlin focuses on a particular role and breaks the resulting talk into speech acts and smaller functional units.

can be controlled by the microworld.

Viability of NLP-Based Microworlds

The ALLP project has produced what Murray and Felshin deem successful demonstrations of NLP-based microworlds. However, efforts to tailor the NLP to the scope and variety of real student input proved overwhelming. Unwilling to retrench the original goals of providing broad communicative practice, these developers decided to focus on interactive video and to shelve the NLP applications until technologies are advanced enough to support the desired levels of coverage, complexity, speed, and portability. Their decision should be interpreted in light of the magnitude of the ALLP undertaking—arguably the most ambitious of the working systems described in this volume.

The intelligence-gathering microworld described by Kaplan and Holland has not at the time of this writing been completed sufficiently to allow testing. A preliminary trial of the English screen-state prototype summarized by Sams (Section I) repeated the finding of Sanders and Sanders (Section II) and to some extent Loritz (Section I): Students were unsure what to say when they entered the microworld. The response of MILT's developers was to promote viability by designing a kind of scaffolding—early verbatim hints that may be withdrawn so that students do not lapse into the copying responses observed by Sanders and Sanders. Moreover, the array of manipulable objects in MILT (around 20) is smaller than the number implemented in the original LINGO (around 40). Finally, second-order constraints on students' input are being considered for MILT as they were not for LINGO. Still, it remains to be demonstrated that the semantic mechanisms being developed for MILT, described by Dorr et al., are sufficient to handle what students type in and link it appropriately to the graphical world.

LingWorlds is judged viable by Douglas and by Tomlin. Their system does not need to analyze free sentence input because the developers decided to start with comprehension, having students respond to commands rather than initiate them. Nevertheless, LingWorlds includes an exploratory mode that accomplishes the dynamic connection of language to graphics: Learners move objects on screen to form new configurations, for which the system generates descriptions in the target language. The NLP-graphics connection is rendered feasible through restriction of microworld actions to manipulating a few spatial relations.

None of these systems addresses the intricate knowledge of the world needed to relate a modeled environment fully to natural language instructions and descriptions. This knowledge includes, for example, the representation of physical properties of objects and their interrelationships and the coordination of plans and goals involved in carrying out requests that have been the subject of considerable AI research (e.g., Wahlster, Andre, Finkler, Profitlich, & Rist, 1993; Webber, Badler, Di Eugenio, Levison, & White, 1992). It is not clear how much world knowledge is needed to support the microworld interactions envisioned by ICALL designers.

Techniques, Optimizations, and Technology Reach

There is considerable computational detail in this section of the book. Hamburger outlines computational mechanisms for implementing the plans and tutorial schemas that coordinate the microworld options in his framework. Douglas describes the object-oriented programming techniques by which she builds microworlds that are fully integrated with the interface. Felshin's chapter is devoted to describing the NLP system developed for the ALLP. It is the only independently published documentation of the project's extensive NLP work and stands as an overview of the manifold problems involved in designing a comprehensive NLP system. Dorr et al. show how theoretical and empirical progress in crosslinguistic studies of lexical semantics, such as Dorr's work on lexical conceptual structure (LCS), support aspects of foreign language tutoring. Consider a few of the technical innovations advanced in these chapters and the surrounding issues:

The possibilites and limitations of LCS representation are discussed by Dorr et al. They focus on its role in MILT to support text-based dialogue, where LCSs link to a knowledge base, and to enable free response questions, where an algorithm diagnoses students' departures from a target answer, following the technique of Levin and Evans (this volume). LCS representation is also used to drive actions in the MILT microworld although the links to animation are not discussed. LCS entails a relatively shallow level of semantic analysis, focusing on argument. It may be compared to the fuller semantics described in Felshin and to the heuristics, selectional restrictions, and concept ontologies built by DeSmedt (Section II). The latter approaches are less principled, however, suggesting a tradeoff between ad hoc utility and principled extendibility. A parallel tradeoff is suggested between the general AI planning mechanisms proposed by Dorr et al. to support dialogue and the task-specific dialogue handling mechanisms developed by DeSmedt.

The coordination of NLP analysis with video is discussed by Murray, as seen in one version of *No recuerdo*. The tie between NLP and video is not intrinsic, as in reactive graphics, but associative. Students view characters on video and then converse with them through typed input. The characters' answers come from canned video or audio segments or from printed messages that the system generates.

Notable in Felshin's chapter is the discussion of penalty assignment to treat ambiguous input during parsing. The idea of ranking interpretations according to how likely a construction or error is in the learner population appears useful, but the initial determination of penalties is likely to be labor intensive, and it is not clear how the project would go about it.

The focus in LingWorlds is not NLP but rather the introduction of computational mechanisms in the manner of intelligent tutoring systems—specifically, direct manipulation interfaces and a principled pedagogical component. The emphasis on formal representations of pedagogy is unique among the working systems in this book.[30] By modeling the human interactions observed in Tomlin's FlatLand, Douglas creates a tutoring control structure that varies the mix of student and tutor initiation of action and that generates

[30] Although the tutors described by Kaplan and Holland and by Sams (Section I) encode sets of pedagogical rules that are independent of other system components, these rules chain exercises through randomization algorithms or local branching decisions. The rules and decision criteria can be modified infinitely and do not represent a central, coherent pedagogical strategy. ICALL systems that build computational models of pedagogy in the manner of intelligent tutoring systems have been developed in Europe and are described in Swartz and Yazdani (1992).

linguistic descriptions differing in complexity along the dimensions found in the human dialogues.

The issue of authorability is ubiquitous in these chapters. The developers recognize that static systems have limited life. Kaplan and Holland describe an extensive authoring front end to MILT that enables nonprogrammers to make new exercises, construct rules for sequencing them, and set criteria for branching to remediation. (The forerunner of this approach is described by Kreyer and Criswell in Section I.) Their system responds to the military's need for a malleable system that can be quickly updated. Dorr et al. demonstrate how LCS analysis facilitates authoring of question-answer exercises that accommodate a range of semantically equivalent answers (cf. Levin & Evans, Section I). Douglas presents a two-level system that offers teachers who want it the power to create their own microworld objects, whereas teachers with less experience can draw on simulations previously stored in a library of microworlds. Felshin describes a control module by which to change the penalties assigned to alternative interpretations of input, permitting the core grammar to be customized to different learners. Murray acknowledges that graphics are superior to video in allowing creation of new configurations and actions and suggests a tradeoff between flexibility (graphics) and cultural authenticity (video).

There are limits to what can be changed by the end user, however. Dorr et al. comment on the difficulties of providing an easily authorable lexicon and knowledge base, reflecting the conclusion of DeSmedt: Better knowledge representation systems are needed to handle the inference problems of dialogue, but such systems are laborious to build even by skilled AI programmers. They cannot be made accessible to nonprogrammers until large common-sense knowledge bases become available to check the potentially unruly ramifications of even a small change to a knowledge system. Hendler, in the workshop preceding this book, cautioned that making a system's computational engines more accessible to the novice entails diminishing their power. At the same time, however, progress is being made in automating the acquisition of lexical and knowledge base components so that they will not all have to be built by hand (see the introduction to Section I; also Levin & Evans, this volume; Dorr, Garman, & Weinberg, 1994).

Assessing Usability and Effectiveness

Given the unfinished status of the systems presented, these chapters offer little information on usage or effectiveness. Murray reports preliminary data about user acceptance of the NLP applications in the ALLP. Focus groups with language teachers indicated strong interest in both LINGO and *No recuerdo*, confirming for Murray the promise of animated microworlds and of designs that associate video with NLP. For the time being, however, interactive videodisc remains for Murray and colleagues the most viable and motivating CALL format. Murray discusses innovations such as menu-based interactive fictions that stretch the capabilities of this technology.

Tomlin's FlatLand protocol, although intended for theoretical research, turned up potentially important data on long-term retention of foreign languages. The data suggest that mastering comprehension of a novel language in a narrow domain promotes high levels of retention even after long periods of disuse. This observation merits further study and has practical implications for programs of rapid train-up that assume zero competence. Unanswered questions about LingWorlds concern the method of modeling the strategies of experienced human tutors. How effective were the tutors selected for observation compared with other tutors? Is the success of their teaching strategies independently validated? Other questions concern whether the basic assumption of the project has merit—that delaying production improves acquisition. A system like LingWorlds can provide a test for such assumptions by allowing comprehension-based acquisition to be compared with acquisition through a mix of comprehension and production. LingWorlds encourages the operationalization and testing of corollary questions about the comprehension approach: At what point should production be taught before proceeding to higher levels of comprehension? Should instruction iterate over an array of domains (i.e., microworlds), first by comprehension, then production? Or should it move from comprehension to production within each domain?

Questions for MILT concern the cost-effectiveness of a fully authorable tutor. It is not obvious that the minute manipulations enabled by the authoring interface are worth the computational cost. Nor is it obvious that instructors or researchers will know how to use this capability, particularly when they are faced with building sequencing rules from the ground up rather than being provided with a few top-level manipulations, such as the variable interaction modes offered by LingWorlds. The approach to authoring in MILT borrows from human factors methods of simulation modeling used in military logistics and resource planning. ICALL, by contrast, may profit from a theoretical predisposition toward the definition of tutoring variables.

An approach to evaluating systems is suggested by Dorr et al. They propose to vary a modular system's degree of dependence on various levels of information, such as LCS, to look at how much knowledge is necessary for tutoring effectiveness. This kind of fine-grained comparison is suggested by MacWhinney (Section IV) as a cornerstone of ICALL evaluation.

References

Dorr, B.J., Garman, J., & Weinberg, A. (1994). *From subcategorization frames to thematic roles: Building Arabic lexical entries for foreign language tutoring.* Manuscript submitted for publication.

Krashen, S. (1982). *Principles and practice in second language acquisition.* Oxford: Pergamon Press.

Lawler, R., & Yazdani, M. (Eds.). (1988). *Artificial intelligence and education. Volume I: Learning environments and tutoring systems.* Norwood, NJ: Ablex.

Searle, J.R. (1969). *Speech acts.* Cambridge, UK: Cambridge University Press.

Swartz, M. L., & Yazdani, M. (Eds.). (1992). *Intelligent tutoring systems for foreign language learning: The bridge to international communication.* New York: Springer-Verlag.

Wahlster, W., Andre, E., Finkler, W., Profitlich, H., & Rist, T. (1993). Plan-based integration of natural language and graphics generation. Artificial Intelligence, *63*, 387-427.

Webber, B., Badler, N., Di Eugenio, B., Levison, L., & White, M. (1992, December). *Instructing animated agents.* Paper presented at the US-Japanese Workshop on Integrated Systems in Multimedia Environments, Las Cruces, NM.

10

Tutorial Tools for Language Learning by Two-Medium Dialogue

Henry Hamburger
George Mason University

FLUENT, a complex, conversational intelligent CALL (ICALL) system, presents many design options for tutorial strategies. The introductory overview in this section, besides serving as an orientation to the system, points out the various access points for the tutorial decision-making that is the focus of this chapter.

The objective of the FLUENT project is to provide one essential form of foreign language learning experience: conversation in the target language, uninterrupted by discussions of grammar, use of first language, and difficulties of other students. Because conversation relates to situations, typically with visual components, the medium of language interaction in FLUENT is tightly integrated with a visual medium consisting of partially animated graphics under shared control of the tutor and student. The availability of the two media, along with situational continuity, can provide to adults the kind of redundancy that seems essential to children in their race to fluent use of their native tongue. The resulting experience—situational immersion—is intended to foster direct association of the words and constructions of the new language to their meanings in the context of use in a situation.

A conversational ICALL system like this requires concepts and techniques from several subfields of artificial intelligence: natural language processing, intelligent tutoring systems, planning, and knowledge representation. These are deployed in the various components of the current FLUENT-2 system, organized as shown in Figure 10.1. The focus of this chapter is the tutorial module and how its decisions can provide a comprehensive and comprehensible series of conversations. Those tutorial decisions involve four sets of tutorial options: microworlds, types of moves in two-medium dialogues, what to say, and what to do. Schemas and relationships that organize these four sets of options include, respectively:

1. prerequisite relationships among the microworlds;
2. interaction types to deal with two-medium dialogue moves within a microworld (involving turn-taking in a conversation and whether to speak or to act);
3. situation viewpoints controlling what aspects of situations to talk about;
4. plan structures that permit coherent successions of actions within a single microworld.

This chapter treats the four respective sets of options, with their organizing structures, from a tutorial viewpoint. After an overview in this first section, the four categories of tutorial options are introduced ("Tutorial Choices"), then issues of design strategy are presented ("Taming the Problem"). In light of the mutual constraints among the

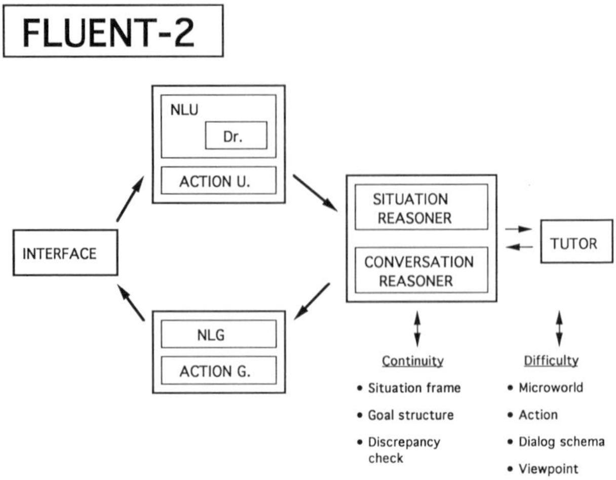

FIG. 10.1. System design of FLUENT-2. Student input goes from the interface either to the natural language understanding (NLU) system with its diagnoser (Dr) or to the action understanding module (ACTION U.). Based on reasoning operations, the tutor determines what to do and/or say. The resulting construction is transformed via the natural language generator (NLG) or the action generator (Action G.) or both. The results go to the student interface.

categories of options, the chapter concludes with proposals for integrative schemas to take advantage of the relationships and avoid incompatible choices.

Hamburger and Hashim (1992) present a declaration of the objectives, rationale, potential significance, and initial organization of the current FLUENT-2, along with a description of its predecessor, the working FLUENT-1 (Maney, 1992). Although the newer system is more ambitious in its conception, the two systems have the same goals and at first glance look similar to a user. In each, there are movable objects in a coherent scene on the computer screen as well as actions that can be carried out by both student and tutor as an integral part of a conversation. For example, Figure 10.2 shows a scene from the Kitchen World of FLUENT-2 in which a hand has picked up a cup and filled it with water from the spout. Each of these actions may have been done by either the student or the tutor. The difference between the two systems can be seen most clearly by noting that whereas an educational unit of FLUENT-1 combines a particular situation, language, and learning activity, these aspects and others are chosen independently in FLUENT-2.

This independence opens the door to additional languages and subject matter without reworking other parts of the system. By taking a generative approach to dialogue management, FLUENT-2 dramatically enhances the linguistic range of the tutor while continuing FLUENT-1's method of imposing conversational continuity on the tightly integrated linguistic and spatial communication between student and tutor

The progress reported here builds on earlier efforts in the project, such as those reported by Hashim and Hamburger (1992) and Hamburger, Tufis, and Hashim (1993).

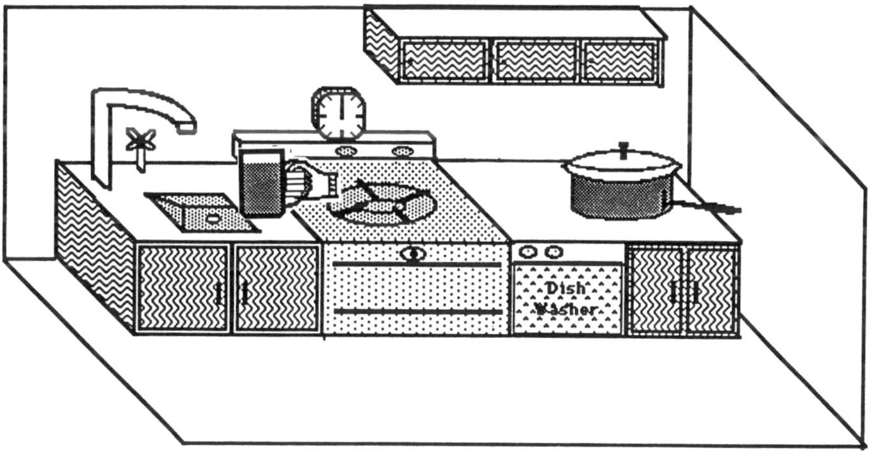

FIG. 10.2. Scene from Kitchen World in FLUENT-2. The system can comment on states of objects (e.g., "the water is on," "the cup is full"). It can also command relevant actions, (e.g., "turn on the water," "pick up the cup").

The current work heeds the cautionary remarks on the competition between conversational continuity and tutorial needs that appear in Hamburger and Maney (1991). It ties specific aspects of system design to successful second language pedagogy and appropriate second language research, such as work by Asher (1977), as reported in Hamburger (1993). The techniques of effective teaching and tutoring that we attempt to emulate are known to be exceedingly valuable, but let it be clear that other, complementary techniques are not meant to be excluded. Relevant to this point is a recent finding of apparent synergy between grammatical knowledge and in-country experience for advanced students of Russian (Brecht, Davidson, & Ginsberg, 1993) .

FLUENT-2 is attached to a large natural language processing system that has been developed by the Athena Language Learning Project (ALLP) of MIT (Felshin, this volume; Murray, this volume; Murray, Furstenberg, & Morgenstern, 1988) and adapted for us. The natural language processing, graphics, microworlds and tutorial reasoning are all in MCL2 Common Lisp with CLOS on a Mac-IIfx with 20MB of main memory.

Tutorial Choices

The tutorial module in FLUENT influences the learning environment by making choices about the four sets of options: microworlds, dialogue turns, what to say, and what to do. This section provides a brief introduction to each of these matters, in turn.

A microworld is an internal representation of the objects, actions, and plans that permit events to happen. For example, the microworld sampled in Figure 10.2 includes a hand that can operate on various kitchen objects in coherent, common-sense ways. In particular, Kitchen World incorporates a plan to boil water involving subplans for filling the pot with water from the tap and then heating it on a burner of the stove. Subplans are further broken down, ultimately into primitive actions such as turning on the water and picking up the pot. The subject matter of all the two-medium conversations in FLUENT is organized into microworlds. The student needs good microworlds and needs to be in the right one at the right time. This latter problem of global navigation is taken up later in this chapter, and the design of good microworlds is discussed in Hamburger (1993).

Each microworld contains representations of its objects and actions, which form the basis of the evolving situations for its particular topics, as well as associated tutorial information. Microworld objects (implemented as programming objects) have a complex structure because of their triple role for language, graphics, and internal representation. Objects are of various types or classes with individual properties (some inherited) and various relationships to each other. Among an object's properties may be one or more images showing it alone and, as relevant, held by a hand and/or in a sequence of animation positions. For example, the full cup held by a hand in Figure 10.2 is only the first in a long sequence of cup-in-hand images at various angles that permit an animation of pouring water out of the cup and restoring it to an upright orientation.

The dialogues that occur within a microworld are made up of moves, or basic communicative acts. To organize the move structure of the dialogues, we introduce the interaction type. An interaction is a short sequence of specified kinds of linguistic and spatial moves by the tutor and student. Choosing an interaction type determines, among other things, whether it is the tutor or the student who momentarily takes the initiative. Besides helping to organize the dialogue, interaction types are a useful tutorial tool because of their wide variation in difficulty, a point elaborated later in the chapter. These definitions are relevant to interaction types:

- agent: one of {student, tutor, a microworld character}.
- move type: one of {action, question, command, statement}.
- move specification: an agent, move-type pair.
- interaction type: a sequence of move specifications.

The simplest useful interactions consist of one linguistic or spatial move by the student or tutor and then a reaction by the other party. A pedagogically useful interaction type for language learning should have at least one linguistic move because purely graphical interaction does not advance the goal of language use. In terms of these definitions and ignoring the possibility of involving the microworld characters directly in an interaction, there are eight possibilities for a move specification: Either the tutor or the student makes one of the four move types—a graphical action or a linguistic question, command, or statement. Accompanying each of these possibilities with its anticipated response (e.g., question-answer, command-action) yields eight interaction types, four with the tutor going first and four at the initiative of the student. With the tutor going first and the student responding, we have

Celebrity:	T acts and S tells about it.
Quizmaster:	T asks a question and S answers it.
Commander:	T makes a command and S executes it.
Narrator:	T says something and S enacts it.

With the student going first and the roles reversed, we have

Movecaster:	S acts and T tells about it.
Oracle:	S asks a question and T answers it.
Servant:	S makes a command and T executes it.
Interpreter:	S says something and T enacts it.

Thus, in the Movecaster type, the student is at liberty to make any possible move, and the tutor then comments; in Celebrity, these roles are reversed; and so on. These names, initially a convenient shorthand for the tutor's roles, evoke motivationally useful and authentic personality traits (Murray, 1992) and suggest a step in the direction of well-motivated situations for language learning (Murray, 1990, 1991, this volume).

To keep matters relatively simple, these definitions omit the fact that the second move in an interaction (as well as the third and later ones if they exist) must be responsive to the move that precedes it. For example, in Quizmaster, the student's answer to the tutor's question should be a sentence in some cases but just a phrase or "yes" or "no" in others, and it should also constitute a relevant response. Another interaction type that includes constraints on student responses is a variation of Commander, in which the student's action is compared to the tutor's command. In this variation (which is under development) a follow-up third move comments on whether the student did in fact carry out the command.

The student has more freedom when going first in an interaction, as in Movecaster. Such freedom gives the student some local control over what to study; this can be beneficial to a student who sees how to take advantage of the situation. In some of the interaction types, however, the design must involve a little ingenuity to help the student make use of what is available. In Oracle, the student can ask questions but might well wonder what to ask. FLUENT-1 therefore includes a readily understood game in which the student must ask distinguishing questions to guess which one of three similar pictures the tutor has in mind (e.g., "Does the picture show a table?" "Is there a cup on the table?").

This list of interaction types does not exhaust the useful possibilities. It omits Tourguide, for example, which consists of three move specifications: an action by the tutor, a description of that action by the tutor, and an acknowledgment by the student. As used in FLUENT-1, Tourguide plays the important role of providing an initial exposure to a new microworld. For example, in a microworld designed to teach contrastive adjectives, the tutor highlights successive objects (e.g., a big black car then a small white car) and follows each with a distinguishing linguistic description. Variations of Tourguide in FLUENT-2 allow the description to precede or follow the action or both, giving a basis for variations in tense.

Within this framework for dialogue moves, the next tutorial problem concerns what to say. To see what is at stake here, suppose that the student has just made something happen in a Movecaster interaction so that the system's role is now to make a relevant comment. The most straightforward way to formulate a comment would be to say what the student did, using a representation of the microworld action that was just carried out. This representation would consist of an operator with its operands, for example, "You placed the cup on the table." Just such a representation is available in the FLUENT-2 action rules and can be transformed to an appropriate input for the ALLP natural language generation module, which outputs the resulting sentence. We do use such a technique, but rather than acting deterministically on only the one action-to-language connection just described, we interpose a wide-ranging choice of different approaches to constructing something to say, depending on the viewpoint assumed. For example, it might also be appropriate for Movecaster to say, "The cup is now on the table" or "You have finished setting the table." These situation viewpoints, as we call them, or simply views, play a key role in providing the linguistic variety that is essential to our conversational approach.

Because there are many views, we give categories rather than an exhaustive list. The categories of views discussed in this chapter include action-oriented views, state-oriented views, plan-oriented views, event-level views, contextual views, object-level views, and rejection views.

One *action* view describes the current action, another notes whether the commanded action was performed or not, and a third contrasts the current action with its predecessor. Among *state* views, the most straightforward is a comment on the new value of an object's attribute (e.g., "The cup is on the table"), but it is possible that it would take the form of a comment on the cessation of the corresponding previous value (e.g., "The cup is no longer in the cabinet"). Another state view is applicable if the new value is the same as the corresponding one for another object. One can then say, for example, that there are two cups on the table or that both cabinet doors are open. *Plan* views refer to, among other things, the completion of a plan or subplan (e.g., "The table is set"), transition from one subplan to the next, and the next action needed in the course of fulfilling the goal of the current plan (e.g., "You are ready to pour the coffee"). All these action and state views, along with some of the plan views, collectively make up the *event-level* views. Such views typically relate a kind of microworld action or relation to some specific arguments, all this being expressed linguistically within a single clause.

Often independently of choices at the event level, one can choose to comment in a variety of ways on broader, contextual aspects. Thus, the comments may occur at various relative times or may be posed in relation to the time of surrounding events (e.g., "You did this before that happened"). These options, along with recasting a proposition as a question, a command or descriptive statement, are some of the possible higher level or *contextual* views. Such views subsume events and are related to tense, aspect, and mood in language.

A third tutorially useful category of views, at a lower level, includes the *object-level* views, typically affecting noun phrases. These views determine what object or collectivity to talk about and how to refer to it in language. With a black and a gray cup, for example, a person can move the black one and then speak of the gray one as "the gray cup," "the other cup," "the second cup," or even "the cup that is still on the table." The fact that such noun phrase level choices can often be made independently of clause level choices makes it necessary to posit view structures, which specify both levels for a single sentence. Here, we continue to speak just of views and let context disambiguate. The operation of the view processor and its integration with the language generator is laid out in Hamburger and Hashim (1992); the operation of the generator itself, in Felshin (1993; this volume).

The next realm of tutorial choices concerns what to do. This means choosing one of the primitive actions in a microworld. These actions are represented as action rules and include things like turning a faucet on or off and picking up a movable object or putting it down onto an appropriate supporting object. To provide motivation and avoid confusion, these actions should proceed toward the completion of recognizable, coherent activities like brushing one's teeth, boiling a potato, or assembling the parts of something. Figure 10.3 illustrates the structure of such an activity.

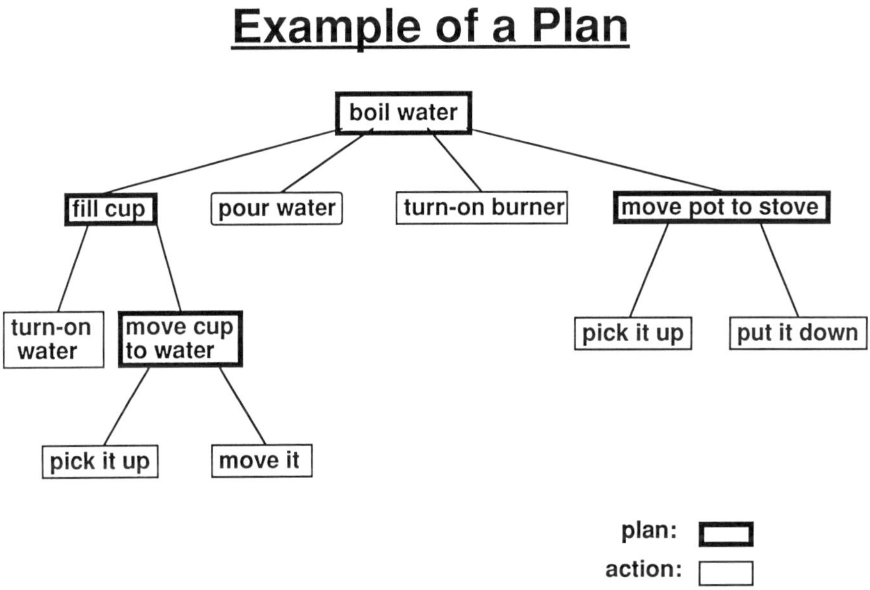

FIG. 10.3. Structure of an activity in FLUENT-2. A coherent sequence of actions is achieved by following the successive primitive actions at the bottom nodes in the tree. The top node is a plan; the nodes immediately below are subplans, and so on.)

The tutorial component must somehow be able to select sensible actions, both for itself to carry out and to form the basis of instructions to the student. Rigid action sequences, even if coherent, would not provide the basis for the tutor to be responsive to student initiative and progress. We therefore propose the use of flexible plan structures to organize actions (elaborated later in "Plans for Coordinated Tutoring"). This achieves the objectives just indicated without demanding that the microworld designer give a finely detailed specification to support a full treatment of common-sense reasoning. Plans can be used not only to select tutor actions but also to form the basis for issuing a coherent set of instructions or requests for student action or to generate sensible comments about student actions. Linguistically, plans allow discussion of discrete actions in terms of more abstract activities (e.g., tying one's shoe in terms of getting dressed) as well as relations like purpose (e.g., hammering a nail in terms of hanging the picture).

Four sets of tutorial options have been introduced. Later discussion focuses on how a tutorial module can integrate the use of these options to discharge its responsibility of managing a two-medium conversation. This management calls for drawing the student to the available variety of language aspects, both syntactic and lexical, in a manner that is consistent with the student's apparent partial knowledge of the situation and that avoids causing confusion by doing or saying things that do not fit the target language. The next section is devoted to reining in that problem.

Taming the Problem

In devising a tutor, it is easy to become ensnared in hard problems, notably cognitive modeling and dynamic tutorial planning. The strategy in FLUENT is to use heavy machinery only as needed. This section first looks at how to whittle down the tutorial problem by engaging the student to take over some of the decisions. The section next looks at how tutorial strategy can minimize reliance on a student model by identifying kinds of student moves that require particular tutorial responses without reference to student attributes. A student model will still be important, but a design of only moderate detail is proposed at the conclusion of this section.

Shared Control

The ultimate stratagem of tutorial management is to turn over decision-making responsibility to the student on the grounds that such active involvement can itself be beneficial. Moreover, the student may know better than the tutor what is needed, wanted, or has been assigned to learn. Degrees of this approach are possible by offering the student control of one or more of the four sets of options at various times. A student can first participate in choosing a microworld (discussed later under "Microworld Navigation"). Within a microworld, the student can be allowed to choose the type of interaction, or at least to declare that the current one is too easy or too difficult in the current situation. In addition to any such accommodations, the student has inherent local control of the evolution of microworld situations whenever the student has the first move in the interaction, as in Movecaster.

For these kinds of student involvement to be beneficial, some self-knowledge and judgment are required. Even then, there is the risk that tutorial planning chores may distract the student from the business at hand or that the student may fail to explore fully and utilize what the system has to offer. In any case, the tutor must be prepared to handle choices on the four tools at all times because the student may choose to relinquish control at any time. Decisions about sharing control constitute a potential fifth province of tutorial decision making.

Views as Tutorial Strategy

One way to keep tutorial strategy simple and to minimize reliance on a student model is to design direct tutorial reactions to particular kinds of situations in which it is clear what needs to be done, regardless of the student's characteristics. A candidate for such a reaction mechanism is what can appropriately be called a *rejection* view. This category of views gives rise to comments on disallowed and discouraged actions, such as, "Putting the cup in the window will not help to set the table." Two possible tutorial uses of these contextual level views are to correct misperceptions and to repair communications. A more whimsical use would apply to the Lingo microworld of devilish deeds (Murray, this volume). The key point with respect to taming the problem of student modeling is that the appropriateness of expressing a specific rejection view follows from the situation and not from the details of a student model.

Two rejection views that can respond to an inappropriate student action in Movecaster are to disallow the action because of an unsatisfied precondition, as in (1a) below, or an unwanted consequence as in (2a). Examples of tutor reactions generated by these views are respectively (1b) and (2b), the latter motivated by the mischievous Lingo character. Additional variants can be obtained by recombining the first part of (1a) with the second part of (2a). To make this recombination work, we put *but* or *because* in the first part of each rule. For the beginning student, views consisting of just *but* plus the second half of (1) and (2) would yield sentences that are easier to understand, such as "But the table would break."

1a. Some preconditions are satisfied, but
one precondition would be violated.
1b. "You can move the book, and it fits on the table, but
the load on the table would exceed its weight limit."
2a. The action is disallowed because
an unwanted consequence would occur.
2b. "You can not put the refrigerator on the table because
the table would break."

Granularity of the Student Model

Detailed student modeling is notoriously difficult for tutoring systems in general, partly because it must cope with the equivalent of the machine learning problem of assigning credit and blame to various pieces of knowledge and misconceptions of them. Beyond that, the thing to be learned in the tutoring system context is the student's cognitive state, which is a moving target. In our case, moreover, the domain is the unusually large and complex one of human language. Although we can reduce this difficult domain to a series of increasing sublanguages (i.e., subsets of the specification of the target language), that stratagem carries the danger of finding fault with a student for having picked up correct bits of the language that are outside the current sublanguage. Another strategic compromise is to diagnose the current input from the student on the basis of a static, generic student model that includes popular misconceptions about language labeled as such. This strategy is used by Malone and Felshin (1992) with a best-first parser (see also Felshin, this volume).

The approach proposed here is to use an individual student model that, per the suggestion of Self (1990), has only as much precision as the tutorial module is going to put to use. The information recorded in the student model reflects performance with respect to the sets of tutorial options. Thus, for each microworld and interaction type, the model records how well the student is doing with respect to each combination of an object/action/plan and a relevant view. For each combination the tutor needs to know whether the student has had Tourguide exposure to it and whether the student's comprehension of it in Commander (where the student acts) has been good enough to warrant trying it with Quizmaster (where the student produces language). Finally, such records provide the basis for a decision to leave the microworld after generally good performance on the most demanding interaction type.

Microworld Navigation

The tutor must be able to decide when to abandon the current microworld and which new one to move to. A student not wishing to make such a shift may be allowed to override this decision. Generally speaking, there are two opposite reasons for leaving: mastery and unpreparedness. A judgment of unpreparedness needs to be made when the student model indicates that the student cannot function well in the current microworld even with the other parameters (i.e., for selecting action, view, and interaction type) at settings that are easy. Interaction type plays a particularly important role in this connection because it varies strongly in difficulty, as discussed in the next section. A judgment of unpreparedness for a microworld also should occur if the student is too slow to succeed in the more challenging interaction types despite adequate exposure to the less challenging types. In contrast, mastery of a microworld is judged only in terms of success in the most challenging interaction types. A student who is well prepared for a microworld can be permitted to make only limited use of the easiest interaction types in that world.

Having decided that the student is to leave a microworld, the tutor must pick a new one. Alternatively, the student may wish to leave but want a recommendation for where to go. In either case, the tutor needs information about relationships among microworlds, particularly prerequisite relationships. A student who departs a microworld when doing poorly can profitably go to an easier environment that permits preparation for the departed microworld. That environment could be either a subworld or some other microworld that provides practice on prerequisite language knowledge. If, on the other hand, the student has apparently mastered the current world, the tutor should change to a more demanding one. This could be one for which the current world provides some prerequisite knowledge and for which any other prerequisites are also met. Alternatively, it might be a super-world of the current world, it might be found on an agenda of microworlds to visit, or it might be next on a default ordering.

Finding easier and harder microworlds has been described in terms of prerequisite language knowledge. The language aspects that constitute that knowledge can be lexical, syntactic, or semantic. To use these aspects in creating a prerequisite structure, we propose to associate with each microworld two lists: the language aspects it requires and those for which it provides exposure, possibly learning, and hence the satisfaction of prerequisites of other worlds. In this way prerequisites induce an implicit AND/OR graph of microworlds (cf. Hamburger and Maney, 1991).

Interaction Type Difficulty

The task demands of the interaction types vary widely. Tourguide and Movecaster are linguistically unchallenging. They allow the student to become familiar with what can be done in a new microworld and gain exposure to what can be said about it. For these interaction types, the student model need only include a record of what the student has been exposed to and how often. Commander is a step up in difficulty, requiring comprehension but not production. The level of difficulty is greatest for those interaction types that require a student to produce the most language, notably Servant and Oracle, for which the student issues full-sentence commands and queries respectively. Although Quizmaster requires the student to produce an answer, that answer can vary from a one-word response to yes/no questions, through noun phrase answers to "what" questions, to full sentential responses to "why" and "when" questions.

The interaction types differ not only in difficulty but also in how informative they are about the student's knowledge. In fact, the more challenging an interaction type, the more informative it can be about what the student knows. However, if the challenge is so great that the student makes several errors, nothing specific can be inferred with confidence about what the student does not know because performance factors may intervene. The need for information about a student's knowledge relates directly to uncertainty levels in the student model. That uncertainty is likely to be high for a new student who already has obtained some knowledge elsewhere. Finally, interaction types differ in the kind of syntactic features they exercise. Most salient are the variations in sentence structure required by declaratives, imperatives, and questions.

Views and Their Relationships

A key pedagogical purpose of views on what to say is linguistic variety, as described earlier. It is also true that views, like microworlds and interaction types, differ in difficulty, thereby providing another tool with which to adjust language output to the level of the student. Not only are some views more difficult than others, but also the mere fact of varying views presents a challenge. It is important to note, however, that although adding views expands conversational flexibility, this very flexibility may cause ambiguity about what is being said. Careful control of the use of views, and/or parallel development of ways to communicate visually the corresponding ideas, is necessary so that ambiguity does not undermine the FLUENT immersion strategy and the student will have a basis for inferring the view in use at any time.

Although numerical evaluations of difficulty have a role to play in tutorial decisions, they cannot serve alone. Selecting combinations of action, view, and interaction type such that the combined difficulty scores come out right will not guarantee sound pedagogy or reasonable dialogue. Moreover, some views do not even apply in certain circumstances. For example, plan views do not make sense in Movecaster, where the student is allowed to initiate arbitrary actions. To impose the necessary constraints on the use of views, we incorporate view selection in a new and slightly more complicated version of interaction types. In particular, a view-constrained interaction type is the result of letting each linguistic move in an interaction type be optionally attached to a single view or set of views, as opposed to permitting random attachments. This modification is necessary anyway because Commander and Quizmaster require the tutor's language move to be a command or question, respectively.

Views and interaction types can also work together to introduce a plan. Once a plan has been selected, a domain plan executor can introduce it using Tourguide along with two simple views: describe action and describe plan (illustrated earlier). As the plan is executed, Tourguide comments on what is happening by using an action view or a plan view, as appropriate, at the level of the overall plan, subplans, or individual actions (see Figure 10.3).

Having related views to interaction types, we turn to coordination of views with plans. Consider what should happen upon entry to a microworld to familiarize the student with what it is about and how to talk about it. Relations in the microworld (*on*, *under*, etc.) can be demonstrated by introducing objects to serve as the arguments of the relation and then performing some action that causes the relation to be satisfied. The support relation is a good example here because it is already satisfied by the process of introducing a movable object. After completion of the plan that achieves the relation in the microworld—say, a table supporting a cup—it is essential that the tutor mention that fact (e.g., "The cup is on the table") as opposed to, say, describing the action that made it hold (e.g., "The cup was placed on the table"); otherwise, the point of the introduction is lost. In other words, the appropriate view for describing relations, a state-oriented view, should accompany the plan that is appropriate for introducing relations.

Views have a more pervasive relationship to microworlds than has been shown in the foregoing comments relating them to plans. To apply across a spectrum of microworlds and situations, views are defined generically, rather than in terms of particular actions, plans, object states, or object relations. Views are thus abstractions of what the tutor can say. For the tutor actually to say something, a view must be fleshed out by particular instances of objects, relations, goal structures, and events in the microworld. It is thus appropriate for the view processor to take as inputs both the current view, selected by the tutorial component, and information from the microworld. The needed microworld information concerns principally the current event but may also involve information about the plan it is part of, the objects it acted on, and the changes it caused.

The relevant information for a view is found in a variety of locations in the microworld representations. Perhaps the most important source of information is the current action, expressed as an action rule object. Its relevant slots for this purpose are its header, goal, and knowledge updates. An object-level view must consult dialogue history as well as object attributes to give phrases like "the rest of the big cups," for which some cup must have already been mentioned and must be one of three or more big ones. A plan-oriented view must consult the plan stack to know the current plan and where the current action fits into it. One kind of plan view, which we call "initial subplan," would generate something like, "To do x, first <agent> does x1," where x1 is the first subplan of x. This plan view anticipates and requires that the execution of the current plan be at a particular kind of node in a tree of plans—specifically, beginning the first subplan. Similarly, a relevant view at the transition from one subplan to the next should produce "Now that <result-state-1>, do <subplan-2>," where <result-state-1> is based on the microworld update slot of subplan-1 and "do" is used to indicate an imperative form for subplan-2.

Plans for Coordinated Tutoring: Programming Specifics

Plans play the key role in organizing microworld activity, but simply executing them is not enough. They must be integrated with the other tutorial tools discussed previously. The next section elaborates on mechanisms by which plan implementation can allow for the needed flexibility and coordination. An important extension to plans then follows.

Plan Flexibility and Integration

Plans are flexible in important ways. First, they can apply to any available objects that meet the type constraints on their operands. Second, a parameterized goal associated with each action or plan makes it possible to detect when that action or subplan can be skipped because its goal has already been met. Finally, plans can explicitly allow for alternative sequencing and alternative subplans wherever the microworld designer finds such options appropriate. Note that microworld design is a factor too. For example, a real person (with two hands) can turn on a water faucet either before or after picking up a bar of soap, but a microworld character with only one movable hand, a constraint in FLUENT-1, should follow a fixed order and pick up the soap first.

The first source of flexibility, that a plan or action can apply to any appropriate available objects, arises from the use of variables. These appear in the header of the action or plan as arguments, along with the name of the action or plan. Each variable is constrained according to what physical things it can be bound to in the microworld. Variables not only occur in the header but are scattered throughout the other slots and get instantiated (bound) on the fly, that is, in the course of execution of the plan or action. For example, a plan may call for filling a cup with water by picking the cup up, putting it under the faucet, and so on. The FILL plan and the PICK-UP action both have a variable that has CUP as its class constraint (and there may be other variables). When the tutor executes the PICK-UP action in the course of executing the FILL plan, the variable becomes bound to a particular cup, and that binding must be respected elsewhere in the plan. The treatment of the scope of binding is analogous to that of logic programming. This arrangement makes it possible for the electronic tutor to reason independently about good plans to invoke and good objects to use within that plan, because the plan execution algorithm can select available objects and bind the variables as it goes along.

Another source of plan flexibility involves associating parameterized goals to detect when an action or subplan may be skipped. Here, an explicit stack of what is left to do in a plan permits tutorial coordination by allowing plan execution to be interleaved with other activities, as in Tourguide or Commander. If the intervening activity is question asking, in Quizmaster or Oracle, the plan can be simply resumed because questions leave the state of the microworld intact. If, however, the intervening activity is a series of actions that disturb the state of the microworld, as in Movecaster, the system must rely on goals, a third contributor to flexibility, to resume the plan smoothly. The original top-level plan in Commander or Tourguide is restored to the plan stack after clearing away all other plans. The plan executor then formally starts all over again, but because it always checks the goal of each action or subplan and skips any whose goals are already met, it appears to be acting sensibly and not reversing or repeating actions.

The third source of flexibility comes from explicit specification of alternative sequencing in the execution of a plan's subplans and actions. The range of orderings give a degree of flexibility consistent with the plan being executed by a single well-organized agent. The value of a plan's subplan slot is a list of the form (<type> <pal>*), where <type> is one of the atoms SEQ, MIX, or ONE, and each <pal> is a simple plan, an action, or (recursively) a list of this same form. An action or a simple plan has the form (<name> <arg>*), just as in a header but with no class constraints. SEQ denotes an ordered sequence, MIX an unordered list, and ONE a choice of exactly one. For example, (seq A1 (mix A2 A3) (one P1 P2)) means to do action A1, then actions A2 and A3 in either order, and finally one of the plans P1 or P2. The plan stack holds subplans of this form, along with lists of variable bindings. When the plan executor pops a subplan with SEQ with at least two <pal>s left, it executes the first and puts back the rest. MIX is handled similarly, but the <pal> selected for execution and removal is random. For ONE there is just a pop and random selection.

Homogeneous Plans

The need to extend the notion of a plan can be seen by considering what happens on entry to a new microworld. At that point, the student needs to be introduced to the contents of the microworld, the actions and events that can happen in it, and how to affect the situation via the interface. Language learning should proceed, of course, during this initial exposure to the microworld. There are various ways to begin, such as introducing the objects, the properties, the actions, and so on. We consider a sequence of introductions of objects, and more precisely, to keep matters coherent, the introduction of an object and then its direct parts (not including parts of the parts). One might choose for this purpose any coherently selected set of objects from a microworld. A coherent set includes all those of some type, all those having some particular property value, or an object and a set of other objects all related to the initial one in the same way (e.g., a person and his or her items of clothing, or a tray and the things on it). These activities may seem very simple, but they are no simpler than what good human tutors do (Douglas, this volume; Tomlin, this volume;).

Each introduction is by definition an action because something that happens in a microworld is always an action. Furthermore, an organized sequence of actions is a plan, so the sequence of introductions described above is a plan—a homogeneous one, in that it consists entirely of a single kind of action (introduction) executed repeatedly over the objects in some list. More generally, a homogeneous plan can iterate over a plan instead of an action. Homogeneous plans can be useful not only for introductions but also for providing practice on a particular verb or construction. Plan specification now also allows (LOOP <name> <pos> <class> <arg>*), where <name> and <arg>* are as defined earlier (see "Plan Flexibility and Integration") and LOOP signifies homogeneity; <pos> indicates the position of the iterative argument in the <arg> list and <class> is its range of values, expressed as a list or a class.

Tutorial Schemas

A crucial remaining issue is how to organize the interplay of these sets of options within a microworld to yield a coherent, flexible, tutorially sound session. We are working on two approaches to organizing options. Each assumes that the choice of microworld itself can be made in accordance with the considerations and specifications offered earlier in the discussion of microworld navigation. In each approach, it is assumed that the various options available at any time have numerical difficulty values that can be used in a computation to ensure an appropriate overall level of challenge without frustration. It is the second approach that introduces tutorial schemas.

The first approach relies on a stability prioritization in which actions change the most frequently, views on what to say are reconsidered less often, interaction types still less often, and microworlds least often of all. When the actions of a plan have been completed, the view regimen (which may be a single view but may alternatively call for some form of alternation among two or three views) is subject to reappraisal to adjust the difficulty level. When the view possibilities attached to the current microworld have been exhausted, it is time for a new and more challenging interaction type or a new regimen involving more than one. Finally, when the relevant interaction modes are finished, it is time to change microworlds. Each change at a higher level in the stability ladder causes a reset at all the lower levels.

The second approach to tutoring decisions within microworlds relies on structures that we call tutorial schemas. The simplest such schema is a (<plan>, <vit>) pair, where <vit> abbreviates view-constrained interaction type. The <vit> may be formed by adding view constraints to an unconstrained interaction type or by further constraining an existing <vit>. A single action or no action (i.e., the null action) may serve in place of a whole plan; these are merely degenerate cases. Each plan variable may be instantiated, subject to its class constraints (except for the iterative argument in a homogeneous plan). Any uninstantiated variable is in effect a parameter of the tutorial schema. The interpretation in this first case, where the schema is simply one (<plan>, <vit>) pair, is that the steps of the plan are to be executed while the <vit> is held fixed. A finite sequence of (<plan>, <vit>) pairs also counts as a tutorial schema. Further flexibility comes readily by letting the <vit> be replaced by a regular expression of <vit>s. Thus generalized, tutorial schemas provide a workable approach to coordinating choices on the three dimensions of tutorial choice within a microworld (i.e., interaction types, views, and actions). Like domain-level plans, tutorial schemas afford flexibility and expressiveness without requiring the system to do excessively detailed reasoning. The level of granularity is intended to be comprehensible to a pedagogical expert, who could be consulted on the construction of potentially useful schemas.

The role and potential benefit of tutorial schemas can be seen in a simple example that pairs the homogeneous introduction plan with the Tourguide interaction type, constrained by an appropriate view. The introduction plan calls for showing the contents of the microworld to the entering student. The list of objects required by the plan corresponds to the one parameter of this tutorial schema. Because any microworld in which a coherent list of objects can be specified can play that role, the schema is microworld independent. The choice of a view to be used in this tutorial schema hinges on some special properties of introduction actions, which should yield sentences like "This is an X" or "An X also has a Y" rather than sentences like "The tutor introduced an X." Further, although the visible action that realizes the introduction may be a movement, the sentence should not be "The X moved to/onto the Y." A view must be used that is understood to call for these distinctions, and the view processor must react to it appropriately.

Whatever is specified in a tutorial schema has the status of being preferred, not required. If the chosen tutorial schema calls for some view that is not possible in the current state of the current microworld, it is understood that some other view can be used instead. Contextual, event-level, and object-level views, as well as view structures consisting of views on more than one of these levels, can all be designated by the tutor as desirable provided that they are possible. The event-level view takes precedence. At each level, the tutor can specify a list of views in priority order.

Although introductions are an important phase of use for a microworld, there are other phases that warrant attention. One of them, the normal use and progress phase, should be readily handled by the tutorial schemas previously defined. However, a third important phase, error recovery, may present different requirements. Although correction is not emphasized in the conversational methods that influence the design of FLUENT, there are times when correction is pedagogically appropriate. Some errors call for immediate correction, without reference to a student model, either because of their seriousness or to repair the conversation so as to avoid damaging misunderstandings. Correction may also become the move of choice after consulting the student model and finding that the current error has occurred frequently for this student, so that immersion is not proving adequate on the particular aspect. Intelligent long-term diagnosis of error patterns may be desirable in other environments (Tasso, Fum, & Giangrandi, 1992). Error correction is a concern here because an error may interrupt or violate an inadequately designed schema. We are currently considering whether the additional overhead of a transition network is needed for error correction. One might then define error-correction subnets that are entered via conditional push arcs. Upon popping from the error-correction net, the system would resume at the appropriate node in the interrupted tutorial schema.

The representation for tutorial schemas allows for the possibility of more than one (<plan>, <vit>) pair, but the examples so far have been limited to a single pair. Now consider a tutorial sequence that alternates between Tourguide and Celebrity in which each occurrence of Celebrity is constrained to use the same action or plan as the Tourguide interaction immediately preceding it. Such a sequence would allow the tutor to carry out an introduction of some sort in Tourguide and then run through the action or sequence of actions in Celebrity, having the student give the description, presumably making use of the language that has just been promoted in Tourguide. For matters to proceed like this, not only must the action or plan be the same with each of the two interaction types, but it must also be instantiated the same way both times. A suitable tutorial schema here although not necessarily with the same variable bindings each time. It may be wise to use a cyclic plan as p1, that is, one that restores the microworld to the state it was in at the start of executing that plan.

Acknowledgments

This work is supported by grant IRI-9020711 from the National Science Foundation.

References

Asher, J. (1977). *Learning another language through actions: The complete teacher's guidebook.* Los Gatos, CA: Sky Oaks Publications.

Brecht, R.D., Davidson, D., & Ginsberg, R.B. (1993). Predictors of foreign language gain during study abroad. *NFLC Occasional Papers.* Washington, DC: The National Foreign Language Center.

Felshin, S. (1993). *A guide to the Athena language learning project natural language processing system* (Athena Project Technical Report). Cambridge, MA: Massachusetts Institute of Technology.

Hamburger, H. (1993, October). *SCIALogie and FLUENT: Pedagogy and microworlds for language immersion and tutoring.* Paper presented at the Workshop on Cognitive Science, Computer Science and Acquisition of Language, Clermont-Ferrand, France.

Hamburger, H., & Hashim, R. (1992). Foreign language tutoring and learning environment. In M. Swartz & M. Yazdani (Eds.), *Intelligent tutoring systems for foreign language learning* (pp. 201-218). New York: Springer-Verlag.

Hamburger, H., & Maney, T. (1991). Twofold continuity in language learning. *Computer-Assisted Language Learning, 4*, 81-92.

Hamburger, H., Tufis, D., & Hashim, R. (1993). *Generating natural language in an immersive language learning system.* Eindhoven, Netherlands: NATO-ASI.

Hashim, R., & Hamburger, H. (1992). Discourse style and situation viewpoint for a conversational language tutor. *Proceedings of the International Conference on Computer-Assisted Learning.* New York: Springer-Verlag.

Malone, S., & Felshin, S. (1991). GLR parsing for erroneous input. In M. Tomita (Ed.), *Generalized LR parsing.* Norwell, MA: Kluwer.

Maney, T. (1992, September). *FLUENT-1: A demonstration.* Presented at the Second International Conference on Intelligent Tutoring Systems, Montreal, Canada.

Murray, J. H. (1990). Emerging genres of interactive videodiscs for language instruction. *Multimedia and language learning.* Institute for Academic Technology, Chapel Hill, NC: Academic Computing Publications, University of North Carolina.

Murray, J. H. (1991). Anatomy of a new medium: Literary and pedagogic uses of advanced linguistic computer structures. *Computers and the Humanities, XXV*, 1-14.

Murray, J. H. (1992). Restructuring time, space, story, and text in advanced multimedia learning environments. In E. Barrett (Ed.), *The social creation of knowledge.* Cambridge, MA: MIT Press.

Murray, J. H., Furstenberg, G., & Morgenstern, D. (1988). The Athena language learning project: Design issues for the next generation of computer-based language learning tools. In F. Smith (Ed.), *Modern technology in foreign language education.* Lincolnwood, IL: NIC Publishing Group.

Self, J. A. (1990). Bypassing the intractable problem of student modelling. In C. Frasson & C. Gauthier (Eds.), *Proceedings of the Montreal Conference on Intelligent Tutoring Systems.* Norwood, NJ: Ablex.

Tasso, C., Fum, D., & Giangrandi, P. (1992). The use of explanation-based learning for modeling student behavior in foreign language tutoring. In M. Swartz & M. Yazdani (Eds.), *Intelligent tutoring systems for foreign language learning* (pp. 151-170). New York: Springer-Verlag.

11

LingWorlds: An Intelligent Object-Oriented Environment for Second Language Tutoring

Sarah A. Douglas
University of Oregon

Oral communication skills—the ability to comprehend and produce oral discourse—are crucial in nearly every educational, business, and scientific setting of language use. Yet the development of oral communication skills remains a difficult theoretical and practical problem, and traditional language teaching approaches regularly fail to help many learners. The central problem addressed by this research project was to design a computer assisted language instruction system that could help beginning language learners develop their aural comprehension abilities. The reasons for targeting beginners as well as listening comprehension were threefold. First, relatively little software is directed at true beginners. Second, relatively little software is directed at improving listening comprehension. Third, the computer environment is best suited to work in teaching listening.

The LingWorlds project, initiated by Russell Tomlin (this volume) and me, draws on two important and innovative approaches to second language learning and teaching: the communicative and the comprehension approaches. Proponents of the communicative approach argue that successful language learning occurs when the student is provided the opportunity to solve nonlanguage problems using the developing second language (Krashen, 1982; Widdowson, 1978). They criticize traditional language teaching for focusing too much effort on the conscious discussion and manipulation of rules of language usage and not enough effort on the acquisition of the second language grammar through using that grammar to solve actual communication problems. This philosophy integrates well with the general spirit of artificial intelligence approaches to education wherein teaching and learning are conceptualized as problem-solving processes.

Proponents of the comprehension approach argue that second language learning is enhanced when beginning stages of language learning are devoted to developing the ability to understand the second language. Both obligatory oral production and reading and writing are delayed until the student is able to understand utterances easily in the second language. Delaying production appears to improve student performance in other aspects of language acquisition (Asher, 1966, 1969, 1977; Postovsky, 1977, 1979; Winitz, 1981; Winitz & Reeds, 1973).

Our project embraces both of these complementary approaches to language learning and teaching. The instructional system we have created, called LingWorlds, involves the student in solving communicative problems interactively with the system. The student participates in problem-solving simulations that allow the student to manipulate objects in a physical scenario or microworld. Information about the problem to be solved and information about the microworld are given orally in the second language. Metalevel commentary by the tutor is also in the second language. The teaching intervention in these simulations can vary from highly directed tutoring, where the tutor issues directions for action, to coaching, to purely student-controlled exploration. LingWorlds uses dynamically generated speech from a digitized phrasal lexicon to produce its side of the tutor-student dialogue. The student's part of the dialogue consists of acts in the microworld. Thus, LingWorlds in its directed tutoring mode conforms to the type of conversational interaction in which the tutor plays the role of Commander, according to the framework defined by Hamburger (this volume) to characterize two-medium (i.e., verbal and visual) dialogues. The chapter by Tomlin in this volume focuses on a precursor to LingWorlds, called Flatland, designed to support research into the discourse structure of tutoring dialogues.

The pedagogical model behind LingWorlds requires many small problem-solving environments as well as many simple tutoring control strategies. These requirements motivated us to create a high-level authoring system. Our general philosophy in constructing this system is that we wanted the microworlds to be very knowledge-intensive and totally integrated with the interface. We also wanted them to be reusable. These two themes have pushed us to envision a sort of library of microworlds and tutoring components. LingWorlds, which is a full object-oriented programming system, offers the teacher a rather large amount of programming power, if the teacher wants to use it, while permitting teachers who have less experience with the facility to build on simple simulations previously stored in a library.

Before the particulars of LingWorlds as a language tutoring system are discussed, an explanation of the pedagogy on which it rests is provided to help readers who may be unfamiliar with these approaches.

Communicative Studies of Human Language Tutoring

Perhaps the most fundamental question for this project was posed early on: What is it that tutors using the communicative/comprehension approach teach, and how do they decide what to do at any given point in a tutorial interaction? An answer to this compound question is needed if the computer tutor is to perform in a way similar to human tutors. The existing literature in communicative language teaching provides only the most general guidelines regarding what is taught and how that teaching is accomplished (see MacWhinney, this volume; Garrett, this volume). Such guidelines are not specific enough to incorporate in any way in the tutor system. Consequently, we have devoted considerable effort to studying the nature of individual foreign language tutoring in specific situations. Before these studies are described, a summary is provided of the general guidance coming out of the literature in communicative language teaching.

Communicative Language Teaching: General Assumptions

The communicative approach (Widdowson, 1978, 1979) views language learning as a social and cognitive enterprise in which the learner entertains multiple hypotheses regarding the structure and function of target language constituents in natural discourse contexts until sufficient contextualized input is encountered to settle on and automate the learner's closest approximation of the native speaker norms. This process of creative construction of an *interlanguage grammar* (Selinker, 1972) is facilitated when linguistic input is comprehensible to the learner (Krashen, 1977, 1982), when it is of sufficient quantity in a variety of discourse contexts, and when the affective environment does not constrain exploration and risk taking (Krashen, 1977, 1982; Schumann, 1978).

This general characterization can be elaborated by a number of tenets of the communicative approach. This approach views language as situated social activity, as an effort of discourse production and comprehension, as *communication.* Thus, in communicative language teaching, systematic attention is paid to functional as well as structural aspects of language. Additionally, classroom work is aimed at the situational and contextualized use of language, and teaching and learning are made observable and transparent through content that is made real to the learner through pictures, sketches, diagrams, and other representations. Attention is focused on the ability to understand and convey information (i.e., on information transfer), and the learner is seen as a responsible partner in learning rather than as an object to be manipulated.

Applying this approach to early language teaching specifically (i.e., starting with a nil-proficiency learner) emphasizes acquisition of linguistic pragmatics, particularly, development of the following aspects:

- lexicon or vocabulary,
- the grammar of spatial relations,
- the grammar of reference including deictic (e.g., in English, *this one, that one*) and pronominal expression (e.g., *it*, *them*),
- basic syntax and word order,
- article systems (e.g., *a*, *the*).

Communicative language teaching represents the effort by the tutor to set up the conditions for learning just described. That is, with more or less finely grained teaching efforts, the tutor seeks to provide to the learner a sufficient quantity of comprehensible input drawn from a wide variety of genuine or authentic discourse contexts (Johnson, 1982; Krashen & Terrell, 1983; Widdowson, 1978) in an affectively supportive environment.

Although these observations represent some of the general principles defining the communicative approach, the general principles do little to tell us exactly what teachers manipulate in tutoring and when and how they do it. In our efforts, then, we developed an approach that yielded concrete understanding of what tutors do when they teach.

Empirical Study 1: Protocols of Face-to-Face Human Tutor-Student Pairs

In the first study we videotaped instances of language tutoring using a constrained semantic domain, employing human tutors and students from the American English Institute at the University of Oregon. The tutors engaged in one-on-one, face-to-face tutorials with learners of English who had nil proficiency in the language and whose native language was not Indo-European. Five of the students were tutored by a master teacher who had many years of experience in the communicative method. Two students were tutored by another tutor who was a relative novice to the method but an experienced teacher of English as a second language. The tutor was directed to teach the English expressions for two-dimensional spatial relations (specifically, *above*, *below*, *to the left of*, *right of*, and *between*) by guiding the student through a series of problem-solving tasks with directions exclusively in English. The task used a set of eight cardboard circles and squares differing in size (large or small) and color (red or blue). The tutor and student sat across from each other with a table between them. Video cameras captured activities on the table and interaction between the participants.

Seven dialogues from these interactions were collected on videotape. The protocols varied in length from 20 to 41 minutes. The videotapes were treated as the transcript, and analysis of the discourse was performed by exhaustive viewing of the tapes. It is important to emphasize that this teaching task was previously unknown to both tutors. They were not allowed time to prepare a fixed curriculum. Our reasoning behind this measure was that not only did we want to capture dynamic, interactive natural language but we also wanted to observe real-time problem solving in a teaching situation.

The analysis of these tutoring sessions followed a discourse model developed by Sinclair and Coulthard (1975) but formally specified and elaborated to provide a sufficient description for an intelligent tutoring system (ITS) for these language tutoring sessions. The complete description of this method of analysis and formalization is published in Douglas (1991). However, a brief description follows to give the reader a general idea of the method.

The tutoring interactions consisted of a number of distinct segments of dialogue, which we have termed exercises, that have a goal of teaching a particular concept of the curriculum, in this case a spatial relation. The length of these exercises varied from 2 to 15 minutes. The more experienced tutor included six or seven of these exercises, which followed a consistent pattern in all her protocols. The novice tutor included nine exercises in each of her sessions but made major changes in sequence between the first and second learner. Within each exercise occurred what we have termed episodes (or alternatively, exchanges) consisting of rhetorical acts. A variable number of acts made up an exercise. No fixed ordering of these acts within exercises was observed, probably due to the dynamic nature of the tutoring situation, where the next act depended on the many factors that made up the control of discourse. A partial ordering was, however, evident. Acts were classified into one of eight classes of common motivating factors, which were formally defined by precondition states of the tutoring goals and curriculum structure, by assumptions about the student model, by the context of the objects on the table, and by the history of student (or tutor) failure and repair.

For example, suppose we wish to explain the following discourse segment, which begins with a context of circles and squares constructed by previous interaction, as shown in Figure 11.1 (in the normal display, black objects would be "red"; white would be "blue"):

Tutor: "Now, take the small red circle"
<pause>
Student: <takes the card and moves it to the side of the table>
Tutor: "and put that below the large red circle."
Student: <hesitates>
Tutor: "Below the large red circle."
Student: <pushes the small red circle to below the large red circle>

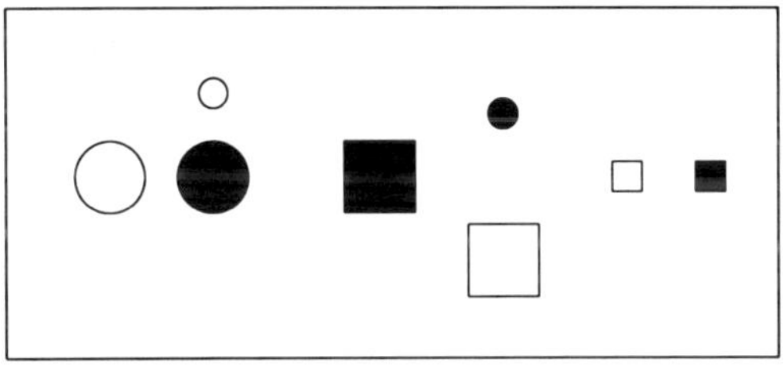

FIG. 11.1. Interim configuration of shapes in a problem-solving task used to tutor English.

The discourse segment consists of three episodes, denoted by the three separate acts of the tutor with corresponding nonverbal responses by the student. The tutor's first two acts (i.e., identifying the object, then requesting the action) are diagnostic, and the third is a repetition of the previous referent phrase (*below the large red circle*) for clarification. What is immediately apparent is that the episodes must be coded at a level below the sentence and clause, usually at the phrase or even single lexical item level. Tutors often strategically break sentences into diagnostic units such as these, with the effect of reducing the complexity of identifying where the student's misconception occurs (e.g., whether it is the noun referent or the verb action that is known or unknown to the student at a given stage). Tomlin (this volume) discusses more about these strategies and how they are reflected in the structure of sentences and dialogue. A second observation from the discourse segment is that many of the interaction cues are nonverbal—consisting of hesitations, intonations, physical actions, and so forth. Tutors observed all student actions intently during their performance to ascertain whether trouble was imminent.

Empirical Study 2: Protocols of Machine-Mediated Human Tutor-Student Pairs

After studying face-to-face human tutors and students and observing the large amount of nonverbal interaction that was present in the interactions, we decided that we needed to study how human tutors adapt to a tutoring situation where the tutor, like the computer, has a much more constrained environment without access to visual information on the movements of the learner's face, hands, and eyes. In the second study we programmed a computer-manipulable version of the previous cardboard circles and squares task, called FlatLand. In this version, the tutor was given a teaching environment consisting of an inventory of eight circles and squares (although black and white) that she or he could move using a mouse. The objects were initially located in a "stock," itself located in the right margin of the screen and separated from the main demonstration area by a vertical line. The student was given a second, separate computer system including a mouse. All actions occurring on both computer screens were equally visible to the tutor and student. Tutor and student had oral access to each other but could not see each other. Six native English-speaking students participated in this study. Three were taught Indonesian and three Japanese. All tutors were native speakers. A complete analysis of this study has been done by Ungar and Smith (1987), who paid particular attention to more refined analysis of the rhetorical acts, event networks, and the role of repetition in teaching with the communicative approach.

From these two studies, we were able to extract significant components and principles of second language tutorials regarding rhetorical acts in communicative and comprehension-based language teaching, control strategy of the tutors, the handling of tutoring and linguistic failure and repair, the role of nonverbal interaction, and the limitations of existing technology to support this method. These studies provided theoretical insights into the linguistic structure of tutoring discourse, explored in the chapter by Tomlin (this volume). Moreover, these studies provided much of the detailed empirical experience that we needed to grasp the basic demands of a computer-based system. Many of these insights are built into the LingWorlds system described here.

Empirical Study 3: Survey of Communicative Language Teaching Targeting Listening Comprehension Examples

Although the previous empirical studies provided us with much-needed knowledge about the process of teaching in the communicative method, we were still relatively uncertain about what constituted a suitable set of exercises for learning a language by means of listening to and carrying out directions for a problem-solving task. We searched the pedagogical and theoretical literature in second language learning and teaching, and we interviewed practicing second language teachers to create an inventory of listening activities. The inventory of activities is organized to reveal necessary prerequisite skills required to perform the target task, learning goals for the task, expected outcomes for the task, methods of presenting or executing the task, and means of evaluating the effectiveness of the task.

Although we conducted no original work in this area, the inventory remains useful in organizing suggestions for practicing teachers who might be interested in using the computer tutor system. These insights are reflected in a number of the LingWorlds exercises and in the LingWorlds teacher's manual.

Combining Communicative and Comprehension Approaches in LingWorlds

Overall Approach

It is clear from the previous descriptions that implementing an intelligent tutor would demand a number of compromises. First and foremost, the computer system would not have the ability to assess students' physical responses beyond the simplistic mouse actions of pointing, dragging, and button pressing. Second, tutoring actions would be confined to focusing students' attention by moving and highlighting objects and by using simple spoken language. Finally, the sophisticated control structure of instruction that we observed in our empirical studies could not be replicated in any existing computer system because present technology lacks full participation, perceptually and socially, in a conversation. For more explanation of these limitations, the reader is referred to Suchman (1987). Despite these difficulties, we still felt committed to exploring a more restricted version of communicative/comprehension instruction of a second language, in which a language could be tutored by presenting objects in a context (i.e., microworld) through linguistic descriptions that varied in noun phrase and speech act complexity, as generated by a simple phrasal lexicon (cf. the visual microworlds described in this volume by Felshin, by Hamburger, and by Murray).

To illustrate the basic concept, let us consider an example of the most simplistic sort. It is well known that for Japanese speakers learning English, the appropriate use of English prepositions is extremely difficult. The following three sentences represent three different states of the world:

(1) Put the baby in the car.
(2) Put the baby on the bus.
(3) Put the baby on the car.

Although (2) could mean to place the baby on the roof or hood of the bus, its more typical meaning, and the one problematic for many learners, is to place the baby inside the bus. A microworld that supports the manipulation of objects (babies or suitcases or whatever) and their relations (e.g., in, on, under) to locations (e.g., cars, buses) permits the student to learn about the semantics of English prepositions through simulated interaction with a physical environment. The student is not told the meanings of *on* versus *in*. Instead the student learns this difference by solving problems that require understanding that semantic difference if the desired outcome (i.e., getting the baby inside the bus) is to be obtained. Even though no oral response is required or expected of the student, the underlying grammar of the second language is directly developed as the student learns to understand the second language.

Although this example may seem a trivial one for native speakers of English, it is by no means trivial to beginning language learners. Similar problems clearly exist for all other languages one might desire to learn. It is possible to build increasingly complex microworlds that challenge the learner with increasingly complex grammar in increasingly complex discourse.

Related Work in Simulation, AI, and Intelligent Tutoring Systems

Our work builds on the idea of simulation microworlds, first proposed by Papert (1980) for LOGO programming. A later paper by Burton and Brown (1982) on reactive learning environments urged the pedagogical value of exploratory learning in domains other than programming. Our work has been greatly influenced by research projects on embedded semantics in microworlds with direct manipulation interfaces: Programming by Rehearsal (Gould & Finzer, 1984), ARK (Smith, 1986), the work on STEAMER (Hollan, Hutchins, McCandless, Rosenstein, & Weitzman, 1986), Thinglab (Borning, 1981), and Envisioning Machine (Roschelle, 1991).

In LingWorlds we build microworlds that are simulations of the world as defined for tutoring purposes. This places our work closer to the work of Programming by Rehearsal than to systems like ARK, STEAMER, Thinglab, and Envisioning Machine, which represent the knowledge of Newtonian mechanics and hydraulics. We are interested in packing as much common-sense knowledge as possible into the microworld. Thus we want to allow the system to derive inferences beyond the facts explicitly declared. For example, we want the system to be able to compute spatial relations dynamically. We have found that artificial intelligence (AI) work on scene analysis and diagram understanding, as well as the literature on spatial reasoning and databases, is related to our work. We have pursued our own research into spatial relations to provide a useful set of spatial pragmatics for the system (Douglas, Novick, & Tomlin, 1987). Additionally, although we wish to continue the basic notion of exploratory learning, we also want to introduce more tutor-controlled strategies and ITS computational mechanisms into the microworlds. This, in effect, turns the microworld into what Wenger (1987) terms a knowledge presentation system (in exploratory mode) and an active knowledge communication system (in tutoring or coaching mode).

Although we have concentrated mostly on developing the microworld concept, we have other shared interests with ITS research. ITSs can be contrasted with traditional CAI (computer-assisted instruction) in the following ways. First, the ITS approach sees learning and, consequently, teaching as a cognitive, knowledge-intensive, and typically problem-solving process rather than as a reinforcement process. Second, ITS control structure is dynamically generated by the interaction of curriculum, student response, and heuristics for diagnosis and tutoring, rather than simply being stored by the program. Third, the domain knowledge taught in ITS is explicitly available (i.e., computationally encoded) for pedagogical decisions rather than being embedded as numerical calculations (as in simulations or drill and practice) or blocks of text/images/sound (as in programmed instruction). Finally, empirical, scientifically conducted studies of students and teachers form the foundation for ITS research, from initial data collection through to evaluation.

Influenced heavily by the cognitive science movement, ITSs represent a significant attempt to model the cognitive aspects of teaching and learning, particularly in providing an individualized approach. Our project's empirical approaches to understanding the cognitive and social bases of comprehension and communicative language teaching place us squarely in this camp. Likewise, the domain knowledge being taught in LingWorlds is explicitly available for pedagogical decisions and not embedded as numerical calculations or blocks of text/images/sound. That is, in LingWorlds the characteristics of the domain objects are declaratively represented. This means that, as each object determines its behavior from its characteristics, so too can the tutoring control system make pedagogical judgments based on direct, explicitly represented domain knowledge.

A LingWorlds Example: Provisioning the Lifeboat

To provide the reader with a concrete idea of how the system works, we present an extended example called *Provisioning the Lifeboat*. In this simulation the student is faced with the nonlinguistic task of provisioning a lifeboat before an ocean liner sinks. The computer displays an introductory animation showing an ocean liner colliding with an iceberg. A simple oral narrative accompanies the animation: "Your ship has hit an iceberg. It is sinking." An on-deck scene of equipment and people near a lifeboat is then presented (see Figure 11.2). At this point, student interaction begins. In tutoring mode, spoken language from the system directs the student to provisions and equipment needed to use the lifeboat successfully. The student responds to the instructions by pointing at or dragging objects with a mouse. Only through successful comprehension of the spoken language will the student be able to complete the tasks required to stock and use the lifeboat.

FIG. 11.2. A screen configuration from Provisioning the Lifeboat simulation.

As an example, an early, easy task posed by the tutor is "Put the anchor in the lifeboat." The student uses the mouse to move the cursor to the anchor, attach the anchor to the mouse, move the anchor to the rope, and release it. The student can see the anchor move, and when it is released on the deck, the screen appropriately updates. With successful completion of the task, the computer provides the oral response: "Okay, let's keep going!" More advanced problems involve the tutor's asking the student to "put the binoculars in the basket in the lifeboat and put the water jug beside them." Note that in this task the student must solve several complicated problems: identifying the objects by name, performing the task in the correct temporal order, selecting which of the two baskets is the correct location, and interpreting prepositions of location (e.g., *beside*, *in*, etc.).

Three versions of the Lifeboat simulation, varying by the mix of student and tutor initiation and control complexity, are described next: an exploratory (student-initiated) version, a coaching version, and a directed tutor version. These control strategies can be combined in a single lesson. These versions demonstrate the kind of versatility that we want to provide, although they are a poor substitute for the kinds of complexity we observed in human tutor-student interactions, as described in the section on empirical studies.

Exploratory lifeboat. In a totally exploratory mode, the student can use the mouse to single-click objects and hear their names ("the basket") or to double-click objects to hear a linguistic description of their locations in relation to another object ("The woman is not in the lifeboat"). The student is also free to drag objects from one location to another to hear the effect of a changed location. Help instructions are available by clicking a question mark (?) icon.

Coaching lifeboat. The coaching mode uses a game format with oral commands that direct the student to locations of provisions and equipment needed to stock the lifeboat successfully, but the system does not otherwise intervene. The sinking of the ship provides time pressure for completion of the tasks. The system keeps a score of successful tasks.

Tutored lifeboat. The directed tutor mode supplements the oral commands of the coaching mode (game format) with remedial intervention. The control strategy that we used is derived from protocol studies of the human expert tutors described previously. The tutor maintains a curriculum of concepts to be taught (e.g., *between* and *beside*) as well as a differential student model to determine state transition information and diagnose types of errors. If the student fails to move any object after a few seconds, the command is repeated. A second such failure causes repetition of the instructions for the overall task; after the third failure the system demonstrates the action. If the student moves an object to the wrong place, it is returned (by the system) to its initial location and the command is repeated. After several failures, the system moves the object to the appropriate location, demonstrating the task. The student is then given another opportunity.

The LingWorlds Simulation System: Software Implementation

The LingWorlds system is illustrated by functional parts in Figure 11.3. The microworld component is essentially all object-oriented, as is the tutor component. The following

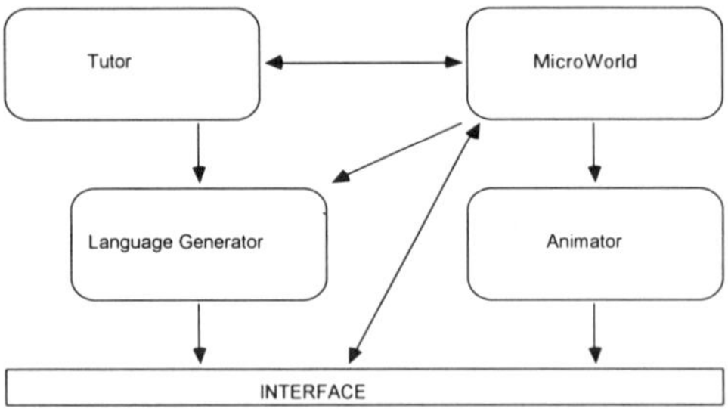

FIG. 11.3. Functional description of LingWorlds.

sections briefly describe how LingWorlds works in terms of software implementation. Readers wishing a more complete and technical description are referred to Douglas (1991).

Contexts and scenes. Each lesson or exercise consists of a sequence of contexts. Each context is either a "movie" sequence or a "scene." Within a context, a series of movies or scenes may occur. Each scene can be composed of subscenes appearing simultaneously in the same window or in recursive windows. A scene is simply a set of problem-solving objects for the student to manipulate and to focus attention on. A scene may have a background that is simply a bit-mapped picture and not a full-fledged object.

Interactors. Each object represented in a scene is a highly specialized object called an interactor. Interactors in the Lifeboat microworld (see Figure 11.2) include the rope, the anchor, the lifeboat, and the question mark (?) icon. Interactor instances have various attributes, actions, and relations with other interactors. Interactors are usually visible as a bit-mapped picture and arranged in x-y locations during the initialization of a scene. They can also be visible or invisible, draggable or not, highlighted or not.

Interactor actions. Interactors can respond to both user actions, such as mouse clicks or dragging, and system actions, such as message passing or tutor-generated events. Interactors can highlight themselves and they can speak. System animation for the interactors can result from following any of three methods: an arbitrary path stored by the designer, a computed trajectory, or a location described by a natural language spatial relation, which allows a description of motion by displacement. It should be emphasized that these interactors, although representing concrete entities in the real world, do not manifest the physical laws of that world. Interactors do not "fall" under the influence of gravity, unless caused by the system designer. In other words, the microworld is more of an imaginary, linguistic world. Each interactor responds to single-click, double-click, press-and-hold, and press-and-drag mouse actions by the user. The designer can choose to enable or disable these events and then write a method using a special language that describes how the interactor should respond. Thus, the system can enable drag actions on some interactors and ignore them on others.

Interactor attributes and semantic properties. Each interactor has a set of attributes that determines whether it responds to different user interface events and also a set of semantic features that defines it for linguistic purposes. These semantic features include whether or not the interactor is animate, a person, an artifact, a vehicle, a vehicle of public transportation, or a container. Any other attribute-value pairs can be added by the designer. For example, an author could specify the interactor's color or the lexical item that designates its name. In a Japanese version of Lifeboat, animacy features were added to interactors for purposes of producing the correct morphemes during speech generation (because in Japanese animacy of noun objects determines agreement phenomena). Each interactor can also be decomposed into a subset of other interactors. This decomposition expresses the *has-parts* relation. For example, a human interactor can be decomposed into further interactors of arms, legs, torso, and head. This relation can be used for generalized possession as well. Interactors can also have ports that cause auto-message passing between them when they are contiguous.

Graphics and spatial relations. Each interactor has a graphic image and an initial position. Interactors are located on planes, with each interactor occupying its own plane. Interactors can swap planes dynamically. This provides the scene with a simulation of three-dimensional reality as interactors are animated by the system or dragged by the user. The animator is a specialized commercially available program for running animation sequences as "movies" of previously digitized data rather than generating them directly in LingWorlds. However, the LingWorlds objects are themselves capable of animated sequences under direct program control of x-y locations and planes.

Probably the most difficult and interesting part of the system is the set of spatial relations that we have very thoroughly studied and built into the system. We focused particularly on the spatial relations used in prepositional phrases: *left of*, *right of*, *above*, *below*, and *between*. These constitute a common-sense description of space. We developed algorithms to compute these relations in a manner similar to native English speakers (Douglas et al., 1987), based on our own intuitions, various psychophysical experiments, and the protocol analyses we conducted of human tutors using simple geometric shapes to teach spatial relations, as discussed earlier. These spatial relations algorithms have been incorporated into LingWorlds. Typically, in tutoring mode the system might move three objects into the main frame and then ask the student to touch one of them, based on salient descriptive characteristics. Although this capability was implemented initially for the pedagogical goal of teaching spatial relations involving prepositions, it has had interesting side effects for the overall design of the system. For example, it allows interactors to locate themselves in a scene in a specific spatial relationship with other interactors (e.g., the water jug might locate itself between the rope and the basket).

Our initial work with spatial prepositions included those in the essentially horizontal and vertical two-dimensional planes. (Because of issues hinted at previously, our simulations are primarily in two dimensions, but because of the possibility of overlapping and movement, they approximate three dimensions. At this time we have yet to implement the depth plane prepositions, *in front of* and *in back of*.) Attempting to develop a complete computational model of human spatial relations language, as most readers know, is as yet an unsolved if not intractable problem (readers wishing more background on this problem are referred to Herskovits, 1986 and Talmy, 1983). However, because of the highly limited spatiality of the computer screen, we were able to develop algorithms that relied primarily upon visual presentation elements of the objects (e.g., their centroid).

To implement spatial relations in our tutor, we compute, on demand for each interactor, several spatial properties: center-of-area (centroid), distance, areas that project from edges, and angular displacements. These properties, as implemented in some rather straightforward message-passing algorithms, have sufficed to compute successfully the relations *left*, *right*, *above*, *below*, and a modified two-dimensional *in*. In some linguistic tasks, proximity becomes a crucial factor for the computation of these relations and appears as the most difficult component to determine in the general case because it is clearly dependent on social and psychological factors as well as cultural convention. For example, whether it is appropriate to describe the woman in Figure 11.2 as *to the right of* the trunk (from the student's point of view) may depend on whether there are intervening objects between the woman and the trunk. In addition to the computed properties, we implement certain spatial properties as features attributed to an interactor. This allows for the specification of a container feature for *in* relations.

This is not to suggest that there were no difficulties. A major problem for us was where to put the deictic origin of the speaker. Is the speaker, in this case the tutor, describing the scene from the position of the student looking at the scene on the CRT screen, or is the speaker sitting opposite the student? An argument can be made for either case. Certainly the voice is coming from an entity seated across from and facing the student. On the other hand, people using deictic expressions can always see the location of the speaker and make the relative orientation adjustments between what the speaker sees and what the hearer sees. In the case of the computer, one is simply not sure where the speaker is. The least ambiguous assumption is that the descriptions are from the point of view of the speaker in a position of the viewer, because the location of the speaker is not known. Thus, spatial relations are computed for a scene from the deictic perspective of the student. In addition to the issue of point of view, judgments of these relations can vary depending on shape, size, discourse task, and contextual arrangement. There also may be prototype positions for some situations.

Because our primary goal is to allow generalized tutors for various languages, it seems reasonable to allow the teacher/author to change the semantics of spatial relations, as these may vary by language. Although this modification might seem trivial to monolingual English readers of this paper, it can be a tricky and difficult problem. For example, imagine a bowl that contains an apple. Both English and Chinese speakers would say, "The apple is in the bowl." Now imagine that the bowl is turned upside down (assuming that you imagined the first one in its canonical orientation). English speakers would now say, "The apple is under the bowl" (even though it is still within the containment of the bowl), but Chinese speakers would still say, "The apple is in the bowl." Clearly, the same problems occur in instances like "Get on the bus" in English, which French speakers would interpret as someone on top of the bus. These semantic differences suggest that the knowledge representations for spatial relations should be open to change by the authoring system. This goal could be exceedingly difficult to achieve.

Speech output. The speech output of LingWorlds is activated by user-generated, tutor-generated, or other internal events directed to interactors. Methods executed in response to these events may contain the "say" programming statement, which must refer to an entry by label in a stored phrasal lexicon. A phrasal lexicon is speech consisting of units as small as a single word or as large as a phrase (Fischer & Lemke, 1988). In developing a LingWorlds lesson the teacher must predetermine what the units of speech will be. Items in the lexicon can vary from entire phrases such as "in the lifeboat" to individual words with varying intonations such as sentence final. For example, in the Lifeboat problem, "the rope," "the woman," and "in the lifeboat" are all entries in the spoken lexicon. Using entire phrases reduces the number of entries in the lexicon and reduces processing time while dynamically concatenating lexicon units during run time. Because interactors can contain semantic features, future extensions of the system include adding a case-frame semantic grammar and processor. A separate processor would be necessary for each language taught.

Because of the demands for speech quality and non-English languages in a language tutoring program, we decided to use digitized human voice recorded under studio conditions, rather than any of the available speech synthesis systems (Streeter, 1990). After preparing the application vocabulary, a trained speaker records each of the lexicon entries, whether they be phrases or single words, in a studio. Care is taken to make voice intensity and inflection as appropriate as possible, often by embedding the desired lexicon in complete, continuously spoken sentences. If differing inflections of the same word or phrase are required, these are all separately recorded in a representative context. For example, "the rope" uttered declaratively, as in "The rope is to the right of the jug," is recorded separately from "the rope" used in a question, such as "Is the jug to the right of the rope?" By means of a commercially available, digital waveform editing program, the recordings are edited to excise the predetermined phrases and words and to remove silent portions between phrases. Items may need to be adjusted to ensure proper amplitude levels among lexicon entries. The edited lexicon is stored on disk as digitized file entries. On output the phrases and words are concatenated and converted from digital to analog form.

Integrating the microworld with the tutor. The preceding description of the microworld components shows how program code is modularized by what is essentially display and control of the interface. Because much of this control is generalizable, it is highly productive to have it available as part of the class definitions. However, as just described, the basic control appears to be primarily student initiated. If the student clicks with the mouse on a particular interactor on the screen, a method is appropriately activated to move the interactor, cause it to say something, and so forth. Because the programming language for these methods has conditionals, it is possible to make an object quite context sensitive in its response to an event. This is the basic flavor of all exploratory learning environments. It is the case, though, that we often want to introduce more teaching intervention into student actions. Thus, ITSs vary along a continuum from totally event-driven exploratory environments to coaches that are embedded within a game structure to goal-directed tutors that have a highly specified control structure. Teaching expertise that is ideally encoded in an ITS approach includes what instructional approach to use and why and how often to tutor the student.

Control from the tutor is introduced into LingWorlds by the tutor *object* (in programming terms), which is global to the interactors in the microworld. In LingWorlds the control is knit together by message passing between interactor objects and the tutor object. A totally exploratory microworld has its control locally defined, with the behavior of each object tied to student actions. A game microworld increases tutor control. Finally, a goal-directed tutor microworld controls most of the interaction through a task-based agenda. Even in the goal-directed tutor, interactors retain individual control over the semantics of their own actions. For example, the tutor can be notified that a particular interactor has been dragged, and through additional message passing with the interactor, determine the location. Thus, the object-oriented paradigm allows an event-driven format that accommodates user-initiated actions as well as internally triggered actions.

The LingWorlds Simulation System: Programming for Authoring

Our system is almost entirely object oriented, as are Programming by Rehearsal, ARK, ThingLab, and STEAMER. In that context, we explore the utility of several important programming concepts: *object-oriented paradigm*, *direct manipulation programming environment*, and *high-level user interface programming language*. We believe that the combination of these features has resulted in a uniquely powerful blend of flexibility and simplicity, allowing nonprogrammers to construct a wide range of complex interfaces.

Object-oriented paradigm. Previous work comparing rule-based with object-oriented ITS tutors (Douglas, 1986) suggested that significant advantages are possible with an object-oriented implementation, not the least of which is the accommodation of event-driven, student-initiated control with event-driven, tutor-initiated control.

In LingWorlds every functioning interface object is an object in the programming sense. Objects were developed using a tool for graphical user interface construction called QUICK (Douglas, Doerry, & Novick, 1992). Unlike most object-oriented languages, the objects in QUICK are prototypical rather than classed (Borning, 1981, 1986; Ungar & Smith, 1987). That is, every object is created with all the characteristics of the basic prototypical object. This prototypical object, called an interactor, has a potential for a graphical image, animated movement, and response to user interface actions. There is no notion of inheritance or class-based specialization. This design choice reflects a decision to support the initial bottom-up design of interface objects from a set of fundamental parts as a construction kit (Fischer & Lemke, 1988), rather than a top-down taxonomic specialization using inheritance. We feel that this approach lends itself to cognitive simplification. At the same time, we provide strong support for the two primary advantages of the class-based approach, abstraction and reuse. Abstraction is supported in that the user may define new classes by aggregating groups of objects, thereby defining a new type of object. Reuse is supported in that objects (simple or aggregate) may be duplicated.

Direct manipulation programming environment. The LingWorlds system is developed as a rapid prototyping environment with an easy switch between run and authoring environments. Typically, the author creates images using a painting program and then imports these into the LingWorlds system to create a background and the images for interactors. The programmer works directly with these objects through a direct manipulation programming environment. Because interactors are visible, they can be positioned in the scene and animated by directly moving the mouse (as opposed to specifying the x-y coordinates symbolically). Figure 11.4 depicts the menu-based programming choices for a selected interactor. Note that in this figure, in addition to options for programming

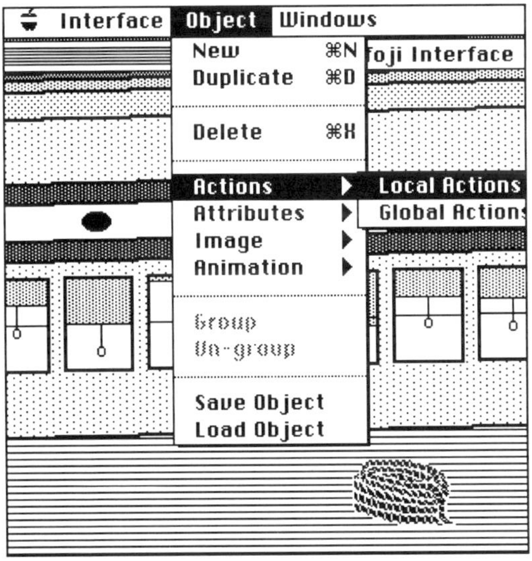

FIG. 11.4. Programming options for developing an interactor.

interactor actions and attributes, there are basic options for creating, deleting, duplicating, saving (to a file), and loading (from a file) any interactor. These options support the reusability of interactors between microworlds.

High-level user interface programming language. Actions for interactors are created using a relatively simple English-like language. Methods for the tutor can be created using the same language. The following are the basic commands, functions, and control structures of the language:

1. Animate <list of objects>
2. Flash <object>
3. Highlight <object>
4. Unhighlight <object>
5. If <test> <then> <else>
6. For-each <list of objects> <code>
7. Set-attribute <object> <attribute> <value>
8. Say <list of sounds>
9. Move <object> <location>
10. Trigger-action <object> <action>

Despite the simple nature of the QUICK language, programming would still be error prone for novice users in a free-form environment. Thus, we provide a hierarchically structured editor that at each stage presents the user with only legal options to choose from. In fact, the only time the user is actually asked to type anything is when an object or a file needs to be named. Figures 11.5 and 11.6 below give the flavor of the structure editor.

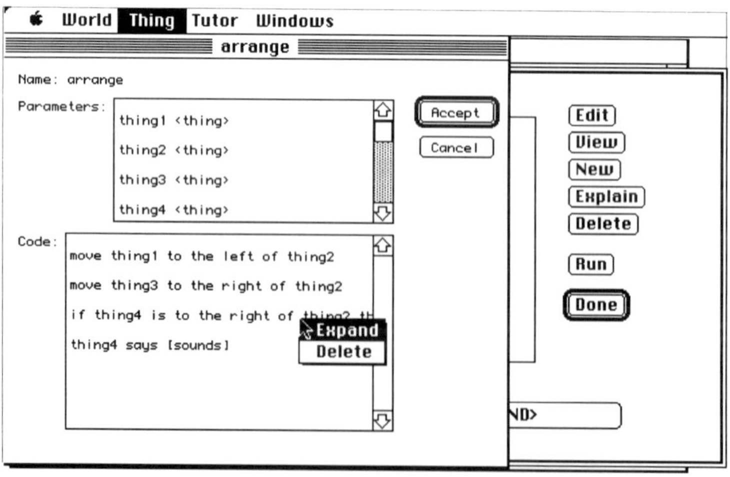

FIG. 11.5. Programming an action in LingWorlds.

The language is fully extensible so that higher level actions can be composed from these elements and added to the system. For example, Figure 11.5 depicts a new action called *arrange*.

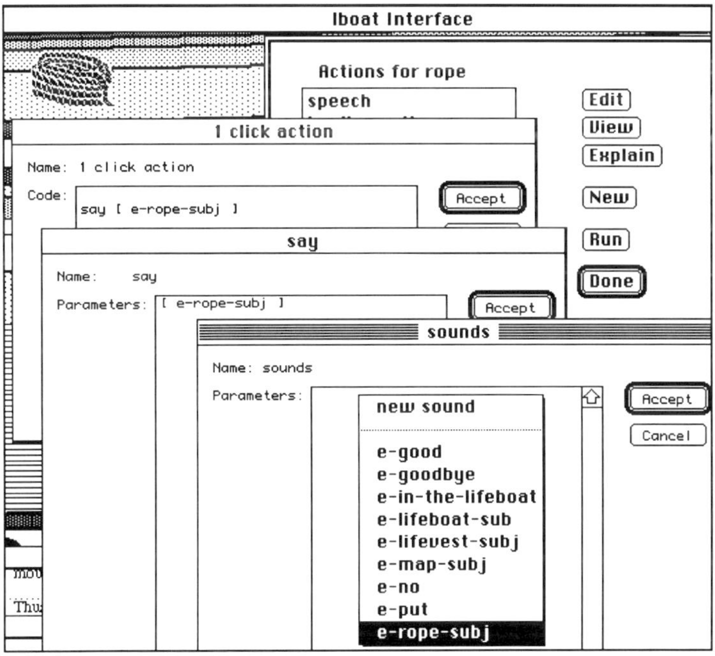

FIG. 11.6. Programming a spoken phrase in LingWorlds

Actions determine the response of an interactor to events generated by user actions (mouse clicks, dragging), other interactors, and the tutor object. In Figure 11.6, we are in the process of programming in the Lifeboat application the *1-click-action* of the *Rope* object to announce its name. The stacking of the dialogues illustrates the hierarchical nature of the editor. The user selects the *1-click-action* to edit, is presented with a code dialogue, selects *say* from a pop-up menu (no longer visible in the figure), is presented with a specialized dialog for *say*, and selects the (initially empty) list of sounds to work on. At the moment of this snapshot, the user has just depressed the mouse to display a pop-up menu of available sounds and has selected the digitized recording of "the rope."

Thus, the structure editor combines the fill-in-the-blanks and multiple-choice paradigms to create a highly constrained programming environment that is easy to use for teachers constructing microworlds.

Other LingWorlds Simulations

We have built both an English and a Japanese version of Provisioning the Lifeboat, with all the expected savings in programming, because interactors and tutors can be reused for any particular microworld. We built the exploratory version first and then added the directed tutor version. A game version has not been programmed but would be trivial.

The Japanese version of Lifeboat is virtually identical to the English except for the addition of animacy features required for speech synthesis, as mentioned earlier. In addition to Lifeboat, we have created an inventory of other pedagogical microworlds that build knowledge of a second language through listening comprehension.

FlatLand. This simulation was introduced in the section in which communicative studies were discussed and is further described in this volume by Tomlin. FlatLand has the student build simple two-dimensional configurations from a limited set of objects: circles or squares, black or white, large or small. The tutor initially trains students to recognize the lexical items needed to identify individual objects. It then introduces the specific spatial relations to be manipulated (*above*, *below*, *left*, *right*, *between*). Finally, the student is directed to build configurations of these objects like the one shown in Figure 11.1. This is done by placing one object at a time in its proper location in response to a single, complex utterance in the target language. The implementation of FlatLand took less than two weeks because almost all the code was reusable from the Lifeboat problem.

Mystery world. This simulation places the student in the position of a witness to some set of events. The events are presented as an animated film. Associated with the film is a descriptive sound track that narrates the actions witnessed by the student. This narration, whose contents are provided by the teacher, can precede, follow, or occur simultaneously with the movie.

The student engages in two kinds of tasks. First, the student practices ordinary listening, matching the narration with the ongoing events portrayed in the movie. Second, and of more interest, the student can interact as witness to the computer tutor's detective to solve a mystery presented in the movie. The detective can interview other witnesses in the scene, and the student must listen and verify the truth and accuracy of those interview responses. In addition, the detective can interview the student directly, through the judicious use of *yes-no* questions. This interaction can take the student through the traditional hierarchy of question types in listening: questions of observed fact, questions of inferred fact, questions of inferred motivations, and questions of evaluation.

Shopping mall. This simulation involves the task of shopping for a list of items by exploring a shopping mall containing different stores. The student is given a limited amount of money to spend. Each store can say its name and be opened into a new window showing the items contained. Each item can say its price. The student can choose to buy an item by dragging it to a shopping cart.

MapTiles. This simulation allows the system to construct a map from tiles containing streets, intersections, houses, and so on. The student is given instructions to follow a particular set of directions in order to find some object. The system can assess the student's understanding by requesting that the student point to a current location.

Build! This simulation gives the student instructions for assembling objects from simple parts. The system points to the object by moving the cursor and highlighting the object. The student builds the object by dragging the parts into position. A simple problem would be to build a house. A more elaborate problem would be to build a plumbing system. Again, each part is an interactor, and the system can always determine the correct (symbolic) position of the part by querying for its spatial relation(s).

Conclusions

For those of us interested in computer-based language teaching, LingWorlds represents a major, comprehensive attempt to integrate available computer technology with a real language-teaching pedagogy, that of the companion communicative and comprehension approaches. From the point of view of the student, we believe that the system we have developed is challenging and interesting. The student cannot accomplish the needed tasks simply through knowledge of the world but must come to comprehend the second language utterances. That is, the student is engaged in true communicative behavior, using the developing second language to solve meaningful, nonlanguage problems—the essence of the communicative approach. The student demonstrates mastery of the linguistic task by physical manipulation of the world rather than by linguistic production. This work in aural comprehension is the essence of the comprehension approach to second language learning.

Future work in LingWorlds will involve extending the simpler semantics of object behavior to issues of common-sense causality as well as time. We are also interested in adding a simple case-frame speech generator. Finally, we need to begin an evaluation period with real language learners.

Acknowledgments

I thank Russell Tomlin, David Novick, Gary Smithrud, Suzanne Shroyer, Kira Carroll, Sue Olivier, Sharon Collins, Joe Clifford, and Brad Tollefson for help in programming, protocol analysis, pedagogical analysis, and imaginative creation of some microworlds. Research for this project was sponsored under Fund for Improvement of Postsecondary Education (FIPSE) Grant No. 84.116C and National Science Foundation Grant DCR-8612578.

References

Asher, J. (1966). The learning strategy of the total physical response: A review. *Modern Language Journal, 50*, 79-84.

Asher, J. (1969). The total physical response approach to second language learning. *Modern Language Journal, 53*, 3-17.

Asher, J. (1977). *Learning another language through actions: The complete teacher's guidebook.* Los Gatos, CA: Sky Oaks Publications.

Borning, A. (1986). Classes versus prototypes in object-oriented languages. In *Proceedings of the ACM/IEEE Fall Joint Computer Conference.*

Borning, A. H. (1981). The programming language aspect of ThingLab, a constraint-oriented simulation laboratory. *ACM Transactions on Programming Languages and Systems, 3*, 353-387.

Burton, R. R., & Brown, J.S. (1982). An investigation of computer coaching for informal learning activities. In D. Sleeman & J. S. Brown (Eds.), *Intelligent tutoring systems.* London: Academic Press.

Douglas, S. A. (1986). Prospects for an ICAI authoring system: A review of computer-based design. In *Proceedings of the IEEE Systems, Man, and Cybernetics Conference*:

Douglas, S. A. (1991). Tutoring as interaction. In P. Goodyear (Ed.), *Teaching knowledge and intelligent tutoring.* Norwood, NJ: Ablex.

Douglas, S. A., Doerry, E., & Novick, D. (1992). QUICK: A tool for graphical user interface construction. *The Visual Computer, 8*, 117-134.

Douglas, S. A., Novick, D.G., & Tomlin, R.S. (1987). Consistency and variation in spatial reference. In *Proceedings of the Ninth International Conference on Cognitive Science*:

Fischer, G., & Lemke, A.C. (1988). Construction kits and design environments: Steps toward human problem-domain communication. *Human-Computer Interaction, 3*, 179-222.

Gould, L., & Finzer, W. (1984). *Programming by rehearsal* (Tech Report No. SCL-84-1). Xerox PARC, Palo Alto, CA.

Herskovits, A. (1986). *Language and spatial cognition: An interdisciplinary study of the prepositions in English.* Cambridge, U.K.: Cambridge University Press.

Hollan, J., Hutchins, E., McCandless, T.P., Rosenstein, M., & Weitzman, L. (1986). *Graphical interfaces for simulation* (ICS Report 8603). Institute for Cognitive Science, UC San Diego, La Jolla, CA.

Johnson, K. (1982). *Communicative syllabus design and methodology.*New York: Pergamon.

Krashen, S. (1977). *Second language acquisition and second language learning.* New York: Pergamon.

Krashen, S. (1982). *Principles and practice in second language acquisition.* New York: Pergamon.

Krashen, S., & Terrell, T. (1983). *The natural approach.* New York: Pergamon & San Francisco: Alemany.

Papert, S. (1980). *Mindstorms: Children, computers and powerful ideas.* New York: Basic Books.

Postovsky, V. (1977). Why not start speaking later? In M. Burt (Ed.), *Viewpoints on English as a Second Language.* New York: Regents.

Postovsky, V. (1979). Effects of delay in oral practice at the beginning of second language learning. *Modern Language Journal, 58*, 229-239.

Roschelle, J. (1991). *Students' construction of qualitative physics knowledge: Learning about velocity and acceleration in a computer microworld.* Unpublished doctoral dissertation, University of California, Berkeley.

Schumann, J. (1978). Social and psychological factors in second language acquisition. In J. Richards (Ed.), *Understanding second and foreign language learning: Issues and approaches.* Rowley, MA: Newbury House.

Selinker, L. (1972). Interlanguage. *International Review of Applied Linguistics, 10*, 209-231.

Sinclair, J. M., & Coulthard, R.M. (1975). *Toward an analysis of discourse.* New York: Oxford University Press.

Smith, R. (1986). The alternate reality kit. In *Proceedings of the 1986 IEEE Computer Society Workshop on Visual Languages.*

Streeter, L. (1990). Applying speech synthesis to user interfaces. In M. Helander (Ed.), *Handbook of human-computer interaction.* Amsterdam: North-Holland.

Suchman, L. (1987). *Plans and situated actions: The problem of human machine communication.* Cambridge, U.K.: Cambridge University Press.

Talmy, L. (1983). How language structures space. In H. Pick & L. Acredolo (Eds.), *Spatial Orientation: Theory, research and application.* New York: Plenum Press.

Ungar, D., & Smith, R. B. (1987). SELF: The power of simplicity. In *Proceedings of the Object-Oriented Programming Systems, Languages, and Applications Conference.*

Wenger, E. (1987). *Artificial intelligence and tutoring systems: Computational and cognitive approaches to the communication of knowledge.* Los Altos, CA: Kaufmann.

Widdowson, H. G. (1978). *Teaching language as communication.* New York: Oxford University Press.

Widdowson, H. G. (1979). *Explorations in applied linguistics.* New York: Oxford University Press.

Winitz, H. (Ed.). (1981). *The comprehension approach to foreign language instruction.* Rowley, MA: Newbury House.

Winitz, H., & Reeds, J. (1973). Rapid acquisition of a foreign language by the avoidance of speaking. *International Review of Applied Linguistics, 11*, 295-317.

12

Modeling Individual Tutorial Interactions: Theoretical and Empirical Bases of ICALL

Russell S. Tomlin
University of Oregon

Curiously, the development of a true intelligent computer assisted language learning (ICALL) system requires that a number of fundamental issues about second language acquisition and instruction be addressed, yet relatively little research is available that links basic questions about acquisition to applied questions about engineering a useful tutoring system. This chapter presents a theoretical model of input and interaction in second language acquisition and a research protocol—the FlatLand protocol—employed to provide some empirical grounding to this model. The model represents an overall picture of how language learning activity involving a single human tutor and a single human learner transpires on an utterance-by-utterance basis, thus providing insight into how one might conceptualize the control structures needed for an ICALL system.

Background of the Project: Goals of LingWorlds

In the mid-1980s, two of us at the University of Oregon (Tomlin & Douglas, 1989) began a project in ICALL known as LingWorlds. We intended to develop a computer tutor that permitted language teachers to design simulated microworlds to support what is called the communicative approach to language teaching. We hoped to escape the electronic workbook format for a more tutor-like—meaning realistic and human-like—learning and authoring environment. Under a communicative approach to second language teaching, learners are to solve nonlinguistic problems that require the use of the second language (L2) for their solution (Allen & Widdowson, 1974; Brumfit, 1984; Canale & Swain, 1980; Johnson, 1982; Piepho, 1983; Widdowson, 1978, 1979).

As described in this volume by Douglas, our model problem targeted developing listening comprehension in beginning learners by asking them to provision a graphically simulated lifeboat on a sinking ship in response to utterances in Japanese. The learner could explore the Lifeboat microworld on his or her own, or the learner could respond to digitized spoken directions from the computer by moving objects around in the microworld. The LingWorlds project attempted to combine communicative language teaching theory with an object-oriented, empirically grounded tutoring model. Whereas the chapter by Douglas describes the development of object-oriented programming concepts for constructing the microworld, this chapter discusses the dialogue interactions on which the tutoring model is based. These interactions are quintessentially the kind of two-medium dialogue described by Hamburger (this volume), in which verbal exchanges are linked to a visual context.

Some Basic Issues in ICALL Design: Constructing Tutorial Actions

One critical problem that we faced in developing the Lifeboat prototype, and a problem of continuing interest for developers of ICALL, is how the computer tutor is to be constructed, how the fundamental control of the system is to be managed; in effect, determining what kinds of action the tutor engages in and how the tutor decides what to do next.

The development of an ICALL tutor is not in any simple way merely an applied engineering problem or a simple extension of human factors studies. It requires that we develop a deep understanding of how one-on-one tutorial interaction transpires. No matter how good our underlying expert system may be, whether it represents the knowledge of a physician or a physicist—or a linguist in the form of a principle-based parser—still an expert system never stands alone as a tutor. The larger system that incorporates the expert always assumes, often implicitly, some view of how instruction is to take place and how that instruction leads to learning. For example, the Japanese parser underlying the ALICE tutor (Evans & Levin, this volume) is a particularly splendid example of a sophisticated expert system. A student can input an attempted sentence in Japanese, and the parser examines that input and determines with a high degree of accuracy the target sentence structure that best matches the student input. The system then displays this preferred target along with a description of the student's error(s). That design decision—to provide immediate grammatical feedback in the form of the corrected sentence plus an explicit grammatical explanation—represents a tutorial decision that such feedback is at a minimum useful to the learner and, ideally, just the right feedback at the right time for language learning. Regardless of whether the expert system is a good one or whether the designers happened on the right kind of tutorial action, there remains a fundamental theoretical and empirical problem: How can we know that the tutorial component, the underlying control structure for the ICALL system, is an effective one, an appropriate one, and ideally a suitably grounded one to incorporate into the ICALL system?[31]

Several important issues cascade from this overarching one. First, we need a theory of second language acquisition (SLA) that is oriented to the individual learner as well as to the fundamental sociocognitive dilemma the learner faces: the development of an L2 grammar, of which the learner is largely unaware, through constrained but overt social interactions with native speakers of L2. Second, our SLA theory must operate within a fine-grained temporal scale that accounts for very local decision-making, because the tutorial episodes presented by ICALL systems are of brief duration (in the LingWorlds applications, for example, language-microworld activities of 2- to 8-second duration are distributed over a 20- to 60-minute session). Third, we must consider how rich or complex our model of acquisition must be—whether and how to include and account for linguistic input, social interaction, representations of the world and context, representations of the learner and tutor, and so on. We want to include those essential aspects of human-to-human tutoring that lead to demonstrably effective and efficient learning.

Recent directions in SLA theory (e.g., Flynn & O'Neil, 1993) focus on acquisition of knowledge representations of L2 grammar as an internal cognitive phenomenon. By contrast, we consider the contribution to cognitive change in the learner of the larger, detailed social and problem-solving situation. In fact, the model of SLA presented here

---

[31] By comparison, it would seem absurd to build an expensive parser without carefully considering which of several competing linguistic theories holds the most promise for an array of language questions.

views acquisition and instruction as a special instance of discourse interaction in general. Acquisition requires the learner to be exposed to appropriate and well-timed L2 input, and such input never occurs independently of either a conceptual context (i.e., what we are talking about) or a social context (i.e., why we are speaking to each other). In terms of conceptual context, decisions made by a tutor, whether computer or human, about what to say, when, and in what form are not determined solely by linguistic matters (e.g., the level of syntactic complexity mastered by the student), but they are constrained in important ways by the task the tutor and learner are engaged in. Thus, the model presented here links input as produced by the tutor and construed by the learner to the shared conceptual representation of the task for which the input is produced. The content, form, and timing of utterances are very much tied to this task representation, and the tutorial actions employed by the tutor are likewise constrained. In terms of the social context, cognitive changes in the learner (i.e., the developing L2 grammar) do not come about through direct intervention by the tutor but through social interactions the tutor sets up. These interactions may not lead directly to cognitive changes in the individual, so we need to build a model of SLA in which we understand how these changes are brought about through social interaction.

We examine three specific tutoring problems that any ICALL system must deal with: lexical acquisition in context, repetition, and selection between grammatically simple versus grammatically complex utterances. It is generally accepted within instructional settings that vocabulary is learned better in context (e.g., Gildea, Miller, & Wurtenberg, 1988), yet we do not know much about how context supports lexical acquisition. It is also generally accepted that repetition is a key instructional action, yet we do not have a clear idea of how it helps the learner or what circumstances call for it during tutorial interaction. Finally, tutors clearly select between grammatically simple and more complex forms in dealing with the same semantic content, but it is not at all clear what circumstances during the time course of a tutorial call for one alternative over another. For each of these problems we show how the tutor and learner cooperate in navigating through a simple task, the FlatLand protocol, in which the tutor selects from a limited set of tutorial actions to provide input useful to the learner.

Insights from Input and Interaction Theory in Second Language Acquisition

The principal theory of language learning embraced here is learning as hypothesis formulation and modification. In this view, sometimes called *creative constructionism* (Dulay & Burt, 1975), the learner formulates hypotheses about the L2 grammar as exemplars of the L2 system are encountered in natural discourse. Initial hypotheses, derived either from the grammar of the first language or from linguistic universals, are then subject to modification over time as the learner encounters additional exemplars of L2 utterances.

However, as noted previously, these exemplars are never encountered independently of a social or conceptual context, and the study of how such exemplars are provided and how they contribute to acquisition is the focus of *input and interaction* research in SLA (e.g., Givon, 1984; Hatch, Flashner, & Hunt, 1986; Klein, 1986; Krashen, 1985; Long, 1985). The basic idea is simple: Providing the right input at the right time sets up the conditions for acquisition to occur. The right input at the right time is input that is comprehensible to the learner. Comprehensible input (Krashen, 1982) is seen to increase *intake*, the information available for further processing.

There are three ways in which input is made optimally comprehensible to learners. First, input can be linked directly to the immediate physical context. This can be done by exploiting the here-and-now principle (Klein, 1986). Attention is drawn to details of the immediate setting as L2 input is provided. Second, input can be modified directly to make it more comprehensible. This can be done by changing the frequency with which particular grammatical forms are encountered, by modifying the length of utterances, by providing shorter utterances, by altering intonation, or by modifying the structural characteristics of the input to make it less complex grammatically at the right time. Third, input can be better situated by modifying interactional features of the input context (Long, 1983, 1985). Tutor and learner may work together, through the use of questions, repetition, requests, and so forth, to clarify how information is to be construed at particular points in time.

Although insights from the research on input and interaction seem useful for developing a model of tutorial interaction, some key questions remain. First, can we specify more precisely what "comprehensible" means? Second, how does the here-and-now principle actually operate? Third, when does the tutor decide to make input structurally less complex? Fourth, under what circumstances does the tutor decide to modify the interactional characteristics of the tutorial dialogue? Each of these questions requires a precise model of the details of the interaction between tutor and learner.

The FlatLand Protocol

The FlatLand protocol was designed to collect observational data on human-to-human tutorial interactions. It permits the consistent collection of comparable discourse data from a variety of learner-tutor pairs. It provides a means, congruent with task-based, communicative language teaching theory, of examining the earliest development of listening comprehension abilities in L2.

In this protocol we paired effective language tutors, each with a minimum of five years' experience in L2 tutoring, with nil-proficiency learners, who had had no prior exposure to the L2 they were to encounter. We then set a simple, observable teaching-learning problem before each pair of participants: The tutor must help the learner construct two-dimensional configurations of geometric shapes using only spoken directions in the new L2—Indonesian (the L2 considered in this chapter), Mandarin, Japanese, Spanish, or English. The tutor was to instill enough of the language so that the learner could build new configurations based on L2 directions (there was no expectation that the learner would be able to *produce* L2 directions). The configurations were constructed piece by piece from a restricted inventory of eight objects, all visible to both participants: large or small, black or white, circles or squares.

Participants were further restricted to the use of a set of five spatial relation terms: *above*, *below*, *left*, *right*, and *between*, and their counterparts in the target languages. We asked the tutor to use only the target L2 and the learner not to speak during the interaction, though both participants were free to manipulate the objects as each chose. Some protocols were collected face-to-face using matte-board counters. Others were collected through a computer-mediated arrangement in which the participants could see and manipulate the same set of objects displayed on different monitors and could freely speak to and hear each other but could not see each other. Figure 12.1 illustrates the beginning state of the display. By videotaping the session, we recorded virtually all the input and

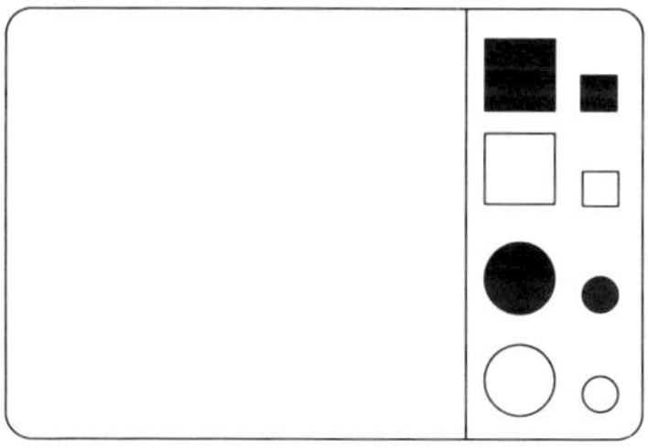

FIG. 12.1. The FlatLand environment: Initial state.

interactions leading to acquisition of this limited sample of the L2. Additional details on design and data collection methodology in the protocol appear in the chapter by Douglas.

The FlatLand protocol gives the researcher a complete record of the initial stages of acquisition. At the beginning of the interaction, the learner knows nothing of L2. (In fact, for the Indonesian data considered here, we know that the learner had never before heard a word of Indonesian.) By the end of the session, we observed that learners uniformly had acquired some measure of listening ability in L2 (albeit limited); they could build configurations of geometric shapes in response to native-like instruction in L2.[32] Moreover, the observed effectiveness of the tutoring appears to have had some durability. After a single 40-minute session, subsequent testing on the same task as long as 18 months later showed learners capable of building novel configurations in response to oral instructions in L2, even though the learner had invested no additional effort with the L2.

Modeling Tutorial Interactions

Interactions from FlatLand: An illustration of the Modeling Problem

At a superficial level, FlatLand interactions are predictable: Tutor and learner work first on establishing the lexical means to identify objects in the display, they then add these one to another to form more complex utterances required to move the objects about, and the tutor ultimately tests the learner's listening ability in L2 by requesting actions of the learner. All the protocols are remarkably uniform in this overall organization, but such a characterization masks their deeper and more fine-grained organization. There is a critical interplay between the structure of the FlatLand task itself and the location within that structure where the participants find themselves, the tutor's estimates of the current linguistic state of the learner, and the kinds of actions taken by the tutor at any given moment during the interaction.

[32] The main difference was one of pace or speed of production on the part of the tutor.

Consider an example that illustrates aspects of this fine-grained organization that are important to model: lexical acquisition. By the end of the protocol, learners clearly can comprehend the key lexical items involved in building FlatLand configurations. It should therefore be possible to model the acquisition of these items in some way. A sequence of protocol events relevant to lexical acquisition is depicted in Figure 12.2.

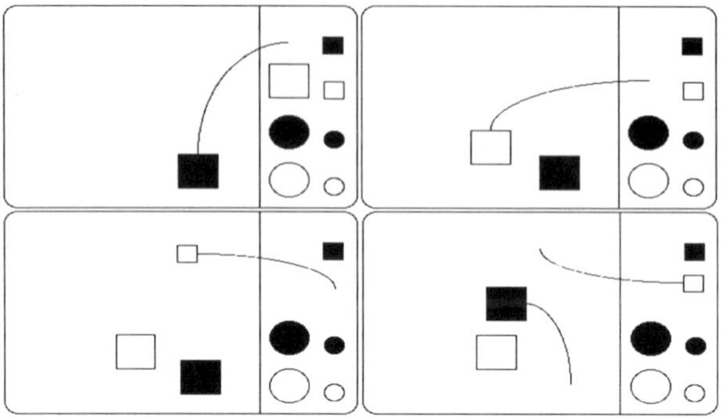

FIG. 12.2. Some early FlatLand events (in sequence from left to right).

In the first tutorial action the tutor moves the large black square to the lower right-hand corner of the working space and utters the expression "kotak" two times. Next, the tutor takes the large white square and moves it into the work space somewhat to the left of the first black square and again utters "kotak." Then, the tutor takes the small white square and moves it onto the work space and for a fourth time utters "kotak." Finally, the tutor moves the small white square back to the home area and picks up the black square and moves it slightly above the large white square and utters "kotak" yet again. At this point, the tutor requests of the learner that she pick out a square, which the learner does successfully. Never again does the tutor do anything that resembles a teaching action involving the lexical item *kotak*.

As we try to model the behavior exhibited by tutor and learner, we want to answer a number of basic questions. What sort of tutorial action is the tutor taking at any given moment during the interaction? What contribution to the learning of Indonesian does each of the utterances of "kotak" make? What is the relationship between the utterances provided by the tutor and the manipulations of the microworld?

Although this particular example is simple, even trivial, it nonetheless is useful for pointing out the design problems we face in building an ICALL system. Somehow the tutor can make decisions about what to say and when in a way that makes a clear contribution to language learning, yet the tutor may not be aware of the reason for these decisions. It is precisely such behavior that we seek to model in building an ICALL system. Note that, according to the framework described by Hamburger (this volume), the primary interaction types observed in these protocols are Tourguide (i.e., the tutor moves and labels the microworld objects) and Commander (i.e., the tutor requests an action of the learner), integrated into a common tutoring purpose. Within these global roles, we want to model the specific kinds of tutoring acts that underlie the behaviors observed in the protocols.

Our general model of tutorial interaction links a limited inventory of tutorial actions or schemata to a conceptual representation of the nonlinguistic task jointly held by tutor and learner. During the course of the interaction, the tutor and the learner each manages a dynamic model of the task. The tutor estimates which component of the task he or she currently believes the learner cannot complete using the L2, a component called the *essential event* (e.g., identifying the object to be moved). The tutor then selects from the inventory of tutorial schemata a particular action that helps the learner complete that essential event. The task network very much and very usefully constrains the L2 input: The tutor provides input to the learner via the chosen tutorial schema, and the learner construes that input against the learner's own estimate of the current essential task event. When these estimates are congruent between tutor and learner, the input provided is comprehensible and contributes to hypothesis formulation or modification in the learner.

Thus, our tutorial model requires three components: tutorial schemata, which represent a limited set of actions the tutor may select from; a task model, a network of simpler action schemata; and action schemata governing both the task model and tutorial schemata. The next section considers the general structure of action schemata.

Modeling Complex Human Actions: A General Schema

From a cognitive point of view, any human action, whether tying one's shoes or driving one's car across town, can be viewed as a network of simple action schemata. Following the work of Baddeley (1986), Shallice (1972, 1982), and Norman and Shallice (1980), a simple action like tying one's shoe can be seen as being composed of a simple action schema, as depicted in Figure 12.3.

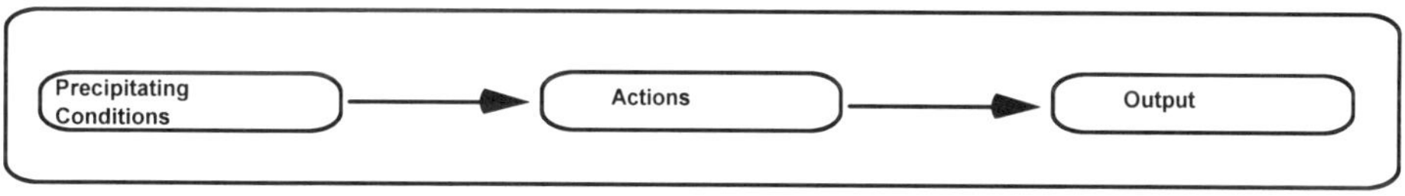

FIG. 12.3. A simple action schema.

A particular action schema is composed of some set of actions that are automatically and fully executed when certain precipitating conditions are encountered in the environment. The output of the actions may be either particular observable behavioral consequences or mental representations that can serve as input to further action schemata. In the case of tying one's shoe, the actions executed—the grasping of the shoe strings in the proper way and the twisting and pulling them through to form a proper bow—are actions run off by adults in a routine and unexciting way whenever certain precipitating conditions are met. For example, walking down the street, one might notice a certain looseness in one's shoe that serves to precipitate the activation of the action schema of tying the shoe. The output of the tying-the-shoe action schema is simply the resulting state of a properly tied shoe. Although the tying-the-shoe example is a trivial one, ideas of action schemata are central to understanding more complex human actions. In this view, all actions, whether simple or complex, are composed of automated action routines, a set of precipitating conditions that trigger those action routines, and the characteristic output of such routines when the actions have been activated.

More complicated human activities can be conceived of as networks of simpler action schemata. The action schema in Figure 12.3 can be thought of as a simple node in a more complex network of action schemata. Thus, any complex activity—like the Flat-Land task of moving geometric shapes around on a computer screen—can be represented as a network of simpler action schemata. As individuals seek to complete a particular task, they move through that network of simple action nodes, working from logically earlier nodes toward completion of the event in some terminal node. Figure 12.4 depicts the memorial representation of some task. The highlighted node, N1, indicates that the problem

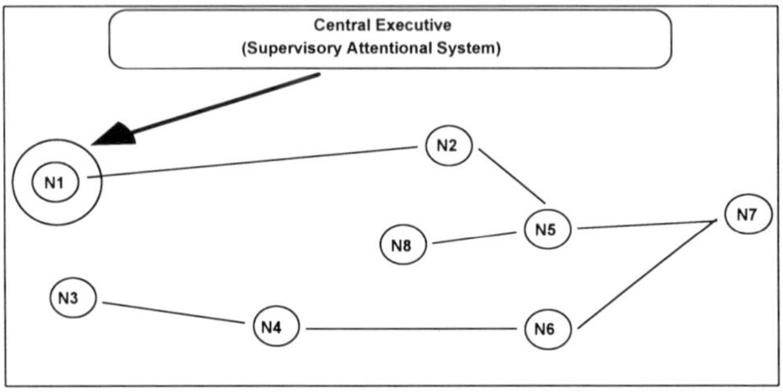

FIG. 12.4. A memorial representation of a task as a network of action nodes, with sequence controlled by a central executive.

solver has selected N1 to work on first, on the way to completing the task that ultimately requires the completion of node N7.

As the problem solver navigates through the action network to complete the task, decisions must be made between two competing nodes. For example, in Figure 12.4 nodes N1, N3, and N8 are all independent of one another and the selection among them must be controlled in some fashion. It is argued by Baddeley (1986), Shallice (1982), and Norman and Shallice (1980), among others, that a central executive serves as the cognitive mechanism that controls selection among competing nodes. The central executive (sometimes known as the supervisory attentional system) biases the problem solver to just one of the sets of competing action nodes.

In addition, the central executive can be employed to deal with problematic aspects of the action network. If any particular node in the network turns out to be difficult for the problem solver, the central executive can be used to unpack the action schema into a more explicit and more complex representation. For example, when teaching a child to tie a shoe, the component steps of the bow-tying process must be brought to the child's attention. Thus, an action schema of tying the shoe, which is easily and automatically executed by any normal adult, is not easily executed by any 4-year-old child. The teaching effort of the parent in part directs the central executive within the child to unpack the complex action schema into a network of simpler actions, which can ultimately be combined to form the complex action of tying one's shoe (see Figure 12.5).

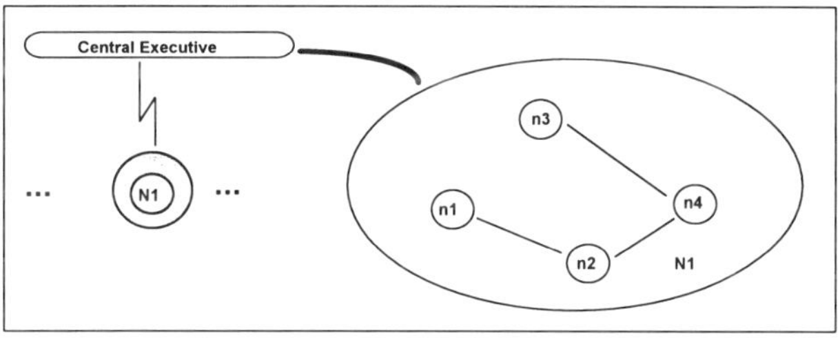

FIG. 12.5. The central executive "unpacks" one node into component action schemata.

Applying the Components of Tutorial Modeling to the FlatLand Protocol

Task Schemata: The Conceptual Model of the FlatLand Task

The task in the FlatLand protocol is a simple one. The tutor helps the learner move eight geometric shapes around a two-dimensional space. Despite the simplicity of the overall task, it, like others, can be viewed as a network of simpler actions. These actions, depicted in Figure 12.6, include those events that must logically be carried out in order for the tutor or learner to move one particular object to its targeted location (e.g., the small black square beneath the large white circle). So, as seen in Figure 12.6, the terminal

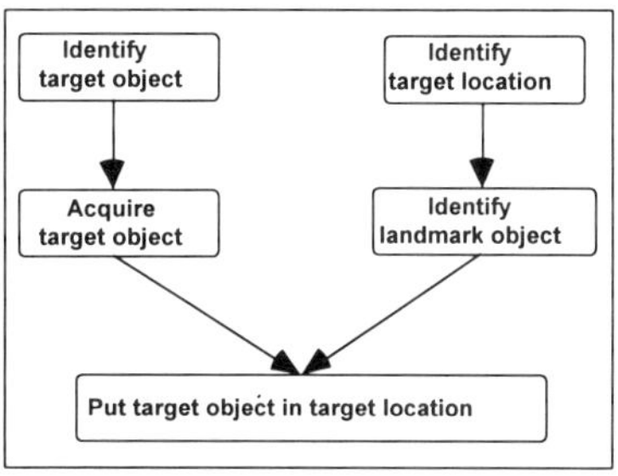

FIG. 12.6. The basic FlatLand task network.

action to be executed by the problem solver is to put the target object in its targeted location. However, in order to carry out that final action, several logically earlier steps must be completed. The problem solver must previously acquire the target object (e.g., the small black square), which in turn requires that the problem solver identify that target object. In parallel, to get the target object in its proper location, the problem solver must be able to identify the target location (e.g., beneath the large white circle), which requires further that the problem solver be able to identify a landmark object (e.g., the large white circle) against which the target location is defined. Failing any of these steps means that the terminal node in this directed graph cannot be completed and the object cannot be put in its proper place.

Under ordinary circumstances, when both the tutor and the learner are native speakers of English, the simple problem of moving a targeted object to its target location is a trivial one, as are the component steps of identifying targeted and landmark objects, acquiring the target object, identifying the target location, and getting the target object to its target location. However, when the learner has zero proficiency in L2, this task cannot be completed in L2 in any simple fashion. The simple network must be made somewhat more complex, as shown in Figure 12.7.

For the nil-proficiency learner, identifying either a target object or a landmark object requires that the learner be able in principle to identify individual objects. In the FlatLand microworld this ability requires that the learner be able to deal with each of the three variables: color, shape, and size. This step is trivial for the native speaker of the language and need not be dealt with explicitly in microworld interactions. But for a nil-proficiency learner, identifying objects is anything but trivial. We do not want to claim here that learners are unfamiliar with the problem of identifying an object or with the concepts of color or shape or size, which they know quite well in their own native language. Rather, the difficulty is in managing these concepts in L2. Thus, the more complex action network for nil-proficiency learners in Figure 12.7 shows an increased granularity of the actions to be carried out (e.g., separate identification of color, shape, and size variables).

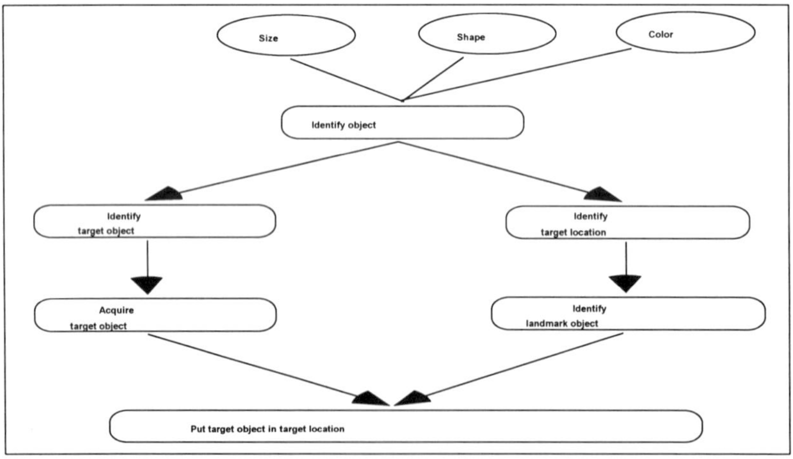

Figure 12.7. The FlatLand task network unpacked (for nil-proficiency learner).

Tutorial Schemata for FlatLand

The FlatLand tutorials can be described in terms of a constrained set of tutorial schemata, which are selected by the tutor during the time course of interaction. Each tutorial schema is distinguished from others by differences in behavioral content, precipitating conditions, intention, and output.[33] The behavioral content of a tutorial schema includes specific manipulations or linguistic activity intended to lead to changes in the learner. The output of these actions is changes to the learner's mental representation of both the task network (see Figure 12.7) and the L2 grammar. The immediate cause for those actions being carried out is the tutor's intention, which is related, in turn, to the occurrence of precipitating conditions in the environment. So, as depicted in Figure 12.8, the precipitating conditions serve as the foundational trigger for an intention in the tutor, which when activated leads to a set of actions being executed, which in turn result in changes in the mental representation of the learner.

This idea can be made most clear through the example used in Figure 12.8, the tutorial schema called *Describe Object* (DescObj). The precipitating conditions for the

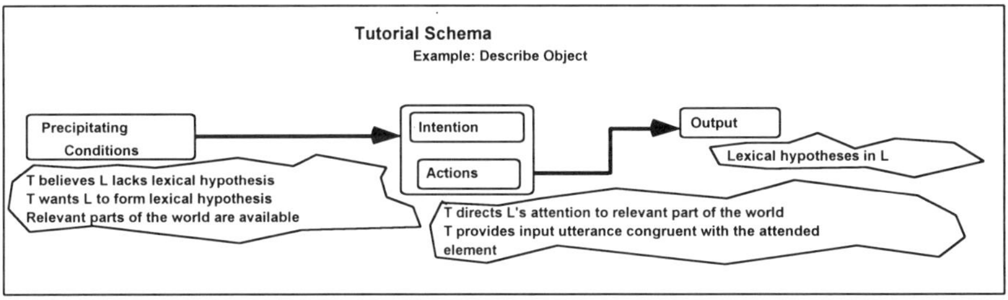

Figure 12.8. A FlatLand tutorial schema (DescribeObject), where T is the tutor and L is the learner.

DescObj tutorial schema are three. First, the tutor believes that the learner lacks a lexical hypothesis (i.e., does not understand the L2 term for *square*); second, the tutor believes that the learner needs the lexical hypothesis to carry out one of the nodes in the FlatLand task network (i.e., needs to understand the term for *square* in order to pick out the small black square that is to be moved); and three, the tutor believes that relevant parts of the world (e.g., squares) are in fact available to the learner. When these precipitating conditions are encountered during the tutorial, an intention is generated in the tutor to generate a lexical hypothesis in the learner. The tutor then carries out a specific set of actions. These include, first, directing the learner's attention to some part of the world, that is, providing an exemplar of the object that the learner needs to identify (e.g., pointing to the square); and second, providing L2 input congruent with the part of the world to which the tutor has directed the learner's attention (e.g., uttering "square" while pointing to the square). When successful, the output is an updated lexical hypothesis in the learner.

It is possible to describe all the interactions occurring in the FlatLand protocols we collected in terms of just nine tutorial schemata. In addition to Describe Object, these

[33] The notion of a tutorial schema developed here is clearly indebted to Searle's analysis of speech acts (Searle, 1969, 1979) as well as to related work on the structure of instructional interactions (Mehan, 1979; Sinclair & Coulthard, 1975).

include, for example, Describe Relation, Repeat Expression, Repeat Focus, and Affirmation. Although it is beyond the scope of this paper to elaborate on this inventory, it should prove amenable to implementation in an ICALL system (see Tomlin, 1994, for details).

Modeling Tutorial Interactions: Lexical Acquisition, Repetition, and Grammatical Complexity

This section looks at the details of modeling FlatLand tutorial interactions. At the outset we can observe that tutor and learner share the same conceptual representation of the FlatLand task, that is, the network of actions presented in Figure 12.7. Both tutor and learner, regardless of the language they speak, complete the FlatLand task by navigating through this task network. It is important to see that although tutor and learner share the network representation for a simple task like FlatLand and that there may be universal components to how tasks are represented, it is by no means necessary that tutor and learner always share a representation of the task (for example, the tutor may collapse those actions that the learner assumes will be unpacked). Differences in their respective task models can lead to difficulties for tutor and learner in providing and interpreting input.

One key problem for the FlatLand participants is to ensure that both are on the same node within the task network at any given moment. The principal means by which this is managed is for the participants to search for the current essential event, that is, the logically earliest node in the task network (such as identifying the target object) for which absence of explicit instruction results in failure to continue the task. Having mutually and successfully located the current essential event severely but usefully constrains the participants. The learner construes current input only as an attempt to deal with the current essential event (rather than, say, the overall task outcome or some task-irrelevant item); the tutor provides input that deals only with that event. In this way, the hypotheses about L2 formulated and tested by the learner are very much limited, drastically simplifying the SLA problem.

The FlatLand task and lexical acquisition. The overall FlatLand task is transparent to both the tutor and learner—an eight-fold iteration of the basic FlatLand network presented in Figure 12.6. In order to place any object in its targeted location, the listener must acquire the object and identify the location, which in turn requires identifying both the target object and the landmark object. Because our nil-proficiency learner cannot yet manage any of this in L2, he or she must first learn to identify any object using L2, which requires identifying either its color, size, or shape. If we assume shape as the most basic cognitive category of these three, we can model the acquisition of lexical items involving shape. Figures 12.9 through 12.11 illustrate the tutorial activity required for our learner to acquire the Indonesian expression *kotak* (square). This analysis provides an explanation of the behaviors overviewed earlier in illustrating the modeling problem and sketched in Figure 12.2. The outset of the interaction, both tutor and learner search for the current essential event, which we assume is the node Identify Object. At this point, the tutor monitors the learner (activity 1 in Figure 12.9). In doing so, the tutor observes that the learner lacks the lexical means to identify any object. Thus, the precipitating conditions for a DescObj tutorial schema are well met. To identify an object, the learner needs a lexical hypothesis, and from the tutor's point of view, relevant parts of the world are available to the learner to build and entertain hypotheses about the Indonesian expressions describing objects. Therefore, the tutor engages in a DescObj action (activity 2). The tutor brings to the learner's attention an exemplar, the large black square, and provides an input utterance congruent with that object, namely, "kotak." The result for the learner is the formulation of a number of hypotheses about what "kotak" might mean (activity 3).

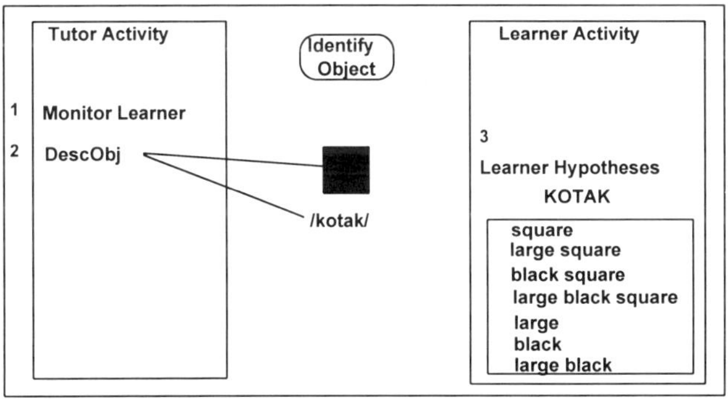

FIG. 12.9. First tutorial move in lexical acquisition of Indonesian *kotak* (square).

The hypotheses entertained by the learner are very much constrained by the task network in which the participants are engaged. That is, the learner does not entertain just any possible meanings for the utterance "kotak" but only those that are congruent with the task node the participants are working on. Thus, the learner will interpret "kotak" as an attempt to identify the object presented in the exemplar and not as any of a number of other things, such as a request for action or a greeting. Given the universe of objects in the FlatLand environment and the specific task node on which the participants are located, the learner's hypotheses about the meaning of "kotak" are severely but usefully constrained. The term might mean *square* or *large square* or *black square*, but it most definitely cannot mean anything else at this moment in this environment during this interaction. (Moreover, for inferring which dimension "kotak" refers to, it may be that mutually held and possibly universal beliefs about the lexicon further constrain hypotheses: Learners may assume that shape will be the first feature mentioned based on its cognitive salience and its greater likelihood than size or color to function as a nominal, e.g., *a square* rather than *a red* or *a big*. This possibility could be tested in further protocols.)

At this point (see Figure 12.10), the tutor continues to monitor the state of the learner (activity 4) and sees that the learner still does not have a unique meaning associated with "kotak." Therefore, the conditions for the tutorial schema DescObj are again met and the tutor again selects DescObj as the appropriate tutorial action (activity 5).

The tutor selects another object, the large white square, and again utters the identifying expression "kotak." The learner, knowing that the current essential event is still to identify the object, now interprets "kotak" in a way that further restricts the associated hypothesis space (activity 6). Thus, hearing "kotak" uttered for the large white square exemplar allows the learner to eliminate four of the seven hypotheses being entertained, leaving only *square*, *large square*, and *large* as possible meanings.

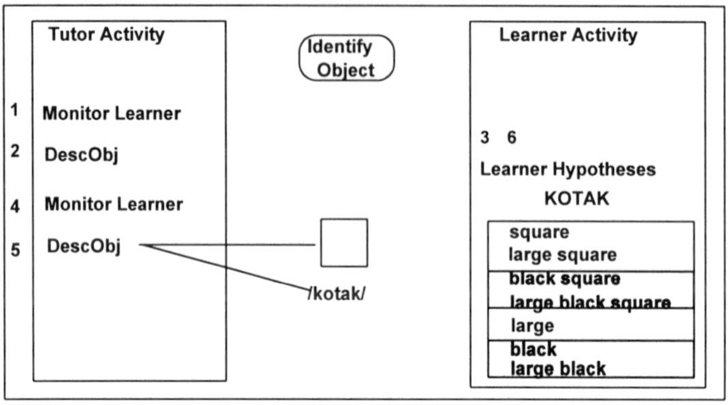

FIG. 12.10. Second move in lexical acquisition of *kotak* (darkened areas indicate hypotheses about meaning eliminated).

At this point (see Figure 12.11), the tutor once again monitors the learner, noticing that the set of hypotheses the learner can entertain for "kotak" is still larger than one (activity 7). Again, this leads to selection of a DescObj schema (activity 8), and the exemplar of a small black square is put forward along with the input utterance. At exactly this point, the learner is able to reduce the hypothesis space to one. Having encountered exactly these three exemplars associated with "kotak" permits the learner to formulate and then reduce the hypothesis space to a single one linked to the meaning *square*.

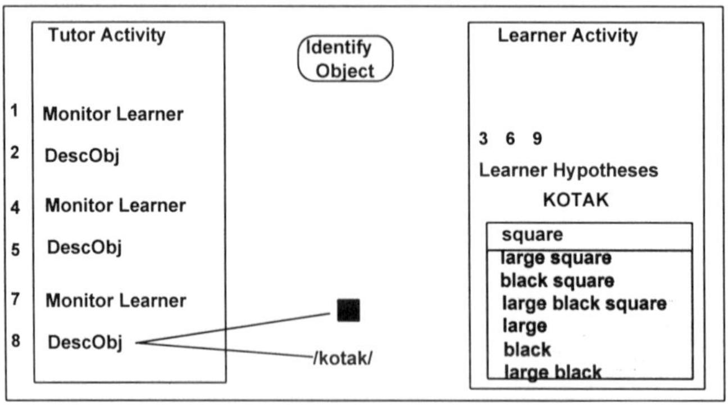

FIG. 12.11. Third move in lexical acquisition of *kotak* (darkened areas indicate hypotheses about meaning eliminated).

We may reasonably hypothesize that this particular moment is the one when the lexical item *kotak* is acquired by this learner (suggesting in general how words are acquired in context). Additional exemplars may be needed to reinforce or strengthen the surviving hypothesis given memory limitations or to overcome problems engendered by mismatches in tutor and learner models of the task or locations within the task. Still, in reviewing the inventory of FlatLand transcripts, we can see, in general, for the learning of all lexical items involving size, shape, color, and spatial relations, that the number of exemplars provided corresponds very roughly to the number of exemplars minimally needed to reduce the lexical hypothesis space to one. At that point, the tutor no longer provides exemplars of the targeted lexical item but instead, tests the learner more directly by requesting actions such as picking up a square. The tutor and learner now incorporate "kotak" into further, more complex utterances involving size and color, which previously the tutor did not attempt at all. In the end, whether or not this apparent key point in lexical acquisition survives as the actual moment of acquisition remains an empirical question. Presumably, research methods sensitive to on-line tasks, such as dual task assays or evoked response potential (ERP) techniques, may permit us to test this hypothesis more directly.

The FlatLand task and repetition. Although it is a virtual truism of second language teaching that repetition is essential for learning, it is not known exactly what role repetition plays (Tomlin, 1994). From the point of view of developing an ICALL system, understanding the conditions under which repetition occurs in natural tutor-learner discourse is essential. The alternative is to repeat randomly or to repeat all the time or to repeat in an ad hoc manner. Yet even a cursory glance at any of the FlatLand protocols reveals that tutors do not seem to repeat utterances randomly, nor do they do it all the time. It is generally assumed that mere frequency or simple repetition makes a significant contribution to learning (cf. Kaplan & Holland, this volume), but in this modeling we will consider whether particular exemplars make different contributions to learning at different times despite structural identity. Repetition is not mere iteration but is treated as a kind of tutorial action selected for particular purposes. This leads to some key questions: How, when, and why does the tutor repeat utterances? What kind of input is repetition, and what contribution does it make to SLA?

In the FlatLand protocols, we identified four distinct kinds of repetition: repeat expressions, repeat focuses, repeat acts, and augmented repetitions. It is beyond the scope of this chapter to examine all these types (see Tomlin, 1994, for a detailed discussion). Instead, consider the function of just one kind of repetition, the repeat expression, or RepExp.

RepExps, exemplified in the protocol fragment schematized in Table 12.1, show two distinct structural characteristics. A RepExp involves a verbatim repetition of an immediately preceding utterance with no change in the associated visual display. Thus, Table 12.1 shows that the tutor first moves the object to its desired location and utters "kotak" (an instance of the tutorial schema of DescObj), and then immediately provides a verbatim repetition of the utterance without making any change in the visual display.

Table 12.1
Opening Moments of an Indonesian FlatLand Protocol
(all objects are in start-up position)

Time	Tutorial Action	Activity on Display/Utterances
00:00		**cursor on LBS (large black square)**
00:06		**LBS —>**
Time	**Tutorial Action**	**Activity on Display/Utterances**
00:08		**LBS lower right screen**
00:08	DescObj	Ko:tak./
00:11	RepExp	Ko:tak./
00:13		**cursor —>**
00:17		**cursor on LWS (large white square)**
00:17		**LWS —>**
00:20		**LWS lower right screen (u/l LBS)**
00:20	DescObj	Ko:tak./
00:21		**cursor —>**
00:26		**cursor on SWS**
00:26		**SWS —>**
00:27	DescObj	Ko:tak./

Further, it is important to note that RepExps occur not only at the beginning of FlatLand protocols and do not deal solely with lexical expressions. RepExps also occur under the same kinds of conditions with entire sentences, as shown in Table 12.2.

Table 12.2
Later Occurrence of RepExp in an Indonesian FlatLand Protocol

Time	Tutorial Action	Activity on Display/Utterances
25:02		**SWS —>**
25:06		**SWS r LBC /l LWC**
25:08	DescRel	Ko:tak (.11) pu:tih KE:CIL (.84) DI:(.11)ANTARA (.21) ling:karan./
25:16	**RepExp**	**Ko:tak pu:tih KE:CIL (.60) DI:ANTARA (.84) DI:ANTARA lingkaran**

Functionally, RepExps are offered relatively early in the interaction and always without overt learner action or request. That is, the learner does nothing to the visual display and makes no verbal or other kind of request for information from the tutor. In addition, RepExps are offered quickly. Over the course of this protocol, they are offered with a mean delay from the preceding utterance of about 2.25 seconds, significantly faster than all other kinds of repetition observed in the FlatLand transcripts.

A number of observations about the FlatLand protocol help one make sense of how these RepExps are being used. First, learners must sustain and rehearse a phonological representation of input in order for that input to be available for further cognitive processing and storage in memory. Second, virtually all the learners participating in the Flat-

Land protocol report difficulty subvocalizing L2 input. Many learners also report that when they stopped trying to subvocalize input utterances, they were astonished that they could still complete the FlatLand task. Third, phonological representations in general decay rapidly without rehearsal. It is argued in the psycholinguistic literature (Cowan, 1988) that phonological representations decay within about two to three seconds without conscious rehearsal. Given these cognitive observations, together with the distribution of RepExps in the FlatLand data, one can hypothesize that the primary function of a RepExp is to provide the learner with input dedicated to sustaining a phonological representation. One can further hypothesize that this function is mutually assumed by tutor and learner.

The tutor, of course, may not know consciously that the purpose of the RepExp is to help the learner sustain a phonological representation, but it seems reasonable to assume that the tutor notices that the learner needs this kind of help whenever the tutor, assuming the learner's perspective, notices that he himself would need a repetition at that point. If these observations are correct, then an ICALL system would benefit from incorporating within it a tutorial schema like the RepExp as a way of helping the learner toward the internal processing required for word learning in real time.

The FlatLand task and syntactic complexity. Human tutors routinely decide between more and less complex expressions when conveying events or actions to second language learners. For example, the actions depicted in Figure 12.12 can be described

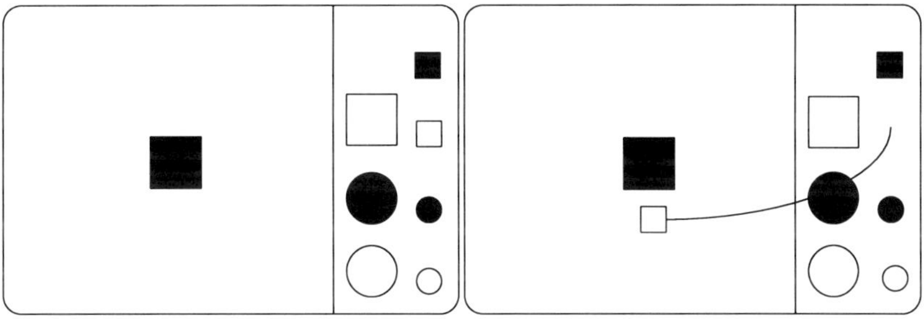

FIG. 12.12. Actions expressed by "The small white square is below the large black square."

either in a single, relatively complex utterance (as in Example 1) or as a series of simpler short utterances (2)a-c that culminate in an expression like (1), as shown in (2)d.

(1) kotak putih kecil dibawa kotak hitam besar
square white small below square black large
'The small white square is below the large black square.'

(2) a. kotak putih kecil
'The small white square'
b. kotak putih kecil dibawa
'The small white square below'
c. dibawa kotak hitam besar
'Below the large black square'

d. kotak putih kecil dibawa kotak hitam besar
square white small below square black large
'The small white square is below the large black square.'

It is, of course, immediately obvious that the set of simpler utterances in (2) is used earlier in the tutorial protocol than (1) is. The human tutor can somehow sense when the learner needs the simpler, decomposed input and when the more complex utterance will do. The ICALL system should in principle mimic whatever that sensing is. It is not enough to specify simplistically that in the beginning of the tutorial the system uses simpler sentences that are replaced later with more complex ones, for this begs the critical question: What are the conditions in the tutorial interaction that call for the use of simpler, decomposed expressions versus their more complex alternatives? How does the tutor decide that just now it is appropriate to use a more complex utterance where several simpler ones had been used previously?

The present model permits one to capture the difference between the simpler and more complex cases. First, there is a link between the clause as an utterance unit and an action node in a task network. Although native speakers must, in a microanalytic sense, navigate through the entire object movement schema in order to place an object in its targeted location (that is, they must identify and acquire the target before moving it, etc.), they can do so almost always via a single complex utterance, such as (1), which expresses the terminal node in the task network. For the native speaker, the terminal event is the essential event, and no action is needed by the tutor to treat earlier nodes in the network as explicit steps in reaching the task goal.

The learner, on the other hand, cannot initially manage the terminal node in the task network—not in L2 at any rate. This requires the tutor to retreat to earlier nodes. In providing input congruent with whatever the current essential event is, the tutor again produce a single utterance for that node. One can therefore see that the set of simpler utterances in (2) is a means of tackling the task by elucidating earlier component nodes in the task network. This is linguistically analogous to the parent unpacking and demonstrating to the child the component actions required to get one's shoe tied. As the component elements of each task become more automated, there is increasingly little reason for unpacking.

How does the tutor decide when to move from less to more complex utterances? In the FlatLand protocols this movement occurs cumulatively as the learner demonstrates the ability to deal successfully with the earlier nodes. Once the learner can manage the identification of the objects involved a particular configuration, the tutor moves toward the identification of the locations. Once the locations are managed well by the learner, the tutor moves to the terminal node in the network. At this point, the tutor reverts to simpler utterances only when the learner demonstrates difficulty completing the task via a more complex utterance. Overall, then, the move from simpler to more complex utterances is not in any simple way merely a linguistic judgment (e.g., a judgment about the level of syntactic competence of the learner). As the tutor and learner interact, the tutor decides to move to more complex utterances based on estimates of what the learner can manage linguistically relative to their joint navigation through the task network. Simpler utterances occur naturally as the reflex of dealing with earlier nodes in the task network;

complex utterances arise naturally as the outcome of accumulating the ability to deal with earlier nodes in the task network.

Conclusions

Utility of the FlatLand Paradigm

The FlatLand paradigm permits a close examination of the very earliest stages of SLA. We can document the time course of acquisition in nil-proficiency learners and examine the protocols to see the contribution of individual utterances to that acquisition. Let us return to the four key questions posed at the beginning of this chapter.

What is comprehensible input? Second language interaction theory argues well that L2 input is most usable to the L2 learner when it is comprehensible (Krashen, 1977a, 1977b, 1982, 1985). However, within the literature it has not been entirely clear what *comprehensible* means. In the model we have been developing through the FlatLand protocol, input is comprehensible just when (a) tutor and learner are on the same node in the task network and (b) that common node is the earliest essential event. When these two conditions are met, input in L2 is comprehensible, and the learner can process that input as intake.

It may be the case that the tutor and learner find themselves on different events in the task model as a result of incorrect estimates on the part of the tutor about which task node the learner is on, or as a result of the task models differing in detail between tutor and learner (e.g., the tutor's model may overestimate the learner's proficiency and lack decomposed nodes). The input provided will thus not be comprehensible to the learner, who will either ignore or question the input or, possibly, incorporate it into false hypotheses about L2. For example, it may be that the learner infers from a longer utterance by the tutor that the tutor assumes a terminal task node, whereas the learner knows that an earlier node is needed; the learner who assumes a cooperative tutor may then indicate confusion or request in L1 that the utterance be repeated or, if the learner is really self-aware, request that it be broken down. Alternatively, the learner may wrongly assume that the tutor's utterance is simply an object-identifying expression. Again, the learner may have assumptions about discourse and about the mapping of utterance length to task nodes that bias toward one or the other interpretation, a possibility that could be tested in further tutoring protocols.

How does the here-and-now principle work to make input more comprehensible? The manipulation of the immediate physical context makes more explicit the task network. As tutor and learner are engaged in configuration building in the FlatLand protocol, the task model takes on dramatically greater concreteness than is the case when the learner is merely observing. For several of the FlatLand protocols, we asked a second individual to observe the interaction from the point of view of the learner and to try to learn to complete the task just as the learner did. This second learner was not able to manipulate the FlatLand world. We found that, whereas the primary learner completed all configurations in the FlatLand task in about 40 minutes and could do so at various later times without intervening practice, the observer always failed to complete the task in subsequent testing episodes.

When does the tutor use structurally less complex forms? Overall, there seems to be a principle at work in the FlatLand protocols that the tutor provide a single utterance with respect to a particular and single action node in the task network (as opposed to linking two nodes in an utterance, as in "Find the X and then move it"). If the tutor provides an utterance vis-à-vis the terminal node, the resulting expression must necessarily be a complex one; for example, "Put the small white circle below the large black square." When the tutor provides an utterance congruent with earlier nodes in the action network, then those nodes, because they unpack and deal with simpler portions of the task, are structurally simpler. For example, the expression for identifying a target location, "above the white circle," is less complex than "Put the small white circle below the large black square." The tutor uses structurally less complex forms exactly when attempting to deal with earlier nodes in the task network.

When does the tutor modify the interactional organization of the protocol? This occurs to ensure that the input can be processed by the learner. For example, the repetition data suggest that the tutor modifies the interaction at particular points to assist the learner in sustaining a phonological representation of the input utterance. Thus, the input provided in a RepExp serves a different function than that of a DescObj schema, for example. A RepExp modifies the interactional organization by shifting the kind of activity in which the participants are engaged; it is designed deliberately to assist the learner in durable lexical learning rather than in completing the task. Other ways in which the interactional organization of the tutoring discourse is systematically modified to serve different purposes are described in Tomlin (1994).

More General Conclusions

ICALL systems require some theory or model of tutorial interaction if they in fact are to be intelligent systems rather than fancy electronic workbooks. At this moment, we are not aware of any ICALL system that is sensitive to the details of how human tutors and learners interact during second language tutorials. Indeed, there are few empirical studies to draw on. Throughout this volume, we see the value of incorporating sophisticated parsers in analyzing the output of second language learners and in providing them with feedback of one kind or another. However, this feedback routinely takes the form of an error report or correction (see chapters in this volume by Levin & Evans, Loritz, Sams, and Weinberg et al.). It is not at all clear that the underlying theory of feedback and correction that implicitly guides these systems aligns well with what human tutors and learners actually do. Therefore, we conclude that ICALL systems ultimately will require designers to pay more attention to basic research in second language learning and teaching. In particular, ICALL designers should not assume that the way they have been taught foreign languages is the best way to teach in an ICALL system. Nor should designers assume that one can come up with governing tutorial principles to serve as control structures for a system without having done the work of examining in detail genuine tutorial interactions between actual tutors and actual learners.

References

Allen, J.P.B., & Widdowson, H. G. (1974). Teaching the communicative use of English. *IRAL*, *12*, 1-21.
Baddeley, A.D. (1986). *Working memory*. New York: Oxford University Press.

Brumfit, C. (1984). *Communicative methodology in language teaching*. Cambridge, UK: Cambridge University Press.

Canale, M., & Swain, M. (1980). Theoretical bases of communicative approaches to second language teaching and testing. *Applied Linguistics*, *1*, 1-47.

Cowan, N. (1988). Evolving conceptions of memory storage, selective attention, and their mutual constraints within the human information-processing system. *Psychological Bulletin*, *104*, 163-191.

Dulay, H., & Burt, M. (1975). Creative construction in second language learning and teaching. In M. Burt & H. Dulay (Eds.), *On TESOL '75* (pp. 21-32). Washington, DC: TESOL.

Flynn, S., & O'Neil, W. (1993). *Linguistic theory in second language acquisition.* Dordrecht, Netherlands: Reidel Press.

Gildea, P.M., Miller, G.A., & Wurtenberg, C.L. (1988). *Contextual enrichment by videodisc: A first report.* Cognitive Science Laboratory, Princeton University.

Givon, T. (1984). Universals of discourse structure and second language acquisition. In W. Rutherford (Ed.), *Language universals and second language acquisition* (pp. 109-136). Amsterdam: John Benjamins.

Hatch, E., Flashner, V., & Hunt, L. (1986). The experience model and language teaching. In R. Day, (Ed.), *Talking to learn: Conversation in second language acquisition* (pp. 5-22). Rowley, MA: Newbury House.

Johnson, K. (1982). *Communicative syllabus design and methodology*. Oxford: Pergamon Press.

Klein, W. (1986). *Second language acquisition*. Cambridge, UK: Cambridge University Press.

Krashen, S. (1977a). The Monitor model for second language performance. In M. Burt, H. Dulay, & M. Finocchiaro (Eds.), *Viewpoints on English as a second language* (pp. 152-161). New York: Regents.

Krashen, S. (1977b). Some issues related to the Monitor model. In H.D. Brown, C. Yorio, & R. Crymes (Eds.), *On TESOL '77: Teaching and learning English as a second language: Trends in reseach and practice* (pp. 144-158). Washington, DC: TESOL.

Krashen, S. (1982). *Principles and practice in second language acquisition.* New York: Pergamon.

Krashen, S. (1985). *The input hypothesis*. London: Longman.

Long, M. (1983). Native speaker/non-native speaker conversation in the second language classroom. In M. Clarke & J. Handscombe (Eds.), *On TESOL '82: Pacific Perspectives on Language Learning and Teaching* (pp. 207-225). Washington, DC: TESOL.

Long, M.H. (1985). Input and second language theory. In S. M. Gass & C. Madden (Eds.), *Input in second language acquisition* (pp. 377-393). Rowley, MA: Newbury House.

Mehan, H. (1979). *Learning lessons*. Cambridge, MA: Harvard University Press.

Norman, D., & Shallice, T. (1980). *Attention to action: Willed and automatic control of behavior* (Center for Human Information Processing Technical Report No. 99). San Diego, CA: UCSD.

Piepho, H. (1983). Establishing objectives in the teaching of English. In C. N. Candlin (Ed.), *The communicative teaching of English* (pp. 8-23). New York: Longman.

Searle, J.R. (1969). *Speech acts*. Cambridge, UK: Cambridge University Press.

Searle, J.R. (1979). *Expression and meaning: Studies in the theory of speech acts*. Cambridge, UK: Cambridge University Press.

Shallice, T. (1972). Dual functions of consciousness. *Psychological Review*, *70*, 383-393.

Shallice, T. (1982). Specific impairments of planning. In D.E. Broadbent & L. Weiskrantz (Eds.), *The neuropsychology of cognitive functions.* London: The Royal Society.

Sinclair, J.M., & Brazil, D. (1982). *Teacher talk*. New York: Oxford University Press.

Sinclair, J.M., & Coulthard, R.M. (1975). *Towards an analysis of discourse*. Oxford: Oxford University Press.

Tomlin, R.S., & Douglas, S. A. (1989). *Beginning second language instruction: computer-based curriculum improvements* (Final Report, Grant No. G008541129). Fund for the Improvement of Post-Secondary Education, FIPSE.

Tomlin, R.S. (1994). Repetition in second language acquisition. In B. Johnstone (Ed.), *Repetition in discourse: Interdisciplinary perspectives* (pp. 172-194). New York: Ablex.

Widdowson, H. G. (1978). *Teaching language as communication*. New York: Oxford University Press.

Widdowson, H. G. (1979). *Explorations in applied linguistics*. New York: Oxford University Press.

13

Lessons Learned from the Athena Language Learning Project: Using Natural Language Processing, Graphics, Speech Processing, and Interactive Video for Communication-Based Language Learning

Janet H. Murray
Massachusetts Institute of Technology

The Athena Language Learning Project at the Massachusetts Institute of Technology (MIT) began in 1983 as an attempt to apply the principles of communicative language learning to the multifunctional interactive medium promised by emerging technologies. The three emerging technologies that the project explored were natural language processing (NLP), interactive video, and speech processing. Graphics were used to create a microworld in which to exchange natural language input and computer generated language as output (Kramsch, Morgenstern, & Murray, 1985; Murray, Furstenberg, & Morgenstern, 1988).

Project methodologies derived from the theories of project cofounder Claire Kramsch (now Professor of German at the University of California at Berkeley). She drew on research in sociolinguistics. Kramsch stressed the importance of language as part of a larger cultural context and as a medium for conveying meaning always embedded in interpersonal exchanges (Kramsch, 1989). This position is in opposition to the pedagogy that sees the acquisition of language solely as the mastery of a set of grammatical rules and the acquisition of discrete vocabulary items. The second cofounder was Douglas Morgenstern, now Senior Lecturer in Spanish at MIT, who was an innovator in the use of simulation methodologies for language learning. Both saw the computer as a locus for communicative exchanges, where the student could practice using language with imaginary interlocutors. Kramsch, Morgenstern and I formed the core group of the project. My own background was in English literature, particularly in narrative structure, complemented by a stint as a systems programmer for IBM. It became my job to translate the goals of the foreign language teachers into programmable designs. Because the teachers themselves had no experience with computers, they were not limited by the existing capabilities of programmed learning. Our designs therefore reflected not the existing computational medium but the one that would emerge as the new multifunctional workstations came into being. This medium is, of course, still emerging almost 10 years later, and we still find that our designs outstrip the available technology.

Suzanne Flynn, Professor of Linguistics and English as a Second Language, participated as the chief investigator of the speech processing system. It was developed for pronunciation practice for Asian and Spanish speakers learning English. Gilberte Furstenberg, Senior Lecturer in French, joined the group to work on interactive video for learning French (Furstenberg, 1988, 1992). For technical advice we consulted Robert Berwick, Professor of Electrical Engineering and Computer Science and expert in natural language processing; Kenneth Stevens, Clarence J. Lebel Professor of Electrical Engineering; Andrew Lippman, one of the founders of MIT's Media Lab; Glorianna Davenport, Associate Professor of Media Arts and Sciences; and Harold Abelson, Professor of

Electrical Engineering and Computer Science and one of the key developers of LOGO, the pioneer of microworld design. We also had extensive involvement from graduate students in MIT's Department of Linguistics who provided the schematic representation of the several languages in our NLP system.

We were able to accomplish more than our level of resources would ordinarily achieve largely because we benefited from an atmosphere at MIT that encourages collaborative interdisciplinary work and smiles upon the process of making something new and useful. By January 1985 our idea had grown into the largest project under the institute-wide initiative for educational software called Project Athena. Our chief funder was the Annenberg/CPB Foundation. As humanists at MIT, we felt a dual obligation to capture the leading technical advances for the purposes of language teachers and to convert our ideas into products that would have the greatest possible usefulness. This involved taking risks with emerging technologies while keeping an eye on the delivery environment in modestly funded language labs.

Designing Exercises Using Natural Language Processing

The Athena Language Learning Project set out to model exercises for the emerging workstation medium. Our initial focus was on NLP research. We set out to build a multilingual system that would support several kinds of microworlds and would generate as well as accept language. We particularly wanted to engage the student in conversations that would adhere to desirable rules of discourse structure. When we started out we had two natural language applications in mind. *LINGO,* authored by Claire Kramsch, is a graphics-based conversation with a poltergeist who can be directed to clean up or mess up an apartment (Figure 13.1 represents a sample screen). *No recuerdo,* authored by Douglas Morgenstern, is an interactive video exercise that allows students to converse with on-screen characters who return the conversation with canned remarks or with spontaneously generated text.

FIG. 13.1. Sample screen from LINGO.

To implement these and projected future exercises in all the languages taught at MIT, we developed a natural language processing system that accepted input and created output in French, German, Spanish, Russian, and English. We later did a pilot project involving Japanese (Hirata, 1986; Tenny, 1986) and a cooperative project with Harvard University that added grammar rules for classical Greek to the parser. In addition to the original two projects, we designed a third based on the Spanish capabilities of the system and not using the discourse and knowledge representation components of the NLP system: *The Intelligent Workbook* was authored by Douglas Morgenstern and includes a series of exercises that allow students to receive grammar correction on sentences created in a limited domain of prestructured conversations based on communicative functions.

None of the three NLP exercises was completed to the point of delivery to students. All three reached the demonstration stage. At that point we concluded that the underlying hardware environment was not yet ready to support such systems at the complexity at which we wanted to work. The range of student input proved to be more demanding than we predicted. Although we saw several ways to improve our own NLP system (see the chapter in this volume by Felshin), we felt the major stumbling block to successful implementation was the speed and capacity of current hardware. We did not see a way to cope with the complexities of the problem within current levels of language processing speed. Therefore, we decided to wait until parallel processing and similar advances increase our ability to process language before attempting to bring these designs to the level of reliability necessary for use with students.

Our NLP system remains functional and is now running on the Macintosh. It has been used at MIT in teaching computational linguistics, and it is incorporated in Hamburger's FLUENT program (see Hamburger, this volume). We are looking into ways of making it more widely available as a general research system. Although we have postponed our work on NLP systems because of the scarcity of funds for humanities applications and because of the need to work on projects that will be of more immediate usefulness, we still have confidence in the pedagogic and design strategies we devised, and we look forward to returning to this research when the hardware catches up to our needs.

Design of the NLP System

The strategy for designing the NLP system was to create a language-independent framework with language-specific modules (see Figure 13.2.). The parser is based on compiler technology and was of the LALR (i.e., look ahead, left to right) type. We had originally used the Marcus parser but found it too inefficient for languages other than English. The LALR parser was designed by Stuart Malone, currently head programmer for the Laboratory for Advanced Technology in the Humanities (LATH). The linguistics programming was done by Sue Felshin, currently head linguistics programmer for LATH. The work was overseen by Robert Berwick. (For a more technical description of the system than the following overview, see the accompanying chapter by Felshin, this volume; see also Malone & Felshin, 1991.)

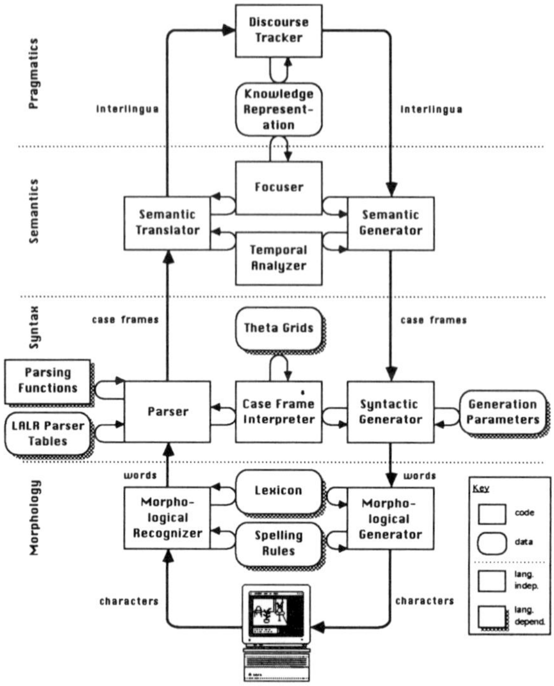

FIG. 13.2. Design of the NLP system in the Athena Language Learning Project.

The NLP system is designed to be multifunctional. Referring to Figure 13.2, the shaped boxes are the only parts that are language specific. Rectangles represent processing components; rounded rectangles represent data. The system has morphological, syntactic, semantic, and pragmatic components for both input and output. Typed input is processed first as strings of characters that are turned into words according to language-dependent spelling rules, which also mark the words with parts of speech (e.g., adjective, noun, feminine, masculine, etc.). They are then parsed by the syntactic system, which refers to language-dependent parsing functions and case frames. This results in a representation of subject, object, verb, participial phrase, and so forth. The result of this processing, expressed as case frames, is passed to the semantic processor, which examines both pronoun reference (focus) and constructions relating to tense and aspect. The result is a representation that is entirely language independent (although the Lisp code looks like English) and represents the idea expressed in the input string. For instance, if the input were in Spanish, "Ponga el libro en la mesa" (Put the book on the table), the interlingua or conceptual representation would be

```
(#S(PARAGRAPH
   REFERENCES
    (#S(REFERENCE
        INSTANCE #<UTTERANCE #XFF0279>
        PHRASE
```

```
#S(V-PHRASE
   PRED :PUT
   VOICE :ACTIVE
   TMA (#S(WARP INFO (:IMPERATIVE)))
   ARGS
   (#S(REFERENCE
       ROLE :AGENT
       INSTANCE #<PERSON #XD881A9>
       PHRASE #S(N-PHRASE PRED :ANIM-PWO
                          NUMBER :SINGULAR)
       HOW :ANAPHORIC-PRONOUN
       VIA :EXOPHORIC)
    #S(REFERENCE
       SNAGS ((0 . #<AMBIGUOUS-SNAG #XFEF931>))
       ROLE :PATIENT
       INSTANCE #<AMBIGUOUS #XFEF909>
       PHRASE #S(N-PHRASE PRED :BOOK NUMBER :SINGULAR)
       HOW :ANAPHORIC
       VIA :EXOPHORIC)
    #S(REFERENCE
       ROLE :GOAL
       INSTANCE #<TABLE #XD886F9>
       PHRASE #S(N-PHRASE PRED :TABLE NUMBER :SINGULAR REL :AT)
       HOW :ANAPHORIC
       VIA :EXOPHORIC
       NODE #<NODE PREPP>
       PROMINENCE :POSSIBLE-FOCUS)))
```

The difference in length between the input and the representation makes clear how much must be specified to represent even simple statements about a narrowly defined world. At this point in the NLP analysis, the system is dealing in pragmatics, which is to say in the microworld that defines an application. The system is designed so that the microworlds can be interchanged. The microworld consists of two components: a knowledge representation, which knows about the poltergeist's room or the amnesiac scientist's secrets, and a discourse tracker that knows about the way to talk to a German poltergeist or a Spanish scientist. These components analyze the input and initiate an appropriate action in the microworld (e.g., moving the book) or create a suitable output string—again in language-independent form. This interlingua representation is passed down through semantic, syntactic, and morphological processors that are designed for generating rather than interpreting language. The result is a grammatical utterance in the target language (e.g., "The book is already on the table").

The system includes error analysis for language-dependent errors such as agreement and for other language-specific errors. It has a set of expected errors, errors based upon our assumption that the learner's first language is English. The parser treats these errors in two ways: with rules for incorrect structures and with relaxed rules for correct structures that assign penalty values to certain expected errors but allow the parse to proceed. Disambiguation is handled with penalties that amount to an *improbability index*, allowing us to choose between two possible interpretations when one is less likely than the other.

The system can also make disambiguating inquiries originating at the pragmatic level, such as "Which book did you mean?"

LINGO

The LINGO world owes something to Terry Winograd's SHRDLU in that it is a world of visible objects that are altered in response to typed input (Winograd, 1972). The dialogue is made more communicative by giving the agent a personality as a cranky poltergeist. Graphics are intended to be culturally authentic, changing depending on which language is in use. Ultimately the system is meant to evolve into an authoring system in which teachers select sets of objects and tasks in order to target specific linguistic skills.

LINGO dialogue. The following LINGO dialogue, which the system runs in German, Spanish, and English, illustrates the functionalities of the system. The utterances of Drulla the Poltergeist are constructed from a language-independent representation by the syntactic, semantic, and pragmatic parts of the NLP system. In addition to a knowledge of the grammar, the system has a schema of the discourse, a picture of the world as it is and the rules by which it can be changed. Drulla can make suggestions as well as respond to input. She has a concept of what is in focus—what object has last been mentioned and is likely to be the referent for a pronoun (e.g., "Open it," says the student, referring to the closet which Drulla has just announced is closed). Throughout the dialogue the screen reflects the poltergeist's actions. Although the graphics included here are generic, the German version includes culturally authentic objects such as furnishings to increase the student's sense of immersion.

> Poltergeist: Hello. My name is Drulla. I am a poltergeist. I can help you to mess up the room. You can ask me to do things or you can ask me questions. Let's start to play now, O.K.?
> Student: No.
> Drulla: Play, please!
> Student: Okay.
> Drulla: Thank you! What should I do?
> Student: You should tell me where the glass is.
> Drulla: The glass is on the table.
> Student: Try laying it inside the fridge.
> Drulla: Very good. I have laid the glass inside the refrigerator. Now what should we do?
> Student: Tell me where the book is.
> Drulla: I don't know which book you're talking about.
> Student: The red book.
> Drulla: The book is lying on the bed.
> Student: Okay, put it upside-down under the bed.
> Drulla: Okay, I have put the book under the bed upside down. What do you think I should do now?
> Student: Look inside the closet.
> Drulla: The closet isn't open. I can't see the contents.
> Student: Open it, then.
> Drulla: Okay, I have opened the closet. [A shirt is visible inside the closet now.] Do something with the shirt.
> Student: Put it in the fridge.
> Drulla: Very good. I have put the shirt in the refrigerator. What should we do now?
> Student: Try putting the closet on the rubbertree.
> Drulla: Are you kidding? The closet is too heavy!

Student: Try the chair, then.
Drulla: I like that! I have put the chair on the poor rubbertree. The poor rubbertree has been killed. What should we do now?
Student: Pour the milk in the vase.
Drulla: There isn't enough space in the vase.
Student: Try the beer then.
Drulla: A wonderful idea! I have poured the beer in the vase. The poor flowers have been killed. I think you have done enough damage now. Good-bye.

Drulla closes the game when the room is messy enough based on an internal score. The same components can be used to create a scenario in which the student neatens the room or looks for a lost object or packs a suitcase, and so forth.

Key functionalities of LINGO. No formal evaluation was done on LINGO because we were not able to use it with students due to hardware-driven graphics speed limitations. However, interest in the design remains strong in focus groups with language teachers and leads us to the conclusion that it is a usable idea, particularly for a multipurpose environment with authoring capabilities. Perhaps the strongest component in LINGO is the concept of the poltergeist itself, which lends psychological verisimilitude to the interaction. The personality quirks of the interlocutor are as motivating as the immediate gratification of seeing the graphics change, based on the responses of those to whom we have introduced it. The challenge in extending the idea is to make more scenarios with involving tasks and appropriate interlocutors.

Assuming that one can master the linguistic domain—a big and as yet unproven assumption—the LINGO model, simple though it is, allows for a number of interlocutor roles that I suggest should form the basis for building interlocutors in an NLP system:

- agent, a personification of the computer's responsiveness in performing tasks set by the student, like the poltergeist's invisible hand;
- interlocutor, a personality who can have specific comic debilities or obstructionist behavior and who could model or demand specific language functions (such as politeness);
- coach, an observer of student activities who suggests actions, gives hints, encourages certain actions;
- informant, who models correct speech and culturally appropriate ideas.

The more one can embody these pedagogical functions in culturally authentic, literally appealing characters, the more one can engage the student in the simulated world within the computer. This engagement allows for the student to form the intrinsically meaningful, motivated tasks that many theorists believe are the basis for successful language learning.

No recuerdo

No recuerdo (I don't remember), written by Douglas Morgenstern, Senior Lecturer in Spanish, is based on a conversational story model. Set in Bogotá, Colombia, the story centers around Gonzalo Restrepo Arenas, an amnesiac microbiologist from Colombia who appears to the student on videodisc. The student's task is to interview him (and a few other key characters) and to move him gradually toward regaining his memory. The plot is dramatic and includes a kidnapping, differing versions of the same event from the protagonist and his lover (who is possibly his kidnapper), and science fantasy elements involving a plague of memory loss linked to recombinant DNA research. The student is motivated in the conversations by a desire to uncover the truth. The system's failures are rendered believable by the amnesia conceit. The conversations progress from simple exchanges about the weather to more pointed exchanges about the kidnapping. The student is meant to learn that in Latin America it is considered impolite to ask personal questions directly. It is necessary to engage in small talk and in discourse strategies that build confidence, such as echoing and expressing empathy. Answers to the student's questions are in the form of prerecorded responses (either in moving video or in audio over a still) or in text responses displayed over a still and created on the fly.

The video increases the motivation of the student and provides for a much greater authenticity and complexity of language than one can capture in an NLP system. The combination of video and NLP technology is particularly promising because it can potentially involve the student directly in a rich linguistic and cultural world. Unfortunately, we were not able to proceed with the NLP version of *No recuerdo* and are now creating a version in which the conversations are held in a menu-driven framework. The menu-driven *No recuerdo* is being built with the aid of an authoring template that should prove useful in creating menu-based interactive fictions with and without video components. The conversation with a fictional character remains a promising avenue even without the NLP component. We look forward to resuming the discourse-based conversational structure that we pioneered in the original *No recuerdo* design when hardware environments are more supportive of NLP work.

The Intelligent Workbook

This is the most currently feasible of the projects that we modeled as demonstrations of the NLP system. Douglas Morgenstern developed a series of lessons based on the functionalities common to foreign language textbooks. The student is given a situation and an English paraphrase of utterances. The student then constructs his or her own Spanish utterances and submits them for immediate feedback in a correction window of the workspace. The feedback includes grammar correction as well as a version of the dialogue created by a native Spanish speaker. The corrected utterance becomes part of a dialogue situation. This design maintains some of the conversational structure while making the input much more predictable. It also emphasizes the grammar-correcting capabilities of the NLP system, which are strong.

This design was successfully modeled but not fully implemented because of the difficulties (described previously) in accommodating the wide range of student input, even for so constricted a domain. It was also clear that such a grammar-checking program was of less pedagogical interest to language teachers than our interactive videos.

Our decision not to pursue the *Intelligent Workbook* at that time (1990) makes clear one of the limitations of NLP work. It is an expensive technology whose chief application is in grammar correction, which is an area that may already be adequately covered by other means, especially for languages close to English, such as French and Spanish. More highly structured or linguistically distant languages, such as Russian, Japanese, or Arabic, may be more appropriate domains for such a system. Nevertheless, even for French and Spanish, language instructors may find it useful to have a correction system that handles free input. At the current time, developers must choose between far more restrictive systems for grammar correction or stepping back and waiting for computational advances that will provide the superior processing power to handle freer and more pedagogically desirable input in real time.

Speech Processing System

The Athena Language Learning Project also created a speech processing system that trained students to identify the differences between sounds such as the *l* and *r* for Japanese learners of English and then used spectrographs to help them produce the appropriate sounds. This project was directed by Suzanne Flynn and Sharon Manual. The project results indicated that display of spectrograms in real time was a valuable technique in learning to produce these elusive differences but that it was probably necessary to have a teacher work with the student at least part of the time at the machine. On the other hand, students could independently learn to differentiate aurally between formerly undifferentiated sounds (including English vowel sounds for native Spanish speakers learning English) by working only with the machine-based exercises.

This is an area in which technology has caught up with our designs in a gratifying way. Although our original system became stranded on now out-of-date UNIX platforms, we plan to move these exercises to the Macintosh, which is now capable of real-time speech processing.

Although these pronunciation exercises are not communication based in the usual sense, they address a crucial problem of adult second language learners, one that often prevents students from using the target language because of embarrassment and frustration. In addition to measured improvement, students who tested our pronunciation workstation were enthusiastic and grateful, sometimes mentioning years of fruitless efforts in mastering these distinctions.

Interactive Video

Finally, we created three interactive video programs that represented original attempts to define two new subgenres: the interactive narrative and the interactive documentary. These programs have been extensively written about elsewhere (Furstenberg, 1988, 1992; Murray, 1990, 1992; Murray et al., 1988), and so I briefly describe them here.

A la rencontre de Philippe was developed by Gilberte Furstenberg and is an interactive narrative. Philippe needs a new place to live or help in making up with his girlfriend who is kicking him out of her apartment. The student accompanies him through the day providing help through interactive conversations, surrogate travel around Paris, use of virtual objects such as a telephone and answering machine, and intensive listening to very rapid, authentic French with the aid of a suite of computer-based comprehension tools.

Dans le quartier St. Gervais is an interactive documentary developed by Gilberte Furstenberg. Students at beginning, intermediate, or advanced levels can explore a neighborhood of Paris, meet the people who live and work there, learn about the history of the neighborhood from the 17th century to the present, and make their own minidocumentaries and multimedia documents based on the material in the program.

No Recuerdo is an interactive narrative with documentary elements, developed by Douglas Morgenstern. It includes the amnesiac scientist adventure described earlier as well as explorations of Bogotá. The student is in the role of a journalist who must report on Bogotá and get the story of Gonzalo's adventures.

All these projects were designed to be exploratory in nature, motivating the students by intrinsic rather than extrinsic rewards. There is not a right and wrong path to the narratives, which both have multiple endings and many ways of threading through the story. However, the microworlds are designed in a way influenced by the work of Seymour Papert, so that they invite engagement and so that engagement is rewarded with consequences (Papert, 1980). The more students explore in Philippe's world the more they can influence the story. But nothing they do is penalized as a wrong answer. The only incorrect response is lack of engagement.

Both interactive fiction and interactive documentary have that build confidence proven to be valuable genres for introducing students to authentic language at all stages of language learning. Narrative is motivating and provides students with a structured experience. These programs are not limited to use as a narrative, either. Furstenberg and Morgenstern have developed several exercises for *Philippe* and *No recuerdo* that students have used successfully without involvement in the entire story. Because the video is on a randomly retrievable medium (currently videodisc, eventually CD-ROM) it can be treated as a data bank and indexed for linguistic functions. An example would be to access every event in which people greet one another. Interactive documentary is more flexible, however, and if done correctly, an excellent corrective to stereotyping of foreign cultures. It is less likely to become dated and, because it is not linked to a story line, it is open to multiple uses. Both genres have a role to play in curricular materials. Both are superior to video shaped in conventional lesson format because they have richer cultural content and can be used in multiple ways.

One of the chief surprises of the ALLP work is the rapidity with which teachers and hardware developers accepted the new interactive video technologies. The ALLP designs were invented in an environment in which there was no software to produce interactive narratives or documentaries—only rigid, lesson-oriented programs. The hardware needed to run the interactive video programs at that time cost as much as $100,000. Currently the ALLP videodisc programs run on a configuration that costs $2,500 and is readily available in secondary schools, colleges, and universities nationwide and even worldwide. More importantly, language teachers have eagerly turned to interactive video to deliver authentic language that is otherwise unavailable or too dense to be comprehensible by students. The match between this technology and the goals of language teaching is clear and widely recognized.

We are only beginning to understand the ways in which the curriculum will be reshaped by the inclusion of video resources. We are finding that we can teach things that could not be taught before with precision and immediacy. There is no reason why the book should be at the center of language courses. It seems increasingly likely that a multimedia environment will take the place of the book, with a corresponding restructuring of what is taught and the manner in which the teaching takes place. At MIT a new teaching environment, the Language Learning and Resource Center, combines multimedia classrooms with carrels so that students can bring their computer-based work into the classroom. Teachers can present computer-based material to large and small groups. Experience with the new materials in the new environments is already resulting in a reshaping of methods and curriculum. We are just at the beginning of this process.

Learning Styles

The formative evaluation of the ALLP videodiscs (Brownfield, 1990) indicated that there are roughly speaking three ways of going through exploratory interactive materials:

- Look first, carefully doing all the previewing exercises and then reviewing the video, with transcription and glossary tools, until you understand every word.
- Leap right in with no previewing and barrel through without reviewing, guessing at the answers and only correcting yourself when you hit a barrier.
- Leap in and try to figure things out, and then look things up as you need.

Clearly, the third method is the preferable one and the one that most nearly models the successful language learner in the authentic situation, where you must try to make do with less than perfect knowledge and correct yourself and obtain more information as you go along. A remaining question is how to encourage this approach in our students.

Because the interactive technologies are intrinsically procedural, they represent the opportunity to model the how of learning as well as the what. A clear future goal as we gain more experience with these technologies is to help students use the materials to learn how to be successful learners.

Future Directions

The Athena Language Learning Project will be over formally when the last evaluative work is done in early 1994. Meanwhile, the original group has grown into a new structure at MIT, the Laboratory for Advanced Technology in the Humanities (LATH). LATH is carrying on interactive video projects in Japanese and in English as a second language and is the home of the Shakespeare Interactive Archive. LATH is meant to provide exemplary applications and building blocks for projects that cannot be supported by existing marketplace technologies.

The major direction for LATH research is interactive video, to be delivered in the short term on videodisk and ultimately on CD-ROM. Current efforts center on the creation of multifunctional archive architecture and the creation of a library of loosely related interactive documentaries for language learning from a variety of cultures. The NLP system has been ported to the Macintosh, but we await future hardware advances before resuming research in this direction.

NLP work remains promising for language learning, especially in the work of analyzing input from a syntactic perspective. NLP systems could provide students with immediate grammar-checking feedback, and more importantly perhaps, they could provide researchers with important information on student errors, which could broaden our knowledge of second language acquisition. In this regard, work currently being done by Robert Berwick and Suzanne Flynn at MIT, including analyzing errors with a principle-based parser, is particularly interesting to us (Flynn, 1987).

NLP systems are more problematic as creators of output. Although it is easier to generate language than to analyze input, computer-generated language raises questions of authenticity. It is important to define tasks narrowly to create microworlds in which the computer-generated language is credible. However, if we limit ourselves to grammar-driven or function-driven language that is too narrowly focused, we risk producing very sterile output.

NLP systems seem to be of most use when tied either to microworlds like LINGO or to targeted Intelligent Workbook applications, like our own or like the ALICE, CALLE, and BRIDGE applications described in this volume (see, respectively, Levin & Evans; Rypa & Feuerman; Weinberg, Garman, Martin, & Merlo). The limitation of the Workbook style exercises is the degree to which they allow free input. Microworlds are even more limited by the current level of responsiveness of NLP systems. In the long run NLP holds considerable promise not just for language learning but for literary purposes as well (Murray, 1991). Even within the limitations of current NLP responsiveness, LINGO-like microworlds can be used to support targeted skills in an environment where students are encouraged to initiate language and receive immediate intrinsic feedback. They can play a role in motivating repeated practice in a meaningful context, substituting genuine involvement for rote repetition of targeted constructions. Much that is worthwhile can be done with only simple sentences, which would provide the most likelihood of success. The FLUENT system, described by Hamburger (this volume), is pursuing this possibility.

Insofar as these microworlds give feedback without native language (L1) intervention, provide extensive practice, and offer the opportunity for student initiation of language, they are promising and should be further explored. But such systems provide only a small part of the functionality language teachers seek in an environment in which students can initiate utterances. Only when they are capable of receiving much freer input will they command the attention of the majority of language teachers. Even then, NLP systems need to be combined with extensive exposure to authentic speech produced not by machines but by native speakers in the culturally appropriate environment. The ideal medium for presenting this input is, of course, interactive video.

One way of avoiding the problems of inauthenticity and of unmanageable input is to limit NLP systems to reference use. To this end our group, Professor Kenneth Hale, and S. J. Keyser of MIT's Linguistics Department are currently designing an advanced bi-directional lexical translation system that allows translation of words in context. This system will provide the correct translation based on context. This project, named CASTLE, or Computer-Aided Semantic Translating Lexicon Experiment, will translate between Spanish and English and between Japanese and English on typed-in short phrases. Such a tool can make up for the deficiencies of traditional dictionaries, which will tell you, for instance, that *preguntar* means "ask" but will not describe how the grammars of the two languages encode the overlapping but not parallel usages of the words. Because the syntax of the input sentences to the translation system is only as complex as necessary to give context, the parser should be able to operate in real time, and grammars can be restricted to a manageable size.

The use of graphics-based animation raises the same issues of functionality versus authenticity as machine-processed language. Graphics microworlds are desirable because they are dynamic and can change with interaction in an exciting and motivating way. Graphics-based interactions can be structured to avoid L1 intervention by illustrating the target language directly rather than translating it. In this regard graphics are superior to video, which is by nature canned and unchanging, though it can be accessed in a flexible manner. Video can never compete with animation in the range of response that it can support. Yet animation is clearly a culturally impoverished reality compared to video.

Even video, which is so much richer than machine-generated language and image, offers the potential for distortion. Pedagogically produced video is notoriously stereotyped, and more sophisticated production often introduces the subtler distortions of broadcast television conventions. In the end we have to remind ourselves that there is no technology or combination of technologies that offer the solution to language learning. The embedding of language in culture requires a humanistic approach, with the teacher as an active participant and with the student exposed to a wide range of speakers and writers in an exploratory, multidimensional learning environment.

Conclusion

Language learning is changing rapidly with the introduction of the new technologies and particularly in response to the availability of interactive video, which provides authentic speech and cultural context in a comprehensible format. Although some may use the new technologies to produce multimedia versions of the old (and discredited) programmed learning, the academic world will continue to stress culture and language as one entity and to resist attempts to automate language learning and off-load it onto machines.

At the same time, the pressures of global coexistence push us to develop the means of fostering cross-cultural understanding rather than merely facilitating instant business-speak. The changes to look for, therefore, are the displacement of the book from the center of the curriculum, the redefinition of the teacher from sole purveyor of the language to orchestrator of tasks, and the reinvention of the student as a discoverer of information in a responsive and demystifying data bank. Of the several technologies that will play a role in advancing these changes, the most important one will be interactive video, with significant roles to be played by speech processing, graphics animation, and—once the hardware base is faster and nimbler—natural language processing.

References

Brownfield, S. (1990). *Methodological issues when using self reports in evaluating instructional videodiscs.* Unpublished doctoral dissertation, Harvard University.

Flynn, S. (1987). *A parameter-setting model of L2 acquisition: Experimental studies in anaphora.* Dordrecht: Reidel.

Furstenberg, G. (1988). Quand une pedagogie rencontre une technologie. *Le Francais dans le Monde,* 158-166. Paris: Hachette.

Furstenberg, G. (1992). Developing comprehension of spoken French through interaction within an authentic cultural context: An illustration of the use of videodisc technology for foreign language learning. In R. B. Kozma & J. Johnston (Eds.), *Educational computing in the humanities.* Ann Arbor, MI: University of Michigan Institute for Social Research.

Hirata, J. (1986). *A Japanese parser.* Unpublished undergraduate dissertation, Massachusetts Institute of Technology.

Kramsch, C. (1989). New directions in the teaching of language and culture. *Occasional Papers of the National Foreign Language Center*, No. 4, Washington, D.C.

Kramsch, C., Morgenstern, D., & Murray, J. H. (1985). Designing materials for the language lab of the future: An overview of the MIT Athena language learning project. *The CALICO Journal, 2*, 31-34.

Malone, S., & Felshin, S. (1991). GLR parsing for erroneous input. In M. Tomita (Ed.), *Generalized LR parsing.* Norwell, MA: Kluwer.

Murray, J.H. (1990). Emerging genres of interactive videodiscs for language instruction. *Multimedia and language learning.* Chapel Hill, NC: University of North Carolina Academic Computing Publications.

Murray, J.H. (1991). Anatomy of a new medium: Literary and pedagogic uses of advanced linguistic computer structures. *Computers and the Humanities, XXV*, 1-14.

Murray, J.H. (1992). Restructuring time, space, story, and text in advanced multimedia learning environments. In E. Barrett (Ed.), *The social creation of knowledge.* Cambridge, MA: MIT Press.

Murray, J.H., Furstenberg, G., & Morgenstern, D. (1988). The Athena language learning project: Design issues for the next generation of computer-based language learning tools. In F. Smith (Ed.), *Modern technology in foreign language education.* Lincolnwood, IL: NIC Publishing Group.

Papert, S. (1980). *Mindstorms.* New York: Basic Books.

Tenny, C.L. (1986). A context free rule system for parsing Japanese. *MIT-Japan science and technology program reports*, Massachusetts Institute of Technology.

Winograd, T. (1972). *Understanding natural language.* New York: Academic Press.

14

The Athena Language Learning Project NLP System: A Multilingual System for Conversation-Based Language Learning

Sue Felshin
Massachusetts Institute of Technology

The Athena Language Learning Project (ALLP) is described in broad view in the chapter by Murray (this volume). The current chapter focuses on the natural language processing (NLP) system developed for the ALLP and in particular, the computational details of the NLP and conclusions reached in the course of its development (further details appear in Felshin, 1993; Malone & Felshin, 1991). Murray gives an overview of the NLP system, including a schematic diagram of its components (Figure 13.2), and these will be expanded here. Extensive work on the NLP in several languages has produced a system that works very well as a prototype but is not sufficiently reliable as a delivery system, largely in the syntactic recognition of students' input. Therefore, although the ALLP has developed a small number of prototypes of NLP applications—such as the LINGO microworld described by Murray—these remain experimental and have not been readied for users.

Scope of the NLP

The NLP system developed in the ALLP supports Spanish, French, German, English, and Russian. The system addresses both recognition and generation of language. The recognition module accepts typed sentential input from students and analyzes its morphological, syntactic, semantic, temporal, and, to some degree, pragmatic structure. For input in a specific language the system produces a language-independent conceptual representation, or *interlingua*. The system can detect errors students make and can construct the best possible interpretation given those errors. Errors in agreement are anticipated by relaxing constraints in the rules that comprise the system. Structural errors such as misorderings are anticipated by addition of extra rules or more flexible rules. The generation module of the system can be used to re-output erroneous input with the student's errors corrected or to output artificially computed responses, as in a simulated dialogue. Because our system is based on linguistic theory (as far as possible given constraints in development time, processing speed, and advances in the field of linguistics), we assume that it is well suited to anticipating, detecting, and correcting probable human errors.

The Spanish implementation of the system can generally process sentences that are input by first through fourth-semester college-level students. The lexicon includes some 3,000 roots from a variety of sources, including popular textbooks. The Spanish system not only detects and recovers from errors, but also analyzes them for the student and outputs corrected versions of the student's language. The French and German systems run at about the second- or third-semester level, include error detection and recovery, and have large, accurate lexicons. The English system runs, with error detection and recovery, at about the level of the Spanish. The Russian system includes a large, accurate lexicon but little semantic information and minimal error detection, and it does not generate output. The Spanish and English systems have nearly complete temporal modules for high-level processing of tense and aspect in students' language; French and German have bare-bones temporal modules.

As a cooperative effort with Harvard's Perseus Project, the ALLP has written a Classical Greek implementation that includes a grammar and semantic information and that accesses the Perseus Project's lexicon. The Greek implementation detects syntactic and semantic errors and is intended to analyze them for the user, but it does not process the input into interlingua or generate corrected output. The Perseus Project's lexicon does not provide for error detection, so no lexical or morphological errors are detected.

Structural Overview

For each language supported by the system, for every level, we store appropriate data or, occasionally, code. Data is generally bidirectional (i.e., used for both recognition and generation), whereas code is most often monodirectional. Because our system works by translating input into a language-independent format and then regenerating in the target language, each language's data is independent of every other language's data. Consequently, adding a language to the system entails only the encoding of information specific to that language. This kind of modular separation of linguistic data from other processes is similarly used to achieve generalizability across languages in tutoring systems such as ALICE-chan (Levin & Evans, this volume).

To use the NLP for a language-teaching application like the LINGO microworld requires the addition of a top-level control module and knowledge representation system. The system lends itself to the addition of any number of control modules, which would allow it to be extended to a variety of language teaching tasks, such as morphological, lexical, syntactic, semantic, and temporal drills, translation exercises, and simulation games. With modification, it could also be used as a natural language interface (e.g., to a database system) or for research in machine translation.

Summary of the NLP Software

The NLP system in the ALLP uses language-independent processors to control both recognition and generation of input and output at every level of analysis. These processors include modules that handle the following functions: spelling rules, lexical lookup in a compacted lexicon, best-first generalized LR (i.e., left to right—rightmost derivation) parsing, case frame interpretation and thematic role assignment, resolution of underspecified noun phrases and other referential expressions, conversion of input to language-independent form, and generation of output from interlingua using generally accepted principles of universal and transformational grammar (see, e.g., Chomsky, 1981, and the discussion of principles and parameters parsing by Weinberg, Garman, Martin, & Merlo, this volume, and by Berwick, Abney, & Tenny, 1991). In addition, modules written in C produce generalized LALR (look ahead, left to right) parsing tables from context-free rules and automatically format parse trees, case frames, and interlingua for screen display.

All parts of the system are designed to facilitate detection, recovery, and correction of ill-formed input.

The system consists of four major categories of software. *Low-level tools* are modules unrelated to natural language processing that are used by the rest of the system, such as debugging aids and memory management tools. *Language-independent modules* include the parser, lexical storage, lookup and generation code, a case frame interpreter, a focuser, temporal processing, syntactic generation, and other minor programs, which apply to any language. *Language-dependent modules* include, for each supported language, a lexicon, a grammar, temporal rules and data, some information for generation, spelling rules, and keyboard layout information (to be described in more detail later in the chapter). *Microworlds* each require a top-level control module and may include some exercise-specific knowledge representation. Our system is written largely in Common Lisp, with a few auxiliary precompilers and debugging tools written in C. The Common Lisp code is completely portable except for file access code and the function `copy`, which is an extension to Common Lisp.

Summary of Language-Dependent Modules

Language-dependent code, specific to each language addressed by the ALLP, includes the following components:

1. *Character sets* allow us to isolate keyboard differences between different machines, to handle customized keyboard layouts for foreign languages, to display what the user types in a font appropriate for the language, and to make it easy to key in and read the lexicon.

2. *Features* describe the inflectional information of morphological and syntactic units (i.e., morphemes, words, and phrases). Features are arranged in a complex hierarchical system. For instance, in Greek, "dual" and "many" are subfeatures of "plural," which combines with "singular" to form "number," which combines with "gender," "case," and so forth, to form the set of inflectional features for nouns, and with "person," "tense," and so forth, to form the inflection features for verbs.

3. The *lexicon* contains words entered in stem form, with information given for finding inflected forms and possibly for forming nouns from verbs, and so forth. Irregular forms are given as subentries. Definitions store inflectional information as features and include pointers to semantic information.

4. *Spelling rules* describe regular spelling changes in the language, motivated by phonological and/or textual requirements rather than by morphological requirements. For instance, English always inserts an *e* before the ending *s* when the word ends in a sibilant (e.g., the plural of the noun *box* and the third person singular present tense indicative of the verb *box* are both *boxes*).

5. *Surface filters* accommodate the fact that a single word in phonological and surface syntactic structure (e.g., *don't*) may be more than one word (e.g., *do not*) in underlying syntactic and semantic structure.

6. *Grammar rules* describe the structure of those sentences of the language that can be parsed by our system. The grammar consists of two parts: context-free productions, which describe simple syntactic structure, and reduction functions, which restrict the structure allowed by the productions, perform agreement and other checks, build the parse tree, and reference the case frame interpreter, which uses semantic information to check the semantic validity of the argument patterns parsed. Reduction functions are allowed access to the parsing stack so that they may perform context-sensitive operations.

7. *Semantic data* for each language describe verbs, nouns, and adjectives according to the argument patterns they take, or *license*. For example, a transitive verb pattern licenses an agent-to-subject argument mapping and a patient-to-direct-object argument mapping ("the three little pigs built houses"). There are also distinct patterns for intransitive and double object verbs. Sets of allowed argument patterns are known as *theta grids* (which specify the allowed thematic to syntactic role mappings, see also Weinberg, this volume). Each language system includes a set of defined theta grids, which the lexicon assigns to individual words.

8. *Semantic code* draws on software hooks used by the focusing module to determine the referential properties (anaphoric vs. exophoric, specific vs. generic vs. typical, etc.) of noun projections as semantic arguments.

9. *Generation information* consists of a set of parameters describing the language, plus a small number of code hooks for cases in which the language has quirks that cannot be parameterized.

10. *Temporal information* is handled by a pair of engines, one for recognition and one for generation, which translate between language-dependent temporal features (e.g., present perfect tense) and language-independent temporal features (e.g., relevant anterior as a universal semantic property of references to time).

A Detailed View of NLP Functions

Representations

This section describes the conceptual representation of language according to the linguistic theory expressed by our system and relates that theory to the concrete representation of language as implemented in the NLP system of the ALLP. Representations will be described at each level of analysis used by the system: phonological, lexical, morphological, syntactic, semantic, and interlingual.

Language is always structured as a tree, but there is more than one way to view this tree structure. On the one hand, we build our tree from segments of language, from the smallest units, sounds or letters, through morphemes, words, phrases, and sentences up to discourse structure. The branches undergo fundamental change as we cross from one level of structure to another—from morphological structure (i.e., words and their components) to syntactic structure (i.e., sentences and their components, which are recursive phrases with words as the leaves), to discourse structure (i.e., sentences combining to form paragraphs, perhaps sections and chapters, and eventually whole narratives, dissertations, and conversations). At every level, and overall, the structure remains a tree.

On the other hand, we can regard the tree structure for any segment of language at different levels of abstraction. Each level can be subdivided into a surface and underlying form, each derivable from the other by some complex transformation. In phonological structure, the least abstract level, phones (on the surface) and phonemes (underlying) form the leaves of the tree, and they build up through syllables, morphemes, and words into the stream of speech. In text, the constraints of the writing system add an additional layer of complexity to the representation. Leaves may interact across boundaries according to various rules of phonology and spelling, as in these examples:

Underlying	Surface
in+possible	*impossible*
won't you	*woncha*
a apple	*an apple*
try+s	*tries*

Recognition processes. Because our system represents language purely in text, we can not strictly follow phonological theory. In our system, the original input to the system is keystrokes on the keyboard by the user. The transliterator converts these from the character set describing keyboard input/output in the current language (e.g., Spanish) to the character set for system-internal representation of the current language and passes the result to the input editor. The input editor computes surface M-structure (i.e., morphological structure) by breaking up the character stream, deterministically, into tokens. The input editor passes each token to the lexical recognizer, which simultaneously converts the surface characters (our surface phonological structure) to underlying characters (our underlying phonological structure) and performs lexical lookup.

Lexical lookup divides each input token into morphemes. A morpheme is the smallest meaningful portion of a word, that is, the smallest portion of a word that can carry meaning or inflection. I introduce the term *kibble* to describe the minimal unit that can carry both meaning and category. For example, the word *recalibrates* can be broken down into four morphemes and three kibbles: (*re caliber* (*ate s*)). Every kibble consists of exactly one meaning-carrying morpheme and any number of inflectional morphemes. A word consists of exactly one base kibble, that is, one kibble that is capable of forming a free-standing word, and any number of satellite kibbles whose meanings modify the base kibble. In *recalibrates*, *caliber* is the base kibble and *re-* (again) and *-ate* (act on, in a specified way) are satellite kibbles. Given this definition, contractions (e.g., *I'd*, *who'll*) must derive from separate words because they would otherwise contain more than one base kibble. The same applies to compounds like *doghouse*. In theory, the recognizer should combine morphemes into a tree of kibbles representing all possible interpretations of the word token. Instead, for implementational reasons, each possible sequence of morphemes is combined into a sequence of kibbles and the kibbles further combined into a single word for each interpretation. This word is implemented in underlying M-structure but still corresponds to a surface word token.

The words (conceptually, kibbles) are passed in a stream to the surface filters. The surface filters' proper function is twofold. First, they allow us to handle cross-word phonological or typographical constraints, such as the a/an alternation in English and the mutation of punctuation adjacent to a quotation mark. Second, they combine kibbles into words. They also cover up for the lack of kibbling in the recognizer by splitting the "words" into real (underlying) words where necessary.

Having built the underlying M-structure, we are ready to move to the next level of abstraction, syntactic structure. In S-structure and D-structure (i.e., surface and underlying syntactic structure, respectively), words form the leaves of the tree, and they build up through cyclical projections into sentences.

The parser uses the grammar to create parse trees out of the words. A parse tree consists of words and nodes and contains all the syntactic information built by parsing. Our parser allows only for the construction of a single tree for each interpretation of the input; it does not allow for the creation of both S-structure and D-structure. Current grammars (e.g., Weinberg, this volume) build S-structure trees, with traces to indicate D-structure.

Syntactic to semantic interpretation is performed during parsing by the case frame interpreter, which creates case frames. Case frames are created for all predictable words by using a case frame pattern, or theta grid, as discussed earlier. The theta grid for a word is obtained through the lexicon and converted into a realized case frame by fitting arguments of the predicate into the case frame according to the patterns licensed by the theta grid. The final interesting result of parsing is a parse tree where those nodes corresponding to what are known as semantic maximal projections (see Figure 14.1) are annotated with complete case frames. The case frames, in turn, contain the next layer down of nodes corresponding to semantic maximal projections. We call this node-and-case-frame tree *CF-structure*. It is the surface semantic structure. In summary, parsing covers three levels of abstraction: the two levels of syntactic structure and surface semantic structure.

CF-structure is in turn transformed into its underlying form, the interlingua, which gives a deeper representation of meaning. Where CF-structure contains nodes and case frames, interlingua contains references and phrases. A phrase represents the textual part of a reference to a predicate—what word was said to represent the predicate, what arguments described it, and so forth. A reference represents the language devices used to refer to the object, such as noun versus pronoun, or reference to an object currently in, versus new to, the conversation. Interlingua contains no syntactic information, and, wherever possible, it contains actual object-in-the-world representations (implemented as CLOS instances, i.e., Common Lisp Object System), instead of just descriptions that might refer to objects. In theory, interlingua is universal and contains no language-dependent information, but idiomatic structures may compromise the structure by introducing language-dependent information. Conversion to interlingua takes place in two steps: (a) simultaneous conversion between CF-structure and phrases and focusing (i.e., production of references to objects) and (b) conversion between language-dependent and language-independent temporal features.

Generation processes. An exercise-dependent module must determine the appropriate output from the system, in the form of interlingua. This output can take two forms. For syntactic exercises, where student errors are corrected, it may simply be a recast version of a sentence the student has entered, with errors corrected. For dialogue exercises, where the system is expected to respond to the student, the output would be some new interlingua structure. Generation of linguistic responses by the system, unlike parsing, translates from interlingua to CF-structure, to D-structure, and to S-structure in three separate steps. In the first step, the focuser chooses how to refer to objects that have been previously mentioned or that are part of a microworld (e.g., should the reference be pronominal or nominal, and with what article, meaning, and arguments?). CF-structure is then built including the chosen elements. Next, D-structure is built by applying the parameters of the current language (head-initial vs. head-final, etc.) to principles of universal grammar. S-structure is produced by applying code transformations to D-structure. Most transformations are language independent but are controlled by the parameters of the current language; a few transformations are language dependent.

The S-structure tree is flattened to produce the M-structure, which is a list of words. This structure is run through the same bidirectional surface filters that were used during recognition and is then run through the morphological generator. The latter performs two actions: lexical lookup to find the underlying representation of the word and spelling rule application to find the surface representation of the word. The M-structure may then be printed, using the character set describing keyboard input/output in the current language. The printed string is what users see as the system's response to their input. As a postpass, we use the S-structure to update the focuser's data structures so that the focuser may properly recognize and generate references to objects in successive sentences.

Error Detection, Recovery, and Analysis

As students enter language into the system, linguistic errors are detected at nearly all levels of representation (e.g., morphology, syntax, semantics). Whenever an error is detected, an object (i.e., a CLOS instance) is created to represent the error, and the object is attached to the language structure. The offending language structure is modified to conform to the correct structure. If the error causes the input to have multiple correct interpretations, the most likely interpretation is chosen. If no interpretation is obviously more likely, an interpretation is chosen at random, but the error object is made to specify that the error could not be uniquely resolved. Therefore, to produce the/a correct version of an interpretable input, one may simply pass the final analysis of the input to the generation component of the system. Error objects contain information about the errors they represent, so it is possible to describe the error to the student. The problem of dealing with multiple possible interpretations when outputting a correct version of what the student has said is discussed next.

Ambiguity of Input: Tailoring Recognition Through Penalty Assignment

Language is frequently ambiguous. So that the NLP can choose the correct interpretation of ambiguous input, the system is nondeterministic at all levels of analysis. To produce the most likely interpretations in the shortest time, all input modules use a best-first recognition algorithm. All error objects are assigned a penalty, which is transferred to the linguistic object to which the error is attached. The penalty of any interpretation is the sum of the penalties of all structures that it contains.

The goal of recognition is to produce the most likely interpretation(s) of the input, not the most correct interpretation(s). A beginning Spanish student who starts by typing *la libro* probably means "the book," with an agreement error between *la* and *libro*, and not "[I] free her," which is the translation of *la libro* assuming no errors. Therefore, penalties are assigned according to how unlikely an error is in the learner population, rather than how severe the error is absolutely. For some errors, the penalty assigned may even be 0. Moreover, when a correct but highly unlikely structure is encountered (e.g., the English verb *putted* as past tense of *putt*) and when that structure is ambiguous with a more common but ungrammatical structure (e.g., *putted* as an error in forming the past tense of *put*), a penalty is assigned to the former structure (*putt*) even though it is grammatically correct. The errorful interpretation is more likely in learner language than the correct one and would take precedence when the system is weighing alternatives.

When an interpretation is too unlikely, the input module discards it. In the case of either severely malformed input or structures beyond the capacity of the grammar, recognition fails entirely. In addition, the input system contains a variety of thresholds that can be used to affect how many interpretations are sought. During recognition, there is always a best partial interpretation. All interpretations whose penalties exceed that of the current best partial interpretation by more than a certain threshold are discarded and recycled immediately, without being completed. When the penalty of even the best partial interpretation exceeds a separately set threshold, the recognition process halts entirely. This prevents the system from wasting the user's time while the parser undergoes last-ditch efforts to discover wildly unlikely interpretations of very bad input.

To make optimum use of the best-first strategy, penalties are assigned to interpretations as soon as possible during parsing. When two elements of the input fail to agree in some way, the penalty is assigned to the first element, if possible, rather than to the dominating element (which may not be constructed for some time), so that the input module will encounter the penalty earlier. The penalties assigned to different interpretations of input can be altered by a control module. For instance, suppose the recognition system is to be used by a control module that processes only simple commands (as might be appropriate for beginning students). In this case, the module could raise the penalty for parsing unexpected clauses, to speed parsing of sentences without such clauses. For example, raising the penalty on parsing participial clauses would speed the processing of "Put on the hat" by causing the parser to avoid applying the rules it would use for "Put on the hat, the pin began to sparkle" (where *put on the hat* modifies *pin*). In this way, the same core grammar could be tailored to accommodate different learner groups.

Penalties may also be modified to fit an individual profile, stored for each user, to tune recognition to anticipate errors common in that individual. Penalties may be modified on the fly. For example, if the user accumulates many errors in grammatical case, then reducing the penalty for case error will speed recognition of input that contains case errors and make it more likely for ambiguous input to be parsed as an interpretation with case errors than without them.

Penalty values now in the system were determined partly by examining sentences produced by learners, partly by consulting with language teachers, and partly by intuition. On these bases, we hand-tuned penalties to cause the system to choose interpretations that appeared more likely. Learner language was obtained from general essays and from paper tests of proposed microworlds to be based on the ALLP NLP, such as *No recuerdo*, the simulation game described by Murray (this volume). We intended that more accurate values be determined when the NLP system was put into extensive use with students.

Mapping Between Syntactic and Semantic Representation

The NLP system uses a simple but powerful representation of syntactic and semantic structure and the relationship between them. (Our approach to semantic representation can be compared to the one described by Dorr et al., this volume). In our approach, all syntactic phrases (XP) consist of a head (X^0), a single bar projection (X') from which depends an argument (a syntactic phrase), and a maximal or double bar projection (XP). The X' projection may be duplicated to allow multiple arguments. The syntactic structure is mapped to a semantic structure via a set of semantic projection rules. All semantic phrases (X^{max}) consist of a head (the predicate), a specifier, a relation, and a set of arguments. The predicate, specifier, and relation are all syntactic heads (X^0s); therefore, every X^{max} consists of exactly three XPs, which fall in a triple projection. The arguments of an X^{max} are the collective arguments of the XPs that comprise it. Figure 14.1 shows the correspondence between syntactic and semantic structure for the three types of semantic projections, which are those headed by verbs (V^{max}s), by nouns (N^{max}s), and by adjectives (A^{max}s). These projections thus correspond to chains in the parse tree that include complement phrases prepositional phrases and adverb phrases.

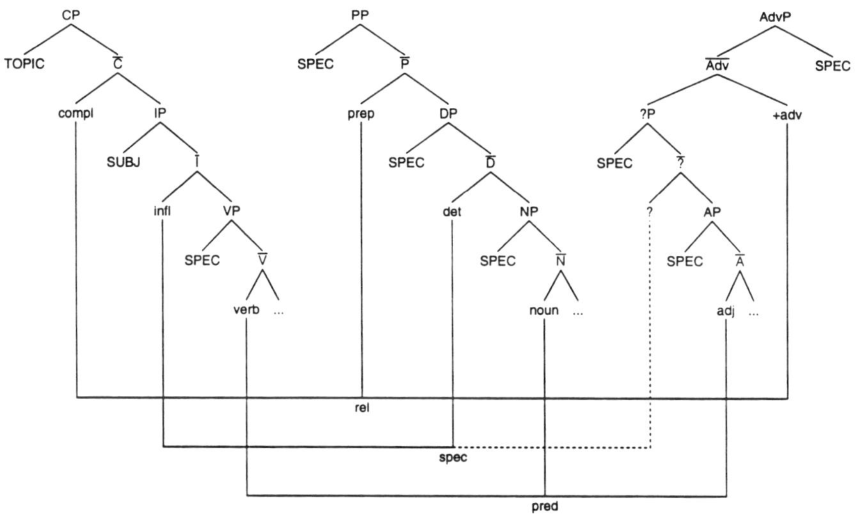

FIG. 14.1. Syntactic-semantic structure of the semantic projections V^{max} (from the verb), N^{max} (from the noun), and A^{max} (from the adjective), in the NLP system. Semantic projection components indicated are the predicate (pred), specifier (spec), and relation (rel).

The semantic predicate (pred) in Figure 14.1 is the head of the semantic projection. Any word that may assign thematic roles is a valid predicate: specifically, the syntactic categories verb, noun, and adjective. (Quantifiers are subcategories of either nouns or verbs. Adverbs in *+ly* are incorporations of adjectives with other material. Proforms are incorporations as well.) The semantic predicate, that is, the noun, verb, or adjective, is the lowest head of the triple syntactic projection.

The semantic specifier (spec) in Figure 14.1 specifies properties of the semantic projection; it corresponds to the middle head of the triple syntactic projection. The specifier of a V^{max} is INFL (inflection). The specifier of an N^{max} is DET (determiner). A^{max}s do not have a lexically apparent specifier in English, as indicated by the "?" label in Figure 14.1. The specifier does exist, though: In Japanese, where adjectives may have tense, it is presumably the position where tense falls (compare verbs' INFL).

The semantic relation (rel) in Figure 14.1 relates the semantic projection to its dominating projection. The relation of a V^{max} is COMPL, or complementizer; the relation of an N^{max} is PREP, or preposition; the relation of an A^{max} is +ADV. (In English the adjective and +adv invariably incorporate.) In semantic structure, the relationship between an argument and its dominating projection is largely indicated by the thematic role that the dominating projection assigns to the argument. The relation position of a projection indicates any additional relationship not covered by the thematic role. For example, in semantic structure, the preposition *by* as in "the mouse was chased by the cat" maps purely to the thematic role AGENT; the relation of the N^{max} "by the cat" is empty. On the other hand, in "the cat jumped onto the box," the preposition *onto* serves to indicate both the thematic role GOAL and the particular orientational relationship of the cat to its goal (*on* rather than *in*, *under*, etc.).[34]

Conjunction can appear at any level and even, apparently, cross-structurally: "this blue and that red book." In semantic structure, deleted and gapped material must be recovered, so that only maximal semantic projections are conjoined. Conjunction structure itself can be considered as a sort of degenerate semantic projection containing a predicate (the conjunction) and arguments but no specifier, relation, or syntactic specifier (SPEC) positions. In generating syntactic structure from semantic structure, redundant material may be deleted. This syntactic/semantic mapping can be used to cover all language structures and to convert all language-dependent structures to interlingua. It does not, however, aid in translating between languages when radically different language structures are used to represent similar speech intentions, as in *hello* versus *buenos días* (literally, "good days").

The representation described here has proved extremely successful for processing language at the level of sophistication required by the ALLP's foreign language teaching applications. It generally processes meaning at the level of words although it does allow for some simple conflation or deflation of a predicate meaning with an argument. Its major drawbacks are that it requires a highly sophisticated algorithm, not yet implemented, to delete and gap redundant material when generating conjoined structure (e.g., to generate "this blue and that red book") and that it does not provide methods to regularize structures that differ across languages in ways other than simple conflation or deflation of predicates with arguments (as compared with the more systematic approach to crosslinguistic description of Dorr et al., this volume). Plans have been mapped out for addition of code to regularize structure. Because of the modular nature of the system,

---

[34] In surface semantic structure, the relation of a semantic projection is simply the head of the top syntactic projection in the triple syntactic projection. Thus, in converting surface structure to underlying structure, the surface relation is converted partially or entirely to a thematic role.

such code would be relatively easy to add, but time did not allow addition of any such code in this project.

Subcategorization Frames

Both syntactic and semantic heads have intrinsic subcategorization frames that describe their allowed arguments. Subcategorization frames of nonpredicates are trivial; for example, a preposition (e.g., *under*) merely subcategorizes for an NP of a certain case (e.g., objective case). Predicates have complex subcategorization frames in both syntactic and semantic structure. In a complete NLP system, it is necessary to store not only syntactic and semantic subcategorization frames but also the rules for mapping between them.

Semantic structure is language independent from the standpoint of argument structure.[35] Language-independent parts of an NLP system can store and process purely semantic subcategorization frames, such as the following frame for an information-transfer verb such as *tell* or a physical-transfer verb such as *give*:

```
((:thematic-role agent)
 (:thematic-role theme)
 (:thematic-role destination))
```

A particular language's lexicon adds language-dependent information to subcategorization frames, largely by specifying the syntax of arguments but also by adding a voice marker (e.g., active, passive, middle) to the subcategorization frame. A subcategorization frame for English *tell* must cover sentences of the type

I told her that he was going.	(I told her [CP [SPEC e] [compl that] he was going].)
I told her he was going.	(I told her [CP [SPEC e] [compl e] he was going].)
I told her who was going.	(I told her [CP [SPEC who] [compl e] was going].)
I told him to go.	(I told him [IP to go].)

The frame must disallow sentences of the type

* I told her that he be/were going.
* I told her if he was/be/were going.

The frame for *tell* that meets these requirements is expressed in Lisp code as follows:

```
(:voice active
(:thematic-role agent
 :syntax ((:case subject :type dp :required-p t)))
(:thematic-role theme
 :syntax ((:case empty :type vmax
           :spec (or indicative infinitive)))
  :required-p t)))
(:thematic-role destination
 :syntax ((:case indirect-object :type dp :required-p t))))
```

---

[35] It does not account for differences due to predicate choice (e.g., "I ate with a fork" vs. "I used a fork to eat") or for figures of speech.

In this code, the case EMPTY (*e* in the above sentence examples) for the theme argument covers *that* clauses (but not *if* clauses) because *that* is semantically null; its presence or absence in syntax follows syntactic constraints alone. The type V^{max} is a supertype of CP (complementizer), IP (inflection), and VP (verb phrase). VPs and subjunctive CPs are ruled out with *tell* because they are neither indicative nor infinitive.

Similarly, a subcategorization frame for English *give* must cover sentences of the type

I gave them the money.
I gave the money to them.

The frame developed for *give* is expressed in Lisp as

```
(:voice active
(:thematic-role agent
 :syntax ((:case subject :type dp :required-p t)))
(:thematic-role theme
 :syntax ((:case direct-object :type dp :required-p t)))
(:thematic-role destination
 :syntax ((:case indirect-object :type dp :required-p t)
          (:case to :type pp :required-p t))))
```

Transformations can be applied to language-dependent subcategorization frames to produce passive frames from active ones, noun frames from verb frames (as when *destroy* becomes *destruction*), and so forth. Expletive arguments (e.g., *it* and *there* as empty subjects) can be marked as semantically null, in which case they are not represented in interlingua. Other arguments can be marked as semantically null to cause them to conflate with their predicate in semantic structure; particle constructions and idioms such as *raining cats and dogs* are handled in this fashion.

Getting the Most out of an LALR Parser

The ALLP uses an LALR (look ahead, left to right) parser with one element of "look ahead." Parsing requires two modules—the parser itself, which is basically a finite state automaton (but with hooks allowing context sensitive operations), and a rule compiler that precompiles productions into a state transition table for the parser.

The parser, which is similar in design to that of Tomita (1986), accepts context-free grammar productions with associated functions in which one may perform context dependent tests (cf. Levin & Evans, this volume). When the parser finds the objects specified in the right side of a rule, it reduces them to the left side. A function associated with the reduce action, called a *reduction function*, is passed the right side objects as arguments and returns a value, which is generally either a new node created from its arguments or nil to indicate failure. The rule compiler is written in C and produces parsing tables in Common Lisp. The parser and rule functions are written in Common Lisp. The rule productions are in a special format that the rule compiler parses.

Although the parser is LALR in design, we support context-sensitive operations by passing the stack to all reduction functions as an argument. Reduction functions are free to access the stack and can even modify it. Modifications are performed by adding substitution pairs for constituents to a substitution table associated with the parse state; all constituents are accessed through this table to obtain the correct copy. By allowing stack access and by performing a large proportion of semantic processing during parsing, we can make many decisions early, eliminating unnecessary processing of incorrect parses. Penalties associated with unlikely parse paths, combined with a best-first algorithm, postpone processing of unlikely parses until more probable paths fail. Semantic processing is performed during parsing only to the extent necessary to determine a minimum semantic penalty for a case frame; other semantic processing is postponed until the final set of parses is chosen.

On the down side, stack access and semantic processing make it impossible to use such optimizations as parse state merging and well-formed string tables because for states to be considered equivalent, their stacks must also be equivalent. This so rarely happens that the bookkeeping for the optimizations takes more time than the optimization saves. Therefore, to speed the parser, it is necessary to take as much advantage of stack access as possible. Typically, this involves examining the stack in these circumstances:

- When creating a trace, the stack is examined to determine the trace's binder; if none exists, the trace is not created or a penalty is marked;
- When parsing a COMP (complement) or TOPIC, the stack is examined to mark a penalty if the dominating predicate does not subcategorize for a clause with the given COMP or TOPIC;
- When completing parsing of any other argument, the stack is examined to mark a penalty if the dominating predicate does not subcategorize for an argument of that argument's type.

In other words, all semantic and context-sensitive tests must be performed as soon as it is possible to determine the type of structure being parsed, in order to avoid partially parsing paths that will eventually be discarded. It is difficult to write general, formalized grammar rules to perform these tests because the numerous small variations that occur in structures require equally numerous, highly specialized rules to test for penalties at the earliest possible point.

By the time we had thoroughly explored the LALR parser's good and bad points, we had invested too much time in writing LALR grammars to switch to a new parser. The current parser is reasonably fast, except for long, highly ambiguous structures (which, fortunately, language students rarely produce). Because most of the work of a grammar is done in Lisp code, it is easy to analyze typical arbitrary natural language structures. Because grammars consist largely of code, big grammars are extremely difficult to modify: Even small changes can have repercussions throughout the grammar. Because all grammar code is language dependent, new grammars must be essentially written from scratch, a process which consumed huge proportions of our time. If we had it to do over, we would try using some more principle-based parser, possibly including unification. Still, it is not clear that for a large, complex grammar that anticipates user errors, any sufficiently powerful grammar can be specified simply.

Morphological Processing

The current NLP system uses a spelling rule system developed from the KIMMO morphological processor (Karttunen, 1983).[36] A preprocessor allows programmers to write individual rules in a somewhat natural format, which the preprocessor converts to finite state automata that are then merged into a single finite state automaton (FSA). In our system, all rules apply simultaneously and so must be written to take each other into account. The rule for *epenthesis*—or insertion—of the letter *e* before the *s* morpheme in certain English words (e.g., *glasses, churches*) is expressed by the following Lisp code:

```
(rule "epenthesis"
      #\+ #\e #\0
      (sequence (or (sequence (or #\c #\s) #\h)          ;churches
                    Sibilant                              ;foxes, glasses
                    (/ #\y #\i)                           ;tries
                    #\o)                                  ;heroes
                 _ #\s))
```

This rule calls for insertion of *e* in place of a morpheme boundary if the environment indicated (e.g., a sibilant like *s*) is matched; otherwise, the morpheme boundary is deleted. Note that the rule must take into account simultaneous application of $y \rightarrow i$ as in *try/tries*.

If conflicts occur when merging FSAs, the system refers to a global specificity table that orders sets. For example, *i* belongs to both the set of front vowels and the set of all vowels. Because the set of front vowels is more specific than the set of all vowels, a rule referring to front vowels takes precedence over a conflicting rule referring to all vowels. Unfortunately, the specificity table is incapable of resolving some conflicts. For instance, *i* belongs to both the set of front vowels and the set of high vowels, neither of which sets is more or less specific than the other.

We have written a new spelling rule system in which rules can be written to apply in parallel, sequentially, conditionally, and in other ways. Thus, the insertion rule can be applied earlier than $y \rightarrow i$ on generation and later than $i \rightarrow y$ on recognition. Because this system works on strings rather than characters, the set Sibilant can be defined to contain *ch* and *sh*. The rule is simply a description of changes:

```
(rule "epenthesis"
     (wherever (sequence (or Sibilant "i" "o") "+"
                         (or (/ "" "e")
                         (error ""))
```

Although the system is still character-based rather than feature-based, it is possible to write rules that very nearly take on the standard rule format used by phonologists by means of tagging related sets (so that each nth element of an input set with a given tag is converted to the nth element of an output set with the same tag). In this system, conflicts are resolved by ordering rules sequentially, thus eliminating the global specificity table.

---

[36] Kimmo Koskenniemi described a morphological generator/recognizer in his doctoral dissertation and elsewhere (Koskenniemi, 1983). The ALLP's morphological analyzer is based on a Lisp implementation of Koskenniemi's system as described by Karttunen (1983) but has been modified and enhanced.

In addition, this system allows any rule or its section to be annotated with a penalty, which will be marked on the word. The older system does not allow penalties to be marked because there is no place in the merged FSA to store them. As with the older system, rules are compiled into a single FSA so the new system is equally efficient at run time. This new spelling rule system is not yet in use because its rule compiler operates too slowly and time and resources have not allowed adequate optimization of the compiler.

Recognition Versus Generation: Instructional Implications

In the ALLP NLP system, recognition and generation use separate algorithms and grammars. This has the disadvantage of requiring more software, but we found it to be worth our while to maintain separate systems because of the huge effect of error detection on recognition grammars. Each recognition grammar requires hundreds of complex rules to meet the needs of error handling. The entire generation system for all languages together requires approximately one tenth the code of a single recognition grammar, and 90% of the generation code is language independent.

The separation of systems does not enforce equal coverage on input and output. Because generation is so much easier to work with than recognition, generation will always exceed recognition in coverage. This is disadvantageous in that users cannot necessarily input any structure they see the program output. However, because the system is designed for language teaching, students are likely to have greater recognition than production abilities, and greater generation coverage is useful and appropriate.

Conclusions

NLP is hard. When we initiated our project, we naively thought that we could successfully build an NLP system in two to three years that could analyze and respond in real time to input to any one of four European languages, up to the level of a fourth-semester student. Instead, it took us five years to build a system that can process second- to fourth-semester level input pretty well and often in something approaching real time. This was accomplished with a software development team consisting of two full-time professional programmers over the entire five-year period, about a dozen linguistics graduate students, and upwards of a score of computer science undergraduates who each contributed a semester or two of work.

Our greatest difficulty, aside from poor equipment, was in implementing grammars. We had thought that to cover fourth-semester language, we could simply cover all language described by a first through fourth-semester set of textbooks. In reality, textbooks designed to teach European languages to Americans describe merely the few differences between the target language and English and omit nearly all information about the target language needed to write a computational grammar. Moreover, by extrapolating from their source language, typical language students produce far more language than is described in their textbooks. Grammar writing eventually expanded to fill all available time, preventing us from implementing more than prototypes of the numerous applications based on the NLP that we had originally intended to create.

References

Berwick, R., Abney, S., & Tenny, C. (1991). *Principle-based parsing: Computation and psycholinguistics.* Dordrecht, Netherlands: Kluwer.

Chomsky N. (1981). *Lectures on government and binding.* Dordrecht: Foris.

Felshin, S. (1993). *A guide to the Athena language learning project natural language processing system.* Cambridge, MA: Massachusetts Institute of Technology.

Karttunen, L. (1983). KIMMO: A general morphological processor. *Texas Linguistic Forum, 22*, 165-186.

Koskenniemi, K. (1983). Two-level model for morphological analysis. In *Proceedings of the 8th International Joint Conference on Artificial Intelligence* (pp. 683-685). San Mateo, CA: Kaufmann.

Malone, S., & Felshin, S. (1991). GLR parsing for erroneous input. In M. Tomita (Ed.), *Generalized LR parsing.* Norwell, MA: Kluwer.

Tomita, M. (1986). *Efficient parsing for natural language.* Boston: Kluwer.

15

Application of Learning Principles to the Design of a Second Language Tutor

Jonathan D. Kaplan and V. Melissa Holland
U.S. Army Research Institute

The Army Research Institute (ARI) is developing an adaptive language tutor that gives job-relevant communicative practice, known as the Military Language Tutor (MILT). The ARI program that engendered MILT is overviewed in this volume by Sams. Our chapter describes the instructional features of MILT and explains how certain of these features are shaped by principles of learning and memory drawn from work in experimental psychology. Some of these principles are presented in MacWhinney's chapter in this volume, as part of the tenets of learning theory and other branches of experimental psychology that have potential relevance to language tutoring systems. Although we agree with MacWhinney's conclusion that these tenets are too vague to connect precisely to features of system design, we have found them useful in guiding our thinking about aspects of the tutor. As psychologists in human factors and instruction, we come at the problem of designing a language tutor from a somewhat different angle than do others in this volume. We and our colleagues have had considerable experience developing training systems in areas other than foreign language, and we have applied general principles from research on motivation, cognition, skills acquisition and retention, and human factors. The application of these principles has resulted in demonstrably effective programs, models, and devices now used in the military as well as, in various transformations, in industry and schools (Berkowitz & Simutis, 1983; Farr & Ward, 1988; Hagman, Hayes, & Bierwirth, 1986; Hagman & Rose, 1983; Kaplan, 1989; Laughery, Dahl, Kaplan, Archer, & Fontenelle, 1988; Oxford, Harman, & Holland, 1987; Psotka, Massey, & Mutter, 1988; Wisher, Holland, & Chatelier, 1987; Wisher, Sabol, & Kern, forthcoming; Yates & Macpherson, 1985).

Application of these principles to a language tutor assumes that language in use shares features with human skills like adding numbers or driving a car, rather than being an exclusive realm of knowledge with unique organizational and acquisitional principles (for a recent articulation of the language-as-skill point of view, see Lawton & Andreson, 1994). Theoretical claims about the nature of language are widely disputed. We do not engage in those disputes here but rather draw on analogies that yield sensible ideas for the design of our tutor.[37]

Some of the principles that underlie MILT derive from behavioristically oriented learning theory. One of the early foundations of experimental psychology, this theory attempts to represent the dynamics of learning, some of which were originally described by Skinner (1938) and others through animal experiments. Although some of these

[37] Even the most extreme ontological position in regard to language—that its structure is innate and universal and governed by laws of acquisition not shared by cognitive and physical domains (Chomsky, 1981)—does not preclude appeal to general cognitive principles to explain the learning of language-specific vocabulary, constructions, and rules of use.

findings and principles are of dubious generalizability, others have become accepted bases for the design of computer-based training and programmed instruction (Anderson, Kulhavey, & Andre, 1971; Gagne & Briggs, 1979). Learning theory has pointed to practice and reinforcement as major dynamics, and these continue as significant constucts in cognitive formulations of learning (Anderson & Schooler, 1991; Newell, 1990; Schmidt & Bjork, 1992), with reinforcement replaced by concepts of feedback and knowledge of results (Schmidt, 1990).

The MILT system draws on ARI's earlier BRIDGE project (Kreyer & Criswell, this volume; Sams, this volume) and will be implemented in both Arabic and Spanish. The tutor exists now as a screen-state prototype with demonstration displays in English, from which the screen examples in this chapter are taken. The tutor will overlie a natural language processing (NLP) engine that uses parsing mechanisms described by Weinberg, Garman, Martin, and Merlo (this volume) and that incorporates semantic and dialogue analysis components discussed by Dorr, Hendler, Blanksteen, and Migdaloff (this volume). A very large Arabic lexicon has been constructed for MILT through reuse of preexisting lexical resources (Dorr, Garman, & Weinberg, 1994).

Principled Design Features of the MILT System

Practice and Intrinsic Motivation

The initial target user for MILT is intelligence linguists in the U.S. Army who have progressed to advanced individual training in preparation for jobs. They can be assumed to have reached a Level 2 in target language proficiency (on the 5-point Interagency Language Roundtable scale). As noted by Sams (this volume), these soldiers are more likely to use a language tutor for optional self-study than as part of a formal program of instruction. For this reason, we wanted the tutor to be interesting enough that students would want to use it on their own time and, moreover, would want to explore the tutoring environment beyond the basic exercises. The learning principle here is straightforward: The more learners use language—to the point of overlearning words and constructions—the better they will retain it. According to learning theory, practice improves performance (Anderson & Schooler, 1991; Schmidt & Bjork, 1992). Learning has been shown to follow some form of the classical learning curve, a power function schematized in Figure 15.1.

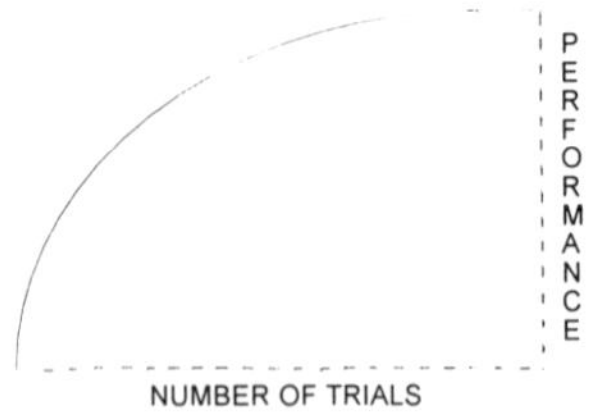

Fig. 15.1. Typical learning curve.

The learning curve indicates that after some amount of practice, performance is as good as it will get, and there is not much point in practicing more. However, this does not take into account a phenomenon called *overlearning*. It turns out that when well-trained people are placed under significant stress, they experience breakdowns in performance. Furthermore, if people do not practice a skill regularly, they tend to forget it. However, if they have practiced that skill many times after they already appear to be performing well, then the stress-related breakdowns and the losses over time are reduced—a result of overlearning (Driskell, Willis, & Copper, 1992; Schendel & Hagman, 1982). Because language training in the military is intended to enable realistic performance in situations that may be stressful and to support retention of language skills over periods of nonusage, it is desirable to push learning beyond the point of asymptote. Therefore, the key to improving performance is to design a tutor that interacts with students to produce successful practice trials even after students manifest mastery of the material.[38]

How could we design a tutor that would motivate students to practice on their own time and to continue beyond basic exercises? We first reasoned that students would be encouraged toward self-study by a system that is intrinsically rewarding.

Intrinsic motivation. It is well established in behavioral research that rewards improve learning (Deese & Carpenter, 1951; Miller, 1963). Typically, people think of reward as some action that occurs upon the successful completion of some behavior. The rat gets to the end of the maze and is given cheese. The language student practices conjugating in the future perfect tense, takes a test, and is given an *A*. This is extrinsic reward. The behavior itself is not rewarding. It is the cheese and the *A*, delivered from an external source, that reinforce the desired behaviors.

Extrinsic reward does not explain the behavior of people endlessly playing computer games that they do not win, artists who paint without hope of selling, or people who do crossword puzzles without being able to finish them. In these examples, people are motivated intrinsically, by the pleasure of the behavior itself. The facilitating effects of intrinsic motivation on learning have been widely demonstrated (Berlyne, 1968; McClelland, 1961; Malone, 1981). The behavior that people find intrinsically motivating appears to be quite diverse. However, much of this apparent diversity has underlying commonality. For example, common elements are exercising control over external objects and engaging in problem solving.

In the case of a language tutor, we interpreted intrinsic reward to mean constructing exercises that offer students the opportunity to practice in the context of doing something that is important or interesting to them and at which they can succeed. We assume that they will be rewarded by some version of controlling their environment and solving problems, but the specific form that these two dimensions will take differs according to who the learners are.

---

[38] The long-term picture is more complicated than the learning curve suggests: After students reach a certain level of expertise, their linguistic performance begins to exhibit characteristic discontinuities and degradations, explained as a wholesale restructuring of linguistic knowledge (McLaughlin, 1990, 1994). We assume that whatever cognitive restructuring eventually occurs, there is still a need for a tutor that promotes practice and automatization of skills in the early stages.

Application of intrinsic motivation in the ARI language tutor. We know that the military linguists who make up our user population are more intelligent than the average person, motivated to learn and retain foreign languages, job oriented, but likely to become bored. Taking these characteristics into account, we developed a design for MILT that can support intrinsic reward through several means. First, the content of exercises reflects what Army linguists do at work. Second, students are given very detailed information as to the level of accuracy of their input, plus a changing score that reflects performance. We assume that information that enables students to view improvements in their performance will itself prove rewarding to them.

Finally, the types of exercises being built into MILT enable realistic communicative interactions in which students solve an interesting problem or execute a simulated job task. Such interactions can be interpreted as applying a communicative approach to language teaching, as discussed by Douglas (this volume), whose LingWorlds tutor provides a precedent for using language to solve nonlanguage problems. In MILT two primary exercise types are designed to motivate students to want to use and improve their language: a simulated dialogue exercise and an animated graphics microworld.

Simulated dialogue. This exercise allows students to practice production and understanding of language embedded in an interview or interrogation task that is central to their job. Students engage the tutor in a question-answer dialogue in the target language as they try to elicit important information, somewhat in the manner of the Herr Kommissar tutor of DeSmedt (this volume), which uses a detective game format to stimulate dialogue. An example of a dialogue interface taken from the MILT's screen-state prototype is in Figure 15.2. (Recall that these dialogues are being implemented in Arabic and Spanish.)

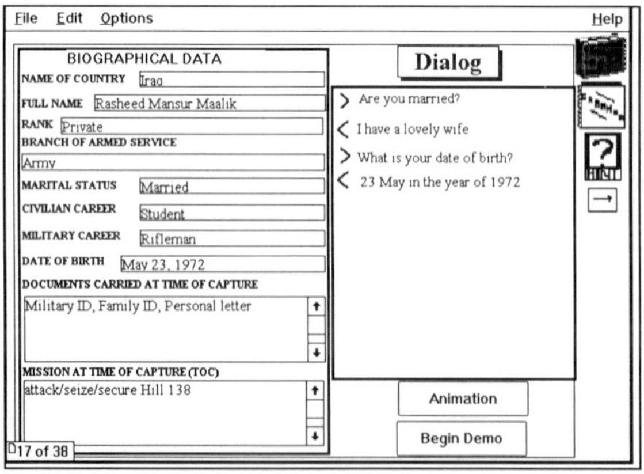

Fig. 15.2. Dialogue exercise screen from MILT design prototype.

Here, the student is seeking biographical information from the system in the role of respondent, to fill out the report form on the left side of the screen. The report form naturally constrains the dialogue, a convention borrowed from real life to render the conversational interactions NLP-tractable within the tutor. The NLP components have been designed to recognize errors without rejecting student input, as described by Weinberg et al. (this volume).

Graphics microworld. This exercise allows students to use language production to manipulate a graphics microworld. The successful manipulation of the graphics lets users control the microworld environment and should therefore be intrinsically rewarding. In addition, the microworld is set in a problem-solving domain, and the problem solving itself should provide intrinsic motivation.

In practice, a student is able to see a graphic scene and enter a natural language command in the target language, such as "open the briefcase," as shown in Figure 15.3.

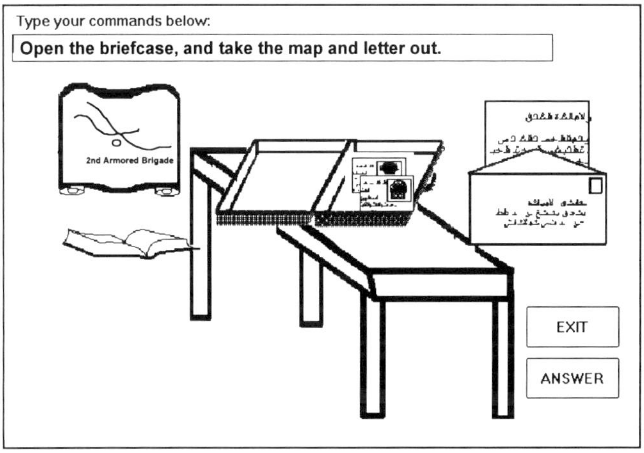

Fig. 15. 3. Microworld exercise screen from MILT design prototype.

The NLP engine analyzes the entry and converts it to an interlingual representation, using the lexical conceptual structure (LCS) discussed by Dorr et al. (this volume). That representation links to appropriate, animated graphics—for example, the briefcase opens. Because LCS analysis can accommodate some kinds of linguistic equivalence, the tutor can handle different forms of linguistic input to accomplish the same action (e.g., "open the briefcase," "make the briefcase open up," etc.).

If the student types a command that appropriately reflects that student's intention—such as "open the briefcase" to see the briefcase opened—then the student will be able to manipulate the microworld successfully. If students use the wrong words or constructions to express their intentions but the entry can still be processed, then the expressed action will take place in the microworld. For example, if the student has not learned the prepositional system in the target language and types "put the briefcase under the table," then that action will occur, even if the student means to request that the briefcase go on top. If the student enters a command that cannot be accomplished in the microworld—if the objects called for are not present or the properties are not legal—then the student will be given conversationally realistic, discriminative feedback, such as "there is no chair to be moved" (for absent objects) or "the table cannot open" (for illegal or unassigned properties). If the command contains grammar errors that do not compromise interpretation or execution, then the requested action will be carried out and the errors may or may not be reported, depending on the reporting strategy chosen by the instructor. If the sentence cannot be parsed due to either garbled or complicated grammar, then the student will be told, "I can't understand you" or "please rephrase."

We are implementing three reporting options for grammatical errors in the dialogue and microworld exercises: informing students of errors as they are made, an expression of form-focused instruction; withholding error reports, an expression of communicatively based instruction; and saving error reports until the exercise is complete, borrowing the tactic of replay and critique used in some intelligent tutoring systems (Kurland & Tenney, 1989). Sams (this volume) calls this tactic as an "after-action review" to echo the military argot.

The microworld will be partially authorable from a short list of objects that can be chosen to inhabit the microworld. The scenario backdrop can be changed as well. Readable objects like books and letters can be rewritten. Moreover, authors will be able to create either free-play environments or game-like scenarios with specified goals, such as determining the identity of the briefcase owner for the scenario in Figure 15.3. However, we do not envision in this tutor going beyond the interactional type that Hamburger (this volume) calls *servant*, in which the system carries out the student's commands within the microworld (as opposed to the system's issuing the commands or playing any of the other roles described by Hamburger).

To provide appropriate feedback, the MILT is being equipped with a number of evaluation mechanisms, specific to exercise types. Syntax and semantics are differentially checked by the parser and the LCS components of the NLP engine. The dialogue exercise uses a knowledge base to retrieve facts requested by the student. An exercise type we have not discussed is the free response question, designed to prompt a single-sentence answer from students, much as in the BRIDGE tutor (Sams, this volume). These exercises will use a matching routine that compares student answers to prestored target answers on the basis of LCS representations, as described by Dorr et al. (this volume).

Knowledge of Results: Variation in Error Reporting

Work in instructional psychology (e.g., Levine, 1975) suggests that learners' performance can be improved with appropriate feedback that points out errors. This finding has received recent support in the area of second language learning (e.g., Ellis, 1994; Lightbown & Spada, 1990). The instructional psychology literature further suggests that informative feedback—telling learners the nature of their error rather than simply that there is an error—works better for most learners (Kulhavey, 1977; Kulik & Kulik, 1988). At the same time, this literature suggests that high-ability learners who are also field-independent (a cognitive style characteristic grounded in research by Witkins, Moore, Goodenough, & Cox, 1977) may do better if they have to figure out their error—that is, if they receive simple, uninformative feedback. Thus, knowledge of results appears to be a useful parameter to manipulate in a tutoring system.

Like other work in intelligent CALL, the MILT system exploits the NLP's capability of delivering precise feedback about users' errors. Misspelled words can be recognized through the computational lexicon. Major classes of grammatical errors can be recognized and differentiated by the parser and its error handler. Some semantic errors can be recognized by the LCS component. Factual errors can be recognized through the matching routines that link with either instructor-entered target answers or with the dialogue knowledge base.

We contend that the pattern of these errors is a key metric of learners' progress and that feedback about these errors is critical to mastering language form and content. We do not in this tutor commit to either a form-focused or a communicative approach; instead, either approach, or compromises between them, can be instantiated through the authoring interface. As pointed out for the dialogue and microworld exercises, one mode of instruction will be to withhold reporting of grammatical errors and respond only to factual and semantic errors, ideally by conventions that occur naturally in conversation. Another mode of instruction is to report all grammatical errors.

For grammatical errors, MILT will follow the principle of informative feedback and will have as a default value the delivery of complete information about each error: its location in the sentence as well as its classification as a subject-verb disagreement, and so forth. Moreover, consistent with the varying effects of knowledge of results, the amount of information about errors will be modifiable through the authoring interface. In effect, instructors will be able to separate simply reporting an error from reporting information about the error and will be able to mask the latter. Researchers can use this manipulation to study how the interaction between field-dependency and knowledge of results that has been observed in other domains generalizes to the domain of language learning.

We are also aware that when students lose confidence in their ability to reduce errors eventually, the resulting situation is punishing to them, and they give up literally or effectively (Maier, 1949). When they literally give up, they stop practicing and learning. When they effectively give up, they continue to practice but not to try, and they stop learning. This suggests that the tutor should be designed to reduce the chances of putting the student in situations where errors are overwhelming. Another reason for trying to curb errors is that students appear to learn best when they produce and practice correct actions (Anderson, Boyle, Corbett, & Lewis, 1990; Skinner, 1957). That is, learners who manage to avoid errors can more efficiently build desired activities (or mental processes) into their repertoires. The learning principle here is to build for success, an idea put to work in the series of tutors for geometry and for programming designed by Anderson and colleagues (Anderson, Boyle, & Yost, 1985; Anderson, Conrad, & Corbett, 1989), following a model of human cognition known as ACT* (Anderson, 1983). These tutors present material in small increments designed to minimize the errors students can make in progressing to the next step. At the first error, the student is corrected.

We considered two approaches to containing errors in a tutoring system. One is to put the exercises in a fixed sequence, such as from simple to complex, that users can ideally traverse without excessive errors at any one point (as occurs in programmed learning). The second is to make the tutor adapt to any current state of the individual user's changing level of performance (as occurs in the ACT* tutors through a process called *model tracing*). The problem with the first approach is that it assumes that the user population is homogeneous and well understood. If this is not the case, then some users will produce excessive errors, whereas others will find the exercises unchallenging and unrewarding. That leaves the second approach as the more viable one. The question is, how does one implement it? We consider this question in the next section.

Adapting Exercises to the Learner's Error Performance

To adjust to varying levels of student ability and performance, we designed MILT to enable faster progress for students who make fewer errors and to enable slower progress, as well as error-specific remediation, for students who make more errors. Our tutor does not attempt the detailed model tracing employed in the ACT* tutors but rather keeps a running count of each type of error made and waits for errors to reach some threshold before branching to remedial exercises (following work by Atkinson, 1976; Goldstein, 1979). When errors of a given type reach a prespecified threshold, a remedial set of exercises is automatically triggered. Moreover, this threshold is easily modifiable through the authoring interface. This logic also underlies the tutoring rules designed for BRIDGE, as discussed by Sams (this volume).

The adaptive branching in MILT can employ rules that range from very simple IF and GOTO statements to computationally complex operations, the building blocks for a formal student model. MILT supports computationally complex operations by linking performance criteria to Boolean (and/or) statements. Error counts are compared to settable thresholds, which can be considered as Boolean combinations. For example, branching to a given kind of remediation can depend on the student's reaching a threshold of subject-verb agreement errors together with a threshold of verb tense formation errors. An example of the authoring interfaces that control this adaptive structure appears in Figure 15.4.

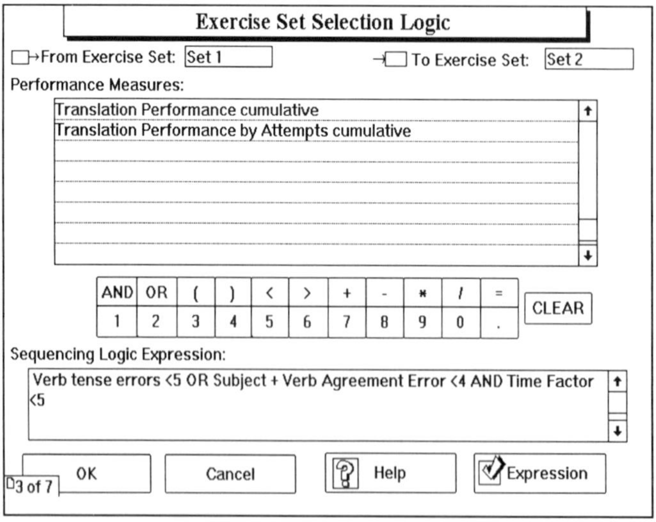

Fig. 15.4. Performance-based sequencing in MILT showing Boolean approach to controlling adaptivity. (Student's performance on various error types is compared with Boolean combinations of error criteria to determine when to branch from one exercise set to another.)

In addition to error-based adaptation, MILT can be modified to allow students to select their next exercise or set, or it can select the next exercise randomly. The screen that permits this modification is shown in Figure 15.5.

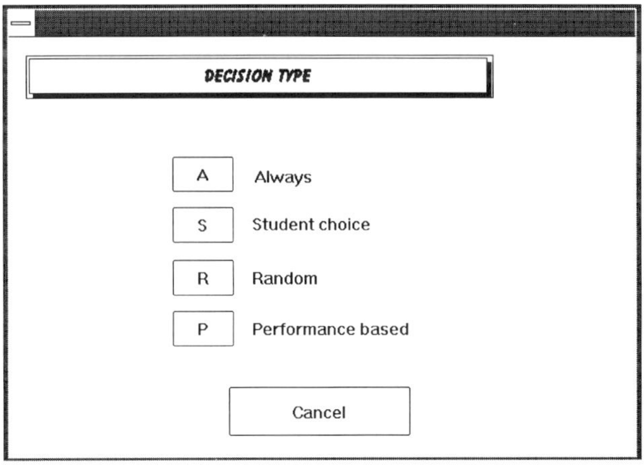

Fig 15.5. Decision type menu controlling the sequencing of exercises in MILT. *Always* avoids alternative sequences, and the student always is sent to the same next exercise. *Student choice* allows the student to pick the next exercise. *Random* picks the next out of alternative exercises according to a random number generator. *Performance based* makes use of performance criteria that are set by the author individually, or in combination with a Boolean editor (see Figure 15.4).

Parts Then the Whole, or Vice Versa

When target skills are complex, teaching component or prerequisite skills to high levels of fluency can lead to faster learning of the complex skill, as found in a variety of tasks (Stammers, 1980). Indeed, if initial presentations are too complex, learners' attempts to practice may result in failure, anxiety, and eventual unwillingness to continue (Farber & Spence, 1953). In such cases, people learn more effectively if they first practice simpler parts of a task, before putting these parts together into the complete task. This approach is known as *part-task training* and is the basis of many of the training simulators used in the aviation community (Knerr et al., 1985; Wightman & Sistrunk, 1987).

At the same time, some current theories of learning call for starting with the whole task, albeit in simplified form, so that learning is always contextualized. This reasoning underlies constructivist approaches such as *apprenticeship learning* (Collins, Brown, & Newman, 1989). It might also be argued to underlie the immersion method of language teaching, which stems from the communicative approach (see Oxford, this volume), whereas the grammar drill and practice and audiolingual methods reflect a part-task philosophy.

Both theoretical directions suggest that a tutor be designed to provide multiple types of exercises for students. These exercises should provide practice in simplified as well as complex versions of the skill being taught. Following these assumptions, we equipped the MILT authoring interface with exercise templates that correspond to progressively more cognitively demanding exercise types. Practice in recognizing written or spoken language is possible using multiple choice questions. Production of words and phrases may be practiced using fill-in-the-blank questions. A kind of proto-sentence production is enabled by exercises in assembling sentences from words in a menu (from a set of methods called *guided sentence production* by Kempen, 1992). The free response questions mentioned earlier elicit full sentence production from students. At the most complex end of this continuum are the microworld and dialogue exercises, which permit more extended communicative interaction.

This exercise variety permits both the part-to-whole and the whole-to-part approaches to be defined operationally within the tutor and then compared and tested. The part-to-whole approach suggests that the student be offered the opportunity to practice relatively simple, fragmentary language input and understanding, then the more complex full sentence version, and finally, complete dialogue. The whole-to-part approach suggests that the student (who has already reached an early level of proficiency) start with dialogue and microworld interactions, then go periodically to simpler exercises to practice vocabulary or syntax found to be not yet mastered. Indeed, the flexibility we have built into this system permits many of the somewhat ethereal notions about language pedagogy (such as contextualized language teaching) to be brought down to earth and defined within the manipulable parameters of the tutor.

Human Factors in the Authoring Interface

For practical applications, a tutor should be designed either with a very large body of exercises and/or with the ability to accept new exercises. Although we are designing a set of demonstration exercises in Arabic and Spanish, we decided not to install a full curriculum but rather to design an authoring interface so that instructors or researchers could build their own lessons. Unfortunately, most authoring systems are so difficult to learn that they require their own tutor. Therefore, the authoring interface being developed for MILT is based largely on templates so as to require no programming expertise or other specialized knowledge on the part of lesson authors.

The MILT authoring system allows foreign language teachers not only to create their own exercises but also to control the sequencing of those exercises. Exercise creation is based on templates for specific exercise types. The template approach has been continued from the BRIDGE tutor, as described by Kreyer and Criswell (this volume.) Figure 15.6 shows the exercise template for a fill-in-the-blank question. The author types desired elements into the question fields, which should require little or no training to understand.

For free response questions, whose answers are NLP-analyzed, the author types in the desired question and a sample answer. The sample answer is analyzed by the parser and the LCS interpreter, and the resulting representation is stored as the target feature set to which students' answers will be compared. The matching routine that performs this comparison is described by Dorr et al. (this volume).

The capability for control of sequencing also follows from the BRIDGE tutor but is aimed at introducing more flexibility, as illustrated by the combination rules discussed earlier (see Figure 15.4). Exercise sequences can be fixed and under the control of the author, fixed and under the control of the student, variable based on student performance as interpreted by rules created by the author, or a combination of these possibilities. The basic authoring interface for sequencing uses a flow chart approach, as shown in Figure 15.7.

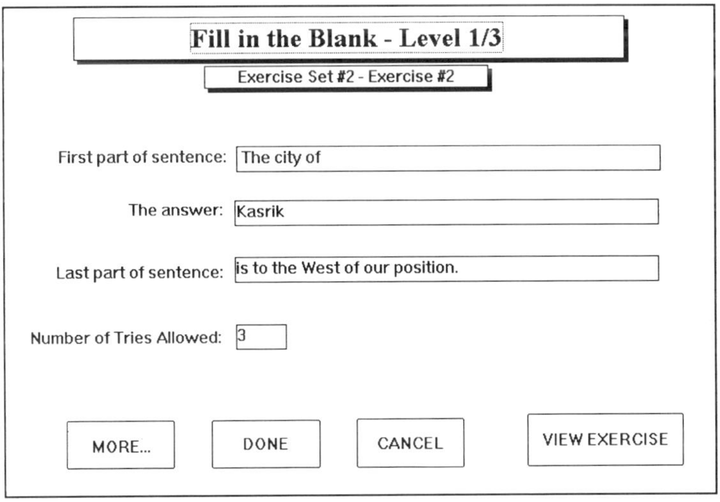

Fig. 15.6. Authoring interface for fill-in-the-blank questions.

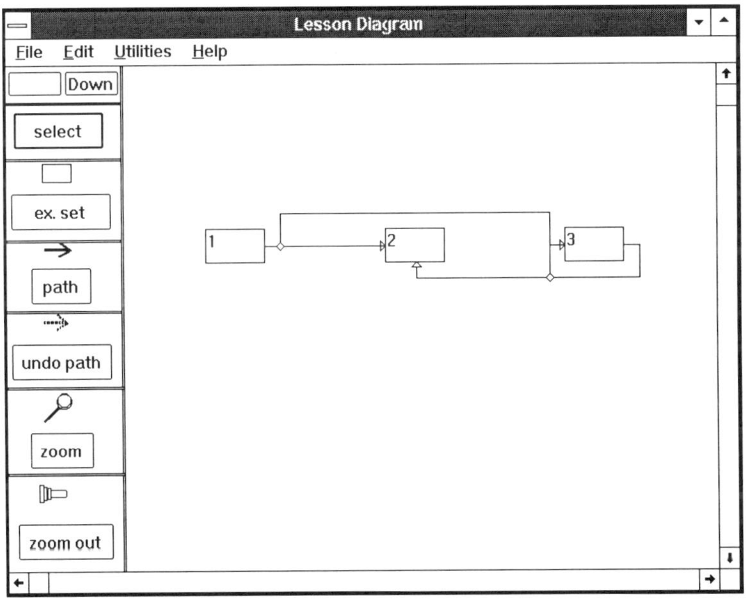

Fig. 15.7. Exercise sequence interface using flow charts to define the progression of exercise sets and decision diamonds to define branching.

The decision diamonds in these flow charts indicate points at which the author has specified branching based on the student's performance. For example, the configuration in Figure 15.7 means that students who make too many errors in Set 1 are branched automatically to Set 3 instead of Set 2. They will continue to redo Set 3 until their errors are below criterion; at that point they will go to Set 2. The threshold that governs the decision diamond is defined through a separate screen (e.g., Figure 15.4). Finally, the author can control the timing and wording of exercise feedback through templates.

This authoring design is based on an intersection of principles. First, we know that little detail exists in current theories of language learning and teaching to guide specific features of a tutor like sequencing of exercises and timing of feedback. We therefore built the authoring interface as a research tool to explore these questions. Second, we tried to build in parameters that have been found relevant in research on learning and instruction generally: Sequencing rules and selection and scheduling of feedback have been implicated in numerous studies (see Park & Tennyson, 1983; Schmidt, 1990). Third, we tried to ease the author's burden by using templates and menus where possible.

Final Thoughts

There have been few serious attempt to link the design of computer-assisted language instruction to learning research in areas outside of second languages.[39] However, there exists a rich empirical literature regarding how people acquire and retain cognitive skills. We feel that a principled tutor should draw on this literature, and we have found its principles selectively useful in shaping our ideas for design. The application of general principles to the design of a particular tutor is open to interpretation, as suggested by MacWhinney (this volume). Indeed, other designers might apply the same principles and come up with a system much different from ours, or they might arrive at the same design from a different set of principles. However the principles we have cited serve as rules of thumb by which we support or cast doubt on what are admittedly common-sense intuitions about design. Further principles from the literature on learning will come into play when we recommend how to use the tutor in language labs. For example, the benefits of distributed over massed practice for long-term retention have been demonstrated in many kinds of learning (Hagman & Rose, 1983; Landauer & Bjork, 1978; Melton, 1967), and on that basis we suggest that students who have some fixed number of hours to give the tutor distribute those hours over days or weeks rather than expending them at once or in a few sessions.

We question Oxford's position (this volume) that behavioristically oriented learning theory has nothing to say to language instruction. Some principles with their origin in behavioral theory have proved useful in guiding our design, as we have demonstrated. Although the novice-expert paradigm and constructivist theory discussed by Oxford have generated useful studies of knowledge and understanding, they serve in our case primarily as justifications after the fact rather than as shapers of design ideas. It is easy enough

---

[39] Frederiksen et al. (this volume) link their design to research on text comprehension processes, a direction expectedly different from ours given their focus on reading assistance in exploratory environments.

to say, and we probably will say in the future, that exercises like MILT's microworld and dialogue agree with constructivist interpretations of how people learn. This justification is nevertheless post hoc, and like much post hoc justification, neither necessary nor sufficient to explain the shape of a tutor.[40]

Acknowledgments

ARI's prime contractor for the MILT project is Micro Analysis & Design of Boulder, CO. The natural language processing components are being developed by the University of Maryland, Institute for Advanced Computer Studies. The views, opinions, and conclusions contained in this paper are those of the authors and should not be construed as an official Department of the Army position, policy, or decision.

References

Anderson, J.R. (1983). *The architecture of cognition.* Cambridge, MA: Harvard University Press.

Anderson, J.R., Boyle, C.F., Corbett, A.A., & Lewis, M.W. (1990). Cognitive modeling and intelligent tutoring. *Artificial Intelligence*, *42*, 7-49.

Anderson, J.R., Boyle, C.F., & Yost, G. (1985). The geometry tutor. In A. Joshi (Ed.), *Proceedings of the Ninth International Conference on Artificial Intelligence* (pp. 1-7). Los Altos, CA: Morgan Kaufman.

Anderson, J.R., Conrad, F., & Corbett, A. (1989). Skill acquisition and the LISP tutor. *Cognitive Science*, *8*, 87-129.

Anderson, J. R., & Schooler, L. J. (1991). Reflections of the environment in memory. *Psychological Science, 2*, 396-410.

Anderson, R.C., Kulhavey, R., & Andre, T. (1971). Feedback procedures in programmed instruction. *Journal of Educational Research*, *62*, 148-156.

Atkinson, R.C. (1976). Adaptive instructional systems: Some attempts to optimize the learning process. In D. Klahr, (Ed.), *Cognition and instruction.* Hillsdale, NJ: Lawrence Erlbaum Associates.

Berkowitz, M., & Simutis, Z. (1983). The development of a hand-held computerized tutor for military vocabulary. *Journal of Computer-Based Instruction*, *5*, 41-44.

Berlyne, D. (1968). Curiosity and exploration. *Science*, *153*, 25-33.

Chomsky, N. (1981). *Lectures on government and binding.* Dordrecht, Netherlands: Foris.

Collins, A., Brown, J.S., & Newman, S.E. (1989). Cognitive apprenticeship: Teaching the craft of reading, writing and mathematics. In L.B. Resnick (Ed.), *Knowing, learning, and instruction: Essays in honor of Robert Glaser* (pp. 453-494). Hillsdale, NJ: Lawrence Erlbaum Associates.

Deese, J., & Carpenter, J.A. (1951). Drive level and reinforcement. *Journal of Experimental Psychology, 42,* 236-238.

Dorr, B.J., Garman, J., & Weinberg, A. (1994). *From subcategorization frames to thematic roles: Building Arabic lexical entries for foreign language tutoring.* Manuscript submitted for publication.

Driskell, J.E., Willis, R., & Copper, C. (1992). Effect of overlearning on retention. *Journal of Applied Psychology*, *77*, 615-622.

Ellis, N.C. (Ed.). (1994). *Implicit and explicit learning of languages.* London: Academic Press.

Farber, I.E., & Spence, K.W. (1953). Complex learning and conditioning as function of anxiety. *Journal of Experimental Psychology*, *45*, 120-125.

Farr, B.J., & Ward, J.S. (1988). The Job Skills Education Program: Technology transfer. In *Proceedings of the 1988 Conference on Technology in Training and Education.* Biloxi, MS: U.S. Air Force.

---

[40] Elsewhere (Holland, 1994) we have argued that the shape of a language tutor comes less from prior principles than from social negotiations among project participants, who may have radically different points of view on what is important in building a tutor.

Gagne, R., & Briggs, L. (1979). *Principles of instructional design.* New York: Holt, Reinhart & Winston.

Goldstein, I.P. (1979). The genetic graph: A representation for the evolution of procedural knowledge. *International Journal of Man-Machine Studies, 11*, 51-77.

Hagman, J., Hayes, J., & Bierwirth, W. (1986). A method for estimating task retention: Research pays off. *Army Trainer, Fall*, 54-55.

Hagman, J., & Rose, A. (1983). Retention of military tasks: A review. *Human Factors, 25*, 199-213.

Holland, V.M. (1994). Lessons learned in designing intelligent CALL: Communicating across disciplines. *Computer Assisted Language Learning, 7*, 227-256.

Kaplan, J.D. (Ed.). (1989). *MANPRINT methods monograph: Aiding the development of training constraints* (Technical report no. 890621). Alexandria, VA: U.S. Army Research Institute.

Kempen, J. (1992). Language technology and language instruction: Computational diagnosis of word-level errors. In M. L. Swartz & M. Yazdani (Eds.), *Intelligent tutoring systems for foreign language learning: The bridge to international communication.* New York: Springer-Verlag.

Knerr, C.M., Morrison, J.E., Mumaw, R.J., Stein, D.J., Sticha, P.J., Hoffman, R.G., Buede, D.M., & Holding, D.H. (1985). *Simulator-based research in part-task training* (Report FR-PRD-85-11). Alexandria, VA: HumRRo.

Kulhavey, R.W. (1977). Feedback in written instruction. *Review of Educational Research, 47*(1), 211-232.

Kulik, J.A., & Kulik, C.C. (1988). Timing of feedback and verbal learning. *Review of Educational Research, 58*, 79-97.

Kurland, L., & Tenney, Y. (1989). Issues in developing an intelligent tutor for a real-world domain: Training in radar mechanics. In J. Psotka, D. Massey, & S. Mutter (Eds.), *Intelligent tutoring systems: Lessons learned.* Hillsdale, NJ: Lawrence Erlbaum Associates.

Landauer, T.K., & Bjork, R.A. (1978). Optimum rehearsal patterns and name learning. In M. Gruneberg, P. Morris, & R. Sykes (Eds.), *Practical aspects of memory.* London: Academic Press.

Laughery, K.R., Dahl, S., Kaplan, J.D., Archer, R, & Fontenelle, G. (1988). *Proceedings of the Human Factors Society 32nd Meeting, 2.* Santa Monica, CA: Human Factors Society.

Lawton, G., & Andreson, J.T. (1994). *Toward a behavior analytic assault on foreign language instruction.* Manuscript submitted for publication.

Levine, M. (1975). *A cognitive theory of learning.* Hillsdale, NJ: Lawrence Erlbaum Associates.

Lightbown, P., & Spada, M. (1990). Focus on form and corrective feedback in communicative language teaching: Effects on second language learning. *Studies in Second Language Acquisition, 12*, 4.

Maier, N.R.F. (1949). *Frustration: The study of behavior without a goal.* New York: McGraw-Hill.

Malone, T.W. (1981). Toward a theory of intrinsically motivating instruction. *Cognitive Science, 4*, 333-369.

McClelland, D. C. (1961). *The achieving society.* New York: Van Nostrand.

McLaughlin, B. (1994, September). *Language aptitude: An information processing perspective.* Paper presented at the Language Aptitude Invitational Symposium, Center for Advancement of Language Learning, Arlington, VA.

McLaughlin, B. (1990). Restructuring. *Applied Linguistics, 11*, 1-16.

Melton, A.W. (1967). Repetition and retrieval from memory. *Science, 158*, 532.

Miller, N. (1963). Some reflections on the law of effect produce a new alternative to drive reduction. In M. R. Jones (Ed.), *Nebraska Symposium on Motivation.* Lincoln: University of Nebraska Press.

Newell, A. (1990). *A unified theory of cognition.* Cambridge, MA: Harvard University Press.

Oxford, R., Harman, J., & Holland, V.M. (1987). Advances in the development of hand-held, computerized game-based, training devices. In D. Crookall & C. Greenblatt, (Eds.), *Simulation-gaming in the late 1980s.* New York: Pergamon.

Park, O.K., & Tennyson, R.D. (1983). Computer-based instructional systems for adaptive education: A review. *Contemporary Education Review, 2*, 121-134.

Psotka, J., Massey, D., & Mutter, S. (Eds.). (1988). *Intelligent tutoring systems: Lessons learned.* Hillsdale, NJ: Lawrence Erlbaum Associates.

Schendel, J.D., & Hagman, J.D. (1982). On sustaining procedural skills over a prolonged retention interval. *Journal of Applied Psychology, 67*, 605-610.

Schmidt, R.A. (1990). *Feedback for skill acquisition: Preliminaries to a theory of feedback* (Final Report, U.S. Army Research Institute Contract MDA903-85-K-0225). University of California at Los Angeles: Department of Psychology Motor Control Laboratory.

Schmidt, R.A., & Bjork, R. (1992). New conceptualizations of practice. *Psychological Science*, *3*, 207-217.

Skinner, B.F. (1938). *The behavior of organisms.* New York: Appleton-Century-Crofts.

Skinner, B. F. (1957). *Verbal behavior.* New York: Appleton-Century-Crofts.

Stammers, R.B. (1980). Part and whole practice for a tracking task: Effects of task variables and amount of practice. *Perceptual and Motor Skills*, *50*, 203-210.

Wightman, D.C., & Sistrunk, F. (1987). Part-task training strategies in simulated carrier landing final-approach training. *Human Factors*, *29*, 245-254.

Wisher, R.A., Holland, V.M., & Chatelier, P. (1987, May). *Portable training and job aiding devices.* Paper presented at the NATO Conference on Military Personnel and Training, Luxembourg City.

Wisher, R.A., Sabol, M., & Kern, R. (in press). Modeling acquisition of an advanced skill: The case of Morse Code copying. *Instructional Science.*

Witkins, H.A., Moore, C.A., Goodenough, D., & Cox, P. (1977). Field-independent and field-dependent cognitive styles and their educational implications. *Review of Educational Research*, *47*, 1-64.

Yates, L., & Macpherson, D. (1985). Analytic prediction of training device effectiveness. In *Proceedings of the 27th Annual Conference of the Military Testing Association* (pp. 515-520). San Diego, CA: U.S. Navy Personnel Research and Development Center.

16

On Beyond Syntax: Use of Lexical Conceptual Structure for Intelligent Tutoring

Bonnie Dorr, James Hendler, Scott Blanksteen, and Barrie Migdaloff
University of Maryland

The chapters in this book result from a workshop that presented a number of state-of-the-art projects in ICALL, or Intelligent Computer-Assisted Language Learning (see Holland, this volume). At that workshop, several different speakers stated that the study of syntactic processing was at a mature enough state that it could be reliably used as a basis for tutoring systems. Semantic knowledge, however, was deemed to be less well understood and not reliable for use outside of extremely limited domains such as graphics microworlds or adventure game level discourse (see, e.g., Murray, this volume). Further, authoring of semantic knowledge was dismissed by many as not currently available.

It is our contention that these views are too narrow. Current advances in lexical semantics make it possible to provide a wide range of new capabilities. In particular, recent work in computational linguistics (Dorr, 1992, 1993a, 1993b; Jackendoff, 1983, 1990) has shown that a lexically based semantics, tied relatively closely to grammatical structures, can be used to create an interlingua that can support activities such as machine translation and language tutoring. Although these lexical structures fall short of providing full semantic inferencing, and knowledge-based systems are still limited in the domains for which such inferencing can be supported, these lexical semantics provide a robust basis for the development of tutoring functions and an analysis that is more useful than syntactic analysis.

A simple example can easily show the need for going beyond syntactic processing in computer-aided language tutoring situations. Consider a syntactically based language tutor such as the BRIDGE system developed by a team of researchers from SAIC (Kreyer & Criswell, this volume), the University of Maryland (Weinberg, Garman, Martin, & Merlo, this volume), and the U.S. Army Research Institute (Holland, Maisano, Alderks, & Martin, 1993; Sams, this volume). Student input to BRIDGE can be analyzed for syntactic correctness but not for whether the answer is appropriate to the question. In one lesson, BRIDGE presents the student with a map and asks the student to provide a sentence in the target language (German in this example) that answers the question

TUTOR> Wie fährt man von Heidelberg nach Frankfurt?
'How does one drive from Heidelberg to Frankfurt?'

The student's answer is processed through a syntactic parser. If the student gives an appropriate answer, for example, "Folgen Sie der Autobahn im Norden" (You take the autobahn to the north), the system attests that the answer is syntactically correct, and the student continues on. If there is a syntactic error, the student is corrected in various ways, and the lesson continues.

However, consider what happens if the student types "Ich bin Berliner" (I am from Berlin) in answer to the question. As there are no syntactic mistakes in the sentence, the student is rewarded for a correct answer! Clearly, the system has missed the fact that the answer was inappropriate for the question asked. Catching such problems is quite difficult, however, because the student can produce many sentences that correctly answer the question, such as: "You take the Autobahn northwards," "You go north on the Autobahn," "You take the Autobahn to the north." Thus, the system must have some model of the semantics of the sentence if it is to correctly recognize the cases where the student's answer has the same meaning as the instructor's expected response.

In the sections that follow, we discuss the semantic models used by a tutoring project that is being developed jointly by the University of Maryland and Micro Analysis and Design, Inc., under sponsorship of the U.S. Army Research Institute. This emerging system, known as the Military Language Tutor (MILT), is described in detail in the chapter by Kaplan and Holland (this volume). The general goal of the MILT is to allow a wide range of lessons to be developed for use in language training. In addition to a number of authoring tools, speech and written display lessons, and various types of language drills, the MILT will offer authorable question answering exercises as well as an animated microworld and a limited-domain dialogue lesson. To support these goals, we are developing a natural language processing system that can encode the wide range of lexical and semantic knowledge that is relevant for understanding utterances, whether they are placed in an overt lesson, a microworld, or dialogue context. The first languages targeted for the system are Arabic and Spanish.

In this chapter we discuss the semantic tools that let us go beyond the capabilities of syntax-based tutors such as BRIDGE as well as the ALICE-chan and CALLE systems described in this volume (respectively, Levin & Evans; Rypa & Feuerman). We start by reviewing the particular lexical semantic model that we use in the section of this chapter entitled "Lexical Conceptual Structure." In succeeding sections we show how this representation supports a question-answering system and a limited domain discourse. An authoring tool for entering the relevant semantic knowledge is described in "LCS Editing Capability." We conclude by discussing future work, particularly focusing on developing a better integration between the lexical semantics and deeper knowledge-based inferencing, which will be needed to improve these capabilities in the future.

Lexical Conceptual Structure

One of the types of knowledge that must be captured in the tutor is linguistic knowledge. At the level of the lexicon, this covers a wide range of information types such as verbal subcategorization for events (e.g., that a transitive verb such as *hit* occurs with an object noun phrase), featural information (e.g., that the direct object of a verb such as *frighten* is animate), thematic information (e.g., that *John* is the agent in "John hit the ball"), and lexical-semantic information (e.g., spatial verbs such as *throw* are conceptually distinct from verbs of possession such as *give*). By modularizing the lexicon, we treat each information type separately. This allows us to vary the degree of dependence on each level so that we can address the question of how much knowledge is necessary for the success of the tutoring system.

The most intricate component of lexical knowledge is the lexical-semantic information, which we encode in the form of lexical conceptual structure (LCS) as formulated by

Dorr (1992, 1993a, 1993b), based on work by Jackendoff (1983, 1990). This representation abstracts away from syntax just far enough to enable language-independent encoding while retaining enough structure to be sensitive to the requirements for multilingual processing. The central idea of LCS is that the human language can be modeled using a uniform internal representation of conceptual information with a few parameters that can be toggled one way or another to obtain various languages. The versatility of the LCS allows us to reuse labor-intensive features of the lexicon across languages. We perform natural language analysis by mapping the syntactic representation of the input sentences into this internal representation. The result is used later as the basis for semantic interpretation. This technique produces more accurate analyses than naive syntactic-tree matching approaches, which tend to be much more limited in coverage.

A central issue that arises with respect to the use of a language-independent representation in any multilingual system is that of defining a set of primitives to represent cross-linguistic phenomena. Because it is generally difficult to define such a set, many researchers have abandoned the use of an intermediate representation in multilingual applications (see, for example, Vauquois & Boitet, 1985). However, recently, there has been a resurgence of interest in the area of lexical representation and organization (with special reference to verbs) that has initiated an ongoing effort to delimit the classes of lexical knowledge required to process natural language (e.g., Grimshaw, 1990; Hale & Keyser, 1986a, 1986b, 1989; Hale & Laughren, 1983; Jackendoff, 1983, 1990; Levin, 1985, 1993; Levin & Rappaport, 1986; Olsen, 1991; Pustejovsky, 1988, 1989, 1991; Rappaport, Laughren, & Levin, 1987; Rappaport & Levin, 1988; Zubizarreta, 1982, 1987). As a result of this effort, it has become increasingly more feasible to isolate the components of meaning common to verbs participating in particular classes. These components of meaning can then be used to determine the lexical representation of verbs across languages.

The LCS approach views semantic representation as a subset of conceptual structure (i.e., the language of mental representation). Jackendoff's approach includes types such as event and state, which are specialized into primitives such as GO, STAY, BE, GO-EXT, and ORIENT. As an example of how the primitive GO is used to represent sentence semantics, consider the following sentence:

(1) a. The ball rolled toward Beth.
b. $[_{Event}$ GO $([_{Thing}$ BALL$]$,
$[_{Path}$ TOWARD $([_{Position}$ AT $([_{Thing}$ BALL$]$,$[_{Thing}$ BETH$])])])]$

This representation illustrates one dimension, the spatial dimension, of Jackendoff's representation. Another dimension is the causal dimension, which includes the primitives CAUSE and LET. These primitives take a thing and an event as arguments. Thus, we could embed the structure shown in (1)(b) within a causative construction:

(2) a. John rolled the ball toward Beth.
b. $[_{Event}$ CAUSE
$([_{Thing}$ JOHN$]$,
$[_{Event}$ GO $([_{Thing}$ BALL$]$,
$[_{Path}$ TOWARD$[_{Position}$ AT $([_{Thing}$ BALL$]$,$[_{Thing}$ BETH$])])])])$

Jackendoff includes a third dimension by introducing the notion of field. This dimension extends the semantic coverage of spatially oriented primitives to other domains such as possessional, temporal, identificational, circumstantial, and existential.[41] Jackendoff argues that spatial primitives are more fundamental than those of other domains (e.g., possessional). Thus, spatial primitives have their own special status as an independent dimension. For example, the primitive GO Poss refers to a GO event in the possessional field as in the following sentence:

(3) a. Beth received the doll.

b. [$_{\text{Event}}$ GO $_{\text{Poss}}$
([$_{\text{Thing}}$ DOLL],
[$_{\text{Path}}$ TO $_{\text{Poss}}$ ([$_{\text{Position}}$ AT $_{\text{Poss}}$ ([$_{\text{Thing}}$ DOLL],[$_{\text{Thing}}$ BETH])])])]

To further illustrate the notion of field, the GO primitive can be used in the temporal and identificational fields:

(4) a. The meeting went from 2:00 to 4:00.

b. [$_{\text{Event}}$ GO Temp
([$_{\text{Thing}}$ MEETING],
[$_{\text{Path}}$ FROM Temp ([$_{\text{Position}}$ AT Temp ([$_{\text{Thing}}$ MEETING],[$_{\text{Time}}$ 2:00])])]
[$_{\text{Path}}$ TO Temp ([$_{\text{Position}}$ AT Temp ([$_{\text{Thing}}$ MEETING],[$_{\text{Time}}$ 4:00])])])]

(5) a. The frog turned into a prince.

b. [$_{\text{Event}}$ GO Ident
([$_{\text{Thing}}$ FROG],
[$_{\text{Path}}$ TO Ident ([$_{\text{Position}}$ AT Ident ([$_{\text{Thing}}$ FROG],[$_{\text{Thing}}$ PRINCE])])])]

Figure 16.1 shows a subset of the types and primitives currently used in the LCS scheme.

Type	Primitives
Event	CAUSE, LET, GO, STAY
State	BE, GO EXT, ORIENT
Position	AT, IN, ON
Path	TO, FROM, TOWARD, AWAY-FROM, VIA
Thing	BOOK, PERSON, REFERENT, KNIFE-WOUND, KNIFE, SHARP-OBJECT, WOUND, FOOT, CURRENCY, PAINT, FLUID, ROOM, SURFACE, WALL, HORSE, BALL, DOLL, MEETING, FROG
Property	TIRED, HUNGRY, PLEASED, BROKEN, ASLEEP, DEAD, STRETCHED, HAPPY, RED, HOT, FAR, BIG, EASY, CERTAIN
Location	HERE, THERE, LEFT, RIGHT, UP, DOWN
Time	TODAY, SATURDAY, 2:00, 4:00
Manner	FORCEFULLY, LIKINGLY, WELL, QUICKLY, DANCINGLY, SEEMINGLY, HAPPILY, LOVINGLY, PLEASINGLY, GIFTINGLY, UPWARD, DOWNWARD, WITHIN, HABITUALLY

FIG. 16.1. LCS primitives and types.

[41] As we will see shortly, the label *Loc* has been adopted to distinguish the spatial field from the nonspatial fields. Note that the spatial field is used to denote the primitives that fall in the spatial dimension.

Figure 16.2 shows the different types of sentences that can be represented by the system of primitives and fields in Figure 16.1. It should be noted that although the LCS representation appears to be somewhat like English, it is only superficially so by virtue of the labels of the primitives (e.g., GO, TO) that are used in the representation.

Primitive	Primitive-Field	Example
GO	GO_{Poss}	Beth received the doll.
	GO_{Ident}	Elise became a mother.
	GO_{Temp}	The meeting went from 2:00 to 4:00.
	GO_{Loc}	We moved the statue from the park to the zoo.
	GO_{Circ}	John started shipping goods to California.
	GO_{Exist}	John built a house.
STAY	$STAY_{Poss}$	Amy kept the doll.
	$STAY_{Ident}$	The coach remained a jerk.
	$STAY_{Temp}$	We kept the meeting at noon.
	$STAY_{Loc}$	We kept the statue in the park.
	$STAY_{Circ}$	John kept shipping goods to California.
	$STAY_{Exist}$	The situation persisted.
BE	BE_{Poss}	The doll belongs to Beth.
	BE_{Ident}	Elise is a pianist.
	BE_{Temp}	The meeting is at noon.
	BE_{Loc}	The statue is in the park.
	BE_{Circ}	John is shipping goods to California.
	BE_{Exist}	Descartes exists.
GO-EXT	$GO\text{-}EXT_{Ident}$	Our clients range from psychiatrists to psychopaths.
	$GO\text{-}EXT_{Temp}$	The meeting lasted from noon to night.
	$GO\text{-}EXT_{Loc}$	The road went from Boston to Albany.
ORIENT	$ORIENT_{Loc}$	The sign points to Philadelphia.
	$ORIENT_{Circ}$	John intended to ship goods to California.

FIG. 16.2. Sentences represented by event and state primitives of the LCS.

These primitives were chosen on the basis of an extensive crosslinguistic investigation, though they may be labeled and used in a fashion that appears to be modeled after a particular language. The verb classes (based on work by Levin, 1985, 1993) that are currently accommodated are shown in Figure 16.3. It is expected that this verb classification scheme will need further refinement as more properties of verbs are identified.

To illustrate the use of this representation in the lexicon, consider the following example:

(6) E: I like Mary.
S: María me gusta..
Mary (to) me pleases

The language-independent representation for this example looks like the following:

(7) $[_{State}$ BE Ident $([_{Thing}$ I$]$
$[_{Position}$ AT Ident $([_{Thing}$ I$],[_{Thing}$ MARY$])],$
$[_{Manner}$ LIKINGLY$])]$

Class of Verb	Examples
position	be, remain, . . .
change of position	fall, throw, drop, change, move, slide, float, roll, fly, bounce, move, drop, turn, rotate, shift, . . .
directed motion	enter, break into, bring, carry, remove, come, go, leave, arrive, descend, ascend, put, raise, lower, . . .
motion with manner	sail, walk, stroll, jog, march, gallop, jump, float, dance, run, skip, . . .
exchange	buy, sell, trade, . . .
physical state	be, remain, keep, leave, . . .
change of physical state	open, close, melt, redden, soften, break, crack, freeze, harden, dry, whiten, grow, change, become, . . .
orientation	point, aim, face, . . .
existence	exist, build, grow, shape, make, whittle, spin, carve, weave, bake, fashion, create, appear, disappear, reappear, persist, . . .
circumstance	be, start, top, continue, keep, exempt, . . .
range	go, last, extend, intend, aim, range, . . .
change of ownership	give, take, receive, relinquish, borrow, lend, loan, steal, . . .
ownership	belong, remain, keep, own, . . .
ingestion	eat, drink, smoke, gobble, munch, sip, . . .
psychological state	like, fear, admire, detest, despise, enjoy, esteem, hate, honor, love, please, scare, amuse, astonish, bore, surprise, stun, terrify, thrill, . . .
perception and communication	see, hear, smell, feel, look, watch, listen, learn, sniff, show, tell, talk, speak, shout, whisper, scream, . . .
mental process	know, learn, . . .
cost	cost, charge, . . .
load/spray	smear, load, cram, spray, stuff, pile, stack, splash, . . .
contact/effect	cut, stab, crush, smash, pierce, bite, shoot, spear, . . .

FIG. 16.3. Linguistic classes from Levin (1985, 1993) implemented in LCS framework.

The representation in (7) roughly means, "I am in an identificational state LIKINGLY with respect to Mary." Both the Spanish and English sentences are based on this representation. The syntactic distinction (i.e., the subject-object reversal) is captured by means of parameterization in the lexicon:

(8) a. **Lexical entry for *like*:**

$[_{\text{State}}$ BE $_{\text{Ident}}$ ($[_{\text{Thing}}$:EXT W],
$[_{\text{Position}}$ AT $_{\text{Ident}}$ ($[_{\text{Thing}}$ W],$[_{\text{Thing}}$:INT Z])],
$[_{\text{Manner}}$ LIKINGLY])]

b. **Lexical Entry for *gustar*:**

$[_{\text{State}}$ BE $_{\text{Ident}}$ ($[_{\text{Thing}}$:INT W],
$[_{\text{Position}}$ AT $_{\text{Ident}}$ ($[_{\text{Thing}}$ W],$[_{\text{Thing}}$:EXT Z])],
$[_{\text{Manner}}$ LIKINGLY])]

The :INT and :EXT markers are examples of lexical parameterization that allow the system to account for the subject-object reversal of the *like-gustar* example. The LCS representation has been developed on the basis of a study of crosslinguistic distinctions such as that shown in (6). This decompositional approach to describing linguistic constructions is consistent with the philosophy behind well-grounded lexical-semantic theories such as meaning-text theory (MTT) by Mel'cuk and Polguère (1987). That is, rather than postulating a set of semantic primitives a priori, the intention is to discover them by means of a "painstaking process of semantic decomposition applied to thousands of actual lexical items" (p. 266). Given that recent research has made it increasingly more feasible to isolate components of verb meaning, this approach to the construction of a language-independent representation is no longer impractical. Note that this is in direct contrast to other approaches that employ primitives that are chosen a priori, such as the conceptual dependency approach by Schank (1972, 1973, 1975) and Schank and Abelson (1977), for which there has never been a crosslinguistic investigation into the applicability of the primitives.

A final point to be made about the current representation is that it is intended to include those aspects of lexical knowledge related to argument structure, not deeper notions of meaning such as aspectual, contextual, domain, and world knowledge. Although these deeper notions are indisputably necessary for a general solution to language understanding, previous approaches that have employed deep semantic representations say very little about how to map the representation systematically to the surface syntactic structure, especially in the context of crosslinguistic distinctions such as that in (6). These approaches pay a high price for incorporating too much deeper knowledge without preserving structurally defined lexical-semantic information. This is not to say that research should head in the direction of shallow representations (see Sharp, 1985). The current approach attempts to achieve a middle ground between representations that encode too much information and those that encode too little. Specifically, the current representation captures parametric information that accommodates cross-linguistic distinctions without losing the systematic relation between the language-independent representation and the syntactic structure. Moreover, the representation lends itself readily to the specification of processing components that operate uniformly across different languages.

Using the LCS for Question Answering Lessons

As discussed in the introduction, the LCS is a critical component of our approach to matching student answers in the context of a question answering lesson provided by the foreign language tutor. This lesson requires the student to answer free response questions about a short foreign language passage. In order to inform the student whether a question has been answered correctly, the author of the lesson must provide the desired response in advance. The system parses and semantically analyzes this response into a corresponding LCS representation, which is then prestored in a database of possible responses. Once the question answering lesson is activated, each of the student's responses is parsed and semantically analyzed into a LCS representation, which is checked for a match against the corresponding prestored LCS representation. The student is then informed as to whether the question has been answered correctly depending on how closely the student's response LCS matches the author's prestored LCS. This matching process is like the one described by Levin and Evans (this volume) for free response questions and other exercises in the ALICE-chan tutor. However, we do not envision in our current system building in the kind of flexibility described by Levin and Evans, in which instructors can tailor the prestored target features. At the same time, our matcher may gain flexibility by comparing on features that are more semantic in nature than the lexical functional features used in ALICE-chan.

The overall processing design used to support question answering exercises is shown in Figure 16.4.

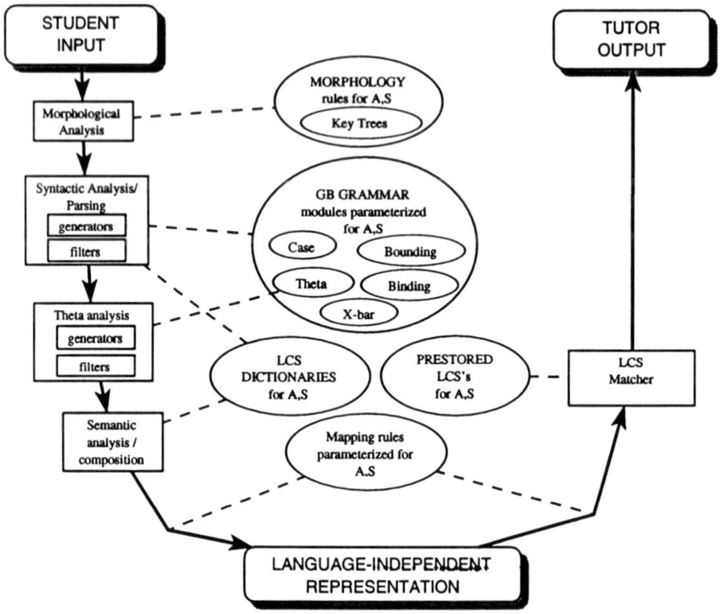

FIG. 16.4. Diagram of processing flow for question answering.

The analysis component of the system includes morphological, syntactic, and semantic processing that transforms the student's input sentence (i.e., the response to the tutor's question) into a language-independent representation. The syntactic analyzer, described by Weinberg et al. (this volume), makes use of government and binding principles (developed by Chomsky, 1981, 1986, and his followers) that are parameterized for the particular language in question. Thus, the analyzer is able to function in both Arabic and Spanish, given the appropriate lexicon. The parse tree produced by the syntactic analyzer is passed to the semantic analysis/composition component, and the language-independent LCS representation is generated. This representation is then passed to the LCS matcher, which checks the answer for a match against the desired answer that was prestored by the author. The degree to which the match succeeds is then determined, and this is used to generate the tutor output (i.e., confirmation of (in)correctness).

LCS Matching

To support question-answering lessons, a student's input must be matched against the instructor's stored answer to see if the answer is appropriate. In this section we briefly describe the matcher and its output. In the next, we discuss how it is used in the question-answering context. The matcher is a relatively straightforward algorithm that performs a recursive descent through two LCSs, determining where they are the same and where they are different. The matcher starts by determining whether two LCS structures contain the same primitive. If they do, it determines for each of the fields whether they are omitted or, if present, whether they contain the same fillers. If all the fields in the stored answer are correctly matched with the student's answer, then the match is said to be correct. If extra information is provided by the student, this is identified as well. The return from the matcher identifies whether the match is correct and what fields are missing or extra.

As an example, consider what happens in a lesson if the teacher has specified that a correct answer is "John ran to the house." This sentence is processed by the system to produce the following LCS:

(9) $[_{\text{Event}}$ GO $_{\text{Loc}}$
  $([_{\text{Thing}}$ JOHN],
  $[_{\text{Path}}$ TO $_{\text{Loc}}$
    $([_{\text{Position}}$ AT $_{\text{Loc}}([_{\text{Thing}}$ JOHN],[Property HOUSE])])],
  $[_{\text{Manner}}$ RUNNINGLY])]

This LCS is stored by the tutor and later matched against the student's answer. If the student types "John went to the house," the system must determine if this matches the teacher-specified answer. The student's sentence is processed and the following LCS structure is produced:

(10) $[_{\text{Event}}$ GO $_{\text{Loc}}$
  $([_{\text{Thing}}$ JOHN],
  $[_{\text{Path}}$ TO $_{\text{Loc}}$
    $([_{\text{Position}}$ AT $_{\text{Loc}}$ $([_{\text{Thing}}$ JOHN],[Property HOUSE])])])]

The matcher compares the two LCSs, and produces a data structure representing the output of the comparison:

Missing :
  MANNER RUNNINGLY
Extra :
  NIL
INCORRECT answer.

This structure identifies the student's response as an incorrect answer because the student has omitted the fact that John was running. If we reverse the situation, with the teacher storing as the correct answer "John went to the house" and the student typing "John ran to the house," the situation would be different. In this case, the matcher would return

Missing :
  NIL
Extra :
  MANNER RUNNINGLY
CORRECT answer.

This time the student has provided information the teacher did not require but omitted nothing that was required. Thus, the system has identified the answer as correct and recognized that the student provided information about the manner of the going, which was not necessary. The returns from the LCS matcher are passed to the tutor, which turns them into appropriate replies to the student (e.g., a reply template could be filled to yield, "Your answer is right but you did not say how John went.")

Question Answering

Question-answering lessons are formulated as sets of free response questions associated with a picture or with a paragraph (or more) of text in the target language. In an authoring session, the lesson designer enters the passages and the questions and types a sample appropriate answer for each question.[42] This answer is processed by the system, and the appropriate LCSs are stored. If the lesson designer wishes to increase the semantic coverage of the system for processing such questions, a LCS editor is provided (discussed in the next section.) At lesson time, the student is prompted with these questions and enters an answer. This answer is processed and matched as described previously. If the answer matches, the student continues to the next question. If the answer is identified as an incorrect match, a diagnostic message is prepared by the tutor and shown to the student.

As an example of the use of the LCS processing and matcher to support a lesson, consider the following example of a Spanish passage the student might be expected to read (with the English translation below):

(11) a. Carlos Perez, propietario de la Pescadería Perez, fue arrestado ayer en su casa por elasesinato de Juan Rodriguez. El Señor Rodriguez fue encontrado muerto en su apartamento el mes pasado con múltiples heridas de puñaladas en el pecho y estómago. Las huellas tactilares del propietario de la tienda fueron encontrados en el arma asesina, el cual estaba tirado en un cercano basurero.

b. Carlos Perez, owner of Perez Fish Market, was arrested yesterday in his home for the murder Juan Rodriguez. Mr. Rodriguez was found dead in his apartment last month with multiple stab wounds in the chest and stomach. The storeowner's fingerprints were found on the murder weapon, which had been discarded in a nearby trash bin.

The student reads the Spanish passage and is then asked questions about it. An example of a typical question might be the following:

TUTOR> Qué pasó a Juan Rodriguez?
'What happened to Juan Rodriguez?'

Suppose, for the sake of illustration, that the lesson author expects the student's answer to convey the fact that Juan died. Any additional information (e.g., that Carlos caused Juan's death or that Juan was stabbed with a knife) would be optionally allowed as well. The author would provide a sample of the expected student response, such as

[42] We currently limit this to only one appropriate answer per question but expect to relax this limitation in later versions of the system.

"Juan murió" (Juan died). This would be syntactically parsed and semantically analyzed into the following LCS representation:

(12) $[_{\text{Event}}\ \text{GO}\ _{\text{Ident}}$
$([_{\text{Thing}}\ \text{JUAN}],$
$[_{\text{Path}}\ \text{TOWARD}\ _{\text{Ident}}$
$([_{\text{Position}}\ \text{AT}\ _{\text{Ident}}\ ([_{\text{Thing}}\ \text{JUAN}],[_{\text{Property}}\ \text{DEAD}])])])]$

This representation would then be stored as the desired response to the current question.

At lesson time, the student would be prompted with the question and expected to type an answer. The student could type any of the following answers:

STUDENT> Juan murió.
'Juan died. '
STUDENT> Carlos le mató a Juan.
'Carlos killed Juan.'
STUDENT> Carlos le asesinó a Juan.
'Carlos murdered Juan.'

The LCS representation corresponding to the first response is the same as the pre-stored answer provided by the author. The last two are, respectively,

(13) a. $[_{\text{Event}}\ \text{CAUSE}$
$([_{\text{Thing}}\ \text{CARLOS}],$
$[_{\text{Event}}\ \text{GO}\ _{\text{Ident}}$
$([_{\text{Thing}}\ \text{JUAN}],$
$[_{\text{Path}}\ \text{TOWARD}\ _{\text{Ident}}$
$([_{\text{Position}}\ \text{AT}\ _{\text{Ident}}\ ([_{\text{Thing}}\text{JUAN}],[_{\text{Property}}\ \text{DEAD}])])])])]$

b. $[_{\text{Event}}\ \text{CAUSE}$
$([_{\text{Thing}}\ \text{CARLOS}],$
$[_{\text{Event}}\ \text{GO}\ _{\text{Ident}}$
$([_{\text{Thing}}\ \text{JUAN}],$
$[_{\text{Path}}\ \text{TOWARD}\ _{\text{Ident}}$
$([_{\text{Position}}\ \text{AT}\ _{\text{Ident}}\ ([_{\text{Thing}}\ \text{JUAN}],[_{\text{Property}}\ \text{DEAD}])])])],$
$[_{\text{Manner}}\ \text{UNLAWFULLY}])]$

In all three cases, the matcher would be able to recognize that these are correct answers (i.e., each matches the base LCS, although the latter two contain extra information), and the student would proceed.

One advantage of the LCS matching becomes clear in this example. It would be a tedious task if the author were expected to specify, in advance, all possible ways that the student might choose to convey the desired information. Our approach to representing the prestored answer allows the author to type in only the first answer (i.e., "Juan murió," which is analyzed into a LCS representation). This representation is general enough to match any number of additional answers.

Another advantage concerns the handling of inappropriate answers. If the student types a completely inappropriate answer, such as "Me llamo Juan" (I am called Juan), the corresponding LCS would be as follows:

(14) $[_{Event}\ BE\ _{Ident}\ ([_{Thing}\ I],[_{Position}\ AT\ _{Ident}\ ([_{Thing}\ I],[_{Property}\ JUAN])])]$

The representation in (14) is identified by the matcher as being in the wrong primitive class and is rejected as an inappropriate answer. The tutor informs the student that the correct answer is expressed differently, and the student tries again.

More subtle errors can also be identified. Consider the case where the student types the following:

> STUDENT> Juan le mató a Carlos.
> 'Juan killed Carlos.'

This answer is almost correct, but the subject and object are wrong. The matcher recognizes this as an incorrect match, but one in which part of the information is correct. In particular, the matcher would recognize that Juan and Carlos occupy inappropriate slots in a representation that otherwise matches the prestored answer. This information allows the student to be informed that the action seems appropriate but the answer is wrong. The student is advised to reread the paragraph and to answer the question again.[43]

It should be noted that the lack of a more complex knowledge representation system underlying the matching makes for some limitations to this technique. For example, consider the following student response to the question as to what happened to Juan:

> STUDENT> Carlos le dio unas puñaladas fatales a Juan.
> 'Carlos stabbed Juan fatally.'

In this case, the system would generate the following LCS:

(15) $[_{Event}\ CAUSE$
$([_{Thing}\ CARLOS],$
$[_{Event}\ GO\ _{Poss}$
$([_{Thing}\ KNIFE\text{-}WOUND],$
$[_{Path}\ TOWARD\ _{Poss}$
$([_{Position}\ AT\ _{Poss}\ ([_{Thing} KNIFE\text{-}WOUND],[_{Thing}\ JUAN])])])]$
$[_{Manner}\ FATALLY])]$

This would not match the LCS generated previously for "Juan murió." The system would need to infer that *Manner FATALLY* implies the death of the subject, but that is beyond the scope of the LCS system. We return to this issue in our conclusions.

In addition to question answering, the usefulness of the LCS framework and the matching algorithm extends to another lesson type provided by the foreign language tutor, in which the student must translate an English sentence into a sentence in either Arabic or Spanish. Again, the author provides a sample question (this time the sentence to be translated) and answer. The answer is parsed, analyzed, and stored as described previously. The student's translation and the prestored answer are matched, and the tutor is able to analyze whether the translation is correct or not.

---

[43] It should be noted that the matcher cannot currently recognize that they are transposed but simply that they are inappropriate names. Thus "Igor killed Fred" would also be judged similarly.

LCS Editing Capability

During lexical-semantic analysis of a foreign language sentence, the intelligent tutor accesses a LCS dictionary for that language. Manual construction of this dictionary is a very tedious task; thus, we have designed and implemented a LCS editor that makes the construction process much faster, easier, and less error-prone. The heart of the LCS editor is the LCS entry window shown in Figure 16.5. This window is where LCSs are built and modified. During editing, the current state of the LCS is continuously updated and displayed in two windows, the tree representation window and the text representation window.

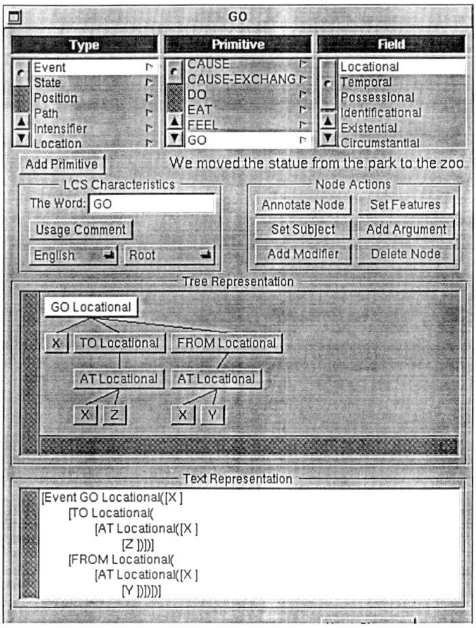

FIG. 16.5. LCS entry window.

The editor also displays sample sentences for various combinations of primitive and field to guide the author with respect to the meanings of the various terms. In Figure 16.5 the words "We moved the statue from the park to the zoo" represent an example of a sentence using a word (i.e., *move*) that has the same type, primitive, and field as the currently selected node.

The LCS of this example contains nodes labeled *X*, *Y*, and *Z*. There are no primitives by these names; rather, these nodes represent variables. Any nodes with the same variable name will eventually refer to the same item in the natural language sentence that this LCS is used to represent. For each type, there is a primitive called *var Type*. For example, under the event type there is a primitive called *var Event*. If this were chosen as a primitive, a window would appear asking for a variable name.

Under the browser is the Add Primitive button. Clicking this button allows the author to add a new primitive to the set that is currently defined as well as to specify which type the primitive belongs to and which fields are applicable.

The next item is a group of controls labeled *LCS Characteristics*. These are items that apply to the LCS entry as a whole. The author enters the word that the entry represents in the text field labeled *The Word*. The Usage Comment button allows the author to enter a comment about the usage of this particular entry for documentation purposes. (It has no effect on the correctness of the entry.) Below this button is a pop-up menu labeled *English*, reflecting the fact that this is the LCS entry for the English verb *go*. Next to this is another pop-up menu labeled *Root*, indicating that this LCS is for a word with root causality. If, for example, the LCS were representing the verb *shove*, then this pop-up would have been set to "Causative."

Next to the group labeled *LCS Characteristics* is another group of controls labeled *Node Actions*. These items apply solely to the node that is currently selected. In the current example, the root node of the tree is selected, so any of the Node Actions items that are chosen apply to the root node. The selection of a node action opens a secondary window (palette) that supports the annotation of LCS items with classifying markers (such as the :INT and :EXT markers given in (8) earlier), semantic and syntactic feature information, and usage comments. If the tree grows large enough, vertical and/or horizontal scrollers appear to allow the author to see different regions of the tree. The LCS Editor is currently being used to enter vocabulary into the dictionaries for Spanish and Arabic in the current tutoring project.

Limited Domain Discourse

Currently under investigation within the context of this research is the development of a tool that will allow the student to interact with a simulated native language speaker in a relatively unconstrained dialogue. In one example of this mode of interaction, the system takes the role of a person responding to questions posed by the student in an interview, debriefing, or military interrogation scenario (cf. DeSmedt, this volume, who uses a civilian interrogation scenario as a context for student-posed questions). Figure 16.6 illustrates a small segment of hypothetical dialogue with the simulated Spanish speaker, whom we have named Diego Ramirez.

The ability to converse in the kind of unrestricted manner shown in Figure 16.6 puts a significant burden on the natural language system. The system must be able to analyze correctly the questions (or statements) the student has produced, and it must be able to generate a correct answer. Generation of an answer can require either a simple knowledge-based retrieval, as in the first three sentences of Figure 16.6, which query simple facts like name and age; or it can require the production of a more complex answer, depending on a full interpretation of the question, as suggested in the remaining sentences in Figure 16.6.

STUDENT> Cuál es su apellido? (What is your name?)
TUTOR> Ramirez.
STUDENT> Su nombre? (Your first name?)
TUTOR> Diego.
STUDENT> Cuántos años tiene usted? (How old are you?)
TUTOR> Yo tengo 24 años. (I am 24 years old.)
STUDENT> Dónde fue la capturada?
(Incorrect sentence: Where was the captured woman?)
TUTOR> No comprendo. (I don't understand.)
STUDENT> Dónde fue detenido? (Where were you captured?)
TUTOR> Durante la redada yo estaba detrás la casa y salí corriendo.
(During the raid, I was in back of the house and ran away.)
STUDENT> Y entonces? (And then?)
TUTOR> La policia me vio y fui arrestado. (The police saw me and I was arrested.)

FIG. 16.6. Sample of small segment of dialogue with simulated Spanish speaker.

When the student's input cannot be analyzed (because of syntactic or semantic error), the system must produce an appropriate response that can keep the dialogue going. For example, in the fourth sentence the student mistakes the inappropriate cognate *capturada* for the correct term *detenido* and asks, "Dónde fue la capturada?" (which translates roughly as "Where was the captured woman?"). If we assume there is no captured woman that the Spanish speaker knows about, the tutor in the role of Diego Ramirez might answer, "No comprendo" (I don't understand you). The student then finds the right word, asks the appropriate question, and the discourse continues.

Efforts to support this type of dialogue interaction require the addition of a planning component with sophisticated semantic representations that can gauge the semantic appropriateness of student input and structure responses that move the dialogue along in a natural fashion. These components are now being added to the already mature syntactic analyzer. Also under implementation is a generation component that turns the output of the NLP interpretation into a response phrased appropriately in the foreign language. Figure 16.7 shows the planned design of the augmented system with generation component.

As an example, consider how the system would understand and produce the answer to one of the questions in the current dialogue. The student types "Dónde fue detenido?" (Where were you captured?) to the tutor, which passes this string to the syntactic parser. The syntactic parser produces a parse tree that recognizes this sentence as a WH clause (in this case, a who-what-when-where type of question), with the appropriate syntactic relations among the words noted.

The parse tree is then sent to the lexical-semantic analyzer, which is responsible for producing a semantic structure that unambiguously captures the meaning of the sentence. This structure is created by combining the meanings of the separate words based on the rules of the language in question (encoded via appropriate parameterization), using the features prescribed in the lexicon for guidance. In this case, the various parts of the parse tree are used to produce the following LCS:[44]

---

[44] Features have been included here for illustrative purposes. The actual LCS is even more complex; we omit some details not relevant to the current discussion.

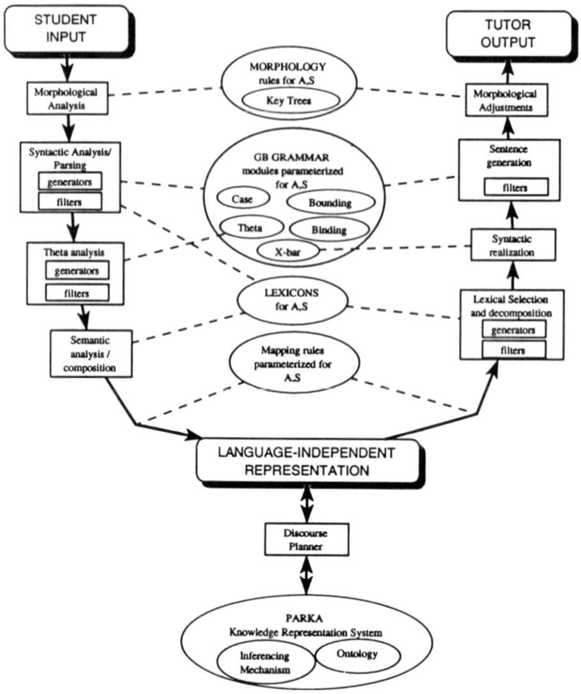

FIG. 16.7. Diagram of augmented natural language processor for tutor project.

$$
\begin{array}{l}
(16)\ [_{\text{Event}}\ \text{CAUSE} \\
\quad ([_{\text{Thing}}\ \text{X +human}], \\
\quad [_{\text{Event}}\ \text{GO}\ _{\text{Poss}} \\
\qquad ([_{\text{Thing}}\ \text{REFERENT +human +sg +p2}], \\
\qquad [_{\text{Path}}\ \text{TO}\ _{\text{Poss}} \\
\qquad\quad ([_{\text{Position}}\ \text{AT}\ _{\text{Poss}} \\
\qquad\qquad ([_{\text{Thing}}\ \text{REFERENT +human +sg +p2}],[_{\text{Location}}\ \text{WH-}_{\text{LOC}}\text{ATION}])])])], \\
\qquad [_{\text{Manner}}\ \text{FORCEFULLY}])]
\end{array}
$$

This LCS roughly corresponds to the question "Where were you when you were caused to be forcefully transferred to someone else's possession?" (Note the WH marker indicating a query regarding location.)

This LCS is then passed to the discourse planner, which attempts to understand it in the context of the current dialogue. Based on information about the situation, the system can infer that this is a question, that it is about Diego Ramirez (the persona the system is imitating), that it concerns his capture, and that the queried aspect is location. These deductions are made via a discrimination network, which efficiently matches components of the LCS against target meanings.

Based on this analysis, the discourse planner is invoked. A number of planning operators may be applicable, each one chosen based on pattern matching against appropriate parts of the LCS. For example, questions about where something has occurred are handled by the following operator:

```
(17) OPERATOR-SCHEMA Where-interrogative
       PRECONDITION: FTYPE(Inst-Frame) ° equiv WH
                     TYPE(Inst-Frame) ° equiv Locative
       BIND: Agent ß*Subject
             Mode ßProcess-clause[*Internal-Clause]
       CONDITIONS:
           Prev-Estab(Agent,?Location,Mode)
               àReply(Already-desc)
           Unknown(Agent,?Location,Mode)
               àReply(Noncommittal,*where*)
           OTHERWISE
               Match-Structure([?Frame,episode = Mode,subj:= = Agent])
```

Roughly translated, this operator states that to answer questions about where an event occurred, we need to check if we have already answered this question and if so, generate a reply to that effect (e.g., "That's been answered already"). If we have not answered it, but we do not know where the event in question has occurred, then we need a noncommittal response (e.g., "I do not know where"). Finally, if we do know where the event has occurred, then we query for the LCS associated with the episode in question.

This query retrieves a set of frames corresponding to episodes in the knowledge base. The knowledge base represents the knowledge of the respondent in the student's dialogue with the tutor. In this application, the respondent is an interrogatee, such as Diego Ramirez. The knowledge base is implemented using the PARKA frame language, a knowledge representation system developed at the University of Maryland (Spector, Hendler, & Evett, 1990). This language provides tools for the creation, editing, and querying of knowledge bases.[45] Associated with each frame is a corresponding LCS that can be used in producing the answer. Thus, for the example we are following, the answer is the following LCSs (where T3 is the time of the raid in the current episode):

(18) $[_{\text{Event}}$ BE $_{\text{Loc}}$
  $([_{\text{Thing}}$ REFERENT +human +sg +pl],
  $[_{\text{Position}}$ AT $_{\text{Loc}}$}
    $([_{\text{Position}}$ BEHIND $_{\text{Loc}}$ $([_{\text{Thing}}$ REFERENT +human +sg +pl],$[_{\text{Loc}}$ation HOUSE])])],
  $[_{\text{Time}}$ T1 overlaps T3])]

$[_{\text{Event}}$ GO $_{\text{Loc}}$
  $([_{\text{Thing}}$ REFERENT +human +sg +pl],
  $[_{\text{Path}}$ AWAY-FROM $_{\text{Loc}}$}
    $([_{\text{Position}}$ BEHIND $_{\text{Loc}}$ $([_{\text{Thing}}$ REFERENT +human +sg +pl],$[_{\text{Loc}}$ation HOUSE])])],
  $[_{\text{Manner}}$ RUNNINGLY],
  $[_{\text{Time}}$ T2 > T1])]

---

[45] One of the most important aspects of PARKA is that it runs extremely efficiently on the massively parallel connection machine. The work in this project uses only the serial implementation (for details about the parallel work, see Evett, Hendler, & Spector, 1993).

These representations roughly correspond to a statement that a REFERENT (a person, in this case) was at a location that was behind the HOUSE (the first LCS) and that this person ran from there to an unspecified location (the second LCS).

This LCS information is passed back to the lexical-semantic component, which uses features in the lexicon to assign words to the variable entries (REFERENT and HOUSE) that must be part of a generated answer based on variables in the student's question. This component determines as well the syntactic structure that best conveys the LCS content in the appropriate language (e.g., Spanish). In response to the first LCS, a syntactic structure is produced that is transformed by the generator into the output response, "Yo estaba detrás de la casa" (I was in back of the house). A similar process is used to interpret the second LCS and produce, "Yo salí corriendo" (I ran away). Following this, time information is used to recognize that the running occurred at the same time as the raid, and thus "Durante la redada" (During the raid) is added to the set of sentences to be expressed. Finally, a generational rule is used to combine these sentences into a more grammatical compound sentence, and the final answer is produced:

TUTOR> Durante la redada yo estaba detrás la casa y salí corriendo.
'During the raid, I was in back of the house and ran away. '

The discourse planner is also invoked when the unification algorithm fails to find a query that matches the LCS produced. For example, following the sentence just given, the student might type

STUDENT> Y entonces?
'And then?'

In this case, no predicted query matches, and a default rule in the discourse planner is used. To handle such cases, the planner tracks the dialogue, keeping account of the context of the discourse. Because the last answer produced focused on running away, this sentence is requesting information about the next temporal event (signaled by *entonces*), and the knowledge base is checked to see what the next event was. Again, an appropriate response such as the following would be produced:

TUTOR> La policia me vio y fui arrestado.
'The police saw me and I was arrested.'

The use of a discourse planner to track the dialogue also allows other behaviors to be introduced via similar mechanisms—for example, responses such as "I told you that already," "I do not know why you want to know that," and "I will not answer that question" can easily be produced.

The examples given so far have assumed a full immersion mode of language tutoring, where the feedback is representative not of a language instructor but of a real respondent in a debriefing or interrogation scenario. However, modes with a lower immersion level can also be envisioned. For example, in order to diagnose that "Dónde fue la capturada" (Where was she captured) is an irrelevant question, the discourse model has to have reported that the discourse does not mention any females being captured. The system might use this information to generate a message telling the student why the interrogatee failed to understand.

Other possible problems the student might have involve lexical-semantic or syntactic errors. For example, the student might make the wrong choice of the Spanish *to be* verbs:

> TUTOR> Era detrás de la casa y salí corriendo.
> 'I took place / am equal to / the back of the house and ran away. '

Here, the student has used a form of *ser* (denoting permanent properties), when the correct verb is *estar*, to mean, "I was in back of the house and ran away."

We expect to be able to configure the system simply to ignore such an error or to tell the student that he or she has used the wrong *to be* verb by pointing to the part of the string where the error has occurred. For selected errors of high priority or high likelihood of occurrence, students can get a grammar lesson (e.g., on the uses of *ser* and *estar*) from a pull-down window. The tutor also keeps track of numbers of errors and can direct the student to exercises of the appropriate style (determined by its tutoring rules) to remediate particular grammatical problems.

Also crucial to running a dialogue are more sophisticated semantic representations that can take information from a knowledge base for the purpose of responding to queries. In particular, two main types of information must be encoded: information about discourse processing and information about the domain of discourse. A number of approaches to encoding these types of information have proven useful when the domain of discourse is limited and controlled, and those approaches will be drawn from in this project. However, how to design a general formal model of discourse processes is still largely an open question.

Conclusions

This chapter has described the use of an LCS-based semantics for free response questions in foreign language training within the MILT system. We started by reviewing the LCS model, and we showed how this representation can be used to support a question-answering lesson as well as a limited domain discourse. An authoring tool for entering relevant semantic knowledge was also described. Although we did not address the role of LCS in the animated microworld lesson of MILT, the LCS representations of students' microworld commands are like those described here, and they connect directly to preprogrammed objects and actions of that world (see Kaplan & Holland, this volume).

An area of current investigation beyond the work described here is that of defining the relation between the lexical-semantic representation and the knowledge representation. Our goal is to understand a sentence whose message involves a spatial relation—in particular, a sentence that conveys information about the location or path of physical entities in the real, physical world. For example, if we consider the status of the sentence, "Daniel drove to the south of Colorado," we quickly determine that the phrase, *the south of Colorado* is ambiguous. One interpretation of this sentence is that Daniel drove outside of Colorado (and south). Another interpretation is that Daniel drove to southern

Colorado; that is, the phrase *the south of Colorado* refers to the region inside of Colorado that is considered its south. The lexical-semantic structure for the part-to-whole relation of the latter interpretation, where the part is the meaning of the entire phrase and the whole is Colorado, is viewed as a place-place relation in the knowledge representation. Thus, the knowledge representation is used to check for a part-whole interpretation when it encounters two place predicates in a lexical-semantic representation.

Another future direction is to explore an extension of this linking of the semantics with a knowledge representation system to handle inference problems, such as the "stabbed fatally" case referred to earlier in this chapter (i.e., *stabbed fatally* must be inferred to mean *killed*). It is clear that to analyze a student's answer fully, we must have an inferencing system capable of understanding both the paragraph shown to the student and the student's response to the query. Providing such a capability on a lesson-by-lesson basis is in theory within the capability of current artificial intelligence (AI) techniques; in essence, a system that enables inferences would require techniques similar to those described in the discourse lesson discussed in this chapter. Unfortunately, this is still a labor-intensive process, and until large, shared common-sense knowledge bases become available, making such a system authorable (particularly, by instructors who are not AI programmers or knowledge engineers) remains a major research challenge.[46]

Acknowledgments

Dr. Hendler is supported in part by grants from NSF (IRI-8907890), ONR (N00014-J-91-1451), AFOSR (F49620-93-1-0065), the ARPA/Rome Laboratory Planning Initiative (F30602-93-C-0039) and by ARI (MDA-903-92-R-0035, subcontract through Micro Analysis and Design, Inc.). Dr. Hendler is also affiliated with the UM Institute for Systems Research (NSF Grant NSFD CDR-88003012). Dr. Dorr is supported in part by grants from NSF (IRI-9120788, IRI-9357731), ONR (N00014-92-J-1929), ARO (DAAL03-91-C-0034, subcontract through Batelle Corporation), and by ARI (MDA-903-92-R-0035, subcontract through Micro Analysis and Design, Inc.).

References

Chomsky, N.A. (1981). *Lectures on government and binding.* Dordrecht: Foris.

Chomsky, N.A. (1986). *Knowledge of language: Its nature, origin and use.* Cambridge, MA: MIT Press.

Dorr, B.J. (1992). Lexical semantics for interlingual machine translation. *Machine Translation, 7.*

Dorr, B.J. (1993a). Interlingual machine translation: A parameterized approach. *Artificial Intelligence, 63.*

Dorr, B.J. (1993b). *Machine translation: A view from the lexicon.* Cambridge, MA: MIT Press.

Evett, M., Hendler, J., & Spector. L. (in press). Parallel knowledge representation on the connection machine. *International Journal of Parallel and Distributed Computing.*

Grimshaw, J. (1990). *Argument structure.* Cambridge, MA: MIT Press.

Hale, K., & Keyser, S.J. (1986a). Some transitivity alternations in English. *Lexicon Project Working Paper 7.* Cambridge, MA: Massachusetts Institute of Technology, Center for Cognitive Science.

Hale, K., & Keyser, S.J. (1986b). A view from the middle. *Lexicon Project Working Paper 10.* Cambridge, MA: Massachusetts Institute of Technology, Center for Cognitive Science.

Hale, K., & Keyser, S.J. (1989). *On some syntactic rules in the lexicon.* Unpublished manuscript, Massachusetts Institute of Technology.

---

[6] Efforts in this direction include the U.S. Knowledge Sharing Effort and the Japanese project NOAH, which both aim to provide tools for building and sharing very large knowledge bases.

Hale, K., & Laughren, M. (1983). *Warlpiri Lexicon Project: Warlpiri Dictionary Entries*. Cambridge, MA.: Massachusetts Institute of Technology.

Holland, V.M., Maisano, R., Alderks, K., & Martin, J. (1993). Parsers in tutors: What are they good for? *The CALICO Journal*, *11*, 28-46.

Jackendoff, R.S. (1983). *Semantics and cognition.* Cambridge, MA: MIT Press.

Jackendoff, R.S. (1990). *Semantics structures*. Cambridge, MA: MIT Press.

Levin, B. (1985). Lexical semantics in review. *Lexicon Project Working Paper 1*. Cambridge, MA: Massachusetts Institute of Technology, Center for Cognitive Science.

Levin, B. (1993). *English verb classes and alternations: A preliminary investigation*. Chicago, IL: University of Chicago Press.

Levin, B., & Rappaport, M. (1986). The formation of adjectival passives. *Linguistic Inquiry*, *17*, 623-662.

Mel'cuk, I., & Polguère, A. (1987). A formal lexicon in meaning-text theory (Or how to do lexica with words). *Computational Linguistics*, *13*, 261-275.

Olsen, M. B. (1991). Lexical semantics, machine translation, and Talmy's model of motion verbs. *Linguistics Working Paper, 3*. Evanston, IL: Northwestern University.

Pustejovsky, J. (1988). The geometry of events. *Lexicon Project Working Paper, 24*. Cambridge, MA: Massachusetts Institute of Technology, Center for Cognitive Science.

Pustejovsky, J. (1989). The semantic representation of lexical knowledge. *Proceedings of the First International Lexical Acquisition Workshop*.

Pustejovsky, J. (1991). The syntax of event structure. *Cognition*, 41.

Rappaport, M., Laughren, M., & Levin, B. (1987). Levels of lexical representation. *Lexicon Project Working Paper 20*. Cambridge, MA: Massachusetts Institute of Technology, Center for Cognitive Science.

Rappaport, M., & Levin. B. (1988). What to do with theta-roles. In W. Wilkins (Ed.), *Thematic Relations* (pp. 7-36). New York, CA: Academic Press.

Schank, R.C. (1972). Conceptual dependency: A theory of natural language understanding. *Cognitive Psychology*, *3*, 552-631.

Schank, R.C. (1973). Identification of conceptualizations underlying natural language. In R.C. Schank & K.M. Colby (Eds.), *Computer models of thought and language* (pp. 187-247). San Francisco: Freeman.

Schank, R.C. (Ed.), (1975). *Conceptual information processing*. New York: Elsevier..

Schank, R.C., & Abelson, R. (1977). *Scripts, plans, goals, and understanding*. Hillsdale, NJ: Lawrence Erlbaum Associates.

Sharp, R.M. (1985). *A model of grammar based on principles of government and binding*. Unpublished master's thesis, University of British Columbia, Canada.

Spector, L., Hendler, J., & Evett, M. (1990). *PARKA: Parallel knowledge representation on the connection machine* (UMIACS TR 90-22, CS Dept. TR 2409). University of Maryland, College Park.

Vauquois, B., & Boitet, C. (1985). Automated translation at Grenoble University. *Computational Linguistics, 11*, 28-36

Zubizarreta, M.L. (1982). *On the relationship of the lexicon to syntax*. Unpublished doctoral dissertation, Massachusetts Institute of Technology.

Zubizarreta, M.L. (1987). *Levels of representation in the lexicon and in the syntax*. Dordrecht: Foris.

Section IV

Theoretical Issues in Language Tutor Design and Assessment

This final section presents discussions of problems and prospects for the field of intelligent computer-assisted language learning (ICALL) from several perspectives: experimental psychology (MacWhinney), linguistics (Bailin), second language acquisition (Garrett), and second language teaching and learning (Oxford, Garrett). The authors tackle the question of what to make of the systems presented in this book: What can they be expected to contribute to practice, to research, to theory?

Contributions to Practice: The Need for Assessment

After reading the preceding chapters, we still know little about how students might respond to and benefit from NLP technology, nor are we sure how to measure the benefits. Thus, assessment is critical. The discussants in this section lead us to question the very assumptions that the designers of many of these systems seem to take on faith. How do we know that error feedback helps? That comprehension should precede production? That creative sentence production is more effective than copied production, or sentence completion, or sentence assembly from word menus? That authentic texts are better than constructed? That viewing parse trees is productive? MacWhinney suggests that prevailing theories, whether of second language learning specifically or of learning and cognition generally, are not precise enough to answer these questions or to determine the myriad other design decisions that face ICALL. Theory is not strong enough to shape technology in its details. MacWhinney outlines a program of evaluation research that can answer such questions in the context of specific tutoring systems and that can in turn strengthen theory.

MacWhinney and Bailin remark that gross comparisons of alternative media—for example, comparing ICALL to CALL or to tapes and workbook—are ill conceived. Rather, we need studies that vary the hypothesized critical features of an ICALL system and compare the variant versions with each other. The only study we know that follows this route is Nagata's (1992) assessment of ALICE-chan, referred to by Levin and Evans (Section I). Nagata varied the presence or absence of NLP-based feedback and found that parser-provided information improves acquisition of certain kinds of syntactic relations in Japanese. Other manipulations are required to clarify this finding. For example, maybe equivalent improvement could derive from workbook exercises that give students ungrammatical sentences to correct, then show them the parser-generated analysis, preprogrammed for each example. This manipulation would separate the benefits of a dynamic parser that can report students' errors as they occur from the benefits of placing parser-based information in a static format. Assessing the effectiveness of ICALL requires untangling a skein of contributing features and confounding factors.

Garrett calls for going beyond these sorts of strict experimental comparisons: For a realistic assessment of benefits, ICALL systems must be examined in their institutional contexts, such as language labs or classrooms, must cover significant portions of a curriculum, and must be used by large numbers of students. Current ICALL systems do not have the scope to meet these criteria, nor do any existing applications fall into Garrett's category of "mandatory-use, central-purpose" technology. To further respect the institutional context, Bailin suggests that assessments consider programmatic measures such as school grades or general proficiency in the target language to complement skill-specific learning outcomes. In addition, Bailin and MacWhinney advocate beta testing of systems to guide successive improvements to the software and the interface prior to experimental and institutional evaluation.

Thus, the levels of an assessment framework, sketched in the introduction to Section I, emerge more clearly. Iterative beta testing is needed to bring systems to the point of formal experimental evaluation, so that easily fixed software bugs and interface confusions do not pollute measures of effectiveness. Formal experimental evaluation follows to explain the effects of specific system features on immediate learning outcomes. Finally, program evaluations determine optimal configurations of system features and reveal the long-term institutional viability of systems in terms of factors like acceptance by students and instructors, adaptability to the larger curriculum, utility in monitoring learner progress, and efficiency of courseware authoring and modification. The cost factors mentioned in Section I enter into program evaluation, as do tools for authoring that can multiply the effectiveness of a delivered system. Pertinent to cost, Bailin's claim that ICALL has not availed itself of ready-made NLP components is becoming subject to challenge, as both production tutors (Dorr, Garman, & Weinberg, 1994) and reading assistants (Myer, 1995) borrow lexicons and other tools from mainstream NLP applications.

A related set of issues concerns what ICALL should teach and thus which learning outcomes should be assessed. There is disagreement here. Bailin and Garrett accept the traditional province of syntax but expand it to include syntax in use. For Bailin this means explaining errors and relating constructions and errors to intentions. For Garrett this means associating forms with meanings, or "psycholinguistic mapping." It is not altogether clear what a system that does these things would look like, but it appears that the detailed analytic capabilities of a parser comes into play in both conceptions.[47] Oxford, on the other hand, assumes that ICALL should realize pure communicative goals, with emphasis on representing meaningful discourse in authentic cultural contexts. In this view, systems that focus on grammar should be refocused. This difference in views implies further disagreement on what assessments of ICALL should measure. The issues of what to teach and what to measure are not indigenous to ICALL but reflect larger tensions in the field of foreign language teaching and research (see Doughty, 1993; Lightbown & Spada, 1990).[48]

Oxford articulates the majority view of progressive language teachers, who tend to espouse the communicative approach. It is evident from her chapter that ICALL will

---

[47] Frederiksen et al. (Section I) and Zock (1992) begin to address Garrett's challenge by presenting semantic structure in the form of propositional trees and conceptual graphs, respectively. Students are then prompted to explore relationships between semantic structure and syntactic expression.

[48] Garrett sees the pure form versus pure communicative distinction as a false dichotomy and seeks a new synthesis in the concept of psycholinguistic mapping.

not find widespread acceptance in this community until it makes its goals clear. Systems that deliberately avoid communicative precepts, instead exploiting the grammar-focused instruction to which parsers are suited, should be explicit about it. Oxford finds such programs lacking personal meaning for students. However, as developers like Levin and Evans and Rypa and Feuerman have stated (Section I), the motivation in the parser-based systems is to select those aspects of syntax that are problematic for learners and can be reliably illuminated by parsing. The intent of these systems is to supplement, not supplant, communicative instruction. Moreover, syntax is a major worry for translators and analysts, who are the primary intended users of ALICE-chan and CALLE, so these systems have ingrained relevance to those users. Whether such systems will be accepted in schools depends upon the teacher's philosophy and how much formal competence is valued as a complement to communicative fluency.

Oxford also finds the abstract visual environments in Tomlin's FlatLand and parts of Hamburger's FLUENT (both in Section III) lacking in cultural relevance. However, these environments were deliberately stripped to essential distinctions to support research on discourse strategies and on computational techniques. These systems in new, practical instantiations could take up Oxford's call for authenticity by modeling culturally valid scenarios in consultation with language teachers. The question posed by Garrett echoes here—how do we know that authenticity is the best criterion for all instructional presentations? Maybe students learn better by starting with minimalist settings to which cultural detail is gradually added. But in the absence of evidence, and to gain teacher approval, microworld environments that seek practical application would do well to reflect aspects of culture.

A topic for programmatic evaluations of ICALL, then, is examining the effectiveness of varying mixes of form-focused versus communicative instruction as distributed over the classroom, the language lab, homework, and immersive events (e.g., movies, radio newscasts). Programs that focus on translation and analysis may emphasize form and combine evaluation criteria differently than programs that focus on conversation.

Contributions to Research and Theory

MacWhinney anticipates that ICALL can contribute to psycholinguistic and learning theories by providing ways to express theoretical principles that are often vague or intuitive and by testing the effectiveness of these principles in the case of language learning. These tests can, moreover, reveal new facts about learning and the designs that enhance it. Such contributions involve research into what Larsen-Freeman and Long (1991) call instructed learning or "second language learning," which is often distinguished from naturalistic development or "second language acquisition" (a distinction blurred by the use of tutoring systems to collect acquisition data, as described later). MacWhinney points out pitfalls in evaluating instructional effectiveness and offers ways around them.

Bailin anticipates contributions of ICALL to linguistic theory in terms of ICALL's obligation to handle errors, potentially spurring an expansion of linguistic models to account for errors, their evolution, their interpretation in context, and strategies for recovering from them. Theoretical linguistics would gain relevance from considering these and other facets of language use, which ICALL must deal with by design.

Bailin and Garrett point out the potential of ICALL to analyze learners' grammatical patterns in the service of second language acquisition research. This research Garrett calls CARLA, for computer-assisted research on language acquisition, a program she has elaborated elsewhere (Garrett, 1991). Current NLP-based systems have not been applied to questions of second language acquisition, given the still incomplete status of most efforts (although Loritz in Section I shows how NLP can be used to develop competency maps of learners' language). However, these systems have obvious relevance to acquisition questions given their capability for recording automatically the constructions learners use and the errors they commit over time. Research programs such as MacWhinney's (1991) CHILDES have demonstrated the profitability of tapping into databases of linguistic usage and error patterns for testing and refining theories of first and second language development.

Garrett holds that ICALL should collect information about the mapping of form to meaning so as to address more valid models of linguistic development. Similarly, Bailin notes the superficiality of raw error data without some theory of the error sources. Nevertheless, the systems featured in this book merely profile performance. They do not attempt to explain it computationally, such as through knowledge bugs, repairs, or qualitative student modeling methods used in intelligent tutoring systems (Wenger, 1987).[49] One justification for avoiding qualitative modeling is its computational expense. A further justification, provided by DeSmedt (Section II), is the current uncertainty of explanatory models of second language acquisition. In any case, as DeSmedt notes, the profiles extracted by ICALL can be used in subsequent longitudinal studies of acquisition, in which theories can be independently applied or constructed to interpret data.

Oxford speaks to the theoretical roots of ICALL rather than to its theoretical contributions. But the pointers to theory in her chapter serve to illustrate MacWhinney's caution about the tenuousness of the links between theory and design. The principles drawn from theoretical frameworks such as constructivism (e.g., cognitive differentiation enhances language learning) may need the quantification and testing provided by tutoring systems at least as much as the systems need the principles. Oxford's suggestions for accommodating individual differences, moreover, are by no means proven and might better be considered design hypotheses: Individual difference measures, even if well defined, could have a number of possibly contradictory implications for a language tutor (see, e.g., the research on instructional effects of individual differences cited in Kulik & Kulik, 1988, and Kulhavey, 1977, as well as the comments of MacLaughlin, 1994, on individual differences in second language learning).

This book bears out Oxford's claim that few ICALL projects attend to theories of how people learn or how they might learn best. Many systems are designed solely or partly by computational linguists, whose focus is NLP, not the psychology of the learner. How that psychology should be addressed—and whether a priori, empirically, or through some interaction—remains the interesting issue.

---

[49] Qualitative student models are found in some European ICALL (see Swartz and Yazdani, 1992).

References

Dorr, B.J., Garman, J., & Weinberg, A. (1994). *From subcategorization frames to thematic roles: Building Arabic lexical entries for foreign language tutoring*. Manuscript submitted for publication.

Doughty, C. (1993, March). *Focus on form: What is it? (Research and pedagogical issues)*. Paper presented at Georgetown University Roundtable on Languages and Linguistics (presession), Washington, DC.

Garrett, N. (1991). CARLA comes to CALL. *Computer Assisted Language Learning*, *4*, 99-104.

Kulhavey, R.W. (1977). Feedback in written instruction. *Review of Educational Research*, *47*, 211-232.

Kulik, J.A., & Kulik, C.C. (1988). Timing of feedback and verbal learning. *Review of Educational Research*, *58*, 79-97.

Larsen-Freeman, D.H., & Long, M.H. (1991). *An introduction to second language acquisition research.* New York: Longman.

Lightbown, P., & Spada, M. (1990). Focus on form and corrective feedback in communicative language teaching: Effects on second language learning. *Studies in SLA*, *12*, 4.

McLaughlin, B. (1994). *Language aptitude: An information-processing perspective.* Paper presented at the 1994 Language Aptitude Invitational Symposium, Center for Advancement of Language Learning, Arlington, VA.

MacWhinney, B. (1991). *The CHILDES database: Tools for analyzing talk.* Hillsdale, NJ: Lawrence Erlbaum Associates.

Myer, R. (1995, May). OLEADA: Using information retrieval tools for language teaching and learning. Paper presented at the 1995 ARPA Workshop on TIPSTER Phase II, Chantilly, VA.

Nagata, N. (1992). *A study of the effectiveness of intelligent CALI as an application of natural language processing*. Unpublished doctoral dissertation, University of Pittsburgh, Pittsburgh, Pennsylvania..

Swartz, M. L., & Yazdani, M. (Eds.). (1992). *Intelligent tutoring systems for foreign language learning: The bridge to international communication.* New York: Springer-Verlag.

Wenger, E. (1987). *Artificial intelligence and tutoring systems: Computational and cognitive approaches to the communication of knowledge*. Los Altos, CA: Kaufmann.

Zock, M. (1992). SWIM or sink: The problem of communicating thought. In M. L. Swartz & M. Yazdani (Eds).

17

Evaluating Foreign Language Tutoring Systems

Brian MacWhinney
Carnegie Mellon University

For adults, the learning of a foreign language is often difficult, sometimes virtually impossible. Systems that promise a way of reducing this language barrier will interest millions of people, if they can really be demonstrated to work. It is not surprising that the enormous breakthroughs in personal computer technology over the last dozen years have led to a renewed interest in the development of computational systems for facilitating language learning. However, the development of these systems is dependent on many types of expertise and requires a great investment of time and energy. If we had a set of basic design principles that could guide the construction of these systems, we could avoid inadequate products and mismatched capabilities. If one looks at work in learning theory, psycholinguistics, and human-computer interaction, there are many signposts or principles that could direct this work. However, to provide a surer grounding for this effort, we need to make direct tests of the pedagogical effects of these principles. Before we examine ways of making these tests, let us review some of the lessons that can be derived from previous work in psychology.

Lessons from Experimental Psychology

On the face of it, one would think that psychology would have a great deal to tell us about the ways in which human beings learn second languages. Ideally, experimental psychology should provide clear principles for designing computational aids and tutoring systems for foreign language learning. Indeed, psychology is rich with theories and principles that have some general applicability to this question. However, few of these principles will strike any of us as surprising or new, and some of them are stated in such a general way that their application to this problem is insufficiently explicit. Consider the following list of basic ideas from learning theory and experimental psychology:

1. *Practice makes perfect.* One of the most well-established principles of learning theory and cognitive science is that the more time one spends on a task, the better one gets at that task (Anderson & Schooler, 1991; Ebbinghaus, 1885; Newell, 1990). This effect is variously known as the learning curve, the power law of practice, or the effect of time on task. We also know that is better to distribute practice across time, rather than massing it into concentrated cram sessions. There is no doubt that the longer one studies a foreign language, the better one gets at that language—at least up to a certain point. How much of the overall variance between learners is accounted for by this principle? Perhaps as much as 30% of the variance can be attributed to this single basic principle.
2. *Rewards work better than punishments.* A robust finding of decades of work with reinforcement training of rats and pigeons led workers such as Skinner (1957),

Mowrer (1960), and Miller (1963) to conclude that learners prefer not to be shocked and beaten while they are trying to learn. It makes good sense to apply this same principle to foreign language tutoring systems.

3. *Success is rewarding.* A slightly more sophisticated variant of the second point was developed in the theory of intrinsic and extrinsic rewards. If the learning process itself can be perceived as rewarding, progress is even swifter. Further elaborating on this theme, McClelland (1961) noted the role of achievement motivation in learning. Most instructors and instructional systems undoubtedly follow these principles even without making a conscious effort.
4. *Feedback promotes learning.* Working within the framework of a hypothesis-testing theory of learning, Levine (1975) and others have demonstrated the importance of feedback in promoting learning. This principle has important potential consequences for the language classroom and computerized language tutors.
5. *Learning strategies can be learned.* Those of us who have learned two or more foreign languages realize that the process of language learning can itself be learned. The notion of learning strategies and learning to learn is a familiar one to psychologists (Hayes, 1981) and can be directly applied to the task of foreign language learning (Atkinson, 1975).
6. *Learning is schema-based.* The recent surge of interest in contextualized bases for language learning matches up closely with an ongoing theme from cognitive psychology. This is the theme that bases all long-term learning on the construction of schemas (Bartlett, 1932; Bransford & Franks, 1971). This view sees the learning of new material as involving integration into old material (Potts, 1978) and emphasizes the role of pictorial cues in information integration (Larkin & Simon, 1987).

These principles from experimental psychology contain certain core truths that help us understand the basic nature of learning. They suggest that computational aids for language learning should be designed to be easy to use, intrinsically motivating, and contextually rich—goals likely to be ascribed to by most of the developers featured in this volume. However, few of these principles speak directly to the specific situation of foreign language instruction or computational aids for language learning.

Lessons from Developmental Psycholinguistics

If we are to discover some finer grained ideas about language learning, we need to turn to the study of first language learning or developmental psycholinguistics. Work in this area has yielded an additional set of findings and principles:

1. *Language is learned in context.* Research on language learning has tended to emphasize the role of the social context in facilitating and determining language learning (Ervin-Tripp, 1981; Ninio & Snow, 1988; Ochs & Schieffelin, 1979; Schieffelin & Ochs, 1987; Vygotsky, 1962). An extreme example of the importance of social context can be found in hearing children of deaf parents in isolated social situations with minimal language input. Although these children may hear many hours of speech on radio and TV, they will not learn to speak until they have the opportunity

to use language in real social contexts. The parallel to the foreign language learner is clear. Children learn language by interacting with people, not passive machines.

2. *Words are the basis of language learning.* Work on the acquisition of grammar (MacWhinney, 1982, 1988) and the development of early vocabulary has underscored the central role that word learning plays in all of language learning. These findings point to a need to emphasize word learning in syntactic contexts (Gleitman, 1990) in systems for foreign language instruction.
3. *Teaching is effective.* Although there is reason to believe that children learn fairly little from overt correction (Brown & Hanlon, 1970), there is also reason to believe that they learn a great deal from scaffolding (Scollon, 1976), modeling (Bohannon, MacWhinney, & Snow, 1990), and recasting (Nelson, 1982).
4. *Errors reflect learning.* A simple but important finding of language acquisition theory is that errors reflect the learning of general patterns (Jespersen, 1922). Some particularly useful models of this overgeneralization process are provided by connectionist models of language learning (MacWhinney, Leinbach, Taraban, & McDonald, 1989; Plunkett & Marchman, 1991). These models stress the extent to which learning is based on generalization, analogy (MacWhinney, 1989), and transfer.
5. *Cue conflicts are crucial for learning.* Work on the learning of both L1 (first language) and L2 (second language) within the framework of the Competition Model (MacWhinney & Bates, 1989) has shown that higher levels of learning require exposure to large numbers of those relatively rare sentences in which cues conflict. Increased exposure to these conflict cases allows learners to tune the weights for conflicting cues properly.
6. *Auditory form scaffolds the learning of articulatory form.* Recent models of the learning of the articulatory forms of words make use of the notion of an auditory template (Houghton, 1990) that can guide the construction of an articulatory plan. This dynamic view of the relation between word comprehension and articulatory production can have important consequences for the design of sound-based language tutoring systems, particularly for those that focus on the lexicon and phonology.
7. *Language learning progresses through a fixed series of stages.* All children move through a one-word and a two-word stage (Brown, 1973). Early sentences always lack auxiliary inversion and display uniform negative positioning. Many of these stages are inevitable consequences of the limited productive abilities of the child, but others reflect consistencies in language learning strategies.

Lessons from SLA Research

These findings from first language acquisition research are bolstered in many ways by parallel findings from second language acquisition (SLA) research. The notion that communication is primary has been supported by studies of second language learning in a variety of real contexts (Broeder, 1991; Klein, 1984; Klein & Perdue, 1989). SLA research also indicates the importance of movement through a series of stages much like those of L1 learning, although there is also evidence of transfer from L1 to L2 (Kilborn, 1989; MacWhinney, 1987; McDonald, 1987; Odlin, 1989; Ringbom, 1987), although this transfer is seldom based on direct translation strategies. The other major finding of this research is that, past a certain critical period, learning of a second language becomes progressively more difficult (Johnson & Newport, 1989, 1991), particularly in regards to the learning of phonology (Oyama, 1976).

The Need for an Interdisciplinary Approach

Although these ideas from experimental psychology, developmental psychology, and SLA research can provide us with some reasonable guideposts in designing foreign language tutoring systems and other computational aids, it would be a mistake to think that these principles are specific enough to determine fully the correct shape of foreign language systems. It is crucial for us to conduct new empirical research that evaluates the role of each of these principles within the context of foreign language tutoring systems. Most important, the process of conducting this evaluation can itself teach us important new facts about language learning.

Designing, engineering, and evaluating effective foreign language tutoring systems is no mean task. At a minimum, this task requires a high level of understanding of computers, programming languages, parser technology, multimedia design, linguistic theory, SLA theory, expert system design, psycholinguistic theory, research methods, and statistical analysis, as well as a thorough working knowledge of the target languages involved. It is unlikely that any one individual would possess full competence in all of these areas. In addition, one can divide the types of linguistic competence targeted by a particular tutor into the standard areas of phonetics, prosody, lexicon, grammar, and discourse. Different systems may rely relatively more or less on techniques for constructing parsers, microworlds, speech generators, speech recognition algorithms, or error analysis programs. Although it is tempting to break up the problem in these various ways, a system designed to imbue a full level of language competence will have to integrate these various diverse components into a general, synchronized approach. In the end, this problem can only be successfully addressed by an interaction between linguists, psycholinguists, language teachers, ontologists, statisticians, and students of human-computer interaction.

Basic Questions to be Answered

We are standing at the very beginning of a challenging and fascinating journey. To guide us in the construction of new systems, there are some very basic empirical questions for which we will have to get solid answers. Previous research in psychology will have to be repeated within this new applied context. Up to this point, system design has proceeded on the basis of a series of hunches and guesses. For us to put foreign language tutor design on a firmer basis, we will need to have real tests of these hunches. Some of the issues that we will need to investigate include the following:

1. *Error diagnosis.* We need to know whether the various error diagnosis or feedback features built into systems such as Herr Kommissar (DeSmedt, this volume), ALICE (Levin & Evans, this volume), or BRIDGE (Sams, this volume) are pedagogically

effective. It makes good sense to imagine that feedback is useful, but we need specific tests.

2. *Parser technology.* Several major projects (Levin & Evans, this volume; Rypa & Feuerman, this volume; Weinberg, Garman, Martin, & Merlo, this volume) place a strong emphasis on parser technology as the core of a foreign language tutor. But there are many ways in which one can deliver foreign language instruction without relying on a full parser. How much does the introduction of a parser improve instruction? Are there practical and attractive alternatives that do not rely on the construction of parsing systems? For example, instead of constructing a complete parsing system to analyze a learner's sentence such as the ungrammatical "Die Schloss Eisenbach stehen in die Stadt Eisenbach," we could just give the right answer, "Das Schloss Eisenbach steht in der Stadt Eisenbach." Or perhaps learners can provide the error diagnosis themselves. Indeed, it might be the case that learning is more effective when the learner provides a self-diagnosis.
3. *Microworlds.* Several projects (Douglas, this volume; Hamburger, this volume; Tomlin, this volume; Yazdani, this volume) assume that microworlds provide an effective framework for contextualized language learning. But how effective are microworlds in facilitating acquisition of basic skills such as lexicon, morphology, and syntax?
4. *Learner models.* Is it important for an intelligent tutoring system (Singley & Anderson, 1989) to have a model of the learner? Does an intelligent system also need a model of the world? Is there any evidence that these models can be used to facilitate learning?
5. *Naturalness.* Current approaches to foreign language tutoring systems make the default assumption that systems that most closely resemble the "real" or "natural" language learning context will be most effective (see Oxford, this volume). Is there any evidence that this is true? For example, the stated goal of Herr Kommissar is "a system that supports meaningful and engaging dialogue with the second-language learner, focused on tasks and interaction that make the exercise and improvement of communicative skills a means, rather than an end in itself." This goal seems entirely reasonable. However, we do not know whether systems designed with such goals in mind are more effective than systems that do not have these goals.
6. *Discourse context.* Frederiksen, Donin, and Décary (this volume) assume that the learning of a foreign language can be strongly facilitated by embedding the learner inside a full rhetorical or narrative context. Is there direct evidence for positive effects of full rhetorical context? What kinds of tests could we use to examine this hypothesis? Do learners need to receive specific instruction regarding the shape of these discourse structures or can tutoring systems simply use these structures as supports for the acquisition of lower level knowledge?
7. *Exploration and interface.* Do students learn better if they are allowed to explore a language through a hypertext-type interface, as in the system by Frederiksen et al. (this volume)? Do students make effective use of help systems or on-line grammars? Can they use structural diagrams to explore sentence patterns in the second language (Frederiksen et al., this volume; Rypa & Feuerman, this volume)?

Can they use a dictionary to explore the conceptual structure of the vocabulary (Swartz, 1992)?

8. *L1 and transfer*. Should L2 systems be designed differently for learners with different first languages? Can the first language be used to promote learning of the second language? Should transfer be encouraged or discouraged and how?

To some of us, the answers to some of these questions may seem to require nothing more than common sense. However, one of the most important lessons we have learned in psychological research is that common sense makes poor empirical predictions. The only way to properly evaluate these various common-sense-based hunches is by detailed evaluation of the instructional effectiveness of the principles being proposed.

Evaluation

The easiest way to evaluate a computational system is to ask students if they like it. If they do, the system receives a high "smile coefficient." Unfortunately, the correlation between evaluations based on the smile coefficient and objective evaluations of the effectiveness of educational systems is not very high. Students might enjoy a particular computer program because it includes a challenging game or nice sound and graphics, not because it does an effective job of teaching Arabic or German. It is a good idea to compute a system's smile coefficient, but we should not confuse this coefficient with real measured effectiveness.

Another level of evaluation for computer systems is that conducted by research in human-computer interaction. If a system is full of bugs, design flaws, and cumbersome options, one can often see easy ways of fixing the system that are sure to improve its effectiveness. If a system is too costly or too low in portability, one can often find ways of addressing these limitations. However, once these obvious flaws are fixed, a further evaluation from the viewpoint of human-computer interaction will require the use of a serious experimental design.

The standard design for measuring educational effectiveness is the pretest-posttest experimental-control design. For example, one could randomly assign students to either an experimental group or a control group. The experimental group would work with a language tutoring system and the control group would spend time reading material in a foreign language and discussing it with a peer. At the beginning of the treatment, all students would take a pretest. After several weeks in the two opposed conditions, all students would take a posttest with items similar in type to those on the pretest. The group that had the largest positive differences on posttest scores minus pretest scores would be declared the winner and the educational treatment given to that group would be considered the better educational treatment.

Applying this conventional design to the study of foreign language tutoring systems raises a lot of problems:

1. What is the correct control group? It is not clear that one really wants to compare a language tutor with a read-and-discuss method. Perhaps this is a comparison of apples and oranges. Perhaps the best comparison is one in which some students stay

in conventional language classrooms and others do not. But is this a fair comparison if computer-assisted instruction is considered enrichment, rather than part of the core curriculum? Moreover, how can the assignment of students to groups be handled in practical terms?

2. Is there a process-neutral posttest? If either the pretest or the posttest are biased toward inclusion of items from either the textbook or the computer system, the results of the evaluation will be biased. There is also the danger that either or both of the instructional formats will start to teach to the test.
3. If the group receiving computational instruction perceives that they have been singled out for special treatment, they may perform better simply in accord with the Hawthorne effect.
4. If the computational system has bugs or design flaws, the basic effectiveness of the method may be underestimated.

Fortunately, there are clear solutions that can be offered to address these problems.

1. Rather than comparing apples and oranges, one can compare apples and apples. In particular, one can compare one foreign language tutoring system with another. The closer the two systems are, the more illuminating positive results will be.
2. The problem of bias in test construction can be minimized by orienting half the items on both the pretest and posttest toward system 1 and half toward system 2.
3. If both treatments involve computational systems, the Hawthorne effect is minimized because both groups will believe that they have been singled out for special treatment.
4. If each system contains internal ways of checking for design flaws, it will be possible to separate out bugs from the real effects of educational designs.

One can push the notion of a direct comparison between two different tutoring systems even further. Instead of comparing two separate groups in terms of the conventional pretest-posttest design, one can construct a series of variants of individual exercises or components of a larger tutoring system. For each component, the experimenter can design the program so that students are randomly assigned to one of two or more conditions right when they log on to the computer. In this way, students will be varied across tests in a Latin-square type of design. Some of the types of modules that can be varied in this way include multiple choice exercises, pointing to a location for an answer, filling in the blanks, sorting items to categories, short answers, pronunciation tutors, morphology tutors, and so on. Here are a few examples of the types of fine-grained by comparing slight variations in individual tutoring systems:

1. In a system such as CALLE (Rypa & Feuerman, this volume), one can compare a teaching module that focuses primarily on the less frequent but "core" or prototypical meaning of Spanish *se* with a module that focuses on its most frequent meaning.
2. When teaching phonology, one can compare a system that teaches phonology without accompanying orthography with one that includes orthography. Of course, this

treatment may have different effects for languages with varying degrees of regularity in their orthographic systems.

3. One can compare a system that promotes transfer by illustrating L2 structures in terms of similar L1 patterns with one that avoids or even blocks transfer.
4. One can evaluate the relative difficulty of teaching different structures by spending a fixed amount of time on Structure 1 in one module and on Structure 2 in another and then looking at how much is learned in the two cases.
5. One can evaluate the value of a hypertext system by allowing student navigation and option selection in one tutor and blocking it in another.

Conclusion

The design of computational systems to support foreign language instruction needs to be grounded in what we know about human learning, language processing, and human-computer interaction. Principles derived from these fields need to be tested and quantified in the context of specific tutoring systems. Evaluation of the pedagogical impact of particular principles can best be achieved by comparing two tutoring systems that differ in controlled and manipulable ways.

True experimental evaluation of foreign language tutoring systems has not yet been attempted. It is difficult to predict at this point how easy it will be to conduct this evaluation. However, the manipulable nature of computer systems makes them ideal testbeds for the evaluation of particular microcomponents of instructional design. Given the great potential commercial market for tutoring systems, it will be important to distinguish between established educational effectiveness, smile coefficients, and simple market acceptance. If these new systems are evaluated carefully, we will learn more not only about computational systems but also about core processes in language learning.

References

Anderson, J.R., & Schooler, L.J. (1991). Reflections of the environment in memory. *Psychological Science*, *2*, 396-410.

Atkinson, R. (1975). Mnemotechnics in second-language learning. *American Psychologist, 30*, 821-828.

Bartlett, F.C. (1932). *Remembering: A study in experimental and social psychology*. Cambridge, UK: Cambridge University Press.

Bohannon, N., MacWhinney, B., & Snow, C. (1990). No negative evidence revisited: Beyond learnability or who has to prove what to whom. *Developmental Psychology, 26,* 221-226.

Bransford, J.D., & Franks, J.J. (1971). The abstraction of linguistic ideas. *Cognitive Psychology, 2,* 331-350.

Broeder, P. (1991). *Talking about people: A multiple case study on adult language acquisition.* Amsterdam: Swets and Zeitlinger.

Brown, R. (1973). *A first language: The early stages.* Cambridge, MA: Harvard University Press.

Brown, R., & Hanlon, C. (1970). Derivational complexity and order of acquisition in child speech. In J. R. Hayes (Ed.), *Cognition and the development of language.* New York: Wiley.

Ebbinghaus, H. (1885). *Über das Gedächtnis.* Leipzig: Duncker.

Ervin-Tripp, S. (1981). Social process in first and second language learning. In H. Winitz (Ed.), *Native language and foreign language acquisition.* New York: New York Academy of Sciences.

Gleitman, L. (1990). The structural sources of verb meanings. *Language Acquisition, I,* 3-55.

Hayes, J. (1981). *The complete problem solver.* Philadelphia: Franklin Institute Press.

Houghton, G. (1990). The problem of serial order: A neural network model of sequence learning and recall. In R. Dale, C. Mellish, & M. Zock (Eds.), *Current research in natural language generation.* London: Academic Press.

Jespersen, O. (1922). *Language: Its nature, development, and origin.* London: George Allen and Unwin.

Johnson, J., & Newport, E. (1989). Critical period effects in second language learning: The influence of maturational state on the acquisition of English as a second language. *Cognitive Psychology, 21,* 60-99.

Johnson, J.S., & Newport, E.L. (1991). Critical period effects on universal properties of language: The status of subjacency in the acquisition of a second language. *Cognition, 39,* 215-258.

Kilborn, K. (1989). Sentence processing in a second language: The timing of transfer. *Language and Speech, 32,* 1-23.

Klein, W. (1984). *Zweitspracherwerb.* Kónigstein: Athenäum.

Klein, W., & Perdue, C. (1989). The learner's problem of arranging words. In B. MacWhinney & E. Bates (Eds.), *The crosslinguistic study of sentence processing.* New York: Cambridge University Press.

Larkin, J.H., & Simon, H.A. (1987). Why a diagram is (sometimes) worth ten thousand words. *Cognitive Science, 11,* 65-99.

Levine, M. (1975). *A cognitive theory of learning.* Hillsdale, NJ: Lawrence Erlbaum Associates.

MacWhinney, B. (1982). Basic syntactic processes. In S. Kuczaj (Ed.), *Language Acquisition: Vol. 1. Syntax and semantics.* Hillsdale, NJ: Lawrence Erlbaum Associates.

MacWhinney, B. (1987). Applying the competition model to bilingualism. *Applied Psycholinguistics, 8,* 315-327.

MacWhinney, B. (1988). Competition and teachability. In R. Schiefelbusch & M. Rice (Eds.), *The teachability of language.* New York: Cambridge University Press.

MacWhinney, B. (1989). Competition and lexical categorization. In R. Corrigan, F. Eckman, & M. Noonan (Eds.), *Linguistic categorization.* New York: Benjamins.

MacWhinney, B., & Bates, E. (Eds.). (1989). *The crosslinguistic study of sentence processing.* New York: Cambridge University Press.

MacWhinney, B., Leinbach, J., Taraban, R., & McDonald, J. (1989). Language learning: Cues or rules? *Journal of Memory and Language, 28,* 255-277.

McClelland, D.C. (1961). *The achieving society.* New York: Van Nostrand.

McDonald, J. (1987). Sentence interpretation in bilingual speakers of English and Dutch. *Applied Psycholinguistics, 8,* 379-414.

Miller, N. (1963). Some reflections on the law of effect produce a new alternative to drive reduction. In M. R. Jones (Ed.), *Nebraska Symposium on Motivation.* Lincoln: University of Nebraska Press.

Mowrer, O. (1960). *Learning theory and the symbolic processes.* New York: Wiley.

Nelson, K. (1982). Experimental gambits in the service of language acquisition theory. In S. Kuczaj (Ed.), *Language development: Syntax and semantics.* Hillsdale, NJ: Lawrence Erlbaum Associates.

Newell, A. (1990). *A unified theory of cognition.* Cambridge, MA.: Harvard University Press.

Ninio, A., & Snow, C. (1988). Language acquisition through language use: The functional sources of children's early utterances. In I.S.Y. Levy & M. Braine (Eds.), *Categories and processes in language acquisition.* Hillsdale, NJ: Lawrence Erlbaum.

Ochs, E., & Schieffelin, B. (Eds.). (1979). *Developmental pragmatics.* New York: Academic Press.

Odlin, T. (1989). *Language transfer: Cross-linguistic influence in language learning.* New York: Cambridge University Press.

Oyama, S. (1976). A sensitive period for the acquisition of a nonnative phonological system. *Journal of Psycholinguistics Research, 5,* 261-283.

Plunkett, K., & Marchman, V. (1991). U-shaped learning and frequency effects in a multi-layered perceptron. Implications for child language acquisition. *Cognition, 38,* 43-102.

Potts, G. (1978). The role of inference in memory for real and artificial information. In R. Revlin & R. Mayer (Eds.), *Human reasoning.* New York: Halsted Press.

Ringbom, H. (1987). *The role of the first language in foreign language learning.* Clevedon, U.K.: Multilingual Matters.

Schieffelin, B., & Ochs, E. (1987). *Language acquisition across cultures.* New York: Cambridge University Press.

Scollon, R. (1976). *Conversations with a one year old: A case study of the developmental foundation of syntax*. Honolulu: University Press of Hawaii.

Singley, K., & Anderson, J. (1989). *The transfer of cognitive skills.* Cambridge, MA: Harvard University Press.

Skinner, B. F. (1957). *Verbal behavior.* New York: Appleton-Century-Crofts.

Swartz, M. (1992). Issues for tutoring knowledge in foreign language intelligent tutoring systems. In M. Swartz & M. Yazdani (Eds.), *Intelligent tutoring systems for foreign language learning* (pp. 219-234). Berlin: Springer.

Vygotsky, L. (1962). *Thought and language.* Cambridge: MIT Press.

18

AI and Language Learning: Theory and Evaluations

Alan Bailin
The University of Western Ontario

The preceding chapters have walked us through the architectures of rather complex teaching machines and have shown us the natural language processing and the knowledge modeling that function as infrastructure. The ingenuity and dogged persistence necessary for such challenging work can only be admired.

Nevertheless, one may well wonder what is the point of all of this work, why one should bother with such complex research. After all, a human teacher can perform all the so-called intelligent tasks that current intelligent computer-assisted language learning (ICALL) software performs and, at present, do a considerably better job in most cases. What then is the point?

Is it to save money? If it is, then the investment is a decidedly long-term one. Clearly all of these projects demand substantial labor to eke out even the smallest amount of so-called intelligence. This might still be a reasonable motivation if one had the feeling that all or most of this work would be adapted on a large scale. Yet, at least at the moment, such a feeling would not be well founded. At the moment, systems such as those discussed in the preceding chapters are used in at most a relatively small number of institutions.

Moreover, I think it is fair to say that even at those institutions that use such software, the impact is, more likely than not, far from overwhelming. As far as I am aware, adding intelligence to computer-assisted language instruction has not allowed any institution to cut back substantially on the number of hours that teachers teach. Computer-assisted language learning (CALL) may be a time-saver, but intelligent CALL (ICALL) has not yet developed to the point where it can make such instruction significantly more effective.

Perhaps we should look in the other direction and regard this work as a form of pure research. But pure research into what? None of the work constitutes pure research into either theoretical or computational linguistics, and none of the presenters has made any claims to that effect. Nor has this work resulted in new theories of second language teaching.

What then is the point? The preceding chapters all consider this question and have tried to supply answers that do not depend on treating intelligent software for language learning as a means either for employing fewer teachers or for developing in isolation theoretical frameworks.

Some of the preceding chapters attempt to address this all-important question as a practical matter. Some of the results have been positive, some not so encouraging. Loritz (this volume), for example, discusses a study that indicates that in one pedagogical context an interactive version of his parser was not particularly successful and suggests that his system may ultimately prove more useful for diagnosis and assessment. Sanders and Sanders (this volume) contend that the "unintelligent" Pilot-Spion is a more effective teaching tool than the "intelligent" Spion. On the other hand, the Carnegie Mellon group, which has produced ALICE (Levin & Evans, this volume), cites a study (Nagata, 1992) indicating that one application of their software can help students to acquire certain language skills more effectively. DeSmedt (this volume) reports that in beta tests, Herr Kommissar was able to detect 92.8% of the student errors and had a false correction rate of 1.1%.

In the discussions, there are also attempts to address the question of purpose in terms of basic research. Frederiksen, Donin, and Décary (this volume) position their project in the context of ongoing basic research at McGill in the area of cognitive science and second language education. The developers of CALLE (Rypa & Feuerman, this volume) have focused on the theoretical basis, both linguistic and pedagogical, of their prototype (see also Feuerman, Marshall, Newman, & Rypa, 1987). DeSmedt (this volume) contends that his program can be used to collect and analyze data for research purposes.

Is, then, the attempt to build intelligent computer programs for language learning a practical or a theoretical matter? Again, what is the point?

Both positions, the practical and the theoretical, have merit, in my opinion. The merit of each position, however, is inextricably bound up with the merit of the other. Intelligent software for language learning can have important practical consequences for teaching and learning to the extent to which it incorporates theory. And it can use theory effectively only if it is used practically. Let me make clear why I think this is the case.

ICALL Research

Computers are slowly but surely being applied to every aspect of human activity, from cooking to driving cars to space travel. They are already used in teaching language, and unless we see a dramatic reversal in social trends, their use will be ever increasing. We can either develop language learning software ourselves or watch others do it. If we take the latter road, we must be prepared to have software that suits the needs of other cultures but may not suit our own. In a world where language skills are increasingly important, this is a rather risky proposition.

Now, if one is going to build software for teaching language, one presumably wants to make it as useful as possible, and making it as useful as possible means trying to use the most cutting-edge techniques we have available. In other words, it means incorporating whatever artificial intelligence techniques we can find.

Considering how time-consuming it is to build these systems, we might well think that the safest and most cost-effective path is to wait until those aspects of artificial intelligence that bear upon the task—that is, natural language processing, knowledge representation, and user modeling—have reached a state of development that makes the building of such systems as easy as possible.

Unfortunately, this path is not feasible for one very simple reason: ICALL software puts demands on artificial intelligence techniques that are often far more encompassing than those of traditional areas to which AI is applied. Not only must the natural language component be able to process well-formed grammatical sentences, but ideally, it must also be able to handle a wide variety of ill-formed input. Not only must the knowledge systems be able to handle very specific contexts (airline bookings, for example), but ideally they must also be able to handle the wide range of changing contexts that are relevant to someone who wants to use a language for everyday purposes. Not only must user models be able to sort users into straightforward taxonomic classes, but ideally they must also be able to identify a variety of different kinds of strengths and weaknesses in different kinds of language learners. Last but not least, ICALL software must have a pedagogical component that may well involve teaching strategies distinct from other academic areas.[50]

We are, of course, a long way from such ideals. Nevertheless, no other existing genre of intelligent system needs all the components that an ICALL system should ultimately incorporate, and among those genres that do incorporate some of the same components, few possess the generalist orientation necessary for ICALL. Note how few of the systems described in this volume use off-the-shelf components developed in other kinds of artificial intelligence (AI) research.[51] This is not to say that ICALL systems cannot use the fruits of other research but rather that, because of its particular requirements, better ICALL is likely to result primarily from research and development in the field of ICALL itself.

A Theory of Language Use

Theory for Practice

ICALL research and development must rely on a significant body of knowledge about what is needed to assist in language learning and how these needs can be met. This knowledge will presumably play a significant role in the construction of software. Why? Computers know only what is specified for them, and if we do not simply wish to base our software on a hodgepodge of heuristics, we must develop detailed models that can be tested to see what works and what does not. Because it is likely to play an important role, let us look more closely at what kind of theory is at issue.

Although theoretical linguistics has clearly played a role in developing the systems discussed in this volume, it deliberately excludes from its domain all issues relating to the way in which language is used. However, ICALL, by its very nature, must focus on use. The goal of ICALL is to help students to become able to use a language, and the primary

---

[50] Germain (1992), for example, noted the limited scope of most NLP applications, whereas Fairweather, Gibbons, Rogers, Waki, and O'Neal (1992) made a similar observation about student models in computer-based training applications. The point here is not that there is no cutting-edge research that can be of use to ICALL but simply that the hope of getting off-the-shelf components from which ICALL applications can be constructed seems, at the moment, quite remote.

[51] The expressed intention of the ALICE project (Levin, Evans, & Gates, 1991; Levin & Evans, this volume) to incorporate the CLARIT indexing system is one of the few exceptions (see Levin et al., 1991, p. 50), as is the use of a preexisting Arabic lexicon in the MILT project (Weinberg et al., this volume).

means by which students learn and language teachers teach is by using the language. I mean here *use* in a quite general way, for both "natural" communication and "unnatural" drills perforce involve language use in the sense I intend.

If this is the case, the most relevant theory for ICALL is a theory, presumably a computationally oriented theory, of language use.[52] I would like to stress, however, that in speaking of a theory, I am not referring to what often gets presented as theory in studies of second language learning, that is, statistical studies that report on how frequently certain constructions, for example, are used (see Chaudron, 1988). Without doubt, such studies fill a need to know what people actually do, but they do not constitute formal hypotheses or models that we can test to see if they have predictive value. Nor am I talking about theories such as the Monitor Theory of Krashen (1981; Dulay, Burt, & Krashen, 1982; Krashen & Terrell, 1983), which, in essence, offers an informal sketch of second language acquisition. When I speak of models, I refer to the kind of predictive hypotheses that we find in at least some work in theoretical linguistics, theories that we can test against data to see the degree to which they have formal predictive value.

Why talk of a theory of language use rather than pragmatics? Because pragmatics treats only those aspects of language use that relate to the use of language in context. It abstracts away those aspects of language use, such as syntax, that are already treated by the core areas of theoretical linguistics (see Horne, 1988). The preceding chapters show clearly that these core areas play an enormously important part in what people need to know in order to use language. A theory of language use must be an integrated model, not because of any great desire to build grand theories but because this is the level of abstraction demanded by the building of intelligent language teaching machines.

At present, discourse models come closest to an integrated theory of this type. Nevertheless, although such models attempt to integrate pragmatics and core linguistics, they tend to be focused on developing systems for limited tasks. Consequently, they do not generally address the issues with which ICALL must be most concerned: error handling, language learning, and language teaching.[53] These areas, however, are important not only to ICALL but also to a more general theory of language use.

Errors

Errors are perhaps the most prominent feature that distinguishes ideal language from actual performance.[54] None of us, when we speak or write, put forward perfectly well-formed texts. Yet despite these errors we can communicate, at least in part because we

---

[52] Discussions of a theory of language use can be found, among other places, in Chomsky (1965, pp.10-15) and Hymes (1972). A computational theory of language use is discussed by Berwick (1983, see especially pp. 28-29). The term "language use" has also been employed by theorists who wish to attack grammatically oriented pedagogical approaches. See, for example, Newmark and Reibel (1968). No such motivation, however, exists here.

[53] See Berwick (1983) and footnote 1.

[54] The role of errors in a theory of language use is noted by Chomsky (1965, pp. 10-15); the discussion is focused on the notions of grammaticality and acceptability.

can figure out what should have been said. In fact, much of this process is done so intuitively that we are completely unconscious of its operation. As evidence, one need only note the ease with which we can pass by typographical errors in a written text, in effect seeing the words in their correct form without even consciously identifying the mistake. The same is true for the mispronunciations, the inappropriate stops and starts, and the agrammatical constructions that characterize normal unplanned conversation.

Effective language instruction must often concern itself not only with identifying ungrammatical constructions but also with identifying intended constructions. ICALL must be able to map the unacceptable onto the acceptable, so that we can not only identify "I slept the baby" as wrong but also, given a particular context of use, construe it as an attempt to say "I slept with the baby." Consequently, a relevant theory of language use must not only identify those errors in a systematic manner but also account for ways in which people can recover from them. This is precisely what language teachers and language users in general are constantly doing.

Errors in language often involve the grammatical system of the language, and for this if no other reason, discussion of ICALL research projects should make clear how a particular linguistic theory has been implemented in the application. It is one thing to note that one has used lexical-functional grammar (LFG), government and binding (GB) theory, or a case-based grammar. It is another to indicate how these theories have been incorporated in the systems and to make clear how the application grammar is used to handle errors.

None of the projects discussed in the preceding chapters have borrowed a preexisting grammar (or grammar fragment) for a particular language.[55] Presumably, the researchers engaged in the time-consuming work of grammar building because no adequate grammars could be found that were compatible with their linguistic theory. If this is the case, a number of interesting questions arise. What constitutes an adequate grammar (or grammar fragment) for a particular kind of project? What areas of the grammar that the project developed were not spelled out in the theory? Are there any aspects of the grammar for which the theory could simply not be applied in its standard form? Do the innovations have any implications for the theory? Answers to these sorts of questions would take us into the nitty gritty of applying theoretical linguistics to matters of language use[56] and in so doing would provide a concrete context in which to understand approaches to error handling.

We might also begin to see ways in which the linguistic theories might need to change so that they could be of use in handling less than perfect input. Linguistic grammars are characteristically intended to account for grammatically well-formed constructions and to identify grammatical errors as violations of the rules and principles that constitute the grammar. For example, "I slept the baby" would be considered a violation

---

[55] In the volume as a whole, the only exception is the FLUENT system (see Hamburger, this volume; Hamburger & Hashim , 1992).

[56] See Berwick and Weinberg (1984, pp. 78-82) for some discussion of the relationship of theoretical grammars and the "cover" grammars used in applications.

of the theta-criterion in GB. The verb *sleep* can assign only one role, and yet the sentence has two noun phrases. Because every noun phrase argument must be assigned a role, the sentence is ungrammatical (see, e.g., May, 1985, p. 28). This, from the point of view of GB, effectively dispenses with the matter. The other principal generative theories, LFG and generalized phrase structure grammar (GPSG), account for this error using different principles, but the result is the same. Once the error is typed as a particular sort of violation, the matter is at an end.

Is all the rest an issue of pragmatics and parsing, in other words, of domains that are not part of what is often known as core linguistics? I do not think so. It is true that the set of ungrammatical structures relative to a language is, strictly speaking, the complement of the acceptable structures in the language and that accounting for this class would place an impossible burden on the grammar for a language. It is not true, however, that the class of errors that learners make is equivalent to that complement. There is, I suggest, a much smaller range of possible errors that a speaker can make. Similarly, there is a restricted class of possible errors that a learner of a language can make at particular point in learning the language.

Language learners, be they first or second language learners, children or adults, do not make mistakes at random. In fact, the range of errors is quite restricted. The restricted range is quite predictable from a basic hypothesis shared by the three major linguistic theories: the assumption that human beings have a set of basic predispositions that come into play when they learn a language, a set of predispositions that is often called "universal grammar." If, indeed, the range of errors is quite restricted, it should be possible to extend the descriptive power of linguistic grammars so that they can be used not only to indicate that a principle or rule has been violated but also to identify the kinds of violations that are possible for particular rules and principles.[57]

This is not a question of simply identifying the invariants, that is, those parts of a grammar for a language that are part of our universal grammar. It is quite clear, for example, that both first and second language speakers of English make all kinds of mistakes related to coordination. For instance, one can find constructions such as "The piano, music sheet, and the tape recorder are all in the other room" and "She made both a speech and she led the group." Some version of a "like matches with like" constraint on coordination is assumed by all three major linguistic theories (GB, LFG, GPSG), and presumably such errors are a transgression of a universal principle.

However, although such errors are relatively common, one rarely, if ever, finds any adult speaker of English transgressing the coordinate structure constraint with a sentence like "What did you see who and?" This structure also transgresses a presumably invariant principle. Nevertheless, the fact that we can transgress presumably invariant principles indicates that invariance is not the only issue.

---

[57] Chomsky (1964) discusses the role of grammars in accounting for ungrammaticality. Chomsky (1986) suggests a grammatical account of gradations of errors (see pp. 1, 28ff, 88).

No doubt the explanation is properly considered part of the study of acquisition. Nevertheless, if we assume that a theory of acquisition should crucially involve the linguistic grammar, the linguistic theory should be rich enough to allow us to point to the particular characteristics that allow one kind of error but not a related one. At the moment, it is not at all clear that linguistic theories have made much headway in this domain. This is where ICALL, which is concerned with the characterization not just of the acceptable but also of the unacceptable, can make demands that may spur theory development.

There are still other areas where ICALL may help to prod and adjust the theoretical linguistic frameworks it needs. The major linguistic theories all assume a notion of sentence as the basic unit of analysis. This comes straight out of traditional prescriptive grammar books. The notion is useful in many respects, but if we wish to use ICALL to help students learn to speak and write more than the standard formal written dialect of a language, then we had better investigate ways to expand our grammars to handle the fragments, asides, ellipses, and nonstandard subordinations that characterize oral and informal written modes of discourse.

Software for ICALL, however, does not have the luxury of remaining within the confines of even an expanded core linguistics. It must consider not only potential but also actual errors, and it must have strategies for dealing with them.

What a language teacher does in helping a student is not all that different from what we normally do, except that the error identification and correction process is far more conscious and deliberate. Language teachers identify mistakes and help students to correct them either explicitly (e.g., "You have not used the right tense; try using the present") or implicitly (e.g., by restating the attempt in an appropriate form).

The intelligent systems discussed in the preceding chapters have, to some degree, imitated this ability, at least in terms of error identification. Two basic approaches, error analysis and construal rules, dominate, both in these chapters and in the field at large. Error analysis routines work on the assumption that there are characteristic incorrect constructions that students will produce when learning specific language skills (cf. Sanders, 1991). Thus, ALICE (Levin & Evans, this volume) searches for such problems as subject-verb agreement and, in a more general way, phrases that do not fit into subcategorization frames. Construal rules work somewhat differently. The intent is to understand what the student is trying to express. In DeSmedt's Herr Kommissar (this volume), for example, if a verb needs a direct object and no noun phrase with the appropriate characteristics can be found, the parser looks for an unassigned noun phrase with characteristics that come close to those required. The intention is not to analyze what went wrong but rather to make sense of the utterance.

To a certain degree, the two approaches mimic two very different human approaches to linguistic interaction. The error grammar approach is at least somewhat akin to the posture of someone concerned not so much with what is being said as with the way it is said. Outside of the traditional language classroom, such situations occur more frequently than one might imagine. They occur, for example, whenever a parent monitors the telephone behavior of a young child. The construal approach, on the other hand, in attempting to accept ill-formed constructions, is similar to our attempts to maneuver around the errors we normally encounter in everyday discourse. Although we are more likely to think of this skill as natural, it can involve abilities that not everyone possesses. Not everyone, for example, can understand the broken speech of a second language speaker, a skill honed by many a second language teacher.

Not surprisingly, the two approaches seem to lend themselves to different types of software. The error grammar approach tends to be used in software that focuses on the form of what the learner produces, such as the formal grammar exercises created with Carnegie Mellon's ALICE (Levin & Evans, this volume) or with BRIDGE (Sams, this volume) and the grammar checkers that identify grammatical and stylistic errors in texts (Loritz, this volume; Sanders, 1991). The construal approach is used in software oriented toward a more communicative or "whole language" style, such as DeSmedt's Herr Kommissar (this volume).[58]

It should be noted that some projects attempt to blend the two approaches (see Felshin, this volume; Hamburger, this volume; Hamburger & Hashim, 1992). Error correction of this sort can sometimes be a difficult business, even for human teachers, because in many cases it depends on inferring from the context and the utterance what the utterance would have been if it had been correct. Construal, as noted previously, only attempts to make some sense of the utterance. Thus, error correction and construal diverge more with more serious errors and with more guesswork necessary to reconstruct the presumably intended construction.

No matter what the strategy, we have only begun to scratch the surface. To use error analysis to identify mistakes does not necessarily mean that we are catching the basic misunderstandings that underlie the mistakes, as, for example, Brown and Burton (1978) attempt to do for basic arithmetic with procedural analysis and the concept of a bug. Understanding these misconceptions could make ICALL far more effective than regular CALL because it would address the roots of problems and not just their surface manifestations (cf. Bailin, 1990b). Nor does the ability to loosen up rules so that the software can process a student's input despite error mean that we have any real knowledge of the principles that underlie such construal. However, such knowledge could allow ICALL software to coach in a far more systematic and consequently effective manner than a human being.

The research we need to achieve these goals will focus on the interaction of performance factors, context, and core linguistics—in other words, research that focuses on an integrated theory of language use. Although, as I have argued, the range of potential errors is presumably constrained by the grammar, the mapping of errors onto intended constructions crucially involves context. Take the simplest of examples—how to con-

---

[58] Mulford (1989, pp. 38-40) also described a construal approach. It should be noted that ALICE can be used to used to create not only formal grammar exercises but also communicative instructional software (Levin & Evans, this volume; Levin et al., 1991).

strue a construction such as "The people wants to go." Clearly, there is a subject-verb agreement problem here. But where precisely does the problem reside? Is it a problem with the verb or the noun phrase? Should the noun phrase be changed to a singular form, or should the verb be changed to *want*? The question can only be answered by examining the context of use and identifying the discourse subject (cf. Sanders & Sanders, 1989, pp. 17-18). Performance issues must also be considered, even in such a simple case of subject-verb disagreement. Is the error a simple slip, or is it systematic? Does it occur every time the construction is attempted? If not, what kinds of circumstances trigger it? The more that we understand the nature of errors and their role in language use, the better our ICALL software will become.

Language Learning

The scope of a theory of language use must also encompass language learning. Language learning outside of the early acquisition process is not simply a pedagogical issue. It is a normal part of our use of language, and it continues throughout our lives, whether this be a matter of learning a language, a terminology in a discipline, or a formal written dialect of a language. If nothing else, ICALL needs a theory of language learning that can be used to map student progress and note both deficiencies and the fossilization of incorrect forms. Student models developed with such theory can be used by ICALL programs to select appropriate materials for individuals who learn in different ways at different rates.

Nevertheless, there has been relatively little discussion in these chapters of such issues, and in the field at large, work in this area is still in its infancy.[59] One major reason may be that available second language theories such as that of Krashen (1981; Dualy et al., 1982; Krashen & Terrell, 1983) are simply too informal to be of much use. On the other hand, psychological and linguistic theories (e.g., MacWhinney, 1987) generally do not take into account the social context in which this learning takes place. However, we use language appropriately not only in relation to the grammar of a language but also in relation to textual and social factors. Learning a language is a matter of not just learning the grammar for a language but also learning the rules for contexts. Whether or not a theory of the acquisition of grammar must take into account the social context of learning, it is difficult to see how a theory that incorporates the acquisition of rules for appropriate use can avoid the context in which the acquisition occurs.[60]

The rules for contexts affect all aspects of language use, even down to what kinds of syntactic constructions are acceptable in given circumstances. Parallel constructions, for example, are often a major source of difficulty for second (and even first) language speakers. In order to use such constructions effectively, speakers need to have some idea

---

[59] See, however, Bailin (1990b) and Swartz & Yazdani (1992, Section 3).

[60] For some discussion, see, among others, Newmark and Reibel (1968), Hymes (1972), Wolfson (1983), and Sperber and Wilson (1988). Please note that I do not stress the importance of language use to attack either generative grammar or pedagogies that use explicit grammars. My point here is that a theory of language use relevant to ICALL research must have a broad scope including, but not restricted to, a theory of linguistic competence.

of the circumstances under which various kinds of parallelism and ellipsis are appropriate. Consider the following case. Someone asks, "How are you today?" as a casual question. On the assumption that there are no other complications, it is generally considered odd to respond, "I am happy, and I am healthy, thank you." The response is grammatically correct but is nevertheless the kind of response we associate with both robots in science fiction and immigrants who have a less than certain grasp of English. On the other hand, shorter, more elliptical responses such as "I'm happy and healthy, thank you" or "Happy and healthy, thank you" are acceptable.

Are there ever circumstances where the nonelliptical parallelism is more appropriate? Indeed, there are. Imagine a context in which the respondent has been accused of being a complaining type of person with an extremely negative attitude. The person in question wishes to change this perception. In response to a sarcastic "How are you today?" the nonelliptical long form will communicate what the shorter forms could not. The crucial factor in this case appears to be the need for an emphatic denial of an implicit assumption.

Clearly, when we learn our mother tongue, we acquire these context-syntax rules. But how? Research into the contexts in which we learn these rules of use may well lead to predictive theory with great utility for ICALL, theory that could, for example, help in setting up scenarios that facilitate the acquisition of certain rules or sets of rules.

Language Teaching

To teach language, we almost invariably use language. So, far from being outside of the domain of language itself, the teaching of language is an important aspect of language use. In fact, language teaching takes place in all societies in all kinds of contexts, both inside and outside of classrooms. We may learn our first language naturally, but it is a mistake to think that there are no self-conscious attempts to help that process along.[61] Moreover, although our earliest language learning may be completely independent of conscious teaching, this does not preclude the possibility that its role in later acquisition may be more significant (see Chaudron, 1988).

The issue here is not just learning a new language. As discussed previously, beyond the early acquisition period, we often acquire and learn how to use different oral and written dialects and registers in different situations for languages that we already know. In many cases, the learning process includes either a formal or an informal teacher.

The presence of informal teaching pervades our use of language in social circumstances. How many of us, for example, have not been given tips on the way we should speak in a new social situation or have not been corrected when we have spoken in a way which was inappropriate? The ubiquity of such coaching gives the lie to the notion that language teaching is in some way unnatural.

More careful examination of the role of informal teaching may also help to understand better the pedagogical roles that ICALL software can play and give us a better un-

---

[61] See Fodor and Crain (1987, p. 48) for a brief discussion and some references.

derstanding of the function of the pedagogical component of ICALL games, such a those designed by DeSmedt (this volume), Sanders and Sanders (this volume), and Douglas (this volume), who attempt to aid language learning by engaging the student in conversation. In such games the coaching element is clearly analogous to the informal instruction we receive outside of the classroom.

The same kind of approach may also help us to understand more formal instruction. Instead of looking at such instruction as a technology that must be understood in terms of how well it works, we should, I believe, try to understand more precisely its function as a social process (see Bailin, 1990a). Such an understanding may well help us to build better instructional systems that, like some of those constructed with Carnegie Mellon's ALICE (Levin & Evans, this volume), use a more traditional teaching approach.

The Role of Evaluation: Practice for Theory

In many ways the software systems discussed in the preceding chapters incorporate incipient models of error handling, language learning, and language teaching. Take, for example, language learning. When Sanders and Sanders (this volume) and DeSmedt (this volume) suggest that a game format may be useful in learning language, they are, at least indirectly, suggesting what may eventually become a quite formal model of adult second language acquisition. Such a model would include the presentation of sentences and constructions and a domain of discourse that requires the student to practice using target constructions and vocabulary in order to communicate for some functional purpose. Similarly, when the developers of CALLE (Rypa & Feuerman, this volume), ALICE (Levin & Evans, this volume), and BRIDGE (Sams, this volume) focus on analytic skills in more classroom-like settings, they are suggesting that very specific conceptual skills may at least aid the language learning process.

None of the programs I have just alluded to incorporate anything like a full language use model of language learning. Each, at best, embodies an aspect of what a full model would include. Nor is it clear that any of these beginnings will lead to good models. However, there is only one way we have of finding out if they have any value, and that is by testing. The kinds of intelligent software discussed in this volume offer the best hope for such testing for two reasons: first, because we can instantiate large portions of the model in the software and second, because we can record very precisely the actions of both the computer teacher and the student learner. Not only, then, is the use of the ICALL software discussed here potentially a practical teaching tool, but it is also an important experimental tool that can push forward the development of the very theory that informs ICALL's development (cf. MacWhinney, 1992).

Nevertheless, by speaking of evaluation here, I am in no way suggesting that we learn much, if anything, from a simple quantitative test of a piece of ICALL software in a language class to see if helps students improve their grades. For evaluation to be useful, it must go beyond "yes, it helps," "no, it doesn't help" information. The evaluative testing should occur in relation to a theoretical model in which the proposed role of the software is clearly understood.

In relation to such a theoretical model, evaluations need to take into account two identifiably distinct roles: the specific role of the ICALL software, that is, the role the ICALL software is intended to perform in helping students to master specific skills; and the general role, that is, the role the skill is supposed to play in developing linguistic ability. When Nagata (1992) evaluates Carnegie Mellon's ALICE program (Levin & Evans, this volume) to see if it is useful in helping students to master the passive in Japanese, her study is focusing on the specific role of the software in mastering skills. Left open is the question of the role that mastery of this particular skill plays in the language development of the student. On the other hand, a study that simply looks at whether or not student performance in a class improved would be looking at the general role of the ICALL software.

The distinction between the two kinds of roles may help to make our evaluations far more precise by making clear the role of the software in the learning process. In effect, it allows us to assess the software, first, in terms of whether it actually succeeds at helping students learn what it is intended to help them learn and, second, in terms of whether the skills that it imparts are in fact useful in the general acquisition process. If, for example, it were found that the students who mastered some skill using an ICALL program did not show gains in the target language, we might need to look at our model of language learning to see if we had correctly assessed the role of such mastery in the learning process. On the other hand, we might find that although the software did not seem to produce any significant effects on the specific targeted skills, it did have effects on general ability with the language. Such a finding might lead us to reassess our assumptions about what the software is really teaching—that is, the specific role of the software.

The difference between the specific role of the software and the general role of the skill is as applicable to open-ended communicative programs as it is to more focused instructional software. No software, no matter how open-ended, presents the students with every kind of construction and vocabulary. There are always choices concerning what is presented and the kinds of feedback proffered. Conscious reflection on the nature of the skills and their role in language development is therefore relevant. Again, however, it must be stressed that the focus should be not on ranking the software but on understanding, in theoretical terms, its successes and failures. By increasing our understanding, the evaluations can help us in quite concrete ways to build better theory and consequently better software.

The testing should be repeated throughout the development process. In this way, presumptions we make about the role of the software in the learning process can be revised. For example, the beta test of the Ms. Pluralbelle parser discussed by Loritz (this volume, 1992) may, among other things, indicate that the assumption is incorrect that students will make hypotheses about grammatical rules based on concrete examples, or at least that this assumption does not accurately reflect how all learners function. It may well be that, contrary to some language teaching theory (Dualy et al., 1982; Hartwell,

1985; Krashen, 1981, Krashen & Terrell, 1983), some students need considerably more intervention from the instructor (in this case, the software) to develop grammatical concepts (see Chaudron, 1988). If Ms. Pluralbelle provides the extra assistance, it may become far more successful at performing its specific role: helping students to acquire and use certain grammatical concepts. Thus, the beta test may lead to a better understanding of the role of parsing in language teaching and learning and allow the software to become an effective classroom tool, given what may only be relatively minor revisions from the viewpoint of the programming. Projects that undergo careful testing can kill two birds with one stone. They can play a constructive role in the development process, and they can function as useful teaching devices.

To say that ICALL software may not yet be much more effective than standard CALL software does not mean that it is not useful pedagogically. Moreover, we can reasonably expect that it will become far more useful than standard CALL when it has had a chance to develop more fully (cf. Underwood, 1989). Even now, when ICALL is only beginning to show something of its potential, it is far more useful than standard CALL as a research device because, unlike standard CALL, it is able to make distinctions in student language behavior that standard CALL, without much analytic capacity, cannot even begin to approach. Using its natural language processing capacities, it can record and analyze responses in a far more sophisticated way. Even at these early stages, ICALL software can identify the syntactic units in a student input, analyze inflections, and note incorrect punctuation. The interactive games have at least the possibility of noting semantic misconceptions. By using student modeling techniques, the software will also soon be able to present us with a far better picture of what students know at particular stages of the instructional process. And its analytic abilities are only part of the story. Because it is able to offer far more varied learning situations than standard CALL, ICALL can provide far richer data about student language behavior. An intelligent game program offers a far wider range of responses than a traditional multiple choice exercise. With the ability to process speech in a flexible manner, it eventually will be able to handle all aspects of language teaching. The potential of CALL as a research tool, which Garrett has argued for so forcefully (this volume; Borchardt et al., 1992, pp. 62-65), comes to fruition in ICALL.

As noted earlier, the developers themselves are aware of this potential. DeSmedt (this volume) writes of the ability of his program to capture and analyze student responses for research purposes. The McGill Language Learning Environment of Frederiksen et al. (this volume) is specifically intended to explore discourse-related issues in second language learning. The developers of CALLE have noted that their project addresses LFG research concerns (Feuerman et al., 1987; Rypa & Feuerman, this volume). The developers of BRIDGE built an authoring interface aimed in part at helping researchers manipulate instructional variables (Kreyer & Criswell, this volume; Sams, this volume). However, the developers of ALICE made the link to ICALL development most clear: "Ultimately, ALICE itself is the tool we need to broaden our understanding of ICALI design and to guide the development of future generations of ALICE" (Levin et al., 1991, p. 53).

Conclusion: Some Caveats in Testing ICALL

In ICALL research, as in so many other things, the devil, as they say, is in the details. For evaluations to be truly useful, we must, among other things, know in detail what content the software is presenting, the way in which the content is presented, and how the lessons are used in the general learning context. If a control is used, then we must have similar knowledge of the control group's learning experience.

If, to take a hypothetical example, we want to compare ICALL lessons with traditional homework assignments, then we must, among other things, know the details concerning the structure of both the software and the assignments and have a procedural map of how each fits in to the learning environment (are they, for instance, both assigned as homework?). Without such information, it is impossible to assess the results. Say, for example, we found no significant difference in achievement between those who used the software and those who used a traditional approach. If the content and presentation of both the ICALL and the traditional assignments are the same, then the study would indicate that the medium (computers versus paper-and-pen) did not significantly affect learning. On the other hand, if the content differed, conclusions would vary depending on the nature of the differences. The details, to a great extent, determine what, if anything, we can conclude. For this reason, in presenting evaluations, we may be better off relying less on the traditional humanities article style (i.e., the style in which most ICALL articles are written) and more on the scientific format, where methodology, results, and discussion are each given their due in separate sections and where no one expects exciting rhetoric anywhere except perhaps in the discussion.

Care must be exercised not only in what is presented but in what we infer from it. For one thing, our testing of the ICALL software can never be a test of ICALL in general. To design such evaluative tests would be about as useful as research to evaluate the utility of books. The implausibility of an evaluation of books as a medium is obvious. How can we possibly evaluate the utility of books without considering their content, their format and, perhaps above all, the particular contexts in which they are used?

No doubt, students of technology and culture can talk about the constraints and potentials of media. But, as professionals investigating computers and language learning, these concerns are peripheral. All that we can test in a meaningful way is particular software or types of software in particular environments. From these tests we may be able to infer something more general about certain models of teaching, learning, and language use, but that is all. The tests cannot evaluate the medium itself.

We must also be careful not to think that we can even evaluate the functionality of a specific piece of software in an absolute sense from one or more specific applications. The functionality of a specific piece of software is dependent not just on its internal workings but also on the context in which it is used. This is particularly important to keep in mind in relation to software intended for instructional purposes. Much of this software does not fit easily or comfortably into the language classroom to which we have become accustomed. This may be, I suspect, the major reason why educators are not banging down the doors to try it out: It is not clear at all how it will fit in.

Is this a deficiency in the design of the software? Perhaps, but it may also indicate that we may need to look at other configurations if we wish to use ICALL software effectively in formal educational situations. I use the word *formal* here deliberately, for software that attempts to check grammar is being acquired by a considerable number of first and second language English speakers. To the limited extent that the current commercial software works (Dowler & McEvoy, 1992; Payette, 1990, pp. 22-27), it is used in much the same way as a calculator—as an aid in performing tasks.

The lesson here is simple. We must be careful to avoid believing uncritically in bureaucratic assumptions about functionality. The point is relevant to more than just formal or informal education. We may make, for example, a very clear division between first and second language instruction in the classroom, but this distinction may really only apply completely to the difference between early childhood acquisition of a first language and the initial steps in the adult acquisition of a second language. It is rather less clear that advanced second language acquisition (including writing in the second language) is significantly different from first language acquisition of the same linguistic tools.

Two software packages that a colleague and I have developed with natural language processing techniques are frequently used at the University of Western Ontario by both first and second language English speakers to improve certain language skills related to writing (Bailin & Thomson, 1988). The skills the packages help with (i.e., the identification of the parts of English sentences and the appropriate use of verb forms) are skills that both groups often need. If we had assumed the software would be useful for only one group or the other, we would have significantly reduced the range of application.

A theoretical perspective on the software, including a clear conceptualization of the specific role of the software and the general role of the target skills, can help us to avoid many limiting preconceptions. In relation to the articulated roles, we should attempt to test the software in as many contexts as possible in which these roles can be realized. The articulation of the roles can help us to see the limiting cases, situations where one's model indicates that the general role of the target skills will play no useful part. For example, there is likely to be no point in using software intended to teach certain fine points of the grammar of a language in a class that focuses only on increasing oral facility.

A too narrow perspective, however, does far more than limit the usefulness of the software. If we apply the software in too narrow a set of contexts, we will learn very little about how people learn language and how computers can be used to help them. And that ultimately is the key to making sense of the apparent successes and failures and using them to guide us on the road to more sophisticated ICALL, a road we have as yet barely begun to travel.

Acknowledgments

I would like to thank Melissa Holland and Oscar Garcia for their helpful comments on an earlier version of this chapter.

References

Bailin, A. (1990a). CALI, artificial intelligence, and the representation of social roles. In M.L. Craven, R. Sinyor, & D. Paramskas (Eds.), *CALL: Papers and reports* (pp. 173-179). La Jolla, CA: Athleston.

Bailin, A. (1990b). Skills-in-context and student modeling. *CALICO Journal, 8*, 7-22.

Bailin, A., & Thomson, P. (1988). Natural language processing in computer-assisted language instruction. *Computers and the Humanities, 22*, 99-110.

Berwick, R.C. (1983). Introduction: Computational aspects of discourse. In M. Brady & R.C. Berwick (Eds.), *Computational models of discourse* (pp. 27-105). Cambridge, MA: MIT Press.

Berwick, R.C., & Weinberg, A. (1984). *The grammatical basis of linguistic performance*. Cambridge, MA: MIT Press.

Borchardt, F., Daetsch, W., Lyman-Hager, M., Garrett, N., Underwood, J., & Foelsche, O. (1992). Technology and academic status. *CALICO Journal, 9*, 57-70.

Brown, J.S., & Burton, R. (1978). Diagnostic models for procedural bugs in basic mathematical skills. *Cognitive Science, 2*, 155-192.

Chaudron, C. (1988). *Second language classrooms: Research on teaching and learning*. New York: Cambridge University Press.

Chomsky, N. (1964). Degrees of grammaticalness. In J.A. Fodor & J.J. Katz (Eds.), *The Structure of language: Readings in the philosophy of language* (pp. 384-389). Englewood Cliffs, NJ: Prentice-Hall.

Chomsky, N. (1965). *Aspects of the theory of syntax*. Cambridge, MA: MIT Press.

Chomsky, N. (1986). *Barriers*. Cambridge, MA: MIT Press.

Dowler, M., & McEvoy, C. (1992). Checking the checkers: Computer editing packages. *Technostyle, 10*, 19-29.

Dualy, H., Burt, M., & Krashen, S. (1982). *Language two*. New York: Oxford University Press.

Fairweather, P., Gibbons, A. S., Rogers, D.H., Waki, R., & O'Neal, A.F. (1992). A model for computer-based training. *AI Expert, 7*, 30-35.

Feuerman, K., Marshall, C., Newman, D., & Rypa, M. (1987). The CALLE project. *CALICO Journal, 4*, 25-34.

Fodor, J., & Crain, S. (1987). Simplicity and generality of rules in language acquisition. In B. MacWhinney (Ed.), *Mechanisms of language acquisition* (pp. 35-64). Hillsdale, NJ: Lawrence Erlbaum Associates.

Germain, E. (1992). Introducing natural language processing. *AI Expert, 7*, 30-35.

Hamburger, H., & Hashim, R. (1992). A foreign language tutoring and learning environment. In M.L. Swartz & M. Yazdani (Eds.), *Intelligent tutoring systems for foreign language learning: The bridge to international communication* (pp. 201-218). New York: Springer-Verlag.

Hartwell, P. (1985). Grammar, grammars and the teaching of grammar. *College English, 47*, 105-127.

Horne, L. R. (1988). Pragmatic theory. In F. Newmeyer (Ed.), *Linguistics: The Cambridge survey, Vol. 1, Linguistic theory: Foundations* (pp. 113-145). Cambridge, UK: Cambridge University Press.

Hymes, D. (1972). On communicative competence. In J.B. Pryde & J. Holmes (Eds.), *Sociolinguistics: Selected readings* (pp. 269-293). New York: Penguin.

Krashen, S. (1981). *Second language acquisition and second language learning*. New York: Pergamon.

Krashen, S., & Terrell, T.D. (1983). *The natural approach: Language acquisition in the classroom*. New York: Pergamon & San Francisco: Alemany.

Levin, L., Evans, D., & Gates, D. (1991). The ALICE system: A workbench for learning and using language. *CALICO Journal*, *9*, 27-56.

Loritz, D. (1992). Generalized transition network parsing for language study. *CALICO Journal*, *10*, 5-22.

MacWhinney, B. (Ed.). (1987). *Mechanisms of language acquisition*. Hillsdale, NJ: Lawrence Erlbaum Associates.

MacWhinney, B. (1992). The Competition model and foreign language acquisition. In M.L. Swartz & M. Yazdani (Eds.), *Intelligent tutoring systems for foreign language learning: The bridge to international communication* (pp. 39-50). New York: Springer-Verlag.

May, R. (1985). *Logical form: Its structure and derivation*. Cambridge, MA: MIT Press.

Mulford, G. (1989). Semantic processing for communicative exercises. *Computers and the Humanities*, *23*, 31-44.

Nagata, N. (1992). *A study of the effectiveness of intelligent CALI as an application of natural language processing*. Unpublished doctoral dissertation, University of Pittsburgh, Pittsburgh, Pennsylvania.

Newmark, L., & Reibel, D.A. (1968). Necessity and sufficiency in language learning. *International Review of Applied Linguistics in Language Teaching*, *6*, 145-164.

Payette, J. (1990). *Intelligent Computer-Assisted Instruction in Syntactic Style* (Tech. Rep. CSRI-247). Toronto: University of Toronto Computer Systems Research Institute.

Sanders, A., & Sanders, R. (1989). Syntactic parsing: A survey. *Computers and the Humanities, 23*, 13-30.

Sanders, R. (1991). Error analysis in purely syntactic parsing of free input: The example of German. *CALICO Journal*, *9*, 72-89.

Sperber, D., & Wilson, D. (1988). *Relevance: Communication and cognition*. Cambridge MA: Harvard University Press.

Swartz, M.L., & Yazdani, M. (Eds.). (1992). *Intelligent tutoring systems for foreign language learning: The bridge to international communication*. New York: Springer-Verlag.

Underwood, J. (1989). On the edge: Intelligent CALL in the 1990s. *Computers and the Humanities*, *23*, 71-84.

Wolfson, N. (1983). Rules of speaking. In J.C. Richards & R.W. Schmidt (Eds.), *Language and communication* (pp. 61-86). New York: Longman.

19

ICALL and Second Language Acquisition

Nina Garrett
George Mason University
and Center for the Advancement of Language Learning

The field of intelligent computer-assisted language learning (ICALL) is still young, and though the various authors in this volume may disagree as to the priorities to be set, we share enthusiasm for its potential. However, beyond the potential of ICALL itself, there are still many extremely complex issues about its integration into the academic reality of language teaching and the theoretical framework of second language acquisition. It is these issues that I address in this chapter.

Teacher Participation in ICALL Development

In terms of the connection between ICALL and language teaching, it must be noted that language teachers have for the most part been little involved in the development of the systems presented in this volume. Although this is regrettable, it is understandable, because foreign languages is a problematic field that for complicated historical, political, and theoretical reasons has not till now been very open to innovation in the teaching of language itself. Most postsecondary departments of foreign languages consider themselves to be primarily departments of literature, and they regard only publications in literature as eligible for promotion and tenure and only *literary* theory as being of intellectual importance to the discipline. Language teaching is still typically seen as the service end of the field, and most language teachers are still trained primarily in methodology, not in linguistics or even applied linguistics.

Furthermore, as regards the uses of technology, in many institutions there is not yet enough support for teacher involvement with technology to make possible the growth of an active corps within language departments of people knowledgeable enough to be active partners in developing ICALL. The average practitioner in the field of language pedagogy is probably not yet convinced that substantial integration of technology is either feasible or desirable. For all these reasons, it is often difficult for ICALL developers to put together teams including appropriate pedagogical expertise. Nonetheless, language teachers have an experiential understanding of language learning and of the nature of the classroom that must be better represented in the development of ICALL.

Common Assumptions About Technology and Language Learning

I first explore some assumptions commonly made (in both ICALL and CALL) about uses of technology in language teaching. After that I discuss some broader assumptions about language learning and teaching in general, which are embedded in the design of many of these systems. Although I am taking a critical stance on many of these assumptions, I do not want to imply that I take them all to be false. I do think they should not be too easily accepted as axiomatic, as basic to the development of language pedagogy generally or ICALL in particular.

Interactivity

The characteristic called interactivity typically has high value in ICALL, indeed in CALL generally. In the context of software evaluation the term is one of approbation. We say, "That's not a good lesson; it's just a page-turner, it's not interactive enough," meaning that the level of interactivity *between the student and the machine* is not high enough to be worthwhile. But the term is ambiguous. When we speak of interactive video or interactive audio, we refer to the interactivity *between the computer and the video or audio device*. But neither of these kinds of interactivity can be simply assumed to be inherently valuable. Does the interactivity between the computer and the video or audio represent some dynamic relationship between textual, aural, or visual aspects of language or language use? When the learner presses keys, manipulates the mouse, chooses responses or new initiatives, does this represent some substantive engagement with the material or only some lively and electronically ingenious interaction with the devices? Interactivity in either sense may be valuable or trivial. These questions are even more important in ICALL than in CALL because ICALL assumes less mediation by the teacher in managing the learning.

Adaptation to Individual Preferences

One of the most important advantages claimed for CALL generally, and even more so for ICALL, is the individualization of instruction—or, more appropriately, the individualization of the learning process—that is possible when students work independently for their own purposes and at their own pace. As Oxford has cogently argued (this volume; Ehrman & Oxford, 1990; Scarcella & Oxford, 1992), learners vary widely in their learning styles and strategies, in their aptitude, motivation, personality, prior language experience, and in many other ways. Technology has the potential to adapt itself and the materials it delivers to many of these variables. However, with all respect for individual learners' rights, I want to sound a note of caution here. We do not really know yet whether accommodating individual learner preferences actually helps them learn language better or whether they would sometimes do better if they were taught to use strategies that do not come naturally.

For example, current methodological mandates insist that learners express themselves spontaneously and without getting hung up on grammatical correctness. Some people do indeed seem to learn best by throwing themselves headlong into a learning activity. They have little anxiety about being wrong or uncertain, and a high level of interactivity provides them with a useful wealth of input data. But some people really do seem to learn better when they have the opportunity to reflect before they speak or respond, consciously forming preliminary hypotheses about the communication going on, using their behavior as a carefully constructed test, and drawing conclusions on the basis of their success in furthering the communication. Do we have any evidence that cautious learners will learn better if they are pushed to abandon their individual proclivities?

On the other hand, research evidence and ample teacher experience tell us that learners tend to overpractice what they already know and underpractice what they do least well. We certainly have ample reason to believe that most learners do not, of themselves, develop what we, as teachers and successful learners, think are the most productive strategies and approaches. The point is that if ICALL is to live up to the promise of individualization, we should not make a priori decisions about which styles and strategies are to be particularly favored or encouraged but should rather use the data collection capabilities of the computer to carry out research that will give us a much better understanding of the problems.

Learner-Centeredness

Closely related philosophically to the idea of individualization is the issue of learner-centeredness, which is widely assumed to have positive value in language learning, in contrast with the teacher-centeredness. In a teacher-centered classroom, the teacher controls all language interactions; almost all dialogue is between the teacher and one student at a time. In a learner-centered classroom, the students talk to each other as much as to the teacher, and they have a fair degree of autonomy in directing and participating in classroom activities. With teacher-centered material design, everything the student does is scripted and anticipated and micromanaged by the teacher in the person of the lesson designer or author. In learner-centered materials the student can make many more choices about what to work on, how to move within and among lesson modules, when and what helps to consult.

The systems discussed in the various chapters of this book show a fair degree of variation along the learner-centeredness parameter, which is entirely appropriate. I would not want to argue against empowering learners to take charge of their own learning, but it may be premature to assume that a high degree of learner-centeredness necessarily benefits language learning. Again, we do not have the research evidence to support such an assumption. If learners themselves do not understand their own styles and strategies, the language learning process, or the relationship between these, then we may not be doing them much good by turning over control of the learning activities to them. Introspection into one's own learning is extremely difficult, especially into language learning, because language is so deeply rooted and for the most part not a conscious kind of knowledge.

Furthermore, learner-centeredness is not likely to bear much fruit for the many students who take foreign languages only to fill a requirement and who are often interested not so much in learning as in getting a passing grade. I do not think we have yet much idea whether ICALL can be designed so as to be of enough interest to motivate such students to take language learning seriously or whether it can be set up to manage the learners' progress through the materials in such a way as almost to force them to learn—or at least to go through the motions.

Limiting the Domain of Processing

One of the most important assumptions on which efforts in ICALL are based is that natural language processing routines can be developed to deal with limited domains of language that plausibly correspond with the expressive limitations of early levels of language learning. This is true in non-technology-based language teaching, too, of course, but the complexities of natural language processing impose very severe constraints on the domain of language in which students can interact. We could hardly do anything interesting in ICALL if we did not accept this, problematic as it is. Unfortunately, the fact that learners have not been taught a given structure does not guarantee against their attempting to communicate an idea that requires that structure in the target language. It appears that several of the systems described in this volume will run into difficulty when learners attempt to use much more advanced language than the systems are prepared to process. There is no obvious solution to this problem, so the best we can do in developing ICALL is probably to help learners become aware of why and how they may have to limit their expressive attempts in certain language activities.

The Value of Help and Feedback

The value of help materials and feedback in CALL and ICALL goes virtually unquestioned. Indeed, ICALL's ability to generate highly specific feedback, whether in the form of error analysis or of responses to learner initiatives, is perhaps its most salient feature, as systems described in this volume illustrate. I would not dream of challenging the idea that feedback can and should be valuable to learners, but our assumptions as to the value rest on some less solid assumptions about how they use it. As teachers and linguists, we often evaluate help and feedback from the perspective that we ourselves had as language learners, forgetting that very few of our learners are likely to grow into linguists and language teachers.

We do not as yet know very much about the extent to which the help and feedback actually contribute to the language development of the average learner. First, there is ample evidence that many, perhaps even most, learners routinely ignore the availability of help materials, even in tasks where we can clearly see that they need them. Second, we do not know, when learners do use them, whether that use results in learning (i.e., a change in their knowledge state) or whether it merely helps them over a momentary difficulty, helps them through the task at hand, by providing a bit of information to be used and immediately forgotten again like a number in the phone book. It could even be argued that the easier the help is to access, the more likely it is to be used in this almost absentminded way.

The development of sophisticated parsers and the effort to tailor their output to provide linguistically precise feedback on grammatical structure for the benefit of learners is one of the best known aspects of ICALL, but I should like to suggest two caveats. The first is that learners doing grammar exercises are quite capable of using linguistically sophisticated error analysis and feedback just as unproductively as they use very crude error analysis and feedback—that is, to get through the task at hand with minimal thought. Second, as linguists and language teachers, we tend to believe that when learners make an error, receive feedback, and correct the error, then they have learned something, have confirmed or disconfirmed an interlanguage hypothesis, and will produce or comprehend that structure differently the next time it shows up.

However, research strongly suggests that all too often learners are operating on a binary correction strategy—If it is not X, it must be Y. If we look closely at the language tasks that most activities ask learners to perform, we realize that in an extraordinarily high proportion of them it is easy for learners to establish a binary choice between two possible responses, even if objectively speaking there are more than two possibilities. In German, for example, if the verb is not weak, it is strong. If negation is not done with *nicht,* it is done with *kein.* If a past action is not rendered with the imperfect, it is likely to be with the present perfect. Even though there are four grammatical cases in German, the learner is almost always choosing between dative and accusative. In multiple-choice questions we often set up such a binary choice. Even if there are four choices, usually only one of them is a genuine distracter to the right answer and the other two are throw-aways. In a large range of language learning activities, therefore, learners are allowed or encouraged to set up a working hypothesis that "it is either X or Y." If feedback, NLP-based or otherwise, tells them that one response is incorrect, they may blithely switch to the other, thus correcting the error without having learned anything at all.

Authenticity

Another assumption commonly held by language teachers but not addressed in most of the projects presented in this volume is that we should make every effort to secure authentic materials for students' use (a view voiced by Oxford, this volume). Authentic, in this context, means textual, video, and audio material that is generated in the country where the language is spoken, for consumption by native speakers of the language, and not constructed for pedagogical purposes. The ability of interactive technologies to give learners access to authentic audio and authentic video is probably its single greatest attraction to most language teachers. I raise this issue not to suggest that ICALL should take authenticity as its mandate. Although there are advantages to giving learners as much contact as possible with authentic materials, there are also serious questions still to be explored about the amount and kind of context and mediation that need to be provided before learners are likely to understand the cultural implications of authentic materials. I only want to suggest that ICALL developers should probably be aware that teachers considering the use of ICALL materials might raise their lack of authenticity as an objection. A case may need to be made as to why authenticity can be held to be unnecessary in some language learning activities.

Pedagogical and Theoretical Issues

At this point I move on to some more fundamental issues in language pedagogy that may not be directly linked to the uses of technology but that underlie and sometimes undermine efforts in ICALL as they do efforts in every other area of the field. Although the projects discussed in this volume represent a wide variety of approaches to language teaching and learning, they can be grouped into two broad categories: those whose primary emphasis is on language as a linguistic system (e.g., in this volume, Levin & Evans; Loritz; Rypa & Feuerman; Weinberg, Garman, Martin, & Merlo) and those whose primary emphasis is on language as communicative behavior (e.g., in this volume, DeSmedt; Douglas; Hamburger; Murray; Sanders & Sanders). This difference in emphasis also characterizes non-technology-based approaches to language teaching. Because the two positions, which ought to be complementary, have become more extreme and have hardened into dogma, the difference has become the basis for a dangerous polarization of the field and is of fundamental importance in the development of ICALL.

Current Bases for CALL and ICALL

The basis for most language materials development today (some ICALL, most CALL, and others) is a body of theory produced in the 1970s and 1980s. This position held that:

- Organizing language learning around a grammatical syllabus (whether explicitly or implicitly) is not only unnecessary but actually counterproductive.
- Language is learned better when learners concentrate on the meaning being expressed rather than on the formal properties of language.
- Second language learning is very similar to first language learning.
- Learners' native language has very little effect on the development of the second language.
- There is a natural order to the acquisition of structure, and therefore there is not much point in trying to teach structure.

I next consider two basic assumptions underlying these points.

Separating meaning from grammar. Much of the theoretical work mentioned previously was undertaken as a reaction against the grammar-translation method of language teaching, which demonstrably did not produce fluent speakers of the languages studied. It went hand in hand with the work of linguists who argued that native speakers' competence in their language went far beyond intuitions about the grammaticality of utterances to include communicative competence—principled and systematic intuitions about the appropriateness of utterances based on considerations of sociolinguistics, pragmatics, semantics, and discourse structure. In its original sense, communicative competence certainly includes grammatical competence, but unfortunately the term *communicative competence* is now widely understood in language pedagogy to mean the ability to communicate, to get meaning across.

Because it is undeniably possible to do that without rigorous concern for grammatical correctness, one could argue that it is possible to teach for communicative competence without teaching grammar. Many in foreign language pedagogy argue, therefore, that the teaching of grammar, as it has always been conceived, has never been shown to have much effect on the learning of communicative competence, and thus there is neither theoretical nor pragmatic reason to teach grammar. At the same time many others continue to insist that we must teach grammar if we are to have any hope that learners will ever express themselves grammatically. This issue fuels an ongoing debate that is both divisive and unresolvable.

It has been said that in the grammar-translation method, we taught for grammatical competence (in the Chomskyan sense) and assumed that the ability to speak and understand language would more or less automatically develop on that basis, at least for motivated students. Nowadays, we teach directly for the ability to communicate and assume that grammaticality will develop more or less automatically, at least for motivated students. In fact, neither of these assumptions holds up particularly well. I think it is crucial to add that neither can it be assumed that if we do a little of each (the so-called eclectic approach), the two will come together satisfactorily.

Instead of just doing lots of communication and teaching a little grammar, we need to give students a principled understanding of the relationship between communication and grammar. Methods training is full of mandates to language teachers about how we should focus on meaning, not on form, as if it were possible to separate them. Until and unless teachers and learners understand that meaning cannot be communicated in language without taking linguistic form, and that linguistic form carries meaning, and that second language acquisition means developing the ability to connect meaning to form in a second language, our pedagogy will continue to be stymied by this artificial polarization. Efforts in ICALL must not simply adopt either a pro- or antigrammar position and thereby recapitulate the counterproductive debate of the field at large, even though it may be necessary and worthwhile to begin with exploring possibilities in one direction or the other. Rather, these efforts must take the lead in showing how grammar can be understood and presented in entirely different ways from the old approaches that "do not do any good."

Making second language acquisition like first language acquisition. Several of the systems described in this volume were shaped by the argument, common in the field, that classroom second language learning by adults (by convention, learners past puberty) should be structured to be as much as possible like nonclassroom first language learning by very young children. It is often claimed that it is "natural" to learn language by listening and making nonverbal responses before speaking or reading. It is said that speaking comes before reading and writing and that certain structures are naturally learned before others. Although these claims are true of toddlers, and although it is certainly true that language learning is a fundamental and universal activity of the normal human brain, it does not follow that the adult human goes about this activity just as the one-year-old does.

Various versions of second language acquisition (SLA) theory differ radically in their perspective on this issue, but it is obvious that adult learners simply cannot set aside their adult cognitive processing and ignore all that they know about language and language use. (Whether they know it consciously is beside the point here.) The influences of their schooling need to be considered too. Even by puberty, students have been thoroughly trained to do most of their learning through reading rather than through listening. Individual learners vary even more in the learning styles and strategies they employ in the classroom than they did as babies—and even in first language acquisition we are coming to recognize that the learning process is enormously variable. I believe, therefore, that the development of ICALL should not be based on any easy acceptance of the notion that adult classroom second language acquisition should be shaped to resemble first language acquisition closely.

A related notion holds that we should try as much as possible to prevent second language (L2) learners from going through their first language (L1), using pictures and graphics to prevent them from thinking in the L1 and then translating into the L2. This is an approach that can be richly supported by technology (see, in this volume, Douglas;

Hamburger; Tomlin). Again, however, I caution against taking it for granted as the best approach for all kinds of learners or learning because we have very little basis for believing that it is possible to prevent learners from thinking first in their L1. Even if we attempt to convey meaning by using pictures, video, or graphics, adult learners are more than likely to attach an L1 label to the visual cue and then to translate that label into the L2. Nor do we have any solid basis for assuming that it would necessarily be advantageous to avoid L1 mediation, even if it were possible.

Granted, we want to discourage attempts to express meaning in the L2 on the basis of superficial word-for-word translation from the L1. However, it seems to me that the way to avoid that is to teach students why superficial translation does not work by showing them how meaning is constructed and conveyed at quite different levels—not to try hopelessly to prevent them from thinking in the L1 and translating. There is nothing wrong with the attempt to construct within ICALL a complex domain in which learners communicate with a strong reliance on visual cues, but I think that a strenuous effort to avoid the possibility of "thinking in the L1" is misplaced.

Theories of Language, Language Processing, and Language Acquisition: The Need for a New Synthesis for ICALL

The most important point I want to make in responding to the impressive array of initiatives in ICALL represented in this volume, however, is not that we need to understand language both as linguistic system and as communicative behavior but that neither of these perspectives, or even both of them together, should be seen as the fundamental basis for developing language learning materials. Whether we take theories of syntax or theories of sociolinguistics, semantics, pragmatics, or discourse to be the most significant ways of understanding language, a theory of language is not per se a theory of language acquisition—nor is a theory of language acquisition to be found in a statement of the most desirable outcome of language study.

The choice of goal or outcome dictates the choice of method, and that is a pedagogical decision, often based on political and ideological grounds. It is sometimes rationalized in terms of prevailing theories of language or of learning (as the so-called audio-lingual method was linked to structuralist theory in linguistics and behaviorist theory in psychology). We need to understand that the identification of a goal is not a theory of how that goal is to be reached. The grammar-translation method aimed to enable learners to analyze grammar and to translate between the L1 and the L2, whereas the communicative method aims to enable learners to communicate in a target-language-speaking environment. Both of them are loosely related to the theories of language prevalent in their eras, but neither of them constitutes, or is directly based on, a theory of language acquisition.

In fact, the most important basis both for theories of language and for theories of language acquisition is a theory of language processing. If we do not understand how people associate meaning with linguistic form and how that association is stored, retrieved, and deployed in communication (i.e., how language knowledge is organized and used by the mind), we have no way of understanding why a linguistic system operates the way it does or how it comes to be acquired. Processing is primary, and the nature of language systems, as well as the shape of language acquisition, must be understood relative to it. But the formal study of processability and learnability undertaken within theoretical linguistics addresses only the logical problem of language processing and acquisition—how must language be organized so that it is possible for the human brain to process and acquire it. It does not address the actual unfolding of processing and learning of real communicative language in real time by real people. That is the problem which concerns us in ICALL, and that is why we have to move in the direction of basing our efforts on psycholinguistic theory rather than on linguistic or sociolinguistic theory.

The contrast between the language-as-system and the language-as-communicative-behavior ICALL initiatives described in this book is clearly seen in the kind of feedback each provides to the learners. The systems based on grammar parsing return, after a learner input error, detailed specifications of the linguistic problem, whereas the systems based on the processing of microworld information return a message about some logical problem with the communicative act. In both categories we have seen extremely sophisticated analyses being carried out and their results communicated efficiently to the learners. However, each of them can give learners only partial understanding of their production or comprehension, a view of one surface or the other but no insight into what thinking underlies that surface.

On the one hand, no matter how detailed and accurate a parser is, parsing is basically an analysis of language form (i.e., what the error is), not an analysis of language processing (i.e., why the learner made that error) or an analysis of language acquisition (i.e., how and why the processing changes over time). Telling learners what their error is does not necessarily tell them anything about why they made it or how to think in order not to make it again. On the other hand, telling learners that they have misunderstood a message or produced a message that cannot be understood does not necessarily tell them how to recognize the meaning of language form or how to choose language form so as to convey what they mean.

No matter what one's theory of language is, describing an error (or tabulating its frequency) is not the same as explaining why the learner made it. Even though the addition of lexical, semantic, and discourse-structure information to the description of language extends and enriches our understanding of language, we know as yet very little about how these kinds of information work in the actual course of acquisition. Neither linguistic feedback nor communicative feedback, nor even both together, can provide the kind of psycholinguistic information that could help learners revise their idiosyncratic hypotheses—their interlanguage rules—about how meaning and form are connected. That is why I suggest that both kinds of ICALL initiatives, the language-as-system ones and the language-as-communicative-behavior ones, should be seen as early stages in the development of ICALL.

If we understand learner errors in these terms, we can see the need for ICALL not only to go beyond assuming that either linguistic or communicative bases for language constitute SLA theory, but even to go beyond adding complex semantic and discourse features to the parsing. We will have to deal with the fact that learners very often do not know what it is that they do not know and therefore find it difficult or impossible to make appropriate use of helps. We will have to develop a much clearer understanding of why they so often cannot use what they know (i.e., what they have been taught) about the target language or even why they so often cannot use what they know about their native language. What transfers, and what does not, and why?

ICALL will certainly need to develop ways of recognizing what level of feedback a learner error requires. When is it an error of form, a surface structure violation, or a mistake within a paradigm? When is it an error of meaning, a problem with the semantic or syntactic concept that should govern the choice of paradigm? When does it show a problem in making the form-meaning connections so as to effect accurate communication? How can tasks and feedback on learner performance be designed to prevent learners from employing the binary correction strategy? Can ICALL make these deeper level distinctions of psycholinguistic processing?

Research

Following these questions takes us, obviously, to the issue of research. It is easy enough and true to say that ICALL can and should serve research goals just as much as it serves language teaching goals. However, we need a clear focus on what kind of research we are talking about (i.e., what kind of theory underlies the particular kinds of research that are designed into ICALL systems). There is no such thing as theory-neutral observation of what learners do. For the linguists active in ICALL, research tends to mean studying the structure of parsers, extending natural language processing, and following linguistic and cognitive theory, and that effort is of great importance in a number of developments. But I assume that in the present context, that of language learning, such research is not taken to be the main purpose.

Efficacy

For most language teachers, in contrast to linguists, research in the technological environment is taken for granted as meaning efficacy studies, that is, evaluation of the pedagogical effectiveness of using technology to assist language learning. This is part of the larger domain of pedagogical research, which involves manipulating some pedagogical variable and tracing its effect on learning. From this perspective, the pedagogical variable in CALL or ICALL is the use of the machinery. I do not take time here to analyze the many problems with research on the general efficacy of technology (for example, the well-documented problems with attempts to compare methods as well as the problem that use of the technology is not itself a method), but I do point out that we must be careful not to transfer these problems wholesale to the possibility of evaluating ICALL generally in comparison to CALL. There are so many uncontrollable variables that evaluating the efficacy of technology across the board is impossible. It is possible to evaluate the pedagogical efficacy of specific features of ICALL for specific learners in specific language learning tasks, but even in carefully delimited studies there is the danger of interpretations based on some of the problematic assumptions I have been detailing.

For example, in ICALL just as in CALL (and as in language pedagogy generally), a study of the efficacy of detailed linguistic feedback (in ICALL automatically generated by a parser) might show very little effect. Language teachers who adhere to the no-explicit-grammar doctrine would be likely to interpret such findings as confirming the claim that teaching students grammar does not do any good and as a basis for arguing against teaching grammar at all. I, on the other hand, respond to such a study by arguing that parser-based explanations of the formal properties of learner grammar errors cannot be expected to do much good if the problem is really with the learners' lack of understanding of the concept that the grammatical form conveys, and that such research shows that we should teach grammar quite differently.

Combining Basic and Pedagogical Research

In some institutions it is important to distinguish pedagogical research from basic research: The latter leads to promotion and tenure whereas the former does not. In such circumstances, the language teacher interested in studying the role of technology in language learning is in a dilemma. Basic research in either literary or linguistic theory has little to do with the nature of the classroom acquisition process, but conventional efficacy research is seen as as merely pedagogical and may not count. It is possible, however, to design research on classroom second language acquisition so that it can appropriately claim to be basic research—by focusing on the nature of the language acquisition process in terms of second language acquisition theory rather than in terms of superficial manipulation of some pedagogical variables. This is a subtle difference but an important one for the field. If the variable of pedagogical treatment is held constant and learning is tracked in correlation with features of the learner (age, learning strategies, cognitive style, native language background, etc.) or features of the learning task according to hypotheses based on one version or another of SLA theory, then we may argue that we are doing basic rather than pedagogical research. Still, the line is not a clear one.

In any case, research on the learning of language is different from research on the learning of any other subject matter precisely because language is not just another body of facts or knowledge but rather a basic function of the brain. In this we might be said to be privileged over other kinds of teachers: Pedagogical research on how chemistry or history is learned is altogether different from basic research in chemistry or history. Research on how language is learned can be either pedagogical or basic depending on where the hypotheses come from. From this perspective we can understand second language acquisition as the basic field of which language pedagogy is the applied arm.

However, even when we are clearly undertaking basic research on second language acquisition, there are so many different theories going by that name that the premises and implications of a given study may be completely misunderstood by those who are nominally in the same field but are operating in a different paradigm. It behooves us in ICALL to be clear ourselves about whether we are conceiving of second language acquisition from a psycholinguistic, a linguistic, or a sociolinguistic/communicative perspective and to make clear the implications of that distinction to those who may be interested in using the research, such as teachers and other theorists.

Whether or not we agree with the strongest version of the communicative position (i.e., that language learning can and should proceed, even in the classroom, with minimal or zero attention to grammar), we need to be aware that teachers who have been strongly influenced by that position are likely to be reluctant to experiment with ICALL systems that are based on a linguistic model of second language acquisition and that provide parser-based feedback focused on grammar problems. There is still a sizable population of language teachers, however, who believe that grammar does need to be taught but who would much prefer to have it taken care of outside of class according to individual learners' own needs. They are likely to be very interested in having their students use parser-based ICALL and in participating in research projects on that use. There are still others who have never relinquished their conviction that teaching language means first and foremost teaching grammar and who will therefore distrust communicative ICALL that does not focus on linguistic accuracy.

Conclusions

The acid test of the development of technology is seen in its use. In this final section I discuss realistic issues in the use of ICALL.

The Partnership of Teacher and Technology

The rapid development of ICALL pushes us towards another fundamental question: How do we envisage the role of the teacher? It is sometimes argued that the ideal experience (at least for nonimmersion foreign language learning) is intensive and extensive one-on-one tutoring by a pedagogically trained native speaker. It is further argued that the use of technology can be considered only a default or back-up to compensate for the more common situation in which there is only one teacher, who is often not a native or even a very fluent speaker or is not experienced in language pedagogy, for a class of 25 or 30 students meeting only 3 or 4 hours a week. Though unfortunately this less-than-ideal situation is the standard one and we can therefore use all the help we can get from technology, most of us would not agree with the assertion that technology is only a backup and that it cannot do anything that the teacher cannot do.

For one thing, multimedia can provide a wealth and a variety of authentic visual and auditory input that no teacher could offer unaided. Moreover, networks and electronic communications allow learners to communicate with each other and access data near and far. Even aside from multimedia and networks, access to a richly supportive technological environment with multiple resources built in can provide the opportunity to individualize learning according to the many variables discussed earlier. On the other hand, teachers, no matter how experienced and flexible, inevitably have their own personal styles and strategies and cannot adapt themselves with infinite flexibility to every different learner. Finally, the computer's ability to record, tabulate, and organize data on the learning history of individual learners goes well beyond a human being's, and it can therefore diagnose individual learning problems far more accurately than even the most attentive teacher. As Bailin has cogently argued (this volume, 1990; Bailin & Thomson, 1988), the student modeling capability of ICALL is the essential tool needed to make the intelligence of the software relevant to the practical business of language teaching.

Nonetheless, there are language learning activities that absolutely require direct interaction with a teacher and always will, most notably spontaneous oral communication, both the practice and the evaluation thereof. The organization and supervision of the whole process of language learning and the integration of technological and human interactions will always require extensive teacher involvement. The design and creation of the materials and activities that the technology supports demands great and growing amounts of teacher time and expertise.

It is politically incorrect even to raise the issue of whether technology can replace teachers, but the issue has to be dealt with. Ray Clifford, Provost of the Defense Language Institute, is widely quoted as saying that although computers will not replace teachers, teachers who use computers well will replace those who do not. That is a sensible and nonthreatening way to look at the future. However, the question has to be taken more seriously than that, not only because so many teachers fear it but also because it would be silly to deny that administrations are interested in using technology to extend teachers' time and to make the time spent more cost-effective (even if the rising demand for foreign language education makes it unlikely that competent teachers will lose jobs). That translates—no matter how carefully it is worded—into using technology instead of teachers to take care of some aspects of language learning.

Surely, in a collection of ICALL work like this book, we have to ask ourselves point-blank, under what circumstances, to what extent, and with what kinds of learners we are willing to experiment with using ICALL as the basis for certain specific language learning activities or purposes rather than as an extra, optional enhancement. Research done to date cannot supply us with empirical justification for supplanting some activities with ICALL because institutions have not yet developed the facilities to make possible the mandatory use of technology in a central role in language learning. Technology-based materials have perforce been designed for optional or limited use. Evaluation of optional uses by limited numbers of students cannot be used as a basis for predicting the efficacy of mandatory central-purpose technology use for all students.

Nonetheless, it is not hard to find theoretical and pedagogical reasons for using interactive multimedia to support, manage, analyze, and evaluate (for the learner's own benefit, not for a grade) a good deal of student work on vocabulary, reading, writing, and listening in a foreign language. I argue, in addition, that good tutorials on grammar concepts and sophisticated grammar practice on-line are likely to be far more effective in getting learners to understand how grammar organizes meaning than any textbook or workbook or—with all respect—most teachers, who have not in the past twenty years been trained to teach grammar and who have for the most part no theoretical background as a basis for doing so. I would even go so far as to suggest that we could, with a clear conscience, experiment with designing a language syllabus in which motivated students (who had undergone a fair amount of consciousness raising about the language learning process) did all their language learning in ICALL except for regular small-group conversation sessions with a teacher. The trouble is we cannot test the hypothesis without going to the enormous work of designing a whole syllabus of ICALL or CALL materials. Leaving aside considerations of cost, I think it is time we asked ourselves seriously how large a scope for ICALL we would want to develop if we had the chance to follow through on the promise of the approaches described in this book, and what advances in theory, programming, and hardware would be required to make such development possible.

Increasing Demand for Language Learning

Posing these questions is not only an intellectual exercise but a necessity, given the rapidly increasing demands of the academy, the government, and economics. In universities, internationalization continues to be a powerful buzzword. Even degree programs outside the liberal arts are now requiring or strongly recommending language study for their majors, such as health-related professions and social work, agriculture, law enforcement, engineering and computer science, and business and international studies. A different kind of demand is also posed by students who come from homes in which English is not the native language—who at George Mason University, for example, comprise nearly 25% of the incoming population. What do we do with students who communicate regularly with family members in Spanish but who are not native speakers and do not read or write it, who do not have native control over the grammar, and who are virtually impossible to fit into conventional courses, but who want to fulfill the language requirement in Spanish? As I see it, the best solution is ICALL work that could, in principle, diagnose their highly individual language capabilities and allow them to focus on those aspects of language learning at which they are weak.

The government needs not only more people who are more competent in more languages but also ways for personnel who have left language training and are on the job around the world to maintain language proficiency on their own. ICALL is one answer, though of course computers are not always available. Distance learning is fast becoming the new imperative. In many fields that means tele-lectures, but those are not interactive enough for language learning. ICALL has to be a large part of the solution.

Integrating Theory, Teaching, and Technology

What these new needs demand of us is not simply a combination of current foreign language pedagogy and technology but rather a principled integration of second language acquisition theory, teaching, and technology, where each of these three is designed and developed in some degree of paradigmatic compatibility with the others. This will not be easy. Second language acquisition theory is still far from unitary. Serious controversy polarizes language teaching, and technology changes so rapidly as to make all of us dizzy. ICALL has to be conceived of as part of a larger research agenda if it is to have the synergistic effect that I think we all believe in. We are really talking about a new discipline here—perhaps we could call it CARLA (computer-assisted research on language acquisition). More power to us.

References

Bailin, A. (1990). Skills-in-context and student modeling. *The CALICO Journal*, *8*, 7-22.

Bailin, A., & Thomson, P. (1988). Natural language processing in computer-assisted language instruction. *Computers and the Humanities*, *22*, 99-110.

Ehrman, M.E., & Oxford, R.L. (1990). Adult language learning strategies and styles in an intensive training setting. *Modern Language Journal*, 74, 311-327.

Scarcella, R., & Oxford, R. (1992). *The tapestry of language learning: The individual in the communicative classroom*. Boston: Heinle & Heinle.

20

Linking Theories of Learning with Intelligent Computer-Assisted Language Learning (ICALL)

Rebecca L. Oxford
University of Alabama

This chapter discusses three current theories of learning that should be considered by designers of intelligent computer-assisted language learning (ICALL). These theories are the novice-to-expert paradigm, constructivism, and the individual differences model.

The state of the art in ICALL is assumed to be well represented by the chapters in this volume. They discuss improvements in natural language parsing, sound and video production, error analysis, and expert systems design, but for the most part they do not mention any underlying theory of learning.

One unknown sage reminds us, "There is nothing as practical as a sound theory." Another warns, "Theory without practice is futile, and practice without theory is fatal." Therefore, it is a good time to ask these questions: What kind of general theories of learning support ICALL either explicitly or implicitly? Is there anything missing?

The three theories of learning in this chapter pervade most of the education in the Western world today, and each has a potentially useful contribution to make to ICALL. In this chapter I do not discuss Far Eastern theories of learning, which are often couched in Confucianism and do not have proven relevance to ICALL, though no doubt a case could be made for them as well. Note that Skinner's behaviorist theory of learning, based on a simple stimulus-response paradigm, is not included here because it does not seem to me to fit with the highly complex activity of learning a second or foreign language. Before discussing the three general theories of learning, let us take a quick detour regarding one theory of second language acquisition as related to ICALL.

Second Language Acquisition Theory

Most ICALL developers, as reflected in this volume, do not cite or describe any underlying second language acquisition theories. Those few that do identify a second language acquisition theory usually mention the ideas of Krashen (1981, 1982). In another place (Oxford, 1990), I have explained that aspects of Krashen's theory have been contradicted by empirical research and practical experience (for example, the Invariant Silent Period Hypothesis and the hypothesis that "learning" can never contribute to "acquisition"). Other elements of his theory are too abstract to be tested (for instance, the "i + 1" or Comprehensible Input Hypothesis). Moreover, the concept that any single methodology focusing on fluency at the expense of accuracy can apply to all students, such as the natural approach of Krashen and Terrell (1983), must be seriously questioned (Oxford, 1990; Scarcella & Oxford, 1992). McLaughlin (1987) outlines the flaws in Krashen's theory and in the resulting natural approach. Clearly, any ICALL developments that are largely based on Krashen's second language acquisition theory need to be reexamined and possibly altered or amplified by additional theories. Many other theories of second language acquisition besides Krashen's—including psycholinguistic, neurolinguistic, sociolinguistic, and social-psychological theories—are available, providing rich offerings to ICALL creators. (For useful information on second language acquisition theories see Beebe, 1988; Brown, 1987; Ellis, 1986; Gass & Madden, 1985; Larsen-Freeman & Long, 1991; McLaughlin, 1987; Oxford, 1990, 1993a, 1994; Phillipson, Kellerman, Selinker, Sharwood-Smith, & Swain, 1991; Scarcella & Oxford, 1992; Van Patten & Lee, 1987). Now I turn to the first of the three general theories of learning that are the primary subject of this chapter.

Novice-to-Expert Paradigm

One of the major theories of learning today contrasts experts with novices in any field. Experts have deeper, more richly connected knowledge structures (*schemata*) to draw upon, whereas novices have shallower, less developed schemata, presumably because of lack of experience (Leinhardt & Greeno, 1986). Well developed schemata allow the expert first to determine what merits attention and then to draw immediately upon relevant information from memory to decide on an appropriate response (Carter, Cushing, Sabers, Stein, & Berliner, 1988). Expertise is characterized by a smooth, flowing, and automatic performance (Dreyfus & Dreyfus, 1986). Reflective-thinking activities can, in some instances, help novices develop schemata that are more like those of experts (Morine-Dershimer, 1989). However, in many cases it is necessary for people to develop their own contextual knowledge through personal experience; novices cannot typically develop expert-like schemata without going through a gradual, experiential learning process.

Let us look at different stages in the development of expertise. Berliner (1987) and Dreyfus and Dreyfus (1986) posited five stages, which could easily be applied to developing foreign or second language ability: novice, advanced beginner, competent, proficient, and expert. Dreyfus and Dreyfus delineated these five steps by studying artificial intelligence and the problem-solving capability of computer programmers.

The *novice stage* is characterized by skill development. The novice learns to recognize various surface features and facts and to determine rules. Novices lack any rational sense of the overall context or organization. They judge their own performance by how well they follow learned rules.

At the *advanced beginner stage*, broad skills and more sophisticated rules are in play. Because the advanced beginner can detect similarities with prior examples, the elements of this stage are situational, as opposed to context-free as they are at the novice stage. Advanced beginners may now determine in which situation one rule works differently from another.

The *competent stage* is exemplified by learners who cope with problems in a highly analytical, hierarchical process of decision-making. This is characterized by identifying a new situation, determining a goal, choosing a general plan to organize the situation, and noting a set of factors that must be considered. The competent performer by now has sufficient experience to determine when given rules will work and when the situation requires an entirely different set of procedures not covered by the rules. At this stage, compared with earlier stages, the learner feels a greater sense of personal responsibility for the outcome.

The *proficient stage* involves not only thinking analytically but also thinking intuitively while attempting to understand and organize the task at hand. The learner's experience is the background for determining how best to manipulate and complete the task. The learner now mobilizes a very large repertoire of patterns that can be used; rules and simple skills are no longer the primary grist for the mill. The learner examines experiences, deliberately considers multiple alternatives, makes some intuitive moves, and feels increased responsibility for the outcome.

At the *expert stage*, the individual shows maturity, practical understanding, and fluidity of performance. He or she does not stop to deliberate but instead immediately, automatically, and fluently performs. Experts are deeply involved in coping with their environment and the task at hand and do not see problems in a detached way. They know by personal feel and familiarity what action to take. Intuition, based on a great deal of practice and on deep understanding, underlies experts' automaticity of response.

How do these stages relate to language learning, especially via ICALL? When individuals first begin to use an ICALL program to learn a given language, they may be at the novice stage. At this stage, they probably lack at least two if not all of the following three kinds of experiential contexts: first, the context of how to learn a language effectively; second, the context of understanding the structure and nature of the target language itself; and third, the context of dealing personally with the target culture. At the novice stage language learners deal almost solely with linguistic facts and rules. ICALL at the novice stage must offer many activities that allow learners to manipulate rules and that push them into the next stage by developing some elements of the three contexts just mentioned. Upon reaching the next stage, that of advanced beginner, language learners make more complex linkages with examples they have already encountered. They have some context, at least in the linguistic realm (and, I hope, also in the realms of the general language learning process and the target culture). ICALL at this stage can deepen the context of both language and culture, explicitly help students understand the language learning process, and encourage many associations through semantic mapping and other exercises.

The competent stage learner analytically organizes plans for attacking a language task, but the proficient stage learner links analysis with intuition, which is well grounded in a wide repertoire of available language patterns associated with a variety of appropriate social situations. At the competent and proficient stages, ICALL can help learners by providing analytic language tasks, by offering diverse global communication tasks that allow the use of patterns, by developing learners' metacognitive (i.e., planning, organizing, evaluating, and monitoring) abilities, and by moving learners into greater use of their intuitive abilities. The language learner who has reached the expert stage demonstrates fluid, automatic performance; language fluency has been attained without destroying precision or falling into fossilization. At this stage, ICALL can help learners by offering challenging language tasks that demand immediate, socioculturally appropriate responses.

All stages except possibly the expert stage can benefit from explicit presentation of possible language learning strategies, which are tools (like planning, underlining, summarizing, or practicing) that learners can use to improve their learning. ICALL provides a perfect venue for training students to enhance their own learning and move themselves through the stages from novice to expert by means of well-targeted learning strategies (see, for instance, Cohen, 1990; Ellis & Sinclair, 1989; Larsen-Freeman & Long, 1991; O'Malley & Chamot, 1990; Oxford, 1990, 1993a, 1993b; Scarcella & Oxford, 1992; Selinker, 1992; Wenden, 1991; Wenden & Rubin, 1987).

The chapters in this volume do not discuss the novice-to-expert paradigm with any specificity. This seems surprising, given that the paradigm comes directly from the information-processing model of learning, a model based on computers and artificial intelligence. It would be useful for ICALL developers to consider whether this paradigm is the theory they want to work with and if so, which levels of learning they desire to target and exactly which kinds of exercises will enhance movement through which stages and at what pace.

Constructivism

The constructivist theory of learning is not explicitly linked with any of the ICALL designs in this volume, yet this theory is sweeping the United States, Canada, Western Europe, parts of Eastern Europe, and Russia. Constructivism, which Yager (1991) called the most exciting idea of the last 50 years and which is one of the major theories in educational psychology today (Mayer, 1993), has roots going back to the 1700s. This theory assumes that students have a purpose for learning and that they are actively engaged in constructing meanings from their learning experiences. Constructivism is an ontological/epistemological paradigm addressing both what is known and how it is known. Ontology refers to the area of metaphysics concerned with the core of things. Epistemology is a branch of philosophy pertaining to the origin, foundation, limits, and validity of knowledge. Prominent constructivist Ernst von Glaserfeld traced the theory of cognitive construction to Neapolitan philosopher Vico, who wrote in 1710 that individuals know only the cognitive structures they put together themselves (Yager, 1991). Vico explained that a person knows something only when he or she can explain it for others to understand and use. One of the most famous constructivists was the cognitive-developmental psychologist Jean Piaget, whose book *The Construction of Reality in the Child* (1954) set the pace for generations of researchers and curriculum designers. In this discussion I follow each basic tenet of constructivism with appropriate implications for ICALL.

Constructivism deals not only with how understanding is constructed but also with how the structure of cognition affects behavior. The theory of constructivism suggests that individuals interpret and act according to conceptual categories in the cognitive system. This theory is like many other cognitive approaches in explaining that an event does not just present itself to individuals in raw form; instead, people construct experience according to the organization of the cognitive system. Constructivism assumes that learners are creative and active. Instead of being acted upon by their situations, people act dynamically and create changes based on how they regulate their activities and how they think. An important implication for ICALL is that language learners must be considered dynamic and self-regulatory. A corollary is that ICALL must teach learners all the metacognitive tools necessary for appropriate self-regulation.

Constructivism is partly based on Kelly's (1955) theory of personal constructs. Kelly suggested that people understand experience by grouping according to similarities and opposites. A construct is a distinction between opposites, such as short-tall, fat-thin, black-white, pleasant-unpleasant, that is used to understand events, things, and people. By employing such distinctions and classifications in constructs, individuals give meanings to what they encounter. Constructs move from relative simplicity and generality to relative complexity and specificity (Werner, 1957). A useful if rather basic implication for ICALL designers is that language tasks must move from simple to complex. Moreover, ICALL activities must allow learners repeated opportunities to group ideas, words, phrases, and concepts (and to label those groupings for themselves).

Constructivism recognizes that constructs have social origins: They are learned through interaction with others. An individual's cognitive system is a direct result of interaction in social groups and cannot be separated from social life (Vygotsky, 1987). Goal achievement is often a social phenomenon involving coordination of goal-oriented strategies by a number of people. Group learning, where pairs and small groups of students learn together through social interaction, is predictably one of the key constructivist techniques. Culture is particularly relevant in determining the meaning of events, people, and things (Applegate & Sypher, 1988) and in helping coordinate goal-oriented efforts. Any moment of behavior reflects each person's social history and cognitive understandings. Behavior follows, at least to some extent, schemata that allow people to interact, because these schemata encode knowledge of the social behavior appropriate to circumstances. Under this theory language learning is largely a social activity, and therefore ICALL tasks must simulate as closely as possible real social interaction (using scenarios of many types). Additionally, ICALL tasks should be woven into a larger learning situation if possible—a situation in which students leave the computer, interact with other people for learning-related purposes, and then return to the computer for further work. Another alternative is to include ICALL activities as part of a student-to-teacher or student-to-student network of computerized communication.

Simulated social interaction is found to a degree in a number of the tutors described in other chapters. This is certainly a step in the constructivist direction and reflects the perspective of language as a social act (Chaika, 1989). For instance, Sanders and Sanders (this volume) provide exciting and authentic interaction through a spy game, DeSmedt (this volume) does it through a detective simulation, and Douglas (this volume) does it through a realistic problem-solving environment. The Philippe simulation (Murray, this volume) evokes the language and ambiance of Paris. Dorr et al. (this volume) emphasize the need for discourse-based language input and output, thus stressing social interaction as part of language learning. Sociolinguistic competence—appropriateness of language use in relevant cultural contexts—is required if learners are to become capable of using the language outside of a hothouse environment or laboratory setting (see Beebe, 1988; Folman & Sarig, 1990; Kaplan, 1972; Olshtain, 1983; Omaggio, 1993). Selected systems featured in this volume—such as those of DeSmedt; Frederiksen, Donin, and Décary; Murray; and Sanders and Sanders—seem to highlight sociolinguistic competence, although they do not employ this term directly. Frederiksen et al. are concerned about appropriateness to a given discourse situation; DeSmedt and Sanders and Sanders focus on communication skills as a means of solving problems in a cultural context; Murray uses socially and culturally charged language activities that require some sociolinguistic adeptness. In contrast, other systems are purely grammar focused (e.g., Loritz, this volume; Rypa & Feuerman, this volume), thus obviating the possibility of social interaction using the language; or they treat sociolinguistic competence in a narrow way, as in ALICE's analysis of honorific Japanese terms of address (Levin & Evans, this volume). The BRIDGE system (Sams, this volume; Weinberg, this volume) presents job-relevant scenarios but offers strictly grammatical feedback to students' language. Moreover, both Hamburger (this volume) and Tomlin (this volume) appear to emphasize the value of more or less minimal visual immersion settings that avoid the complexity of culturally based contexts.

Although constructivism recognizes social interaction and culture, it remains primarily a psychological theory of learning dealing with cognitive (construct) complexity. The idea of cognitive complexity was originally developed by Crockett (1965) and elaborated by Schroder, Driver, and Streufert (1967). Individuals with highly developed constructs make more discriminations than those who see the world simplistically. Constructs in adult knowledge differ widely in their cognitive complexity. Different parts of the cognitive system of a single person can also differ in complexity, so an individual might have very elaborate, complicated constructs about cars but not about languages (or vice versa). Complexity or simplicity of the cognitive system is a function of the relative number of constructs and the degree of differentiation one can make between the elements of experience; these are sometimes jointly referred to as cognitive differentiation. Assuming that differentiation enhances language learning, ICALL creators should seek ways to encourage it, as through semantic mapping, flow charts, tree diagrams, and other graphic organizers. Content-based ICALL that deals with the career needs of the learner—containing career-related language themes (categories) and tasks—is valuable both for heightening motivation (Brinton, Snow, & Wesche, 1989; Hutchinson & Waters, 1987; Oxford, 1994) and for expanding learners' networks of cognitive associations (Scarcella & Oxford, 1992). The themes in the BRIDGE tutor (Sams, this volume) are job-related and therefore should be easy to associate to learners' prior knowledge, as should Hamburger's construct of time and the familiar spy and detective themes of Sanders and Sanders and of DeSmedt. The intelligent tutor's roles differ depending on the construct of interest: In Project Athena (Murray, this volume; Felshin, this volume) the tutor serves as agent, interlocutor, coach, informant, and companion; in the plans for FLUENT (Hamburger, this volume) the tutor is envisioned as tour guide, movecaster, commander, servant, oracle, and celebrity; and in the LingWorlds implementation (Douglas, this volume) the tutor directs the student's action. The more grammar-oriented systems (e.g., Levin & Evans, this volume) as well as deliberately artificial microworlds like FlatLand (Tomlin, this volume) do not typically deal with the kinds of motivating, personally meaningful, and easily related categories that would make constructivists happy.

Yager (1991) provides a helpful list of constructivist teaching techniques that may be directly applicable to ICALL (see also Nunan, 1988, 1989, 1992; Richards, 1990). Among these techniques are (a) seeking out and using student questions to guide lessons, (b) accepting and encouraging student initiation of ideas, (c) promoting student self-regulation and action, (d) using students' experiences and interests to drive lessons (and thus offering multiple branches for learning), (e) encouraging uses of alternative sources of information, (f) using open-ended questions and encouraging student elaboration when possible, (g) encouraging students to suggest causes for events and situations and to predict consequences, (h) seeking out student ideas before presenting ideas from the text, (i) allowing adequate time for reflection and analysis, and (j) facilitating reformulation of ideas in light of new experiences and evidence. All of these techniques could be used in one way or another in ICALL.

One further point deserves mention. As explained previously, constructivism posits that advanced learners have highly complex constructs linked by many rich associations. In contrast, the novice-to-expert paradigm described earlier proposes that experts have automatic, fluid behavior. Although these two theories of learning do not necessarily contradict each other, they do focus on the development of somewhat different phenomena at higher levels of learning: Constructivism underscores the development of rich, complex constructs built on interactions with the world, whereas the novice-to-expert paradigm emphasizes the development of intuition and unconscious automaticity. Even though the end results of these two theories appear slightly different, the theories are alike in positing gradual, experientially, personally engaged development of ability through the learning process. These theories provide a wealth of helpful implications to ICALL.

Individual Differences Theory

Individual differences theory suggests that learners learn in different ways and that no single methodology is useful for all. At its most fundamental, the theory is that each person is an individual, composed of a unique combination of personality traits, perceptual differences, and cognitive tendencies known as *individual differences* (Skehan, 1989). Other individual differences involve cognitive needs, beliefs, values, attitudes, and skills (DeFleur & Ball-Rokeach, 1989). These differences, taken together, form a particular *type* or *style* (Myers & McCaulley, 1985), and there are certain learning strategies related to that type or style (Scarcella & Oxford, 1992).

Furthermore, the theory suggests that because each person is somewhat different, instruction must take these contrasts into account and provide a learning environment that optimizes the educational benefit of the contrasts. Based on the theory, individuals typically have initial style preferences, but some of these preferences might alter a little over the course of a lifetime. Moreover, people can learn to use new strategies that do not fit into their initially preferred style. Thus, individual differences are not static; they may change through experience or instruction.

The theory of individual differences comes partly from the work of the Swiss psychologist Jung (1923). However, systems claiming to analyze human beings into different types have existed since the Middle Ages (remember the differences between choleric and sanguine personalities, for example). Even before that the ancient Sufi enneagram divided all people into nine clearly defined groups and helped individuals understand their strengths and weaknesses. The Jungian system, widely used now by psychologists, educators, chief executive officers, and personnel managers throughout the Western world, suggests that each person is composed of four primary dimensions. Various combinations of these dimensions produce 16 types or styles. The four dimensions are extroversion versus introversion, indicating the source of the individual's energy; sensing versus intuition, related to the individual's way of dealing with stimuli, either concretely and sequentially or futuristically and randomly; thinking versus feeling, indicating how the person makes decisions; and judging versus perceiving, linked to the individual's need for rapid closure or for greater openness. Ehrman and Oxford (1988, 1989, 1990) found that these individual-difference elements have a significant impact on adult language learning.

Jung's ideas, although extremely valuable, do not touch on several other aspects of individual differences that are also related to language learning. These include analytic versus global processing, related to breaking things down into details or synthesizing them into a whole picture; reflection versus impulsivity, concerning not just the rapidity with which an answer is reached but also the accuracy of that answer; visual, auditory, kinesthetic, and tactile sensory preferences; and learning strategies, which are the specific learning behaviors that often directly reflect the preferred style or type.

As a whole, the authors in this volume do not, regrettably, consider most aspects of style (as covered in Oxford & Ehrman, 1993; Oxford, Ehrman, & Lavine, 1991). For example, there is no overt mention of reflection and impulsivity in students, although presumably the self-pacing of ICALL has something to do with this aspect of learning style. There is no explanation of extroversion and introversion and how these dimensions influence choice of activities in ICALL. No discussion exists of the hugely important difference between the analytic style of language learning (i.e., focusing on details of grammar, pronunciation, and spelling) and the global style (i.e., emphasizing main ideas, guessing, and general cultural awareness). There is no exploration of the possibilities for using ICALL to link students with each other through a network of extended communication, capitalizing on multiple learning styles and strategies.

Some authors in this volume explicitly state that they are not concerned with a student module, which is one way to accommodate individual differences. In one particular respect, however, almost all of this volume's authors are involved in designing interfaces that can potentially deal with individual differences. For example, whenever there is an allowance and concern for choice of sensory preferences (visual, auditory, kinesthetic, or tactile), the designers are thinking about how students learn most efficiently and effectively. Many of this volume's authors demonstrate interest in the visual learning style (e.g., Murray; Rypa & Feuerman; Tomlin) and how to couple it with an auditory style (e.g., Douglas; Hamburger).

If learners learn in different ways, the instructional assistance they need is *mutatis mutandis* likely to be different. The concept of assistance comes from the Russian psychologist Vygotsky (1987), who believed that learners have a *zone of proximal development* (zone of potential growth) that they can traverse with just the right assistance coming at the appropriate time. As Scarcella and Oxford (1992) suggest, instructional assistance might take the form of error correction, which appears to be the main focus of assistance to learners found in many of the systems described in this volume (see, for instance, Levin & Evans; Sams; Yazdani). However, many other forms of assistance are possible: a useful learning strategy suggested by a teacher or by an intelligent tutor, a full explanation, a schematic/partial explanation (e.g., Rypa & Feuerman, this volume), a leading question that provokes thought, a pictorial representation of a verbal expression (e.g., Douglas, this volume), a cooperative learning activity, or an encouraging word at just the right moment. Research on styles (see Oxford, Ehrman, & Lavine, 1991) suggests that different learners need different modes of assistance. Concrete-sequential learners want to be told what to do and exactly how to do it, whereas intuitive learners want to find their own answers in their own (often ingenious and random) ways. Thinking-oriented learners want factual feedback, whereas feeling-oriented learners require greater emotional support. Analytic students enjoy an emphasis on accuracy and detail, whereas global students desire an emphasis on meaning and breadth. Knowing more about styles, especially as they relate to the assistance needed by students, would certainly enable ICALL designers to produce more useful systems.

A variety of materials is available on CALL that would be useful for ICALL developers to know intimately because these materials offer a vast range of activities and ideas applicable to students of almost all styles: Ahmad, Corbett, Rogers, and Sussex (1985); Brumfit, Phillips, and Skehan (1985); Celce-Murcia and Hilles (1988); Crookall, Coleman, and Oxford (1992); Crookall and Oxford (1990); Hardisty and Windeatt (1989); Higgins (1988); Jones and Fortescue (1987); Legenhausen and Wolff (1987); Pennington (1989); Phillips (1986); Underwood (1984); Wyatt (1984); and Zetterson (1986).

Conclusion

This chapter shows the need for greater clarity about the theories of learning supporting new developments in ICALL. After a brief discussion of one theory of second language acquisition, three general theories of learning are explained: the novice-to-expert paradigm, constructivism, and the individual differences model. For each theory, implications for ICALL are explained, often with reference to the other systems described in this volume, even though the designers of these systems rarely reference particular theories of learning.

Designers must be aware of the theories of learning that relate to their ICALL products. Unless ICALL creators know exactly what they are trying to develop, why they are attempting to develop it, which theories support the development, and to what degree these theories are sound, it is entirely possible that ICALL will be less than successful. After all, as noted earlier, practice without theory can be fatal. Armed with an understanding of appropriate theories of learning, ICALL designers have a far better chance of creating innovative systems that truly serve the needs of the learners.

References

Ahmad, K., Corbett, G., Rogers, M. & Sussex, R. (1985). *Computers, language learning, and language teaching.* Cambridge, UK: Cambridge University Press.

Applegate, J.L., & Sypher, H.E. (1988). A constructivist theory of communication and culture. In Y.Y. Kim & W.B. Gudykunst (Eds.), *Theories of intercultural communication* (pp. 41-65). Newbury Park, CA: Sage.

Beebe, L.M. (Ed.) (1988). *Issues in second language acquisition.* New York: HarperCollins.

Berliner, D. (1987). In pursuit of the expert pedagogue. *Educational Researcher, 15*, 5-13.

Brinton, D., Snow, M.A., & Wesche, M. (1989). *Content-based second language instruction.* New York: HarperCollins.

Brown, H.D. (1987). *Principles of language learning and teaching* (2nd ed.). Englewood Cliffs, NJ: Prentice-Hall.

Brumfit, C.J., Phillips, M., & Skehan, P. (Eds.) (1985). *Computers in English language teaching: A view from the classroom* (ELT Documents 122). Oxford: Pergamon.

Carter, K., Cushing, K., Sabers, D., Stein, P., & Berliner, D. (1988). Expert-novice differences in perceiving and processing visual classroom information. *Journal of Teacher Education, 39*, 25-31.

Celce-Murcia, M., & Hilles, S. (1988). *Techniques and resources in teaching grammar.* New York: Oxford University Press.

Chaika, E. (1989). *Language: The social mirror.* New York: Harper & Row.

Cohen, A.D. (1990). *Language learning: Insights for learners, teachers, and researchers.* New York: HarperCollins.

Crockett, W. (1965). Cognitive complexity and impression formation. In B.A. Maher (Ed.), *Progress in experimental personality research* (pp. 47-90). New York: Academic Press.

Crookall, D., Coleman, D., & Oxford, R.L. (1992). Computer-mediated language learning environments: Prolegomenon to a research framework. *CALL, 5*, 93-120.

Crookall, D., & Oxford, R.L. (Eds.). (1990). *Simulation, gaming, and language learning.* New York: HarperCollins.

DeFleur, M.L., & Ball-Rokeach, S. (1989). *Theories of mass communication.* White Plains, NY: Longman.

Dreyfus, H.L., & Dreyfus, S.E. (1986). *Mind over machine.* New York: The Free Press.

Ehrman, M.E., & Oxford, R.L. (1988). *Ants and grasshoppers, badgers and butterflies: Qualitative and quantitative exploration of adult language learning styles and strategies.* Paper presented at the Symposium on Research Perspectives on Adult Language Learning, Ohio State University, Columbus, OH.

Ehrman, M.E., & Oxford, R.L. (1989). Effects of sex differences, career choice, and psychological type on adults' language learning strategies. *Modern Language Journal, 73*, 1-13.

Ehrman, M.E., & Oxford, R.L. (1990). Adult language learning strategies and styles in an intensive training setting. *Modern Language Journal, 74*, 311-327.

Ellis, G., & Sinclair, B. (1989). *Learning to learn English: A course in learner training.* Cambridge, UK: Cambridge University Press.

Ellis, R. (1986). *Understanding second language acquisition.* New York: Oxford University Press.

Folman, S., & Sarig, G. (1990). Intercultural rhetorical differences in meaning construction. *Communication and Cognition, 23*, 45-92.

Gass, S.M., & Madden, C.G. (1985). *Input in second language learning.* New York: Harper & Row.

Hardisty, D., & Windeatt, S. (1989). *CALL.* New York: Oxford University Press.

Higgins, J. (1988). *Language learners and computers.* New York: Longman.

Hutchinson, T., & Waters, A. (1987). *English for specific purposes: A learner-centred approach.* Cambridge, UK: Cambridge University Press.

Jones, C., & Fortescue, S. (1987). *Using computers in the language classroom.* New York: Longman.

Jung, C.G. (1923). *Psychological type.* New York: Harcourt Brace.

Kaplan, R. (1972). Cultural thought patterns in intercultural education. In H. Allen & R. Campbell (Eds.), *Teaching English as a second language: A book of readings* (pp. 294-310). New York: McGraw-Hill.

Kelly, G. (1955). *The psychology of personal constructs.* New York: North.

Krashen, S.D. (1981). *Second language acquisition and second language learning.* New York: Pergamon.

Krashen, S.D. (1982). *Principles and practices in second language acquisition.* New York: Pergamon.

Krashen, S.D., & Terrell, T.D. (1983). *The natural approach: Language acquisition in the classroom.* New York: Pergamon & San Francisco: Alemany.

Larsen-Freeman, D.H., & Long, M.H. (1991). *An introduction to second language acquisition research.* New York: Longman.

Legenhausen, L., & Wolff, D. (Eds.) (1987). *Computer-assisted language learning and innovative EFL methodology.* Augsburg: Universitat Augsburg.

Leinhardt, G., & Greeno, J.G. (1986). The cognitive skill of teaching. *Journal of Educational Psychology, 78*, 75-92.

McLaughlin, B. (1987). *Theories of second-language learning.* London: Edward Arnold.

Mayer, R.E. (1993). Educational psychology—past and future: Comment on Derry (1992). *Journal of Educational Psychology, 85*, 551-553.

Morine-Dershimer, G. (1989). Preservice teachers' conceptions of content and pedagogy: Measuring growth in reflective, pedagogical decision-making. *Journal of Teacher Education, 30*, 47-52.

Myers, I., & McCaulley, K. (1985). *Manual: A guide to the development and use of the Myers-Briggs Type Indicator.* Palo Alto, CA: Consulting Psychologists Press.

Nunan, D. (1988). *The learner-centred curriculum.* Cambridge, UK: Cambridge University Press.

Nunan, D. (1989). *Designing tasks for the communicative classroom.* Cambridge, UK: Cambridge University Press.

Nunan, D. (Ed.) (1992). *Collaborative language learning and teaching.* Cambridge: Cambridge University Press.

Olshtain, E. (1983). Sociocultural competence and language transfer: The case of apology. In S. Gass & L. Selinker (Eds.), *Language transfer in language learning.* Rowley, MA: Newbury House.

Omaggio, A. (1993). *Teaching language in context.* (2nd ed.) Boston: Heinle & Heinle.

O'Malley, J.M., & Chamot, A.U. (1990). *Learning strategies in second language acquisition.* Cambridge, UK: Cambridge University Press.

Oxford, R.L. (1990). *Language learning strategies: What every teacher should know.* New York: HarperCollins.

Oxford, R.L. (1993a). Language learning strategies in a nutshell: Update and ESL suggestions. *TESOL Journal, 2,* 18-22.

Oxford, R.L. (1993b). Research on second language learning strategies. *Annual Review of Applied Linguistics, 13,* 175-187.

Oxford, R.L. (1994). Progress in tertiary content-based ESL instruction. *TESL Canada Journal.*

Oxford, R.L., & Ehrman, M.E. (1993). Second language research on individual differences. *Annual Review of Applied Linguistics, 13,* 188-205.

Oxford, R.L., Ehrman, M.E., & Lavine, R.Z. (1991). Style wars: Teacher-student style conflicts in the language classroom. In S.S. Magnan (Ed.), *Challenges in the 1990s for college foreign language programs* (pp. 1-25). Boston: Heinle & Heinle.

Pennington, M.C. (Ed.) (1989). *Teaching languages with computers: The state of the art.* La Jolla, CA: Athlestan Press.

Phillips, M. (1986). *Communicative language learning and the microcomputer.* London: British Council.

Phillipson, R., Kellerman, E., Selinker, L., Sharwood-Smith, M., & Swain, M. (1991). *Foreign/second language pedagogy research.* Clevedon, Avon: Multilingual Matters.

Piaget, J. (1954). *The construction of reality in the child.* New York: Basic Books.

Richards, J.C. (1990). *The language teaching matrix.* Cambridge, UK: Cambridge University Press.

Scarcella, R., & Oxford, R. (1992). *The tapestry of language learning: The individual in the communicative classroom.* Boston: Heinle & Heinle.

Schroder, H.M., Driver, M.S., & Streufert, S. (1967). *Human information processing: Individuals and groups functioning in complex social systems.* New York: Holt, Rinehart & Winston.

Selinker, L. (1992). *Interlanguage.* New York: Longman.

Skehan, P. (1989). *Individual differences in second-language learning.* London: Edward Arnold.

Underwood, J. (1984). *Linguistics, computers, and the language teacher: A communicative approach.* Rowley, MA: Newbury.

Van Patten, B., & Lee, J.F. (1990). *Second language acquisition—foreign language learning.* Clevedon, Avon: Multilingual Matters.

Vygotsky, L.S. (1987). *Collected works.* (R.W. Rieber & A.S. Carton (Eds.), N. Minick, Trans). New York: Plenum.

Wenden, A. (1991). *Learner strategies for learner autonomy: Planning and implementing learner training for language learners.* Englewood Cliffs, NJ: Prentice-Hall.

Wenden, A., & Rubin, J. (Eds.). (1987). *Learner strategies for language learning.* Englewood Cliffs, NJ: Prentice-Hall.

Werner, H. (1957). The concept of development from a comparative and organismic point of view. In D.B. Harris (Ed.), *The concept of development.* Minneapolis: University of Minnesota Press.

Wyatt, D.H. (Ed.). (1984). *Computer-assisted language instruction.* New York: Pergamon.

Yager, B. (1991). The constructivist learning model. *The Science Teacher, 51,* 52-57.

Zettersen, A. (1986). *New technologies in language learning.* New York: Pergamon.

Author Index

—J—

—K—

—L—

—M—

—S—

—T—

Subject Index

—A—

—B—

—C—

—D—

—W—

—Z—